POLITICAL THEORIES
for Students

POLITICAL
THEORIES
for Students

Matthew Miskelly and Jaime Noce,
Editors

GALE GROUP

THOMSON LEARNING

Detroit • New York • San Diego • San Francisco
Boston • New Haven, Conn. • Waterville, Maine
London • Munich

Political Theories for Students

Staff

Editors: Jaime E. Noce and Matthew Miskelly.

Contributing Editors: Kathleen E. Maki-Potts, Rebecca Marlow-Ferguson, Christine Maurer, Jeff Sumner.

Managing Editor, Content: Erin E. Braun.

Managing Editor, Product: Amanda C. Quick.

Technical Specialist: Paul Lewon.

Permissions: Maria Franklin, *Permissions Manager.* Margaret Chamberlain, *Permissions Specialist.*

Manufacturing and Composition: Mary Beth Trimper, *Manager, Composition and Electronic Prepress.* Evi Seoud, *Assistant Manager, Composition Purchasing and Electronic Prepress.* Rhonda Williams, *Buyer.*

Imaging and Multimedia Content: Barbara Yarrow, *Manager.* Randy Bassett, *Imaging Supervisor.* Kelly A. Quin, *Image Editor.*

Product Design: Cynthia Baldwin, *Manager.* Pamela A.E. Galbreath, *Senior Art Director.*

Copyright Notice

Table of Contents

Advisors and Contributors

Advisors

The contents of Political Theories for Students *were devised in cooperation with the following individuals who were consulted based on their awareness of student social studies needs.*

Chris Ford: Teacher, Northville High School, Northville, Michigan.

Christine Godin: Librarian, Northwest Vista College, San Antonio, Texas.

Contributors

The following writers are the primary contributors to *Political Theories for Students.*

Bob Catley: Professor, School of Business, Northern Territory University, Darwin, Australia. Contributed the entries on Imperialism, Liberalism, and Socialism.

Barbara Lakeberg Dridi: Ph.D.; Political scientist and educator. Founder and Director, Concordia International Research. Philadelphia, Pennsylvania. Contributed the entry on Nationalism.

Alison Graham: Freelance journalist. Evanston, Illinois. Contributed the entries on Capitalism, Communism, and Marxism.

Lauri R. Harding: Attorney and freelance writer. Melbourne, Kentucky. Contributed the entry on Conservatism.

John Higgins: Freelance writer specializing in fields of psychology, social issues, and politics. Kirkfieldbank, Scotland. Contributed the entry on Fascism.

Jonathan Marks: Ph.D.; Visiting Assistant Professor, Political Theory and Constitutional Democracy, James Madison College, Michigan State University, East Lansing, Michigan. Contributed the entry on Republicanism.

Amy H. Sturgis: Ph.D.; Editor in Chief, *Humane Studies Review*, Institute for Humane Studies. Lebanon, Tennessee. Contributed the entries on Anarchism, Federalism, Feudalism, Libertarianism, Populism, and Utopianism.

John C. Yoder: Ph.D; Professor, Comparative Politics and Peace Studies, Politics and History Department, Whitworth College, Spokane, Washington. Contributed the entries on Pacifism, Patron–Client Systems, and Totalitarianism.

Introduction

Political Theories for Students has been designed to provide in depth information about political theories and systems in use throughout the world, both in past and present times. While the book was designed to fulfill specific curricular needs and meet curriculum standards for high school and undergraduate college students and their teachers, it also serves the needs of the general reader and researcher. Nineteen theories and systems are presented in comprehensive essays that provide an overview of the theory or system, its historical context, analysis and critical response, and examples of the theory or system in action, as well as information about significant people whose ideas or actions contributed to the development or refinement of the system. Each essay includes supplementary sidebars, which include biographical information about major individuals involved with a theory or system, significant writings attached to the theory, and a chronology of key dates. Potential study questions and research topics, in addition to bibliographic citations and suggested further readings, guide readers to relevant subjects and other helpful research materials.

The list of topics for *Political Theories for Students* was selected by teachers and librarians regarding student research needs in their studies of political systems and government. Additionally, the editors accounted for the curriculum standards in place for high school social studies in compiling the required content for each essay. The nineteen theories presented in *PTfS* include the most–studied individuals, philosophies, and thoughts connected with post and present day systems and governments. Where appropriate,

theories and systems that are closely related or that are rooted in another theory have been combined in one essay.

How Each Essay is Organized

Each essay contains the following elements:

- **At a Glance:** Essays begin with key factual information in a "question and answer" format, found at the start of the Overview section. This allows the reader to quickly answer fundamental questions such as who controls the government, the powers held by the people, and major figures associated with the theory or system.

- **Overview:** This section provides a brief and general description of the theory.

- **History:** This section describes the background and history of the theory, including its origins and evolution, its main tenets and individuals associated with its development and practice, and a discussion of places and periods where it has been used in government.

- **Theory in Depth:** This section outlines the philosophy of a theory and expands discussion of its main tenets with examples and explanations. It describes the political system's general view on such topics as economics, civil liberties, and the military.

- **Theory in Action:** This section describes the application of the theory in countries throughout the world and explains its effect. Examples and details about ruling bodies and individuals, political parties and factions, and elections, compare and contrast the theory's use in different parts of the world. Additionally, this section includes perspectives from economic, humanitarian, and social points of view, as well as scope of the theory's impact.

- **Analysis and Critical Response:** This section analyzes the theory's strengths and weaknesses and offers insight as to its success or failure. The critical response presents reaction from political leaders and historians.

- **Topics for Further Study:** This section suggests related research topics and invites readers to expand upon ideas presented within the essay.

- **Bibliography:** This section lists sources consulted and cited within the essay, as well as suggested further readings and sources for additional information.

- Cross–references to related essays are found at the end of each essay.

In addition, essays in *PTfS* contain one or more of the following supplementary sidebars:

- **Chronology:** This sidebar lists major dates and events associated with a theory.

- **Biography:** This sidebar provides biographical and career details about an individual whose role was pivotal in developing the theory, producing major writings or ideas on the theory, or instituting the theory into practice.

- **Major Writings:** This sidebar describes major works connected with the theory, and outlines their contents, creation, purpose, and impact.

Additional Features

Political Theories for Students provides the following tools to assist the reader in understanding ideas and terminology, and to compare and contrast the nineteen theories and systems that are presented:

- **Comparison Table of Political Theories:** The table serves as a one–stop comparison tool to identify differences and similarities among the major theories and systems. It is organized by theory and graphically presents the information found in the *At a Glance* section

- **Glossary:** The glossary contains 125 terms used throughout the essays.

Comments and Suggestions

The editors of *Political Theories for Students* welcome your comments and ideas. Please contact the editors at:

Editor, *Political Theories for Students*

Gale

27500 Drake Rd.

Farmington Hills, MI 48331

Telephone: (248) 699-4253

Toll-Free: (800) 347-4253

Fax: (248) 699-8052

Comparison Table of Political Theories

The purpose of the Comparison Table is to allow for comparison and contrast of the political theories and systems presented in *Political Theories for Students*.

The Table details the following information about each system or theory:

Who controls government?

How is government put into power?

What roles do the people have?

Who controls production of goods?

Who controls distribution of goods?

Major figures

Historical example

Political Theory	Who controls government?	How is government put into power?	What roles do the people have?
Anarchism	No government, the people rule	Not applicable	Keep informed; challenge any authority
Capitalism	Elected officials	Elected by the masses	Sustain the free market
Communism	The state	Revolution	Work for state's benefit
Conservatism	Elected officials, with some appointed	Popular vote of the majority	Vote for representatives
Fascism	Dictator	Overthrow or revolution	Not interfere with the state
Federalism	Elected officials, majority of power in national leaders	Popular vote of the majority	Vote for representatives
Feudalism	Nobility	Birth; feudal contract	Work for nobles' benefit
Imperialism	Nation–state	Conquest	Provide military and labor services
Liberalism	Individuals supported by the people	Popular vote of the majority	Vote; Bring about social change
Libertarianism	Restricted officials	Group dissatisfied with previous powers	Enjoy rights while not infringing on others
Marxism	Society	Revolution	Work for all individuals
Nationalism	State officials	Crisis situation	Support the nation
Pacifism	Officials supported by the people	Peaceful removal of unjust regime	Protest peacefully unjust laws or actions
Patron–Client Systems	Wealthy officials	Overthrow or fall of previous regime	Obey leader
Populism	Elected officials	Elected by popular vote	Pressure big business if unfair or unethical
Republicanism	Elected officials, majority of power in state leaders	Popular vote of the majority	Vote; serve the state in a crisis
Socialism	Society	Revolution or evolution of other theories	Share capital and means of production
Totalitarianism	Dictator	Overthrow or Revolution	Devote life to dictator and the state
Utopianism	State supported by the people	Cooperative founded by dissatisfied group	Tolerate differences; conform if needed

Who controls production of goods?	Who controls distribution of goods?	Major figures	Historical example
The people	The people	Emma Goldman; Mikhail Bukunin	Anti–globalization movement of late 1990s
Owners of capital	Owners of capital	Adam Smith; John Locke	United States
The state	The state	Joseph Stalin; Mao Tse–tung	China, 1949–present
The owners of capital	The owners of capital	Edmund Burke; Ronald Reagan	Great Britain in the 1980s
The state	The state	Benito Mussolini; Adolf Hitler	Italy, 1922–1943
The market	The market	James Madison; Alexander Hamilton	United States
Nobility	Nobility	William the Conqueror; Eleanor of Aquitaine	Medieval England
Nation–state	Nation–state	Genghis Khan; Hernán Cortés	Mongol Empire, 1206–1368
Private citizens	Private citizens	John Stuart Mill; William Gladstone	Great Britain, 1870–1900
Private individuals	Private individuals	Ayn Rand; Russell Means	Austrian School of Economics
The people	The people	Karl Marx; Vladimir Lenin	Soviet Union, 1917–1924
Owners of capital	Owners of capital	Ernest Renan; Johann Gottfried Herder	Republic of Turkey, 1923–present
The people	The people	Mohandas Gandhi; Martin Luther King Jr.	U.S. civil rights movement in 1960s
Government and wealthy businesspeople	Government and wealthy businesspeople	Pope Adrian IV; Juan Perón	Zaire, 1965–1997
The people	The people	William Jennings Bryan; George Wallace	People's Party in U.S. South in the 1890s
The owners of capital	The owners of capital	Niccolò Machiavelli; John Jay	Ancient Sparta
Society	Society	Pierre–Joseph Proudhon; Julius Nyerere	Tanzania, 1964–1985
The state	The state	Friedrich Nietzsche; Adolf Hitler	Egypt, 1952–present
The people, managed by state	The people, managed by state	Sir Thomas More; Robert Owen	The Farm

Anarchism

WHO CONTROLS GOVERNMENT? No government, the people rule

HOW IS GOVERNMENT PUT INTO POWER? Not applicable

WHAT ROLES DO THE PEOPLE HAVE? Keep informed; challenge any authority

WHO CONTROLS PRODUCTION OF GOODS? The people

WHO CONTROLS DISTRIBUTION OF GOODS? The people

MAJOR FIGURES Emma Goldman; Mikhail Bukunin

HISTORICAL EXAMPLE Anti–globalization movement of late 1990s

OVERVIEW

The political theory of anarchism revolves around the ideal of noncoercion. Born with the rise of the nation-states in the eighteenth century, anarchism has developed four major strains including muualism, anarcho-individualism, anarcho-socialism, and anarcho–communism. In the late twentieth century, anarchism has been adapted to the student, women's, and environmentalist movements, among others. Anarchism has spawned experimental communities, peaceful protest, violent rebellion, and a wide and varied literature dedicated to the achievement of human liberty.

HISTORY

Popular use of the term "anarchy" tends to portray an image of chaos, of bombs and fires and looting, of crisis overtaking order. Hollywood dystopias and fringe rock bands have played into this stereotype with glee. Although some anarchists desired political revolution over political reform, many advocated peace. Equating anarchy with chaos obscures a rich and serious tradition of political thought and the subtle variations that have evolved from it.

The ideas of anarchism began in the distant past. When Plato (428–348 B.C.) wrote his *Republic* in the fourth century B.C., he advocated a centralized government coordinating a communist society; his fellow

CHRONOLOGY:

1793: William Godwin's *Enquiry Concerning Political Justice* is published.

1840: *What Is Property?* by Pierre–Joseph Proudhon appears.

1843: Phalanx, New Jersey, becomes the first Fourierist experimental community.

1852: Josiah Warren's *Practical Details in Equitable Commerce* appears.

1879: Peter Kropotkin founds the journal *Le Réolté* in Switzerland.

1881: Benjamin Tucker founds the newspaper *Liberty, Not the Daughter but the Mother of Order.*

1882: Mikhail Bakunin's *God and the State* is published.

1923: Emma Goldman's *My Further Disillusionment with Russia* appears.

1927: Nicola Sacco and Bartolomeo Vanzetti are executed in the United States.

1973: *For A New Liberty* by Murray Rothbard appears.

1982: Murray Bookchin's *Ecology of Freedom* is completed.

William Godwin. (The Library of Congress)

Greek philosopher Zeno (c. 335–c. 263 B.C.), founder of the Stoa school, responded by championing a stateless society as the ideal way for humans to live together. The absence of government described by Zeno might be called one of the earliest articulations of anarchism. This theme found repetition among different peoples and eras for centuries.

A later precursor to anarchism developed after the English Civil War in the form of the Digger Movement. The founder of this dissenting group was Gerrard Winstanley (c. 1609–1660), an unorthodox Christian who identified God with reason. In his 1649 pamphlet *Truth Lifting Up Its Head Above Scandals*, Winstanley proposed principles for the Diggers, principles that later served as foundational assumptions for many anarchists. He noted the following: power corrupts, property hinders freedom, authority and property cause crime, and freedom requires the opportunity for people to live without laws or rulers according to their own consciences. He and his followers also taught nonviolent activism. In 1649, they occupied an English hillside, created a communist community there, and offered passive resistance to local landlords. Although local opposition eventually crushed the movement and forced Winstanley into obscurity, the Diggers provided a direct antecedent to later anarchist thought and practice.

The term "anarchy" was not used to describe the nonexistence of governmental coercion until 1703, however, when the French traveler Louis Armand de Lahontan (1666–1715) in his book *New Voyages in North America* described Native American societies that functioned without a state apparatus. He noted that they lived without governments or codified laws: in other words, "in anarchy." Thus the modern sense of the term was born.

William Godwin

Anarchism as a political theory and movement appeared in the late eighteenth century and paralleled the rise of nationalism tied to the era of great nation–states. The British philosopher and novelist William Godwin (1756–1836) offered the first systematic treatment of anarchist thought in his 1793 work *An Enquiry Concerning Political Justice and its Influence on General Virtue and Happiness*. In this book he argued that humans were evolving toward increasing perfection, but institutions such as the government hindered individuals' use of reason. By removing such hindrances as the state, enlightened and educated people could live peacefully in small, cooperative communities and devote themselves to self–betterment. Godwin's work found resonance in the political theory community. It also influenced the literary establishment; Godwin's daughter by the feminist leader Mary Wollstonecraft (1759–1797) was Mary Shelley (1797–1851), author of *Frankenstein* and wife of Romantic poet Percy Bysshe Shelley (1792–1822). Percy Shelley adopted Godwin's theme in his own work and gave anarchism an influential, poetic voice.

Godwin's concept of small, cooperative communities thriving in the absence of government control inspired French theorist Charles Fourier (1772–1837). Many of his concerns about the coercion, mechanization, dehumanization, and class schism of society previewed concerns later raised by critics of the Industrial Revolution. His belief in channeling humans' natural passions to achieve social harmony, and the practical means he suggested for achieving it, became known as Fourierism.

Fourierism

Unlike other collectivists of the era, who believed the state needed to own the means of production in the economy, Fourier called for anti–authoritarian socialism based on private property ownership and individual needs and desire. He simply wanted a well–ordered agricultural society, one based on cooperation and gender equality. Fourier devised with almost mathematical precision his plan for achieving harmony: the phalanx, an economic unit of 1,620 people who divided labor among themselves according to ability. He wrote and spoke about his blueprint for utopia, and followers and newspapers responded enthusiastically. Unfortunately, Fourier did not live to see his ideas applied in concrete settings. After his death in 1837, adherents such as Albert Brisbane (1809–1890) and Horace Greeley (1811–1872) transplanted Fourierism to the United States and in 1843 founded Phalanx, New Jersey, the first of almost thirty experimental communities based on Fourier's vision. Christian, but nonsectarian, these colonies organized themselves as cooperatives with equalized wages and supported themselves by the work of members and funds from non–resident stockholders. The communities encouraged traditional values such as monogamy and family, but also encouraged gender equality: several directors or presidents of Fourierist communities, in fact, were women.

BIOGRAPHY
William Godwin

The English William Godwin originally studied to be a minister but, after several years of practicing the profession, left his preaching due to religious doubts and set out to be a writer. During his day he was known as much for his personal life as for his political views. He was married to Mary Wollstonecraft, a political theorist in her own right, and also an early activist for women's rights. She died in childbirth in 1801; the child she bore grew up to be Mary Wollstonecraft Shelley, author of the 1818 horror classic *Frankenstein*. The daughter Mary tested her father's liberal views when she fell in love and ran away with Percy Bysshe Shelley, the Romantic poet, who at the time was a married man. The couple was ostracized due to their scandalous behavior. After his wife's suicide, Shelley married Mary, however, and the scandal quieted. Shelley credited his father–in–law with opening his eyes to anarchism; in turn, Godwin's influence gained entrance into the world of poetry and literature.

Godwin's *Enquiry Concerning Political Justice* (1793) explored his belief that humans were rational creatures and, through reason, could live together in peace without the need for institutions such as the law and the state. He asserted that humans were perfectible, and any mistakes they made could be traced to mistaken beliefs. With proper information backing true beliefs, he continued, humans would better and eventually perfect themselves. He criticized the state and other coercive institutions for keeping citizens ignorant and thereby denying them the opportunity to become more than what they are. His novels such as *Adventures of Caleb Williams* (1794), *St. Leon* (1799), and *Fleetwood* (1805) illustrated his political views and moral theory. Godwin died in London in 1836. His works remain the first comprehensive articulation of anarchism.

The best symbol of Fourierism was Brook Farm, an experimental community in West Roxbury, Massachusetts. The community began in 1841 as a Unitarian venture but converted to a Fourierist phalanx in 1844. Brook Farm gained international celebrity status thanks to its membership, which included some of the era's intellectual elite, including Nathaniel Hawthorne, Ralph Waldo Emerson, Margaret Fuller (1810–1850), and Orestes Brownson (1803–1876). The Fourierist newspaper *Harbinger* began publication at Brook Farm as well. After the central building was destroyed by fire, the colony fell into economic hardship and eventually disbanded. Its fame lived on, however, in the works and lives of its former members. Though certainly not the only attempts to create utopia through experimental communities, Fourierism did represent one of the earliest and most successful attempts at implementing the kind of non–coercive framework Godwin advocated.

Pierre–Joseph Proudhon

After Godwin's theory and Fourier's practice, the next dramatic step in the story of anarchism appeared with the French journalist Pierre–Joseph Proudhon (1809–1865).

The Frenchman Proudhon was haunted by the spectre of poverty all of his life. Born to a poor family, Proudhon worked hard to obtain scholarships in order to continue his education, but eventually was forced to abandon them in order to work. His later life found him once again with little income or economic opportunities. His experience with financial hardship helped to form his view of property as an exploitative system. He first gained public recognition writing about the abuses inherent in the institution of property and his anarchist solutions to these inequalities in the 1840 work *What Is Property?* He followed this publication with many other works, the highlights among which are *System of Economic Contradictions; or The Philosophy of Poverty* (1846), *General Idea of Revolution in the Nineteenth Century* (1851), and the three–volume *Of Justice in the Revolution and the Church* (1858). In his writings he gave the words anarchy and anarchist their modern meaning and opened the door for an identifiable anarchist movement across the West.

Proudhon's activism began as a vocal member of the Constituent Assembly in France, in which he voted against a constitution for the simple fact that it was a constitution. His 1840 *What Is Property?* used the term "anarchy" to mean the absence of sovereignty and "anarchist" to mean one who advocates anarchy. His later works further explored the subject. Proudhon made waves with his attack on the state in general and representative democracy in particular. To replace these systems, he advocated the cooperation of industrial and agricultural communities and the commercial use of labor checks instead of money; labor checks, he explained, would represent how much labor went into the

production of a given product, and thus would assure that the exchange rate of products would be determined by the labor they represent, to the benefit of the workers. He termed this cooperative system with its corresponding labor theory of value "mutualism."

Mutualism

After the Revolution of 1848 in France, Proudhon, who had worked his way up to the editorship of a successful newspaper, was elected to the Constituent Assembly. He sensed an historic opportunity to make changes on behalf of the workers, and therefore proposed establishing a national bank to reorganize the credit system to liberate and empower the working class. His efforts failed. He went on to think outside of the French system and imagine a replacement, one with loosely federated communities uniting by free choice around certain common assumptions about the labor theory of value and the endeavor to reach common societal goals. His work criticized legal government's centralization of authority in officials and fixed, general rules that discouraged individual judgments and broke down communal ties—in short, stunting individuals' growth and their opportunity to cooperate with others for mutual benefit. He is best known as the father of mutualism, the variety of anarchism in between individualism's reliance on private property and collectivism's wariness of it.

Proudhon's mutualist anarchy, with its focus on laboring classes and their emancipation from economic coercion, contrasted with another contemporary version of anarchism, individualism. Individualist anarchists emphasized the emancipation of the individual from the political coercion of the state. Two pioneers of this variation of anarchism included Max Stirner (1806–1856) and Benjamin R. Tucker (1854–1939). The German philosopher Stirner came to the conclusion that the state should not exist because it deprives individuals of the qualities that make them unique. Any time people are treated as collectives rather than different individuals, he argued, violence is done against them. In order to rule, the state requires servants who obey. Without this obedience, people become individuals and the state ceases to exist. In his 1844 work *The Ego and his Own*, Stirner set out his views on individuality, collectivity, the will of the state, and the way in which individuals could break free of submission and thus rid themselves of the institutions of coercion such as the state.

Anarchism in the United States

Anarchism crossed the ocean in the nineteenth century and came to the United States in the persons

BIOGRAPHY

Lysander Spooner

Lysander Spooner was a reformer by nature. Born in Athol, Massachusetts in 1808, Spooner worked on his father's farm until the age of twenty–five. He then began to study law under two prominent Massachusetts jurists, John Davis and Charles A. Allen. When he learned that the law required non–college–educated candidates to the bar to study law for an extra three years above what was required for university students, he campaigned against the statute and ultimately achieved its repeal. As a young lawyer, he took part in the free thought campaign of the times and wrote a popular tract against religious orthodoxy, *The Deist's Reply to the Alleged Supernatural Evidences of Christianity* (1836).

Spooner's greatest contribution to anarcho–individualist thought was his critique of the U.S. Constitution—and, by implication, all constitutions—as a mechanism of special privileges through which minority groups could exploit others. After the U.S. financial panic of 1837, Spooner observed how political and governmental bodies inserted themselves into private banking through complicated restrictions and legal escape mechanisms. His 1843 work *Constitutional Law Relative to Credit, Currency and Banking*

offered a lasting addition to free banking literature and the anarchist cause. His interest in individual liberty also led him to oppose slavery and write for the abolitionist cause.

He attacked the U.S. government's monopoly on the mail system by noting that the Constitution did not provide the state the sole and exclusive right to establish postal service for the nation. He viewed it not only as a financial evil, but a moral one as well, noting the power it gave the state to be the only conduit for information. Spooner then established a competing business in 1844, the American Letter Mail Company, which promptly proved it could deliver mail faster at a lesser cost. In 1845, a congressional act imposed heavy penalties for independent mail companies and Spooner was forced to close his doors. Spooner continued to publish books and pamphlets prolifically on a number of topics, as well as contribute articles to Benjamin Tucker's anarchist newspaper *Liberty*. Until his death, his writings on an expansive number of issues and his activism in concert with his publishing ventures made Spooner one of the most important anarcho–individualists in history.

---

of Josiah Warren (1798?–1874), Lysander Spooner (1808–1887), and Benjamin R. Tucker (1854–1939). Warren had followed the socialist utopian teachings of Robert Owen (1771–1858), but soon became convinced of what he called "the sovereignty of the individual" against the claims of the group. Like Godwin before him, Warren believed that products should be valued by the amount of labor it took to produce them. Based on this conviction, Warren opened several so–called "equity stores" where goods could be exchanged based on the labor they required to produce. Cost, in effect, served as the limit of price. His efforts led him to found several experimental colonies based on his anarchist principles, including the highly visible Modern Times, which endured on Coney Island, New York from 1851 until approximately 1860. He published his views on anarchist theory and practice in his 1852 *Practical Details in Equitable Commerce*, his 1863 *True Civilization*, and other works.

Lysander Spooner Lysander Spooner, like Warren, was both an activist and a political philosopher. A critic of the U.S. system and its legislative process, Spooner believed the Constitution created opportunities for minority groups to exploit others through the use of special privileges. His training and practice as an attorney afforded him the tools to dissect the finer points of statutes. In 1843, he warned that artificial restrictions were closing the door to private, competitive credit in *Constitutional Law Relative to Credit, Currency and Banking*, which influenced the free banking movement in the United States for decades. He noted that acts of incorporation helped individuals to escape their contractual obligations by hiding behind the fictional face of a corporation. When Spooner formed the American Letter Mail Company in 1844 to compete with the U.S. Post Office, he proved that a private company could deliver mail faster and at a lower price than could a government monopoly—and the United States promptly outlawed his venture. His two–part *The Unconstitutionality of Slavery* in 1845 and 1846, among his many other publications, explored his understanding of natural law, justice, and government, and set the stage for his criticisms of the institutions of majority rule. His pamphlet series *No Treason* and 1882's *Natural Law* further cemented him as a giant of American anarchism.

Benjamin Tucker American journalist Benjamin R. Tucker drew inspiration from Josiah Warren's "sovereignty of the individual" idea and in turn led a publishing venture that supported and galvanized a flourishing anarchist movement in the United States. Tucker's individualist anarchist newspaper *Liberty, Not the Daughter but the Mother of Order*, with its title taken from a quote from Pierre–Joseph Proudhon, ran from 1881 to 1908. As editor, Tucker wrote for the paper, but he also published the work of Lysander Spooner, Victor Yarros, J. William Lloyd, Vilfredo Pareto (1848–1923), and many others. Diverse and visible readers such as Walt Whitman (1819–1892), George Bernard Shaw (1856–1950), and H. L. Mencken (1880–1956) praised *Liberty* for providing a quality forum for American radicalism. The paper served to unify American individualists and had a great impact on U.S. libertarianism through the twentieth century. Due to its popularity and longevity, *Liberty* remains one of the most thorough and wide-ranging collections of individualist anarchist writing in existence.

Russia

The nineteenth century also brought anarchism to Russia. Mikhail Bakunin (1814–1876) helped to take anarchist thought from the theory books to the street. He prized human freedom and dismissed its enemies, which he believed included the state—even when it appeared as a representation of the people—and all forms of religion. He predicted that the future of Europe included increasing state powers and economic monopoly unless someone took action. Bakunin tried; he advocated revolution and organized secret societies under the conviction that a few people could change the system and liberate all individuals. His goal was to create a society arranged from the bottom up through collective, social property; he opposed the centralized state necessary for the implementation of communism, however, and instead supported free association. His theories put him in direct opposition to another revolutionary thinker, Karl Marx, and inspired socialist movements in France, Italy, Switzerland, and, most notably, Spain, where it impacted the country's civil war in the late 1930s.

Peter Kropotkin Unlike Bakunin, fellow Russian Peter Kropotkin (1842–1921) was an anarcho–communist who believed in the coordination of industry and agriculture; like Bakunin, he feared the power of the centralized state, and so he believed that small communities should control their economies. Kropotkin's main interest rested in finding a scientific justification for anarchism. His 1902 *Mutual Aid: A Factor of Evolution* challenged Charles Darwin's (1809–1882) assumptions about evolution and suggested that mutual aid played as important a role in society as the struggle for survival. He saw cooperation as a fundamental aspect of human nature, and expected that any process of self–realization would lead an individual not to isolation, but to greater harmony and solidarity with others. Kropotkin was not impressed with the final result of the Russian Revolution of 1917 and criticized the fact that power continued to be centralized in an impersonal authority, the party dictatorship, rather than in the councils of the workers, peasants, and communities. Kropotkin's voice brought anarchism into the twentieth century.

For a short time at the turn of the century, a phenomenon known as anarcho–syndicalism existed. Based on the French *syndicat*, or union, the idea was to infuse the movement with stabilizing organization by infiltrating the union system and taking over its infrastructure. The most successful example of anarcho–syndicalism was Fernand Pelloutier's *Fédération des Bourses du Travail*. These French labor exchanges provided workers the opportunities to seek jobs and, at the same time, receive anarchist propoganda. Beginning in about 1895, this had great success in moving anarchism in a positive direction. The French model inspired similar organizations in Spain and elsewhere. By the time of World War I, however, this movement began its decline everywhere but Spain, where it played a key role in that country's civil war.

Germany

In Germany, Gustav Landauer, a generation younger than Kropotkin, felt the impact of the German School of Romanticism as embodied in figures such as Arthur Schopenhauer (1788–1860), Friedrich Nietzsche (1844–1900), and Henrik Ibsen (1828–1906). Landauer's contribution to anarchism was the blending of Romantic sensibilities with anarchist politics. He was fascinated by the notion of the human psyche resting beneath consciousness, and he prioritized the spiritual need for rootedness and community that pulled individuals together. He believed the society of the times—cold, mechanical, industrialized, impersonalized, and centralized—could not replace the relationships that had been lost, and he called for an uprising to replace the authoritarian state with the wholeness of folk community. The revolution he supported was not a violent cause of politics, however, but an internal change of attitude, a rebirth within individuals. In his words: "The state is a condition, a certain relationship between human beings, a mode of human behavior; we destroy it by contracting other relationships, by behaving differently." Landauer did participate briefly in the Bavarian Revolution of 1917–1919, but later in 1919 was stoned to death by state troops in Munich.

Emma Goldman

Emma Goldman's (1869–1940) activist anarchism is more difficult to assign to a specific country. A native of Lithuania, Goldman immigrated to the United States in 1886 and was deported to Russia in 1919. She took part in the Spanish Civil War in 1936 and died in Canada in 1940. This woman of the world is best known for introducing feminism to the anarchist tradition. Her controversial views included promoting birth control and obstructing the draft. Together with Alexander Berkman (1870–1936), Goldman published the short–lived but highly visible anarchist paper *Mother Earth*. Goldman based her activism on Kropotokin's anarcho–communism but admitted that the theory might be less than successful in actual practice. This did not dissuade Goldman, however, from her attacks on the concentration of political and economic power. She urged women in particular not to be satisfied with a vote that meant little in a system stacked against the individual. In the process, her controversial and public protest brought new sensibilities to the movement.

Sacco and Vanzetti

Often when anarchism is discussed, Nicola Sacco (1891–1927) and Bartolomeo Vanzetti (1888–1927) are the first names mentioned. The seven–year trial of Sacco and Vanzetti was perhaps the most famous trial in U.S. history; it certainly was the most famous trial of the first half of the twentieth century. One of the keys to the emotions and politics surrounding the case rested in the fact that both Sacco and Vanzetti were anarchists.

Both Sacco and Vanzetti were Italian emigrants who came to the United States to practice their trades. Sacco was a shoemaker and Vanzetti was a fishmonger. Both became involved with the American anarchist movement and avoided the draft for World War I. On April 15, 1920, in Braintree, Massachusetts, a shoe company's paymaster and his guard were shot and killed by two men who stole over $15,000 from their victims' company. Local police investigated and linked a car with the crime. When Sacco, Vanzetti, and two others arrived at the garage to claim the car, the police arrested them and charged them with the crime.

The case seemed problematic: Sacco and Vanzetti were armed when arrested, but neither had a criminal record and no sign of the stolen money could be traced to them. Sentiment against such so–called "radicals" as anarchists ran high, however, and circumstantial evidence—much of which was later discredited—mounted against Sacco and Vanzetti. The trial received further controversy due to the conduct of Judge Webster Thayer. Nonetheless, the Massachusetts State Supreme Court stood behind the conviction of Sacco and Vanzetti and the governor chose not to pardon them. Despite worldwide sympathy demonstrations and political protests, Sacco and Vanzetti were executed on August 22, 1927. Their true guilt or innocence remains uncertain. Their death made them anarchist martyrs, however, and their story was translated into songs such as Joan Baez's "The Ballad of Sacco and Vanzetti" (an anthem of the 1960s U.S. counterculture), plays such as Maxwell Anderson's *Gods of the Lightning*, novels such as Upton Sinclair's *Boston*, and poems such as the sonnets of Edna St. Vincent Millay.

The Twentieth Century

The twentieth century brought feminist and environmental variations on the anarchist theme, among others. Longer–lived strains such as individualist anarchism also gained a second wind. Murray Rothbard (1926–1995) was one of the theorists who brought individualist anarchism to public attention in the late twentieth century. Rothbard came of age intellectually in the Austrian School of Economics, which was pioneered by Carl von Menger (1840–1921) and Ludwig von Mises (1881–1973) in the late nineteenth and early twentieth century. He took that school's emphasis on human unpredictability and spontaneous order, as well as its condemnation of centralized planning, and followed it to an anarchist conclusion. Believing that all state intervention is not only disastrous but also based on unconscionable force, Rothbard produced such works of theory as *Man, Economy and State* (1962), *Power and the Market* (1970), *For A New Liberty* (1973), and *Ethics of Liberty* (1982). His work brought him great prominence in the emerging American Libertarian Movement before his death in 1995.

From its roots in ancient times through its development in France, England, and the United States, as well as its relationship with revolts such as the Russian Revolution and Spanish Civil War, anarchism has been a theory of many manifestations. As a coherent movement, however, anarchism is relatively young, which has meant that theorists and activists have influenced each other significantly, even when writing or working in other countries and situations. As new concerns such as environmentalism confront individuals, the tradition evolves to encompass new voices and positions. Despite the movement's adaptability, the repudiation of coercion holds all of anarchism's diverse strains together across the years and miles.

THEORY IN DEPTH

Anarchist theorists have covered the spectrum from those who believed property is theft to those who believed property is an inalienable natural right, from those who wished to stir revolution to those who embraced pacifism. Others incorporated the agendas of other movements: anarcho–feminism appeared in hand with the women's suffrage movement, and anarcho–environmentalism emerged with the Green Movement. At its core, all strains of anarchism deal with the question of how to eliminate coercion. The four principle divisions of anarchist theory that sprang up in answer to this question were individualism, mutualism, socialism, and communism.

Godwin and Noncoercion

The first systematic exploration of the anarchist theme of noncoercion appeared in William Godwin's 1793 English work *An Enquiry Concerning Political Justice and its Influence on General Virtue and Happiness.* Any examination of anarchism must begin there. The former minister set out his vision of the ideal community and explained that its existence implied the dissolution of government. Godwin's vision of societies based on consent, cooperating with one another, and working and sharing the wealth equally, sounded almost utopian. With the members in agreement, no external state or mechanism of law would be necessary:

> Government can have no more than two legitimate purposes, the suppression of injustice against individuals within the community, and the common defence against external invasion. The first of these purposes, which alone can have an uninterrupted claim upon us, is sufficiently answered, by an association of a jury, to decide upon the offences of individuals within the community, and upon the questions and controversies, respecting property, which may chance to arise.... But there will be no need of any express compact, and still less of any common center of authority, for this purpose. General justice, and mutual interest, are found more capable of binding men, than signatures and seals.... This is one of

the most memorable stages of human improvement. With what delight must every well informed friend of mankind look forward, to the auspicious period, the dissolution of political government, of that brute engine, which has been the only perennial cause of the vices of mankind...

Anarcho–individualism

Anarchist individualist theory begins with the individual as the building block of the world. Individualists believe that each person has rights—some would call these natural rights—that no other person or group of people can ever violate. These often include rights such as the individual's right to live, to control his or her body, and to speak his or her mind. Theorists in this tradition also believe that people have rights to certain actions around them, including the rights to be creative and to own what they have produced. If people are independent thinkers and producers, then, the main way individuals interact socially is through exchange—buying, selling, and/or trading—and contract, where two or more individuals agree to an action with reciprocal duties, responsibilities, and gains.

Warren's Vision

Josiah Warren's vision of anarcho–individualism may have been the first fully articulated version of the theory, but it was not indicative of the tradition as a whole for two reasons. First, Warren argued that the individual should follow his or her wishes only; other individualists recognized that religious, moral, and social rules might have a part to play in individuals' decision making. Second, Warren remained tied to the labor theory of value and its idea of using cost to determine just price for items.

Josiah Warren was concerned with the inequities and imbalances of power created by property ownership. In his 1852 book *Practical Details in Equitable Commerce,* he offered a different interpretation of legitimate property: individuals owned the products of their own labor. This eliminated more passive earnings such as rent on lands or interests on loans and leveled the playing field for individuals within the framework. Warren reiterated that his blueprint for a new system held individuality as its highest goal:

> I will not now delay to detail the reasonings which led to the conclusion that SOCIETY MUST BE SO RE-CONSTRUCTED AS TO PRESERVE the sovereignty of every individual inviolate. That it must avoid all combinations and connections of persons and interests, and all other arrangements, which will not leave every individual at all times at LIBERTY to dispose of his or her person, and time, and property, in any manner in which his or her feelings or judgement may dictate, WITHOUT INVOLVING THE PERSONS OF OTHERS.

There must be:

Individuality of Interests,

Individuality of Responsibilities,

Individuality in the deciding power; and, in one sense,

Individuality of action.

The idea of the sovereignty of each over his own property made it necessary to determine what is truly and legitimately one's property. The answer would seem to be, *the whole product or results of his own labor.*

Other individualists alternately ignored or refuted Warren's understanding of economics. Benjamin Tucker, Lysander Spooner, and Murray Rothbard better represent the consensus of anarchist individualist theory. Tucker, for example, put some restraints on a person's liberty. In his 1893 collection *Instead of A Book*, he explained that an individual should exercise the greatest possible amount of freedom that allows an equal amount of freedom to all other people.

Tucker's Liberty

Tucker remains best known for editing the anarchist newspaper *Liberty*, but he also wrote works independent of the publication. His 1888 book *State Socialism and Anarchism* demonstrates the breadth of the anarchists' attention; whereas Spooner was concerned with close legal readings of the Constitution, for example, Tucker explained how a broad belief in noncoercion might affect the most intimate relationships between adults and their families. Even the relationships that form the building blocks of society were liberated, according to Tucker, by anarchist theory:

In the manner of the maintenance and rearing of children, the Anarchists would neither institute the communistic nursery which the State Socialists favour, or keep the communistic school system which now prevails. The nurse and teacher, like the doctor and the preacher, must be selected voluntarily, and their services must be paid for by those who patronize them. Parental rights must not be taken away, and parental responsibilities must not be foisted on them. Even in so delicate a matter as that of the relation between the sexes the Anarchists do not shrink from the application of their principle. They acknowledge and defend the right of any man and woman, or any men and women, to love each other for as long or as short a time as they can, will, or may. To them legal marriage and legal divorce are equal absurdities. They look forward to the time when every individual, whether man or woman, shall be self–supporting, and when each shall have an independent home of his or her own, whether it be a separate house or rooms in a house with others: when the love relations between these independent individuals shall be as varied as are individual inclinations and attractions; and when the children born of these relations shall belong exclusively to the mothers until old enough to belong to themselves.

Spooner and the Constitution

Spooner's view of anarcho–individualism led him to celebrate private property as one of the natural rights of individuals. He explored contemporary authorities and questioned their legitimacy. One source of illegitimate power, the American believed, was the U.S. Constitution. He often explained that the Constitution was used by the few who were favored by its founders or who had discovered its loopholes in order to accumulate more power for themselves. In the sixth tract of his *No Treason* series, entitled "The Constitution of No Authority" and published in 1870, Spooner went further by pointing out that the Constitution as a contract was impotent, since the past generation could not bind future ones without their express consent. Since Spooner himself and his contemporaries had not agreed to the contract, he argued, it did not apply to them:

The Constitution has no inherent authority or obligation. It has no authority or obligation at all, unless as a contract between man and man. And it does not so much as even purport to be a contract between persons now existing. It purports, at most, to be only a contract between persons living eighty years ago. And it can be supposed to have been a contract only between persons who had already come to years of discretion, so as to be competent to make reasonable and obligatory contracts. Furthermore, we know, historically, that only a small portion even of the people then existing were consulted on the subject, or asked, or permitted to express either their consent or dissent in any formal manner. Those persons, if any, who did give their consent formally, are all dead now. Most of them have been dead forty, fifty, sixty, or seventy years. *And the Constitution, so far as it was their contract, died with them.* They had no natural power or right to make it obligatory upon their children.

All of the anarcho–individualists criticize monopolies, especially those created and upheld by the state, for wielding coercive power against individuals and limiting their decision–making capabilities. Despite some of the earlier individualists' sympathies with socialism, many later individualists have looked to the free market for models to follow. Since they support the expansive right of the individual to obtain and sell goods in the marketplace, some call themselves anarcho–capitalists rather than anarcho–individualists, thus focusing attention on the metaphor of the market as a key to their philosophy. These anarchist individualists often have taken part in the movement of libertarianism, which is based on similar claims of individual rights and distrust toward centralized state authority.

Mutualism and Pierre–Joseph Proudhon

Mutualism, the second version of anarchism, splits the difference between individualism on one side and socialism and communism on the other. Pierre–Joseph Proudhon coined the term to describe the economic system he devised. He did not do away with private property; instead, his model allowed individuals to own the tools of production. In the case of manufacturing, these tools might be the equipment used to make products. In the case of agriculture, these tools might be the land itself as well as the implements necessary to plant and harvest crops. Proudhon believed that individuals should only be rewarded for their labor, however. This eliminated rewards such as rent or profit and maintained a form of equality among all people regardless of what they owned.

Proudhon took Godwin's theory of noncoercion a step further. Where Godwin focused on consent, Proudhon asserted that there could be no consent while property, a great inequalizer and therefore oppressor, existed. He advocated changing the nature of private property and holding all goods in common. Proudhon was not a traditional communist, however. He believed that communism failed to recognize independence and proportionality, and without those balancing instincts the theory became tyrannical and unjust. He concluded that communism's focus on equality could be saved by infusing it with the individualism often provided by property: by mixing the two, he created mutualism. He described this combination in his 1840 work *What Is Property?*:

> Anarchy—the absence of a master, of a sovereign—such is the form of government to which we are every day approximating, and which our accustomed habit of taking man for our rule, and his will for law, leads us to regard as the height of disorder and the expression of chaos... Then, no government, no public economy, no administration, is possible, which is based on property. Communism seeks *equality* and *law*. Property, born of the sovereignty of reason, and the sense of personal merit, wishes above all things *independence* and *proportionality*. But communism, mistaking uniformity for law, and levelism for equality, becomes tyrannical and unjust. Property, by its despotism and encroachments, soon proves itself oppressive and anti–social. The objects of communism and property are good—their results are bad. And why? Because both are exclusive, and each disregards two elements of society. Communism rejects independence and proportionality; property does not satisfy equality and law. Now if we imagine a society based on these four principles—equality, law, independence, and proportionality... this third form of society, this synthesis of communism and property, we will call *liberty*.

Rather than bargaining for profit, as many did and do in the marketplace, Proudhon imagined individuals would bargain only for direct equivalents to what they were offering—he called this "ethical" exchange. As so often happened in anarchist thought, much of the implementation of his ideas required a different kind of

banking. Proudhon imagined a kind of mutual credit bank, a non–profit institution, which would lend money to producers at a rate of interest high enough to cover the bank's operational costs only. Although Proudhon's experiments did not succeed, his vision of mutualism continued to have currency in France for some time. Nonetheless, anarcho–mutualism became perhaps the shortest–lived of the various forms of anarchism.

Socialist Anarchism

Socialist anarchism did not make the same concessions to property as mutualism did, but it retained the sense of voluntary cooperation absent in the more coercive forms of state–centralized socialism experienced across the globe. Charles Fourier's experimental communities in the United States did allow some property ownership, and these small agricultural colonies fit the bill as attempts at socialist societies, complete with collective decision making and communal work for the community's maintenance and upkeep. Participation in such societies remained voluntary.

Mikhail Bakunin   Under Mikhail Bakunin, anarcho–socialism became the dominant form of anarchist thought, at least for a time. Bakunin and his compatriots had experienced too much centralized control and coercive force under the old Russian regime of the tsars—they did not wish to wield the same kind of control over individuals by forcing them into a socialist system. If, after the Russian Revolution of 1917, control could have been divided among community groups such as representatives of the workers and peasants, and these bodies could have devised collective governance led by free association, Bakunin and his contemporaries would have considered the rebellion a success. Instead, another form of government, Marxist communism, became just as coercive as the former had been.

Mikhail Bakunin represented the collectivist end of the anarchist spectrum. In his influential 1882 work *God and the State*, he questioned the nature of power and set out why universal authorities—whether they come from the government, the church, or other institutions—did not deserve submission. He relied on his reason to determine when he should be subordinate, and to whom. His dismissal of state, religion, and even family hierarchy fed anarchist rebellions across Europe:

> I bow before the authority of special men because it is imposed upon me by my own reason. I am conscious of my own inability to grasp, in all its detail, and positive developments, any very large portion of human knowledge. The greatest intelligence would not be equal to a comprehension of the whole. Thence results, for science

as well as for industry, the necessity of the division and association of labour. I receive and I give—such is human life. Each directs and is directed in his turn. Therefore there is no fixed and constant authority, but a continual exchange of mutual, temporary, and, above all, voluntary authority and subordination. This same reason forbids me, then, to recognize a fixed, constant and universal authority, because there is no universal man, no man capable of grasping in that wealth of detail, without which the application of science to life is impossible, all the sciences, all the branches of social life. And if such universality could ever be realized in a single man, and if he wished to take advantage thereof to impose his authority upon us, it would be necessary to drive this man out of society, because his authority would inevitably reduce all the others to slavery and imbecility.

Unlike the Russian variety of Marxist communism, anarcho–socialism, had it been instituted, would have been a voluntary system, because even communist anarchists believe in the rule of non–coercion. Peter Kropotkin, among others, argued for communities to hold resources in common instead of privately, so each member of the society could draw upon these resources according to his or her need. In such a system, Kropotkin believed, people would work without the need for material incentives to motivate them; moreover, without scarcity, crime would all but disappear and, with it, the need for centralized institutions such as the law. Workers would unify of their own free will to do work, and each community would determine what work was necessary for the good of all. Large infrastructure projects—roads, bridges, railroads—would evolve due to the voluntary cooperation of smaller communities working together for a common goal.

Anarcho–communism

Peter Kropotkin, a Russian like Bakunin, followed a scientific program to arrive at anarcho–communism. Despite his reasoned approach, however, he was also an inspirational and emotionally charged leader. This side of Kropotkin appeared most clearly in his 1895 work *The Commune of Paris*, in which he described the rise and fall of revolutionary protest and experimental communities in Paris. The work captured a snapshot of anarchism in action and the brutal force of the state used to combat and subdue it. By writing his book, Kropotkin helped to create and remember martyrs for the anarchist cause.

> The Commune of Paris, the child of a period of transition, born beneath the Prussian guns, was doomed to perish. But by its eminently popular character it began a new series of revolutions, by its ideas it was the forerunner of the social revolution. Its lesson has been learned, and when France once more bristles with communes in revolt, the people are not likely to give themselves a government and expect that government to ini-

BIOGRAPHY
Mikhail Bakunin

Mikhail Bakunin was a revolutionary. Although he was born into a wealthy family, he left the Russian aristocracy behind in order to push for new systems of government to replace the old. In 1848 and 1849 he participated in the revolutions in France and Saxony. When he was sent back to Russia, his home country exiled him to Siberia. He escaped in 1861 and went to London, where he met Russian revolutionary leader and writer Aleksandr Herzen (1812–1870). Herzen believed the peasant communes of the Russian countryside foretold a new socialist society soon to dawn on Russia. Bakunin was greatly influenced by Herzen. Bakunin articulated his own political views in the 1882 work *God and the State*. He argued that human nature was inherently good, and cooperative socialist anarchism, without the interference of the state, would allow people to better themselves. If it required revolution to overthrow the current system in favor of socialist anarchism, so be it. Bakunin devoted himself to the creation of secret societies for the purposes of future revolution, and experimented with their organization and makeup.

Bakunin's thought further solidified in contrast to the communism of Karl Marx. In 1864, the International Workingmen's Association, also known as the First International, formed in London in order to unite all workers for the achievement of political power. Both Marx and Bakunin imagined using the apparatus of the First International as a conduit for revolution, but each wanted something very different from a revolution. As a result, the association became a battleground between Marx's totalitarian communism and Bakunin's socialist anarchism. Eventually, the power struggle spelled the end to the group in 1876. The debate about the role of the state and the individual helped Bakunin to articulate his position, though it never appeared in any completely systematic kind of way. Interestingly enough, the debate also led to fame for Bakunin, who in the nineteenth century managed to offer an insightful and prophetic critique of the potential consequences of Marxist communism applied to the real world, foresight not proved correct until the twentieth century. Bakunin is best remembered as one of the most famous advocates for anarchists and the inspiration for numerous revolutions around the world.

BIOGRAPHY

Peter Kropotkin

Peter Kropotkin was born into the Russian nobility and even went into the service of Tsar Alexander II (1818–1881) as a young man. His travels away from court, especially in Siberia, helped to cement his views about the failures of centralized government. He traveled to Western Europe and then returned to Russia to join the radical Chaikovsky Circle political group; this association landed him in prison in 1874, but he escaped to Western Europe in 1876. He immediately joined the anarchist movement and founded the anarchist paper *Le Révolté*, for which he wrote articles outlining the foundational ideas of anarcho–communism. He was imprisoned for his political views again, this time in France in 1883, and after release he relocated to England. He wrote several works on anarcho–capitalist themes, including the well–known *Mutual Aid* (1897). He returned to Russia right before the revolution and died shortly thereafter; his funeral, in fact, was the last occasion at which opponents of the Bolshevik regime were allowed to demonstrate in public.

Unlike Bakunin, who devised secret cells with an eye toward revolution, Kropotkin believed his role was to discuss theory. He believed that the ideas he and others explained would take hold of the people and dovetail with their revolutionary tendencies almost spontaneously. He focused on exploring the basic tenets of anarchism in general and the specific case for anarcho–communism. Kropotkin had a scientific mind, and he looked to justify the political theory he advocated through scientific means. He challenged Darwin's assumption that the struggle for survival was the primary theme of society; instead, Kropotkin believed that cooperation, mutual aid, and social interaction formed just as strong an impulse in the human animal. He counted on this cooperative drive, in fact, to motivate people to produce once all property belonged to the commons and material incentives for work disappeared. Kropotkin's efforts cemented his place as the father of anarcho–communism.

tiate revolutionary measures. When they have rid themselves of the parasites who devour them, they will take possession of all social wealth to share according to the principles of anarchist communism. And when they have entirely abolished property, government, and the state, they will form themselves freely, according to the necessities indicated by life itself. Breaking its chains, overthrowing its idols, humanity will march onward to a better future, knowing neither masters nor slaves, keeping its veneration for the noble martyrs who bought with their blood and suffering those first attempts at emancipation which have enlightened our march toward the conquest of liberty. At the heart of the main opposition in the anarchist tradition, that between individualism and collectivism such as socialism and communism, rests a fundamental disagreement over the core of human nature. Individualists assume that the primary motivation that moves people to act is self–interest, and that people will naturally choose to interact with others when this interaction benefits them. When an impersonal mechanism such as the market exists, a number of individuals can act for their own self–interest and these decisions will form a natural harmony of interests that allows everyone to benefit. Collectivists assume that individuals are drawn to interact with each other naturally, and the desire for cooperation and fellowship is the primary motivation that moves people to act. Individualists hold that the state or any other institution or group should not coerce people because this coercion infringes on individual rights. Although most collectivists would agree with the notion of rights in some limited way, they would argue that coercion is wrong primarily because it interferes with the harmony of free association and the opportunities for cooperation.

Emma Goldman and the Russian Revolution

Just as Kropotkin captured his memories of Paris, Emma Goldman wrote of what she witnessed in Russia after the revolution. The United States deported Emma Goldman to Russia in 1919; she could only bear to stay for two years. Two years after she left, she published *My Further Disillusionment with Russia*. This critique of the revolution was all the more poignant for the fact that Goldman seemed to see an opportunity for greatness after the abdication of the tsar and the overthrow of the monarchy. Instead, she witnessed another kind of tyranny. Her warnings about the means of rebellion matching the ends of rebellion resonated in the anarchist movement and particularly were repeated in the 1960s and 1970s during the first phase of anarcho–feminism.

> Today is the parent of tomorrow. The present casts its shadow far into the future. That is the law of life, individual and social. Revolution that divests itself of ethical values thereby lays the foundation of injustice, deceit and oppression for the future society. The means used to *prepare* the future become its *cornerstone*. Witness the tragic condition of Russia. The methods of State centralization have paralysed individual initiative and ef-

Emma Goldman. (The Library of Congress)

fort; the tyranny of the dictatorship has cowed the people into slavish submission and all but extinguished the fires of liberty; organized terrorism has depraved and brutalized the masses and stifled every idealistic life, and all sense of dignity of man and the value of life has been eliminated; coercion at every step has made effort bitter, labour a punishment, has turned the whole of existence into a scheme of mutual deceit, and has revived the lowest and most brutal instincts of man. A sorry heritage to begin a new life of freedom and brotherhood. It cannot be sufficiently emphasized that revolution is in vain unless inspired by its ultimate ideal. Revolutionary methods must be in tune with revolutionary aims.

After Emma Goldman's disillusionment with the Russian Revolution, it seemed as if anarchism had lost its moment. Then the Austrian School of Economics, which moved from Europe to the United States due to World War II, infused anarcho–individualism, also known as a form of libertarianism, with a new vitality. One of the most prolific writers to come out of this reemergence was Murray Rothbard. He published a number of books, the most notable of which is 1973's *For A New Liberty*. He used the terms "individualist" and "libertarian" interchangeably to refer to those who sought to live without coercion. His work attacked the state as the chief agent of corruption and called for a dissolution of all state apparatus:

> The State! Always and ever the government and its rulers and operators have been considered above the general

BIOGRAPHY
Emma Goldman

Emma Goldman was more of an activist than a theorist. She is best known for introducing feminism to anarchist thought and leading a famous and remarkable life in the process. As a woman, a Jew, and an anarchist, Goldman was a minority to the third power. Born in Lithuania, Goldman came to the United States at the age of seventeen and worked in clothing factories. Three years after her arrival, she began participating in the anarchist movement. Her passionate speeches attracted a great deal of national attention; in 1893, she was arrested for inciting her audience to riot. In 1906, she partnered with Alexander Berkman to publish the anarchist paper *Mother Earth*. Her repudiation of institutionalized coercion went hand in hand with her feminism, and in 1916, after a speech urging women to bear children only when they wanted to be mothers and not before, she was arrested for advocating birth control in public. The next year she was imprisoned again, this time for obstructing the draft.

After Goldman's numerous arrests for promoting various political positions in public, the United States deported her to Russia in 1919. Disappointed and disillusioned with the Bolshevik government that came to power after the Russian Revolution, she left in 1921. In 1926 Goldman married James Colton, a Welshman. The United States finally allowed Goldman reentry into the country in 1934 on the condition that she did not discuss politics in public. In 1936, Goldman took part in the Spanish Civil War, which offered a unique living experiment in anarchist philosophy. She died four years later. Goldman's articles and treatises could not compete with her persona: she was the most widely–known anarchist and feminist of her era, whose speeches and statements were years ahead of their time in terms of sexual culture and politics. Her outspoken ways made her notorious—at one time, she was even implicated in the assassination of U.S. President William McKinley in 1901—and she used that notoriety to express her ideas about noncoercion and liberty.

moral law. The 'Pentagon Papers' are only one recent instance among innumerable instances in history of men, most of whom are perfectly honorable in their private lives, who lie in their teeth before the public. Why? For 'reasons of State.' Service to the State is supposed to excuse all actions that would be considered immoral or criminal if committed by 'private' citizens.... In fact, if you wish to know how libertarians regard the State and any of its acts, simply think of the State as a criminal band...

Although they originated in different assumptions and carried with them different conclusions, the variations on the theme of anarchism all embrace noncoercion as the highest political and social value. In practice, anarchism has appeared violent and peaceful, secretive and overt, male and female, and informed other movements during their development. Its many faces make anarchism a dynamic and living political theory even in the twenty–first century.

THEORY IN ACTION

Anarchism has always been something of a fringe theory, meaning that at any given time its proponents never led a regime or successfully held majority power in any nation. Much of this is due to the theory itself: if anarchists did come to power, their goals would not be to force specific policies into action, but rather to end force altogether. In general, manifestations of anarchism have differed due to the individuals involved—the influence of Spooner, for example, or Bakunin—as opposed to the regions in which they were practiced, although the broad tendency has been for anarchism to be increasingly individualistic the further west it traveled and increasingly collectivist the further east it traveled. Exceptions to this trend do exist, however. Scattered anarchists have thrown bombs, plotted assassinations, preached peace, and practiced nonviolent protest. Few anarchist actions have been well–coordinated enough, lasted a significant amount of time, or drawn enough individuals together to warrant calling them an example of theory in action.

The Spanish Civil War

One exception might be the case of the Spanish Civil War, which took place from 1936 to 1939. Spain had been an eager recipient of the French model of anarcho–syndicalism, and Spanish anarchists looked for ways in their own country to use the infrastructure of trade unions to provide stability and order for the movement. The *Confederación Nacional de Trabajo*, for example, formed in 1910. Thanks to organizations such as these, anarcho–syndicalist groups began to

gain a wide following, especially among lower classes in places like the industrial Catalonia, rural Andalusia, and mining Asturias districts. The revolutionary form of anarchism and socialism of the time had the flavor of Mikhail Bakunin and his secret societies.

The Spanish–American War in 1898 marked the end of Spain's empire era, but this defeat spawned a new moment of self–reflection and cultural rebirth. When World War I erupted, King Alfonso XIII (1886–1941) kept Spain neutral. The wartime economy flourished and the industrialists' profits swelled. The anarchist and socialist workers responded with strikes and uprisings, which the state beat down often with brutal force. The church sided with the landowners and prompted bitter anti–clerical feelings among the revolutionaries. Even greater unrest occurred after the end of the war. Rebellions flared. One movement in Catalonia in 1923 resulted in a military dictatorship over the area, but massive opposition eventually led to his resignation, followed by municipal elections. In 1931, Alfonso XIII was deposed and the second republic was born. Alcalá Zamora became the new president and enacted reforms meant to please the anarchist and socialist groups; for example, church property was redistributed to the people. These reforms were only skin deep, however, and more anarcho–syndicalist uprisings followed in Catalonia. By 1934, the new government behaved as the old one had, quelling revolt with force and bloodshed.

The anarchists had more than rebellion, however; they, along with republican, socialist, and communist allies, had a majority in Spain. Together they won the 1936 Spanish elections and chose a new government under Manuel Azaña (1880–1940). Before the newly–elected administration could act, however, a military rebellion led by General Francisco Franco (1892–1975) swept the nation and instigated civil war. On the one side was social and political change—anarchists, socialists, communists—and on the other was the establishment—the military, the church, the landowners. The Nationalists under Franco received military support from Germany and Italy. France and England both observed noninterventionist policies toward Spain, so the Popular Front, including the anarcho–syndicalists, had little support save meager aid from Russia. Anarchist leaders from across the world, including Emma Goldman, traveled to Spain to lend support. The Popular Front made determined stands, especially in central Spain, but eventually fell to the Nationalists' superior military forces. Many of the survivors fled to France as Franco's government took control of Spain.

The experience of the Spanish Civil War was important for several reasons. First and foremost, it showed how popular the principles of anarchism could be to a widespread audience. The financial inequities in Spain led to a schism between labor and landowners/producers, and anarchism appealed to the laboring class due to its emphasis on equality, especially as reflected in the labor theory of value. The Bakunin–inspired rhetoric of revolution against the institutionalized interests such as the aristocracy and clergy also played well with the masses; not only did they listen, but they also participated. The Spanish example further proved the staying power of anarchism once it was organized. By using the trade union structure to create anarcho–syndicalist societies, anarchists were able to reach and mobilize a number of people effectively.

Moreover, these anarchist leaders proved to be practical in mindset, willing to compromise the rigidity of their political beliefs in order to ally themselves with similarly minded activists from the socialist and communist camps. The resulting coalition sacrificed some anarchist principles, but managed to move a fair portion of anarchist thought, if ever so briefly, into the mainstream. Finally, the response from anarchists outside of Spain who joined in the efforts either in person or through the power of the pen underscored the close anarchist community that transcended national boundaries and united theorists across the miles.

Since the Spanish Civil War, other movements, although perhaps less visible on the world front, have continued to demonstrate the adaptability and energy of anarchist thought. Toward the end of the first half of the twentieth century, anarchist thought often fueled the work of pacifists, who were concerned with military build–up at the onset of the Cold War. Refusal to serve in the military, as well as civil disobedience, was common in the pacifist wing most allied with anarchism.

Other Movements

The second half of the twentieth century offered three specific examples of anarchist variations across the world: the student movement, anarcho–feminism, and anarcho–environmentalism. The first of these appeared in the 1960s in the form of the student movement.

The student movement The student movement stretched across the globe from the United States to France to Japan to Mexico. After World War II and the escalation of the Cold War between the United States and the Soviet Union, interest in communism waned. In the United States, for example, some students found fault with the Students for a Democratic Society (SDS) organization due to its strong links with communism. These students wanted to distance themselves from the dogmatic, centralized activism of the SDS and other such groups and link their protests of

the establishment and the Vietnam situation with issues of lifestyle, including experimentation with sexuality and drugs.

When the antiwar movement and the counterculture movement united in the United States and elsewhere, the agenda broadened to include not only new attitudes toward sex and drugs, but also new exploration of mystical religions and rock music. Those involved criticized the nuclear family, the corporate economy, the consumer ethic, the bigotry of sexism and racism, and the hierarchies of university, church, and career life; in short, they rebelled against what they saw as agents of coercion in favor of freedom and equality. The values of community and spontaneity manifested themselves in gatherings such as the Woodstock music festival of 1969 in New York and the creation of communes such as The Farm in Summertown, Tennessee.

The revolution discussed by such youth usually contained a pacifist, nonviolent tone, although a terrorist fringe also existed. The United States' Weathermen faction of the SDS and Italy's Red Brigade, among other groups, had collectivist predecessors in anarchism. Daniel Cohn–Bendit (born 1945) gained notoriety for the mini–revolution of May 1968 in France, in which students liberated their schools and called for student, black, woman, and gay power as ends to traditional hierarchies. He wrote in his 1968 work *Obsolete Communism: The Left–Wing Alternative* that he saw this action in the tradition of Nestor Makhno's (1889–1934) uprising in the Ukraine and the Kronstadt revolt against the Bolshevik Party, both of which were primarily anarchist movements. As the personal became political, few youth overtly called themselves anarchist, but the movement's concern with obliterating coercion against the individual made the 1960s brand of collectivism a distinctly anarchist moment.

Feminism On the heels of the student movement came the feminist anarchists. The momentum behind their cause grew out of the sexual experimentation and freedom of the 1960s. Some called themselves "anarcho–feminists" up front as they criticized what they perceived as the two faces of coercion: male–dominated government in the public sphere and male–dominated family in the personal sphere. They believed the aggression in the world sprang from the aggression in nations' states and homes. Inherent in their protests was the assumption that men objectified both nature and the Other—regardless if the Other's difference came from gender, race, religion, or beliefs—and thus coerced them; women's approach to relationships on grand or intimate scales was more egalitarian, empathetic, and cooperative.

Anarchy symbol spray painted on a sign outside of The World Bank during protests in Washington, DC in April of 2000. (Getty Images)

Anarcho–feminists sought to counter male dominance even in the anarchist movement itself and highlighted past women leaders such as Emma Goldman as true embodiments of the anarchist ideal.

Following the anarcho–feminist strain of anarchism that emerged in the West in the 1960s and 1970s came anarcho–environmentalists, also known as eco–anarchists. These thinkers moved beyond the mindset of many communists, for example, who leaned on industrialism as the main window into the world. In contrast, these anarchist thought in post–industrialist, information age terms about global economy and society of the twentieth and twenty–first century. Unlike traditional environmentalists who saw humans and nature often in unfortunate opposition, eco–anarchists viewed the world as an interdependent whole including animal and plant life, humanity, and its setting.

Murray Bookchin American anarchist Murray Bookchin (born 1921) authored two key texts in this movement: 1971's *Post–Scarcity Anarchism* and 1982's *The Ecology of Freedom: The Emergence and Dissolution of Hierarchy*. With a scientific approach reminiscent of Kropotkin, Bookchin criticized authoritarian reason and its coercive tendency to view the

world in hierarchies, to objectify and to dominate. He called for a more symbiotic relationship with nature and each other, nurturing and cooperating with the ecology of the planet and society. On a more radical note, green groups such as Earth First! have developed a form of anarchist eco–terrorism to support their environmentalist agenda around the world. Though they, too, have clear roots in anarchist activism, theorists such as Bookchin denounce them as coercive in their own right.

In practice, anarchism has collaborated with other similar political theories for momentary success, as in the case of Spain before and during that nation's civil war, and also split apart from other movements to focus criticism on a particular form of coercion, as in the case of the student movement, anarcho–feminism, and eco–anarchism. The adaptability of the tradition and its applicability to new issues ensures that the young theory will endure in a number of variations for years to come. Perhaps the latest incarnation is the anti–globalization movement.

The Anti–Globalization Movement

Many of the young activists at the heart of the current anti–globalization and anti–corporate movements consider themselves anarchists, but as Barbara Epstein writes in her article "Anarchism and the Anti–Globalization Movement" in the September 2001 *Monthly Review*, "these circles might be better described as an anarchist sensibility than as anarchism per se." The current radical ideology holds decentralized organizational structure, decision–making by consensus, and opposition and/or suspicion of authority as its key principles. They are more aligned with socialist thought than the individualist strains of anarchism envisioned by Benjamin Tucker.

The activists connected with the anti–globalization movement express their perspectives through action. For perhaps the best example of this, one can look at the mobilization against the World Trade Organization (WTO) that took place in Seattle in late November and early December of 1999. Over the course of several days, the activists blocked the meetings of the WTO, fought with police, and aligned themselves with trade unionists and environmentalists, groups with similar aims. They succeeded in bringing a great deal of media attention to their cause.

Similar demonstrations—against the WTO, the International Monetary Fund, and the World Bank—have taken place elsewhere. In addition, stronger ties are being forged between the movement and like-minded individuals and groups. The anti–globalization movement and the anti–corporate movement are beginning to overlap, particularly in protest against the Free Trade Area of the Americas, the use of sweatshops by major corporations, and the destruction of natural environments. Viewpoints on how to deal with corporations vary. Some activists want regulation of large companies, while others would like to see them destroyed altogether.

Perhaps the biggest issue in the current movement is the question of violence to achieve desired ends. Some factions in the anti–globalization movement believe violence toward corporate property and police authority furthers the cause. There was violence in Seattle as well as at demonstrations in Quebec City in May 2001. What must be determined by these activists is if the violence they carry out is according an ethical vision, rather than simply an expression of frustration or rage.

ANALYSIS AND CRITICAL RESPONSE

Anarchism must be analyzed and judged on two criteria: as a theory in the abstract, and as a political plan in action. The first of these categories, as a theory in the abstract, is somewhat difficult, considering the fact that individualism, mutualism, socialism, and communism, the four contributing wings of the theory, start from different philosophical assumptions. All forms of anarchism hold coercion as wrong and undesirable, but on other fundamental issues—the natural perfectibility or depravity of humanity, the sociability or independence of human nature—diverge greatly.

Nonetheless, certain things can be said of the theory of anarchism. First, it seems at times to be more about what it denounces, namely coercion, than what it espouses. In other words, it is sometimes difficult to gain a concrete vision of what world anarchists would prefer to substitute for the one in which they live. Cooperation and harmony sound like good things, but what, exactly, do they mean? What do they look like? When, in the defense of these values, would coercion be justified? If the anarchist theorists wanted to reform the world, they needed to provide clear recipes not only for how to dismantle a contemporary system, but what to erect in its place.

When descriptions were forthcoming, they often seemed more like utopias, or ideal communities, than real blueprints for actual life. For example, the collectivist anarchists' vision included communal property and work without material reward, but the theorists insisted that these societies would be based on free will and consent. What, then if someone in the

community chose not to give up private property? Would that person be relocated so that those who agreed could live together in harmony? Removing an individual would be coercion, however. What if an individual was not motivated by neighborly feelings and therefore did not work, but instead became a freeloader on the labor of others? How could the system be implemented without some kind of force mechanism? Collectivists assumed that everyone would be in agreement and see the wisdom of the anarchist model. This seems idyllic at times, not practical. What if agreement and cooperation never appeared?

Coordinating Communities

The problem of coordinating multiple communities posed another obstacle to tranquil life in free association societies. Theorists assumed that groups of communities would work together for the common good, from the establishment of trade to the construction of roads, bridges, and other forms of infrastructure. What mechanism ensured that each community agreed or, if they agreed, carried its own weight in the arrangement? What if one community decided to take over another? These small communities, communist or individualist, for that matter, offered the opportunity for outside groups that had opted out of the communal lifestyle to divide and conquer them due to their lack of centralized force. In the same way that feudal era Western Europe found itself vulnerable to invasions from the south, north, and east, these communities faced difficulty in provided a common action or a common defense.

The communes and experimental communities engaged with this theory solved these problems by founding small settlements of like–minded people located away from others. They did not face the challenge of incorporating many individuals of dissimilar backgrounds and convictions in preexisting societies. Even then, infighting, philosophical disagreements, and economic challenges threatened and often ended the fledgling groups. Imagining the harmony of many such communities banding together across countries and continents out of natural agreement seems somewhat naïve.

Anarchists on the individualistic side of the anarchist spectrum faced comparable problems. According to these theorists, individuals primarily relate to one another in terms of contracts. If institutions such as governments and laws wither away from disuse, however, what mechanism would enforce contracts? Who would settle disputes about them? Without some manner of protecting the private property and transactions of individuals, a list of "playing rules" everyone one must observe, the very foundation of the free market might crumble. What system would protect individuals from theft, fraud, and abandonment in the face of contractual obligations? Again, the theorists seem to rely on a naïve belief that everyone would choose to live in the same way and behave themselves while doing so. Like the collectivist anarchists, anarcho–capitalists face difficulties in explaining how to get there from here and how to maintain the ideal system once it is in place.

Misinterpretations

The generality or elasticity of the idea of anarchy also has led it to be misused and stretched beyond all proportion. When the British band the Sex Pistols begged for "Anarchy in the U.K." in 1975, anarchy seemed to mean rebellion—and scandalous, dangerous rebellion at that, they implied, as they rhymed "anarchist" with "antichrist." A listen and look at the band suggested that they in fact did not subscribe to anarchism as much as nihilism, the conviction that life is useless and senseless. When they screamed or sang or wore t–shirts proclaiming anarchy, what did they mean? Why did they choose that term? The symbol for anarchy remains a punk staple and has filtered into the underground of other forms of music and art, but what does it mean in this context?

The term has been modified by casual use to such a degree that "anarchy" has become synonymous with chaos, destruction, and bewildering confusion. Newscasters use it to describe natural and planned disasters, and pundits use it to forecast doom if the wrong policy is adopted. Certainly this is not the anarchy desired by the anarchist political theorists. The very vagueness and open–endedness of the theory, however, leaves the term susceptible to being appropriated and misused by others. In other words, if the theory were more concrete, perhaps the term would not have been available to take on multiple, misleading meanings.

Conversely, the breadth of the noncoercion foundation of anarchism has allowed the theory to evolve in new and relevant directions across the years. Not only has the coercion in question been that of authoritarian states, but it has also been understood to mean the coercion of the institution of slavery, according to Lysander Spooner, organized religion, according to Mikhail Bakunin, gender discrimination, according to Emma Goldman, and ecological domination, according to Murray Bookchin. The open–endedness of anarchism has allowed it to be adapted to the concerns of agriculture, manufacturing, students, and those who wished for the freedom to experiment with sexuality, drugs, and alternative lifestyles. The same vagueness

that can be the Achilles' heel of anarchism also allows the theory its longevity.

Anarchy in Practice?

Anarchism in practice has yielded mixed results. One could say anarchism proper has never been practiced, except perhaps in small, temporary, experimental communities outside of the mainstream West. The actions of activists, however, can be judged. On the one hand, the legacy of anarchism in action is one of compassion, egalitarianism, and nobility. In challenging coercion, anarchists have championed the oppressed, the ones against whom the weight of the social, economic, and/or political system rested. In trying to liberate the laborers, empower the women, and preserve the ecology, among other things, anarchists have approached heroic status. The strand of anarchist thought opposing all violence in principle fed the pacifist tradition and helped to inform the practice of civil disobedience; again, the scales tip favorably on the side of anarchy.

The popular image of anarchism is not that of pacifism, however. In the late nineteenth century, some anarchists across the world adopted the notion of "propaganda by the deed," meaning that the anarchist message could be communicated best by taking dramatic, public action. This often translated into violence. On May 4, 1886, for instance, anarchists in Chicago staged a protest for an eight–hour workday. When policemen tried to disband the crowd of approximately 1,500 people, a bomb exploded and killed seven policemen and four crowd members and wounded more than 100 people. Although individual guilt was hard to determine in the case, four anarchists were executed, and four others were imprisoned. Other bombings, fights, and assassinations followed. On September 6, 1901, for example, anarchist Leon F. Czolgosz shot and killed U.S. President William McKinley, saying he was "an enemy of good working people." Such violence occurred in Europe as well and became linked with anarchism in the popular mind. Revolutionaries like Bakunin encouraged this perspective.

Arguably, the U.S. execution of Nicola Sacco and Bartolomeo Vanzetti in 1927 for murder had less to do with evidence beyond a reasonable doubt presented against them than with the stereotype of the violent, bloodthirsty anarchist that had grown in the public mind by that time due to bombings, assassinations, and attempted violence across the West. Anarchist terrorists reveal how the theory could derail into something destructive. In the case of Sacco and Vanzetti, unfortunately, the anarchist violence of others returned to haunt possibly innocent anarchists.

The Future

Though the many faces of anarchism make analysis challenging, they also ensure that the theory will adapt itself to new issues and eras. If the pattern holds, theorists will propose ideas that inspire new anarchist variations and inform other movements in the process. As some activists find constructive ways to use the theory, however, others will wield it in more destructive ways. The diversity of anarchism remains its strength and its weakness.

TOPICS FOR FURTHER STUDY

- What other twentieth and twenty–first century movements besides feminism and environmentalism reflect some form of anarchist thought?

- In what ways did Lysander Spooner's postal business embody the anarchist ideal? What kind of enterprise today might be similarly symbolic?

- Investigate the Romantic poets and novelists. How did Percy Shelley and other Romantics reflect anarchist thought in literature?

- Read about the Transcendentalists in the nineteenth century such as Henry David Thoreau and Ralph Waldo Emerson. In what ways did their beliefs in civil disobedience and spirituality have roots in anarchist thought?

BIBLIOGRAPHY

Sources

Boaz, David, ed. *The Libertarian Reader: Classic and Contemporary Writings from Lao–Tzu to Milton Friedman.* New York: The Free Press, 1997.

Brown, L. Susan. *The Politics of Individualism: Liberalism, Liberal Feminism and Anarchism.* New York: Black Rose Books, 1993.

Epstein, Barbara. "Anarchism and the Anti–Globalization Movement." *Monthly Review*, September 2001, 1.

Godwin, William. *The Anarchist Writings of William Godwin.* Peter Marshall, ed. London: Freedom Press, 1986.

Goldman, Emma. *Anarchism and Other Essays.* New York: Dover Publications, 1969.

Heider, Ulrike. *Anarchism: Left, Right, and Green.* San Francisco: City Lights, 1994.

Martin, James J. *Men Against The State: The Expositors of Individualist Anarchism in America, 1827–1908.* Colorado Springs: Ralph Myles, 1970.

Miller, David, ed. *The Blackwell Encyclopedia of Political Thought.* Cambridge, Blackwell, 1991.

Sonn, Richard D. *Anarchism.* New York: Twayne, 1992.

Sturgis, Amy H., Nathan D. Griffith, Melissa English, Joshua B. Johnson, and Kevin D. Weimer, eds. *Great Thinkers in Classical Liberalism: The LockeSmith Review.* Nashville: The LockeSmith Institute, 1994.

Wiener, Philip P., ed. *Dictionary of the History of Ideas: Studies of Selected Pivotal Ideas.* Volume I. New York: Charles Scribner's Sons, 1968.

Woodcock, George, ed. *The Anarchist Reader.* Atlantic Highlands, NY: Humanities Press, 1977.

Further Readings

Avrich, Paul. *Sacco and Vanzetti: The Anarchist Background.* Princeton: Princeton University Press, 1991. An anarchist historian takes a new look at the famous 1920s trial.

Bakunin, Mikhail. *God and the State.* Mikhail Bakunin's 1882 work sets out to dismiss universal authorities such as the government and the church.

Bookchin, Murray. *To Remember Spain: The Anarchist and Syndicalist Revolution of 1936.* San Francisco: AK Press, 1994. A history of the anarchist revolutionary movement in a Spain on the brink of civil war.

Glassgold, Peter. *Anarchy! An Anthology of Emma Goldman's Mother Earth.* Washington, D.C.: Counterpoint Press, 2001. A fine collection of important pieces that appeared in the radical periodical *Mother Earth* from 1906 through 1917.

Wolff, Robert Paul. *In Defense of Anarchism.* Berkeley: University of California Press, 1998. Wolff attempts to break through the stereotypes and present a clear explanation and analysis the anarchist philosophy.

SEE ALSO

Communism, Marxism, Pacifism, Utopianism

Capitalism

OVERVIEW

Capitalism is more than an economic system. It's an entire ideology centered around the idea of the individual's right to choose his work, his goals, and his life's details. Capitalism is based on the relationships between the capitalists, the consumers, and the laborers. Capitalists essentially acquire or create goods for less than they sell them. Capitalism has dominated the Western Hemisphere since the Roman Empire began to tumble and, following that, the feudal system disintegrated. Markets determine the production and distribution without government involvement, and the economy and the government remain separate. Its development began, officially, in the 16th century, but the idea started in the ancient world and there have been healthy capitalistic niches ever since. The first major work on capitalism was written by Adam Smith in 1776, *Inquiry into the Nature and Causes of the Wealth of Nations,* and along with his detailed analysis of capitalistic theory began a more structured and formally recognized ideology.

WHO CONTROLS GOVERNMENT? Elected officials

HOW IS GOVERNMENT PUT INTO POWER? Elected by the masses

WHAT ROLES DO THE PEOPLE HAVE? Sustain the free market

WHO CONTROLS PRODUCTION OF GOODS? Owners of capital

WHO CONTROLS DISTRIBUTION OF GOODS? Owners of capital

MAJOR FIGURES Adam Smith; John Locke

HISTORICAL EXAMPLE United States

HISTORY

Capitalism could not exist without the presence of a market. Marketplaces have existed for several thousand years. There are documented markets and trading relationships between the pharaohs of Egypt and the ancient Levantine kingdoms around 1400 B.C.

CHRONOLOGY

c. 1400 B.C.: Trading relationships exist between the pharaohs of Egypt and the ancient Levantine kingdoms

c. 400 B.C.: Marketplaces exist in Greece and Rome

c. 1200: The Reformation begins in Europe

1776: Adam Smith's *An Inquiry into the Nature and Causes of the Wealth of Nations* is published

c. 1800: Industrial Revolution begins in Europe

1929: Great Depression begins

1933: The New Deal begins

1935: The Social Security Act is passed.

1936: John Maynard Keynes' *The General Theory of Employment, Interest and Money* is published

1947: The Taft–Hartley Act is passed

1956: For the first time in world history, the number of people performing services is greater than the number producing goods

1989: The Berlin Wall falls. Germany is reunified and becomes an important economic power.

In 400 B.C., there are records of a rich trading network and commodity exchange in addition to a complicated market in classical Greece and Rome.

These healthy market and trading systems show the historical basis of money, mercantile groups and the idea of profit, but there was not a market system like exists today. Markets joined suppliers and demanders but what was supplied did not change based on the details of demand. Markets existed to provide luxuries to those who wanted them but did not satisfy the essential needs of society. The essentials were taken care of according to tradition, with slavery as the labor source. Living one's life to benefit another was looked down upon for the free man, however, as articulated by the philosopher Aristotle.

Capitalism as it is today is relatively new, but the ideas of markets and profits have been in place for thousands of years. Formally, capitalism began during the Middle Ages with the mercantilist period. The ideology has been around since before the philoso-

phers Aristotle and Plato, however. Plato (428–348 B.C.) began to outline some of the structural ideas of capitalism in terms of freedom and liberty, but subscribed more to communist and community based ideology then to the individualism that defines capitalism. Plato argued that guardians were needed to protect people from injustice and from invasion. He felt that they should share the state's wealth by keeping properties public to ensure equality. He also thought that by allowing people to privately own their own homes and properties they would necessarily become enemies rather than neighbors in mutual protection of one another. The theory of communal living continued but the beginnings of individualistic capitalism were sprouting as well, growing with along the ideas of freedom and liberty.

The idea of capitalism grew from individualistic notions. In religion, this led to the Reformation. In politics, this led to democracy, and with the economy, this led to the capitalistic system. Capitalism has its origins in Rome, in the Middle East, and in Europe in the Middle Ages. Its earliest organized form was called mercantilism, the production and distribution of goods to make a profit.

Mercantilism

Mercantilism began in Rome in its simplest form. The merchants bought goods for less than they sold them. The Roman Empire expanded, and mercantilism grew along with it. As the empire began to shrink in the fifth century, however, so too did mercantilism. By the 700s it was only a small slice of the culture of Europe. During this same period, though, capitalistic practices were thriving in Arabia. The Arab culture existed in the trade routes between three empires: Egypt, Persia, and later, the Byzantium. Islam spread across the Middle East, Asia, Spain, and North Africa in the 700s. Mercantilism spread along with Islam, and its success is evidenced by the number of economic words derived from Islam such as traffic and tariff.

In Europe, the medieval culture relearned the ideas of mercantilism and capitalism from its Arabic neighbors. By the 1300s, Europe had fully absorbed mercantilism and was starting to expand through mobility and mercantilism. Europeans and Arabs alike began to explore the globe. These voyages were inspired by mercantilist thoughts and dreams.

St. Thomas Aquinas St. Thomas Aquinas (1226–1274), one of the most important writers and theorists of the Middle Ages, believed in individuality more than his predecessors. The Reformation was beginning. The Catholic Church was very powerful and equally corrupt. People wanted change and were calling for reform. His economic notions accompanied a new wave of thinking that remained until the Mercantilist time in 1600. Aquinas thought that it was natural for men to hold private property. He argued that there were three reasons for this to be the case, rather than public ownership. His first point was that men will more reliably attempt to secure something for themselves than they would for the public use. Secondly, people conduct themselves more orderly and responsibly when it concerns their personal effects and properties. Thirdly, if everyone is happy with his own lot that he's gotten for himself, peace will ensue much more securely than it would were everyone sharing and feeling, possibly, a lack given their inability to have power over their acquisitions.

St. Thomas Aquinas also argued that when things are in private hands they are easier to share with those who have less. He thought that private property was just and advantageous, provided it was shared with those who didn't have it. This belief made it acceptable for men to be richer than others and to separate their wealth. It became acceptable and even respectable to have things. Aquinas even said that there should be a limit to the amount that any one person should have to give to the poor so as to ensure that one may live as necessary for one's status. He thought that wealth was wonderful if it helped one to live a virtuous life. He also felt that poverty was equally desirable if it was the lack of wealth that helped one to live virtuously. His idea that it was natural for men to have different status levels in life was new, and allowed an individualistic branch of thought to take root.

Aquinas also wrote about more detailed economic ideas. The clergy writers who preceded him had written that a "just" price was that at which the buyer and seller benefited equally. Aquinas said that the "just" price was actually a price range, within which both parties would benefit but allowing for external details to be included in price. He said when figuring the price of an item, the seller should take into account his amount of loss. For example, if the seller had a personal attachment to something that he was going to sell, he could charge more than expected for it for this reason. This opened the door to a lot of subjective reasoning, a door which is still open.

Aquinas' ideas about wages were based on the same principles. A worker's wage should be enough to allow him to live decently without raising the cost of labor enough to raise the price past a "just" level. The cost of labor was very important in determining an object's cost. Aquinas' ideas have become widely used in price determination.

An engraving of St. Thomas Aquinas.

Aquinas touched on money lending as well. He anticipated the idea of interest payments by stating that if a lender could prove that he had missed another financial opportunity because he hadn't had the money that he had lent to someone else, he could charge interest rates for the money that he had lent. He could also charge interest if the borrower was late in his repayment, and he could charge a compensation fee if he could show that he had suffered a loss of some kind.

St. Thomas Aquinas also wrote about the state's needs. He said that in order for a state to have what it needed, it could either produce everything for itself or it could trade. To trade, he realized that merchants were needed and this paved the way for exploration through searches for trading partners and resource suppliers. It was only two hundred years after St. Thomas Aquinas' death that Christopher Columbus set sail to the Indies.

During this same period (roughly 1215 to 1545), the Reformation was gathering speed. Europe went through many artistic, political and social changes resulting from opposition to the Catholic Church. The Church had become very powerful and very corrupt. The official Reformation began in 1517 when Martin Luther, a German Augustinian friar, posted his "Ninety–Five Theses," a list of criticisms against the Catholic Church. People began to take charge of their own salvation since they couldn't trust the Church. Individualism swelled.

Aquinas' ideas took hold and mercantilism was back with a passion in 1500 with continued popularity until the 1700s. The main belief was that a nation's wealth could be expanded upon by exporting products which would bring in gold and silver. This monetary wealth could then be used to build up armies and armadas; the more gold one had, the more one could buy with it. It was this desire for gold that led to exploration on a global scale.

Further developments As an economic system, capitalism has had more recent success. The system's development dates from the 1500s as the areas of mercantilist activity in Europe began to spread. The English clothing industry led a movement toward capitalism in the 16th, 17th, and 18th centuries. People began to realize that they could produce goods and sell them to gain a profit.

In the 16th century, the Protestant Reformation furthered the ideas of individualism. The distaste for material acquisition decreased as the desire to attain went up. Frugal behavior and hard work gained status, and the differences in distributions of wealth began to be justified by the idea that one earned as much as one deserved with the fruits of his labor.

Though there were many details of mercantilism that the philosophers and economists of the day did not agree upon, there were a few essentials that were universally accepted. All of the resources needed for the production of goods were to be created within the host country. If this proved impossible, then only the raw materials would be imported to allow the production to take place domestically. To further the political and economic benefit to a nation, the maximum amount of effort would take place within the borders rather than outside where added payment would be necessary.

Because of the state's desire to provide for itself all of the needed materials both to exist and to export, colonization became increasingly attractive. Colonies could provide free resources for the colonizing country. The colonizer wouldn't have to pay for them from another independent source. Exploration became more than just a search for trading partners; it became a chance to find new areas to exploit and claim for one's own state.

Another effect of mercantilism was the improvement of technology and the need for mathematicians and engineers. In order to travel more successfully than the competitors, a nation needed more advanced navigational equipment. States began to create areas of study for cartographers and mathematicians. In addition to navigational equipment, weapons were improved to facilitate colonial take over. There grew an interdependence of mutual benefit between the state and the merchants, without the state controlling the actions of the merchants and their markets or the markets controlling the actions of the state. Thus, the seeds of capitalistic separation of state and market were planted.

Decline Mercantilism as an idea began to drop in popularity as inflation rose. Given that the more gold a country has decreases the value of all of it, the acquisition of new gold did not necessarily create greater wealth. Since the value is lower, the prices increase. When these now more expensive goods are exported, they are rejected for the cheaper ones available from the other trading partners. This was perhaps best evidenced by the decline of the Spanish Empire, where inflation quadrupled prices in a century due to massive gold intake.

Mercantilism also declined because people began to feel that they were not being provided for adequately by the state. They wanted the state to withdraw further from their lives rather than remaining on top of them and, consequently, stifling their activities. People began to suspect that individual interests led to communal gain for many of the same reasons stated by St. Thomas Aquinas hundreds of years before.

The Rise of Individuality

From mercantilism until the time of Adam Smith (1723–1790), the founder of capitalistic theory, individuality continued to grow. The English philosopher John Locke (1632–1704) believed that a man's place in society was not necessarily a struggle against his neighbors. He disagreed with Plato that private property would necessarily create enemies. Locke claimed that people are born with equality and freedom, and if this turns competitive and ugly, it is because of their actions. Governments form to ensure peace and freedom between people. This creates the possibility of economic freedom that is unregulated by the state, provided one does not harm one's neighbor, people are at liberty to do as they please.

Locke felt that the government had no place in the economic sector. He also believed in private ownership. He believed that the world was created by God to be used by the people and that once one had labored to some end, the end was his to claim. If a man cultivated a field, the products from the cultivation were his. Locke went further to explain the use of money as a substitution for direct labor. He said that men have agreed to money as a means of exchange. Money is paid for something that one man has that another wants. If a man cultivates a field and has more than he needs for himself, since the products are his because he produced them, he may sell them to someone who has need for those products. This exchange allows the producer to earn money he can then use to buy goods he himself is not able to produce.

Locke said that men should be allowed to regulate their own commerce. Governments should exist only to protect people from injustice against the state and against the people, whether from outside sources or from threats within their borders. Locke also explained why some members of society were able to amass such a state of wealth; it was through their own labor that they were able to make enough to sell and, consequently, gather their money.

The Reformation also claimed that people were responsible for themselves and that if they did not reach salvation they had only themselves to blame. People did not necessarily have to go to the Catholic Church in order to have a relationship with God. Everyone was his own priest. These ideas became dominant in the Western world as feudalism collapsed. Much of the production was privately owned and markets began to dictate product and income distribution.

In addition to the mercantilist beginnings and the individualism of the Reformation, Europe's increase of its supply of precious metals sparked a rise of capitalism. Prices inflated because of the supply, though wages did not rise at the same rate. The capitalists benefited greatly from this inflation. They also benefited from the increase of national states which occurred during the mercantilist era. The national policies created legal codes and a regulated monetary system which were necessary social conditions in order for the economic development to be such that a shift would result from public to private ownership and control.

Adam Smith

As time went on, industry began to take the place of commerce. In the 18th century in England, the capital that had been building for centuries was used to develop technology. This in turn fueled the Industrial Revolution. Adam Smith (1723–1790), an early theorist of capitalism, wrote his book An Inquiry into the Nature and Causes of the Wealth of Nations in 1776 which, though not immediately a success, became the first publication having to do with capitalistic theory. Smith recommended allowing the market to make economic decisions through self–regulation rather than allowing the government to control commerce and industry.

An engraving of Adam Smith. (Corbis Corporation)

The main idea of his book was that there is a natural progression through four stages that humans follow, from the crude caveman to more organized agriculture, then to feudal farming and finally to capitalistic independence and commercial wealth. He explained the evolution of society into a market–determined existence free from government interference. Smith called this the system of perfect liberty. He wrote that "Civil government, so far as it is instituted for the security of property, is in reality instituted for the defense of the rich against the poor, or of those who have some property against those who have none at all." This phenomenon and the end result later became known as *laissez-faire* capitalism.

Smith also talked about the invisible hand, which works within the final stage of society. A system of complete freedom, given the drive and intellect of human kind, will create an organized society. He explained this with examples of individual commodity pricing and a regulated legal code. This order would be produced by the two pieces of human nature, the passionate and the impartial. The passions would keep morality up front while the sensibility and apathy would promote organization and cleanliness. Smith argued that competition would result from the marriage of these two bits of human nature. The passion and drive to improve one's condition and the sensibility to

BIOGRAPHY:

Adam Smith

Adam Smith is known mainly for his book *An Inquiry into the nature and causes of the Wealth of Nations* written in 1776. Born in Kirkcaldy, Scotland on June 5, 1723, he lived a scholarly life in Scotland, England, and France. He was born to Margaret Douglas and Adam Smith. He went to elementary school in Kirkcaldy and was said to have been carried off by gypsies when he was four, tracked down by his family and then abandoned by the gypsies.

When Smith was 14, he began study at the University of Glasgow. He graduated three years later, having studied moral philosophy and economics. He then won a scholarship to Oxford. He spent several years there in relative isolation learning more about classical and contemporary philosophy.

After he'd finished his schooling, he gave several lectures in Edinburgh which publicized his name and his studies. In 1751 he began to teach logic at the University of Glasgow and, later, moral philosophy. He was elected dean of the faculty in 1758. He published his first work, *The Theory of Moral Sentiments*, the next year. This work was the foundation for his later book, *The Wealth of Nations*.

In 1763, Smith left the university to tutor a young duke in France. He spent four years with the Townshend family and, when he left in 1767, he had the beginnings for his book. He spent the following nine years finishing the manuscript and *The Wealth of Nations* was published in 1776.

There is some debate as to whether or not the book was an immediate success. Smith went into semi–retirement after its publication and became the commissioner of customs and salt duties for Scotland. He never married and, as was the custom in respect for privacy, many of his files were destroyed when he died in 1790. Whether or not he knew the importance of his theory, his ideology became reality.

---

do it by trying to get the market to work in one's favor leads to a competitive arena.

According to Smith, the invisible hand regulates the economy through this competitive fight for self–improvement. Competition for consumer demand drives the prices down to levels that Smith deemed natural. These prices would be just about the cost of production; enough to make a profit and low enough to be affordable. Smith also theorized that competition creates frugality and efficiency. For the same reason that prices are kept at natural levels, Smith argued that so too will wages, profits, and rents.

Smith's arguments for *laissez–faire market* freedom were as much against monopoly as they are against government. He wrote that competition is essential and he sited the dangers of a monopoly. In addition to that, though he spoke of a capitalistic ideal, he often referred to the actions of the capitalists with contempt and scorn. He did not necessarily approve of the nature of the system, but rather pointed out the benefits that make it so appealing. He also stated that the division of labor reduced the laborer to a robotic being, as he "becomes as stupid and ignorant as it is possible for a human being to become."

A good portion of *The Wealth of Nations* centered around the idea of natural liberty. He points out that this system cannot work with the interference of government. He says that "the monopolizing spirit of merchants and manufacturers, who neither are, nor ought to be, the rulers of mankind" cannot affect the government's actions. If the government heeds the market and reacts to it, all will go sour.

Smith's *Wealth of Nations* also spent a good deal of time analyzing economic growth. Smith thought that the market was self–repairing. Not only did he believe the market would adjust to the economy around it, he also thought that with a free market the national affluence would continually rise.

The backbone of his theory rests with the idea of the division of labor. The book begins with a passage describing a pin factory. Ten people could produce 48,000 pins a day because of the division of labor; if each were producing the entire pin himself, each worker could only produce a few pins a day. This division of labor can only occur, Smith said, after the acquisition of capital. This capital is in the form of machines and tools, and also includes the resulting profits used to pay the workers.

This dramatically improved production has results of its own. Since there is so much being produced, the manufacturer begins to build stock and therefore needs more workers to continue this trend. To attract them, he raises the wage offer. When he hires the workers, he ends up making a smaller profit proportionally. To counteract this, the employer may come up with a more intricate system of labor division in order to continually maximize profits.

Smith's growth predictions did not depend solely on human nature. They also included the necessary lack of government intervention and regulation which would temper the competition, thereby keeping everything as equal as it could be.

Other Influences

The French Revolution and the Napoleonic Wars effectively dissolved the remaining remnants of feudalism. Smith's ideas were increasingly put into practice. In the 19th century, politics were liberal and began to include the gold standard, free trade, relief for the poor and balanced budgets.

Charles Darwin published his *Origin of the Species* in 1859. His ideas were directed toward science rather than toward economics, but were similar to capitalistic ideology. Darwin described the process of natural selection that occurs in evolution. Those who are able to adapt survive while those who cannot will expire. This idea was shared by capitalists. Those best adapted to their environment and market were the most likely to survive and make a profit. Though Darwin didn't suggest or subscribe to the idea of social Darwinism, it became a way to explain why certain groups were less affluent than others; they simply hadn't adapted as well as the upper class. This carried on to economics as well and, though Darwin never actually said "survival of the fittest," the phrase became an accepted explanation of the distribution of wealth in the economy.

World War I, spanning the years 1914 to 1918, was another important time in the history of capitalism. When the war was over, the gold standard was discarded and replaced with separate national currencies. The banking hegemony switched from Europe to the United States, and the barriers to trade grew as the international markets shrank. In the 1930s, the Great Depression ended the *laissez–faire* (hands–off) policy of governments toward economy in many countries. These events cast a shadow on capitalism and people wondered if it could succeed as a system.

Despite these obstacles, capitalism has survived and continued to flourish in the United States, the United Kingdom, Germany, and Japan. It is beginning to gain stature in many other countries as well, and much of the first world subscribes to its belief in freedom from government control of the economy.

THEORY IN DEPTH

The two main ingredients of a capitalist society are the capitalists and the laborers. The capitalists are the people who are in control of the capital, or means of production. They cannot reach their end without productive labor, however, which brings in the rest of society. The human labor needed to produce goods from raw materials is paid labor. People work for money rather than for a part of the product. The workers are not invested in the product and are more detached than if they were receiving goods rather than wages. The work becomes more efficient because of the division of labor. Each worker has a specific job to do and may become very adept at it since his area of expertise is relatively small. This lowers the value of the individual worker, however, since his area of expertise is so specific.

Factors for a Capitalist Society

Individualism   One of the most important traits of capitalism is individualism. Individuals, rather than the state, own the means of production such as land, machinery, natural resources and factories. Public ownership is possible, such as with the postal service and public utilities, but it is the exception rather than the rule. The state may own land as well. In the United States, for example, the government owns roughly one third of all land, mainly in the West and in Alaska.

This bias toward individualism is based on two things. First, ownership of production means having control over people's lives, and it is preferable to have this power spread out amongst many players rather than concentrated in bulk with the government. The capitalists themselves may be regulated by the government, which provides added protection for the consumers and capitalists alike. If the government were in control of the capital, there would not be a second power to curb its actions. The second argument for individualism is that progress is more easily attained when people have personal incentives to reach their goals and the freedom to set the goals in the first place.

Market economy   Another trait of capitalism is the market economy. Before capitalism, families were more self–sufficient they produced what they needed to exist, with any extras being bartered for any supplies they themselves could not produce. This was a sort of primitive market on a small scale. Families bartered with other families in their locality. There was no division of labor because the families took care of all of their needs themselves. In contrast to the time when these families generally produced everything for themselves, the capitalist system ensured that no one would have to master so many different tasks. In capitalism, each person specializes in one task.

Each person creates and supplies only a small portion of what they need to live, relying on others to

MAJOR WRITINGS:

Wealth of Nations

The first major writing in the field of capitalism was Adam Smith's *The Wealth of Nations* in 1776. The main topic that Smith tries to resolve in his book is the problem of the struggle between the passionate side and the impartial side in man. Smith describes the four stages that a society will go through, unless blocked or altered by war, lack of resources, or poor government. The first stage is hunting, followed by nomadic agriculture, feudal farming, and finally, commercial interdependence.

Each stage is accompanied by whatever institutions are needed. The hunter stage, for example, does not include ownership of property and does therefore not need an intricate law code to protect property. Tradition–bound peoples solve their economic problems by migrating to adapt to seasons and climate, supporting themselves by gathering, hunting, and farming. With nomadic farming, social organization becomes more complicated. Rules are needed to distinguish between goods and a primitive form of law and order begins.

Though *The Wealth of Nations* was immediately championed by Smith's friends and colleagues, there is a debate as to whether or not it was quickly accepted by society as a whole. Whatever the case, Smith was the first to write a book so completely dedicated to the idea of capitalism:

> The whole annual produce of the land and labour of every country, or what comes to the same thing, the whole price of that annual produce, naturally divides itself, it has already been observed, into three parts; the rent of the land, the wages of the labour, and the profits of the stock; and constitutes a revenue to three different orders of people; to those who live by rent, to those who live by wages, and to those who live by profit. These are the three great, original and constituent orders of every civilized society, from whose revenue that of every other order is ultimately derived. (Book One, Chapter X).

> The subjects of every state ought to contribute towards the support of the government, as nearly as possible, in proportion to their respective abilities; that is, in proportion to the revenue which they respectively enjoy under the protection of the state. The expense of government to the individuals of a great nation, is like the expense of management to the joint tenants of a great estate. In the observation or relect of this maxim consists, what is called the equality or inequality of taxation. (Book Five, Chapter II).

Smith wrote his work before the Industrial Revolution and made no mention of its possible arrival. Some of his feelings and predictions may have been different if he had imagined the industry waiting in the wings and the progression from an industrial economy to a service economy that was to occur.

---

produce what else they need. Wages earned from this labor goes toward the purchase of other necessities. Because of this difference in direction, a worker produces not for himself but for the market. Supply and demand determine the prices paid for the goods produced. The government may regulate to some extent; in the United States, the government intervenes to break up monopolies, promoting competition and lowering prices.

Decentralization   In contrast with other systems that are dictated by a central body that attempts to keep up with the economic and social intricacies, capitalism is broken into so many different pieces that, in theory, each piece is expertly managed by the person in charge of that slice of the pie.

This lack of central regulation is a very important ingredient of capitalism. The state does not tell people where and when to work, how much to charge for their labor, what to do with their money, and what they should be producing at their job. The government may direct the market subtly with its budget, interest rates, and taxes, and it may break monopolies into smaller pieces. However, the direct economic control remains in the hands of the masses and the government serves only as a referee to promote fair play in the game.

Links between supply and demand   Another feature of capitalism is the sovereignty enjoyed by the consumer. He chooses both what will be produced and how much of it will be available through his demand or lack thereof. The number of televisions produced, for example, is not a result of a government limit or quota but rather a direct result of how many televisions sold the year before and whether or not there was a surplus or a shortage. The government may increase interest rates to discourage borrowing for the purpose of business expansion, but the decision is ultimately up to the capitalist who is willing, or unwilling, to pay the price. United States President Richard Nixon (1913–1994), for example, set wage and price controls in his economic policy of 1971. He did not, however, forbid action of any kind; he encouraged the market to act in ways better for the consumer. Thus, the government may protect the consumer by creating standards for wages or by encouraging competition when a monopoly has formed.

Competition   Competition is another essential aspect of capitalism. Competition means that it is the interactions between the buyers and sellers that determines the price of goods and services rather than the state or a private monopoly. Research, for example, has become one of the largest competitive arenas. By performing research today, companies can anticipate the goods and services consumers will desire in the future. Research has become a very competitive area; when one company researches and then produces a product first, all of its competitors who were working on similar products have lost out. Their goal has been realized by someone else and all of the resources they have expended to that end have been, relatively speaking, wasted. For example, as soon as someone designs a smaller cell phone, the others working on a similar project must then think of something else to design. Competition creates fervent researchers. Research fuels competition not only between companies, but between entire economies. In the 1970s the United States began to relax its research endeavors both publicly and privately. Japan and Germany have since grown enormously in strength due to their research, taking part of the success away from the United States.

Profit   Another principle idea of capitalism is profit. A special level of freedom is created in capitalism that is not found in other systems. It guarantees freedom in several important areas: contract, property, trade, and occupation. In contrast, when prices are established by the state, there is a limited amount of profit to be made and, therefore, less incentive to enter the market.

Capitalism is a system based on profits and, consequently, on losses. When one person, company, or state makes an enormous profit, there is always some-

one who has lost out. In any given year, forty percent of corporations will report losses. Fifty percent of firms close down within two years of opening, and eighty percent close within ten years of opening. The closures are usually due to continual financial losses.

THEORY IN ACTION

There are many examples of capitalism. Germany, the United States, and Japan are countries where capitalism is the driving economic force but which are, at the same time, very different from one another. While Japan is more specifically designed like itself, both the United States and Germany are universalistic. Germany is community oriented and the United States revolves around individualism. The United States is analytical and Germany integrative.

Before World War II, which lasted from 1939 to 1945, the capitalist economies were plagued by dips and swings, depressions and peaks. There has been a huge change since the Great Depression of the 1930s, however. Welfare policies and available aid have curbed the slumps. The economy has also changed from an industrial economy to a service economy which has created greater stability in supply, demand, and in the job market.

Capitalism in practice was very much like capitalism in theory through the mid–nineteenth century until the Great Depression. One thing that has happened is a change in proportion of the population in the labor force. With technological development, under capitalism or any other economic system, the industrial working class increases constantly at the expense of the tradesmen: carpenters, blacksmiths, bakers, and plumbers, for example. These potential tradesmen choose jobs in factories instead. As time progresses in industrial development, however, the numbers working in industry begin to go down again in proportion to the population. Their absolute numbers keep growing, but proportionally the numbers are shrinking.

The United States

Since the advent of the twentieth century, the technological working class in the United States has consistently grown while the proportion of people working in industry has steadily gone down. This has occurred for two reasons. The first reason is the switch from blue collar work to white collar work. There has been a steady shift as technology increases. Automation and machinery do the work that the blue collar workers used to do. There are more white collar

American women working in a rifle factory during World War I. (The Library of Congress)

workers needed to manage the technology, but the overall number of workers goes down.

Rise of the service economy   The second reason for the steady decline in workers proportional to the population is the growth of companies to provide service rather than goods. From 1950 to 1985, the number of people employed more than doubled from 60 million. The number of white collar workers rose from 22 to 53 million. The new white collar workers were employed in government, retail and wholesale trade, schools, insurance, communications, entertainment, health services, finance, and real estate. Government in particular has grown enormously.

The change from producing goods to providing services has led to a shift in the nature of most employment. In 1950, more than half of the labor force was blue collar. Today, white collar workers outnumber blue collar workers by more than two to one. The production line has given way to the office and the product has become a service. This is called the service economy to prevent confusion with the industrial economy that it replaced.

The two–tier labor market has largely been created by the advent of improved technology which separates white collar and blue collar workers more distinctly. Generally speaking, blue collar workers lack the education, pay raises, health insurance and other benefits that common in the white collar sector. In fact, since 1975, the majority of the household income gains have gone to the upper 20 percent. From 1994 to 1999, inflation was low and unemployment fell to below 5 percent. In 2001, the economy moved into a downswing, however, and the long term troubles with a lack of economic investment, medical cost increases with the aging population, trade deficits, and family income stagnation for the lower income families became problematic.

An important year in American capitalism history related to the rise in the service economy was 1956. For the first time in world history, the number of people performing services was greater than the number producing goods. The same change has since occurred in Sweden, Great Britain, and Canada. This switch has been significant politically because the salaried members of society identify more strongly with the upper and middle classes than with the working class. This white collar group generally produces children who continue in this social stature. The new members of society are better educated and more wealthy than their blue collar counterparts, and because of this, they're better suited to remain in that position.

In comparison, Russia saw a huge increase in industrial workers, both skilled and unskilled. As its industrialism increased, however, the same phenomenon occurred and there were increasing numbers of white collar members of society. Class lines have become defined despite the communist ideology. The social status of the blue collar worker is distinctly different than that of the white collar worker. These new upper classes are rising at the expense of the lower. In communism as well as capitalism, industrialism breeds this shift in the populous.

The new service economy has greatly affected the strength of the capitalist economies. In a goods-producing sector of the economy there are large shifts of employment and of demand. When there is excess supply, it can usually be stockpiled and the surplus saved. With the service economy, however, the services cannot be saved if there is a surplus in supply. There is necessarily a better balance between supply and demand for this reason and this in turn creates a more reliable and predictable job market.

In countries that practice capitalism, the economic levels are high enough to allow for welfare policies and payment. With other economic systems, however, though there are often welfare policies existing in theory, there is often not enough money to pay for them and they become obsolete. Under capitalism the constant increase of goods and services allows for enough wealth to be able to be distributed to the people who

are struggling. Since the market is permitted to adjust to itself and is in control of all of its own intricacies, it is able to be much more efficient than if the state tried to regulate all of the details.

It is interesting to note, however, that despite the success of capitalism and the relative economic boom in the United States, there is still a poverty problem and an uneven distribution of wealth. Many people are in debt, and the United States itself has a huge debt to repay to its lenders.

Non-Profits Another change in the structure of capitalism has been the increase in the non–profit sector. In the United States, the non–profit sector is made up of private not–for–profit organizations and the government. This section of the economy is growing at a faster rate than the for–profit sector in the United States. Non–profit means that there is a direct, or indirect, contribution back to society. Since the non–profit sector doesn't invest their earnings in themselves, what would have been profit goes back into circulation.

The non–profit sector has grown for several reasons. The government has continued to expand in the areas of defense, health, education and welfare. Private non–profits have also grown in both health and education. The service economy has helped the non–profit growth as well. As the industrial economy advances and grows, a service economy slowly replaces the industrial economy. When this happens, the production of goods is replaced by services for both for profits and non–profits, such as health, community, welfare and education services.

Finally, as a nation's economy advances and evolves, there is a greater demand for provision of services that not everyone is getting. Health insurance, educational aid and transportation are considered essential but unobtainable. More socialist governments like those in Scandinavia and Britain have concentrated their socialization programs on service areas like health and education rather than controlling economic activity.

The government steps in There have been many successes with capitalism, but there have also been many problems as well. Capitalism has not always gone according to the theory. The Great Depression was an unexpected event. It was responsible for the welfare system which has come to characterize so many capitalist countries, including the United States, Canada, the United Kingdom, and much of mainland Europe. The population believed that *laissez–faire* economics was ideal and that even when the market

BIOGRAPHY:

Franklin Delano Roosevelt

Franklin Delano Roosevelt was born on January 30, 1882 at Hyde Park, New York. He was the only son of James and Sara Roosevelt. Under the guidance of his mother, Roosevelt received a private education until the age of 14, when he left home to attend Groton. After completing Groton, Roosevelt attended Harvard, where he majored in history and political science.

During his college years, Roosevelt courted his distant cousin Eleanor Roosevelt, and they married on March 17, 1905. He enrolled in Columbia University's law school, passed the bar after a little more than two years of study, and joined a noted law firm. Roosevelt was elected to the state legislature in 1910.

In August 1921, Roosevelt's world was changed forever. While vacationing at his island retreat off the coast of Maine, he was stricken with polio. Roosevelt survived the near–fatal attack, but was paralyzed from the waist down for the rest of his life. Roosevelt didn't let his condition get him down. He continued to devote his time to his law practice, his hobbies, and some business ventures. He returned to politics at the end of the 1920s, when he was elected governor of New York in 1928. He served two terms as governor.

During Roosevelt's second term, he dealt with effects of the Depression that had hit New York. Along with a group of advisors, he devised a program that was in many ways similar to the New Deal. The plan included unemployment relief, farm relief, old–age pension, tax increases, and various other reforms. The roots of the New Deal were a big part of his campaign for the presidency in 1932. Roosevelt won the election, and shortly after his inauguration on March 4, 1933, the New Deal became reality. His plan included regulation of credit and currency, reduction of federal salaries, the allocation of grants to cities and states for relief purposes, agricultural subsidies, and regulation of the stock market. Roosevelt regarded the National Industrial Recovery Act (NIRA) of 1933 as the key to the entire program. The purpose of the act was twofold. It devised codes of fair competition in industry and it also guaranteed labor the right to organize and bargain collectively. Unemployment relief came in the form of various work relief agencies.

After 1935, the most important legislation of the New Deal was focused in the area of reform. The National Labor Relations Act was passed by Congress on July 5, 1935. It guaranteed the right of workers to organize and bargain with their employers. On August 14 of that same year, the Social Security Act, which provided old–age retirement payments and benefits for widows, orphans, and the needy, was passed. The Fair Labor Standards Act of 1938 was the final achievement of Roosevelt's New Deal; it set a federal minimum wage and outlawed child labor.

After 1938, foreign affairs became the focus of the Roosevelt administration as the threat of war loomed in Europe and the Far East. Roosevelt, despite protests from the majority of Americans and Congress, involved the United States in the growing war. Roosevelt's involvement in the Allied effort was crucial. He worked on strategic negotiations with the Allied leaders and pursued his dreams of a United Nations.

Sadly, Roosevelt would not survive to see the war end or the implementation of the United Nations. He died from a massive cerebral hemorrhage while on vacation on April 12, 1945. After four terms as President, Roosevelt had successfully realized the social and economic reforms of the New Deal.

---

plunged it would be able to fix itself again without outside influence. When the economy dipped to the point where one quarter of the population was out of work, enterprises were going bankrupt and couldn't pay their employees, and farmers couldn't sell their products without taking a loss, something had to give. The welfare state was created. While not an entirely natural step in the progression of capitalism, it became necessary for the crippled economy.

U.S. President Franklin Roosevelt began the New Deal in 1933. It outlined emergency measures to help people back onto their feet after the Great Depression. The Agricultural Act (May 12, 1933) provided aid for farmers in return for lowered production, thus raising prices due to a decrease in supply. This allowed them to buy the industrial products to which they had become accustomed.

The National Labor Relations Act (July 5, 1935), also known as the Wagner Act, changed the nature of relations between employers and employees. Before the act, employers had been at liberty to recognize, or to ignore, unions in their midst. They often fired workers for being involved in union activities and the workers had no means of protection from this. The Wagner Act promoted bargaining between the unions and the employers. It could not force the two sides to agree, but it prohibited both strikes and lockouts, the scare tactics of both sides. The result was a distinct decline in violent labor disputes.

The Social Security Act (August 14, 1935) was another major step in the welfare system's creation. Private efforts to protect individuals from poverty in old age had proved largely ineffective and the Social Security Act sought to create a public provision for everyone through taxation of wages. This act was of particular importance because it showed the United States' belief that it was partly responsible for the monetary security of its citizens.

In 1947, The Labor–Management Relations Act, also known as the Taft–Hartley Act, replaced the Wagner Act. Some provisions of the Wagner Act were altered for the Taft–Hartley Act, but the principle upon which it was founded, bargaining between the two sides, remained unchanged.

In 1965, Congress took the Social Security Act even further to include health care for people over the age of 65. The health insurance covered both doctors' bills and hospitalization. Medicare, the insurance program, existed for senior citizens, but the government also gave grants to the states to provide aid to families unable to cover their medical costs. Many states followed suit by setting up Medicaid, programs set up to deal with federal grants and distribution of money to the families it was designed to reach.

The Elementary and Secondary Education Act in 1965 was another important step. The government made grants directly to school districts with families with low incomes. The Higher Education Act from that same year gave both grants and loans to institutions to improve their facilities. It also gave aid to millions of students in the form of federal loans, federally guaranteed private loans, work–study aid, and grants for students with disadvantages.

The main mechanism for funding the social welfare systems is taxation. Through federal taxation the income is more evenly distributed than it would be if the economy was entirely *laissez–faire*. This distribution of wealth has led to a higher minimum allowance for many. This allows a greater proportion of the population to remain active economic players which ultimately keeps the economy more stable than it would be if the wealth were more distinctly separated. Government taxation is structured to compensate for economic dips and swings. The government has stores of money from taxation from which to continue its wel-

fare programs regardless of the state's economy. Through social welfare, the government is able to retain relative stability.

The debate over public vs. private With his New Deal, Roosevelt essentially changed the relationship between the public and private sectors. He supported farmers and farm prices, protected unions, created a social security system for the elderly and retired, gave aid to the unemployed, and regulated the market. His advocates called him a savior, while his opposition labeled him a traitor.

Initially, everyone seemed in favor of the welfare state in the United States. President Lyndon Johnson (1908–1973) proposed "the Great Society" to this end. This trend continued with Democrats and Republicans alike. The conservatives tried to buff up the existing programs, and President Nixon did just this with welfare and education. With his "New Economic Policy," Nixon also set up price and wage controls.

After 1970, however, attacks on the welfare system became more direct and biting. As time went on, opposition of the welfare system grew. Support and dissent split onto different sides of the fence. Liberals argued that the government should be expanded even further, wrapping its protective, paternal arms even more tightly around its citizens. Two important political changes occurred in the Western world. Margaret Thatcher was elected as the Conservative Prime Minister of Great Britain in 1979, and Ronald Reagan (born 1911) was elected as the Republican President of the United States the next year. Both administrations held strong opposition to the welfare state. Policy shifted and challenged the existing system. Margaret Thatcher privatized even more of Britain's functions including the post office, and she became known as "Maggie Thatcher, the milk snatcher" for revoking free school lunches.

The conservatives had several gripes. They emphasized decentralization of the government, deregulation of the economy and privatization of public entities. After Adam Smith in 1776, capitalism promised free market growth uninhibited by government regulation. The economic advances were coupled with problems, however, such as monopolies, swings of booms and recessions that affected the economy's growth, disregard for the environment by the companies producing waste, and an uneven distribution of wealth, which left many without the means to provide health care, retirement funds and other needs for themselves. These troubles led to government aid and action. Governments began regulating the economy and disbanding monopolies, providing social welfare through taxation, and creating restrictions and guidelines for company waste production.

The conservatives believed that the market economy would correct itself and that government should step back. Distribution of wealth would be unchecked, branches of the government such as the U.S. Environmental Protection Agency wouldn't be able to monitor and control emissions of various kinds and people would be entirely responsible for their own livelihood. The conservatives believed that the economic differences are justified; people reap what they sow and create their own wealth or their own poverty.

The decentralization of government is another concern of the conservative opposition. They argue that national policies are less effective than local policies because the localities are better suited to address specific needs. A national minimum wage, for example, ignores the differences in cost of living between New York City and rural Wisconsin. The concentration of power also means more bureaucrats in the capital, which raises the cost of running the government, which in turn raises taxes. As economies encounter problems, the trend is to deal with them on a national scale if they are affecting the entire country. The right wing feels this is a poor remedy, however, and argues that government should be broken up into smaller bits and pieces.

They also contend that the conditions that spurred much of the governmental growth and attention to social welfare are different than they were when the changes occurred. The Great Depression was seventy years ago. There was an economic crisis. John Maynard Keynes' (1883–1946) ideas of necessary government aid were adopted and Franklin Delano Roosevelt's New Deal began a wave of change. There are problems with social welfare; the people meant to receive the aid don't always get it.

Another contention is the belief in the need for privatization of public functions. The United Kingdom did a lot of privatization under Margaret Thatcher, but the United States has shown more resistance and continues to have many large public arenas. Liberals advocate public welfare for the poor while conservatives want taxes lowered and programs cancelled. The right wing feels that public functions do not operate under market pressures and have no drive to be efficient and successful. The same argument goes for social welfare; the conservative viewpoint is that the allocation of aid prevents self–help and, through apathetic acceptance, promotes long–term poverty and complacency.

The conservatives also feel that the publicity of functions deters the freedom of those functions.

Churches, schools, and museums should be private to protect their individuality. In regard to schools, both the United States and United Kingdom have the option of state funded or privately funded schooling.

There are now two sides of the fence. Views on capitalism have split with the liberals on the left, the conservatives on the right, and many stages in between the two. The liberals support increased government spending and centralization, social welfare and national regulation of the economy. The conservatives want to decrease the size and budget of the federal government, distribute power on a local level, and leave the market to its own devices.

Today, the United States has, arguably, the most diverse and technologically powerful economy in the world with a per capita gross domestic product of $33,900. Private individuals and businesses make the economic decisions with little guidance from the state and the government spends an large sums buying its supplies from private American corporations. Business firms in the United States have much greater freedom to make their own decisions than do their competitors in Japan and Western Europe. They may expand capital, lay off large numbers of workers, and create new products. They do, however, face more obstacles in exporting their goods than do outside firms when exporting to the United States. U.S. firms are technologically competitive and are leaders in computing, aerospace, military equipment and medicine. The technological advantage has continued to narrow since the end of World War II, however.

Germany

The German model of capitalism is somewhat different from that of its Western siblings. Because of the discrepancy between the United States, Britain, and France's definition of democracy and that of the Soviet Union, when the Allies invaded Germany and set up democracy after World War II, there was some debate over which model to install.

Both "democracy" and "capitalism" are ambiguous words and have different meanings for different people and for different countries. The United States, Britain and France have a different meaning of democracy then do the Soviets and Chinese. The former associate democracy with freedom of press and speech, free elections, equality, the right to choose one's job and to criticize the government, the right to travel within one's country as well as internationally, and the right to create trade unions to protects one's rights in the work place. Russia and China, however, consider that version the formal definition. In their view, democracy under communism is the true democracy, with freedom of everything with certain provisions; freedom of speech so long as it is in favor of communist theory and freedom of the press provided the writing is in favor of the government. To clarify, it seems that capitalism and the democracy favored by the Western world go in tandem.

This western view of democracy includes several themes which are used as a basis for reality, whether or not it lives up to them. Individualism, rationality, voluntary choice, the law, means, consent, and equality are the standards behind the democratic machine. The government is by and of the people.

After World War II, the two definitions caused trouble within the Allied Powers. What resulted was the split of Germany down the middle. West Germany was set up with a western idea of democracy and East Germany with that of the Soviets and communism. Since the Berlin Wall came down in 1989, the two halves of Germany reunified, and Germany has emerged as an economic leader with stability that is envied.

Germany has become a model for much of the European Union's development. Like the European Union, Germany's states unified through the Zollverein, the customs union, before there was political unity. The German bank, separate from the woes of politics, is a model for the economics of the European Union. The state and private corporations create business regulations together in a way which would not be possible in the United States due to the individualistic attitude. Germany is more community oriented than the United States. Decisions are made at levels of interaction between the labor, industrial, government, and financial groups.

The German system is almost a merger between the democratic and communist ideals that split the country for so long. Though its politics are not utopian, its economics are almost that. West Germany was able to attain the same Gross National Product (GNP) that she had before World War II by 1950, just five years after the installation of democracy. Germany has trade surpluses today and is in a good position to buffer the collapse of the communist states which border it.

As the United States and Russia distance themselves from Europe, Germany fills the void. Companies like Volkswagen are able to expand, provide more jobs, and produce more cars in order to meet increasing demand. Germany has come from behind and may be winning the race.

Historically, Germany got a late start, about thirty–five years after the United States and seventy–five years after Great Britain. Though the states had begun economic unity in Germany by the mid 1830s, the revolutions of 1848 failed in Germany and, twenty years later, Germany was still in economic chaos. Budding capitalism was intertwined with feudalism. There were not entrepreneurial notions or free markets as there were in Great Britain and the United States. In 1871, the Franco–Prussian War and France's defeat gave rise to the creation of one Germany. Thus, Germany joined the race during the second industrial Revolution: machinery making and steel. Germany's chancellor Otto Von Bismarck, after having banned the Social Democratic Party, began an early model of welfare in the 1870s. His "marriage of iron with rye" was designed to bring German produce to his armies by train and, ultimately, to unite Germany. His workers were well–provided for, and after Germany had become industrialized, its economy fell into place. Though it was still politically and militarily confused, its economics were beginning to stabilize.

Germany surpassed Great Britain economically in the beginning of the twentieth century, but plummeted again due to high inflation and occupation of the Ruhr. Germany had a brief recovery before the Great Depression and rose again before the complete crumble that happened during World War II. Once she was reestablished, however, Germany rose again and, in the early 1950s, grew by eight percent annually economically.

After the United States and Japan, Germany has the third most technologically powerful economy. Its capitalism has begun to struggle, however, due to its welfare system. There is a high social contribution on wages, which has raised unemployment levels. Taxes may be too high and unemployment benefits too tempting to encourage many to work. At the same time, Germany's population has grown older, using the resources set aside from social security while fewer in the younger generations are working and contributing to the bank of funds. There is also a continued integration of East Germany which is very costly for the country as a whole. There are annual transfers of roughly one hundred billion dollars. In 1999, growth slowed to 1.5 percent economically, due to lowered export and even lower confidence in the business sector.

New business, combined with tax cuts and increased Asian demand, may boost the growth higher again but the future of Germany is more uncertain than is has been for many years. The adoption of a common currency for the European Union and other communal integrations have affected Germany as well, though the specifics of the effects are still too young to analyze accurately.

Japan

The Japanese idea of capitalism is rather different than that of either the United States or Germany. The Japanese view capitalism as a way that communities can serve their customers, rather than a system to enable individuals to make a profit. This community logic has created a different, and equally successful, example of capitalism.

Companies in Japan not only take responsibility for their employees but also for the way its employees behave toward others. If an employee and his family had a fire, for example, their relatives and coworkers would help them rebuild what they had lost. In the United States, the family would be more likely to take a loan from the bank or to collect insurance money than to ask for collective help. In Japan, employees are paid more if they have larger families, whereas in the United States the size of someone's family is irrelevant.

The Japanese subscribe to *amae* (indulgent love), meaning that they treat their best customers as royalty. Giving can become intensely competitive. The idea of *sempai–gohai* is also popular: elder brother, younger brother relationships played out in the work place in the form of mentors and apprentices. A manager in Japan is likely to help his employees with their work lives and home lives. Work is all–encompassing rather than just time in an office where one spends part of each day.

Japan is a different kind of capitalist country. There is strong cooperation between industry and the government. There is also a very strong work ethic, an excellent technological sector of creation and research, and a relatively small defense spending allocation, as specified by rules set up after World War II. Japan only spends one percent of her Gross Domestic Product (GDP) on defense. The combination of qualities have helped Japan compete strongly with China and the United States for the largest economy on the planet and have given it a second place slot in the most technologically advanced category of economics.

An important asset that Japan has is its *Keiretsu*, a philosophy of a tightly knit working unit made up of manufactures, suppliers, and distributors. Another ingredient is the guarantee of lifetime employment that Japan gives to much of its urban work force. Both of these assets are beginning to wane, however. There are several reasons for this. Industry is the most important sector of the Japanese economy, and industry is extremely dependent on imports of fuels and materials. The agricultural sector is much smaller and heavily protected and subsidized by the government. Japan is usually self–sufficient in rice but must import half of its grain and fodder needs. Japanese fishing makes up about fifteen percent of the world's catch.

For thirty years, Japanese economic growth had been outstanding. It has boasted a ten percent average in the 1960s, a five percent average in the 1970s, and a four percent average in the 1980s. In the 1990s, economic growth slowed remarkably. By 1995, the effects of over–investing and contradictory domestic policies which were meant to bring excess from the markets caused enormous economic shrinkage instead. In 1996, growth picked up a bit to under four percent due to stimulating monetary and fiscal policies and low inflation rates, but by 1998 Japan was in the middle of a taxing recession created by real estate, rigid corporate structure, labor markets, and trouble with the banking system. In 1999 the output began to correct itself with emergency government measures and an improvement in business confidence from increased government spending. The overcrowding of livable land continues to be a burden, however, and the relative aging of the populous is another concern, similar to the social security troubles in Germany and the United States.

Germany and Japan are similar in many ways, though as a group are very different from the United States and the United Kingdom. The latter two were early industrializers and they developed their economies through entrepreneurship. Their governments have only interfered after the fact, to curb adversarial wealth holders. Germany and Japan, however, were late bloomers and have played "catch–up" in the sectors of technology that they deemed most valuable. Their governments are up to date on the strengths of other economies and cooperate constructively with industrialization before the fact.

Comparisons

The United States and United Kingdom have very broad and sweeping education strategies which stress science and management. Their economics are split between macro (the entire economy) and micro (individual firms). Their social policies have been somewhat left behind and the governments may try to impose social burdens on businesses. Germany and Japan, in comparison, focus their education on technology and science. Their economic system is mainly meso, focusing on the dynamics of specific sectors of industry. The social policies are involved in industrialization efforts and the government considers social benefit crucial to its longevity.

The labor relations in the United States and United Kingdom are generally poor due to pressure on labor costs. In Japan and Germany, relations are still good because wages continue to rise. The American and British development philosophy is *laissez–faire*, free trade, whereas in Germany and Japan it is managed, protected, and targeted.

Historically, the western transition from feudalism was slow and complete. Industry was built on the values of individualism. In Japan and Germany, the conversion is still in progress. Industry is built on communal ideas of reciprocity. The countries differ in ideas of industry financing as well. While the United States and United Kingdom have short term equity markets and many risk takers in the stock market, the markets in Germany and Japan are dominated by banks and low–risk industrial institutions.

The many countries that are capitalistic are very different in their details and, though they share the capitalistic ideals on some level, what that means from border to border varies quite a bit.

ANALYSIS AND CRITICAL RESPONSE

There is a notable relationship between capitalism and democracy. Throughout the world, the successful capitalistic countries tend to be democratic. Great Britain is a good example of this relationship given the fact it is the birth place of both capitalism and democracy. Through the majority of the nineteenth century, Britain kept its international leadership role as a politically democratic and economically capitalistic nation. These qualities transferred to the United States in the twentieth century.

An absolute democracy which entails unlimited rule by the majority is not compatible with freedom and, likewise, with capitalism. Rights would be arbitrary because they could be voted away with the next meeting of leaders. The accepted definition of democracy has come to mean a democracy that is constitutionally limited in its power. The idea behind this kind of democracy is to choose who is in power and how that power is used, but exactly what power the leaders will have remains unchanged because it is outlined in the constitution. A bill of individual rights is also necessary.

Materialism

An interesting development in capitalism is that of materialism. The main object of capitalism is just that, an object. Capitalism relies upon consumers and their every whim, a majority who consumes without producing. Capitalism is based on distributing these goods, though the consumers have no relationship

with the producers or the distributors other than meeting eyes with someone at the counter as they purchase their item. In the internet age, however, the middle man is cut out altogether and people order goods with a click of the mouse.

The only relationship consumers have is with the object itself. This gives the objects more relative importance. Part of capitalism is the mind set of these consumers, that they begin to identify themselves in terms of the objects they have purchased rather than by things that they have themselves produced.

Morality

Regarding morality, there is some debate about capitalistic virtues. Some argue that a capitalist nation is just because everyone is considered equal. Possessions are earned and the distribution of wealth is, in theory, fair. In the 1980s, Reaganomics, United States President Ronald Reagan's trickle down theory of economics, became popular. President Reagan predicted that even though much of the wealth was in the hands of few, through their spending and existence as people of their stature, their wealth would trickle down through society, remain in circulation and reach the less wealthy. What actually happened was financial investment rather than trickle down economics. Money was put in the bank and in stocks where it could not be reached by the rest of society. Trickle down economics did not work.

Many argue that capitalism is functional but not fair, and others feel that the opposite is true; capitalism is the only fair system to choose. Capitalism allows a division of wealth that would not be possible under communism where everything is communal and personal properties are limited. Because of the economic freedom, wealth is unevenly distributed among the players. So perhaps capitalism is practical, but if this is the case, why is the state increasingly involving itself in the market details? Federal taxes are proportionately higher than they have been since the Second World War, and federal regulations on the register are expanding by 60,000 pages each year. Even the recent tax cut will only have a small effect on the government revenue.

Advocates on both sides, the left and the right, seem to agree that capitalism is immoral but practical. They agree that the free market be kept in some sort of check by the government; it is only in the scope of that check that they differ. Is capitalism moral? Immoral? It allows for great discrepancies in the distribution of wealth, and depending on the explanation, whether one earns one's due or lucks into it, the feelings of fairness differ. In *Capitalism: Opposing*

Viewpoints, Michael Parenti argues that capitalism is immoral and quite exploitative:

> The apologists for capitalism argue that the accumulation of great fortunes is a necessary condition for economic growth, for only the wealthy can provide the huge sums needed for the capitalization of new enterprises. Yet a closer look at many important industries, from railroads to atomic energy, would suggest that much of the funding has come from the public treasury—that is, from the taxpayer—and that most of the growth has come from increased sales to the public—from the pockets of consumers. It is one thing to say that large–scale production requires capital accumulation but something else to presume that the source of accumulation must be the purses of the rich.

Some argue that capitalism, however, is very moral indeed. Because of capitalism, we have all the products that are available today. There is an abundance of food, whether it reaches the corners of the earth or not. The life expectancy has doubled because of capitalistic driven research. We have air travel, air conditioning, aerospace technology and computers. It is the capitalist who envisions a product, researches it, and turns it into a saleable product.

Capitalism allows people to think freely and enables them to work out their thoughts. If the businessman cannot act on his own volition, his decisions will be limited as may his production and success. An important idea of capitalism is that everyone has the fundamental right to do with their life and property as they please. A government rampant with regulations can thwart this development, as evidenced by the many third–world nations and the fall of the Soviet Union. The free market drives the community to succeed by way of personal ambition. Adam Smith touched on this in his philosophy by saying that capitalism necessarily meant mutual agreement and mutual benefit.

The advocates of the moral defense of capitalism ask if capitalism is selfish, if it is selfish to take one's own lives seriously and to pursue happiness. A system that revoked some of the personal freedoms would take away some of this liberty and the option to follow a dream, however fantastic. Perhaps for these reasons capitalism is on higher moral ground than it gets credit for.

Modern Realizations

In the material world, there are a lot of problems with modern capitalism. The reality of capitalism was the closest to its theoretical self during its classical period from the middle of the 1700s to the end of the 1800s. Since 1900, capitalism has changed in several ways.

The corporate role The corporate form of business is partly to blame. This form allows for the separation of the ownership of a business from its management and financial control; a company sells its stock and becomes public. The shareholders are only liable for the company in so far as the number of shares that they own. Before the corporation, partnerships involved the complete responsibility of the partners for business operations. Partnerships were small and each member had a sense of moral, financial, and personal involvement with the company.

In the modern world, 100 million shareholders may jointly own a corporation. The connection between these owners and the managers is thin. The corporation may or may not even be in the same country as its owners, and generally less than one percent of the shareholders attend the annual business meetings to elect officers and managers.

Management, rather than owners, decides who runs the elections, who is up for election, what policy proposals are needed, and how salaries should be altered. When these propositions are put to a vote the result is usually over ninety–five percent in favor of the recommendations of management. In political elections, in comparison, the majority usually wins with fifty–two percent. The other forty–eight percent of the population votes the other direction. For this reason, there is a lot of skepticism about the level of democracy within corporate management.

With the government, the people who hold power are accountable to those who gave them this power through elections, assuming the country is relatively democratic and holds elections. The government is the agent of the people, created by and from the population. In theory, political power is in the interest of the people rather than based on what politicians want. With corporations, however, the management makes continual decisions which affect the shareholders. The management is not accountable to them, however, nor does it have any obligation to seek their approval beforehand.

Like other forms of empires, industrial empires fall prey to the same fate. They become increasingly conformist and bureaucratic, leaving the ideology and spirit of capitalistic competition and freedom in their wake as they forge ahead into impersonal rules and enterprises. In many ways, large–scale capitalist enterprise is similar to large–scale socialized enterprise. As corporations become bigger and bigger, they swallow the smaller businesses and the populous is left with fewer and fewer choices.

This has happened in the United States. When on the outskirts of a city it is difficult to tell what city

With marquees on both sides, this building is an example of corporate presence in a capitalist world.
(Corbis Corporation)

one is in because the surroundings are the same. There will be a Walmart and a Target, a McDonalds, a Taco Bell, a Bed Bath & Beyond and a local State Farm Agent. Free–enterprise is changing to become safe enterprise and the corporate giants are sweeping the country and leaving their mark across the planet. It is difficult to drive fifty miles without seeing the telltale blue roof of an International House of Pancakes or a Perkins flag.

The same phenomenon has occurred with personal individuals. Fewer than one tenth of a percent of the population own one fifth of all the stock, and though the number of persons owning stock has been increasing, this is still quite a discrepancy in wealth distribution, paralleling the big business ingestion of the smaller.

Competitive opportunities There is another side to the coin, however. There are still many opportunities for small businesses, provided they aren't in competition with large corporations; quite often, the existence of big business creates opportunities for small businesses. General Motors, for example, produces half of the passenger cars in the United States. Their domination of the market, however, creates opportunities for small mechanic shops, parts stores, dealerships, and gas stations. The corporations are still in

some amount of competition amongst themselves as well. Target is pitted against Walmart. Linens & Things competes with Bed Bath & Beyond. General Motors competes with Ford, and there is also competition between its various divisions: Chevrolet, Pontiac, Buick and Oldsmobile. There is some debate, however, on the compatibility of competition and big business. It is less difficult, for example, to compete with one other company rather than having to compete with thousands of other companies who offer similar products. The drive to produce superior products may decrease.

Given the rapid change of technology and, likewise, people's desires and wants, there is a continual opportunity for new business. However, there is also a continual failure of businesses that are no longer relevant in the marketplace. Arguments for big business include greater stability for the employees due to less risk. Labor rights are safeguarded by the labor unions.

In big business, however, the profits need not be shared with the shareholders or with the consumer. If two companies merge, their combined assets may be profitable for management only. There are not regulations for this sort of wealth distribution, and monopolies benefit the owners at the expense of the consumer.

Critical Views

Structurally, there are some problems with capitalism. Because growth is driven by the desire for profit, it fluctuates according to the number of opportunities and openings. When an opportunity appears, capitalists hurry to take advantage of it and, consequently, there is an economic boom. Eventually, however, the market will be saturated and the boom will end, beginning a recession. Investment ends and the economy takes a dive.

Karl Marx published his criticisms of the ups and downs of the market in his 1867 work *Das Kapital*. Marx said that the growth was not only unsteady because of opportunities seized and missed, but also because of the natural progression toward industrialization and big business which, as explained earlier, makes the booms and recessions of the market more stark and profitable or, in the case of a recession, painful. Big business is not only encouraged by the advent of technologies which allow improved efficiency, but with recessions as well. When the market goes down, some firms will do better than others. The companies that have fared well usually swallow those that have not and become even larger and more successful than they were before.

John Maynard Keynes, an English economist, published *The General Theory of Employment, Interest and Money* in 1936. In his book, Keynes not only agrees with Marx that the ups and downs of a market economy are problematic, but goes further to say that it is possible for an economy to remain in a recession without periodic booms to balance it out. In terms of unemployment, Keynes felt that communal investment was the best way to fight this stagnation.

Another criticism of market–driven growth is the products produced by the capitalists can cause as much harm as good. Since the products are generally regulated only by customer demand, negative side effects often go hand in hand with production of goods. Toxic waste, unnecessary products, wasteful packaging, and poor working conditions are all side effects that accompany the products consumers demand.

There is heavy debate on how to deal with the apparent evils of capitalism. Some argue that the problems are not with capitalism but are actually lodged in the attempts to fix it. Well–meaning measures to curtail the market may lead to problems. The market should be left as independent as possible to ensure optimal operation. On the other hand, others advocates intervention and social welfare to distribute wealth more fairly, promote competition and deal with undesirable products of the market such as pollutants. Today, there are no advanced capitalistic countries that allow complete market freedom without social welfare to compensate for pockets of poverty. In the United States, these transfer payments for health benefits and pensions comprise ten percent of the total consumer income. In Europe the percentage is much higher.

In making his case for capitalism in *Capitalism: Opposing Viewpoints*, Howard Baetjer Jr. writes:

> This is the virtue of the free economy. The whole fabric of economic interactions is freely chosen, cooperative, and generally beneficial. Each party to an exchange believes he is benefiting. This point bears emphasis because so many believe that in capitalism the rich get richer at the expense of the poor or that the seller of a good exploits the buyer, or vice versa, so that one is better off and the other worse off. When one is free to exchange in a transaction or not, he does so only when he believes he will be better off for it. Think about your trips to the ice cream shop: you put your money down for the ice cream; they put down the ice cream for the money. You care for the ice cream more than the money at that point, and they don't want the ice cream, they want the money. Everybody goes away content. There is a mutual 'thank you' as you exchange goods and money, because you both are better off...

> People ought to be free economically as well as every other way. *Laissez–faire* is a great system, both practically, because it works to the increasing, as well as the well–being of all, and ethically, because it suits basic principles of decent interpersonal behavior. It is a system that deserves our hearty support.

TOPICS FOR FURTHER STUDY

- There is a similarity between the changes that occur with capitalistic production and Marxist theory. The material basis of production goes through a series of shifts under both systems that alter the structure of civil institutions and the laws that govern them. Compare and contrast Marxist theory with Adam Smith's theory of capitalism.

- How will the European Union affect the capitalism within its borders? Will the common currency promote a common capitalism, or will countries retain their beliefs and practices regardless of their neighbors' differences? Will Germany's economic strength remain, or will it lose its stature as it joins with the rest of the continent?

- James Madison wrote in the *Federalist Papers* that governmental power might one day become less of a threat than that of the effects of freedom and personal liberty. Are his predictions are coming true? His checks and balances system protect us from the government, but we do not have a similar system to protect us from the corporations that provide us with goods and services.

BIBLIOGRAPHY

Sources

Beatty, Jack, ed. *Colossus*. New York: Broadway Books, 2001.

"Capitalism Theory: Frequently Asked Questions." Available at http://www.ocf.berkeley.edu/shadab/capit–2.html.

CIA World Factbook. United States, 2000.

Commire, Anne, ed. *Historic World Leaders* vol. 5. Detroit, MI: Gale Group, 1994.

Ebenstein, William and Edwin Fogelman. *Today's Isms: Communism, Fascism, Capitalism, Socialism*. New Jersey: Prentice–Hall, Inc., 1985.

Galbraith, John Kenneth and Stanislav Menshikov. *Capitalism, Communism and Coexistence*. Boston: Houghton Mifflin Company, 1988.

Hampden–Turner, Charles and Alfons Trompenaars. *The Seven Cultures of Capitalism*. New York: Bantam Doubleday Dell Publishing Group, Inc., 1993.

Hooker, Richard. "Capitalism," The European Enlightenment Glossary. Available at http://www.wsu.edu/dee/GLOSSARY/CAPITAL.HTM.

Kronenwetter, Michael. *Capitalism vs. Socialism; Economic Policies of the U.S. and U.S.S.R.* United States: Michael Kronenwetter, 1986.

Leone, Bruno. *Capitalism: Opposing Viewpoints,* Minnesota: Greenhaven Press, Inc., 1986.

Martella, John. "Philosophy, Economic History, and the Rise of Capitalism." Drury University, 1992.

Tracinski, Robert. "The Moral Basis of Capitalism," The Center for the Moral Defense of Capitalism, 1998. Available at http://www.moraldefense.com/Philosophy/Essays/The_Moral_Basis_of_ Capitalism.htm.

Further Readings

Helpful internet sites include: http://www.capitalism.org; http://www.CapitalismMagazine.com; http:// www.moraldefense.com; http://www.sharedcapitalism.org; and http://www.naturalcapitalism.org. These sites give current information on how Capitalism operates in the world today.

Marx, Karl, *Capital: A Critical Analysis of Capitalist Production*. 1886. Provides a critique of capitalist theory and practice.

Pryor, Frederic, *A Guidebook to the Comparative Study of Economic Systems*. 1985. Provides general information on capitalism.

Smith, Adam, *The Wealth of Nations*. 1776. This is the original text of capitalism.

SEE ALSO

Conservatism, Liberalism, Marxism

Communism

OVERVIEW

Communism is a political and economic system in which citizens share property and wealth based on need. Private ownership does not occur. The idea of communism was set forth by Plato in *The Republic* in the 300s B.C. Plato's ideas were followed by those of Sir Thomas More, who in the sixteenth century described utopias based on common ownership. Communism did not become a formal political system until the nineteenth and twentieth centuries when Karl Marx brought communistic ideas to center stage. It was further developed and implemented by Vladimir Lenin and Joseph Stalin in the Soviet Union, and after World War II, began to spread to countries such as East Germany, China, and Poland.

As the twentieth century drew to a close, communism began to experience problems. Though the most oppressive form of communism, known as Stalinism, had become obsolete, the state–owned systems were not able to provide for the public. One–party systems seemed to disturb personal freedom and create massive unrest. China began to allow private ownership in the 1970s and 1980s. Mikhail Gorbachev reformed the Soviet Union in the 1980s, and other communist regimes began to crumble in the 1990s. Many of these countries are still feeling the pains caused by decades of mandatory communism.

WHO CONTROLS GOVERNMENT? The state

HOW IS GOVERNMENT PUT INTO POWER? Revolution

WHAT ROLES DO THE PEOPLE HAVE? Work for state's benefit

WHO CONTROLS PRODUCTION OF GOODS? The state

WHO CONTROLS DISTRIBUTION OF GOODS? The state

MAJOR FIGURES Joseph Stalin; Mao Tse–tung

HISTORICAL EXAMPLE China, 1949–present

CHRONOLOGY

1848: *The Communist Manifesto* is completed

1917: Bolsheviks gain control in Russia

1924: Joseph Stalin becomes leader of Soviet Russia

1945: Soviet communists take control of Eastern European countries

1949: Mao Tse–tung's Chinese Communist Party gains control of China

1956: Soviet Premier Nikita Khrushchev denounces Stalin at Twentieth Party Congress

1958: Mao Tse–tung introduces the Great Leap Forward in China

1959: Fidel Castro and the Communists are empowered in Cuba

1966: Mao Tse–tung strives to bring China into the modern age with the Cultural Revolution

1989: The Berlin Wall falls in Germany

1991: The Soviet Union collapses

HISTORY

Communism is not a new idea. Industrial and political power was used for thousands of years to control the masses. Social prophets were born from this inequality, and they began to imagine a better system. The ideas that they came up with were communal.

Utopian Ideas

Amos, Hosea, and Isaiah of the biblical Old Testament all examined the possibilities of a different existence, free from control and exploitation and full of life, equality, and vigor. Jeremiah, born in 650 B.C., imagined a new beginning. Everyone would be provided for equally, young and old would commune together, and justice would be the fabric to hold everything together. Similarly, Jesus Christ suggested a utopia as well, created from love. Jesus felt that a communal life would arise naturally from spiritual and social development. It would lack selfishness and cruelty and would thrive with the spirit of humility, service and communism.

Plato The Greek philosopher Plato (428–348 B.C.) had more detailed ideas about how to improve upon reality. Plato lived during a war between Athens and Sparta and was inspired to invent a world without war. After having seen corruption thread its way through society, he became suspicious of any idea that allowed an individual to have greater importance than society as a whole. It was this sentiment that gave birth to his book, *The Republic.*

Plato's ideas were based upon a desire for justice and equality that he longed to see in his society. . All necessities would be provided, but wealth would be prohibited. He argued that wealth creates negativity and laziness and that poverty begets apathy and a general distaste for life. He predicted that his perfect society would eat corn, wine, barley, and wheat. They would sleep on yew beds, wear garlands, and sing while they drank their wine. Plato's Republic would consist of three classes: the artisans would build and produce food and clothing; the warriors would protect the city from whatever threats it encountered; and the guardians would preside over the city. The guardians were the smallest and most important group and should therefore be very carefully chosen and vigorously trained.

In the early centuries A.D. there were several Roman writers who focused on the ways in which society could be improved. They wrote about the evils of corruption and class struggle. They argued that community and shared material would foster a better system. The poet Virgil (70–19 B.C.) described a utopia with no fences or boundaries. Everything was shared.

During the reign of Henry II, towns sprouted up all over England. The towns needed to be able to provide for themselves, so the surrounding land was of great value to the inhabitants. However, gradually the nobility began to claim this land for its own purposes. Land that had formerly been communal for pasture was falling into private hands. The peasants, accustomed to cooperative production and communal living, were horrified by the nobles' appropriation of the land. In 1381, communal ideals were asserted in the Peasants' Revolt as the common folk demanded the return of the land.

Sir Thomas More Sir Thomas More (1478–1535) was affected by the tales of exploration that he had heard in his childhood. He was intrigued by the description of the people on the islands in Northern Africa who had no property but shared all the riches and despised the idea of personal property and status. These travel tales inspired More's *Utopia.*

More wanted a new social organization. *Utopia* contains a slightly different version of communism than earlier works. It described a sailor who found the island of Utopia (the Greek word for nowhere.) The people of Utopia lived in harmony and communion without the crime and indignity so common in England.

Through his explanation of the sailor's experiences on Utopia, More criticized the English legal system, inequality, and described the evils of private property. Utopia was an agrarian state, supporting itself with its agriculture. Many citizens conducted trade during part of the year but returned to the land to help during the harvest. Each person had his own specialty.

On Utopia, each day was divided into eight hours for sleeping and six hours for work. The remainder of each day was spent freely. Any surplus labor was used to repair highways. There was a monthly exchange of goods through communism. Families gave away everything they were not using and took whatever they were in need of. Though no one owned anything, everyone was rich in that they were entirely provided for. Money and the collection of gold or riches were forbidden. Formerly valued items were used in the most common way possible. Gold and silver, for example, were made into utensils and chains rather than coins.

Utopia's government was made up of its people. Each group of thirty families elected a magistrate. Each ten magistrates elected an "archpilarch," and they elected a prince. Criminals were sentenced to slavery and the slaves would do the work that no one else in the community wanted to do. *Utopia* was the most substantial communal idea written since Plato's *Republic*.

Utopia became an English word to describe a flawless society. There were more examples and ideas of utopian communities, and these ideas spread throughout Europe. In the seventeenth century, John Locke (1632–1704) argued with other philosophers about whether or not communism existed in nature. Locke felt that it did not.

Other utopian writers and social reformers continued to speckle the seventeenth and eighteenth centuries with new ideas about equality. Each had his own ideas of how to organize a perfect existence, and each thought that he had finally figured it out. Peter Chamberlen (1560–1631), a social reformer, introduced the idea that the backbone of any society was the worker who owned nothing. He made up the army, did the work, and had as much of a claim on the earth as did the noblemen. The abolition of wealth, he said, would simultaneously end poverty. If the rich were honest and strong of heart, the poor would not exist.

Owen In 1817, Robert Owen (1771–1858) began to tackle the problem of unemployment with his theo-

ries. England had recently gone through a year of overproduction, and the need for relief grew until the House of Commons created a Committee on Poor Laws. Owen wrote a paper for this committee, explaining that the world had been taken over by wealth. Machinery had decreased the need for labor and the common man was not able to earn enough to buy what he needed to support his family. Owen felt that the best solution was communism and cooperative creation. He advocated self–contained communities, though not isolated from the rest of the world.

Anxious to attempt his own utopia, Owen bought Harmony, Indiana in 1824. He came to America and tried to create perfection in his colony, New Harmony. It failed. The failure was blamed on absolute equality of payment, regardless of the work put out. Despite the failure, Owen continued to write and publish works advocating communism. Utopianism swept through the United States and the idea of community gathered momentum in Europe.

The Beginnings of Marxism

Karl Marx (1818–1883) started as an advocate of communism and eventually developed his own theory with the help of Frederick Engels (1820–1895). Karl Marx founded the Communist League in 1847. When he published *The Communist Manifesto* in 1848 with Frederick Engels, a new brand of communism arose. The *Manifesto* explained that communism was the natural last step in the progression of society In order to get to this socialist state, a country must first evolve through slavery, feudalism, and capitalism. It was the dissatisfaction with capitalism and the realization of the working class of its lot in life that would spark the revolution needed to overthrow the former way of government and begin anew. Marx and Engels argued that industry and power would fall into fewer and fewer hands and that, at the breaking point, revolution would bring properties back to a base at which they would be shared. A central committee would govern over a society of equal members. Marx described this as socialism, using the word communism only to describe the perfection eventually achieved after the wrinkles of socialism were ironed out.

The French Revolution in 1848 created massive socialist excitement. Government had been so thoroughly corrupted that people revolted against the minority that had been controlling them for so long. A provisional government was set up in Paris, promising employment and a new standard of living for all. Democracy began to appeal to more people than communism, and over the next century Karl Marx's ideas lost importance in much of Europe, giving way to the beginnings of democracy and reform.

Vladimir Lenin.

The Soviet Union

At the same time, however, communism was gathering speed in Russia. Vladimir Lenin (1870–1924), the leader of an underground communist movement and a devout Marxist, became the leader of Russia when his Bolshevik party overthrew the provisional government in 1917. By this time, communism had become somewhat different than the utopia described by Plato. It was a totalitarian system with a single political party controlling the government and the means of production and distribution. The new regime, the Comintern, held its first congress in 1919. The Comintern established 21 conditions by which it would define itself. The communists wanted to set themselves apart from all other political movements. They wanted to be seen as unaffiliated with other related ideologies such as the older Social Democratic parties.

After Lenin's death in 1924, a power struggle ensued between Joseph Stalin (1879–1953), the general secretary for the Comintern, and Leon Trotsky (1879–1940), the commander of the Red Army. Stalin eventually won the struggle and Trotsky was expelled from the Soviet Union in 1929. Stalin followed some of Lenin's ideals, including economic policy and his interest in strengthening the Soviet state. Stalin completed the transition from marxism to communism, altering industry and agriculture to become communal.

Stalin and Lenin agreed upon the need for industrial advances, but this is where their similarities ended.

Stalin felt that, rather than waiting for revolution to come to pass in capitalist countries, the Soviets could stand on their own. He believed in a one–country system and structured his regime accordingly. Communist policy changed dramatically when Russia and Germany entered a ten–year peace agreement in September 1939. Adolf Hitler, chancellor of Germany, was free to wage war against France and England. Until Hitler invaded the Soviet Union in 1941, the Communist parties were told to condemn the allied powers of Western capitalism.

Stalin also required the other Communist parties to conduct purges similar to his own. The purges were designed to eliminate disloyalty and skepticism in the ranks and resulted in the deaths of many members of the Soviet party. Stalin asserted his power through personal agents and through the secret police rather than through party channels, as Lenin had. Police violence quashed objections and this oppressive version of communism became known as Stalinism. Because of this change in policy, the party structure weakened. Internationally, other Communist party leaders mimicked Stalin's hierarchy and it became the defining nature of Communism.

When Hitler invaded the Soviet Union, much of the world expected a quick Soviet defeat. Stalin held his ground, however, and many of the evils of his rule were forgotten as he impressed the international community with his military prowess.

The Spread of Communism

While the Soviet Union and Germany were at war, Yugoslavia's Communist movement, led by Marshal Tito (1892–1980), fought its way to power. Communism in Yugoslavia was modeled after the strict Stalinism. In other countries, Communist ideology was slowly replaced with anti–Nazi ideals. In 1943, the Comintern dissolved. It was no longer a tool for Stalin's control, and its end gave weight to Stalin's claim that the Soviet Union had abandoned its revolutionary ideas in favor of nationalism and security.

Stalin's political and military superiority led him to create new policy. He decided to establish political regimes in the countries bordering the Soviet Union and that his country should be internationally recognized as the authority on Communism. His army, still in Poland, Bulgaria, Romania, Hungary, and East Germany when World War II ended in 1945, installed regimes similar to its own. Communism was also implemented in Czechoslovakia and North Korea. Yugoslavia and Albania also became Communist, but on their own accord rather than under the fist of Soviet Russia.

There were three phases under which the countries adopted Communism. The first was a coalition of Communist and Socialist parties in the name of genuine improvement, which lasted for several years in Romania, Hungary, Bulgaria, and Czechoslovakia. In East Germany and Poland, there was a much weaker coalition that gave deference to the Communist parties. Yugoslavia and Albania had even less Socialist party freedom. The Communists required fusion of all other Socialist parties and silenced opposition with varying degrees of legality. By 1949, all of the Communist countries existed in the third phase, without freedom of parties and subject to oppression and violence. The Socialist and peasant parties were attacked and extinguished.

Yugoslavia was different. The Communists, led by Tito, were heavily supported because of their role in the war. The People's Democracy set up in the country was more closely related to Communist political structure than to other democratic countries.

In European countries outside of the Soviet bloc, the Communist parties had trouble clinging to the status they had held during the war. The parties in Italy and France retained relatively high percentages of support, but never held high office. Their power was limited to acts of disorder in line with Soviet policy.

After the war, several Communist parties had evolved in Asia because of the Western resistance to nationalism. In 1948, Communist movements erupted in Malaya, Indonesia, and Burma. After the surrender of Japan in September 1945, the communists under Ho Chi Minh (1890–1969) collected power in Indochina. By the end of 1946, the Communists in the north were fighting the south. This was the beginning of the Vietnam War, which lasted until 1975. India's Communist party gathered momentum after having supported Britain and experimented with Soviet–style violence after India's independence but refuted this policy in 1950.

In China, Mao Tse–tung (1893–1976), also known as Mao Zedong, led the Chinese Communist Party to power in 1949. Though his party had developed with the help of the Soviets, Mao was not interested in being recessive. His party had won after a long guerrilla war. Stalin was unhappy with Mao's autonomy and had planned to treat China as he treated the other countries in the Soviet bloc. Geographically and economically, however, China was in a stronger position to become its own entity and, furthermore, to become the Communist standard by which the rest of Asia measured itself. Other Southeast Asian countries

Joseph Stalin. (AP/World Wide Photos)

did follow China's example. North Vietnam became communist in 1954. In the 1970s, South Vietnam, Laos, and Cambodia also became communist.

There was increasing dissension between the Soviet Union and China. In essence, both countries wanted to be the international Communist leader. On the surface, they fought over doctrine and details.

The Struggle for Power and Reform

Stalin continued to purge his population and those of the border countries. His expansion provoked a counter–offensive from the West, including the formation of the North Atlantic Treaty Organization (NATO) in 1949, which created a permanent defense for Western Europe, and the creation of the atomic bomb which, from 1945 to 1949, remained in sole possession of the United States. Stalin refused the offer of the Baruch Plan, calling for international control of atomic weapons. Instead, he finally succeeded in creating his own atomic bomb in 1949, and the Cold War between the Soviet Union and the United States had begun.

Trouble was brewing between the Soviet Union and Yugoslavia. Tito was unwilling to succumb entirely to Soviet control, and Stalin was unwilling to allow the Communist country to remain autonomous. The Yugoslav Communist Party was expelled from the Cominform, the new group of Communist parties.

Yugoslavia's independence created a new ideal—it had survived its challenge to the Soviet Union. The Yugoslavian Communists could now speak more freely about Soviet Communism.

Reacting to Yugoslavia's breach, Stalin tightened his grip on the remaining countries and renewed the force with which he purged his population of anything anti–Stalin. The countries in the Soviet bloc were overflowing with anti–Stalin sentiment by the time he died in 1953, largely because of his quest to eliminate such feelings.

In the east, Korea was having a struggle of its own. After the defeat of Japan, Korea had been split in two with a Communist government in the north and a non–Communist government in the south. Both claimed to be the government for the whole country, and when North Korea invaded South Korea in 1950, the United Nations condemned the aggression and approved American assistance to South Korea. There were now Communist struggles under way in Vietnam, Korea, and Eastern Europe.

When Stalin died in 1953, another power struggle ensued in the Soviet Union. Nikita Khrushchev (1894–1971), the first secretary of the Communist Party, ultimately won control. He wanted desperately to undo what Stalin had put in place and to create a Communism not synonymous with misery and mass murder.

Undoing Stalinism   Khrushchev developed a policy of cooperation and integration with the satellite Communist countries. This replaced Stalin's policy of exploitation. He established economic and political freedoms as well. He also tried to reconcile with Tito and Yugoslavia. The Soviet Union signed an agreement with Yugoslavia in 1956, stating that each Communist country was its own entity with none having the right to subject authority over others.

Also in 1956, Khrushchev delivered a speech critical of Stalin. Though this speech was not published in the Soviet Union, its text was published by the United States and was widely circulated among Communists worldwide. His comments sparked a feeling of freedom in the Soviet Union and began a wave of public criticism that had been suppressed for 25 years.

Internationally, Khrushchev's statements began a wave of criticism toward Stalin–like leaders in other countries. Hungary's leader was unseated and revolution began. The Soviet Union invaded Hungary in 1956 to end the revolution. After this seemingly contradictory act, Communists began to question Soviet leadership.

In 1957, Communist parties met in Moscow. At China's insistence, the Soviet Union retained its leadership and, for a while, the rift between China and the Soviet Union seemed to evaporate. In 1959, however, the chasm widened. China grew suspicious of Soviet talks of "peaceful coexistence" with the United States, and the Soviet Union did not support China in its attacks on India. Economic relations were severed and the Sino–Soviet split continued.

In 1961, the Soviet Union began a public criticism of China. The struggle increased and destroyed the idea that Communism was a single viewpoint. The Soviet claim of leadership was weakening, and Communist parties divided themselves into pro–Soviet or pro–Chinese factions. The fact that there was a dispute at all allowed greater debate and freedom within the Communist movement. Soviet control steadily declined. When the Soviet Union tried to swallow Romania into its bloc, Romania resisted and remained outside.

When Khrushchev lost power in 1964, his successors tried to reunify the Communist movement. In 1969, 75 Communist parties met in Moscow. However, only 9 of the 14 parties in power were there. Asia and Africa were not well represented, and Cuba sent an observer rather than a representative. The conference was unsuccessful at rejuvenating the Communist union.

Reform was a reoccurring problem in Communist countries. The only country to attempt reform with mild success was Yugoslavia, who allowed its collective farms to fade away after their creation. Yugoslavia also created the Workers' Councils to provide a voice to the factory workers. Furthermore, Yugoslavia argued that revolution was not necessary for Communism, that the Communist party did not need to be a one–party system, and that war grows from multiple powers in conflict, not simply from threats from the United States.

In Czechoslovakia, reform was chaotic. Alexander Dubcek (1921–1992) came to power in 1968 and tried to liberalize the country. He wanted to install civil liberties, a judiciary, and other democratic ideas. The Communists asserted their intentions to remain in the system, but Soviet leaders responded by invading Czechoslovakia in 1968 to protect against reform. This invasion surprised the international community and was seen as a Communist attack against other Communists.

Hope of *détente*, or peaceful coexistence with the West, gathered momentum in the 1970s. The international community began to envision acceptance between the Communist and non–Communist states.

However, the Soviet leadership stated that it had no intention of changing its position, and countered this with its 1979 invasion of Afghanistan.

Eventually, the Soviet Union began to face trouble. Its economic growth slowed down, and criticism of its policies thrived in the intellectual community. Mikhail Gorbachev became the general secretary of the Soviet Union in 1985 and the president in 1988. He supported structural reform. Gorbachev announced that the Communist revolution had no place in his country, and his relaxed policies allowed increased freedom in the satellite countries.

Though Communism was waning in Europe, the Soviet Union, and Africa, it was gaining speed in Cuba, North Korea, China, and Vietnam. The Tiananmen Square student demonstrations in China in 1989 were violently suppressed in an attempt to prevent anarchy. Though China had also reformed some of its policies, advocating foreign investment, relaxing collective agriculture, and expanding personal freedom, its Communism remained relatively unchanged.

Communism has not succeeded in many ways. It is synonymous with the Cold War, Castro's oppression of his people, the Tiananmen Square uprising, and of the continual struggle of the countries in Eastern Europe. It is difficult to say what lies ahead, and whether or not Communism will yet prove itself to be a viable system or if it will continue to lose ground.

THEORY IN DEPTH

Communism is a very general idea. Of ancient origin, communism means a system in which society owns property collectively. Wealth is shared according to need. Specific ideas on communism have evolved over the years, ranging from the utopian versions of Plato and Sir Thomas More to the more dictatorial creation of Joseph Stalin.

Marxism

The first utopian communities were founded in the nineteenth century, but communism took a different road when examined by Karl Marx and Frederick Engels later in the century. Their *Communist Manifesto* was the first book identified as such, explaining the differences between the classes and the need for revolution to bring equality and, ultimately, Marxism.

Marxism has three main areas—philosophy, history, and economics. Philosophically, Marx agreed with George Hegel (1770–1831), a philosopher that he studied while he was creating his own theory. He

believed that history was a series of conflicts arising from two opposing forces, a thesis, and an antithesis. When the two forces collided, they formed a third entity, the synthesis. This synthesis then became its own thesis, inspired an antithesis, and spawned a new synthesis.

Marx also felt that philosophy had to become real. He did not feel that it was enough to be an observer, He argued that, though observation was useful, little would happen until someone actually did something. One must attempt to change the things that he or she was unhappy with, rather than continually philosophizing about them.

Marx felt that history was made up of different methods of provision. He identified five: the slave state; the feudal state; capitalism; socialism; and finally, Marxism. The slave state exploited the slaves too much to succeed indefinitely, the feudal state did not allow enough freedom, capitalism created too much inequality, socialism would begin to iron out the wrinkles, and Marxism would step in as the ultimate social achievement.

He also explained that the most important aspect of society was the way in which it provided for itself. Its economic means could include hunting and gathering or grocery stores and factories. The tools used and the groups who owned the modes of production were also important aspects to any given society.

Economically, Marx discussed class struggle. He focused on capitalism, arguing that it stole freedom from its citizens and created false feelings of security and equality. He felt that the blue collar workers focused on the ways in which they were not exploited rather than on the ways that they were.

Marxism included the idea of alienation as well. With capitalism, a worker produced goods. He was paid the same wage regardless of the profit his product generated for the capitalist. Marx felt that this separation from the direct profit of the good alienated the worker. He also felt that by selling one's labor as a commodity, one was alienated from oneself. Workers were not paid for their value, but rather were given an amount which would allow them to provide for themselves.

When Lenin took power in Russia in 1917, communism had become a fusion of Marxism, Russian revolutionary tradition, and the personal ideas of Lenin. Lenin's version of marxism came to be known as Marxism-Leninism, and was a sort of transition step between marxism and communism. The general idea of communism remained the same, that is that wealth is shared and that no one takes precedence over another.

MAJOR WRITINGS:

The Communist Manifesto

The Manifesto, written by Karl Marx and Frederick Engels, was published in 1848, right before the French Revolution. The Communist League, during its second Congress in 1847, commissioned Marx and Engels to write their new program. Marx and Engels responded with *The Communist Manifesto*.

The manifesto covers many areas. It begins by describing the bourgeoisie and their role in capitalism. It compares this class with the proletariat, the working class, who sells its labor in order to support itself.

The book explains the progression of capitalism, from world interdependence to centralization where the property becomes heavily concentrated in fewer and fewer hands. The world market is next, creating new opportunities, which, in turn, increase the scope and power of the capitalist. This is followed by the crisis that plagues capitalism—recession.

The manifesto describes the development of the proletariat. The working class slowly realizes that it is not happy with its lot, and will begin to appreciate how it can work collectively to change its situation. Through its struggle with the capitalists, the proletariat forms unions against its oppressors and learns to work in combination with one another. They become revolutionary and, eventually, succeed in ousting the government. They begin again, with their own brand of thought: communism.

Democratic Socialism

The Frankfurt Declaration of International Socialism in 1951 identified the goals and tasks of democratic socialism. The Declaration includes several ideas. It argued that socialism is international and does not demand rigid guidelines. Without freedom, socialism cannot exist, and socialism can only be reached through democratic channels.

The Declaration specifies that socialism would replace capitalism to ensure full employment, increased productivity and standard of living, equality of property, and social security. Public ownership might occur through nationalization or through private coop-

eratives. Trade unions were needed and economic decisions did not rest solely in the hands of the government.

Finally, the Declaration insisted that workers be compensated for their efforts. Socialism attempted to erase discrimination between social groups, races, and sexes. Imperialism was rejected, repression and oppression were shunned, and peace was reached through freedom. It was these ideas that defined the socialist movement in the twentieth century.

THEORY IN ACTION

The Soviet Union

Russia under Lenin Vladimir Lenin brought marxism to the Soviet Union. While Russia was in the middle of the World War I, civil unrest swept through the country. The monarchy was forced out, and Tsar Nicholas II was ousted during a peaceful revolution. The tsar was replaced with a Provisional Government designed to promote democracy and capitalism. Lenin was against capitalism and desperately wanted to bring communism into his country. Lenin's Bolshevik party encouraged peasants to seize land. The Bolsheviks infiltrated trade unions, political parties, and local governments. They slipped in through the cracks. At the end of 1917, though they had only won twenty–five percent of the vote in the free elections the previous summer, they took control by force. The Bolsheviks removed the Provisional Government and claimed power for themselves.

Lenin turned the land over to the peasants and began negotiations to get the newly created Soviet Union out of the war, and his popularity jumped. However, his practices gradually began to differ from marxist theory. Soon after he took power, he began to silence opposition and eliminate threats. He justified political and social atrocities and seemed willing to ignore the ideals of a Marxist communist, equality and freedom, in order to reach his goals. He closed newspapers that were not pro–Bolshevik and he got rid of the Constituent Assembly, which had been elected in 1917.

Lenin collectivized agriculture and confiscated goods and products from the peasants. He redistributed the materials to his troops. He felt that this was a first step to socialism, but the peasants revolted and civil war sprouted up all over the country. The Bolsheviks changed their name to the Communist Party in 1919. Civil war continued until 1921. It was between the Bolsheviks and virtually everyone non–communist, the Whites. The Whites received support from Britain, France, and the United States. Under the direction of Leon Trotsky, Lenin's Red Army won, and by 1921 the civil war had ended.

A massive famine killed 5 million Russians from 1921 to 1922. Lenin's confiscation of goods had left the peasants without provisions and without the desire to create more. Lenin reevaluated his policies and decided that his people would starve if he didn't change his confiscation practices. He had hoped that his ideals would be easily put into place, but was finding it harder than he had anticipated.

In 1921, Lenin began his New Economic Policy, a concession to capitalism. It allowed for limited private property and compensation for goods taken from the peasants. Lenin wanted to stimulate production in workshops and farms through profit and efficiency incentives. This policy allowed Russians to support themselves for seven years, through Lenin's death and the power struggle between Leon Trotsky and Joseph Stalin.

Before Lenin died in 1924, he was concerned about corruption in the party. He had believed the Marxist ideal that, under socialism, there would be no crime or greed because everyone would be provided for. His party leaders, however, had become intoxicated with the power and fear that they held over the people. Communism had begun in earnest. There were frequent abuses of power and Lenin was terrified for the future of his country.

Stalinism   When Lenin died, there were two contenders for his position. Leon Trotsky was the head of the Red Army and the favored man for the job. Joseph Stalin was the crafty general secretary for the Communist party, who eventually won the power struggle through his cunning and political backing.

Stalin created a new theory that he called "socialism in one country." Both Karl Marx and Vladimir Lenin had thought that revolution would be contagious and that the movements in neighboring countries would feed off each other. Stalin saw no evidence of this, however, and felt that the Soviet Union could stand on its own. In order to succeed, he felt that his country needed to substantially improve its technology and industry.

By 1928, Stalin was controlling the government. He decided to alter the economic policy initiated by Lenin and instituted the first of many Five–Year Plans. His goal was to collectivize agriculture and to bring Soviet industry up to speed. The state already had control of the railroads, mines, large factories, and banks. Stalin took control of the smaller factories and peasant farms. He declared a need for communism in or-

der to protect the Soviet Union from its capitalist enemies.

His first Five–Year Plan began in 1929. He ordered heavy industry to grow by 330 percent and general industry to grow by 250 percent. He also collectivized agriculture. Stalin felt that agricultural production would be increased on large, collective farms with machinery. Private ownership went against communist principles and was outlawed. Stalin needed to increase agricultural efficiency so that he could transfer some of the agricultural labor to his industrial labor needs.

Small peasant farms were closed and their land and tools confiscated. Stalin forced his ideas and, when he met opposition, he snuffed it out. Roughly seven million peasants were killed between 1929 and 1933. Many peasants slaughtered their livestock instead of giving their animals to the state. The productivity at the collective farms was poor. The peasants didn't want to be there. They were paid little and they worked little. Famine swept through the country in the early 1930s. Stalin called it "war by starvation."

In time, perhaps because Stalin realized that if everyone died there would be no one left to work, the peasants were allowed to farm small personal plots. Though these plots amounted to only three percent of Soviet farmland, they produced one third to one half of the potatoes, vegetables, meat, and eggs. Stalin had expected the collective farms to produce surplus, which he could export in exchange for machinery. Given that there was no surplus of goods, Stalin directed virtually all of the Soviet resources to industrial advances, leaving the collective farms to fend for themselves.

Stalin's second Five–Year Plan was similar to his first. Though the plans did not achieve the agricultural success that Stalin had projected, they did make remarkable gains in industry. Steel and oil production tripled, with electricity and coal production close behind. The standard of living had plunged, however, for the Soviets that were still alive.

During the second half of the 1930s, Stalin began the Great Purge. Both he and Lenin had conducted purges to eliminate dissent and unrest, but the Great Purge was a much larger murder campaign than anything that had come before it. Millions of citizens were killed or sent to the labor camps where they were worked to death. Stalin eliminated three–quarters of the Communist Party leadership and crippled the economy as the military silenced dissension at every level. The Great Purge ended abruptly in 1938, after at least eight million deaths, and things returned to business as usual.

When Germany invaded the Soviet Union in 1941, the international community expected a quick Nazi victory. When his troops held their own, Stalin gained international respect for his military prowess. The Red Army defeated Germany, and pushed the Germans across its borders. It kept pushing throughout eastern Europe as well, and while occupying the region, installed puppet communist governments in Poland, Romania, Bulgaria, Czechoslovakia, and Hungary.

Communism spread along with Soviet power. When Stalin died in 1953, the Soviet Union was the world's second military and industrial power after the United States. Millions of its citizens were either locked in labor camps or living in extreme poverty, but Stalin had created a superpower with the blood of his people.

Reformation in the Soviet Union After Stalin's death, reform came almost immediately. Attempts were made to increase food and consumer supplies. Party leaders spoke of the need to improve the standard of living, and Nikita Khrushchev, a peasant who had become an important Communist, became the new leader of the Soviet Union. He challenged the ideas of both Lenin and Stalin and tried to set his country on a new path.

On February 25, 1956, Khrushchev denounced Stalin and his methods in a secret speech which lasted four–and–a–half hours. His speech triggered mayhem. His "Destalinization" was designed to remove Stalin's ideology from the previous communist theorists.

Khrushchev declared that, despite marxist claims, capitalism and communism could coexist. He argued that war was not necessary to choose a winner, but that the system better able to provide for its citizens would prevail. He felt that communism would be that system and, after 1956, spent much of his time trying to increase the standard of living so that communism would be the victor. His housing program was more successful than his farming program, but overall he won support. He reduced censorship and increased freedom. He insisted on communism, however, and power remained in the Communist Party exclusively.

Khrushchev also tried to improve foreign relations. He wanted to end the Cold War, the period of time after the World War II when the United States and the Soviet Union were relentlessly competing to outdo the other militarily. In 1962, however, the two countries almost went to war. The Soviets tried to put missiles in Cuba to aim at the United States. The United States threatened war, and Khrushchev backed down. His countrymen were furious at this embar-

rassment and he never fully recovered. The Communist Party leadership removed him from power and he was voted out of office by its Politburo in 1964.

Khrushchev was replaced by Leonid Brezhnev (1906–1982), one of the men who had unseated him. Brezhnev led the Soviet Union for 18 years until his death in 1982. He reversed Khrushchev's economic decentralization program and tried to reinstate Stalin's reputation. He continued to try to curb tensions with the United States and signed a nuclear arms control treaty in 1972.

Regression Many Soviets wanted a return to Khrushchev's reforms, calling for increased freedom and reduced state control. They began to resent communism, and a few Soviets openly criticized the limited freedom. Andrei Sakharov (1921–1989), the leading Russian nuclear scientist at the time, wrote a letter to the Soviet government in 1968. He argued that freedom was imperative and that, without it, the Soviet Union would cripple itself. He was put under house arrest and sent into exile. Not until Gorbachev's *glasnost policies* in 1986 was Sakharov allowed to return to Moscow.

Also in 1968, the government issued the Brezhnev Doctrine, which stated that the Soviet Union would forcefully stop any of its satellite countries from turning to capitalism. The Doctrine claimed that socialism was irreversible—but the vow to forcefully stop any capitalist uprising seemed to be a contradiction of the Marxist doctrine of inevitable and everlasting communist revolution. Protests broke out, particularly among the minorities.

The Soviet economy was flagging and military spending usurped money that could have been used elsewhere. During the Khrushchev era, appliances common in the American home were almost nonexistent in the Soviet Union, particularly because these goods were not only rarely produced, but also almost never imported. It wasn't until the late 1960s and early 1970s that an effort was made to produce great quantities of refrigerators, washing machines, and televisions. And yet, even when these things became common in the Soviet home, it took forever to get them repaired. Moreover, the United States and other Western countries were almost half a century into the transportation age before a car on the streets of Moscow became something other than a rarity.

Everyday services Americans took for granted were woefully poor in Soviet Russia in the 1960s. Since the government controlled the economy, there was no supply and demand. Thus, there was no incentive for people to provide quality service. *Today's*

Isms illustrates the typical frustration of a Soviet consumer: The Soviet shopper had to stand in line three times to buy something—in one line to see if an item was available, in a second line to pay, and in a third to exchange a receipt for the item. "A few supermarkets and self–service stores opened during the late 1960s, and more appeared during the 1970s," note the authors, "but these made little dent in traditional Soviet methods of retailing."

As frustrations mounted for Soviet citizens, bartering and bribery went on behind closed doors—indeed, sometimes the authorities knew but looked the other way. Quality items smuggled in from the West sold at outrageous prices. Domestic prices were kept low by the government, but the ordinary citizen didn't have very much money anyway and there wasn't always a huge selection of things to buy. Furthermore, union workers couldn't address grievances because unions were expected to follow communist policy. The conditions of Soviet workers, in terms of worker's rights and fringe benefits, were only a step or two above the conditions of workers in capitalist countries before the Industrial Revolution. Government housing favored intellectuals and government officials before the ordinary citizen. It wasn't until the early 1970s that the Soviet government came out in favor of private home ownership. During this time, alcoholism grew as a means to escape prolonged misery.

When Brezhnev died in 1982, his country was struggling to keep itself alive. Millions of Soviets had ceased to believe in communism and felt its corruption rather than its ultimate goals of equality. Brezhnev was then replaced by Yuri Andropov (1914–1984) who died after fifteen months in office. Andropov was followed by Konstantin Chernenko (1911–1985) who tried to keep the country afloat. Chernenko died in 1985 after a year in office and Mikhail Gorbachev (1931–) stepped onto the Soviet stage.

Collapse of the Soviet Union   Gorbachev believed in Marx's and Lenin's ideas. He felt that his country needed reform but was not past the point of no return. He called for restructuring (*perestroika*), openness (*glasnost*), democratization (*demokratizatsia*), and new thinking (*novoye myshlenie*). Gorbachev met strong Communist Party opposition to his ideas of reform, but he decided to continue in spite of it.

In 1987, Gorbachev announced a list of changes. His reforms allowed citizens to establish private businesses. He lessened state power over factories and even began converting some of the military factories into civilian factories. In 1989, he allowed farmers to rent land for private business. Censorship dissipated

Mikhail Gorbachev. (Archive Photos, Inc.)

and Soviets gained access to banned books and films. They learned the lies that the government had used to mislead them and saw themselves from a different perspective.

Also in 1987, Gorbachev signed an arms control agreement with U.S. President Ronald Reagan (1911–) The agreement eliminated medium–range nuclear missiles from Europe and did wonders for relations between the two countries. Gorbachev publicized his intent to cooperate with the West. He removed Soviet troops from Afghanistan to deflate increasing anti–communist activism.

In 1989 the first Russian elections since 1917 were held, and non–communists replaced communists all over the country. The Congress of People's Deputies became the new governing body. Boris Yeltsin was elected to the Congress after having lost his job for criticizing Gorbachev. The mood in the Soviet Union grew more restless—there were strikes, and calls for independence from republics such as Armenia, Azerbaijan, and Georgia. Gorbachev remained in power, but was coming under heavier and heavier fire, particularly in the Congress.

Things were even worse in other areas of society. The communist economy imploded before a capitalist economy could replace it. Shortages plagued the country and prices flew upward for the items in the free market. Food rationing began and workers went

MAJOR WRITINGS:
Animal Farm

Animal Farm was written as a parody of the communist revolution in Russia. Written by George Orwell and published in August 1945, this work illustrates some of the potential problems of communist theory. The story follows the political actions of the animals on the Jones' Farm.

At the beginning of the story, the animals begin to notice injustice between the humans and the animals at the farm. Led by a group of pigs, the animals rebel and set up their own farm based on equality. This revolution parallels the Bolshevik revolution in Russia. As with Russia, the communist dream begins to breakdown. One of the pigs gains power through propaganda spread by another pig, much as communist propaganda was spread in Russia through the Russian paper *Pravda*.

The pigs gain control of the farm and the other animals find themselves working just as hard as they did for the humans. The corrupt leaders sleep in the house, justifying their superiority by claiming that, "All animals are equal, but some are more equal than others." *Animal Farm*, though not intended to attack the concept of communism, paints a dismal picture of how communism can breed corruption as successfully as any other system.

---

on strike. Russians began to organize non–communist parties and non–Russians, who made up almost half of the Soviet population, grew weary of their poverty.

Gorbachev's popularity took a nose dive. Conservative communists criticized his reforms, and reformers, including Boris Yeltsin, who had left the Communist party in 1990, argued that his changes were too gradual. Communism began to crumble in many of the Eastern European satellite countries as well. On November 9, 1989, the Berlin Wall came down in Germany. The following day, the Bulgarian communist government fell. Czechoslovakia installed its first non–communist government since 1948, and other countries followed suit.

The Soviet bloc collapsed, leaving only Yugoslavia and Albania to represent its communist

power. Yugoslavia's communism ended with its civil war in 1991, and the government of Albania disintegrated the same year. Gorbachev did not try to stop communism from crumbling. Reformers were still furious with the limitations of his reforms, and conservative communists were equally irate with the changes he had made.

On August 18, 1991, a group of conservative communists tried to return to the former version of communism. They took control of the government and put Gorbachev under house arrest. Though the coup failed, hundreds of thousands of Russians took to the streets in protest. Boris Yeltsin, who had been elected as the president of the Russian republic two months prior, led the resistance.

After three days of mayhem, Gorbachev was back in Moscow as the president of the Soviet Union. He didn't last long, however, and the remaining shards of communism were swept away. Communist party officials were forced out of office and their documents were confiscated. Statues of communist leaders were knocked down and towns and streets were renamed. Gorbachev resigned his post and allowed Boris Yeltsin to take his place.

As communism ended in the Soviet Union, the country itself collapsed. Latvia, Lithuania, and Estonia had been trying to secede since the late 1980s. The Soviet government gave them independence. In December, Boris Yeltsin met with the leaders from Ukraine and Belarus and created the Commonwealth of Independent States, a lax union of states independent from one another. Communism had died, and had taken the former Soviet Union along with it.

China

The Rise of Mao Tse–tung Communism crept into China after World War I. The successful Bolshevik revolution in the Soviet Union and the government that followed gave hope to a similar creation in China. Also, China had supported the Allies in World War I. The Chinese expected the German occupied zones of China to be returned to them, but the Western powers allowed Japan to gain control of them. The Chinese were furious and they lost faith in the Western powers and in their democracies.

The Chinese Communist Party (CCP) was founded in 1921, with Soviet help. The party leadership was shared between Chen Duxiu (1879–1942) and Li Dazhao (1889–1927). The CCP took direction from Moscow. Moscow ordered the CCP to fuse with the *Guomindang*, the nationalist party, to form a "united front" that would unify China and effectively drive the Western powers out of Asia. In 1927, however, the leader of the Guomindang turned against the CCP and murdered thousands of its members. The alliance ended, and the communists who survived fled to the countryside to restructure. Mao Tse–tung was among them.

Mao Tse–tung (1893–1976) was the son of a peasant farmer who went against family wishes and attended primary school. He became interested in revolutionary literature and became a Marxist in 1921. He was a founder of the CCP and, after its victimization in 1927, decided that his party would never again be unable to defend itself. He felt that Chinese revolution would need to be based upon the peasantry rather than the proletariat, as Western Marxists argued.

The CCP party leaders did not agree with Mao's ideas, and continued to take their direction from Moscow. Mao and his supporters were out of reach on their mountain base, however, and did as they pleased. In order to win the support of the peasantry, Mao and his followers treated them with respect. By 1931, Mao had amassed enough support to declare the independent state of the Chinese Soviet Republic. It was an island in the middle of the Republic of China, run by the Guomindang government led by Chiang Kaishek (1887–1975). Mao controlled his republic however, seizing properties from landlords and giving the reigns to the peasants.

Chiang Kaishek tried to crush Mao's regime. He succeeded in 1934 and the communists fled China in what was to be known as the Long March. In a year, they walked over 6,000 miles. One hundred thousand began the march, but only 10,000 finished. When they ended the march in northeastern China, Mao became the party leader and built his new headquarters.

In 1937, Japan invaded the Chinese region of Manchuria. The war crippled the Guomindang forces. Chiang Kaishek was forced to sign a second agreement with the CCP in order to drive the Japanese out. During World War II, Mao developed the "Yanan Way," named after his party's base town. The Yanan Way comprised several ideas. The first was the "mass line," meaning that the peasants were not second class. The party leaders needed to live and learn with the peasants in order to make decisions in their best interest while leading them toward socialism. The Yanan Way included a system of rigid control over the troops, as well as intense training. Nationalism was important as well.

By 1943, Mao was the chairman of the party. Communists were studying his writings and he was called the "Great Savior of the People." When the Japanese were finally defeated in 1945, Mao and CCP had increased their stronghold to 90 million people

Mao Tse–tung.

and hundreds of thousands of square miles. The CCP was much more popular than the Guomindang, and by 1949, the CCP controlled the whole of mainland China. The Guomindang fled to Taiwan where it had American support. Mao was named the chairman of the People's Republic of China.

Life Under The CCP Initially, Mao followed Stalin's example, but within two years began to deviate from the Russian model. In 1953, Mao instituted his first Five–Year Plan. His plan included the collectivization of agriculture, though different from that of the Soviet attempt. Peasants were asked to join collectives voluntarily. Those who did not join voluntarily were persuaded with threats of violence and execution.

Within four years, 90 percent of the country's peasants were working on collective farms. The CCP began to divide, however, and when peasants had to give up their land, they resisted. Organizational problems spawned from lack of experience, and Liu Shaoqi led a movement to slow down the collectivization. Mao was bitterly opposed. Eventually, Mao continued at his pace but with some concessions, such as peasants being permitted to keep their own animals and personal farming plots.

The Five–Year Plan included industrial growth as well. Steel, electricity, and coal grew quickly,

BIOGRAPHY:

Mao Tse–tung

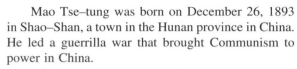

Mao Tse–tung was born on December 26, 1893 in Shao–Shan, a town in the Hunan province in China. He led a guerrilla war that brought Communism to power in China.

Mao was the son of a peasant who had been successful as a farmer dealing grain. His family felt that education was only necessary to teach bookkeeping. He went to school in his village and learned a general knowledge of Classic Confucius. When he was thirteen he left school and began to work on his family's farm. In a rebellious move, young Mao then left his family to attend the primary school in a nearby county, and went on to study at the secondary school in his provincial capital. It was there that he learned of Western ideas. While he was in school, revolution broke out in Wu–chang against the Manchu dynasty and spread quickly to his area.

Mao enlisted in the revolutionary army was a soldier for the next six months. A new Chinese Republic was born that spring, and his military service was over. He drifted through schools for a year, experimenting with law school, police school, and a business school. He studied history and read liberal tradition classics.

In 1918, Mao graduated from the Firs Provincial Normal School in Ch'ang–sha. He went to Peking University and worked as an assistant in the library. He was still at the university during the May Fourth Movement in 1919, which was student protests against giving former German holdings in the Shantung Province to Japan rather than returning them to China. The Chinese radicals turned to Marxism and founded the Chinese Socialist Party in 1921.

In 1920, Mao became the principal of the Lin Ch'ang–sha primary school and he organized a Socialist Youth League branch there. He married Yang

K'ai–hui, the daughter of his ethics teacher. In 1921 he attended the First Congress of the Chinese Socialist Party. Two years later when the party joined Kuomintang, the Nationalist Party, Mao was one of the first people to work for the Kuomintang. He, his wife, and their two sons moved to Shanghai.

Mao began to appreciate the revolutionary potential of the peasant class. He began to try to concentrate the peasant dissatisfaction into revolutionary vigor. After having fled his home from the governor of Hunan, Mao went to Canton and became the head of the Kuomintang's propaganda bureau. When he returned home, he falsely predicted an imminent peasant uprising.

In 1930, the Central Committee ordered the Red Army to occupy major cities, but Mao felt that this would only cause losses to the Red Army and disobeyed orders. His wife was murdered by the Kuomintang and he married Ho Tzu–chen, the woman he'd been living with since 1928.

The Chinese Soviet Republic was founded in November 1931 in a section of the Kiangsi Province. Mao was the chairman. The best hope of victory throughout the country seemed to be to start with a stronghold and to expand outward. Mao led the Red Army on the Long March in October 1934. His army arrived in Shensi Province in the following year. China became involved in a war with Japan, and Mao took the opportunity to expand his army.

From 1936 to 1940, Mao spent much of his time writing. He wrote *Strategic Problems of China's Revolutionary War,*, *On Protracted War,* and *On the New Stage.* By the winter of 1939–1940, Mao could adopt a stronger strategy. He became the socialist leader. He also divorced his second wife and married an actress, Lan P'ing.

---

contrasting with the slow growth in agriculture, similar to the Soviets' example. The population grew faster than the grain production. In order to combat some of the problems, Mao created the Great Leap Forward. He tried to tap into the revolutionary excitement of the populace to create a stronger work ethic.

Communes replaced collectives. The average commune farmed 100,000 acres with 25,000 workers.

In order to promote equality, people were paid the same wage regardless of the work they did, and the peasants were asked to build factories on their communes so that they could work on industry after hours. Mao promised "hard work for three years, happiness for a thousand." The Great Leap Forward was a dramatic failure. China lost Stalin's economic aid. The commune factories produced worthless steel, equal wages created apathy, and China's economy lurched downward. As

Mao continued as the party chairman but lost his post as the president. He was replaced by Liu Shaoqi who reversed many of the changes made by the Great Leap Forward. The communes were divided into "production teams" similar to collective farms. Peasants were once again allowed to farm small personal plots and within three years, China's economy had righted itself. The road to recovery was paved with famine, however, and more than 20 million people died along the way.

The Reds The CCP split into the Reds and the Experts. Mao's Reds subscribed to socialist ideals and communal living. Liu's Experts argued that personal farming plots did not undermine socialism but, in fact, created successful workers.

When Joseph Stalin died in 1953, the gap between the Soviet Union and China began to grow. Mao had been unwilling to succumb to Soviet control, and China continued to create its own version of communism instead of following the Soviet model. Mao opposed Stalin's successor, Khrushchev, and disliked his methods and ideas. Mao felt that Khrushchev was infected with capitalism and wanted nothing to do with him. In 1960, Khrushchev withdrew all aid from China. In 1962, Mao criticized Khrushchev for recalling his missiles from Cuba during the Cuban Missile Crisis. Antagonism between the two continued unabated.

In 1966, Mao launched the Cultural Revolution and restored himself to power. Mao felt that Liu had been corrupted by capitalism, and he created the Red Guards, an organization of teenagers who had done poorly in school and welcomed an opportunity to act out their frustrations. His Red Guards grew to 11 million youths. Under Mao's direction, the Red Guards attacked everything that was foreign, including Western art, books, and intellectuals infested with foreign ideas.

Plays, ballets, and operas were banned. China was enveloped by chaos. Hundreds of thousands of Chinese were killed. Though he withdrew from the public eye in 1969, Mao remained in control until his death in 1976. After a failed attempt to gain control by the "Gang of Four," Communist radicals, he was succeeded by Deng Xiaoping (1904–1997), a supporter of Liu's Experts.

Beginnings of Communist Decline Deng began to unravel the sweater of communism. He instituted "The Four Modernizations," allowing competition, incen-

tives, farming independence, and management autonomy. Deng allowed economic freedoms based on capitalist ideals, but still cracked down on basic rights such as freedom of speech. Nonetheless, the Chinese economy improved as private enterprise was introduced. Moreover, Deng's policies sought foreign investment and the creation of a thriving tourist industry. Western styles and customs began to appear in the youth culture.

A push for democratic reforms increased in strength during the 1980s. By the end of the decade, things had reached their breaking point. In May 1989, during a summit meeting between Deng and Soviet Premier Mikhail Gorbachev, student protesters were such a vocal presence that the long–awaited summit turned into an embarrassment.

When the summit ended, thousands of students and other citizens congregated in Beijing's Tiananmen Square to protest corruption and call for reforms. After officials failed to convince the students to disperse, Deng declared martial law. The government pulled the plug on foreign broadcasts of the demonstration; many observers felt China was on the brink of civil war. Then, on June 3, 1989 the military was brought in to clear the students from the Square. Hundreds died as tanks rolled through the streets and bullets. The uprising was supressed, but China's reputation in the international community suffered.

China has been trying to rebuild its reputation following Tiananmen Square. In the years preceding and following Deng's death in 1997, Chinese leaders have been committed to opening up the country's economy, even at the expense of introducing more capitalist aspects. Communism has started to decompose in modern day China. Deng's legacy is that of a leader who was draconian in the area of human rights, but also of one who did a great deal to raise the standard of living and bring the Chinese economy into the modern world.

Today China more closely resembles the West in terms of the bustling street–side shops, lifestyles of teenagers, and relative economic freedom than any communist country in history. But the government has learned that their concessions to economic freedom have come with a price: the citizens begin to want other freedoms, too. However, it must be made clear that, although capitalist reforms have been introduced and have improved the economy, China is still a *communist* country.

Cuba

Fidel Castro (c. 1926–) brought communism to Cuba. In the fall of 1958, Castro led a revolt against

Fidel Castro. (The Library of Congress)

the government of Fulgencia Batista. Batista fled the country at the beginning of 1959 and, within a week, Castro and his Fidelistas were in control of the capital, Havana. Initially, many Cubans were happy with the revolt. They had been frustrated with the corruption of Batista's government and looked to Castro to wipe the slate clean. However, it soon became clear that Castro intended to bring communism to Cuba.

Regime of a Dictator Castro became the head of the armed forces and, within months, the president. Castro had gained support through his promises of a restored constitution, civil liberties, and honesty. Once in power he was more radical, however. Castro created a dictatorial one–party government. He instituted a centrally planned economy, nationalizing Cuba's commerce and industry. He organized collective farms and cooperatives to produce sugar cane, confiscating land owned by foreigners to do this. The international community and the Americans in particular were outraged by Castro's land confiscation. Under Castro, only Cubans were permitted to own land, and they were restricted in how much they could have. At the same time, Castro expanded social services to all Cubans regardless of stature. Employment was guaranteed and education and health care were made available to everyone. Cuba's economy struggled, however, and Castro was an unsuccessful economic

manager. Cuba depended on the Soviet Union for many of its necessities.

In May of 1959, Castro's government signed the Agrarian Reform Bill. The bill was designed to change the ownership of the agricultural land. Less than 10 percent of the Cuban landowners owned over 70 percent of the land. The bill set a 1000–acre limit of ownership. Another Agrarian Reform Bill in 1963 changed the guidelines to allow for only 167 acres per landowner. Roughly 100,000 Cubans were given 67–acre plots to farm. Most of the land confiscated from the foreigners was turned into collective farms. Communism had begun in earnest.

In 1960, the First Deputy Premier of the Soviet Union, Anastas Mikoyan, visited Cuba. He gave Cuba a loan of 100 million dollars and pledged that the Soviets would purchase 5 million tons of sugar. China offered trade and loans, followed by the Soviet satellite countries.

Cubans who did not support the new regime were killed or imprisoned. Thousands of dissenters went underground or fled Cuba, often to the United States. Castro denounced the United States and accused the country of planning to invade Cuba. American citizens lost enormous investments that they had made in Cuba. Castro confiscated property and though he promised to compensate those he took from, he often did not.

Reactions to Castro For two years, other Western governments tried to establish friendly relations with Cuba. At the beginning of 1961, the president of the United States, Dwight D. Eisenhower (1890–1969), ended the camaraderie. Castro accused Havana's United States Embassy of plotting activities against his revolution. Eisenhower ended diplomatic relations and implemented a complete export embargo. He canceled sugar importation and closed the door to Cuba. Other countries followed suit. Except for Mexico, the other Latin American countries cut their ties with Cuba. In a 1962 conference of the Organization of American States, Cuba was voted out of the organization.

The United States, working with Cuban refugees who wished to overthrow Castro's regime, planned an invasion of the island nation. The Central Intelligence Agency launched an attack of 1500 Cuban refugees on April 17, 1961. They landed at the Bay of Pigs, 90 miles from Havana. Over 1000 of them were imprisoned and their attempted coup was a failure.

In 1962, United States president John F. Kennedy (1917–1963) imposed an embargo on virtually all

BIOGRAPHY:

Fidel Castro

Fidel Castro was born on August 13, 1926 or 1927 near Biran, Cuba. He created the first communist regime in the Western hemisphere and has become infamous in the political world.

Castro was born on the easternmost side of Cuba. His father was a Spanish immigrant and a successful sugarcane farmer. His father had two children with his first wife, and five children, including Castro, with his cook, Lina Ruz Gonzalez. Castro's brother, another son of the cook, became Castro's chief associate.

Castro went to a Roman Catholic boarding school in Santiago de Cuba, and then to Catholic high school in Havana. He was an excellent athlete. In 1945, Castro began to study at the University of Havana in the School of Law. He was very active politically and, in 1947, joined a failed attempt to invade the Dominican Republic to oust Generalissimo Rafael Trujillo. He participated in riots in Bogota, Columbia the following year.

He graduated in 1950 and began to practice law. He joined the reformist Cuban People's Party and became their candidate for the House of Representatives seat in 1952. Before the elections could take place, however, General Fulgencio Batista, the former president of Cuba, overthrew the leadership and cancelled the elections.

Unable to unseat Batista through legal channels, Castro organized a rebel force. On July 26, 1953, he led roughly 160 men on a kamikaze mission on the Moncada military barracks in an attempt to ignite an uprising. Most of the men died, and Castro was arrested. He was sentenced to fifteen years in prison but was released with his brother Raul two years later. The two men went to Mexico to continue their fight against Batista. Castro created a revolutionary group of exiles called the 26th of July Movement.

On December 2, 1956, Castro led 81 armed men to Oriente, Cuba. All but 11 of the men died, but Castro and his brother survived. Revolutionary sentiment grew in Cuba and, after a series of victories, Castro triumphed over Batista's forces and Batista fled the country. Castro's 800–man guerrilla army had beaten Batista's 30,000–man force.

Castro's daughter came to the United States in 1993 and publicly denounced her father's oppressive policies. The largest anti–Castro demonstration in 35 years followed her remarks and Castro lifted his restrictions on Cubans wishing to leave the country. In 1988, Castro allowed the Pope to visit Cuba for the first time. Castro continues to cling to Cuba's political power, and the United States to its anti–Cuban policies.

---

trade with Cuba. The Soviet Union signed a massive 700 million dollar trade arrangement with Castro, however, the Cuban economy was decaying. The industrial plants that Castro confiscated had broken down for lack of materials to keep them running. Agriculture waned and there was a food shortage. In March 1962, Castro began to ration food.

The Soviet Union began to ship military goods to Cuba, claiming that the goods were only for Cuba's defense. The Soviet Union also said that it was sending only technicians to Cuba, not military personnel. In October 1962, tensions between the United States and Cuba came to a head as the Cuban Missile Crisis unfolded. U.S. intelligence began to suspect that the Soviet Union was bringing missiles to Cuba to aim at the United States. Photographs from spy planes confirmed the presence of missile silos being constructed in Cuba. President Kennedy felt a threat to his coun-

try and called for a "quarantine" on the Soviet ships carrying the missiles and military cargo to Cuba. He stated that a Cuban attack anywhere in the West would be interpreted as a Soviet attack on the United States and that he would retaliate with nuclear weapons.

The United States was ready for war. The United States Navy hovered in the Caribbean until the Soviet ships turned away with their cargo. Nikita Khrushchev, the Soviet Premier, sent a letter to Kennedy offering to remove the missiles in exchange for Kennedy's assurance that he would not invade Cuba. Kennedy agreed, the missiles were withdrawn, and the crisis settled.

Conditions between the United States and Cuba improved slightly. At the end of 1962, Castro offered to trade the prisoners he had taken at the Bay of Pigs for over 50 million dollars worth of food and drugs. In 1965, Castro allowed Cubans with American relatives to migrate to the United States. Many Cubans left the country in what became known as the "Freedom Flights." Over 300,000 Cubans came to the United States between 1965 and 1973.

Soviet support for Cuba continued at roughly one million dollars per day. Cuba's industrialization went poorly, and Castro continued to focus on agriculture.

Relations between the Soviet Union and Cuba began to sour in the later 1960s. After Joseph Stalin's death in 1953, the Soviet leadership had become more moderate and democratic. Castro continued his dictatorship, however, despite Soviet displeasure. In 1968, several Cubans in the Communist Party were arrested for siding with the Soviets. Relations improved for part of the 1970s, and the Cubans supported the Russians in the Angolan civil war in 1975 and 1976.

In 1976, Cuba instituted its first socialist constitution. A National Assembly of the People's Power was led by the Council of States and the position of Premier was annulled. Castro was elected to be the president of the Council of States in 1976. In 1977, relations between Cuba and the United States continued to improve. The countries signed agreements on fishing rights and boundaries.

In 1980, almost 10,000 Cubans sought asylum in the embassies of Havana. When Castro loosened his emigration restrictions and opened the port of Mariel, 125,000 Cubans scrambled to the United States. The Americans tried to send them back, but Castro resisted. In December 1984, an immigration policy was developed between the two countries and the Cuban exiles were deported back to Cuba.

Later that year, Cuba suspended the immigration agreement after the United States began broadcasting radio programs to Cuba. When Soviet premier Mikhail Gorbachev began to reform the Soviet Union, Castro refused to change his policies to meet those of the new Soviet leader. In 1989, Gorbachev visited Castro and outlined cutbacks in Soviet aid. The Soviets had been giving five billion dollars annually and needed the money for their domestic struggle. When the Soviet Union dissolved in 1990, the aid stopped completely. Castro was left without his largest supporter and trading partner. Shortages grew worse in Cuba and rationing became tighter. The Cuban economy flagged and Castro was forced to relax his economic policies to allow capitalistic ventures. However, he kept his tight grip on politics. Castro continues to enforce communism, and Cuba continues to struggle.

Korea

In June 1918, the Korean People's Socialist Party was begun in Siberia. The party wanted freedom from

Japanese control. The Koreans felt that the Soviet Bolsheviks would be able to help them with this cause and in 1919 changed their name to the Korean Communist Party.

Lenin contributed financially but did little else to help the Korean communists. On April 25, 1925, the new Korean Communist Party (KCP) was formed by a group of young intellectuals. The Japanese arrested as many communists as they could find between 1925 and 1928 and almost eliminated the communist support in Korea.

By the 1940s, the Japanese had so completely usurped control of Korea that communism dwindled. When the Japanese surrendered at the end of World War II in 1945, the KCP tried again to increase its numbers. There was a struggle among the communists between the "domestic faction," Kim II Sung's (1912–1994) section, and the "Yan'an returnees" from China. Kim's section accompanied the Soviet army to Korea.

In September 1945 the domestic faction began to rebuild the KCP. Kim II, however, began a branch of the KCP in North Korea and became its secretary in October 1945. In December, the group became known as the North Korean Communist Party (NKCP.) The NKCP merged with the NDP in August 1946. The NDP had been concentrating on the middle class, while the NKCP had focused on the peasantry and working class. Together, the parties became known as the North Korean Workers' Party (NKWP).

Soon after, the KCP merged with the NDP in South Korea to form the South Korean Workers' Party (SKWP). The SKWP struggled during the United States' occupation after 1946. The riots and strikes that the party staged helped to keep some cohesion, but the SKWP became a guerilla party. At its peak, it may have had 370,000 members.

The South Korean government squashed radical leftists, driving many of the prominent communists into North Korea. In June 1949, the SKWP merged with the NKWP and formed the Korean Workers' Party (KWP) chaired by Kim II Sung.

The communists began the Korean War in June 1950. The Northern army had occupied most of the South by August, but the United States' intervention prevented a victory. The truce in 1953 prevented the North from forcing communism on the South. Kim II Sung purged his ranks in 1956 and 1958 and got rid of all of the opposition that he could find.

Kim focused on a need to "koreanize" communism. He wanted to establish self–determination and nationalism. By the late 1970s, the KWP had an estimated 2.5 million membership. The party was organized similarly to Soviet party organization. The Politburo governed the party, followed by the Central Committee.

In 1973, Kim began the Three Revolution Team Movement. His goal was to speed economic development and eliminate old ideas. He sent teams of young intellectuals to factories and businesses to guide them into modernity until 1975.

Kim continued to rule until his death on July 8, 1994. His son, Kim Jong II, became the next leader in North Korea. In the 1990s, many high officials left the country and the economy struggled. There were also serious food shortages. U.S. sanctions decreased when a summit between North and South Korea improved their relationship. North Korea is still communist.

ANALYSIS AND CRITICAL RESPONSE

Twentieth century communism has had disappointing results. The Soviet Union, her satellite states, China, Vietnam and East Germany have all gone through massive bloodshed in the name of communism. There are several speculations on why communism has met with so much trouble.

When the Bolsheviks came into power in the Soviet Union in 1917, the Soviets were weary from their tsarist history. They were poor, uneducated, and desperate for food. Their economy and industry was in the gutter and they were tired of losing their sons to war. Lenin pledged to change all of that, bringing goods to those who needed them and ending the war. He did get his country out of the war and he tried to create collective agriculture which provided for the country, but a shortage of resources meant that the little produce that existed was confiscated and given to his Red Army.

Many communist governments' programs of forcing socialism or modernization on its people met with disastrous results. In China, Mao's Great Leap Forward was a nightmare for many areas of society, particularly the education sector. The government interfered with teachers in the universities, and revolutionary ideals and nationalism replaced the standard curriculum.

Modern day China, with its economy thriving largely due to concessions to capitalism, is perhaps one of the strongest indictments against communism. Even the most dedicated Marxist would have a tough time arguing that the capitalist reforms of Deng haven't been good for China. With continuing pressure from abroad regarding the government's human rights policies and with Tiananmen Square still fresh in the minds of the people, many analysts feel Chinese communism won't survive the twenty–first century.

And yet, there are many communist thinkers today who believe China is on the perfect Marxian path, that its economy was never truly socialist in Mao's time, but rather an updated version of feudalism. With its introduction to capitalist reforms in the late twentieth–century, these communist thinkers say that China's economy will become more capitalist until it has fully matured and will then make way for the true socialist revolution.

In the summer of 2001, Chinese President Jiang Zemin announced that the Communist Party would begin to accept private entrepreneurs as party members. However, even a small step toward democracy such as this probably had ulterior motives; it remains to be seen.

Another problem with communism could be the justification of the end by the means. Lenin, Stalin, Mao, and other leaders proclaimed a desire for communism that would provide equality and freedom for the people. In order to reach such a state, however, the leaders ignored equality and freedom. They forced compliance with their decrees and crushed anything in their path. Millions of people were killed in order to reach utopian socialism, which has yet to occur.

The violent tactics used by most communist leaders have created a worldwide distaste for communism. The word conjures up images of East Germany misery, of the Tiananmen Square uprising in 1989 when protesters were killed, and of Fidel Castro's control of Cuba. Communism has seemed to come in tandem with dictatorship. This has meant a lasting dictatorship and an abuse of power rather than an ideal state which provides for everyone and exists without crime.

Marx felt that with marxism, crime would dissolve. He argued that criminals were driven to act because of their poverty and misery, but that with socialism there would be no such misery and, therefore, crime would dissipate. Rather than a lessening of crime, communism seemed to create a justification for heinous abuses of power. Because of dictatorships and forced compliance, leading members of the Communist parties were able to induce fear and acquire virtually anything they wanted. Their control allowed them to do as they pleased, and many of them did.

Marx also argued that the ruling class would only surrender after violence. Because of this, marxism and communism came to power after bloody struggles, both to overthrow the previous government and to convince the population of the need for communism. Violence is not the only option, however. All over

Europe, slavery was abolished on paper and the ruling class allowed the slaves to improve their positions without a violent fight. Perhaps the bloody beginnings of communism led to its bloody future.

TOPICS FOR FURTHER STUDY

- What are the similarities between the versions of communism set down by Plato and Joseph Stalin? Are there more differences than there are commonalities? How would Plato feel about communism as it evolved over the centuries? How would Stalin feel about Plato's *Republic?*

- Would Plato have been in favor of Mao's Great Leap Forward and Cultural Revolution?

- Will communism survive in Cuba after Castro?

BIBLIOGRAPHY

Sources

Binyon, Michael. *Life in Russia,* New York: Berkley Books, 1983.

Ebenstein, Alan, William Ebenstein, and Edwin Fogelman. *Today's Isms,* Upper Saddle River, NJ: Prentice Hall, 1985.

Feinberg, Barbara Silberdick. *Marx and Marxism,* New York: Franklin Watts, 1985.

Hudson, G.F. *Fifty Years of Communism: Theory and Practice, 1917–1967,* New York: Basic Books, Inc., Publishers, 1968.

Kort, Michael G. *China Under Communism,* Connecticut: The Millbrook Press, 1994.

Kort, Michael G. *Marxism In Power—The Rise and Fall of a Doctrine,* Connecticut: The Millbrook Press, 1993.

Laidler, Harry W. *History of Socialism,* New York: Thomas Y. Crowell Company, 1968.

Martin, Joseph. *A Guide to Marxism,* New York: St. Martin's Press, 1980.

Marx, Karl and Engels, Frederick. *The Communist Manifesto,* New York: Verso, 1998.

The Latin American Alliance, "Cuba." Available at http://www.latinsynergy.org/cuba.html, 1997.

Further Readings

Barker, Ernst. *Political Thought of Plato and Aristotle,* New York: Holt, 1915. Gives a detailed analysis of the thought behind Plato's works and those of his teacher, Aristotle.

Binyon, Michael. *Life in Russia,* New York: Berkeley Books, 1983. A journalist from the West chronicles Russian culture and the life of the ordinary Soviet citizen during his time in Moscow from 1978 to 1982.

Davies, John Llewellyn and Vaughan, David, translators. *The Republic of Plato,* New York: A.J. Burt Co., many editions. Plato's idea of a utopia, and the first such example to be written down so extensively.

SEE ALSO

Marxism, Socialism, Totalitarianism

Conservatism

OVERVIEW

Conservatism is generally more reactive than proactive. It is more the presentation of collective responses to other principles and tenets than a collection of its own pure ideologies. Politically, opposing forces are most often called liberal, or favoring reform, and conservative, favoring the preservation of existing order or law and/or cautiously regarding proposals for change. Either term generally refers to an orientation toward facts, laws, policies, or events.

Conservative political tenets vary by country. Whereas socialism and fascism imply certain universal principles, conservatism promotes more parochial continuation. British conservative Lord Falkland once said, "When it is not necessary to change, then it is necessary not to change," begetting the more common, "If it's not broken, don't try to fix it." More moderate conservatives might cautiously change any practice or policy that seemingly has worked successfully for so long. In the alternative, conservatism supports returning to "traditional" or inherited political platforms and tenets as an argument for change.

But historical repetition itself defines what is considered "traditional." Therefore, political conservatism can survive only where governments have been established long enough to secure social, economic, or political traditions. General characteristics include support for the "status quo"; cautiously considering or resisting change; and relying upon traditional values. Conservative ideology has been called "the right" or

WHO CONTROLS GOVERNMENT? Elected officials, with some appointed

HOW IS GOVERNMENT PUT INTO POWER? Popular vote of the majority

WHAT ROLES DO THE PEOPLE HAVE? Vote for representatives

WHO CONTROLS PRODUCTION OF GOODS? The owners of capital

WHO CONTROLS DISTRIBUTION OF GOODS? The owners of capital

MAJOR FIGURES Edmund Burke; Ronald Reagan

HISTORICAL EXAMPLE Great Britain in the 1980s

CHRONOLOGY

1215: Magna Carta (The Great Charter) established under King John at Runnymede, England, giving birth to English political and civil liberties.

1787: "Great Compromise" at Constitutional Convention in 1787, establishes U.S. House of Representatives and Senate as representing national and federal principles, respectively.

1790: Edmund Burke's "Reflections on the Revolution in France" forms the basis of conservatism.

1854: Republican Party, evolved from the Whigs, forms in the United States to oppose the Democratic Party.

1940: Winston Churchill becomes prime minister of Great Britain and will lead country through World War II.

1940s–1950s: "McCarthyism," a period of intense conservatism in the United States marked by anti–Communist fears and criticism of liberal social policies, named after Senator Joseph McCarthy.

1955: The periodical *National Review* emerges, directed by Yale University graduate William F. Buckley, Jr., with anti–Communism, anti–federalism, individualism, and libertarianism its central issues.

1979: Margaret Thatcher of the Conservative Party, urging a reversal to Great Britain's economic decline and a reduced role of government, becomes prime minister.

1980: Ronald Reagan, campaigning on such traditional themes as family and American pride, elected U.S. president and serves two terms.

2000: George W. Bush elected U.S. president.

"right–wing" segment of a theoretical political continuum which radical, reformative, and "liberal" elements define on the left.

Conservative or liberal inclinations are products of one's educational, social, and political environment. Conservative or liberal bias in the media, educational institutions, the courts, and global affairs can greatly affect daily life and one's independent beliefs. One does not often hear about socialistic, communistic, fascist, collectivist, or totalitarian biases in schools or media. One may often hear, however, that conservative or liberal bias has affected a certain policy, rule, decision, vote, or presentation of facts. Under such polarization, there is a tendency to label all political ideas wanting reform or change in government as "liberal." Conversely, any notion that supports continuing the controlling force or government is considered conservative, even if it means maintaining the status quo of an existing "liberal" government: Everything is relative. In any group of two or more persons discussing or arguing the merits of change, the voice of cautious resistance will be deemed conservative.

Historically, political conservatism in the United States has been most often associated with the Republican Party in an essentially bi–partisan system. On the other hand, and although other political parties have appeared sporadically, the Democratic Party has been most often identified with liberals wanting substantive government change to accommodate social needs. Labels, however, are deceptive. In an effort to capture more votes, political candidates have increasingly muddied partisan political waters. Thus, the constituency may often have to decide whether to elect an apparent liberal Republican or conservative Democrat. There are conservative liberals, liberal conservatives, progressive Republicans, and reactionary Democrats, so party labels often reflect political strategy more than ideology, generating more confusion.

U.S. President George W. Bush (1946–), attempting to bridge political gaps, has extolled "compassionate conservatism." In this century, partisan politics and "labels" may diminish as the U.S. attempts to establish parameters of conservative and liberal policies and principles.

HISTORY

Since conservatism generally does not involve strict adherence to tenets but rather the continuation of those in place, there is no tangible origin. Still, in every country in which government has existed long enough to establish social, economic, or political traditions, there will most likely be some form of conservative element in its legislative or executive ruling bodies, or in opposition. The emphasis here is on the Western Hemisphere.

Several world figures, such as Aristotle (384–322 B.C.), Cicero (106–143), Saint Augustine (354–430), Saint Thomas Aquinas (c. 1224–1274), Richard Hooker

(1554–1600), and John Locke (1632–1704), have pioneered conservative political thought. But Edmund Burke (1729–1797) is considered the founder of modern conservative thought. His "Reflections on the Revolution in France" (1790) form the basis of conservatism as a distinct political ideology. Burke's form, however, has been, and remains, a Western phenomenon, and continues to defend most values of Western society. Thus, over the years, the United Kingdom and the United States have become the greatest proponents of conservatism, and even between these two great powers, conservative principles have differed substantially.

Great Britain

The United Kingdom consists of England, Scotland, Wales, and Northern Ireland; the first three constitute Great Britain. Following the collapse of the Roman Empire and the Norman invasion of England in 1066, the area was politically organized under the old feudal system, which entailed large–scale grants of land by William the Conqueror (c. 1027–1087) to his Norman followers. These followers were to become the dominant element of the country's nobility. But the Anglo–Saxon influence contributed to the establishment of English political and civil liberties granted by the Magna Carta (The Great Charter) under King John (1167–1216) at Runnymede in 1215. As one provision in the Carta declared, "The barons shall elect twenty–five of their number to keep, and cause to be observed with all their might, the peace and liberties granted and confirmed to them by this charter."

England's Parliament is descended from the original councils of these barons, feudal landlords, and high–ranking clergy who advised the king on various matters. In the late thirteenth century, additional members of the Great Council were elected from town shires. A bicameral "Parliament" evolved, consisting of members appointed by the king (House of Lords), and elected tradesman, noblemen, guilders, educators, and merchants (House of Commons). From those councils and sessions came the differences in opinions that eventually led to further factions and parties within the House of Commons.

Great Britain's Conservative Party traces to the founding of the Tory Party in 1689. Ironically, the term first applied to Irishmen who, dispossessed by the English in the mid–seventeenth century, became bandits. It then became, sequentially, a term for any marauder, an Irish Catholic royalist, and a supporter of James II (1633–1701). After 1689, it applied to any member of the English party that initially opposed the "Glorious Revolution" during which King James II was dethroned in a bloodless battle, and his daughter and son–in–law, William (1650–1702) and Mary

(1662–1694) of Holland, were invited to assume the throne. Thus, Tory resistance to this change in events may have contributed to their eventual association with conservatism. The Tories were to grow into the party that always supported the monarchy and opposed political reform. Their fear of having the French Revolution repeat itself in England directly relates to their conservative stance of upholding law and order. The Tory Party eventually split into Liberals and Traditionalists, losing their political hold to the Whigs for many years. The terms Tory Party and Conservative Party are often used interchangeably.

The Whigs, short for "Whigamore," one of a body of seventtenth–century Scottish insurgents, were formed in the 18th century as opposition to the Tories. They favored high tariffs, more parliamentary control, and liberal interpretation of laws and charters. Britain's Liberal Party is the heir to the old Whig Party. Following World War I (1914–1918), the Labour Party displaced the Liberal Party as the main opponent to Britain's Conservative Party.

The Roots of Conservatism in America

In the United States, one must look to its founding fathers to understand American political theories, institutions, and moral order. Eventually, as an America independent of England began to form, so also did the rudiments of conservative versus liberal political thought, and their association with certain political parties. Party names and affiliations shifted, mostly the result of conflicting conservative and liberal opinions within.

In colonial America, anyone who could read was certain to have one book: the Bible. This unified New England pilgrims who may have otherwise differed. They established their commonwealth according to the Ten Commandments and it is fair to say that contemporary American democratic society rests upon inherited Puritan and Calvinistic influences. As Clinton Rossiter observed in *Seedtime of the Republic: the Origin of the American Tradition of Political Liberty,* from this Christian heritage comes "the contract and all its corollaries; the higher law as something more than a brooding omnipresence in the sky; the concept of the competent and responsible individual; certain key ingredients of economic individualism; the insistence on a citizenry educated to understand its rights and duties; and middle class virtues, that high plateau of moral stability on which, so Americans believe, successful democracy must always build." The influence of New England Puritan Christianity and the work ethic of later immigrants from Western Europe were the underlying forces in establishing the rudiments of

BIOGRAPHY:

Edmund Burke

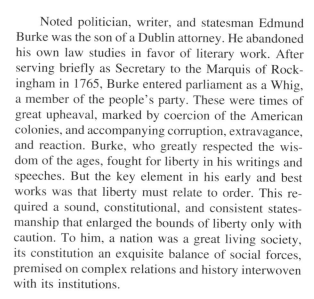

Noted politician, writer, and statesman Edmund Burke was the son of a Dublin attorney. He abandoned his own law studies in favor of literary work. After serving briefly as Secretary to the Marquis of Rockingham in 1765, Burke entered parliament as a Whig, a member of the people's party. These were times of great upheaval, marked by coercion of the American colonies, and accompanying corruption, extravagance, and reaction. Burke, who greatly respected the wisdom of the ages, fought for liberty in his writings and speeches. But the key element in his early and best works was that liberty must relate to order. This required a sound, constitutional, and consistent statesmanship that enlarged the bounds of liberty only with caution. To him, a nation was a great living society, its constitution an exquisite balance of social forces, premised on complex relations and history interwoven with its institutions.

In the mid–1770s, Burke spoke against proposals to tax the American colonies and to regulate the government of Massachusetts. He did not dispute that the imperial government had the right to take such actions, but he did question the worthiness of such rights. To make his point, Burke delivered two impassioned speeches in the House of Commons: one dwelt on the matter of American taxation by duties and the other urged a reconciliation between the imperial Parliament and the colonies. When the American War for Independence did come, Burke opposed it; he perceived it a danger to the liberties of the colonies, and, therefore, of all English subjects.

The French Revolution, which began in 1789, was the most conspicuous development to coincide with Burke's career. In 1790 he published *Reflections on the French Revolution* as a warning to fellow English subjects and admirers that the loss of monarchy and liberty could also occur in England, as it had in France, if preventive action was not taken. This most famous of his works went into an eleventh printing before the year ended and served to create an English response to the French Revolution.

Burke retired from political life soon after his son Richard died of consumption (tuberculosis) in August, 1794. In 1796, he opened a neighborhood school school for foreign and immigrant children who would not otherwise have been educated. Early the next year his health began to decline, and he died on July 9, 1797. Despite a move to have him interred, with public honors, in Westminster Abbey, Burke's own will stipulated he be buried in the yard of the parish church of Beaconsfield.

Because the balance and tranquility of a great nation took so many years and so many components to achieve, Burke always argued against hasty change. He believed that only cautious and delicate adjustment to accommodate pressing events should be attempted, lest the unraveling of latent or unknown components that contributed to the whole would inadvertently cause its demise. Burke's writings inspired many monarchs and leaders through their own confrontations with revolution or reform. His defense of preserving existing institutions and orders became the foundation for Western conservative thought.

---

the America's capitalist democratic republic. It also served to influence the ordered liberty and principles found in the U.S. Constitution.

The Constitutional debates Yet, there were early political and cultural divides. This is apparent from the constitutional debates between the Federalists, who were essentially nationalists, and the Anti–Federalists, who rallied against strong central government in favor of state power. Both sides, however, were concerned with preserving liberty, having just fought a war to protect it. The Federalists believed there were enough checks and balances in the Constitution as written to

protect liberty. The Anti–Federalists wanted the Constitution to spell out specific liberties. Between 1787 and early 1788, five states (Delaware, Pennsylvania, New Jersey, Georgia, and Connecticut) had ratified the Constitution as written. Massachusetts was the first holdout. The Federalists penned a series of 85 papers composed for publication in New York newspapers under the title of "The Federalist," hoping to sway public opinion. Of the papers' three main authors, Alexander Hamilton (1755–1804), James Madison (1751–1836), and John Jay (1745–1829), Madison, in "The Federalist No. 10," argued persuasively for a strong federal government. They said:

The influence of factious leaders may kindle a flame within their particular States, but will be unable to spread a general conflagration through the other States: a religious sect, may degenerate into a political faction in a part of the Confederacy; but the variety of sects dispersed over the entire face of it, must secure the national Councils against any danger from that source: a rage for paper money, for an abolition of debts, for an equal division of property, or for any other improper or wicked project, will be less apt to pervade the whole body of the Union, than a particular member of it; in the same proportion as such a malady is more likely to taint a particular country or district, than an entire State.

But the Anti–Federalist Patrick Henry (1736–1799) of Virginia rebutted:

The first thing I have at heart is American liberty, the second thing is American Union. The rights of conscience, trial by jury, liberty of the press, all your immunities and franchises, all pretensions to human rights and privileges, are rendered insecure, if not lost, by this change so loudly talked of by some . . . You are not to inquire how your trade may be increased, nor how you are to become a great and powerful people, but how your liberties can be secured; for liberty ought to be the direct end of your Government.

The Bill of Rights   The Anti–Federalists wanted a Bill of Rights written into the Constitution. Ultimately, the Federalists proposed ratifying the Constitution as written, with adding a Bill of Rights the first order. This compromise enabled Massachusetts and all other states, except Maryland, to ratify. The document took effect June 21, 1788, when New Hampshire became the ninth state.

George Washington (1732–1799) himself understood well the importance of his Anti–Federalist adversaries. He wrote,

Upon the whole, I doubt whether the opposition to the Constitution will not ultimately be productive of more good than evil; it has called forth, in its defence (sic), abilities which would not perhaps been otherwise exerted, that have thrown new light upon the science of Government, they have given the rights of man a full and fair discussion, and explained them in so clear and forcible a manner as cannot fail to make a lasting impression....

The Constitution of the United States of America had its first ten amendments, now commonly called the Bill of Rights. So much contention and debate had occurred among the States that Benjamin Franklin (1706–1790), asked by a citizen what kind of government the Constitutional Convention had proposed for the country, replied, "A republic . . . if you can keep it." America's political system invites the free expression of opposing and diverse views, a right so fundamental that liberty would have little meaning without it. As Washington said in 1789, "The sacred fire of liberty and the destiny of the republican model of government are . . . deeply and finally staked on the experiment entrusted to the hands of the American people."

Neither the Constitution nor its framers contemplated separate political parties as playing a role in the legislative process. Under the "Great Compromise" reached at the Constitutional Convention in 1787, the delegates agreed that a House of Representatives would represent the "national principle," while the Senate would be an expression of the "federal principle." The Federalists had succeeded in having their proposed Constitution ratified, with the addition of the Bill of Rights; Washington was unanimously voted in as a non–partisan first president, and Federalist sentiments controlled the nation's first Congress. John Adams, the second president, was a strong Federalist. But starting with Thomas Jefferson, the third president and an Anti–Federalist, many of America's first presidents were "Democratic Republicans," including James Madison and James Monroe after Jefferson. It was not until 1828 that the Democratic and Republican parties split into two under Andrew Jackson, who called himself a Democrat and the Federalist Party was dissolved.

Hamilton's views   Fundamental differences even ran through Washington's cabinet, between Jefferson, the secretary of state, and Alexander Hamilton, the treasury secretary. Jefferson, an aristocratic Virginia planter and landowner, considered himself a progressive proponent of the "European Enlightenment" movement and fully supported the French Revolution. He defended local government and viewed rural society as the bearer of democratic sentiment in a struggle against the commercial aristocracy of cities. Jefferson became increasingly conservative in his political sentiments, remaining essentially against centralized government and eventually, international commerce.

Hamilton, by contrast, admired the British constitution and staunchly opposed the French Revolution. The House as well as the Senate, upon receiving Hamilton's first financial plan, began to exhibit a spirit of partisanship. Hamilton and his followers banded together as Federalists, and their opponents, representing agrarian (land–owning) aristocracy, led by Jefferson and Madison, became known as Democratic Republicans in 1792.

Hamilton and his followers, meanwhile, inspired the eventual creation of Henry Clay's National Republicans and Whigs. Decades later, a formal Republican Party was formed from the Whigs in 1854 to

National Review editor William F. Buckley.

(Archive Photos, Inc.)

oppose the Democratic Party. This ended the American factions of Whigs and Tories, inherited from England. American Whigs supported the Revolution; American Tories opposed it. Since 1832, the Tories were considered the conservative party, and remained so in England (opposite the Whigs, and later, the Labour Party). In America, however, the Republicans (the prior Whigs) eventually became known for their conservatism.

Progressive movement   Later in that century, a group calling themselves "populists," or "People's Party," most prominently led by William Jennings Bryan, made Jefferson their hero, even though they advocated such policies as public ownership of utilities which would have horrified Jefferson. The Populist Party formed to represent agrarian interests in the presidential election of 1892. They advocated a more equitable distribution of wealth and power, big business and small independent businesses, a graduated federal income tax, and an increased currency with free coinage of gold and silver.

The Progressive Movement also aligned with Jeffersonian Populists, particularly in the Midwest and South. Jefferson had previously interpreted "Whig" to represent those in favor of change, and "Tory" to mean those opposed to change, that is, conservative. Those

supporting change do so in the name of progress, hence the term "progressive." Throughout the late nineteenth century, the Progressive Movement fought for state ownership of railroads and utilities, hoping to break up monopolies and cartels hostile to rural farmers who relied on rail for shipment of their grains and produce. They also tended toward isolationism, non–interference in world affairs, and opposed imperialism on both moral and practical grounds. They promoted support for local government as a means to prevent wealth and political power from concentrating.

In the early twentieth century, however, the Populist and Progressive movements again splintered. A new progressivism, associated with Theodore Roosevelt and eventually Woodrow Wilson, was taking hold. This more liberal progressivism tracked similar events and times occurring during the Industrial Revolution in England. It promoted nationalism and imperialism, and saw American involvement in World War I as an opportunity to centralize economic control.

Later, during the lengthy period when President Franklin Delano Roosevelt (1882–1945) controlled a Democratic administration, anti–New Deal conservatives and old–time Progressives united again in their opposition of World War II. They also wanted the repeal of the income tax amendment and passage of an amendment to prohibit deficit spending. The Roosevelt administration opposed them and attempted to rally support by labeling them German sympathizers and "Copperheads." But the attack on the United States at Pearl Harbor on December 7, 1941, nearly ended the argument for isolationism and the increasing threat of Communism sent the isolationists into decline. The only part of conservatism that continued after the New Deal and World War II was a suspicion of big government and big business. This thinking was eventually referred to as the post–war "Old Right."

Conservatism After World War II

Still another shift occurred when Ohio Republican Senator Robert Taft (1889–1953) took over as the political leader of the Old Right. Taft was anti–Communist, favored free enterprise, and opposed most of New Deal social welfare legislation. Because the American conservative movement had changed ideologically so many times, the post–war Old Right stood out for its commitment to local liberties and local government, and a concerted dislike for the "collectivist" modern state. American conservatism of the 1940s and 1950s attracted big–business Republicans and other heirs of Alexander Hamilton, but was still under libertarian influence that opposed war, conscription, and imperialism.

From the turn of the century to the 1950s, there had been an increase in administrative consolidation. Government now controlled wages; the national civil service had grown tremendously; executive and congressional authority had empowered labor unions; and federal and state taxes had steadily increased to pay for all this. It appeared to conservatives that old–fashioned libertarianism had become endangered in its own country of origin. Big Government and Big Brother now ruled. The turn of events in post–war England was even more dramatic, when socialists swept to power in the summer of 1945. The newly elected Labour government entered Parliament and sung the "Red Flag" and other songs the revolutionary left had popularized starting in the 1930s.

Anti–Communism and opposition to Soviet imperialism became the driving forces of post–war conservatism. In 1955, the periodical *National Review* appeared. Directed by Yale University graduate William F. Buckley, Jr., the periodical's central issues of anti–Communism, anti–federalism, individualism, and libertarianism were to shape American conservative politics during through the 1960s and beyond.

Post–war conservatism began during these years and coincided with the Cold War against the Communist Soviet Union. Clearly the galvanizing influence of this conservatism was American anti–Communism, generally called the "Red Scare." President Harry Truman (1884–1972) used the Communist threat to justify his administration's Marshall Plan, the European recovery program following World War II and an economic boost for American industry. Truman concurrently appeared before Congress to request extra funds to create congressional subcommittees to investigate and round up Communist insurgents within U.S. borders.

In a 1962 editorial for *National Review,* Buckley defended the House Committee on Un–American Activities and other congressional investigations by appealing to the notion of a "clear and present danger" to America were Communism left unchecked. Buckley balanced libertarian constitutional rights of freedom of speech with the threat of atom bombs and Marxist revolutionaries. Likewise, *National Review* writer Will Herberg, a Jewish theologian, wrote, "It is only when 'un–American' propaganda becomes a part of a conspiratorial movement allied with a foreign enemy, bent on the destruction of our nation, of freedom, and of Western civilization that it becomes a proper subject for congressional inquiry, disclosure, and legislation." Thus, the influential Buckley and his colleagues actually helped promote the conservative premise of maintaining the free–enterprise system against the Communist threat.

Civil rights movement As the conservative movement entered the 1960s, it widened its focus and became more polarized against the growing civil rights movement. To diehard conservatives, the movement represented the destruction of communities that to date had been free of bureaucratic control. They resented government social engineering and considered it an abridgement of their private rights of contract and association.

But separating principle from policy created yet another splintering. There was internal dissent over civil rights, particularly feminism and what was seen as black radicalism. Orthodox libertarians also differed over strong laws regarding pornography. A "fusion" and alignment of issues occurred. Conservatism in America came to represent all of these: economic libertarianism, cultural traditionalism, strong local government, and militant anti–Communism. This fusionist concept united both libertarian and traditionalist factions and became the vital center of what came to be known as neo–conservatism.

This time marked the era of the new Campus Right as well. By the late 1950s, Yale had become a breeding ground such conservative activists as Buckley. In his first published book, *God and Man at Yale* (1952), Buckley protested the pervasive liberalism of Yale's professors. Catholic universities such as Fordham, Notre Dame, and St. John's in New York became important centers of conservative activity. The Catholic component of the intellectual right defended anti–Communist and anti–secularist views and promoted activism to stamp out these threats. They assumed strong positions of political and global involvement to save America Communism's threatening spread. These views separated them, however, from the Southern and Midwestern Protestants, whose foreign policy views were still isolationist. The abortion controversy surfaced in the 1960s after mothers who had taken thalidomide drugs gave birth to deformed babies. Again, the Catholic and Protestant conservatives splintered over this issue, the Catholics being patently anti–abortion. Irish–American Catholics also rallied against liberal social policies such as forced busing. Racial tensions, court–ordered busing, and violent crimes during the 1960s started to move traditionally Democratic Catholic communities in the North toward the conservative Right. Concerned about the expanding welfare system, they demanded harder eligibility tests for welfare recipients.

The conservative movement of the 1960s promoted economic deregulation, a strong military commitment, and a vigorous struggle against Soviet power. Republican Party presidential candidate Barry Goldwater's (1909–1998) ultra–conservative platform

Barry Goldwater. (The Library of Congress)

included notions of a "breakdown of moral fiber in the United States," a big–government conspiracy theory, and an ominous forecast of a Communist takeover of the country. Big business, nonetheless, withheld support from Goldwater–type purists, fearing the loss of lucrative contracts with an expanded federal government and civil service. In 1964, big business backed the more liberal Republican, Nelson Rockefeller (1908–1979). Goldwater won the Republican nomination that year, but lost the November election to incumbent Democratic President Lyndon B. Johnson (1908–1973), who was completing the term of assassinated President John F. Kennedy (1917–1963). About this time, the Christian libertarian, Frank Meyer, who continued to prophesize until his death in 1972, warned that a conservative political majority would again rise in America when its citizens realized the harm liberal policies had caused to their constitutional and moral legacies.

The next political crisis was the Vietnam War, which also started in the mid–1960s. Involvement in the war had divided the nation, torn between conservative and liberal sentiments. A liberal Democrat had gotten the U.S. into the war, it was argued, so Republican President Richard M. Nixon (1913–1994) would end it. Nixon, however, resigned in 1974 during preliminary impeachment hearings following the Watergate scandal. The old conservative distrust of

big government returned, but this time, it involved one of their own.

The Reagan era For the 1980 presidential race, California Republican Governor Ronald W. Reagan (1911–) was the conservatives' dream candidate. As president, he was optimistic and humorous, his manner easy. Amid recession, he spoke of economic growth and hope. Reagan spoke firmly about containing Soviet and Communist expansionism. He was comfortable with his traditional views of family and American pride. He revived national pride and helped unite an economically troubled people. The economy during his administration (1981–1989) embarked on a twenty–year growth pattern that did not slow down until after the millennium, and big business supported him all the way. Conservatism was back in vogue.

Reagan, like Goldwater, spoke of a "moral crisis of our times," and during his administration extreme right conservative organizations such as the "Moral Majority" surfaced. Ironically, for all the great things that Reagan did for the name "conservative," the term became increasingly associated with the extreme religious right, a stereotype that also carried into the millennium.

Reagan's rise also spawned different kind of populism, according to Richard Viguerie, publisher of *Conservative Digest*. In a commentary for the *National Review* in 1984, Viguerie wrote, "To say that every populist is a demagogue is as wrong as accusing every conservative of racism," he wrote. "The 1980s–style populists I describe in *The Establishment vs. the People* are anti–racist, compassionate, anti–Communist, future–oriented, and grounded in traditional values while sympathetic to libertarianism."

George Herbert Walker Bush (1924–), vice president under Reagan, was elected in 1988. Although there was no scandal associated with Bush's term, liberal forces were brewing. Out of virtually nowhere came Arkansas Democratic Governor Bill Clinton (1946–). From 1993 to 2001, Clinton occupied the White House during continued economic prosperity. Many of his liberal policies, however, such as admitting China into the World Trade Organization, drew fire from conservatives, and his intentions for a national health plan never materialized.

In the contested presidential election of 2000, Republican George W. Bush, son of the former president, defeated Clinton's incumbent vice president, Al Gore (1948–). Bush pledged to govern with "compassionate conservatism," a call to return to the private sector, in voluntary social and faith–based settings, the business of social welfare. Priorities rapidly shifted, however, on September 11, 2001, when the World Trade Center in New York was destroyed, killing several thousand people in the worst act of terrorism known to America. The Pentagon building outside Washington D.C., in a simultaneous attack, was also severely damaged.

THEORY IN DEPTH

True political conservatism argues that the survival of any institution such as marriage, the pledge of allegiance, or free enterprise, means it has successfully served a need. Accordingly, its continuation is necessary for that society or government. Conservative statesman Benjamin Disraeli once argued that constant change should at least defer to "the manners, the customs, the laws, the traditions of the people." That notion is at the heart of true conservatism. Conservatism is acutely sensitive to the cost of radical change or reconstruction; until the full consequences are understood, such changes may lead to harmful, unintended consequences or other negative or unanticipated effects.

Conservatism vigorously defends the premise that not all people are equal. It supports the idea that all people are created equal with regard to personal freedoms and rights. But it argues strongly for the inherent inequality in talent and initiative. Conservatism considers it a folly to try to level society by social engineering. Accordingly, attempts to distribute wealth evenly or give equal say to those who have earned no vested interest in a matter are clearly suspect.

Persistent themes of traditional conservatism include a universal moral order sanctioned by organized religion, the primary role of private property and a defense of the social order. On the other end is the criticism that true conservatism is interested only in maintaining existing inequalities or restoring lost ones.

The Conservative Split

Traditionalists and reformers differ on issues, but still consider themselves overall conservatives. As President Ronald Reagan once quipped after being confronted with differences among his aides, "Sometimes our right hand doesn't know what our far–right hand is doing."

Traditionalists and libertarians splintered following World War II. One of the key thinkers of that period was Richard M. Weaver (1910–1963), who defended the old, agrarian hierarchical values of the antebellum South. The agrarians argued that a strictly commercial society and civilization, divorced from the land and from tradition, lacked the necessary traditional and spiritual roots to survive. "Southern" conservatism took on its own character, still resenting a strong central government that had taken away states' rights to secede from the Union, to maintain a slave population and to engage in commerce without federal interference. They would have concluded similarly on their own, they argued, but the issue was the federal government telling them what to do. As Reagan said, "The nine most terrible words in the English language are 'I'm from the government and I'm here to help.'"

Russell Kirk (1918–1994), who admired Weaver, attempted to define American conservatism as having existed and sometimes dominated Anglo–American culture since the late eighteenth century. Kirk's conservatism paralleled the nineteenth century British version in proclaiming that social hierarchy was necessary for world order. There were also re–affirmations of the divine sources of traditional morality, and a strong belief that property and freedom were inseparable. Kirk adopted and re–promoted many of Edmund Burke's original views about the natural law doctrine. Kirk found further support in the writings of two Harvard University alumni, Irving Babbitt and Paul Elmer More. Ultimately, a shared distaste for social engineering and manipulation united traditionalists and libertarians; their shared beliefs included economic libertarianism, social/cultural traditionalism, strong local government, and militant anti–Communism.

Their most common theme was the moral and social good of private property. There was a general support for private enterprise. By the mid–1950s, libertarians and traditionalists regarded personal liberties as virtually incompatible with a welfare state. Communism, therefore, became their nemesis.

John Kekes, in his book, *A Case for Conservatism,* calls the source of conservatism "a natural attitude that combines the enjoyment of something valued with the fear of losing it." According to Kekes, all political theorists agree that certain political conditions are necessary to benefit citizens. Those include general civility and equality, freedom, healthy environment, justice, and peace. Kekes argued that even though these conditions are important to all political theories, liberals and conservatives differ by priority. The conservative premise that there are latent effects of social, economic, and moral policies not always readily apparent, and that changing them without understanding their relationship to the whole system may inadvertently alter things for the worse.

Common to conservative thinking has been affirming the need for an orderly, disciplined, unequal society that benefits from appropriate leadership. All political ideologies, arguably, would desire an orderly, disciplined society. The "unequal" element separates conservatism from liberal socialism. Differences among conservatives have focused on exercising "appropriate leadership." For free–market conservatives, society consists of a hierarchy of talent and achievement, in which an entrepreneurial minority reaps the rewards of its hard work, which gives the minority the incentive to continue creating the prosperity that ultimately will benefit many. Former British Prime Minister Margaret Thatcher (1925–) called this the "trickle down" effect.

Patrician conservatives Patrician conservatives, by contrast, might argue continuing the hierarchy of privileges and obligations, but also safeguarding the majority from capitalistic excess. This requires a delicate balance of laws and protections, because "hand–outs" discourage individual responsibility and negate work incentive. Likewise, those who work hard and succeed would lose the incentive, were their wealth distributed to those who did nothing to earn it.

Both views, however, support the need for a solid framework of law and order which counteracts human weaknesses. These flaws weaken society and tear it apart. The key to rewarding capitalistic venture is apparent. But it is harder to find just the right formula to provide minimum protections for the less fortunate without removing their incentive to change their lives. Thus, social welfare programs or a "welfare state" in which government takes on the responsibility for caring for the needy is viewed narrowly and cautiously. For patrician conservatives, each man is responsible for his or her own life, and only those incapable of earning an honest living should receive economic aid.

Some critics challenge that conservatives are also more likely to resist changes to the U.S. Constitution—one dedicated to the proposition that all men are created equal. Conservatives, believing in responsibility for one's own life, resent shifting such responsibility to government. Pure conservatism supports the idea of equality in man's basic inherent rights, but not in talents, resources, or in benefits achieved through hard work.

Over the years and mostly as a result of twentieth–century immigration and urbanization, the country's growing diversity contributed greatly to disparate views about government's role. One can start to see the connection of these events to the development of American conservatism and liberalism. What is also apparent is the fallacy in trying to attach labels to partisan political views. America's early Republicans were reformers and revolutionaries. But in the early twenty-first century, the Republicans were generally viewed as the more conservative of the two major parties. Historians have attempted to attach such categories as "neo–conservatism," "American conservatism," "the New Conservatism," and "the New Right." Each term, however, relates to a period when the issues of the time were redefining political conservatism. But conservatism more recently has usually referred to economic conservatism and social traditionalism.

The Essentials of Conservatism

Conservatism endeavors to preserve the existing order or the continuance of existing institutions, principles, and policies. Its cautious resistance to change is premised upon the belief that would–be reformers do not fully comprehend the interrelationship and interdependency of their proposed change upon other elements of the larger system in which it is a component. English statesman Edmund Burke is most often credited with inspiring the form of conservatism that has its roots in the Western Hemisphere. American conservatism, although vacillating on a continuum, is generally characterized by economic conservatism (maintenance of a free–enterprise system without government interference) and social traditionalism (the upholding of values and principles as envisioned by the founding fathers).

THEORY IN ACTION

Perhaps nowhere has conservatism established deeper political roots than in the Western Hemisphere. Wherever the politics of tradition, wealth, and aristocracy have been a historic force, one will find a strong conservative presence in government. Examples include the Tories or Conservative Party of Great Britain, the Republican Party of the United States, the prior Gaullists of France, the largely dominant Liberal Democratic Party (LDP) of Japan (which, despite its name, is conservative), and the Swatantra Party of India.

Similar polities exist in other countries. In Italy's May 2001 general election, the right–of–center alliance known as the Casa delle Liberta (House of Freedom) prevailed over the center–left coalition which had ruled the country for the five previous years. In Switzerland, run for more than a century with the Liberals governing and the Conservatives in opposition a four–party coalition known as the "magic formula" now runs the government. Since the fall of the Soviet Union in 1991, Russia has created a parliament. Its two main political forces are the conservative right's Yabloko and a loose coalition of liberal parties known as the Union of Rightist Forces (URF). Iran has suffered relatively bitter power struggles between conservatives and reformers since 1989.

Conservatism in Great Britain

Britain produced the most famous conservative statesman of the twentieth century, Sir Winston Churchill (1874–1965). Twice elected prime minister of the United Kingdom, Churchill conveyed the image of invincible strength and carried his nation through World War II with admirable resolve. He distinguished himself from pre–war Conservative leaders who wanted to negotiate appeasement policies with Adolf Hitler (1889–1945). Churchill refused Hitler's offers and organized one of the boldest military strategies ever. Together with Allied forces, Britain held off the Germans.

The war, however, had devestated Britain. Then, in one of the most striking reversals in political history, Churchill's Conservative Party was soundly defeated by the Labour Party in the general election in July, 1945. Rather than a personal vote of censure against Churchill, the defeat was probably a reaction against twenty years of Conservative rule, a desire for social reconstruction, and uncertainty about the aggressive international policies espoused by the Conservatives. He easily won a seat in his new district of Woodford, which he held for the last nineteen years he spent in Parliament. He immediately resigned as prime minister. The resulting Labour government passed a National Insurance Act and a National Health Service Act.

Churchill, as leader of the opposition from 1945 to 1951, continued to enjoy a worldwide reputation and warned the Western democracies to stand firm in the face of the growing threat of the Soviet Union. Churchill's speeches created a storm of protest and controversy in the West, but events soon confirmed his views of world events and the rapidly developing Cold War. The Conservatives won a narrow victory in 1951, and Churchill was returned to his position as prime minister.

One positive aspect of conservatism was that Britain's Conservative Party did not alter any of the social welfare programs enacted by the Labour Party in the late–1940s—although the Conservatives probably did not do so because they had no mandate, not

Sir Winston Churchill. (The Library of Congress)

much money to spend, and the programs were popular and were working in the relative prosperity of the early–1950s. More so than the Labour Party, however, the Conservatives wanted to maintain a colonial presence on many of Britain's possessions around the world, but economic problems at home and the waves of independence ferver rendered this impossible, and the British Empire continued its rapid decline.

Prime Minister Margaret Thatcher's leadership in the Conservative Party enjoyed a clear majority from 1979 through 1990. Thatcher vowed to reverse Britain's economic decline and reduce government's role in the economy. Her policies included abolishing free milk in the schools, curbing trade union power, expanding private–sector roles in health services and pensions, and deregulating some sectors to break up monopolies. Thatcher is also remembered for her strong position over the Falkland Islands, which Argentina and the United Kingdom both claimed during a crisis in 1982. When Argentine forces occupied the islands, Thatcher's government sent troops to defeat them. Thatcher, despite high unemployment rates, led the Conservatives to a sweeping victory in the parliamentary elections of 1983, bolstered mostly by her successful Falkland Islands policy.

Eventually, even influential figures in Thatcher's Conservative Party resisted some of her changes, es-

BIOGRAPHY:
Sir Winston Churchill

Winston Leonard Spencer Churchill, the famous British prime minister, soldier, and author, was the quintessential conservative. Churchill, born into a military family and educated at private schools in England with unremarkable academic achievement, was first commissioned as an officer in the 4th hussars and served his time in India and the Sudan. After resigning his commission, he made a name for himself as a journalist after writing about his own capture, imprisonment, and escape from the Boers. He was elected to Parliament in 1900 as a Conservative, but switched to the Liberal Party and was appointed, respectively, as undersecretary for the colonies, president of the Board of Trade (1908), home secretary (1910), first lord of the admiralty (1911), minister of munitions (1917), secretary of state for war and air (1918), and colonial secretary (1921), where he helped negotiate the treaty that created an Irish Free State.

Churchill eventually returned to the House of Commons and became prime minister in a Conservative government. He enjoyed great success and faced harsh criticism for many of his ideas and policies. He was a great orator and war leader whose resolve and refusal to appease Adolf Hitler was an important fortifier for European resistance, and ultimately contributed to the Allied victory in World War II. Churchill despised all forms of totalitarian and Communist governments, and steadfastly believed in the moral superiority of democracy and its eventual triumph. He warned the House of Commons in 1935 not only of the importance of "self–preservation but also of the human and the world cause of the preservation of free governments and of Western civilization against the ever advancing sources of authority and despotism." Churchill, who coined the expression, "Iron Curtain," was the first to warn the U.S. of the threat of Soviet expansion. An eloquent and talented literary writer, Churchill won the Nobel Prize in Literature for *The History of the Second World War.* He resigned from office in 1955 due to poor health and died ten years later. Churchill remains the most admired hero of many politicians, including U.S. President George W. Bush and New York Mayor Rudolph Giuliani.

pecially the controversial poll tax and her negative attitudes toward the then European Community (EC). John Major, a New Democrat, replaced her in 1992. Ultimately, the reign of the New Democrats was short–lived when the Labour Party, downtrodden and traditionally identified with the poor and the public–housing tenants, built a more dynamic image around new leader Tony Blair (1953–). His party remained in control in 2001.

America's Own Breed of Conservatism

Democracy and industrialism proved more potent forces than Edmund Burke's principles. And America had its own signature conservative, Henry Ford (1863–1947). The quintessential capitalist and automobile manufacturer was the most conservative of men in his personal habits and opinions. Known for his anti–union labor policies, he employed spies and company police to prevent workers from unionizing his Ford Motor Company in Dearborn, Michigan. He promoted Christian values and principles among his laborers, and monitored personal habits and lives, such as discouraging smoking and alcohol, and providing family housing, counseling, and community events. He also published a weekly journal, the Dearborn Independent, which contained several anti–Semitic articles in its first issues. Ford, however, won respect as an inspiration for change.

McCarthyism

Forever linked to extreme post–war conservatism is Wisconsin Republican Senator Joseph R. McCarthy (1909–1957), the man ultimately responsible for the label "McCarthyism." His U.S. Senate tenure occurred during the Cold War and America's fight to rid itself of Communism. In her book, The Age of McCarthyism: A Brief History With Documents, author Ellen Schrecker described the shift from American tolerance for Communism to American antagonism. She noted that comparative tolerance grew out of a World War II alliance with the Soviet Union, but turned into an aggressive stance against Communism, premised mostly upon the growing hostile relationship with the Soviet Union following the war. In the first five years after the war, the Soviet Union attempted government takeover of the countries it had helped liberate from Hitler's regime during the war. It overtook Poland's government in 1945, pressured Turkey and Iran in 1946, partly instigated the Greek Civil War in 1947, caused the Communist coup in Czechoslovakia and the blockade of Berlin in 1948, and detonated an atomic bomb one year later. Peaceful coexistence no longer appeared viable, and the United States remained the only free nation strong enough to stave off

U.S. Senator Joseph McCarthy during a hearing. (AP/Wide World Photos)

Communist aggression. The world actually hovered on the verge of another world war. Moreover, the threat of internal infiltration of Communist party members and spies caused near panic in America.

As Schrecker wrote, "An important element of the power of a modern state is its ability to set the political agenda and to define the crucial issues of the moment, through its actions as well as its words." This is particularly important when we consider the difference between conservative versus liberal interpretation of the perceived "Communist threat" to the world or to America in the 1940s. In any event, the threat was real, and based on real evidence, and it is true that individual Communists who had infiltrated the government did steal secrets. It is also true that Communist agitators had infiltrated America's labor unions. However, the response to the threat bordered on frenzy and serious violations of civil liberties. In the late 1940s, for example, the Immigration and Naturalization Service began to round up foreign–born Communists and labor leaders for deportation and detention without bail. It has been argued in retrospect that the Truman administration, fearing a Republican Congress that might not allocate enough funds for anti–communist activities or the Administration's foreign policy programs, exaggerated the Communist threat. In March 1947, the president went before a special session of Congress and pled the case for the as-

sessment of Communist infiltration within American society. Congress then created the House Un–American Activities Committee (HUAC) to investigate the extent of the perceived threat. The institutions which best exemplify the McCarthy era were these congressional investigative committees.

Red Scare begins Politically, the move backfired. In 1947, FBI Director J. Edgar Hoover (1895–1972) testified before the HUAC and created such fear of an internal Communist threat that the Republican–dominated Congress launched an all–out attack on anti–American sentiment and activity. Communists were summarily dehumanized and transformed into ideological criminals. Protecting the nation from this danger became the American political theme of that era, which continued well into the 1950s.

The First Amendment's freedom of speech and press does not protect those preaching the violent overthrow of the government. Therefore, Congress, under the HUAC, began a concerted effort to investigate, expose, and prosecute Communist sympathizers. Communist labor leaders were involved in many highly publicized strikes in U.S. defense industries. Although the Communist–dominated Fur and Leather Workers union posed little threat to national security, the United Electrical, Radio and Machine Workers of America (UE) as well as various maritime unions, were of more concern. The politically left–led union leaders became the subjects of investigation and exposure, and many, along with other party leaders, were prosecuted and incarcerated for alleged anti–American activity. The government also implemented an anti–Communist loyalty–security program for government employees in March 1947. Major prosecution trials of espionage agents such as Alger Hess and Ethel (1915–1953) and Julius (1918–1953) Rosenberg received enormous publicity and enhanced the credibility of a real threat to the country. The notorious spy cases of the early Cold War period seemed to punctuate J. Edgar Hoover's contention that "every American Communist was, and is, potentially an espionage agent of the Soviet Union." The Smith Act trials of the top leaders of the American Communist Party in 1949 helped the U.S. government unify all the anti–American themes to bolster its contention that the Communist Party represented an illegal conspiracy under Soviet control and direction.

Using these events to punctuate their criticism of the liberal social policies of the New Deal during the previous Franklin Delano Roosevelt administration, conservative politicians, mostly Republican, accused the Democrats of being soft on Communism. Congressional investigating committees, such as McCarthy's Permanent Investigating Subcommittee of the Government Operations Committee, and Senator Pat McCarran's Senate Internal Security Subcommittee, paralleled the activities of the HUAC. But "McCarthyism" stood for the publicizing or directing of accusations of disloyalty, regardless of evidence.

McCarthy goes too far McCarthy directed his attention to the media and the educational systems because they were viewed as shapers and molders of public opinion. One by one, Hollywood producers, actors, and artists, as well as college educators, were subpoenaed to testify before the congressional subcommittees about their knowledge of and/or affiliation with the Communist Party. Hollywood blacklisted actors who named their colleagues. Witnesses who refused to testify were prosecuted for contempt of Congress, labeled "unfriendly witnesses," and stigmatized equally. The work of the Congressional subcommittees trickled down to state and local levels with their own Un–American Activities Committees. Private employers cooperated in the probes, resulting in public exposure of Communist sympathizers, who then lost their jobs and generally faced ostracism from a patriotic public.

The official manifestations of McCarthyism— public hearings, FBI investigations, and criminal prosecutions—ultimately proved mild compared to the horrors of Stalin's Russia. Nonetheless, in retrospect, they have negatively represented conservatism in the extreme. The government's characterization of the Soviet/Communist threat invoked the criminal justice system and enhanced the American public's perception of domestic Communists as criminals. However, according to Schrecker, even at its peak, the Communist Party had a high turnover rate, and by the early 1950s, most party members had actually quit. The "Red Scare" resulted in numerous violations of civil liberties and freedoms of those whose ties with Communism may have been only incidental or not threatening to the United States.

Here again, is another application of conservative versus liberal sentiment. Extreme conservatism may favor incidental or mild abridgments of civil liberties as a necessary price to secure free enterprise and a way of life that nurtures such freedoms. Alternatively, liberalism believes personal freedom and liberty trump the needs of national freedom from foreign or internal threat. In retrospect, McCarthy–era critics call it the worst kind of conservatism. On the other hand, conservative politicians argue that such tactics would not have been necessary but for the lax policies of liberal politicians and/or the socialistic policies of the New Deal. They argue that such policies ultimately created an environment in which workers felt they were entitled to equal shares of economic prosperity, regardless of personal input. The ultimate fall of Communism and the Soviet empire during the late twentieth century, and a commensurate rise in global free–enterprise systems and governments, emphasize their point.

Ultra–Right Conservatism

Important to the application of the freedom of speech and association to extremist groups, such as the Communist Party, is that they may enjoy First Amendment protections, even if their views are repugnant to some or outside the mainstream. If Communism is associated with liberal socialism near one extremity, then ultra–conservative groups such as the Moral Majority and John Birch Society might occupy the other end. These groups have grown over the years, particularly stimulated into activism during periods of comparative liberal political thought. Many of them have targeted a growing federal bureaucracy and the recovery of perceived lost liberties and/or freedoms (not to be confused with the work of the ultra–liberal American Civil Liberties Union).

Private citizen Robert Welch (1899–1985) founded the John Birch Society in 1958 to preserve and promote America as it was originally established:

a Constitutional Republic. It embodies what is perceived as extreme right–wing conservatism, even though many Americans not part of the Society's membership agree with its principles. Because the Society refers to the country's Judeo–Christian heritage and moral values, it is often criticized as having a religious agenda or representing the Christian Right. Yet, looking to the country's history, the values the Society promotes are similar than those the new republic promoted in the late 1700s: a belief in the family as the primary social unit, a support for a free–market system and competitive capitalism, and a protection of the personal freedoms the original framers of the Constitution contemplated.

John Birch (1918–1945) was a Christian missionary the Chinese Communists killed following World War II. His death symbolized for the Society a unified resistance to a "new world order," a love for freedom, and the rejection of totalitarianism "under any label." According to the Society's Internet website (http://www.jbs.org), its members believe "that the rights of the individual are endowed by his Creator, not by governments..."

In America's early days, the John Birch Society may not have been able to accommodate the number of persons clamoring to join such an organization. But in the twenty–first century, the multiplicity of cultures, values, and religions within the United States has alienated the Society from those who favor diversity. Despite the Society's invitation to "individuals from every walk of life and from all ethnic, racial, and religious backgrounds" who share a love for liberty, the Society remains stigmatized as representative of an ultra–right minority attempting to turn back the clock. For example, attitudes toward the "family" as a primary social unit have changed tremendously, particularly in the last century, when single parenthood, one–parent families, and homosexual marriages affected many lives. Another issue polarizing the Society against more "liberal" conservatives is the Christian theme, admittedly representing the majority of citizens and the country's heritage, but no longer considered "politically correct" within a diverse contemporary citizenry. This serves as a good example of the changing nature of conservatism and its relevance to time along a continuum: what was once considered mainstream thought later becomes threatened and must be defended.

Media Bias

Another important consideration affecting the balance of conservatism versus liberalism in the U.S. is the presence or absence of media bias. Over the years, various accusations have been directed at both sides, claiming that the media attempts to advance its own political agenda by slanting the news. There is apparently some truth in this, straight from the media itself. In *The Media Elite*, authors S. Robert Lichter, Stanley Rothman and Linda S, Lichter summarized the results of their interviews with 238 journalists from the entire spectrum of mass media. This included reporters, editors, executives, anchors, correspondents, and department heads from America's most influential media outlets: *New York Times, Washington Post, Wall Street Journal, Time, Newsweek, U.S. News & World Report,* CBS, NBC, ABC, and PBS, among others. The results, though dated, (1990), tend to support what many have claimed for years. A majority, 54 percent, described themselves as left of center. Only 17 percent described themselves as right of center. While 56 percent responded that they believed their colleagues were on the left, only eight percent responded that their colleagues were on the right.

Moreover, journalists' descriptions of themselves on a wide range of social and political issues revealed the following: 90 percent believed in abortion rights; 75 percent believed homosexuality is not wrong; 53 percent believed adultery is not wrong; and 68 percent believed government should reduce the income gap.

The criticism against a biased media is, of course, that the American people deserve to know all, and not select, facts on any given issue, and that journalists should be compelled to impartially present them. Eva Thomas, Washington bureau chief for *Newsweek* magazine, commenting on House Speaker Newt Gingrich's (1943–) charge that the media was biased, noted, "Particularly at the networks, at the lower levels, among the editors and the so–called infrastructure, there is liberal bias." And Bernard Goldberg, CBS News correspondent, wrote in an editorial for the *Wall Street Journal,* stated that the liberal bias in the media is so "blatantly true that it's hardly worth discussing anymore." It's usually not something the media plans to do—or is necessarily even conscious of doing. Goldberg added that bias is something that comes out of reporters naturally, whether they like it or not.

According to a 1996 Freedom Forum/Roper Center survey of 139 Washington–based bureau chiefs and congressional correspondents, 89 percent voted for Democrat Bill Clinton. (Figures for the 2000 election were not yet available.) Richard Harwood, former assistant managing editor and ombudsman for the *Washington Post*, also noted in 1996 that, while the majority of American journalists do their best to remain impartial, "the journalist without those allegiances is rare indeed…"

Conservatism in the Courtroom

One of the most important ways in which conservatism affects the daily lives of Americans is reflected in political appointments to judicial posts, particularly those by U.S. presidents of justices to the higher federal courts and the U.S. Supreme Court. Since these are appointments for life, they are not taken lightly.

Only federal judges, and a handful of state judges, are appointed for life, barring impeachment. In all other states and in local governments, most judges are elected and reelected by popular vote, and for a specific term. In the abstract, it has always been the desire to make judges, in the words of John Adams's Massachusetts constitution, "as free, impartial and independent as the lot of humanity will admit." But in a political system where social issues define party politics—and where jurisprudence largely affects social issues—alignment and/or labeling is inevitable. A judge, whether elected or appointed, assumes his or her post based on how others perceive he or she will run the bench—conservatively or liberally. Nowhere is it more important that a justice stay politically independent than on the U.S. Supreme Court, for the "supremacy clause" of Article VI of the U.S. Constitution makes the Constitution and treaties "the supreme law of the land; and the judges in every state shall be bound thereby." The top court has the final opinion on Constitutional interpretation.

A president's conservative or liberal leanings, however, may greatly affect his judicial selections. Of course, the Constitution provides a check and balance power of review and confirmation by the Senate for each presidential selection.

The Supreme Court decides some of society's most profound issues, and its ideological makeup during any era may affect decisions on sensitive matters: rights and protections of the unborn, rights of minorities, rights of speech and personal freedom, employee rights, the rights of the accused, rights of the incarcerated, and rights of non–citizens and aliens, among others. Although conservative or liberal leanings may suggest bias in interpreting a law or constitutional provision, a minimum of four other justices would have to agree in order to carry a majority in a decision.

Although a Supreme Court decision may be labeled conservative or liberal, there is a distinction between political conservatism and judicial conservatism. Politicians make the laws; justices interpret

them. When the terms refer to court decisions, conservatism usually means a narrow interpretation of existing law, limited most often by the plain or express language contained therein. This is sometimes called "strict constructionism." Conversely, courts rendering what may be labeled as a liberal opinion in any matter have broadly interpreted the plain language of a law in order to fit the specifics of the case before them.

Conservatism of justices   In one sense, the conservatism of justices parallels true conservatism more so than that of politicians. Justices and judges are extremely hesitant to interpret a law in such a way that it undermines the original legislative intent; in fact, they will often go beyond the arguments made by attorneys in the case, and take it upon themselves to seek the legislative history of the law in question. This is true even if a more liberal or broad interpretation may be more just or favorable under the certain sets of facts before the Court. A court of law has no power to alter or amend existing law, and many times it will state in its opinion that the litigants need to seek legislative rather than judicial relief, i.e., consult their local state representatives or senators to discuss amendments to the written law. However, courts may and often do find certain laws to be unconstitutional under state or federal constitutions, and such a decision by the highest court with jurisdiction over the matter renders the previous law void. And if, in retrospect, a court deems an earlier decision has had far too liberal or conservative effects when applied to other situations, it will attempt to delineate or contain that decision in a subsequent one.

Thus, often in subsequent cases that would require the application of the same law or decision, but with a different set of facts, the Supreme Court will chip away exceptions to the general rule, resulting in a more narrow application of its earlier decision. Although the Supreme Court is empowered to reverse its own decisions, it rarely does. The justices take ultimate care that their decisions are legally and constitutionally sound.

Miranda rights   Take, for example, the case of *Miranda v. Arizona* (1966), in which a liberal Supreme Court held that confessions or responses accused persons gave when law enforcement officials interrogated them could not be used as evidence in court unless the accused had first been advised of such legal rights as not speaking and having legal counsel. These have since been generally called "Miranda rights." While this decision may have been constitutionally sound at the time, the reality of its sweeping effect and/or its application to real cases convinced many Americans that perhaps the Court had been a little too liberal in its constitutional interpretation of the rights of the accused. As a result of the Court's decision, repeat offenders and many persons accused of violent and/or heinous crimes were being released from custody or incarceration. This could have been because of some minor technical oversight or stress–induced mistake on the part of an arresting officer who may have failed to fully advise an accused person of his or her rights.

Since 1966, the Supreme Court has invoked *Miranda* many times, making exceptions or clarifying the general rule. In the 2000 case of *Tankleff v. Senkowski,* the Supreme Court rejected an appeal by Martin Tankleff, convicted of murdering his parents in Belle Terre, New York. Tankleff claimed that his confession, given after he was read his Miranda rights, was nonetheless tainted by police questioning that occurred before they advised him of his rights. This case established no legal precedent.

Supreme balance   Conservatives and liberals try to affect the Supreme Court through congressional pressure to increase the number of justices on the Court. Since justices are appointed for life, members of Congress often want to neutralize the effect of sitting justices. The most recent attempt came during the Clinton administration. Even though Clinton had already nominated two justices during his tenure, liberals Ruth Bader Ginsburg (1933–) and Stephen Breyer (1938–), Congress considered a measure to add two more. Ostensibly it was argued as a measure to reduce a backlog of cases, but in reality it was an attempt to affect the conservative/liberal balance. Congress has the constitutional authority to fix the number of associate justices on the Court; the current number under the chief justice is eight. This most recent attempt to increase the number failed.

In fact, the nine justices who sat on the court going into the new millennium may represent one of the most balanced groups of justices ever to sit concurrently. Three are known conservatives, three are known liberals, and three often provide the "swing vote," which may carry the Court one way or the other in a given case.

William Rehnquist, originally appointed as associate justice in 1971 by a conservative President Nixon, was nominated chief justice by Reagan in 1986. He is known for his hard–line conservative position on most constitutional matters. Another conservative is Clarence Thomas (1948–), whom Bush the elder nominated in 1991. Antonin Scalia (1936–), nominated by Reagan, took his oath in 1986. He is the

third traditionally conservative justice sitting on the top court.

Ginsburg, nominated by Clinton in 1993, is widely known as a liberal. So is Breyer, appointed in 1994 to replace Harry Blackmun (1908–1999). The third liberal justice is John Paul Stevens (1920–). Conservative President Gerald Ford (1913–) nominated him to the top court in 1975. After his appointment, however, he shifted to the left.

Although Reagan appointed justices Sandra Day O'Connor (1930–) and Anthony Kennedy (1936–), in 1981 and 1986, respectively, they have, in fact, proved to be middle–of–the–roaders, often taking moderate stances independent of any other justice. This has also been true of David Souter (1939–), a Bush nominee in 1990. Souter, Kennedy, and O'Connor, therefore, play particularly important roles in delicate decisions the public may erroneously perceive as conservatively or liberally biased.

The Court faced such an accusation following its decision in the Bush–Gore presidential campaign of 2000 involving as many as 15,000 absentee ballots from Florida's Seminole County. The U.S. Supreme Court found that the manual recount of votes ordered by the Florida Supreme Court violated the equal protection clause of the Constitution by treating voters' ballots differently and by conducting it erratically and arbitrarily without proper standards. The media wasted no time labeling judicial players by race, party, and political and personal preferences. Over the years, Democratic governors had appointed all seven Florida Supreme Court justices. But the U.S. Supreme Court comprised a mix of Democrats and Republicans, liberals and conservatives. When the majority ruled against the Florida court, some liberals in the media were openly skeptical about an undercurrent of a "results–oriented" majority seeking a high–minded legal rationale to front their own political leanings. The Supreme Court, however, simply but firmly denied the inference.

ANALYSIS AND CRITICAL RESPONSE

In his essay entitled, "Conservatism Is a Vital Political Ideology," found in *Politics in America: Opposing Viewpoints*, Heritage Foundation president Edwin J. Feulner Jr. attributed to conservatism the conquering of Soviet Communism, the promotion of democracy throughout the world, and the strengthening of the U.S. economy. Feulner argued in his essay that the governments of Eastern Europe were turning to conservative Americans and their free–market ideas

U.S. President Ronald Reagan (left) with British Prime Minister Margaret Thatcher, First Lady Nancy Reagan, and Lord Dennis Thatcher at a White House State Dinner in 1983. (Corbis-Bettmann)

for advice. In Warsaw and Prague, Feulner said, the people wanted capitalism, not lectures on capitalist exploitation.

In an opposing viewpoint entitled, "Conservatism is a Declining Political Ideology," Democrat David Dinkins, former New York mayor (1989-1993), argued that with the fall of the Soviet Union, conservatism lost its cause, i.e., in Dinkins's words, "No Enemy, No Energy." He also blamed the fear of Communism for "block[ing] the path to progress here at home." Said Dinkins:

> The conservatives regaled us with tales of resurgence while the rest of the world went whizzing by. So now we can remember the touching speeches and sentimental images of the 1980s while we travel across roads and bridges that are crumbling, to take our kids to schools that aren't teaching, to prepare them for life in a global economy that suddenly threatens to leave them behind...Military might [has become] the sole measure of national security, leaving no room in our calculation of American strength for infant mortality, literacy, or economic opportunity.

Conservatism ran into some problems in the 1990s, particularly in the United States. It was a belief held by many people—many registered voters—that conservatism was an ideology of the rich, and the 1992 election of Democratic presidential candidate Bill Clinton was in part a rejection of conservative politics.

When the Republicans gained control of Congress in 1994 it often led to policy standoffs with the president which resulted in government shutdowns, and opinion polls showed that people sided with Clinton. "Given the political excitement in the 1980s, the governmental failings of conservatism in the 1990s are nothing short of astonishing," wrote Alan Wolfe in an article in the June 7, 1999 issue of *The New Republic*. Conservative figures such as Pat Buchanan (1938–), Newt Gingrich, and Bob Dole (1923–) were stereotyped as politicans who looked out for big business while not showing much concern for ordinary people facing economic hardship. Sometimes the stereotype was justified, often it was not, but it stuck. Indeed, when George W. Bush campaigned for president in 2000, his platform called for the toned–down version of conservatism which he labeled "compassionate conservatism." This softening of the conservative image may have given Bush the extra boost he needed in one of the closest elections in American history.

Out of Touch?

Of course, the most consistent criticism of conservatism is that its resistance to change has resulted in it being outdated and out of touch with the real world. Liberals may argue that a demand for change is simply a corrective measure to bring forward a lag-

BIOGRAPHY:

Ronald Reagan

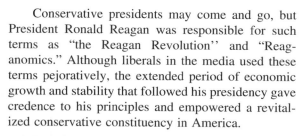

Conservative presidents may come and go, but President Ronald Reagan was responsible for such terms as "the Reagan Revolution" and "Reaganomics." Although liberals in the media used these terms pejoratively, the extended period of economic growth and stability that followed his presidency gave credence to his principles and empowered a revitalized conservative constituency in America.

Born in 1911 in Tampico, Illinois, Reagan won a scholarship to Eureka College, where he majored in economics. He was president of his student body, played football, and was captain of the swimming team. After graduation, Reagan became a radio sports announcer in the Midwest and eventually moved to film acting. In over a quarter of a century of acting, Reagan played in more than fifty films and served as a television host. As president of Hollywood's Screen Actors Guild, he became embroiled in disputes during the McCarthy years over communism in the film industry, and his political views shifted from liberal to conservative. He tried to purge suspected Communists from the movie industry and took a strong anti–Communist stand when testifying before the House Committee on Un–American Activities. Promoting American conservatism around the country, Reagan was elected California governor in 1966 by a winning margin of nearly a million votes.

In 1980 Reagan was elected president, winning 51 percent of the public vote and a ten–to–one margin in the Electoral College. He was perceived as a forceful leader who called for a return to patriotism and traditional morality, and who would restore prosperity to an economically ailing nation. After taking office, Reagan made good on his promises to cut back on big government and taxes, strengthen national defense, curb inflation, overhaul the income tax code (1986) and stimulate economic growth. He shepherded the 1981 Economic Recovery Act. His "supply–side" economics policy intended to stimulate citizen spending on goods and services with money saved from reduced taxes. At the end of his administration, America was enjoying its longest recorded period of peacetime prosperity without recession or depression. Reagan's administration, however, was marred by the "Iran–Contra" affair, a political scandal involving secret weapon sales to Iran in return for support in freeing U.S. hostages held by Lebanese terrorists friendly to Iran. Ostensibly, the moneys earned from the weapon sales were diverted to Contras fighting the Sandinista government in Nicaragua. Reagan denied any knowledge of these secret activities.

When he left office in 1989, opinion polls confirmed Reagan as one of the most popular presidents of the twentieth century. However, when a recession hit the United States in 1991, many critics blamed the policies of Reaganomics in the 1980s. In 1994, Reagan announced that he was battling Alzheimer's disease, and by doing so brought much attention to the illness.

---

ging conservatism that has been left behind. For example, the British public, through the media, expressed its wish for a more personable and approachable monarchy, especially during the time immediately following the death of Princess Diana (1961–1997). Conversely, a majority of the British public confirmed its continued belief in the monarchy, its heritage and tradition, and its maintenance as a British institution.

In economic policy, the general conservative attitude toward a *laissez–faire* capitalism or free enterprise system has always been under attack by a concerted minority. The problem has been that both conservatives and liberals support such a system, and the dissenting minority is also comprised of both con-servative and liberal elements of political following. This mingling with the opposition has manifested on other fronts as well—on issues such as abortion, affirmative action, foreign policy, social welfare, and taxation.

The New Right

Historians and partisan politics have attempted to rectify these muddles by creating subgroups and attaching newer names to the ideology, such as "neo–conservatism," "American conservatism," "the New Conservatism," and "the New Right." However, each of these terms ultimately relates to a particular historic period when the tenets of political conservatism were again being re–defined by, and re–oriented to, pressing issues of the time. For example, critics have argued that following the fall of Communism in the Soviet Union (a declared victory for conservatism), there was no cause celebre to unite conservative forces anymore. But to twenty–first century American conservatives, high crime rates and financial returns on investments were of greater concern than Communism. The fall of the Soviet Union was remote and not palpable, perhaps of more interest to their aging parents than to them.

Moreover, although conservatives have historically been referred to as the political "right," this can no longer be true because those that want to maintain the status quo actually oppose radical "neo liberals" who want to establish a world–wide system of laissez–faire capitalism. Still further, some conservatives actually support and defend certain institutions of a welfare state. The distinction between conservative and liberal views must now necessarily be made on an issue–by–issue basis. General stereotypes and labels have become increasingly less accurate, and characteristic parameters of conservative ideology continue to shift.

This, in turn, pressures political parties in a bipartisan or multi–partisan political system to more clearly distinguish themselves from their competitors or opposition, which, in turn, creates a more adversarial campaign and election system. In a government such as that enjoyed in the U.S., free speech allows two or more sides of an issue to be freely argued, though with special–interest lobbying. But the system has checks and balances. A conservative or liberal president has veto power over Congress, and Congress can override a presidential veto. Judicial rulings of constitutional provisions ensure that no radical new law abridges the rights of the people.

The National Motto

Perhaps a poignant example of the ebb and flow of conservative versus liberal forces in the United States is the sometimes anecdotal, sometimes vociferous arguments over the country's motto. In 1956, the U.S. Congress enacted a law declaring the national motto of the United States to be "In God We Trust." Although the motto had existed de facto for more than one hundred and fifty years prior, it had never been officially codified into law. The motto is now codified at 36 U.S.C. 302. In fact, America's history is replete with other references to God and Providence, only some of which have come under such attack.

Our country, undeniably, was formed on Christian principles. For about two hundred years, this cre-

ated no palpable problem, as the majority of Americans were primarily of Western European Christian heritage. Any protest directed at the symbol or motto of America would have been unthinkable. But the great immigration influx of the twentieth century has made America more consisting of multiple cultures, races, and peoples. Conservatives would argue that it does not matter where you came from, that now you are an American, and you must live according to American tradition and heritage. Liberals would argue that the freedoms guaranteed by the Constitution require that America accommodate the cultural heritages of its newcomers and minorities, who may find such references to God as contrary or even repulsive to their own beliefs. But the real bitterness centered on a majority of Americans still identifying with Christianity in the twentieth century, and resenting a small but vociferous minority attempting to usurp their American heritage. The tensions created when applying old traditions to a newer multi–ethnic, multi–cultural population are all too apparent.

The U.S. Supreme Court has never expressly ruled on the constitutionality of our national motto. When asked to rule, however, it has let stand the decisions of several U.S. Circuit Courts of Appeal (one level down from the Supreme Court) that have upheld the constitutionality of the motto, essentially on grounds of historical significance and heritage.

Still, on April 25, 2000, a three–member panel of the U.S. Circuit Court of Appeals for the 6th Circuit ruled 2–1 that the official motto of the State of Ohio, "With God All Things Are Possible," was unconstitutional. The motto, which was unanimously adopted by the state in 1959 (Ohio Revised Code Section 5.06), existed for years without ado, along with the state wildflower, the state animal, the state coat of arms, and the state song. However, the American Civil Liberties Union (ACLU), representing a single plaintiff, Reverend Matthew Peterson, had challenged the motto in 1997.

Extreme conservatism can be as harmful as radical liberalism. Unbending or uncompromising attitudes, whether conservative or liberal, have limited appeal in any society. It has been partly a media phenomenon that has been responsible for creating stereotypes of conservative Americans as ultra–right–wing religious fanatics. In reality, that is as far from the truth as promoting the perception that all liberals are revolutionaries who wish to agitate Americans toward socialistic totalitarianism. Both extremes do not speak for the vast majority of Americans (and politicians) who vacillate along a continuum of association according to their own views and beliefs.

TOPICS FOR FURTHER STUDY

- Both conservative and liberal governments have enjoyed extended periods of economic wealth and prosperity. In the United States, both Republican and Democratic parties have produced successful administrations. During such times, dissention between conservatives and liberals has often been exaggerated or instigated only to accommodate the need to polarize political platforms. Nothing in the U.S. Constitution either requires or suggests the need for partisan politics. How is it, then, that partisan politics have come to be inextricably bound to the American political system?

- Semantics have always played a role in defining conservative or liberal leanings. The media has the power to create, enhance, or otherwise influence the popularity or unpopularity of certain political views. For example, it may draw more attention to a political view by referring to it as "leftist" rather than "liberal." It may choose to refer to those favoring abortion as "family planners," and abortion clinics as "family planning clinics." In recent times, the mere insertion of the word "Christian" immediately connoted an affiliation with "the right." The public may view something according to how impartially facts have been presented. There have been previous demands by the public for more unbiased news coverage and a demand that "equal time" or "equal press" be given for the presentation of opposing views.

BIBLIOGRAPHY

Sources

"Bicentennial of the United States Constitution." Printed by the Office of the Special Consultant to the Secretary of the Army. 1989.Reprinted in part from *The People Consent: Revisiting the Ratification of the United States Constitution.* Courtesy of Edith R. Wilson & J. Goldman. New York: 1987.

"Biography of Ronald Reagan." 2000. Available at http://www.whitehouse.gov/history/presidents/rr40.html.

"Biographies: The Political Philosopher, Edmund Burke (1729–97)." Available at http://www.blupete.com/Literature/Biographies/Philosophy/Burke.htm.

"CBS Profile: Supreme Court Justices." 2000. Available at http://cbsnews.com/now/story.

"Churchill, Sir Winston Leonard Spencer." *The Canadian & World Encyclopedia.* Available at http://tceplus.com/churchill.htm.

Davies, Stephen. "Margaret Thatcher and the Rebirth of Conservatism." 1993. Available at http://www.ashbrook.org/publicat/onprin/v1n2/davies.html.

Dionne, E.J., Jr. *Why Americans Hate Politics.* New York: Simon & Schuster, 1991

Dole, Bob. *Great Political Wit.* New York: Doubleday, 1998

Encarta Encyclopedia. Available at http://encarta.msn.com.

Forse, Don T., Jr. "Media Bias?" 1997. Available at http://www.afatexas.org/document/news/other/mediabias.htm.

Gottfried, Paul. *The Conservative Movement.* New York: Twayne Publishers, 1993.

"Initiatives for Access: Treasures – Magna Carta." Available at http://www.bl.uk.diglib/magna–carta/overvoverview.html.

International Institute for Strategic Studies. "Country Profiles." Economist Intelligence Unit of the U.S. Military, 2001.

"In Their Own Words: Journalists and Bias." Available at http://www.aim.org/publications/special_reports/bias.html.

Johnson, Stephen D. and Joseph B. Tamney. "Social Traditionalism and Economic Conservatism: Two Conservative Political Ideologies in the United States." *Journal of Social Psychology*, April 2001.

Johnston, Joseph F. "Conservative Populism— a Dead End." *National Review*, October 19, 1984.

Keegan, John. "Sir Winston Churchill." Available at http://www.rjgeib.com/thoughts/britain/winston–churchill.html.

Kekes, John. *A Case for Conservatism,* Cornell UP: 1998.

Kirk, Russell. *The Roots of American Order.* Washington: Regnery Gateway, 1991.

Marlantes, Liz; Scherer, Ron; and Alexandra Marks. "To New Yorkers, He's Churchill in a Baseball Cap." *Christian Science Monitor,* September 12, 2001.

Olasky, Marvin. *Compassionate Conservatism.* New York: The Free Press, 2000.

"Questions and Answers About the John Birch Society." Available at http://www.jbs.org/about/weareask.htm

Ross, Kelley L. "Conservatism, History, and Progress." 1996. Available at http://www.friesian.com/conserv.htm

Rossiter, Clinton. *Seedtime of the Republic: the Origin of the American Tradition of Political Liberty.*

Schrecker, Ellen. *The Legacy of McCarthyism.* Boston: Bedford Books of St. Marvin's Press, 1994.

"The Rise and Fall of the Conservative Party." Available at http://britishhistory.about.com/library/weekly/aa042001a.htm.

Further Readings

Busch, Andrew E. *Ronald Reagan and the Politics of Freedom.* New York: Rowman & Littlefield, 2001. This book supports the premise of Ronald Reagan's enduring legacy as a dominant force in American politics, and the effects his brand of conservatism has had upon contemporary politics.

Dillard, Angela D. *Guess Who's Coming to Dinner Now?* New York: New York University Press, 2001. Author Dillard argues that political conservatism in the U.S. is no longer the domain of white, wealthy males, but instead involves persons of all races, ethnicities, gender, and sexualities.

Kelly, Charles M. *Class War in America.* Santa Barbara: Fithian Press, 2001. In this critical observation of conservative politics in action, author Kelly sub–titles his book: "How Economic and Political Conservatives are Exploiting Low– and Middle–Income Americans."

http://www.heritage.org. The Heritage Foundation is a well–known conservative think tank in Washington, D.C., and actively promotes conservative views through its website and various publications.

National Review. In the ten years between 1955 and 1965, subscriptions to *National Review* increased from 30,000 to well over 100,000. This was primarily due to writer–editor William F. Buckley, Jr., whose opinions and editorials came to define American post–war conservatism.

SEE ALSO

Capitalism, Federalism, Liberalism, Republicanism

Fascism

OVERVIEW

Fascism is a twentieth–century political ideology and movement based on nationalism and militarism, which emphasizes the importance of the state and the individual's overriding duty to it. It opposes communism and liberalism, and seeks to regenerate the social, cultural, and economic life of its country by instilling its citizens with a powerful sense of national identity and an unquestioning loyalty to the state and its leader. Agencies of state control, such as secret police, and sophisticated propaganda techniques are important factors in the suppression of opposition and the advancement of fascist doctrines.

Drawing on nineteenth century theories, such as those of Friedrich Nietzsche and Georges Sorel, fascism arose out of the political and social destruction which followed World War I (1914–1918) and the Russian Revolution (1917), and reached its peak in the inter–war years between 1922–1939. Fascism was officially founded by Benito Mussolini, whose Fascist regime controlled Italy between 1922 and 1945, and derived its name from the *fasces* of ancient Rome, an axe tied up in a bundle of sticks which symbolized authority and justice. Italian Fascism proved to be the model for subsequent movements throughout Europe, most notably that of Germany. Under the dictatorship of Adolf Hitler, Nazism developed the nationalist principles of fascism into a blueprint for conquering Europe and establishing a racial hierarchy. The Third Reich's attempts to create a "new order" led directly to the carnage of World War II, and to the German "mas-

WHO CONTROLS GOVERNMENT? Dictator

HOW IS GOVERNMENT PUT INTO POWER? Overthrow or revolution

WHAT ROLES DO THE PEOPLE HAVE? Not interfere with the state

WHO CONTROLS PRODUCTION OF GOODS? The state

WHO CONTROLS DISTRIBUTION OF GOODS? The state

MAJOR FIGURES Benito Mussolini; Adolf Hitler

HISTORICAL EXAMPLE Italy, 1922–1943

CHRONOLOGY

1918: First World War ends. Its aftermath creates the ideal conditions for Fascism's development

1919: Benito Mussolini and the "Fascists of the First Hour" meet in Milan to form the Italian Fascist Party (PNF)

1921: Adolf Hitler becomes leader of the NSDAP (Nazi Party)

1922: Following the "March on Rome," Mussolini is installed as Italian Prime Minister

1923–1924: Hitler is imprisoned for treason. While in Landsberg prison he writes *Mein Kampf*

1933: Hitler becomes German Chancellor. Almost immediately he passes the Enabling Act which awards him dictatorial powers

1936: Germany reoccupies the Rhineland and signs the Rome–Berlin Axis that unites Germany and Italy as allies. Outbreak of the Spanish Civil War, in which Germany and Italy provide support for General Franco's forces

1939: Italy invades Albania and signs the "Pact of Steel" with Hitler. Germany invades Poland provoking the outbreak of World War II

1941: Hitler and Mussolini declare war on the United States

1943: Allies invade Italy and Mussolini is removed from power

1945: Mussolini is shot dead by Italian partisans, Hitler and other Nazi party members commit suicide and Nazi Germany surrenders unconditionally to the Allies

ter race" inflicting terror and genocide on those who it deemed to be inferior.

Although the era of fascist domination ended in 1945, with the Allied victory over Italy and Germany, the influence of its ideology, as documented in Hitler's *Mein Kampf* ("My Struggle") and Mussolini's *Dottrina del Fascismo* ("Doctrine of Fascism"), continues to exist on the political fringes of all Western democracies.

Within this common framework, however, there are certain characteristics which, although figuring prominently in some fascist movements, are absent in others. Arguably the most important of these differences lies in the militarist and nationalist doctrines of the various regimes, which range from an intense pride in national unity and traditions, through to a belief in racial superiority, ending ultimately in the overt racism, anti–Semitism and ethnic cleansing adopted by the Nazi regime under Adolf Hitler. These ideological inconsistencies have resulted in constant debate as to whether the authoritarian and nationalistic movements that arose in countries such as Spain, Romania, Austria, and France can be accurately described as fascist, or were merely foreign models of the original Fascist regime of Italy. If taken to its most basic and literal meaning, the term *fascism* applies only to the Italian regime which was founded and named by Mussolini although it is generally extended to encompass all comparable ideologies and movements. What is indisputable, however, is that to most people, fascism is primarily associated with the regimes of Benito Mussolini in Italy and Adolf Hitler in Germany. Unfortunately, the well–documented manner in which its regimes mercilessly persecuted their national, political, and racial enemies has replaced much of fascism's political meaning with more common use as a term of abuse and a generic symbol of evil and violence.

Despite this widespread demonization, and fascism's inability to regain the political dominance it enjoyed from 1922 until the defeat of Germany and Italy in World War II in 1945, it would be foolish to dismiss its continuing influence and potential. The resurgence, especially in Eastern Europe, of authoritarian regimes with strong nationalist support, and the existence of fascist and neo–fascist movements on the political fringes of most Western democracies, only serves to highlight the need for continued study of fascism, in the hope of gaining greater understanding of its ideology, aims, and appeal.

HISTORY

Although fascism, as a political system, did not thrust itself upon the world until after World War I, the roots and influences of its political theory stretch back as far as the early nineteenth century. As a reaction to the values and ideals created during the Age of Enlightenment and the French Revolution that had swept across Europe during the eighteenth century, many intellectuals developed philosophies and con-

Nazi youth march in Berlin, 1933. (Archive Photos, Inc.)

cepts which would later be adapted to form the foundations of fascist ideology. Among those who opposed the new prevailing attitudes of rationalism, democracy, and liberalism, were the writers Johann von Goethe (1749–1832) and Friedrich von Schelling (1775–1854), who denied the claims that human nature could be explained in terms of general laws and dismissed the growing belief that politics and economics should aim for greater democracy and universalism. Along with other thinkers, known collectively as the Romantic Movement, Goethe and Schelling placed great emphasis on the importance of nationalism and tradition, and displayed a fervent hostility

towards society's increasing adoption of material values.

The Romantic Movement's philosophy was developed into a rejection of democracy as the ideal form of decision making by thinkers who adapted the works of Jean Jacques Rousseau (1712–1778), in particular his belief in the "general will." Rousseau, a Swiss political philosopher, claimed that a natural, harmonious decision will emerge within a society on any issue, but this decision is not necessarily the one that would be chosen by a democratic majority. He added that, on certain occasions, the people may not be aware of this "general will" and it was the duty of those in authority to invoke it. This theory has been linked to the fascist ideology of the strong, authoritarian state, making all decisions on behalf of its people and in the interests of the nation. In fairness to Rousseau, however, it is doubtful whether he intended for his theory to be interpreted in this way—his other assertions, in contrast to fascism, were that mankind was not inherently evil, and that ordinary people had the right and ability to bring about changes within their society.

During the course of the nineteenth century, the embryonic ideology of fascism gathered momentum and support in many European countries, with the continued rejection of liberal and democratic systems in favor of a return to traditional values and nationalism, under the guidance of a powerful, authoritarian state.

In France and Germany, nationalism progressed beyond its positive function of providing individuals with a shared heritage and a common identity and tradition. By coloring reason with emotion, and by selective interpretation of scientific and intellectual developments, the desire for national unity shifted sharply in the direction of racism. In France, Maurice Barres (1862–1923) introduced his theory of *enracinement*, which essentially suggested the existence of a mystical link between a country's living and dead citizens, placing great emphasis on the importance of a nation to uphold the traditions and values of their ancestors. The views of Barres, along with those of his compatriots Comte Joseph de Gobineau (1816–1882) and Charles Maurras (1868–1952), founded the ideology on which *Action Franqis* (AF), considered by many historians to be the first fascist movement, was based. Formed in June 1899, AF united support from all sections of French society against the liberalism and universalism of the Republican government. With the influence of leading members, such as Georges Sorel (1847–1922) and Georges Valois (1894–1945), AF sought to reinstate the monarchy as the means of reuniting the nation and thereby placing France in a stronger position to defeat external and, more importantly, internal enemies. In France at this time, just as in other Western European countries, the major internal enemy was considered to be the Jews. Viewed as the materialistic and scheming epitome of capitalism, Jews became the convenient focus of the growing nationalist movement and proved an effective common enemy, upon whom society could blame their economic and political failures and disillusionment. However, neither AF nor any of its subsidiaries were able to turn this strong nationalist support into political success. What they had achieved was the setting in motion of a chain of ideas and events which, only a few years later, would see their ideology of extreme nationalism and strong control of the state become the

foundations of a new and powerful political system. Ironically, it would be not in France that fascism eventually obtained its political power, but in Italy and Germany (thus, the fascist regimes that French thinkers had so greatly influenced, almost succeeded in destroying France during World War II).

In Germany, as in France, the path of nationalism had moved from a healthy pride in their heritage and traditions to one of racism, anti–Semitism, and, ultimately, to fascism. The route of German fascism, however, would be influenced by thinkers who placed greater emphasis on the values of national and racial supremacy and military strength.

Before 1870, Germany was divided into many smaller states, the most important of which was Prussia. It was not until after the Prussian armies had defeated France at the Battle of Sedan in 1870 that the unification of Germany was realized, and Otto von Bismarck (1815–1898) became the first Chancellor of the new Imperial German Federation. Yet, as far back as the sixteenth century, Germany possessed a strong sense of nationalism, evident in the popularity of the philosopher and religious reformer, Martin Luther (1483–1546). These values were later expanded upon by thinkers of the Romantic Movement, and by 1873, when German journalist Wilhelm Marr (1819–1904) published his highly successful book, *The Victory of the Jew over the German*, the seeds of anti–Semitism and the desire for racial purity were becoming generally promoted and accepted. The breakthrough, in terms of electoral support, came in 1887 when the independent, anti–Semitic candidate Otto Bockel was elected to the *Reichstag* (German parliament). Yet, his election was not as influential, in terms of fascist ideas, as the manner in which he carried out his campaign. In place of the normally low–key affair, Bockel organized mass rallies, consisting of marching bands and torchlight processions, all accompanied by the singing of nationalist songs and Lutheran hymns. This was a method that would be further developed and successfully employed by future fascist leaders.

Growth In the Twentieth Century

Germany The arrival of the twentieth century still found the growing number of nationalist and militarist movements relegated to the fringes of political power. Even the formation of the Pan–German League, with such popular commitments as emphasizing the will of the people and increasing German economic prosperity by expanding into Eastern Europe, led to minimal electoral support. After the elections in 1912, it was the socialists who had succeeded, for the first time, in becoming the German parliament's largest party. The majority of right wing groups, moderate and extreme, felt that radical measures were required to revive their popularity. Suggestions ranged from the establishment of a new, popular party to the setting up of an authoritarian regime; some activists even advocated the creation of a dictatorship. Two years later, with the onset of World War I, the nationalist and militarist movements seemed to have lost their momentum, as Germany united behind their government in expectation of a glorious victory, and the increased political and economic power that would inevitably follow in its wake. Indeed, had a swift victory occurred, then the course of world history may well have been very different. This was not the case, however, and as the war continued the German people faced increasing hardship, which in turn led to signs of unrest and dissent. The nationalist movements seized on this as their opportunity, and in September 1917 witnessed the formation of the German Fatherland Party (GFP), the first mass party within Germany to be founded on the developing fascist ideology. By proposing the annexation of states along Germany's eastern borders, and by deflecting criticism from the government and military by blaming the ailing war effort on the Jewish population, the GFP had, by July 1918, amassed a membership of 1.25 million.

By October 1918, the leaders of the German military were aware that defeat was inevitable and, in order to shirk from the responsibility of their failure, plans were drawn up which transferred the reins of power from the Imperial hierarchy to a new, democratic government. On November 9, 1918, one day after Kaiser Wilhelm I (1859–1941) had been secretly escorted to Holland, Germany was officially declared a republic. The first duty of the new leadership was to unconditionally surrender to the victorious Allies and, two days after succeeding to power, Matthias Erzberger (1875–1921) signed a formal armistice on behalf of the new government. The humiliation felt by the German people and military was intensified by the conditions imposed on their country by the Allies in the Treaty of Versailles. Among the requirements was that Germany must accept full responsibility for starting the war, and that the regions of Alsace and Lorraine should be returned to France. It also ordered major demilitarization and limitations of the German armed forces, changes to Germany's eastern boundaries, the removal of all German colonies, and a commitment to the paying of restorative compensation to the Allies. The war had shattered German society and they now required someone on whom to place blame, both for the defeat and for the humiliating aftermath. The Germans found two convenient scapegoats in their newly formed democratic government and the Jews. What the German people now sought was the rebirth of their country and the restoration of their national identity and pride, but they no longer believed that the politics of liberalism and democracy would provide this. The German state was collapsing and the people demanded radical changes.

Italy Ironically, one of Germany's enemies in the war, Italy, experienced a similar feeling of national despair and frustration. Although Italy had emerged on the winning side, the cost of their victory had been a national, social, and economic crisis that resulted, just as in Germany, in the desire for a strong, nationalist political party to lead them out of the post–war chaos and confusion. The combination of intense public disillusionment and the general collapse of the old political order contributed to a rapid growth in the popularity of the developing Fascist movement and its leaders. The head of one such movement was quick to observe that a political void now existed, and within one year of the war's conclusion, Benito Mussolini (1883–1945) had added the term Fascism to the political dictionary, and laid the foundations of the first Fascist political party.

Just as in Germany, the political, economical, and social effects of World War I proved to be the most significant factors in the development and popularity of Italian fascism. However, the political ideology of the National Fascist Party, and the reasons for its subsequent rise to power, had roots which lay far deeper in Italy's history.

Corresponding very closely to the development of Germany, Italy as a unified nation did not exist until 1870. Prior to this it had consisted of an assortment of independent city–states, interspersed with several kingdoms under the control of autocratic foreign dynasties. The first half of the nineteenth century had spawned a national independence movement, known as the *Risorgimento*, which sought to establish a united and independent Italian state. The major figures of this nationalist movement were Camillo Cavour (1810–1861), Giuseppe Garibaldi (1807–1882) and Giuseppe Mazzini (1805–1872). Garibaldi and his Redshirts, a renowned army of one thousand red–shirted volunteers, conquered the major kingdom of Naples in 1861 and throughout the 1860s Italy gradually moved closer to unification. The process was completed, under the guidance of Cavour, in 1870. Unfortunately, although Italy was now officially united, in terms of politics, economics, and geography a great deal of division remained. Italy was, in effect, a dual economy, with the more advanced, industrialized areas being concentrated in the north, while the rural economy of the south was beset with problems of illiteracy and underemployment. Politically, Italy was governed by a succession of elitist coalitions, which were unstable and short–lived, causing the people to feel increasingly alienated and resulting in major public unrest. The instability of the new political system was intensified when the Vatican, who objected to losing the Papal States during the unification process, refused to cooperate with the new state, and announced a papal ban which prohibited any participation in politics.

Italy's defeat by the Ethiopians at the Battle of Adowa in 1896 further exposed the weakness of the Italian state, and proved yet another blow in their quest for national glory and stability. The Italian people's discontentment with their leadership became increasingly apparent and, in the years immediately preceding World War I, there was a rapid development in the popularity of both socialism and a new, organized nationalist movement.

While the Italian Socialist Party (PSI) was establishing itself as the largest political party within the coalition government, a small group of intellectuals and writers were laying the foundations of the Italian Nationalist Association (ANI). Officially formed in Florence in 1910, and containing key figures such as Gabriele D'Annunzio (1863–1938), Enrico Corradini (1865–1931) and Giovanni Papini (1881–1956), the ANI adopted a doctrine which focused on the creation of a strong, authoritarian state and a commitment to providing rapid economic growth. At the outbreak of war in 1914, the ANI and their nationalist beliefs were gaining support from all sections of society, including many disillusioned socialists. One of these was Benito Mussolini, whose conversion to nationalism and decision to support, rather than oppose, the war resulted in him being dismissed as editor of the socialist party newspaper, *Avanti!*. Upon returning wounded from the war, Mussolini set up his own newspaper, *Il Popolo d'Italia* (The People of Italy), in which he criticized the government and opposition political parties, while promoting his own nationalist and militarist views.

Birth of Fascism

The official birth of fascism is generally accepted as occurring on March 23, 1919, when Mussolini met with the "Fascists of the First Hour" at the Piazza San Sepolcro in Milan. This gathering, which brought together elements from the extreme right and left of Italian politics, including groups such as the Italian National Association and the Futurists, led directly to the formation of the *Fasci di Combattimento*, the first self–styled Fascist movement. As its symbol, the group adopted the *fasces*, an ancient Roman emblem of authority and punishment, consisting of a bundle of rods bound together with a protruding axe head. Although the membership of the *Fasci di Combattimento* was drawn from all points of the social and political spectrum, most had served in the war, which was of crucial importance to Mussolini, who firmly believed that only a "trenchocratic" regime would be capable of creating a regenerated Italy. He was also of the opinion that the use of violence was necessary to achieve major political goals, whether directly or as a means to suppress the opposition. The *Fasci di Combattimento* was controlled by an elected central committee, the order of the hierarchy being determined by the number of votes gained by each successful candidate. Mussolini secured the number one position. This, however, was his only successful election in 1919, as in the November national elections the newly formed fascist movement attracted minimal support. Mussolini and the Fascist Central Committee, attributed their failure to the electorate's distrust of policies which advocated extreme left– and right–wing measures. In order to redress this imbalance, the Fascist movement distanced themselves from many of their left–wing programs and embarked on a definite shift towards the right.

This further drift towards extremism manifested itself most visibly in the increased level of violence, and in the para–militarism of these attacks. Originally employed on a small scale, in order to intimidate opposition groups and defend those attending Fascist meetings, these tactics soon changed with the setting up of the *squadristi*. These were fascist squads, composed mainly of disillusioned ex–servicemen, who increasingly took on a paramilitary role and favored the use of more threatening tactics. To visually reinforce their militarism, the *squadristi* adopted the black–shirted uniform and the one–armed salute employed during the war by the *arditi*, who were the elite troops of the Italian army. Although Mussolini exercised overall command, at a local level each of these squads was under the control of Fascist leaders known as *ras*, the name being taken from the Ethiopian word for chieftain. By early 1921, Mussolini had growing concerns about the ruthless tactics being employed by the *squadristi*, and the power and influence that certain of the *ras* had achieved. Although he was in favor of using violence to achieve specific goals, Mussolini was, at that time, attempting to portray Fascism as a stable and credible political force, and was concerned that the excessive brutality of many squads would undermine his plans. His solution was to formalize the status of the *Fascis di Combattimento* as an official political party.

When the *Fascis di Combattimento* was first formed, Mussolini deliberately avoided setting it up as an official political party for two reasons. First, Italy's recent political past had caused most Italians to become disillusioned with traditional party politics and the ineffectual parliaments that they consistently created. This persuaded Mussolini and the Central Committee to seek an alternative, less rigid, vehicle for their policies. Secondly, an unofficial and flexible nature of the organization had been able to attract disaffected members from other political persuasions, which allowed Mussolini to present Fascism as an inclusive and holistic political movement. With this achieved, and with the *ras* now threatening his position, Mussolini convened a meeting of the Fascist Constitutional Congress in Rome and, after some shrewd negotiations, successfully pushed through his plan to envelop the Fascist movement within an organized political party, the National Fascist Party (PNF). With Mussolini at the helm, the PNF rapidly attracted mass support from all sections of Italian society and, in particular, the armed forces. There was also an underlying sense of cooperation between the fascists and those in political authority, which led to many of the *squadristi* attacks on socialists going unpunished, even quietly applauded by those with business interests. This newly found acceptance of Fascism was further enhanced when the Prime Minister, Giovanni Giolitti (1842–1928), invited Mussolini and the PNF to join the nationalist electoral coalition, which allowed them to compete in the May 1921 General Election as a respectable, parliamentary–style party. As a result, the PNF won thirty–five seats in the Chamber of Deputies (Italian parliament), providing them with a great deal of political influence and, more importantly, the appearance of a constitutionally respectable political party. At the end of 1920 the *Fascis di Combattimento* and its associated fascist movements had a total membership of just over 20,000, but by December 1921 the PNF had boosted this to almost 250,000. After centuries of intellectual and political development, Fascist ideology had finally secured itself a stable, organized, and united political base; a powerful, charismatic, and politically astute leader; and an increasing body of electoral support comprising a cross section of society. For the first time, Fascism appeared to be on the threshold of political power.

Fascists Gain Control

Throughout 1922 Italy suffered continued political and economic instability, culminating in a general strike which threatened to cripple the Italian economy and invoke considerable public unrest. Mussolini seized on this as the opportunity to strike at the heart of the weak, divided government and secure Fascist control of Italy. In a carefully prepared exhibition of strength and showmanship, Mussolini and the PNF threatened to overthrow the existing regime by dispatching Fascist squads to simultaneously occupy key sites and buildings in all the major cities, while Mussolini, at the head of 30,000 *squadristi*, led the "March on Rome." However, on the morning of October 28, 1922, the date set for the threatened coup, King Victor Emmanuel III (1869–1947) struck a deal with the Fascists and, instead of his proposed march into Rome, Mussolini arrived at the royal palace by train on October 30, 1922 and was duly appointed the youngest prime minister in Italian history.

The Fascist regime that took control of Italy that day would remain in power for more than two decades, and throughout that time, as the regime sought to consolidate its authority and achieve its vision of a powerful, regenerated Italy, the underlying Fascist ideology underwent considerable evolution. Its vision of a new dawn, where the Fascist state would provide strong leadership, economic and social development, and a renewed sense of national pride was replaced by the nightmare of human tragedy and inhuman atrocities which were carried out in the name of fascism. When that evil chapter of history was finally brought to a close in 1945, Italy's Fascist regime had been removed from power and Mussolini had, for a time, been installed as a Nazi puppet ruler in northern Italy, before being captured and shot by Italian partisans on April 28, 1945. In effect, Italian Fascism became a victim of its own success. The theories and achievements of the PNF between 1922 and 1936 became the model for subsequent fascist movements and Mussolini's charismatic style inspired future Fascist leaders. Unfortunately, one of those movements was Nazism, and one of those leaders was Adolf Hitler (1889–1945), and due to a favorable combination of circumstances, fascism was able to assume a far greater degree of unchecked power and dominance in Germany than it had done in Italy.

Fascism's Development in Germany

Although German fascism had been greatly influenced by its Italian counterpart, its origins and development were firmly rooted in German history. The aftereffects of World War I were particularly embarrassing for a nation with such a proud military past as Germany, especially the humiliating conditions imposed on them by the Treaty of Versailles. In addition, post–war problems such as massive unemployment and crippling inflation placed the ruling Weimar Republic under increasing pressure from both left and right. The political opposition to the democratic leadership was comprised of two totalitarian parties, the

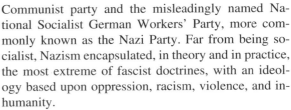

MAJOR WRITINGS:
Mein Kampf

Adolf Hitler composed *Mein Kampf* (My Struggle) while in Landsberg Prison for his part in the unsuccessful attempt to seize power from the Weimar government in 1923. Later to become the bible of Nazism, and a major influence on fascist movements everywhere, *Mein Kampf* was a powerful compilation of fascist theory, propaganda techniques, racist thought, and plans for the creation of the Third Reich, which Hitler declared would first conquer Germany and then Europe as it embarked upon its one–thousand–year reign.

Originally titled *Four and a Half Years of Struggle Against Lies, Stupidity and Cowardice*, *Mein Kampf* was not "written" in the conventional sense, but was dictated by Hitler to his fellow inmate and confidante, Rudolph Hess (1894–1987). In his book, Hitler declared the racial superiority of the German people, warned of the threat posed by the Jews, communists, and liberalism, and explained the need for a strong, authoritarian state which was willing to use war to achieve military and economic greatness for Germany. It outlines, in great detail, his belief in Aryan supremacy, anti–Semitism and the importance of conquering those who do not recognize their racial inferiority to the German race. *Mein Kampf* also specified the military conquests that Hitler would later attempt in order to expand the German nation and described the fates of those who were conquered.

Published in 1925, *Mein Kampf* initially attracted little interest from the public, due in part to its length and the labored style of its writing. However, upon Hitler's ascension to Chancellor, and ultimately Führer, its popularity soared and millions of copies were sold. Although rarely read from cover to cover, the majority of German households possessed a copy of *Mein Kampf*, as did followers of fascism everywhere, and the influence it exerted is evidenced by the devastating events that followed.

Communist party and the misleadingly named National Socialist German Workers' Party, more commonly known as the Nazi Party. Far from being socialist, Nazism encapsulated, in theory and in practice, the most extreme of fascist doctrines, with an ideology based upon oppression, racism, violence, and inhumanity.

By 1923, the economic and social crisis in Germany had virtually destroyed the authority of the democratic Weimar government and, on November 8, the Nazis organized an unsuccessful attempt to gain power. Under the leadership of Adolf Hitler, the Nazis and 600 armed storm troopers raided a Munich beer hall, in which several leading government figures were addressing a public meeting. However, the Nazis' military and popular support was insufficient to succeed with their *coup d'etat* and, following a violent clash with armed police, Hitler was arrested and subsequently sentenced to five years in prison. He served only nine months in Landsberg Prison, and it was during this time that Hitler formulated and dictated his book *Mein Kampf* ("My Struggle"). Upon his release from Landsberg, Hitler discovered that economic conditions had improved, resulting in an increased air of confidence in the democratic leadership and a sharp decline in popular support for fascism. Hitler and his associates, presumably heeding the lesson learned in Munich, acknowledged that the time was not right and quietly set about rebuilding and reorganizing the party. It was not until the national election of 1930 that they achieved any notable electoral victories, their cause aided by Germany having almost been brought to its knees by the economic crisis and crippling unemployment that resulted from the Depression that swept over Europe and the United States.

In the years between 1925 and 1929 Hitler reinforced his position as the *Führer*, or irrefutable leader, of the Nazi party and continued to develop the radical fascist doctrine which would shape the Third Reich. Hitler held dictatorial power over the party and set about creating a paramilitary wing, known as the *Sturmabteilung* (SA), drawing recruits from the unemployed, criminals, and down–and–outs of Bavaria. This period also witnessed important changes in the functions of the *Schutzstaffel* (SS) who were originally formed to act as bodyguards for Hitler but, under the guidance of Heinrich Himmler (1900–1945) assumed responsibility for supervising and policing the party, and for ensuring that Hitler's patriotic propaganda was able to permeate every area of German society with little resistance. It was becoming apparent that German fascism intended to control all aspects of national life, yet its proposals to restore Germany's economic and military pride proved extremely popular with the electorate, and seemed to instill the nation with a re-newed sense of purpose. Therefore, when economic disaster struck again following the Depression, and the democratic Weimar Republic was unable to resolve the crisis, it was the Nazi Party's stable, unified appearance, its commitment to German rebirth, and its powerfully charismatic leader, which helped them become Europe's second fascist government. Adolf Hitler was appointed Chancellor on January 30, 1933, and the Third Reich began its twelve–year reign of terror and oppression, during which time its "achievements" included plunging Europe into a war which cost over thirty million lives.

The Third Reich, which had been created to reign for a thousand years, effectively ended with the suicide of its *Führer* on April 30, 1945 in Berlin, with the victorious Soviet troops only streets away. The triumph of the Allies in World War II and the deaths of Adolf Hitler and Benito Mussolini effectively brought the era of fascist rule to a close. In an attempt to eradicate the memory of fascism in Europe, and to ensure that it could not rise from the rubble, the Allies banned Fascism in Italy and set up a program of *de–Nazification* and re–education for the German people. Fascism had to be seen to be punished, and in addition to the Nuremberg Trials of 1946, which imposed death sentences or incarceration on many of the surviving Nazi leaders across Europe, there was a desire for retribution, resulting in tens of thousands of fascists and fascist sympathizers being summarily executed. Germany, having come so close to conquering the rest of Europe, stood defeated and helpless as it was divided into the German Democratic Republic (East Germany) under the control of the Soviet Union, and the Federal Republic of Germany (West Germany) which was initially controlled by the western Allies of Britain, France, and the United States. It would remain a divided nation, tainted by the shadow of Nazism, until its celebrated reunification in 1990.

Fascism In Other Countries

Outside of Germany and Italy, fascism was unable to convert its significant influence and public support into political power. Many regimes and movements were denied the political space in which to fully develop their fascist ideas, but did incorporate specific aspects of fascist theory into their doctrines, with varying degrees of success. Yet again it was the aftereffects of World War I, coupled with the rise to power of Mussolini and Hitler, that encouraged many of these movements to emerge and develop during the 1920s and 1930s. In Spain the fascist *Falange* Party, founded in 1933 by Ramiro Ledesma Ramos (1905–1936), wielded sufficient influence to become incorporated

into General Francisco Franco's (1892–1975) regime, which emerged victorious from the Spanish Civil War in 1939. The *Falange* was later subordinated to Franco who, although the dictator of a brutal and totalitarian state which ruled until 1975, is more accurately described as being an authoritarian conservative rather than fascist. France had always possessed a strong sense of nationalism, so it came as no surprise that many fascist movements evolved from the extreme right of French politics. However, unlike Italy and Germany, French fascists formed and supported several movements, rather than focusing their energy and ideas into promoting a single, united fascist party. As a result, groups such as *Le Faisceau* ("The Fasces"), the *Francistes*, and the *Croix de Feu* ("Cross of Fire") (which was banned in the same year as its formation only to be reformed as the *Parti Social Francais*) each separately attracted a great deal of political and popular support, but no individual movement was able to amass a power base capable of threatening the political establishment. British fascism, in the form of the British Union of Fascists (BUF), was viewed as a novelty by the public, and posed no threat to the liberal democratic traditions. After its formation in 1932, the BUF and its founder Sir Oswald Mosley (1896–1980) attracted significant publicity, but a government ban on the wearing of paramilitary uniforms was enough to ensure the BUF's collapse. Despite differing in many respects, the movements that evolved in Spain, France, and Britain shared an ideology that mimicked that of Italian Fascism and sought to bring about change through the use of nationalist and militarist policy. However, in eastern and southern Europe, the path of fascist thought was following the route taken by Nazism, with the emphasis on racism and anti–Semitism.

The Iron Guard was a violent fascist movement in Romania that developed and promoted its ultra–nationalist and anti–Semitic beliefs from 1930 until its destruction by the Romanian army in 1944. In Hungary, the nationalist dictator Miklos Horthy de Nagybanya (1868–1957) ruled from 1920 and, when the country came under German control in 1944, the reins of power were handed to the radical fascist Arrow Cross Party, albeit only briefly. From 1932 onwards, Antonio de Oliveira Salazar (1889–1970) established a dictatorial regime in Portugal, into which he incorporated many fascist characteristics such as the one–party state, a secret police force, and widespread propaganda. However, the virulent anti–fascist period that followed the defeat of Germany and Italy in 1945, and the disclosure of the atrocities that had been carried out in the name of fascism, ensured that any party or movement holding a similar ideology came to be viewed with a mixture of loathing, fear and suspicion. Even those regimes who remained in power after the war, such as in Spain and Portugal, diffused their fascist traits and adopted a style more akin to authoritarianism than totalitarianism. It appeared that fascism had not only been discredited, but any movement acquiring the label of "fascist" became instinctively despised and relegated to an existence on the most extreme of political fringes.

Political Landscapes Change

The socioeconomic recovery after 1945 removed many of the conditions that had been such a major factor in the rise and advance of fascism, and the consensus among historians was that fascism had simply been a phenomenon of the inter–war years, a case of a political movement being in the right place at the right time. What no one could foresee was the rapidity with which the world's political landscape would change. Within a few years of their united triumph, the wartime Allies became absorbed in their own ideological battle, the Cold War, and the eradication of fascism was no longer their priority. The superpowers' preoccupation with each other allowed fascists the political space to regroup, develop new ideas and strategies, and emerge as a significant influence in many European countries. The first instance of this re–emergence, known as neo–fascism, occurred as early as December 1946, when former members of Mussolini's regime developed the Italian Social Movement (MSI) which, in the 1948 general election, secured six seats in the Chamber of Deputies. At around the same time, in Germany, the link with fascism was maintained, firstly by the Socialist Reich Party (SRP), and then by the National Democratic Party (NDP) which continued to promote its extreme nationalistic views into the 1980s. In recent years many neo–fascist movements have infiltrated extreme right–wing groups in an effort to gain wider support and increased influence. *Front National*, under the leadership of Jean–Marie Le Pen (1929–), executed this tactic so successfully that they established themselves as a legitimate third party in French politics, obtaining widespread support for their fascist program, in particular their anti–immigration policy. In Italy, Gianfranco Fini (1951–) guided the National Alliance (AN) into a coalition government in 1994 and two years later Fini had become Italy's most popular politician. This trend in the upsurge of neo–fascism has been mirrored in many countries, as witnessed by a widespread increase in extreme nationalist groups and racial violence against ethnic minorities, immigrants, and asylum seekers. Although racism and fascism are not synonymous, many of

these movements do possess a core fascist ideology, based on promoting national identity and pride, and on singling out racial scapegoats for any social and economic difficulties. To reach its political pinnacle, the fascism of Hitler and Mussolini required the political and economic instability that arrived in the wake of World War I, and unnerving comparisons may be made with the horrifying policy of "ethnic cleansing" that was carried out following the collapse of the former Yugoslavia throughout the 1990s. Fascism, as an identifiable political theory, has existed for less than a century, yet the violence, murder, and brutality for which it is already held directly responsible make it essential that close study is made of its causes and its future development. In the words of Primo Levi (1919–1987), a writer, chemist, and survivor of Auschwitz, from his work, *If This Is a Man*: "We cannot understand it, but we can and must understand from where it springs, and we must be on our guard. If understanding is impossible, knowing is imperative, because what happened could happen again."

THEORY IN DEPTH

Although strands of fascist ideology had been evolving throughout the eighteenth and nineteenth centuries, it was the First World War and the destruction left in its wake, that proved to be the active catalyst that fused these fragmented ideas into a coherent and powerful political theory. In most countries this emerging philosophy was confined to several extreme nationalist movements, which existed on the political fringes, and in a few others it exerted varying degrees of limited influence within major political parties. However, within a handful of countries, where socio–economic crisis was combined with strongly held national traditions, disillusionment with the existing leadership, and the emergence of an inspirational figurehead, the core components of fascist ideology were adopted to develop a radical and powerful political system. The unrestricted power enjoyed by fascist regimes, and the illiberal policies they introduced, while ultimately remembered for the mass atrocities to which they led, also reshaped their societies, resulting in the majority of their citizens enduring an everyday life which came to be dominated by oppression, fear, and violence. However, such was the appeal of the fascist philosophy and propaganda that, in Germany and Italy in particular, the majority of people were willing to sacrifice their individual freedoms and ambitions for the greater good of their nation.

Nationalism

The ability to convince each individual that the nation belonged to them, and that they in turn belonged to the nation, was one of the doctrines which lay at the heart of the fascist political system. In fact, it could be argued that this is the central tenet of fascist ideology. Fascist philosophy is anti–liberal, in that it views the nation as the most important political and social unit, and that the individual's value is measured only by the extent to which he contributes towards the well–being and success of the national community. In all fascist writings and speeches, the recurrent message is one of national rejuvenation, rebirth, or regeneration, and it is this belief in *organicism*—that a nation is an entity in its own right, an organism that can decay or be revitalized—that instilled in a nation's people a sense of duty to protect and nurture their nation, irrespective of the cost to themselves. This "illiberal nationalism" exploited the basic human desire to conform and belong, and provided individuals with a sense of importance and purpose, believing that they would be the generation that would restore the nation to its rightful place of prominence and glory. This type of nationalism breeds powerful emotions and feelings of kinship between those who view themselves as being ethnically and culturally united in their endeavors, but inevitably generates equally intense feelings of hostility and distrust towards those considered as outsiders. Therefore, racism was an inherent factor of fascist ideology, and although this did not necessarily have to result in the persecution of specific groups or races, unfortunately, that is exactly what happened in the countries where fascism was able to gain political control. In Germany, the Nazis systematically victimized and murdered countless Jews, Gypsies, blacks, homosexuals, and anyone who did not conform to the fascist regime's definition of "ethnically pure" was subjected to abuse, oppression, and violence, not only from the authorities, but also from within the community, including their neighbors, work colleagues, and even those whom they had considered as friends. In Italy the Fascist regime conducted a less extreme campaign of propaganda and violence aimed, more generally, at persuading all immigrants and foreigners to return to their own nations.

The extreme nationalism contained in fascist ideology was at the core of its main aim, that of creating a "new order." This was the term used by fascists to describe their vision of how they would implement their doctrines and values in order to transform society. Regardless of how the theory and practice of fascism varied from regime to regime, and from country to country, the total commitment to establishing some form of "new order." was inherent to all. The typical fascist view, most notably implemented within Italy, was that the creation of the new order, and the new Fascist man which it would cultivate, should be an inclusive process, instilling into as many of its citizens as possible strong feelings of national pride and a desire to work together towards restoring their nation to a position of greatness. Unfortunately, both for its own people and for the world at large, the Nazi regime took a very different approach towards creating the "new" Germany, and enforced programs and policies that went far beyond the basic fascist premise of asserting national virtues, traditions, and superiority.

Nazism

The Nazi model of fascism was contaminated by a pseudo–scientific component, developed from the theory of Social Darwinism, which was used to promote and justify its overtly racist, anti–Semitic, and morally reprehensible policies. Although Charles Darwin's (1809–1882) principle of "survival of the fittest" had long been a recurrent theme in fascist theory, the Nazi regime replaced natural selection with their own criteria for deciding who was, or was not, fit to survive within their "new order." Society in fascist Germany therefore became multi–layered, with the regime and its agencies at the pinnacle, followed closely by all individuals who were considered to be racially pure (that is, Aryan) and who enjoyed the social and financial rewards which this status bestowed. However, for those who were placed lower down this discriminatory hierarchy there was no inclusion into the proud national community, only the misery of continual oppression, persecution, and terror. The most appalling and barbaric treatment was reserved for those unfortunates who found themselves in the lowest classification and whom, not only the fascist regime but also many of the German people, considered to be sub–human. This ill–fated group, including Jews, Gypsies, and the mentally handicapped, among others, were so despised that they were commonly labeled "the useless eaters." By use of indoctrination, which was an another important facet of all fascist movements, this depersonalization of the nation's "internal enemies" was accepted by the public who, either through fear or through consensus, condoned the systematic abuse, torture, and murder of countless innocents, whose only crime was to differ racially, culturally, or physically from the fascist blueprint of the "new man."

Bringing About a "New Order"

In order to successfully implement the societal changes necessary for the creation of a "new order," fascism relied heavily on its commitment to a strong, authoritarian state and to the widespread use of indoctrination and propaganda. Both of these factors were mutually advantageous, the propaganda helping to ensure the continued dominance of the totalitarian regime, which in turn applied its absolute control over the lives of individuals to maximize the effectiveness of the indoctrination. Fascism has often been accused of containing more style than substance, yet its mastery of propaganda techniques and its skill in the art of political theater provided it with a greater mandate for the implementation of its policies than most other ideologies could ever hope for. The techniques employed by fascism, to ensure public conformity and to inspire enthusiasm for the creation of a "new order," were highly sophisticated, both in their conception and their execution.

Drawing on psychological theories, such as Gustave Le Bon's (1841–1931) study of crowd behavior, and the primitive, but highly persuasive, effects of symbolism and tradition, fascism was able to convert vast numbers of people to its ideals and values without having to present a rational and coherent body of ideas. Instead, it spawned charismatic leaders who commanded total obedience and assumed grandiose titles, such as *Führer* and *Il Duce*, thereby acquiring an air of infallibility. To cultivate this sense of hero–worship towards its leadership, fascism was responsible for the introduction into politics of stage–managed public appearances and carefully written speeches which contained powerfully emotive slogans and "catchphrases" designed to reinforce national unity and support for the state, while imploring every individual to offer greater sacrifice and effort in the struggle to achieve a "new order." The success of this approach was assisted by programs of indoctrination, which permeated every section of society through the education system, youth groups, the workplace, the frequent public mass rallies, and the extensive presence of fascist symbolism. State control of the media provided fascism with yet another valuable method of exerting its influence, and it made full use of the opportunity by transmitting powerful propaganda films and radio shows, and ensuring strict pro–fascist censorship of the press. From dawn until dusk, those who lived under the power of fascism found that every activity involved in their daily life was, in some way, influenced or controlled by fascist ideology and policies. Many willingly welcomed this as being necessary for the eventual success of their nation, while others, who were less committed to the values of the regime or the concept of a "new order," accepted it, though rather less eagerly.

Then there were those who were not persuaded by the propaganda, and refused to accept fascist au-

thoritarianism, whether on political, moral, or racial grounds, and opposed it, either openly or within their private circles. Fascism, however, was eventually well prepared for this with state controlled secret police and an extensive network of official and unofficial informants enabling it to suppress most incidents of opposition by means of fear and violence. The secret police organizations, such as the SS and the Gestapo in Germany, had full access to an individual's private life, and they were quick to assault, imprison, or even murder, anyone who dared to denounce the regime or its leadership. It was a fearful and lonely existence for those who opposed fascism and for those not considered worthy of inclusion into the "new order," as most citizens supported and obeyed the leadership and would readily report any acts of disobedience or denunciation. There were frequent instances of teachers informing on their students and traders reporting on their customers, but what illustrated the immense control that fascism exerted over its subjects was the distressing number of dissenters who were reported by friends, neighbors, and, in some cases, their own families. This coercion proved successful in suppressing a great deal of the resistance to fascist policies, although it also made it impossible to accurately assess the levels of dissent that existed. Did the majority of German and Italian people genuinely support their fascist regimes, as some commentators profess, or were they merely reluctant to oppose it for fear of the terrifying consequences?

Eliminating Opposition

Fascism's commitment to eliminating all opposition was only one manifestation of its intense hostility towards all forms of liberalism. The fascist state was a rejection of all that liberal democracy stands for, and involved the abolition of the principles of pluralism, individualism, parliamentary democracy, and the concept of *natural rights*. The centralized, single–party state was the foundation on which fascism sought to rebuild the "new order" and, within this reorganized society, there was no place for opposition parties or democratic elections. All other political parties were banned, and in the case of the Communists and Socialists, many of their members were imprisoned, tortured, and executed. Fascism had long held a deep–rooted hatred and fear of communism, as exemplified by this comment, made by Heinrich Himmler, the man who led the SS, during a lecture to his officers in 1937: "We must be clear about the fact that Bolshevism is the organization of sub–humanity, is the absolute underpinning of Jewish rule, is the absolute opposite of everything worthwhile, valuable and dear to an Aryan nation." Yet, without communism, it is unlikely that fascism would ever have gained political power in either Germany or Italy, as it was the fear of the threatened spread of Bolshevism from post–revolutionary Russia, westward into Europe, that increased the electoral support for fascist movements. Many people believed that fascism's strong authoritarian and militarist approach was their nation's prime hope of protection. The electorate were proved correct and fascism emphatically extinguished any threat posed by those on the political left, and continued this violent persecution throughout the duration of their dominance. Yet, beneath the intense hostility, fascism and Communism shared a common ideological enemy—Capitalism—and it was this opposition to both Communism and Capitalism that has seen fascism sometimes referred to as the "Third Way."

Third Way

This "Third Way" was most apparent in the economic thought and policies of fascist regimes which, although exhibiting slight variations, tended to follow a similar model, that of corporatism. Unlike Marxist theory, fascism did not concur with the belief that class antagonism was the primary agent of social change, neither did it agree with the capitalist emphasis on economic motives as the basis of a nation's success. Fascist theory sought to eliminate class conflict and bring about social change by creating a national unity based on the shared values of language, culture, race, and tradition, and by glorifying traits such as heroism, bravery, and strength, rather than materialism. It allowed the ownership of private property, and developed its economic policy along the lines of a partnership between the owners, the workers and the state, through the setting up of syndicates and corporations. In practice the workers interests were given low priority and they received little support from their unions, which had become state–run organizations following the abolition of all free trade unions, while the employers were rewarded with the granting of state investment and government contracts. Notwithstanding this unsuccessful attempt at corporatism, fascism possessed no stable or coherent economic policy, but instead relied on a series of temporary, short–term measures, while state intervention continued to escalate, as fascist economies increasingly relied on the work provided by their rearmament policies. War, therefore, was not only an important political and ideological factor of fascism, but was also crucial economically.

In economic matters, as in many others, fascism displayed its tendency towards male chauvinism. With the ideology's emphasis on war, strength, and heroism, it followed that women were relegated to the role of home–maker and mother of the nation's future workers and warriors. Germany, in particular, adopted an extremely repressive attitude towards women, excluding them from all leading positions within the party and prohibiting them from becoming judges or public prosecutors. After 1933, the regime extended these restrictions and dismissed many married female doctors, teachers, and civil servants to concentrate on, what Nazi propaganda minister Joseph Goebbels (1897–1945) described in 1934 as "the task of being beautiful and bringing children into the world."

Militarism

Militarism and fascism are often considered to be synonymous, which is unsurprising considering the events and atrocities for which their unholy alliance will forever be remembered. To fascists, military strength and victory in battle lay at the very core of their personal and national identity. It encapsulated the ideals and virtues which they glorified above all others, and would ultimately, in their opinion, lead to the successful creation of an heroic "new order." Only through war, against internal and external "enemies," could fascism assert its core values and ensure continued public support as it strove to achieve its ideological goals. All fascists agreed with Mussolini's view that war was inevitable and often preferable, and believed that the annexation of weaker nations by the strong, to form powerful empires, was the highest form of human development. In addition, the military values of patriotism, unity, and discipline could equally be applied to fascism, and military symbolism was widespread in fascist societies. By putting them into uniform and involving them in organized movements, fascism gave individuals a sense of belonging, and reinforced the belief in a national cause that was of far greater importance than their individual lives.

Fascist foreign policy, therefore, tended to be extremely aggressive, driven by the desire to expand their territory and assert the superiority of their nation. In Italy, where Mussolini was aware that his army had serious weaknesses, they used shows of military strength as a means of manipulating public opinion, whereas the German fascists possessed the capability and the conviction to expand their "new order" throughout Europe, and were ruthless in pursuit of their goal. The consequence of this determination to create a great and glorious Germanic empire was the attempted genocide of the Jewish race, a barbaric program of ethnic cleansing and racial war, and the brutal butchery of over 30 million soldiers and civilians in World War II. That fascism came so close to succeeding in its mission is terrifying to contemplate, especially when considering that this destruction was only the first phase in the blueprint of the "new order." Subsequent plans for fascist domination included the deportation of millions of Slavs to Siberia to provide the German people with increased *Lebensraum* (living space), and the extension of the fascist model of Social Darwinism to include the areas of health and social welfare, the level of assistance to be determined on the grounds of race and fitness. Although the Allied victory in 1945 successfully halted these developments, the extent of public acceptance and support for such abhorrent policies served to illustrate the ever–present danger of underestimating the influence and appeal of fascist theory.

Although the end of World War II saw the defeat of fascism's political power and the widespread condemnation of its illiberal and racial theories, it has continued to exist as a political undercurrent, as numerous groups have modernized and adapted its ideology in an effort to revive its popularity. Unlike the movements of the inter–war years, neo–fascism and neo–Nazism has to compete with a relatively stable, liberal democratic Europe, not one that is in political and economic crisis. So, although the fundamental ideology remains the same as it was before 1945, neo–fascists have had to repackage their ideas and promote them in a far subtler manner than their predecessors. This often involves the infiltration of mainstream political parties and movements, especially those on the extreme right, where they attempt to introduce their nationalist and racial values into areas such as anti–immigration policy and the issue of asylum seekers. Fascism has become a marginalized and fragmented movement, which has, in general, lay dormant since its military defeat in the Second World War, but as the campaign of ethnic cleansing in the former Yugoslavia in the 1990s illustrates, if given the correct political or economic stage, fascism will be waiting in the wings.

THEORY IN ACTION

The failure of many democratic governments to effectively tackle the political, social, and economic consequences of World War I, the Great Depression, and the perceived threat from the spread of communism fueled the creation and development of fascist movements throughout the world. The *Falange Espanola* in Spain, the Iron Guard in Romania, and the Arrow Cross Party in Hungary all shared many of the fascist doctrines and displayed much of its political style. In one of Europe's most well established and advanced democracies, that of France, it was estimated that, in 1934, almost 370,000 people were members of the various French fascist movements and, in

Britain, support for Oswald Mosley's BUF was sufficient to bring about a government ban on the wearing of paramilitary uniforms. Yet, despite this widespread influence and depth of support, fascist ideology only managed to manifest itself in the form of a truly fascist government in two countries, Italy and Germany, and the era of its dominance would last only twenty–three years.

Fascist Italy

The "March on Rome" in October 1922 was a demonstration rather than a glorious bid for power, but it resulted in King Emmanuel III inviting Mussolini and his party to form the world's first Fascist government. It was a relatively smooth takeover and, due to the limitations on their power invoked by a coalition government, the Fascists made very few changes to the Italian state in the first three years. Upon becoming prime minister, Mussolini successfully secured a parliamentary vote allowing him to rule by decree for a year. It was during this time that he established the Fascist Grand Council, a forum with the official function of coordinating the activities of the party and the government, but which Mussolini intended to eventually supercede the parliament as the center of power. The gradual move towards absolute control continued with the introduction in 1923 of the Acerbo Law which granted two–thirds of parliamentary seats to any party that obtained a majority of the vote in a general election providing they had polled at least 25 percent of the total votes. Mussolini and the PNF duly obtained control of two–thirds of parliament at the next general election, in April 1924 and, with Fascist membership having spiraled from 300,000 in 1922 to 783,000 by the time of the general election, the initial limitations to Fascist power were disappearing. Having already outlawed the Communist Party, immediately after taking office in 1922, Mussolini then abolished what little remained of the socialists and trade unions after their crushing electoral defeat, before introducing further measures designed to increase the authority of the PNF within the parliament, and to strengthen his position as *Il Duce*.

The year 1925 witnessed the creation of two major agencies of state control. First of all, Mussolini, in order to maintain control over the blackshirted *squadristi*, incorporated them into the Fascist Voluntary National Militia (MVSM), a paramilitary force whose main function was the violent oppression of left–wing opposition, but who also assisted in the theater of Fascist politics by performing in ceremonial events. Shortly afterward, in response to several assassination attempts on his life, Mussolini created a state–controlled secret police force, the OVRA, who

BIOGRAPHY:

Benito Mussolini

The founder and leader (*Il Duce*) of Italian Fascism, Mussolini was born in Predappio, Romagna, on June 29, 1883, the son of Alessandra, a blacksmith, and Rosa, a schoolteacher. Following in his father's footsteps, Mussolini joined the Socialist party in 1900 then entered his mother's profession by qualifying as a schoolmaster in 1901. In 1910 he became secretary of the local Socialist party in Forli, and his reputation as a prominent socialist was further enhanced the following year when he was jailed for his opposition to the war that Italy had declared on Turkey. Upon his release, Mussolini was appointed editor of *Avanti!*, the Socialist newspaper based in Milan, establishing him as one of Italy's leading socialist activists.

When World War I broke out in 1914, Mussolini denounced it as "imperialist" and argued for Italian neutrality, even threatening to lead a proletarian revolution if the Italian government took the decision to fight. Within a few months, however, he had totally reversed his position, and called for Italian intervention on the side of the Allies, resulting in his expulsion from the Socialist party. On November 15, 1914 he founded his own newspaper, *Il Popolo d'Italia* (The People of Italy), in which he expounded his support for the war, and introduced the embryonic ideology of the Fascist movement.

He formed the *Fasci di Combattimento* in March 1919 and, with the support of industrialists and landowners who saw him as their protection against communism, he entered the *Chamber of Deputies* in 1921. Following the fascists' symbolic "March on Rome," King Victor Emmanuel III, invited Mussolini and his now formalized Fascist Party (*Partito Nazionale Fascista*), to form a government on October 30, 1922. Mussolini had become the youngest prime minister in Italian history and quickly became the most powerful.

He linked Italy to Nazi Germany with the Rome–Berlin Axis in 1936, closely followed by the "Pact of Steel" in 1939, and committed the military of Italy to the Nazi war effort in 1940. After many Italian defeats, a meeting of the Grand Fascist Council was called on July 25, 1943, and Mussolini's colleagues turned against him. King Victor Emmanuel III first dismissed him from power, then had him arrested.

Rescued by German parachutists in September 1943, Mussolini set up a puppet regime, under the control of Nazi Germany, in the Republic of Salo in northern Italy, where he "ruled" until April 1945. As the Allies approached Milan, Mussolini and his mistress, Clara Petacci, attempted to flee into Switzerland, but were discovered at a roadblock near Lake Como. On April 28, 1945, Mussolini was shot by his Italian partisan captors, and his body was strung up publicly in Milan.

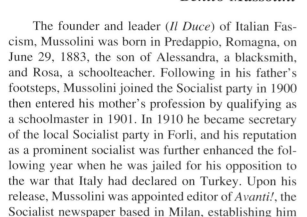

were responsible for monitoring Italian society for evidence of dissenters, who were then tried by the Special Tribunal for the Defense of the State. Although this illustrated the repressive nature of the Fascist state, the vast majority of dissidents were sentenced to exile, with relatively few being incarcerated and even less condemned to death. Unlike the Nazi regime which would later gain power in Germany, the development of the centralized fascist state in Italy was based more on acceptance than it was on fear and, except in the case of left–wing political opposition, there remained a degree of toleration of criticism and dissent.

By 1930, most of the political opposition had stood down or been abolished, and Italy had become a single–party state, with Mussolini at the helm. To fortify his position as *Il Duce*, Mussolini granted additional powers to the Fascist Grand Council, and any members of the PNF who were perceived as a threat were removed and replaced by impressionable sycophants. However, throughout his reign, Mussolini's authority over the state was limited by the country's economic weakness, his reliance on the backing of the king and his political advisers, and the need for continual compromise with the existing establishment. Although he overcame these constraints in creating a dictatorship, he was never able to achieve the level of absolute power and control which was later to be enjoyed by Hitler in Germany. To ensure his continued supremacy, and to advance the implementation of Fascist policies, Mussolini therefore had to rely more on the force of persuasion than on the power of coercion. In his development of propaganda techniques and

Benito Mussolini decorates the battle flag of the Royal Air Corps. (The Library of Congress)

political theater, Mussolini created what was to become a familiar pattern for subsequent dictatorships, elements of which have evolved to become incorporated and accepted into most areas of modern mainstream politics.

Il Duce

An extremely charismatic leader who was highly skilled in the use of propaganda, Mussolini ran most of the important government offices himself and made use of any opportunity to reinforce his revered public image. Such was the importance he placed on public persuasion and manipulation that, in 1935, he set up an official governmental ministry for the promotion

and development of propaganda. Influenced by Gustave Le Bon's theories of crowd psychology and Friedrich Nietzsche's (1844–1900) belief in the "will to power" and the *Ubermensch* (*overman* or *superman*), Mussolini displayed a charismatic style and dynamism that proved a convincing advertisement for his rejuvenation of Italy. Mass rallies, orchestrated military displays, the renaming of Labor Day to Birth of Rome Day, and the resetting of 1922 to *Anno Primo* (Year One) all instilled the Italian people with the belief that their nation was destined to return to the glorious days of the Roman Empire.

On a smaller but no less significant scale, Mussolini placed great emphasis on his personal image in order to elevate his status as *Il Duce* to that of an all–powerful and all–knowing ruler of his people. Every public appearance was carefully choreographed to ensure his physical appearance and gestures were appropriate for each specific situation, and experts were employed to ensure the correct use of setting, lighting and music, especially for photographs, which were invariably taken from below to disguise his diminutive stature.

Fascism Permeates Life

Throughout Italian society the ideology and symbols of Fascism were inescapable. It appeared that almost every official, from local to government, wore a different uniform each day, and all street corners were clothed in nationalist images and the painting of Fascist slogans. The teaching of Fascist values and ideals and the promotion of the qualities required to create the new Italy invaded all aspects of daily life—in schools, at work, in leisure pursuits, in the press, and in the media. The principal target of manipulative policies were the young, who embodied the desired Fascist attributes of strength, energy, and loyalty, and they were exposed to indoctrination, not only in school but also in the Fascist promotion of sport and physical fitness, and in political youth organizations, such as "Little Italian Girls" and "The Sons of the She Wolf." For these groups, the focus was on cultivating the importance of militarism and conformity, with boys as young as seven receiving training in military drill and gun skills, and the program's popularity resulted in over five million young members by the 1930s. Sport also played an important role in the advancement of Fascist propaganda with its wide appeal, its ability to divert the public's attention from other matters, and its manifestation of Fascist belief in national pride and a sense of belonging. These sentiments were echoed in the media, who were tightly controlled and prohibited from printing or broadcasting anything which the Fascist censors considered would shed a poor light on the image of either Mussolini or his regime.

One area of policy that could not disguise its consequences with censorship or propaganda was the complex relationship that existed between the Fascist regime and the economy. Initially, the inconsistent economic and social policies introduced by Mussolini failed to address the deep–rooted crisis that consumed Italy in the aftermath of World War I. The continual rise of unemployment was exacerbated by the Fascists' unsuccessful attempts to manipulate the value of the *lire*, which they carried out in the hope of improving their economic competitiveness. The arrival of the international depression in 1929 deepened Italy's problems and, by 1932, wages had halved in real terms, becoming the lowest in western Europe. Although Mussolini readily acknowledged the drop in the Italian standard of living under Fascism, his response of "fortunately, the Italian people were not used to eating much and therefore feel the privation less acutely than others" did not fill his supporters with any measure of confidence.

The decision amongst the PNF was for an increase in government intervention, with the immediate result that strikes became illegal, and in exchange employers were forced to offer improved wages and conditions to their workers. Italy then moved towards becoming a corporate state, in which each industry came under the control of a corporation consisting of representatives of employers, workers, and government officials, though ultimately these corporations were under the control of Mussolini. In practice, the labor force received very little consideration and the state effectively stepped back and encouraged employers to manage their own affairs, the only apparent measure of intervention occurring when the state rewarded big business with state investment and government contracts.

There then followed a period of consolidation, during which measures introduced by the Fascist Regime—such as the "Battle for Grain," in which offering farmers incentives to increase production ensured almost total self–sufficiency in wheat production—created substantial improvements in the country's economic and social conditions. Mussolini also introduced a vast program of public works, under which the Pontine Marshes were drained, public buildings were improved, ancient monuments were restored, and hydro–electric power was developed to counterbalance Italy's lack of coal and oil. This phase of Fascism also witnessed the creation of the *autostrada* (motor ways), and the improvements he made to the railways and airlines gave rise to the myth that Mussolini's power was so great that he could even make the trains run on time.

Italian Foreign Policy

One of the most significant and enduring legacies of Italian Fascism was Mussolini's signing of the Lateran Treaties with Pope Pius XI (1857–1939) in 1929. This gave official recognition of the Vatican as an independent state and confirmed Catholicism as the state religion, in the process bringing to an end a half–century of discord between the state and the Church. These successes, and the growing confidence that they instilled in Mussolini's regime, led to the development of an aggressive foreign policy, beginning with the invasion of Ethiopia in 1935 and culminating in the "Pact of Steel," signed in 1939 to cement the alliance between Italy and Nazi Germany.

Militarism, and the belief that war was essential to the creation of the new order, was a central element of Italian Fascist ideology and figured highly in Mussolini's plans from the moment he secured power. He temporarily seized the Greek island of Corfu in 1923, but it was his invasion of Ethiopia in October 1935 that won him acclaim from within all sections of Italian society and inspired him to proclaim the beginning of the new Italian Empire. However, some of the barbarous methods employed to secure victory included chemical warfare and mass executions of native tribesmen, a radical departure from previous campaigns. Shortly afterwards, the sanctions imposed on Italy by the League of Nations, in response to Italian military aggression, led to Mussolini forging closer links with Germany, who had stood by Italy over the Ethiopian invasion. The "brutal friendship" was affirmed by the signing of the Rome–Berlin Axis in 1936 and later tightened by the "Pact of Steel" in 1939. Both countries joined in supporting Francisco Franco's nationalist revolt in the Spanish Civil War and, as the specter of World War II rapidly approached, it was apparent that Mussolini and Italian Fascism were becoming increasingly influenced by the ruthlessness and success of Nazism.

Adopting Hitler's belief in its purely nationalistic nature, Mussolini curtailed his promotion of "universal fascism," in which he had invested a considerable amount of capital and effort to encourage foreign forms of fascism, including the British Union of Fascists. Of greater concern to the Italian people, and to governments throughout Europe, was the introduction, in 1938, of anti–Semitic laws into official Italian policy. Until this development, anti–Semitism had no place in Italian Fascism, with the PNF including a number of Jews among their membership, and its introduction proved unpopular throughout Italian society and provoked opposition from many organizations, including the Vatican. By the time the Second World War broke out, a great deal of division existed within Italy—and within the PNF—over the association with Germany, and cracks began to appear in *Il Duce's* veneer of invincibility.

World War II

When war broke out in September 1939, Mussolini, who was fully aware of his country's military weakness, initially reneged on the "Pact of Steel" because he had previously informed Hitler that Italy would not be prepared for war before 1942. This declaration of neutrality only lasted until June 1940 when Mussolini, exhibiting his capacity for opportunism, sensed that a German victory was imminent and feared missing out on a share of the spoils. Still

harboring hopes of extending his Italian Empire into the Balkans and Africa, Mussolini's aspirations had outgrown his military capabilities and German forces had to come to the Italians' rescue, both in Albania and North Africa. For the remainder of the war, Italy tagged along as the weaker member of the Axis partnership, with Italy's interests becoming subordinate to those of Germany, resulting in the erosion of Mussolini's authority.

Support for the Fascist regime collapsed in the face of constant military defeats and, with the invasion of Sicily and southern Italy by the Allies in 1943, there was a rapid growth of partisan resistance throughout Italy, plunging the country into civil war. As a result, many of the Fascist Grand Council turned on their leader and, on July 25, 1943, King Victor Emmanuel III dismissed, then arrested, Mussolini, and surrendered Italy to the Allies. In an attempt to regain control over Italy, Hitler rescued Mussolini from imprisonment and installed him as the puppet ruler of a brutal Social Republic in the north of Italy. With the aid of the Black Brigades, which were the vicious secret police force controlled by the Nazi SS, Mussolini endeavored to recreate his original vision of a Fascist state, but his personal stature had now crumbled and there was a total lack of support for his philosophy. The demise of *Il Duce* and Italian Fascism reached a violent conclusion when, on April 28, 1945, while fleeing from the approaching Allies, Mussolini was captured and shot by Italian partisans, who then strung his body upside down in Milan as a powerful symbol of the death of Italian Fascism.

Fascist Government Rule in Germany

The only other fascist regime to assume the power of government was the *National–sozialistische Deutsche Arbeiterpartei* (National Socialist Party of German Workers), who became universally known as the Nazis. After rising to power through democratic means in January 1933, the party wasted no time in diminishing the authority of the Reichstag, and establishing the creation of a Nazi state. One month after the elections the parliament buildings were destroyed by fire and Communist agitators were accused of arson. Using this as vindication, the Communist and the Social Democratic parties were subject to mass attacks and violent suppression, with neither offering any resistance. By the time the Enabling Act was passed in March 1933, removing all legislative powers from the Reichstag and passing them to Hitler's Cabinet, all opposition parties had been abolished and it became a criminal act to even *attempt* the creation of any new party. The Enabling Act, which had effectively granted dictatorial powers to Hitler and signified the

BIOGRAPHY:

Adolf Hitler

The architect of the Third Reich, Adolf Hitler was born on April 20, 1889 in Braunau on the River Inn, Austria. The son of an Austrian customs official, Hitler followed an undistinguished school career at Linz and Steyr, with an equally unremarkable spell as a would–be art student in Vienna. By 1914, he had cultivated a lifelong hatred for academics, Jews, and socialists, while his voracious reading had instilled him with a fervent belief in German nationalism and anti–Marxism.

Hitler moved to Munich and, on the outbreak of World War I, enlisted in a Bavarian regiment. Acting as a messenger between Regional and Company Headquarters on the Western front, he was wounded twice and received the Iron Cross for bravery in action. Germany's defeat, and the humiliating conditions imposed by the Treaty of Versailles, reinforced Hitler's anti–Semitic and racist ideology, while strengthening his belief in the greatness of Germany and the virtue of war. In September 1919, Hitler joined and became the seventh member of the German Workers' Party, a group founded by Anton Drexler (1884–1942) in order to promote a nationalist program to workers. By 1920 the party had changed its name to the National Socialist German Workers' Party (*Nazis*) and in July 1921, when Hitler became party chairman, its membership had increased to 3,000.

In November 1923 he made his first attempt to seize power when he tried to violently overthrow the Bavarian state government, in the Munich *putsch*, or bid for power. The attempt failed and Hitler received a five year jail sentence for treason.

Hitler contested the presidential election of April 1932, narrowly losing to the incumbent, Paul von Hindenburg (1847–1934). However, the relentless growth of support for the Nazi party resulted in President Hindenburg appointing Hitler as chancellor of Germany on January 30, 1933. To national acclaim, Hitler pursued a policy of expanding German territory, an act which sparked the horrific death and destruction of World War II.

Throughout the war Hitler pursued his desire to build a "new order" in Europe, one that centered on the creation of a master Aryan race. Hitler's *Final Solution* to rid the world of the Jewish population was an event of such incomprehensible horror and inhumanity that it has left the German nation a legacy that will haunt them for generations to come.

Although he remained popular with the masses, one group of army officers and civilians, under the guidance of Col. Claus von Stauffenberg (1907–1944), attempted to assassinate Hitler in July 1944 but failed, and paid with their lives. By then, however, the Allied forces were closing in and Hitler, who was deteriorating both physically and mentally, acknowledged defeat but planned to reduce Germany to rubble for failing him. At this final hour his lieutenants turned against him and refused to carry out his orders. On April 30, 1945 Hitler and his wife of a few hours, Eva Braun (1912–1945), committed suicide in his Berlin bunker, their bodies then being taken into the Chancellery gardens and burned.

end of the German Weimar Republic, was reinforced in December 1933 with the passing of a further law, which declared the Nazi party "indissolubly joined to the state." Hitler's development of the Nazi state involved eliminating all working class and liberal democratic opposition, so he exploited the aftermath of the Reichstag fire not only for the suppression of the Communist and Social Democratic parties, but also for abolishing many constitutional and civil rights.

Thereafter, the Nazi party and the state became indistinguishable and Germany was under the control of a totalitarian regime. Party members who were of

"pure" German blood and were over eighteen years of age were required to swear allegiance to the *Führer* after which, according to Reich law, they became answerable for their actions only in special Nazi Party courts. At its peak, the Nazi Party had an estimated membership of seven million and although the majority had willingly joined, a great many more were forced to join against their will, including many civil servants who were required to become members.

As with Mussolini in Italy, Hitler's powerful personal charisma, aided by his meticulously organized public appearances and the saturation of everyday life

Joseph Goebbels, Propaganda Director for the Third Reich. (AP/Wide World Photos)

with Nazi symbols, posters, and indoctrination, established him as the infallible, hero–worshiped savior of the German people. Despite the fact that his repressive totalitarian regime had abolished many of their basic liberties, and that just about every area of their lives was pervaded and controlled by state police organizations, many of the German people responded with uncritical loyalty to their leader and a frightening willingness to obey all state–issued directives. The *Nazification* of German society was greatly assisted by the efforts of the Ministry of Public Enlightenment and Propaganda under the control of Joseph Goebbels, which was highly effective at promoting the Hitler regime as a "well–oiled Nazi machine," by means of mass rallies, military parades, and sophisticated manipulation and censorship of the media.

That being said, the ordinary German citizen still lived a relatively normal life—as long as that ordinary citizen didn't happen to be a Jew or a gypsy and didn't question the policies of the Nazi regime. Most people in Nazi Germany did not live in constant terror. Many had normal families, satisfying careers, and social lives closely resembling that of 1930s Americans. Author Walter Laqueur, in *Fascism: Past, Present and Future*, notes that people were "not told what games to play, what movies to watch, what ice cream to eat,

or where to spend their holidays." In other words, a person could feel "free" as long as he kept his mouth shut and did not show much of an interest in politics. Conversely, if most people kept quiet and did not cause trouble, there was not really a need for the regime to risk agitating the populace by interfering in every aspect of life.

State agencies The principle auxiliary organization of the Nazi regime was the *Brown Shirts* or SA , often termed the "vanguard of National Socialism," whose functions included the official training of the German youth in the ideology of National Socialism. The SA was also responsible for the organization of the Nazi program against the Jews in 1938, and throughout World War II they ensured the indoctrination of the German army and coordinated the Reich's home defenses.

Another organization to prove crucial in maintaining state control was the SS, whose special combat divisions were invariably called upon to support the regular army in times of crisis. Assisted by the *Sicherheitsdienst* or SD, the espionage agency of the regime, the SS controlled the Nazi party in the latter years of the war, while the SD also operated the concentration camps for the victims of Nazi persecution. Other auxiliary agencies included the *Hitler Jugend* (Hitler Youth organization) who prepared teenage boys for membership within the party, and the *Auslandsorganisation* (Foreign Organization) who promoted propaganda and the formation of Nazi organizations among Germans abroad. However, the most brutal and oppressive of all the state agencies was the infamous *Geheime Staatspolizei* (secret state police), known as the Gestapo, which was formed in 1933 to suppress all opposition to Hitler's regime. Upon its official incorporation into the state, in 1936, the Gestapo was declared to be exempt from all legal restraints and was responsible only to its chief, Heinrich Himmler, and to Hitler.

By 1935 the last remnants of Germany's democratic structure were replaced by the Nazi centralized state. The Reichstag no longer performed any legislative functions, but was retained to be used for ceremonial purposes, and the autonomy which provincial governments had previously exerted had been removed and replaced with local governments which were nothing more than strictly controlled instruments of central government. The process of coordination (*Gleichschaltung*) ensured that all private organizations, such as business, education, culture, and agriculture were also subject to party direction and control. Not even the church escaped the pervasive domination of Nazi doctrines.

Economy Upon taking control of the German economy, the most pressing problem to face the party leadership was unemployment, which at that time was in the region of six and a half million. Included in this figure were large numbers of Nazi party members who rapidly became disillusioned when Hitler failed to fulfill his anti–capitalist pledge to put an end to large businesses and cartels and to rejuvenate German industry by promoting the extensive growth in small businesses. The party rank and file demanded a "second revolution" and Hitler was faced with a choice between appeasing the working classes or forging an alliance with Germany's industrialists. He decided on the latter course of action and, on the evening of June 30, 1934, which would come to be known as the *Night of the Long Knives* he issued orders for the SS to assassinate members of the SA, a group who had a mainly working–class membership and who Hitler now feared would attempt to threaten the social stability and agitate the *Reichswehr* (the regular army), with whom they sought a closer affiliation. A number of prominent SA members, including their leader Ernst Rohm (1887–1934), and over 400 of their followers were killed, most of whom had no intention of opposing Hitler.

Although it proved a powerful warning to other agitators, this ruthless display of state terror did not solve the underlying cause of the unrest, the problem of unemployment. To resolve this issue, Hitler had to regenerate German industry, and he proposed to accomplish this with the creation of the "new order." In common with the Italian vision, the German "new order" was based on the premise of regenerating the Germany nation and restoring it to a position of strength and leadership in world politics, industry, and finance. In addition, Hitler sought it necessary to ensure that he possessed an adequate merchant fleet, and that he constructed modern air, rail and motor transport systems. To achieve total implementation of his plans required Hitler's reversal of the economic and political restrictions imposed on Germany by the Treaty of Versailles, which he was aware would ultimately result in war. Therefore the Nazi economy, by stockpiling raw materials and resources, and insulating itself from the international economy, was reorganized essentially as a war economy. Hitler's reputation was enhanced when, in the years 1937 and 1938, the German economy made a dramatic recovery and the country achieved full employment, due mainly to the increasing level of rearmament, introduced in preparation for war, and to enable his policy of *Lebensraum*, which advocated the eastward expansion of German territory.

The creation of the new order also resulted in the banning of strikes, the abolition of trade unions

Adolf Hitler gives the Nazi salute. (United States Holocaust Memorial Museum)

(including the confiscation of their assets), and the termination of all forms of collective bargaining between workers and their employer. In their place, a team of government officials, appointed by the Minister of National Economy, adjudicated on any issues relating to wages and conditions of employment. Official directives also empowered the Ministry of Economy to expand any existing cartels and introduce policies designed to merge entire industries into powerful conglomerates. Private property rights were preserved and previously nationalized companies were "re–privatized," which returned them to private ownership but subjected the owners to rigid state controls. The introduction of these measures eliminated competition and ensured that the new order was economically dominated by four banks and a relatively small number of huge conglomerates. One of those to prosper was the notorious *Interessengemeinschaft Farbenindustrie* (I.G. Farben), an enormous consortium composed of over four hundred businesses, many of which exploited millions of prisoners of war and immigrants from conquered nations as slave labor. These cartels also readily supplied the materials and expertise that were employed in the systematic and scientific extermination of millions of innocent people under Nazism's racial doctrines.

Expansions and Expectations

Above all, Nazism was a nationalist movement, and Hitler's plans for the *Thousand Year Reich* were based on the construction of a greater German state that would initially include Austria and the other German–speaking people who had been lost to Poland and Czechoslovakia in 1919, but would ultimately unite all of Europe's Germans and rise to world supremacy. From 1933 to 1939, Hitler continually proclaimed that he was merely asserting the national rights of Germany, and most Germans agreed with his declaration that the imposed terms of the Treaty of Versailles had been a "shame and a disgrace." Even those who despised the Nazi party methods, and much of its doctrine, supported its nationalist policies and acclaimed Hitler's militarist program, which resulted in the reoccupation of the Rhineland in 1936, the *Anschluss* or union with Austria in 1938 , the occupation of Czechoslovakia in 1938 and ultimately the start of World War II.

Genocide and Destruction of Lives

The most destructive aspect of German fascism was its racial and anti–Semitic doctrine. Drawing on the roots of German nationalism and anti–Semitism, which dated back to the nineteenth century, Hitler's regime developed a hierarchy of "racial value" which was placed at the core of their vision of national re-birth and the creation of a "new order." Human breeding programs were developed, called the *Lebensborn experiment*, in which SS members were used to sire Aryan (racially pure) children. Legislation was introduced which excluded Jews from the protection of German laws, and the Nuremberg Laws (1935) were passed, which withdrew citizenship from non–Aryans and forbade the marriage of Aryans to non–Aryans. Although several state–sponsored programs were implemented before 1939, such as the notorious *Kristall-nacht* (Night of Broken Glass) in November 1938, it was during the course of World War II that the Nazi regime displayed the full extent of its disregard for human rights and its capacity for murderous efficiency.

Although there is no evidence of a written order by Hitler authorizing the Holocaust, it is believed that he either issued a verbal order or, at the very least, made it clear to leading Nazis that this was his intention for the *Final Solution*. He did, however, officially endorse The Law for the Prevention of Hereditary Diseased Offspring which, by 1944, had enforced sterilization on over 400,000 women who were either mentally handicapped or considered at risk of passing on a hereditary illness. He also personally introduced a program of euthanasia which "put to sleep" more than 70,000 people, mostly children, who suffered from serious physical or mental disabilities. Of course, even

these atrocities were overshadowed by the policy of genocide which was pursued against all those considered "without value" by the Nazis. When the Allied forces finally brought the war to an end in 1945, the human cost of German fascism's attempt to create a "new order" was the extermination of tens of millions of innocent lives and the infliction of terror and torture on countless others, while Europe had been reduced to rubble, and the political, economic, and geographical scars would remain for decades to come.

ANALYSIS AND CRITICAL RESPONSE

What perceptions and images come to mind when people consider the word fascism? Among the most common replies would probably be Hitler, the swastika, the Holocaust, inhumanity, and racism. These all appear to be perfectly rational and understandable reactions, based on what is known about fascist regimes, and their political, social, economic, and humanitarian ideology. Yet, understandable though they may be, these responses are wholly inaccurate, as what they affirm is the widespread confusion that has long existed between fascism and its notorious cohort, Nazism. The tendency to attribute the evils of Nazism to fascism in general paints a misleading picture of the values and motives of many fascist movements who denounced much of what Nazism advocated. It is important, therefore, when conducting an overall evaluation of fascism, that the abhorrent acts of inhumanity committed by Hitler's regime do not affect the objectivity of the analysis.

Fascism as a political system was discredited and condemned after the Allied victory over the German and Italian regimes in 1945, and has since been unable to achieve any significant level of political power in its own right. However, considering its once dominant position, it is unsurprising that elements of fascist ideology have continued to exert a major influence in political movements and governments throughout the world. Yet, because of the lingering images of the human destruction and atrocities carried out in its name, these movements seek to avoid the label of "fascist" for fear of being perceived as guilty by association. This has resulted in neo–fascism and extreme nationalism devising far subtler and less apparent means of promoting their values and beliefs to a wider audience, in the hope of regaining a foothold on the ladder of political power. In order to identify and prevent any of these disguised strains of fascism from re–emerging from the shadows, it is important to construct a detailed understanding of its strengths and weaknesses, the conditions that are required for its growth, and the techniques it employs to infiltrate society to attract support.

Fascism's Limited Spread

Despite inspiring the development of countless groups and movements, fascism has only risen to power on two occasions, the Italian Fascists of Mussolini and Hitler's Nazi party in Germany. Although it exerted varying degrees of influence in other countries, such as George Valois' *Le Faisceau* in France and Oswald Mosley's BUF in Britain, fascism consistently failed to convert this influence into significant political power. There were a number of reasons for fascism's inability to successfully cast its net outside of the two Axis states, one of these factors being that, in the years between the First and the Second World Wars, Italy and Germany possessed the ideal combination of political, social, and economic conditions considered necessary for fascism to prosper, and their existing governments were too weak and unstable to provide effective resistance against the growing fascist bandwagon. In addition, the profound dissatisfaction with the apparent decline of their nation, and an intense fear of the threat posed by Communism had already established a desire, within the Italian and German public, for stronger and more nationalistic leadership.

In contrast, the fascist movements that arose in other European countries in the aftermath of World War I were denied the political space in which to develop, due to the long–established liberal traditions within these nations and the relative stability of their governments. However, before Nazism's inhuman methods had caused fascism to become primarily associated with the atrocities of World War II, it was neither loathed nor condemned in those countries who had resisted it, but was accorded a certain degree of respect. Winston Churchill (1874–1965) is recorded as stating that, if he was Italian he would have been glad to be living under Mussolini's Fascist regime. Even as late as the mid 1930s, many of Europe's leaders continued to accept Italian Fascism as being a legitimate right wing reaction to Communism. Indeed, until Mussolini allowed Italian Fascism to become influenced by Hitler's philosophy, the state was no more oppressive or violent than it had been under the liberal regime in the years leading up to 1922. It was those near–civil–war conditions that had led to the significant rise in Fascism's support and enabled it to seize power from the previous government.

Also, at that time, Italian Fascism was strictly opposed to both anti–Semitism and biological racism, and even when Mussolini's alliance with Hitler persuaded him to adopt these principles in 1938, the majority of his fascist regime and the Italian people rejected it, and on several occasions, the Italian military deliberately sabotaged the carrying out of anti–Jewish campaigns. During World War II the Italian General, Mario Roatta, disobeyed a German order to round up Jews because he viewed this as "incompatible with the honor of the Italian Army" which, in stark contrast to the German military, had pledged equality of treatment to all civilians.

These contradictions portray fascism as an extremely fluid ideology and one which enabled the modification of specific characteristics to accommodate the diverse nature of national traditions and values. Therefore, although all fascist movements asserted the importance of the nation, the need for strong authoritarian leadership, and the desire to create a "new order," they frequently differed in regard to the methods they employed and the promises they made in order to attract support. Indoctrination and propaganda were other central tenets of fascist ideology, and these were also adapted to target each regime's specific objectives. Italy tended to focus on promoting the "Italian national spirit" as being a tangible entity, relying on each individual's support and effort for its survival and, in return, providing them with a sense of belonging and purpose. The majority of Italians did not view themselves as being governed by the state, to them it was a natural and integral organ of their existence, and in pledging their lives to pursue its success, they were willing to sacrifice their individualism. German fascism added a twist to this philosophy which, although in retrospect is viewed as evil and barbaric, at the time was an adaptation intended to reflect the German people's cultural history of racism and anti–Semitism. For the German fascists it was not enough to simply become a unified nation with a greater standing within the world—they also focused their efforts on asserting German dominance within their own nation, through biological racism and ethnic persecution. This single modification of the classic fascist ideology led directly to the deaths of more than 30 million people. Although many fascist groups, who became generically termed *the fifth column*, assisted Nazism in these atrocities, a great many more opposed and condemned it just as strongly as those in liberal democracies.

Aims and Goals

The ultimate aim of fascism was to create a "new fascist man," who would possess the desired strength and courage to earn the right to exist within a "new order." A major element in the ideology behind this aim was the belief in the necessity and glorification of war, and it was this principle which ultimately led to the defeat of Italy and Germany, thereby ending the era of fascism. In only twenty three years, from Mussolini's seizing of power in 1922 until the Allied victory in 1945, fascism had indeed succeeded in reshaping society, though not with the outcome that they had intended. The reality that had been produced by fascist ideology included worldwide destruction, the senseless loss of millions of lives, the reduction of the major cities of Europe to rubble, and the permanent alteration of the political and geographical landscape of Europe. But what of the culpable nations? What had fascism achieved within its own countries that could justify the rest of humanity paying such a high price? The answer is...very little.

Economically, fascist countries did show some improvement as the government prepared for war. Many people came to compare the economies of Fascist Italy and Nazi Germany to capitalist countries such as the United States, but this is inaccurate. There's a big difference between a free–enterprise economy and one run by a government to achieve its own ends before those of its people.

Italy's "national spirit" quickly disappeared, revealing a country which still possessed both class and regional divisions, while the introduction of corporatism had failed to shield the economy from the massive cost of the war effort. It had, however, left behind an improved relationship between politics and the papacy, the construction of the countries motor ways, and an increased level of self–sufficiency in food production. Under the Hitler regime, Nazism had succeeded in creating improved economic and social conditions for those groups in the upper levels of the racial hierarchy, but only at a huge humanitarian cost to the remainder of German society. As the full extent of the Nazi atrocities began to emerge in the aftermath of the war, the German people became the focus of the world's hatred and condemnation. In his attempt to unite Germany and restore it to greatness and glory, Hitler and his regime had achieved the exact opposite and condemned his nation to years of control by their conquerors, during which time it became divided, both politically and geographically, for almost half a century.

There are, however, certain elements of the fascist style of government which have been incorporated into mainstream politics throughout the world. Every government and regime today acknowledge the importance of image in modern politics, and have developed the techniques used by Hitler and Mussolini to manipulate their audience. The carefully worded speeches, the stage–managed appearances, and the effective use of technology and the media have all been updated and employed with increasing sophistication. The majority of governments, even those in the ad-

vanced western democracies, favor a charismatic leader who will be considered an international statesman and the singularly authoritative spokesperson for his nation, and even the fascist's use of symbolism and party slogans has gained widespread imitation.

Neo–fascism

Since 1945 no country has yet experienced a replica of the conditions which predisposed both Italy and Germany to the rise of fascism, but with the end of the Cold War and the collapse of the Soviet Union have there has been a negative effect on the political stability of recent decades. In the 1990s there has been an increase in the support of neo–fascist movements and political parties with extreme nationalist agendas. *The National Alliance* led by Gianfranco Fini became part of an Italian coalition government, in France Jean–Marie Le Pen's *Front National* regularly polls 20 percent in national elections, and the *Austrian Freedom Party* have amassed up to 28 percent of their country's electoral vote. Other neo–fascist movements prefer to infiltrate established right–wing parties and exert their influence on immigration policy and on the increasingly popular platform of Euro–fascism, which advocates the strengthening of the European Union into a closely unified "super–state."

Fascism has no concrete ideology, it has the ability to quickly adapt to changing circumstances to further its own aims. This capacity for improvisation assisted it to gain power in Italy and Germany, and it now allows neo–fascists and neo–Nazis to avoid the damaging associations of the past by disguising themselves in the cloak of the New Right and other mainstream havens of respectability. The need for political vigilance is succinctly stated in the words of Roger Eatwell: "Beware the men—and women—wearing smart Italian–style suits...the material is cut to fit the times, but the aim is still power."

TOPICS FOR FURTHER STUDY

- Compare the political ideology, style of government, and propaganda techniques employed by Saddam Hussein's dictatorship in Iraq with those that exemplified Hitler's Nazi regime before World War II.

- In 1945, Hitler and Mussolini both lost their lives in the final days of World War II, and after the Allied victory the fascist movements in Germany and Italy rapidly collapsed. Consider which of these two events, the loss of the war or the loss of their idolized dictators, was of greater significance to the disintegration of fascism in those countries.

BIBLIOGRAPHY

Sources

Berwick, M. *The Third Reich.* London: Wayland Publishers, 1971.

Eatwell, R. *Fascism: A History.* London: Vintage, 1996.

Griffin, R. *Fascism.* Oxford: Oxford University Press, 1995.

Laqueur, Walter. *Fascism: Past, Present and Future.* New York: Oxford University Press, 1996.

Thurlow, R. *Fascism.* Cambridge: Cambridge University Press, 1999.

Woolfe, S.J. *European Fascism.* London: Weidenfield and Nicolson, 1981.

Further Readings

Adamson, W. *Avant–Garde Florence: From Fascism to Modernism.* Boston: Harvard University Press, 1993. A comprehensive study of the ideals and methods of the new nationalism.

Koon, T. *Believe, Obey, Fight: Political Socialization of Youth in Fascist Italy 1922–43.* North Carolina: University of North Carolina Press, 1985. Study of indoctrination and propaganda as used in education, sport, and other areas of interest.

Koonz, C. *Mothers in the Fatherland.* New York, 1976. A detailed and interesting account of life for women under the Nazi regime.

Lyttleton, A. *The Seizure of Power: Fascism in Italy 1919–1929.* London: Weidenfeld and Nicolson, 1997. A broad explanation of fascism's formative years.

Federalism

OVERVIEW

Federalism divides sovereignty between a centralized state and regional or local states. This authority might be equal or hierarchical, shared or separate. Different republics, confederations, and unions have experimented with federalism across the years. The United States remains the most striking and enduring example of federalism; its system has changed radically as the relationship between state and national authority seeks to gain or regain balance.

WHO CONTROLS GOVERNMENT? Elected officials, majority of power in national leaders

HOW IS GOVERNMENT PUT INTO POWER? Popular vote of the majority

WHAT ROLES DO THE PEOPLE HAVE? Vote for representatives

WHO CONTROLS PRODUCTION OF GOODS? The market

WHO CONTROLS DISTRIBUTION OF GOODS? The market

MAJOR FIGURES James Madison; Alexander Hamilton

HISTORICAL EXAMPLE United States

HISTORY

The term federalism can be difficult to pin down. People discuss the federal government, but also talk the national, state, and local government. Which one is federal? At one point in the history of the United States, Federalists were those who supported the ratification of the U.S. Constitution. At another time, Federalists were members of a political party that advocated strong, centralized governmental authority. Some who were Federalists in the first case were not Federalists in the second. Add Anti-Federalists and definitions become more confusing.

The Earliest Years

Federalism dates to approximately 1200–1400 A.D., when the Senecas, Onondagas, Oneidas, Mohawks, and Cayugas ended their war and formed a fed-

CHRONOLOGY

1603: Johannes Althusius, the father of modern federalism, publishes *Politica: Politics Methodically Set Forth and Illustrated with Sacred and Profane Examples.*

1776: British colonies in North America declare independence.

1781: Articles of Confederation are ratified as the new government of the American states.

1787: Constitutional Convention meets to discuss alterations to the Articles of Confederation. The first of *The Federalist Papers* appears in newspapers to support ratification of the U.S. Constitution.

1789: U.S. Constitution is enacted.

1819: U.S. Supreme Court, in *McCulloch vs. Maryland*, establishes that the powers of the United States were not limited to those expressly in the Constitution, thus expanding the power of the national government.

1831: In the Fort Hill Address, John C. Calhoun advocates the theory of nullification by citing Madison's language from the Virginia Resolution.

1848: Federal Constitution of the Swiss Confederation is adopted.

1933–1939: President Franklin Delano Roosevelt creates the New Deal.

1963–1969: President Lyndon Johnson begins the Great Society.

1991: The Treaty on European Union creates the European Union.

---

eral union known as the Iroquois Confederacy. The constitution uniting these North Americans was called *Kaianerekowa*, the Great Law of Peace. Recorded and preserved in wampum, a beaded "text," this document codified laws for each nation, rules for the confederacy, and consistent rights protection for all citizens. National membership remained open, and other peoples joined the confederacy. The northeastern body became known as the Six Nations after adding the Tuscaroras in approximately 1714.

Hiawatha, addressing a group of nations.

(Corbis Corporation)

In the West, the concept of federalism dates to the German political theorist Johannes Althusius and his 1603 work, *Politica: Politics Methodically Set Forth and Illustrated with Sacred and Profane Examples.*

"Althusius' *Politica* was the first book to present a comprehensive theory of federal republicanism rooted in a covenantal view of human society derived from, but not dependant on, a theological system," wrote Daniel J. Elazar, a professor at Temple and Bar–Ilan universities. "It presented a theory of polity–building based on the polity as a compound political association established by its citizens through their primary associations on the basis of content rather than a reified state imposed by a ruler or an elite." Elazar added, "The first grand federalist design, as Althusius himself was careful to acknowledge, was that of the Bible, most particularly the Hebrew Scriptures or Old Testament. For him, it was also the best— the ideal policy based on the right principles."

Seventeenth–century Puritans, in the earliest known use of the word "federalism," referred to the covenant between God and the American settlers as "federal theology." The term was probably borrowed from Latin via French. In Latin, *foederatus* means "bound by treaty," derived from *foedus*, or treaty, and *fidere*, meaning "to trust." Although governments developed various divisions of power across the years

BIOGRAPHY:

Hiawatha

Hiawatha, Ojibwe for "he makes rivers," was a member of the Onondaga Nation. His legend is far better known than his true history. According to myth, Hiawatha was not only a great chief, but also the living incarnation of progress and civilization. His magical abilities allowed him to manipulate for good the natural forces that threatened humanity; thus, he taught his people medicine, agriculture, navigation, and art. Henry Wadsworth Longfellow's popular epic poem *Song of Hiawatha* (1855) created an even greater chasm between the man and the myth.

An historical Hiawatha did exist. According to oral history and other sources, Hiawatha collaborated with a Huron named Deganwidah to help end a bloody war among the five nations of the Finger Lakes region of what became New York State. With Deganwidah's plan and Hiawatha's diplomacy, leaders of the nations came together for a summit. The result was *Kaianerekowa*, the Great Law of Peace, the document ending war and creating a confederal alliance among the Onondagas, Senecas, Mohawks, Cayugas, and Oneidas, allowing free entry and exit for those nations and others. The resulting League of Five Nations, later Six, practiced dual federalism, with a League Council and Great Law applying to all—including a Bill of Rights—on one level, and national constitutions among each member group on another.

The Iroquois Confederation survived intact well into colonial times; vestiges remain in the twenty–first century. The league of nations remained at peace after the compact took effect. The Great Law of Peace eventually was translated into other languages. The example of the stable and long–lived federalist system inspired many, including Benjamin Franklin, who discussed the league in his writings on the 1754 Albany Plan of Union, the precursor to the Articles of Confederation.

since then, some by default rather than design, the first conscious, systematic, and extended experiment with federalism took place in the United States. Five periods highlight the evolution of American federalism:

the founding through the Civil War (1776–1865); post–bellum expansion and the Progressive Era (1866–1920s); the New Deal, World War II, and post-war prosperity (1930s–1960); the Great Society and war in Vietnam (1860s–1970s); and the age of new federalism (1970s onward).

Founding of American Federalism

The Articles of Confederation In 1754, Benjamin Franklin offered a sketch of a federal government for the colonies, known as the Albany Plan of Union, to organize common defense and achieve other collective goals. Though the colonial leaders and the crown both felt little interest, the plan anticipated the later Articles of Confederation. In 1776, the British colonies in North America declared their independence from Great Britain. After winning the War of Independence, the former colonies debated how they should arrange their new government. Their experience with Great Britain had soured colonists on the idea of monarchy, thanks to the king, and distant representational government, thanks to parliament. Many of their frustrations with Great Britain stemmed from decisions and enforcement coming from people who treated the colonists' situation as low priority.

Leaders of the former colonies decided to organize the new states as a loose confederation. Under the Articles of Confederation, ratified in 1781, the individual states maintained most of the government's power, including the all–important power to tax. The national leadership consisted of a committee, and its important decisions required state representatives to agree unanimously. The government began at a disadvantage thanks to the tremendous governmental and private debts accrued during the War of Independence; with no power to tax, a bad economic situation grew worse. By 1787, a Constitutional Convention formed to try to alter the Articles so that the government might stay afloat. The men who gathered to adjust the Articles threw them out altogether and creating a new system. The U.S. Constitution was born.

The U.S. Constitution Founders such as James Madison—the chief architect of the U.S. Constitution—Alexander Hamilton and John Jay believed that the new system required more centralized authority than the Articles of Confederation had offered. A strong national government could cope with the economic challenges of debt and international trade, they argued, and provide the necessary political and social cohesion to maintain independence. The U.S. Constitution, therefore, offered a system of dual federalism, with clear divisions between the responsibilities of

James Madison, fourth president of the United States.

(National Archives and Records Administration)

state and national governments. Madison called this system a combination of a national government, in which the national branches make decisions, and a federal government, in which the people of the states make decisions through the state apparatus.

These proponents of the new Constitution, called Federalists, received opposition from the Anti–Federalists. Leaders such as Patrick Henry and George Mason worried that if the states adopted the new Constitution, they would have been trading one tyranny, Great Britain, for another. The doubted that an extended republic could exist with a heterogeneous population; republics, they argued, needed to be small and include people of similar background, faith, lifestyle, and economic interest. Otherwise, they believed, the states would quickly lose power to the national government, with its consolidated authority and decision–making from a distance. They feared the lack of term limits would spawn an aristocracy, that the vagueness of the Constitution in phrases such as "necessary and proper" and "general welfare" would invite abuses of power, and that the absence of a Bill of Rights left individual liberties unprotected.

"Given such deep–seated devotion to local self–[government], it would be wrong to assume that

the Founders were satisfied to exchange the kernel for the husk," wrote author Raoul Berger. "What they sought was to preserve an independent, 'inviolable' sphere of action, underscored by repeated assurances that the federal government sphere was limited."

Eventually, some Anti–Federalists agreed to support the U.S. Constitution provided a Bill of Rights be included. In 1789, the United States left behind the confederacy of the Articles in favor of the federalism of the U.S. Constitution.

The first parties After the U.S. Constitution was ratified, the new nation elected its first president, George Washington. Political parties began to form almost instantly around the issue of federalism; the likes of Alexander Hamilton and John Adams, who favored the natural balance of power to shift in favor of the nation were called Federalists, while those who favored more power in the hands of the states were called Democratic–Republicans. The first two presidents, Washington and John Adams, were Federalists.

The first change of parties in the White House came when Thomas Jefferson, a Democratic–Republican, won the presidency in the so–called Revolution of 1800. This "revolution" occurred in part as a reaction to the concentration of power in the national government during Adams' administration. Adams had used the Alien and Sedition Acts, intended as rare wartime options, to quiet his political opposition. The Virginia and Kentucky legislatures, in turn, passed resolutions nullifying what they believed to be unconstitutional acts. Jefferson succeeding Adams signaled the young nation's first transition between competing theories of federalism.

Decisions of the Supreme Court The decentralist position advocated by the Democratic Republicanism faced new obstacles thanks to Supreme Court decisions in the 1810s. Led by Chief Justice John Marshall, a Federalist, the Supreme Court made decisions that defined its own position as equal to the executive and legislative branches. The Court then went on to read the supremacy, commerce, and contract clauses of the U.S. Constitution to give broad economic authority to the national government. In 1814, the Court held that U.S. powers extended beyond those expressly written in the Constitution, thus opening the door for a dramatic expansion of governmental authority. In the 1819 *McCulloch vs. Maryland* case, the Court upheld the creation of a national bank by reading the Constitution's "necessary and proper" clause liberally. Marshall viewed the Constitution as a compact among the people of the nation, and not the states. Through the Court's decisions, Marshall drew more

BIOGRAPHY:

James Madison

James Madison served the United States in many ways; he was a U.S. representative, secretary of state under Thomas Jefferson for eight years and president for eight more. He remains important to federalism for three specific reasons. First, he helped coordinate the Constitutional Convention that produced the U.S. Constitution. Second, he served as the primary architect for the Constitution. Third, he penned part of *The Federalist Papers* supporting ratification of the Constitution, including the key Federalist #39 regarding the federal and national nature of the U.S. system.

When the Articles of Confederation were clearly in trouble, Madison convinced states' rights advocate John Tyler to call the Annapolis Convention of 1786. He knew the message would seem less threatening from someone of Tyler's persuasion. Madison then guided the Annapolis Convention to produce the Constitutional Convention of 1787. When it began, Madison already had a plan for a new government sketched out. Presented as the Virginia Plan, Madison's ideas became the blueprint for the U.S. Constitution. In particular, Madison believed in controlling a strong government through checks and balances; he chose federalism to balance the government.

After the Constitution was drafted, Madison and his fellow founders had to convince the people to rat-ify it. Madison joined with Alexander Hamilton and John Jay to write a series of articles in favor of ratification called *The Federalist Papers*. Madison wrote 29 of the 85 articles, including a detailed discussion of federalism in Federalist #39. Their efforts helped form a new government. One of Madison's first actions as a member of the new House of Representatives was to keep a promise made to Anti–Federalists and sponsor the first ten amendments to the Constitution, the Bill of Rights. The Tenth Amendment further illuminated the federalist structure of the government by reserving all unenumerated powers for the states. Madison's fingerprints appear all over the U.S. system.

"Despite the Marshall Court's interpretation of the Constitution as authorizing the exercise of significant federal power, Madison's predictions that (as a matter of public preference) the states would remain predominant proved accurate at least until the Civil War," wrote David L. Shapiro.

> The growth of national power and its exercise since then, especially in this century, have been primarily the product of the post–Civil War Amendments and their implementation, and the expansive reading that the federal courts have been willing to give to congressional authority over commerce and over the purse, including the authority to condition grants to state and local governments.

---

power to the national government and away from the states.

"Marshall's opinions continue to have real influence, in part because he had the great good fortune to set precedents rather than follow them," wrote Marshall biographer R. Kent Newmyer, a University of Connecticut law professor. "But his opinions carry weight because of his reputation as a republican statesman." Newmyer added, "Marshall persuaded his colleagues to abandon the old way in favor of a majority opinion written by one justice, most often Marshall himself. This was perhaps Marshall's greatest accomplishment, because it's the institutional foundation of judicial review." Because of a resurgent states' rights movement, Marshall, ironically, considered himself a failure when he died in 1935, according to Newmyer.

Civil War and Reform

After Andrew Jackson became president in 1829, Northern and Southern states battled over tariffs and slavery. When Northern interests passed increasingly high tariffs that injured the Southern economy, former vice–president–turned–senator John C. Calhoun argued that the U.S. Constitution gave each state the power to nullify federal legislation that was dangerous to its interest. He returned to his native South Carolina, called a state convention, and directed the passage of an ordinance of nullification.

Like the Anti–Federalists before him, Vice President John C. Calhoun found his interpretation of the United States' federalism to be in the minority in 1831, when he delivered his "Fort Hill Address on the Relations of the States and Federal Government." In this speech, Calhoun explained his theory of nullification,

The signing of the U.S. Constitution.
(Bettman/Corbis)

based on the idea that the Constitution was a compact among the states instead of citizens, using James Madison's language from the Virginia Resolution. A year later, Calhoun's message convinced South Carolina to adopt an Ordinance of Nullification and threaten to secede from the union; the state reversed its position after President Andrew Jackson threatened to use troops against it, and the issue of nullification was postponed for a few more decades. Calhoun continued to argue for nullification for the rest of his political career. The "Fort Hill Address" remains one of his most famous speeches:

> The question of the relation which the States and General Government bear to each other is not one of recent origin. From the commencement of our system, it has divided public sentiment. Even in the Convention, when the Constitution was struggling into existence, there were two parties as to what this relation should be, whose different sentiments constituted no small impediment in forming that instrument. After the General Government went into operation, experience soon proved that the question had not terminated with the labors of the Convention....

> The great and leading principle is, that the General Government emanated from the people of the several States, forming distinct political communities, and acting in their separate and sovereign capacity, and not from all of the people forming one aggregate political commu-

nity; that the Constitution of the United States is, in fact, a compact, to which each State is a party, in the character already described; and that the several States, or parties, have a right to judge of its infractions; and in the case of a deliberate, palpable, and dangerous exercise of power not delegated, they have the right, in the last resort, to use the language of the Virginia Resolutions, 'to interpose for arresting the progress of the evil, and for maintaining, within their respective limits, the authorities, rights, and liberties appertaining to them.' This right of interposition, thus solemnly asserted by the State of Virginia, be it called what it may—State–right, veto, nullification, or by any other name—I conceive to be the fundamental principle of our system, resting on facts historically as certain as our revolution itself, and deductions as simple and demonstrative as that of any political, or moral truth whatever; and I firmly believe that on its recognition depend the stability and safety of our political institutions.

I am not ignorant, that those opposed to the doctrine have always, now and formerly, regarded it in a very different light, as anarchic and revolutionary. Could I believe such, in fact, to be its tendency, to me it would be no recommendation. I yield to none, I trust, in a deep and sincere attachment to our political institutions and the union of these States. I never breathed an opposite sentiment; but, on the contrary, I have ever considered them the great instruments of preserving our liberty, and promoting the happiness of ourselves and our posterity; and next to these I have ever held them most dear.

President Jackson, though he ran on a states' rights platform, offered a strong proclamation against nullification and threatened to use armed force if necessary against South Carolina. A compromise tariff rushed through Congress did not end the problem. The stop–gap measure simply postponed the question of the relationship between the states and national government in the federal system. The national government, by winning the Civil War, finally settled the doctrine of nullification.

In the post–bellum and Progressive Era after the Civil War, the national government took on a broader economic more, while states concentrated on issues of police power and services such as sanitation and health. Reform engulfed both levels of government with the goal of making processes more democratic; secret ballots, initiatives, and antitrust legislation all came from this pro–democracy impulse. Progressivists began at the local and state levels to try to initiate reforms that addressed the new realities of industrialization, urbanization, and immigration, but the most successful of these agendas ended up at the national government level for application and implementation. States, for example, attempted to regulate railroads but the Supreme Court struck them down in 1886, and this led to the Interstate Commerce Act of 1887.

What the state governments could not do, the national government could. The first cash grants to states from the national government appeared during this time, as did the Sherman Antitrust Act of 1890, which, along with the Interstate Commerce Act, expanded national authority over commerce. Perhaps the greatest expansion of national power came in 1913 with the Sixteenth Amendment, which established the income tax. This created the foundation for the federalism of the twentieth and twenty–first century by emphasizing intergovernmental transfers and the use of the power to tax and spend to further national policies.

"Over the past two centuries, the American system of federalism—one in which the states have always played a significant role—has contributed to the Nation's growth and health in different ways at different times, often advancing and sometimes hindering that growth and prosperity," author David L. Shapiro wrote. "But the overall balance is a favorable one, and on the economic front in particular, that balance continues to hold."

"The case for federalism from the perspective of economic and related policy issues is more complex and harder to summarize," Shapiro added.

It rests on three related premises: first, that a well–conceived and smoothly operating federal system is one

Alexander Hamilton, one of the first American Federalists. (Smithsonian Institution)

in which policy emerges as part of a process and from the interplay of a multiplicity of sources; second, that competition among states is bound to enhance the production of capital and labor in the long run; and third, that the states not only can serve, but have served, as experimental laboratories for the development of a wide range of social and economic programs.

Centralization

The New Deal, World War II, and postwar prosperity period essentially brought an end to federalism as the founders had intended, meaning dual federalism. A new federalism merged the responsibilities of the nation and states; the nation, however, always came out on top. Two world wars mobilized the nation, and the Great Depression between them led to President Franklin Delano Roosevelt's New Deal. The Supreme Court rejected the policies of the New Deal at first, but then reversed and agreed to the unprecedented centralization when Roosevelt threatened to add judges to the court until he had a majority. The New Deal established a national welfare state and allowed the national government to control economic development and regulation of labor relations and agriculture, previously within the states' authority.

During this time the Court ceased to define the nation's role in overseeing commerce, effectively is-

BIOGRAPHY:

Franklin Delano Roosevelt

Franklin Delano Roosevelt was the only U.S. president elected to office four times (1932, 1936, 1940, and 1944), leading the United States through the Great Depression and World War II, and connecting with the U.S. citizenry in an unprecedented personal way, thanks to his "fireside chats" that American families listened to on radio. In relation to federalism, however, he is best remembered as the father of the New Deal.

The New Deal attempted to remedy some of the problems caused by the Great Depression, but also aimed to balance conflicting economic interests through government regulation. Roosevelt's program included reforms in industry, agriculture, finance, waterpower, labor, and housing. The national government oversaw the reforms in these areas; this new responsibility tipped the scales of dual federalism in the United States. State governments did not possess their own sphere of authority after the New Deal spanned 1933–1939; instead, states shared functions with the national government, usually in a subservient role. By shifting the balance from dual federalism to cooperative federalism in a centralized welfare state, Roosevelt altered the workings of the United States' system. When the Supreme Court argued the unconstitutionality of some of his programs, he threatened to add justices until he had a supportive majority. After the crisis passed, the nation never regained the original balance of dual federalism. Roosevelt's presidency was a watershed era for federalism.

---

suing a blank check for the national government to expand its own power. Although some social service programs existed under state control, the national government set the guidelines. With new grant–in–aid programs and national spending, especially on highways, the 1950s became another decade of centralization. Although President Dwight Eisenhower established the Commission on Intergovernmental Relations to identify and return programs to the states, no changes ever came. States' rights advocates launched one more unsuccessful campaign called "interposition," the twentieth–century version of nullification, temporarily defying federal orders to desegregate state schools.

Creative Federalism

The Great Society and Vietnam Era brought yet another period of growth in national authority over state governments. As states challenged the likes of crosscutting grants that tied aid for one policy to the performance of another, coercive taxes, and federal mandates, the Court upheld their constitutionality. "Creative federalism" included dramatically more federal money to localities, sometimes bypassing the states. These actions forged intergovernmental links. The practice of partial preemption also developed, allowing the federal government to take over in any state that did not meet the requirements of a given act.

Although the federal government's role increased, this sometimes meant more power for local leaders. As programs overlapped and even opposed each other, the national apparatus became increasingly mired in its own red tape; this gave the opportunity for state administrators to control programs in the absence of clear lines of hierarchy and communication. When oversight did exist, however, conflict often followed. The war in Vietnam and the oil crisis of the 1970s shattered confidence in the national government.

New Federalism

This backlash spawned a movement to reduce national control over grants–in–aid programs and revise the federal role in general welfare spending. Beginning with Richard Nixon in the early 1970s and increasing steadily, especially in the years of Ronald Reagan's administration (1981–1989), the national government attempted to streamline its services, decentralize programs, and redirect funds to the states. Under this "new federalism," however, new restrictions plus other strings came attached to funds earmarked for states. The Supreme Court effectively overturned the Tenth Amendment and admitted that no barriers existed to the federal regulation of state functions in its 1985 *Garcia v. San Antonio Metropolitan Authority* ruling, which was another blow to those who wanted to help balance the federalist structure. The small loss of power the national government endured did not create an equal rise in the authority of the states.

One exception marked a possible reversal in the trend of nationalism. The Supreme Court, in its 1995 *United States v. Lopez* case, said the national government had usurped state police powers regarding guns near schools. This move to define and separate spheres

---

of authority marked a change in the Court mindset and perhaps a return to an older federalism rather than the creation of yet another one.

"At the threshold we are met by the question, why should we, at a remove of 200 years, look to the Founders for guidance; why should a nation of 220 million souls spread from ocean to ocean feel found by an instrument fashioned for the governance of three million people sparsely scattered along the East Coast," wrote constitutional author Raoul Berger. "Why, an instrumentalist has asked, should the Founders rule us from their graves? We are not, of course, 'bound' by the Founders; rather the issue is who may revise the Constitution—the people by amendment or the judges, who are unelected, unaccountable, and virtually irremovable."

THEORY IN DEPTH

Federalism in theory merely means dividing governmental authority between a centralized whole and a decentralized region. All forms of federalism share certain characteristics. First, the independent states subsumed into a union recognize a rule of law as supported and reinforced by common institutions. Often a constitution defines this law and the relationship between national and state laws. Second, law enforcement bodies with independent powers and responsibilities ensure the rule of law. Executives and judiciaries are examples of law enforcers. Third, the law of the union applies to all member states and citizens. Fourth, the union has some form of independent legislative or policy institution that remains separate from those of member states. Fifth, the institutions of the union and its member states have democratic characteristics. Last, a formal mechanism exists to establish the powers and responsibilities of each member and the union as a whole; constitutions usually fill this role.

Despite these similarities, different forms of federalism divide this authority in different ways. In some cases, as in the example of the United States, the form of federalism changes over time. Just as there are different forms of federalism, there are also different ways to explain them.

Dual Federalism

In the first theory, three basic organizational structures of intergovernmental relations illustrate federalism. The first is a *dual* or *coordinate* system of federalism. In this model, the different levels of government have separate, autonomous spheres of au-

thority. In other words, issues are either of national or state concern, but are mutually exclusive. This model reflects the system the U.S. Constitution originated. The articles established national powers and the Tenth Amendment reserved the rest for the states. The division was clear and, perhaps more important, equal; this was one of the "balances" of the "checks and balances" system Madison, Hamilton, Jay, and their fellow founders designed.

Chief Justice Harlan Fiske Stone wrote of the Tenth Amendment in the 1941 *United States v. Darby* ruling:

> The amendment states but a truism that all is retained which has not been surrendered. There is nothing in the history of its adoption to suggest that is was more than declaratory of the relationship between the national and state governments as it had been established by the Constitution before the Amendment or that its purpose was other than to allay the fears that the new national government might seek to exercise powers not granted, and that the states might not be able to exercise fully their reserved power.

Compound Federalism

Compound systems of federalism occur when interdependent governments overlap in authority. Neither is superior, so both sides must bargain. Governments can handle the bargaining in different ways. These usually lead to either a *cooperative* relationship among levels of government or a *competitive* one.

Unitary Federalism

Both dual and compound systems assume the different levels of government converge on a fairly level playing ground. That is not always so, however. *Unitary* systems of federalism, also called *centralized* or *national* systems, support the national government's primacy. The relationship is hierarchical. At times in the history of the United States, the balance of *dual* federalism appeared to tip in favor of *centralized* federalism.

The *dual/compound/unitary* model is one way for scholars to understand the different faces of federalism. Another frequent model is *confederal*, *federal*, and *unitary* federalism. In this model, *unitary* federalism is the same as in the first model: the national government retains power and states remain inferior. In a *federal* system, the states and the nation each possess certain powers, and the two remain distinct, much like in the *dual* system. In the *confederal* system, the states are sovereign. This was illustrated in the Articles of Confederation, the first constitution to unite the states after the American War of Independence.

John Jay, a founding father of American federalism.

(*National Archives and Records Administration*)

These two models offer broad categories of federalism to explain the theory behind how the state, with its multiple levels of government, is organized. These are ideal forms, however. Real–world federalism rarely runs as smoothly as the simple models. More descriptive terms help explain federalism in practice. David B. Walker, in his 1995 work *The Rebirth of Federalism*, labeled the different ages of U.S. federalism.

Walker's Classifications

From the birth of the United States to the Civil War (1789–1861), Walker says the United States practiced *dual federalism of the rural republic*. This dual federalism rested on the foundation of enumerated powers—the responsibilities of both layers of government were spelled out in the U.S. Constitution—and sovereign and equal spheres of power.

From the Civil War to Roosevelt's New Deal (1861–1933), the United States had *dual federalism serving commerce*. In this model, government grew at both levels. The state government grew to provide police power and services, while the national government grew to regulate commerce. Both strived to "to perfect the free economy."

The New Deal brought a tremendous shift in federalism. Walker calls the federalism that existed roughly from the New Deal to Lyndon Johnson's Great Society (1930–1960) *cooperative federalism*. No longer did each governmental layer possess authority in its own sphere. The two shared roles and provided services together.

According to Walker, this was followed by *creative federalism*, which lasted until Ronald Reagan took the White House in 1981. *Creative federalism* meant the advent of intergovernmental money transfers, sometimes from the national government to the local government, bypassing the states entirely. It also meant the states oversaw the implementation of federal mandates. The national government ruled and the state governments followed directives in order to receive funding or avoid federal intrusion.

Walker calls the era beginning with Reagan's administration *cooptive federalism and the reaction*. As government tried to downsize and deregulate itself, to devolve, federalism got lost in the mix. Although the national government tried to offer some powers back to the states, it attached new strings. Walker leaves U.S. federalism in a muddle, imbalanced with weight to the national government, unsure of how to proceed in the future.

Several theorists and teachers have described dual federalism as *layer-cake federalism*. Each "ingredient"—state and national government—has its own job to do. Compound federalism is *marble-cake federalism*, where the flavors compete with and complement each other, mixing in the same bite, much as the layers of government work together to achieve a goal. Considering the "plums" the national government gives states through grants and funds, complete with regulatory strings attached, some call the fiscal system of centralized federalism *fruitcake* or even *birthday-cake federalism*.

Any way it is sliced, federalism seeks a balance, either equal or unequal, that allows the national and the regional government to contribute to the lives of citizens. As the scales tip one way or another, new varieties of federalism evolve. Political theory in this case follows reality, as the nations who adopt federalism become the laboratory.

THEORY IN ACTION

Elements of Federalism

Although different examples of federalism in action exist in various nations and times, all of them seem to share certain characteristics. First, these governments are established and maintained through some formal process, usually a written constitution. This provides a kind of stability and permanence to the system, but it also promotes longevity by allowing for means of altering the government as new challenges and decisions arise. For instance, this procedure often includes an opportunity to add amendments to the constitution; a process that, although feasible, is extraordinary, complicated and involved enough to make certain the document is not changed constantly or lightly. Not only do these compacts include the people, the intermediary bodies such as states, and the national government, but they also usually provide that the intermediary bodies reserve their own constitution–making powers as well.

A second element to federalism in practice is noncentralization; power is diffused among several essentially self–contained and self–sustaining centers so that it cannot be centralized without the consent of the many. This noncentralization taken to the extreme loses the idea of a national government altogether and becomes another system known as a confederation. The United States under the Articles of Confederation, which ordered the nation after the War of Independence and before the U.S. Constitution, is an example of this system.

The third common element is known as territorial democracy, and is also called the *areal* division of power. This means that divisions within the nation ensure a degree of neutrality and equality of groups at the national and local levels. This allows for changing demographics within nations, for example, by giving new and emerging interests the opportunity to vote in relatively equal territorial units and enjoy representation according to their numbers. This also preserves stability of federalism by allowing different interests their own bases of power; they can coexist rather than compete for survival. Canada offers a good example of this through Quebec, a province built on citizens of French descent who maintain their French tongue.

Canada

The Canadian example of federalism, in fact, illumines many interesting aspects of the system. The nation's constitution began as the British North American Act of 1867, which was penned by Canadian leaders in Canada as they witnessed a tragic Civil War to their south in the United States. The Constitution Act of 1982 formally transferred the constitution–making power from its official seat, the United Kingdom, to Canada, thus making Canada an independent and sov-

BIOGRAPHY:
Lyndon B. Johnson

Lyndon Johnson was vice president under John F. Kennedy and became the thirty–sixth president in 1963, after Kennedy's assassination. Although celebrated for signing into law the Civil Rights Act of 1964, the most comprehensive civil rights legislation since the Reconstruction era, Johnson was also criticized for greatly expanding the United States' military involvement in Vietnam. After completing Kennedy's term and one of his own, Johnson did not seek reelection to the White House. He died four years later.

Johnson's impact on federalism was noteworthy. His Great Society, second only to Roosevelt's New Deal in scope, unleashed many social welfare programs designed to combat poverty and racism. Much of the campaign appeared in the form of grants, some of which extended from the national government to local governments. Other grants came with restrictions and regulations attached, furthering the national–state power imbalance. Overlapping a conflicting programs begot friction between state and national officials, although some state employees exploited the confusion to wrest back some control. The result moved traditional federalism another step away from its original dual form and left the new creative federalism in its place. This creative federalism remained until the Reagan administration took the White House in 1981.

---

ereign polity and added a Charter of Rights listing the rights retained by all citizens.

The Canadian system attempted to prevent the perceived problems in the U.S. form of federalism—problems that allowed the U.S. Civil War to erupt—by inverting the U.S. Tenth Amendment. Whereas the U.S. reserved all unenumerated powers for the states, the Canadian system established that all powers not assigned exclusively to the provinces belonged to the federal government. Despite this provision, Canadian provinces managed to retain a significant amount of power across the years, making it a relatively decentralized system in practice. Several of its machinations have enhanced its stability.

For example, by promoting direct lines of communication between citizens and all levels of government, Canada has managed to evolve a sense of community and nation in order to hold divergent populations together over time; Canadians have exploited the common experience of bordering the United States as one particular means of creating an identity as a people. Another aspect of Canadian federalism has contributed to the system's success by allowing for the cultural survival of multiple traditions. The constitution allows for a decentralized mixture of judicial systems; common–law and civil–law mechanisms exist side–by–side in a complimentary, competitive relationship. This legal duality in part has enabled the survival of French–Canadian customs.

As in the United States, Canada enjoys a noncentralized party system. Unlike the U.S. two–party system, which allows for a number of different interests to cooperate loosely for common purposes in order to elect presidents, the Canadian parliamentary system requires that a given party must be much more cohesive and unified in order to win and maintain power. This means that leaders must transcend provincial, factional differences and find areas of consensus to push forward through policy. This push for truly national issues, then, enhances the stability of the federal structure and assists in the creation of unity across the provinces.

Unsuccessful Manifestations

Other systems have not been as successful as Canada or the United States in maintaining a federal structure. Many of the destructive problems faced by these governments appeared when one region or section of the nation gained too much power over the others and, in effect, could enforce its citizens will against the citizens of other states. The experience of nineteenth–century Prussia illustrates this point well; in that case, Prussia became so dominant that no other states could gain the chance to offer national leadership or even contribute an alternative voice to public policy. The king and his decisions reflected the values and views of Prussia. Similarly, the Soviet Union faced the same concerns during the twentieth century. Despite the question of communism, the overwhelming power of Russia dominated the nation. The Russian Soviet Federated Socialist Republic represented three–fourths of the country's territory and three–fifths of the country's population. No other group—linguistic, ethnic, or geographic, not to mention political—could possibly compete with it for dominance in policy, and the federal system had little chance of survival.

The Canadian illustration of success and the Prussian and Soviet examples of failure are not the only windows into federalism in practice, however. The theory continues to evolve and develop across the globe from Brazil to Switzerland, from Nigeria to Malaysia.

Balance

Federalism not only has different manifestations in different places, but it also has different manifestations in the same place over time. The United States is a prime example of a nation that has experienced dual federalism, cooperative federalism, creative federalism, and several new federalisms in its history. The relationship between the states and the national government involves a healthy amount of gray area. Take, for example, the issue of medical marijuana in the United States.

According to the federal Controlled Substances Act, marijuana is an illegal substance regardless of the conditions under which it is used; in other words, marijuana use for medical reasons and for personal pleasure are equally against the law. Between 1978 and 1996, however, legislatures in thirty–four states passed laws recognizing marijuana's medicinal value. California, Arizona, Alaska, Oregon, Nevada, and Washington went a step further. Their state legislatures adopted initiatives that exempted patients who used marijuana under a physician's care from facing criminal penalties relating to the possession and cultivation of marijuana for medicinal use. A tug–of–war developed between the states and the national government. The national government would not legalize the drug, but states said they would not prosecute certain offenders. The states pressured the national government to change its policy and vice–versa. There was no resolution.

Other controversial subjects offer similar examples. Some states recognize gay marriages while others do not, yet the U.S. Constitution seems to require a national standardization so that all states give "full faith and credit" to practices in other states; in short, a legally recognized marriage in Vermont, according to the Constitution, must also be so in Kansas. What is the role of the state? The nation? The changing relationship among government levels in the federalist system makes answers challenging.

Nations other than the United States also have explored the balance of federalism in their own systems. The Swiss Confederation, for example, united twenty–six cantons, the equivalent of states, and about three thousand communes together into a nation. The Federal Constitution of the Swiss Confederation was adopted in 1848 and revised in 1874 and 1999 with amendments in the interim. It established the federal government's responsibilities as those dealing with external and internal security, transportation and communication affairs, forestry, water, money, and social insurance programs. Each canton, however, had its own constitution, justice system, and infrastructure. Although the national law trumped canton law, much variation remained among laws in different cantons. Managing this balance, and also administering the army of this neutral country, remains a dynamic experiment in federalism.

Supreme Court rulings in the United States   More than a century after Calhoun explained his vision of states' rights federalism, the U.S. Supreme Court offered an opinion 180 degrees in the opposite direction, effectively overturning the Tenth Amendment. In the 1985 *Garcia vs. San Antonio Metro Transit Authority*, in which the top court reversed a district court ruling and favored a federal agency's ruling that a state mass transit authority was not immune from federal minimum wage and overtime requirements, Justice Harry Blackmun delivered the court opinion that no constitutional barriers limited federal regulation of state matters; if the national government were constrained, he said, it was by the political process, not by the letter of the law:

"...As a result, to say that the Constitution assumes the continued role of the States is to say little about the nature of that role. Only recently, this Court recognized that the purpose of the constitutional immunity recognized in National League of Cities is not to preserve 'a sacred province of state autonomy.'" *EEOC v. Wyoming*, 460 U.S., at 236. With rare exceptions, like the guarantee, in Article IV, 3, of state territorial integrity, the Constitution does not carve out express elements of state sovereignty that Congress may not employ its delegated powers to displace. James Wilson reminded the Pennsylvania ratifying convention in 1787: "It is true, indeed, sir, although it presupposes the existence of state governments, yet this Constitution does not suppose them to be the sole power to be respected." *Debates in the Several State Conventions on the Adoption of the Federal Constitution* 439 (J. Elliot 2nd ed. 1876). According to Elliot:

The power of the Federal Government is a "power to be respected" as well, and the fact that the States remain sovereign as to all powers not vested in Congress or denied them by the Constitution offers no guidance about where the frontier between state and federal power lies. In short, we have no license to employ freestanding conceptions of state sovereignty when measuring congressional authority under the Commerce Clause....

MAJOR WRITINGS:
The Federalist Papers

James Madison describes the U.S. system as part national and federal; this complements the theory of dual federalism that balances national and state authority without giving either the upper hand. Madison's explanation comes from his work with Alexander Hamilton and John Jay in support of the ratification of the U.S. Constitution, *The Federalist Papers*, from 1787–1788. In Federalist #39, Madison writes:

First.—In order to ascertain the real character of the government, it may be considered in relation to the foundation on which it is to be established; to the sources from which its ordinary powers are to be drawn; to the operation of those powers; to the extent of them; and to the authority by which future changes in the government are to be introduced....

If we try the constitution by its last relation to that authority by which amendments are to be made, we find it neither wholly *national* nor wholly *federal*. Were it wholly national, the supreme and ultimate authority would reside in the majority of the people of the Union; and this authority would be competent at all times, like that of a majority of every national society to alter or abolish its established government. Were it wholly federal, on the other hand, the concurrence of each State in the Union would be essential to every alteration that would be binding on all. The mode provided by the plan of the convention is not founded on either of these principles. In requiring more than a majority, and particularly in computing the proportion by *States*, not by *citizens*, it departs from the national and advances towards the *federal* character; in rendering the concurrence of less than the whole number of States sufficient, it loses again the *federal* and partakes of the *national* character.

The proposed Constitution, therefore, even when tested by the rules laid down by its antagonists, is, in strictness, neither a national nor a federal Constitution, but a composition of both. In its foundation it is federal, not national; in the sources from which the ordinary powers of the government are drawn, it is partly federal and partly national; in the operation of these powers, it is national, not federal; in the extent of them, again, it is federal, not national; and, finally in the authoritative mode of introducing amendments, it is neither wholly federal nor wholly national.

In short, the Framers chose to rely on a federal system in which special restraints on federal power over the States inhered principally in the workings of the National Government itself, rather than in discrete limitations on the objects of federal authority. State sovereign interests, then, are more properly protected by procedural safeguards inherent in the structure of the federal system than by judicially created limitations on federal power.

The effectiveness of the federal political process in preserving the States' interests is apparent even today in the course of federal legislation....

We realize that changes in the structure of the Federal Government have taken place since 1789, not the least of which has been the substitution of popular election of Senators by the adoption of the Seventeenth Amendment in 1913, and that these changes may work to alter the influence of the States in the federal political process. Nonetheless, against this background, we are convinced that the fundamental limitation that the constitutional scheme imposes on the Commerce Clause to protect the "States as States" is one of process rather than one of result. Any substantive restraint on the exercise of Commerce Clause powers must find its justification in the procedural nature of this basic limitation, and it must be tailored to compensate for possible failings in the national political process rather than to dictate a "sacred province of state autonomy." *EEOC v. Wyoming*, 460 U.S., at 236.

U.S. federalism is not stagnant, however. Only 10 years after the *Garcia* decision, the U.S. Supreme Court set a limit on the reach of the Commerce Clause for the first time in 60 years, carving out a constitutional space for states' rights. Chief Justice William Rhenquist delivered the 1995 opinion on *United States vs. Alfonso Lopez, Jr.*:

We start with first principles. The Constitution creates a Federal Government of enumerated powers. See U. S. Const., Art. I, 8. As James Madison wrote, "[t]he powers delegated by the proposed Constitution to the federal government are few and defined. Those which are to remain in the State governments are numerous and indefinite." The Federalist No. 45, pp. 292–293 (C. Rossiter ed. 1961). This constitutionally mandated division of authority "was adopted by the Framers to ensure protection of our fundamental liberties." *Gregory v. Ashcroft*, 501 U.S. 452, 458 (1991) (internal quotation marks omitted). "Just as the separation and independence of the coordinate branches of the Federal Government serves to prevent the accumulation of excessive power in any one branch, a healthy balance of power between the States and the Federal Government will reduce the risk of tyranny and abuse from either front." *Ibid.*...

These are not precise formulations, and in the nature of things they cannot be. But we think they point the way to a correct decision of this case. The possession of a gun in a local school zone is in no sense an economic activity that might, through repetition elsewhere, substantially affect any sort of interstate commerce. Respondent was a local student at a local school; there is no indication that he had recently moved in interstate commerce, and there is no requirement that his possession of the firearm have any concrete tie to interstate commerce.

To uphold the Government's contentions here, we would have to pile inference upon inference in a manner that would bid fair to convert congressional authority under the Commerce Clause to a general police power of the sort retained by the States. Admittedly, some of our prior cases have taken long steps down that road, giving great deference to congressional action. See *supra*, at 8. The broad language in these opinions has suggested the possibility of additional expansion, but we decline here to proceed any further. To do so would require us to conclude that the Constitution's enumeration of powers does not presuppose something not enumerated, cf. *Gibbons v. Ogden, supra*, at 195, and that there never will be a distinction between what is truly national and what is truly local, cf. *Jones and Laughlin Steel, supra*, at 30. This we are unwilling to do.

Author David L. Shapiro points to *Garcia* in asserting that even on a national level, state considerations will be recognized.

When the Supreme Court held in *Garcia* that state employees were, after all, subject to federal minimum wage requirements, Congress was quick to respond with at least some relief—including permission to the states to afford compensatory time off instead of paying costly overtime rates that would otherwise be required by federal law. And the complaints voiced by many states that they are being forced to pay too large a share of the cost of many programs are clearly being heard in the halls of Congress.

The European Union

One of the most interesting federalist experiments is the European Union, an organization of western European nations that oversees the states' economic and political integration and provides a framework for unified action in security and foreign policy matters. The European Union (EU) is the grandchild of the European Economic Community (EEC), which formed in 1957 in order to organize and integrate the economies of the western European nations. In 1967 the EEC merged with the European Coal and Steel Community and the European Atomic Energy Community to form the European Communities (EC). The financial success of the trade policies adopted by the EEC and then the EC persuaded member nations to consider further integration. In 1991, the Treaty on European Union created the EU out of the EC. Member states include Belgium, France, West Germany, Italy, Luxembourg, the Netherlands, Denmark, Ireland, the United Kingdom, Greece, Portugal, Spain, Austria, Finland, and Sweden.

The Commission of the European Communities, led by twenty commissioners with at least one representing each nation in the Union, initiates and implements the Union's legislation. The European Parliament (EP) acts as the EU's legislative branch, and the European Court of Justice (ECJ) serves as the EU's judicial branch. The EU, then, serves as the highest level of government in this form of federalism, and the nations' governments serve as the second level; in other words, the EU, were it compared to the U.S. system, would mirror the national government and the nations' governments would parallel the states' governments.

The EU's judicial branch has been innovative in its federalism. As Nathan Griffith pointed out in his article "Between A Rock and A Hard Place: Political Safeguards, The Federal Majority, and Judicial Nullification" in the fall 2001 *Humane Studies Review*, the relationship between the ECJ and the national courts has opened the door for what John C. Calhoun would have loved: nullification. Whereas Calhoun imagined legislative nullification—a state's legislature might declare the law the nation's legislature made was unconstitutional—in the case of the EU, a national court such as Germany's *Bundesverfassungsgericht* (BVG) might exercise judicial nullification. The BVG's own judgments have opened the door.

Also, according to the BVG's past judgments, as Griffith pointed out, Germany is bound by the EU's laws because Germany binds itself. The opportunity for secession, the same withdrawal the Southern U.S. states attempted in the nineteenth century, remains open for EU members. Interestingly enough, the BVG recognized the older EC as a supranational government; it recognizes the EU as a federation of states. The growth of the nations' power, then, contrasts with the opposite experience in the United States. The possibilities for judicial nullification and secession on the part of the member states further suggests that the balance of power would not soon shift away from the member nations to the EU itself.

Asked about the expected state of European Unity in the future, Oxford University historian Timothy Garton Ash said,

> I think we will not have a clearly defined federal United States of Europe. We will muddle through as we are at the moment with a European law covering a single market, competition policy—broadly speaking economic Europe—and a strange mixture of intergovernmental and supranatural authority in other areas. It will be extremely mess. No schoolchild will be able to understand it in ten pages, but I think it will still be done.

Urgency, however, hastens many an agenda. The terrorist attacks on the United States on September 11, 2001 may force EU officials to more quickly address common criminal justice concerns.

BIOGRAPHY:

Johannes Althusius

Johannes Althusius is remembered as the father of federalism and a champion of popular sovereignty. The German political theorist studied philosophy and law in Switzerland before becoming a professor at the University of Herborn in Nassau. He wrote several works on law including an analysis of Roman legal thought, but his chief work was the 1603 *Politica: Politics Methodically Set Forth and Illustrated with Sacred and Profane Examples*, which explored forms of human association. He determined there were five primary building blocks to human interaction: the family, the voluntary corporation, the local community, the province, and the state.

Althusius noted that each level existed independently. He described different arrangements of associations, and in the process articulated the first real theory of federalism. He believed federalism, with people sovereign through their associations, would best achieve national stability and unity. Associations, he continued, would only add to the happiness and quality of life of each member. The people, not the institutions, were his first concern.

Althusius rose to public office in Emden, East Friesland, later known as Germany, and died there in 1638. For some years his work disappeared from the minds of the academy, but his work was rediscovered and reprinted in the early twentieth century. His articulation of the theories of federalism and popular sovereignty remain milestones.

And, some of today's more modern political systems bear the fingerprints of Althusius. "The revival of interest in Althusius in our time has accompanied the revival of possibilities in confederation," professor Daniel J. Elazar writes.

> The European Union is the leading example of postmodern confederation; there are now three or four others as well. Although Althusius himself does not develop a theory of confederation *per se*, his particular kind of federal thinking in which he sees his universal association as constituted by comprehensive organic communities has clearly had something to contribute to an emerging postmodern theory of confederation.

The attacks on America, wrote F. T. McCarthy in *The Economist* magazine, "have utterly changed the atmosphere." He added:

> National sensitivities about protecting old ways of doing things suddenly seem self–indulgent. Spurred on by this new mood, integrationists eager to set up a European police force and a European prosecutor and keen to agree on shared definitions of *Euro–crimes* suddenly sound more plausible.

Shortly after the attacks, Antonio Vitorino, the EU's new justice commissioner and former deputy prime minister of Portugal, received the blessing of the EU governments to make provisions for a single European arrest warrant. The 15 member governments must ratify the changes.

"It does not burn my lips," Vitorino says of the word federalism, though he quickly asserts his interest lies in criminal justice, not theory. While terrorism poses an immediate concern, Vitorino is said to be targeting cyber–crime, environmental infractions and financial–services fraud.

The experiences of the United States, the Swiss Confederation, and the European Union show how the dynamism and adaptability of federalism make its precious balance unstable; it also, however, ensures its longevity in some form.

ANALYSIS AND CRITICAL RESPONSE

Like many political theories, federalism is prettier in the abstract. Ideal forms do not encounter sectional divide, war, or depression. Federalism is delicate, history messy.

The theory of federalism has much to recommend it. Federalist theorists asked a number of important questions that some other theories do not take into account. How can unity be created out of many different groups? How can disparate people work together peacefully? How can a distant state know the needs of a local community? How can local communities provide large–scale services such as defense? How can individual rights be assured? How can citizens be protected from those who rule? How can the opportunity to abuse power be limited?

The theory's Achilles' heel lies in keeping the system once it is devised. Madison realized that striking the perfect balance between the state and national governments was only half the trick; the other half came in maintaining it. If a constitution divides sovereignty between nation and states, who ensures that neither side oversteps its boundary? Who watches over the federal balance? Neither side could be trusted to do so, because either might take the opportunity to claim more power. Both sides require watching, but if both are suspect, who plays judge? The so–called "who watches the watchers?" dilemma lies at the heart of the federalist model.

Aspects of federalism, practically speaking, make sense. The division of sovereignty allows different levels of government to specialize, which creates efficiency. The national government can exploit economies of scale to provide services such as defense without being sidetracked by regional issues a distant government would not understand, and vice–versa.

Two practical problems affect federalism. If balance is delicate, how can a people be sure they haven't tipped the scale too far one way or another? Even if the balance is workable, how can it be righted once the scales have tipped? Consider the Articles of Confederation. After their colonial experience with Great Britain, the former colonists understandably did not want to face the same problems with their new government. They tipped the balance of federalism toward the states' authority. At the time, each of the provisions of the compact seemed reasonable.

Imposed Limitations

The Articles provided for a loose confederation united by one house of Congress. Since the British authorities had been too distant, then this government, by focusing power in the states, would remain close to home, able to interact with the people and see their needs. Only one house was needed because, frankly, there was not going to be much for it to do. One state received one vote in Congress because the Articles was a compact between states, not individuals, and no state wanted to be represented less than the others just because fewer people happened to live there.

Congress could request funds from states, but states maintained the power of the purse. After being taxed without representation, and for reasons unrelated to the colonies, the people believed granting the taxation power to a national government would lead to a repeat of the same grievances. Virginians did not want New Yorkers spending their money. By keeping taxation a state matter, Congress would have to prove the worth of its need beyond a shadow of a doubt before any state agreed to give funds, and in the meantime those who kept the coffers were the ones who had the locals' best interest at heart.

"The taming of the continent's vast distances by modern technology makes it difficult today to appreciate how the primeval wilderness appeared to the colonists," constitutional author Raoul Berger wrote.

"When William Houston was sent from Georgia to the Constitutional Congress in 1785, he thought of himself as leaving his 'country' to go to 'a strange land amongst Strangers'."

"There are several responses available to a defender of a strong federal system—a system based on the states as presently constituted as at least an appropriate starting point for a diffusion of governmental authority that increases democratic participation and that recognizes individual and small group preferences," wrote David L. Shapiro of federalism today.

> First, California is, of course, the most populous and thus a highly atypical state. At the other end of the scale, such states as Wyoming and New Hampshire are sufficiently small that electors are likely to know their representative personally—at least their representative in the larger chamber of the state legislature—and are likely to have met and discussed issues with that representative on a number of occasions.

Under the Articles of Confederation, amendments required unanimous agreement of representatives from all states. Again, this is understandable; the colonists had rebelled against a system in which they did not feel represented. In the new system, everyone's voice would be heard, and nothing would be done that would impact one group adversely. The Articles provided for no single leader; the Committee of States was the de–facto executive. In a society wary of monarchs, this solved the problem. Term limits, too, lessened fears that representatives would become an aristocracy. The decisions made in creating the Articles of Confederation followed from the experiences and concerns of the people.

Overall Failure

The federalist model, however, did not work. Many circumstances conspired against it, not the least of which was the terrible public and personal debt the War of Independence brought. The government began bankrupt; it never had a chance. Some historians and political scientists claim the Articles would have failed anyway, however, because the system tipped the balance too far in the direction of the states. Instead of unifying the states in post–victory camaraderie, the Articles allowed sectional conflict and petty jealousy swell while key problems affecting all the states remained unresolved. By the time it was obvious that change was imperative, leaders had given up on the government. The former colonists tried to strike the proper federalist balance, but it proved too delicate to find on the first try, and so difficult to repair that the entire compact was abandoned. The Articles of Confederation illustrate the practical difficulty of a system that requires a careful balance in order to succeed.

United States history offers other illustrations of the failure of federalist experiments. The Civil War came about when the balance of sectional interests at the national level destabilized and tore apart the nation. The "devolution revolution" of the 1980s proved that, even when the national government sought to limit its own power and return authority to the states, the old balance, once lost, could not be regained. The schizophrenia of the *Garcia* and *Lopez* decisions reflects an underlying uncertainty about what federalism really means when applied to the real world.

TOPICS FOR FURTHER STUDY

• How did the "interposition" of the 1950s resemble "nullification" of the 1830s?

• In what ways did the Great Society differ from the New Deal?

• How is the European Union like the states under the Articles of Confederation?

• Look at the Federal Constitution of the Swiss Confederation, especially the section on the army. What federalism label best describes the Federal Constitution of the Swiss Confederation?

BIBLIOGRAPHY

Sources

Althusius, Johannes. *Politica*. Frederick S. Carney. Trans. and Ed. Indianapolis: Liberty Fund, 1995.

Anti–Federalist Papers. Available at http://www.constitution.org/afp/afp.htm.

Berger, Raoul. *Federalism: The Founders' Design*. Norman: University of Oklahoma Press, 1987.

Calhoun, John C. *Union and Liberty: The Political Philosophy of John C. Calhoun*. Ross M. Lence, ed. Indianapolis, Liberty Fund: 1992.

Cayton, Andrew, Elisabeth Israels Perry, and Allan M. Winkler. *America: Pathways to the Present*. Needham, Massachusetts: Prentice Hall, 1995.

Diamond, Martin. "What the Framers Meant by Federalism." From *A Nation of States* (Chicago: Rand McNally, 1974). In O'Toole, Lawrence J. Jr., ed. *American Intergovernmental Relations*. Washington: CQ Press, 1993.

Elazar, Daniel J. "Althusius' Grand Design for a Federal Commonwealth." In Althusius, Johannes. *Politica*. Frederick S. Carney. Trans. and Ed. Indianapolis: Liberty Fund, 1995.

Griffith, Nathan. "Between a Rock and a Hard Place: Political Safeguards, The Federal Majority, and Judicial Nullification," *Humane Studies Review*. 14:1 (Fall 2001). Available at http://www.humanestudiesreview.org.

Hamilton, Alexander, James Madison, and John Jay. *The Federalist Papers*. Clinton Rossiter, ed. New York: Mentor, 1961.

Hamilton, Christopher and Donald T. Wells. *Federalism, Power, and Political Economy*. Englewood Cliffs, NJ: Prentice Hall, 1990.

Johansen, Bruce E. *Forgotten Founders: How the American Indian Helped Shape Democracy*. Cambridge: The Harvard Common Press, 1982.

Kazin, Michael. *The Populist Persuasion: An American History*. New York: HarperCollins, 1995.

McCarthy, F.T. *"Europe: Antonio Vitorino."* The Economist, September 29, 2001.

Miller, David, ed. *The Blackwell Encyclopedia of Political Thought*. Cambridge, Blackwell, 1991.

Nagorski, Andrew. "Towards a Europe of 27: Timothy Garton Ash on Enlarging the EU." *Newsweek*, January 1, 2001.

Newmyer, R. Kent. *John Marshall and the Heroic Age of the Supreme Court*. Baton Rouge: Louisiana State University Press, 2001.

Shapiro, David L. *Federalism: A Dialogue*. Evanston, Illinois: Northwestern University Press, 1995.

Storing, Herbert, ed. *The Anti–Federalist*. Chicago: University of Chicago Press, 1985.

Sturgis, Amy H. "'Liberty in Perfection': Freedom in Native American Thought," *The Freeman* (September 1999): 42–45.

Walker, David B. *The Rebirth of Federalism: Slouching Toward Washington*. Chatham, NJ: Chatham House Publishers, Inc., 1995.

Further Readings

Althusius, Johannes. *Politica*. Frederick S. Carney. Trans. and Ed. Indianapolis: Liberty Fund, 1995.

Buchanan, James M. "Federalism and Individual Sovereignty," *The Cato Journal*. 15:2–3 (Fall/Winter 1996). Available at http://www.constitution.org/afp/afp.htm. This work illustrates the ties between the idea of personal freedom and the political theory of federalism.

Drake, Frederick D. and Lynn R. Nelson, eds. *States' Rights and American Federalism: A Documentary History*. Westport, Connecticut: Greenwood Press, 1999. This book looks at the history of federalism in the United States and the contested nature of the relationship between the state and national governments.

Durland, William R. *William Penn, James Madison, and the Historical Crisis in American Federalism*. Lewiston, New York: E. Mellen Press, 2000. This work explores the Madisonian model of federalism and the theory's crucial early years.

Ostrom, Vincent. *The Meaning of America Federalism: Constituting A Self–Governing Society*. San Francisco: ICS Press, 1991. This book weighs the U.S. experience with federalism as an illustration of the theory in action.

Racheter, Donald P. and Richard E. Wagner, eds. *Federalist Government in Principle and Practice*. Boston: Kluwer Academic Publishers, 2001. This book contrasts the ideal of federalism with the way it has evolved in actual institutions.

SEE ALSO

Liberalism

Feudalism

OVERVIEW

Few political systems have shown the adaptiveness and longevity of feudalism. This system, based on personal relationships, local administration, and defined hierarchies, touched several continents for more than 1,500 years. In some places it filled the void left by other political organizations; in others, it represented the next stage in the evolution of government. In both cases, feudalism grew out of practice and precedents. Theory followed experience. In all cases, a parallel code of values and aesthetics-chivalry in the West, *bushido* in the East—complemented and reinforced the system. Feudalism relied on personal and/or family honor as well as self–interest to work. Its informal and varied methods required a balance between superiors and dependents, rights and responsibilities. Though not in practice today, feudalism and the legends it inspired continue to fascinate many people.

WHO CONTROLS GOVERNMENT? Nobility

HOW IS GOVERNMENT PUT INTO POWER? Birth; feudal contract

WHAT ROLES DO THE PEOPLE HAVE? Work for nobles' benefit

WHO CONTROLS PRODUCTION OF GOODS? Nobility

WHO CONTROLS DISTRIBUTION OF GOODS? Nobility

MAJOR FIGURES William the Conqueror; Eleanor of Aquitaine

HISTORICAL EXAMPLE Medieval England

HISTORY

Modern individuals often equate feudalism with the image of King Arthur and his Knights of the Round Table. Medieval Arthurian legends sprang from the feudal tradition and its code of chivalry, and as fruits of the system, do reflect on the values of feudalism itself. But the contemporary, Hollywood–inspired image of a strong king uniting a close–knit Camelot is not an accurate picture of feudalism. In fact, feudal-

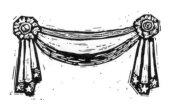

CHRONOLOGY

410: Rome falls to Visigoth invasion.

507: The Frankish Merovingian Dynasty is established. The *precaria* develops during this time.

751: The Frankish Carolingian Dynasty is established. The benefit develops during this time.

1086: William I institutes the Oath of Salisbury, forcing vassals to swear fealty to the King.

1095–1291: Europeans forced join the Crusades to place Jerusalem under Christian control.

1138: Geoffrey of Monmouth completes *History of the Kings of Britain*.

1215: King John signs the Magna Carta.

1603: Ieyasu Tokugawa becomes shogun in Japan.

1945: The end of emperor worship erases the last vestige of Japanese feudalism.

---

ism grew because empires fell and kings were not strong. Local, decentralized, informal decision–making among individuals in the absence of powerful authorities led to the evolution of feudalism.

A Chaotic Time

The feudal system emerged out of a time of chaos in Europe. The rise of Augustus as the first Roman emperor had marked the beginning of the Roman Empire in 27 B.C. For 500 years, the empire provided stability and peace across a vast territory spanning three continents. Carefully constructed public works such as roads, bridges, and aqueducts united the lands physically, while personal allegiance and sometimes worship of the emperor united the people psychologically. Roman law became a universal standard, applicable even to commerce with non–Romans, and professional law schools ensured its uniformity and longevity. The death of Roman Emperor Theodosius I in 395 A.D. and the fall of Rome to the Visigoths in 410, however, spelled the beginning of the end for what had once been a unified West; the great Roman Empire and the peace it provided was no more. By 771, Charlemagne became ruler of a less vast but nonetheless impressive empire that stretched through France, Germany, and Italy, with the blessing and sup-

port of the Pope, but bitter civil wars after his death plunged Europe into disorder once again. Though the Church, based in Rome and led by the Pope, tried to fill the void left by the empire and provide central authority, protection, and law to the different peoples, it often faced internal strife and external obstacles. Invasions from the north, south, and east posed further threats to stability. This period is sometimes known as the Dark Ages, or, more properly, the Early Middle Ages.

Developing Order

As a response to the void of centralized authority, local areas began to develop or renew customs to help people live together in some kind of order. These customs included rules about duties and obligations: who owed what to whom, and when they owed it. Many of these customs were not new. For example, the Germanic peoples had developed a system known as the *comitatus*, or war band, by the time of the Roman Empire. In this group, the war chief owed his followers food for sustenance and spoils from the battles the group fought together. In return, the leader's companions owed him their loyalty and fighting prowess without question. The *comitatus* system had never really disappeared, but it grew in practice in the Early Middle Ages as authority dissolved elsewhere. These customs had several key features: they were localized, not centralized; they were based on personal relationships; and they outlined hierarchies of people, from superiors to subordinates. These features represented the first forms of feudalism in practice.

Another example of an arrangement of this kind was practiced during the Merovingian era. The Merovingian dynasty began with Clovis I, a tribal chieftain who by 507 had built a Frankish, or French, empire stretching to Germany. Clovis united the Gallic clergy and institutionalized Christianity in his dynasty and lands. Though Clovis was a powerful ruler for his time, the authority he and his successors wielded was extremely limited. Most decisions about property and justice were decided locally by informal means. One such means, the proto–feudal legal custom of the *precaria*, developed under Merovingian rule. The *precaria* was an agreement under which one individual would give another the right to live and work on a piece of land for a limited amount of time, after which the land reverted back to the original owner. Clergy and lay people used the *precaria* for a variety of reasons, from escaping tax liabilities to rebuilding a home economy after a crop failure. This kind of temporary commendation, or vassalage, was a contract, and as such came with its own set of duties and obligations.

By 751 Charlemagne's father, Pepin the Short, had replaced the Merovingians and founded the Carolingian dynasty of kings with the Pope's blessing. The Carolingians also relied on decentralized means of maintaining order and therefore fostered the evolution of the feudal system. During the Carolingian period, the *precaria* developed into the benefit. Just as men had duties and obligations to their lords—providing protection, arms, etc.—the lords also had duties and obligations to their men. Those in superior conditions had to provide for the sustenance and maintenance of their pledged dependents, or vassals. Some lords took in their dependent men as members of their households; others granted them land to work so they could support themselves. These positions or lands or offerings became known as benefits, the tangible evidence of the lord's faithfulness and his recognition of his man's loyalty. Under the Carolingians, a variation on this theme also evolved. A king might give the lord who supported him land from royal holdings, but the king might also ask other vassals—for instance, the Church—to grant his man some of their property. This became known as the *precaria verbo regis*, or grant at the king's command. A vassal who received this *precaria* would owe service not to the most recent landholder, such as the Church, but to the king who arranged for the benefit. The complexity and characteristics of local duties and responsibilities—feudalism itself—took shape in the last years of the Carolingian era.

If local customs of duties and obligations anticipated the content of what would become feudalism, then certain events before the chaos of the Early Middle Ages anticipated the ceremony of what would become feudalism. One example is that of Tassilo's commendation. Pepin the Short was uncle to Tassilo, a young boy and Duke of Bavaria. Though the Bavarian people did not wish to be under Carolingian rule, and Tassilo's father had led an unsuccessful revolt against Pepin earlier, Pepin defended Tassilo's duchy of Bavaria from usurpers and protected the young nobleman. In return, he demanded that Tassilo formally commend himself to Pepin in a public and permanent manner. In 757, Tassilo took his nobles to the general assembly meeting in Compiègne, and swore his loyalty to Pepin and Pepin's successors. The ceremony was a complex one. Tassilo took Pepin's hands in his and promised lifelong devotion. He touched religious relics—reportedly the bodies of Saints Denis, Germanus, and Martin, among others—as he promised his dedication to Pepin. Even the members of the Bavarian aristocracy who came with Tassilo had to swear loyalty oaths to Pepin and his sons. In this way, Tassilo showed he was subordinate and faithful to Pepin,

MAJOR WRITINGS:
History of the Kings of Britain

Geoffrey of Monmouth provided the feudal system with a set of heroes. A native of either Wales or Brittany, Geoffrey had a scholarly bent and became a bishop of St. Asaph in 1152. His major work was a chronicle of history called *Historia regum Britanniae*, or *History of the Kings of Britain*, which he completed in 1138. In this work he claimed to be translating a much older document brought by the Archdeacon of Oxford from Brittany, and he presented his book as an accurate portrayal of times past. In reality, however, scholars believe there was no older document and much of Geoffrey's *History* came straight from his imagination.

This does not make his achievement any less important, however, for the popular *History* was read widely at the time (and still is today). Geoffrey provided readers with a list of larger–than–life figures, great kings and their great warriors, who related to each other in feudalistic ways. The heroic vassals performed their duties for their lords, and the lords in turn provided for their dependents. They embodied the chivalric virtues of courage, faithfulness, and loyalty. Geoffrey's *History* included an account of King Arthur and his followers, described as if they were members of the Germanic *comitatus*, a war band bound together by mutual oaths and obligations. Another work attributed to Geoffrey, *Vita Merlini*, also influenced later tales of Arthur and Merlin.

Geoffrey influenced a generation of chroniclers in the Middle Ages such as Wace (1100?–1174) and Layamon (unknown, late twelfth, early thirteenth century) to preserve history and their perceptions of it. More importantly, however, he gave his audience a popular and enduring cast of characters who reflected the best of feudalism and its chivalric code. By blurring the line between fiction and non–fiction, he also started the mystery over the nature and truth of the historical King Arthur, the fact on which the legends were based. As one of the fathers of Arthurian literature, Geoffrey's influence lives on today.

and Tassilo's Bavarian nobles, by following his example, proved their dependence not only on their lord, Tassilo, but also on his lord, Pepin. Thirty years later, Pepin reenacted this commendation, this time pledging his loyalty to Charlemagne. This early ceremony of commendation served as the prototype for later ceremonies of vassalage, in which a man willingly recognized his subordinate status and pledged his loyalty to his lord, in return for the protection and stability the lord provided.

The Role of the Church

Beyond the local customs of duties and obligations and the public ceremonies of commendation, the blending of secular and religious authority offered another foundation for what would become feudalism. The separation of church and state didn't exist in the Early Middle Ages. Christianity, once a persecuted Jewish sect in the Roman Empire, gained converts and momentum and finally became the dominant faith of the West. Constantine, ruler of Rome from 306 to 337 A.D., did a lot to encourage the growth of Christianity, including convening ecumenical councils for religious leaders to discuss theological issues and dedicating his capital city of Constantinople to the Virgin Mary, the mother of Jesus. When Charlemagne was crowned in 800, the Pope placed the crown on the new emperor's head, symbolizing the cooperation and interrelationship between the two leaders. Of course, the fact that the secular and religious worlds seemed to blur together also led to a power struggle between the two groups, as each leader claimed that he had the superior authority. In many instances, however, the lines dividing the two all but disappeared.

For example, as feudalism developed, lords gave tracts of lands to vassals, who in turn pledged loyalty and accepted duties to the lord. One of these vassals was the Church; as the Church accepted land from kings and lords, the Church also accepted the obligations of faithfulness and defense that came with them. The Church, then, could enter into what became feudal contracts. A given church official therefore could be the servant of the Pope at the same time he also was the vassal of a king. The Church did have one special benefit due to its unique status as an institution rather than an individual. When vassals died, their lands returned to their lords. The Church, however, did not die—only representatives of the Church did. So the Church gained from this feudal loophole and continued to accumulate land throughout the Middle Ages, and with it, power.

The Church also influenced the character of feudalism as it developed. While local, secular leaders made decisions regarding the kind of lands given and military service expected and other duties and responsibilities attached to feudal relationships, and these decentralized decisions over time set precedents and became customary, the Church took the opportunity over the years to explain what values the feudal individual—be it lord, vassal, or lady—should embrace. The Church helped to develop an informal code known as chivalry centered around the ideal virtues of love, beauty, courage, and truth. This code implied that might should be used for right; thus knights were exhorted to protect the virtue of damsels in distress, and capture and ransom foes, if possible, rather than kill them. Doing one's Christian duty also meant doing one's feudal duty. In a sense, the Church painted God as the greatest lord of all, with every person on earth as vassals owing Him honor and service and loyalty. Not only did the chivalric code enforce the tenets of feudalism, but it also gave the Church even greater unifying authority in an age of otherwise decentralized, local power.

For example, the Church played upon the feudal ideas of duties and responsibilities and the chivalric notions of justice and honor to call knights and soldiers from various countries together to try to liberate the Kingdom of Jerusalem, one of the key places in Christianity's Holy Land, from Moslem rule and place it under Christian ownership. The repeated attempts at the military takeover of Jerusalem were known as the Crusades, which began in 1095, continued to 1291, and were ultimately unsuccessful. The Crusades nonetheless highlighted the blurry line between secular and religious worlds: kings, emperors, and lords joined together beneath the cross to push for Christian control of a holy city, while popes and church leaders rallied knights and soldiers and planned military strategies. The rhetoric and practice of faith and law, church and state, were inextricably linked as feudalism developed.

Feudal Europe

The high point for feudalism in the West was the High Middle Ages (approximately 1050–1300). The rise of Otto the Great in Germany in 936, the foundation of the Kievan state in Russia in approximately 950, and the Norman Conquest of England in 1066 all served to cement feudal practices from England to Russia. But although the German tribes, the Merovingian and Carolingian kings, and the Church influenced its development, feudalism remained at heart a decentralized, local, informal system. It grew from decisions and customs that endured through time and became precedents for accepted behavior between different pairs of superiors and dependents in social, economic, and religious hierarchies. Political theory,

BIOGRAPHY:

Marie de France

Marie de France is something of a historical mystery. Scholars believe the Frenchwoman was educated in Latin, French, and perhaps English, but was not a nun, although she lived in an era when few women save those in the monasteries or on the royal throne could read. She published poetry and fables of her own and translated other works from Latin. Evidence suggests she knew and was encouraged in her work by Eleanor of Aquitaine, first queen of France by marriage to Louis VII and later queen of England by marriage to Henry II. Eleanor was a great patron of the arts, and she supported authors and songwriters who extolled the virtues of chivalry and values of feudalism. One of Marie de France's most well–known works did just that.

"The Fable of A Man, His Belly, And His Limbs" describes how lords and vassals worked together in a balance of dependence. The lord (the belly) might be wealthy, but he was nothing if his men did not support and defend him; likewise, the vassals (hands, feet, and head) might have the greater numbers, but without the justice and stability provided by the lord, their world crumbles. Together, the superior and his subordinates created a unified whole. Marie de France borrowed from Livy's *History of the Romans* and Aesop's fables to mold a classical parable into a modern poem about feudalism. "The Fable of A Man, His Belly, And His Limbs" appeared in approximately 1160. Its popularity was compounded by the fact that she wrote it in the common language of the people instead of in Latin, and thus made it accessible to a wider audience.

The Fable of A Man, His Belly, And His Limbs

Of a man, I wish to tell, As an example to remember, Of his hands and feet, and of his head—they were angry Towards the belly that he carried, About their earnings that it ate. Then, they would not work anymore, And they deprived it of its food.

But when the belly fasted, They were quickly weakened. Hands and feet had no strength To work now as they were accustomed. Food and drink they offered the belly But they had starved it too long. It did not have the strength to eat. The belly dwindled to nothing And the hands and feet went too.

From this example, one can see What every free person ought to know: No one can have honour Who brings shame to his lord. Nor can his lord have it either If he wishes to shame his people. If either one fails the other Evil befalls them both.

In her widely–read poetry, as well as other works, Marie de France instructed readers on the nature of feudalism and chivalry. She also paved the way for other women to take part in the renaissance of arts and letters that accompanied the High Middle Ages.

---

therefore, did not dictate political practice; on the contrary, it took centuries for scholars to try in writing to articulate the assumptions behind feudal practice. Between the twelfth and fourteenth centuries, authors such as Marie de France, John of Salisbury, Thomas Aquinas, Giles of Rome, Marsiglio of Padua, and Christine de Pizan were exploring feudal ideas of reciprocal obligation and contract theory and ensuring their importance in the Western tradition long after the Middle Ages had ended. None used the term "feudalism," however; the term is a modern one devised to describe the system.

The balance between vassals and lords, who were in turn vassals to other lords, and the complex system of obligations owed in both directions could not hold past the High Middle Ages. The centralized state threatened the loose organization of localities; proto–nations could pay salaried officers and hire mercenary armies. The relationship between subject and sovereign replaced that of vassal and lord. Towns, with their growing economies and emerging middle class, grew into nearly self–sustaining worlds providing for their own protection and needs with little use for knights. For some time, a phenomenon known as "bastard feudalism" appeared, in which the aristocracy wielded its manpower—military might owed to the lords by feudal contract—to gain power and impose its will. These efforts in effect used feudal means toward non–feudal ends, and spelled the last breath for feudalism in the West. The rise of the nation–states meant the end of the Middle Ages.

Feudalism Outside Europe

The phenomenon of feudalism was not limited to Europe. Pre–Columbian Mexico developed a variation of feudalism. The East had its own versions of feu-

Japanese samurai.

dalism in India, China, and, most notably, Japan. Japan's system was based heavily on aspects of Zen Buddhism and Confucianism. Like Western feudalism, the Japanese system included reciprocal duties and responsibilities between lords and vassals. European feudalism borrowed from its religious tradition to create the chivalric code; Japanese feudalism did the same to create *bushido*, the way of the warrior. Like chivalry, *bushido* emphasized honor, loyalty to one's lord, self–sacrifice, courage, and indifference to pain. The two versions of feudalism were nearly contemporaries: the code of *bushido* developed during the Kamakura period in Japan (1185–1333), which roughly correlates to the High Middle Ages. Like its western counterpart,

Japanese feudalism evolved in practice long before theorists committed it to the page; the code was not written down until the sixteenth century, or even termed *bushido* until the seventeenth century. Unlike feudalism in the West, however, Japanese feudalism survived into the modern era. The *daimyo* and *samurai* warriors of the Tokugawa shoguns followed the code, and state schools taught it as a prerequisite for public service. *Bushido* even served as the basis for emperor worship in Japan until 1945.

Today the *samurai* and knights of the feudal system remain potent images in our mythology, but the impact of feudalism extends beyond the codes of chivalry and *bushido*. In constitutions and laws and contracts, and the ideas of obligation, mutual duties, and responsibilities that they contain, the legacy of feudalism has spread and survived throughout the world.

THEORY IN DEPTH

Feudalism seemed to be either evolving or devolving over a period of centuries. It is nearly impossible to pinpoint when full feudalism arrived as a discrete, self–contained phenomenon. The essence of feudalism can be extracted from its historical examples, however, to reveal the theory behind the system.

Gender Roles

Feudalism was largely a male–dominated system. As lords and vassals, property holders at some level of the feudal pyramid, the relationship between superior and dependent almost always included only male parties. Women did not own land; instead, they were considered property by most legal systems. Only a few women monarchs such as Eleanor of Aquitaine (1122–1204) were exceptions to the rule. The military nature of the feudal order with its emphasis on personal combat and training further excluded women from the feudal system's hierarchy. For the most part, feudal decisions were male decisions.

That is not to say that women were not involved in the feudal order. From agricultural workers among the serfs to heroines of song and story, women's lives, like men, were woven inextricably into the feudal fabric. Although they did not hold specific official decision–making positions within the feudal hierarchy, women were indispensable in the related code of chivalry that supported and complemented feudalism. For example, the chaste and pious dictates of courtly love celebrated exemplars of feminine virtue by using them as the inspiration for quests, jousts, and good knightly deeds, as well as the focus for the protection of innocents. The Arthurian legends, which explored and refined chivalric themes, recognized women as powerful figures capable of extraordinary—and sometimes superhuman—acts of faith, magic, and even statecraft. Perhaps most importantly, the chivalric code opened opportunities for real women, as opposed to ideal or fictional ones, to gain fame as poets, artists, songwriters, and authors. The rebirth of arts associated with the age of chivalry allowed some gifted and visible women new opportunities for artistic recognition and self–expression.

Nevertheless, feudalism itself wore a distinctly male face. At its most basic, feudalism was local, per-

BIOGRAPHY:
Eleanor of Aquitaine

Perhaps the best–known woman of the feudal era, Eleanor of Aquitaine was the queen of two of the most powerful countries of the world in the Middle Ages and used her wealth and influence to patronize poets, artists, balladeers, and authors who created new interpretations of the code of chivalry.

Eleanor was the daughter and heiress of William X, Duke of Aquitaine. She married Louis VII and became queen of France. Strong–willed and adventurous, she convinced her husband to allow her to accompany him and his troops to the Holy Land during the Second Crusade (1147–1149). In 1152, Eleanor and Louis received an annulment to their marriage and Eleanor wed Henry, duke of Normandy and count of Anjou, who soon became Henry II of England. Among their sons was Richard I, also known as Richard the Lionhearted, and John I. After an unsuccessful revolt against her husband Henry in 1173, Eleanor was held under house arrest until 1185. She backed Richard's bid for the throne after his father's death and helped maintain his position when he was captured during the Third Crusade (1190–1194). She also helped to orchestrate his eventual ransom and release. After Richard's death, Eleanor supported John's bid for the throne. She was active in court politics throughout her life and died five years after John took the throne of England.

Though a powerful political presence in the reigns of four different kings, Eleanor is best known as an enthusiast of the chivalric code, a patron of the arts and, as such, an inspiration in the development of the music, art, and literature of the feudal era. The queen supported authors such as Wace, Chrestien de Troyes, and quite probably Marie de France, among others, in their endeavors to glorify courtly manners and chivalric virtues. Through her example and her benevolence, Eleanor of Aquitaine became one of the chief architects of and inspirations for the feudal renaissance of arts.

sonal, and hierarchical. All three of these characteristics sprang from the fact that the feudal system relied on the land as its basic building block. In feudal society, the monarch owned the land, but divided it

Eleanor of Aquitaine. (Archive Photos, Inc.)

among his nobles, who in turn divided it among their supporters, who in turn divided it among their workers. This is known as a manorial system.

The Manorial System

The feudal contract   In the manorial system, the land granted by a superior to his dependent was known as a fief. The dependent, or vassal, pledged his loyalty to his superior, also known as lord or suzerain, in a ceremony of homage. In this ceremony, like the earlier commendation, the vassal put his hands in his lord's hands and pledged his loyalty via an oath of fealty. In turn, the lord kissed the vassal and accepted his pledge. This practice served to make public the personal relationship between the lord and his vassal and sealed the feudal contract between the two. By pledging his loyalty, the vassal promised to fight for and defend his lord and lands, and also offer the lord part of his earnings from the land through gifts, percentages of crops, etc. The contract also bound the lord to give the vassal a fief for his sustenance, the individuals attached to the fief, and the promise of order (in this decentralized system, the lord served as the main instrument of justice, and thus heard disputes and decided sentences).

This feudal contract had several important characteristics. First, it was reciprocal. It bound both par-

ties so each had duties and responsibilities toward the other. If one side did not follow through, the mutually beneficial relationship fell apart. Second, it was informal. The contract relied on self–interest—since each party had good reason to live up to the agreement—and an understood code of honor for enforcement. The values of chivalry, then, played a part in socializing lords and vassals to become good contract–keepers. Third, and perhaps most important, the contract was not exclusive: in fact, feudal contracts were stacked upon each other to create the feudal pyramid. In other words, the fact that one individual was lord to a vassal did not keep that same individual from being vassal to a greater lord at the same time, and so on.

The feudal pyramid   This pyramid ended at its top with the king. Beneath him were his tenants–in–chief, counts and barons who had received their fiefs from the sovereign. Below the counts and barons were mesne–tenants, or vassals who received their fiefs from the counts and barons. Several levels of mesne–tenants might exist, each swearing oaths of fealty to the lords who gave them their fiefs. At the bottom of the pyramid were the villains, or serfs. The serfs remained attached by heredity to the land either by custom or law; they performed agricultural labor on the land where their ancestors had worked, in the sections the serfs claimed as their own with the lord's permission, and the demesne, or the land the lord set aside for his own use. On the demesne, they owed their lords work in two forms: week–work, a specified number of days per year, and boon days, or periods of extra effort such as harvest time. Free serfs could move to another fief of their own accord if they chose, but servile serfs had to receive permission if they wished to leave the fief; most serfs remained on the same land for generations.

The heart of the feudal system rested not at the top of the pyramid, with the king, but at the pyramid's base, on the land. Most people during the feudal era were peasants, either free or servile serfs. Their world, and the world of their immediate lords, revolved around the fief. The fief in its smallest form consisted of a manor. The lord retained the manor house and its surrounding demesne for the use of himself and his family. The rest of the fief land was divided. Serfs held the arable, land divided in a system decided by each individual lord (usually in small strips given to individual peasants on which to live and work). Serfs usually held the meadow in common. The lord traditionally retained ownership of the woodland, but allowed serfs to hunt, fish, and cut wood on the land as long as they compensated the lord when they used this privilege. In this manner, peasant and aristocrat, vassal and lord, coexisted on the land.

The legal system   The manor served as the political and economic unit of the feudal system. Politically, the manor offered justice, protection, and administration. Each fief developed a set of manorial courts where disputes about property or crimes could be heard. The local lord or his agent presided over the justice system. The decisions made over time became precedents and served as a form of common law. In this way, the law evolved locally, tailored to address the specific concerns of the peasants, servants, and free people of a given fief. Each manorial court and its decisions might be somewhat different, but within each court, practices evolved and became standardized. Even if a king or overlord transferred a particular manor to another lord's control, the infrastructure of that manor, with its courts and conventions, remained intact. The king also maintained courts, but these heard only a small fraction of the cases in the land. The legal system of the Middle Ages, like feudalism itself, was largely decentralized and personal.

Terms of the feudal contract   This system also provided for the rights of those on the land. Lords and vassals, by virtue of the feudal contract, had specific claims against each other: the lord had to provide sustenance and the vassal loyalty and protection. Serfs, too, had such claims. Even the servile serfs were not in fact slaves. Through the implied contract between manor lord and serf, recognized by the manorial court system, the lord expected goods from his workers—labor, loyalty, dues, payment for use of the lord's woodlands, etc.—but the lord also owed the serfs safety, sustenance, and basic human rights. In a sense, the manor system acted like a primitive insurance policy. In the good, productive times, serfs owed the lord of the manor fees, payments, and part of the fruits of their labors. If crop failure or illness plagued the manor's lands, however, the lord was expected to liquidate assets to provide for those who served him. A lord faced shame and public censure if he turned away from the chivalric code and behaved inappropriately; moreover, if he lost his work force, he also faced financial ruin. Content and motivated serfs brought honor and material success to the lord.

The manor therefore served as the economic unit of the feudal system, as well. The economy of the Middle Ages revolved primarily around agriculture, and the manor oversaw and organized the farming of the land. Internal improvements—the building and repair of roads, bridges, dams, and other pathways for people and information—also took place at the manor level. Taxes and surveys, when taken, were funneled through the manor, as well. Many manor economies also included modest forms of small manufacturing such as the production of cloth, ironwear, and other staples needed for daily life. Self–sufficiency was a goal of the system, for at any time war or disease could cut the manor off from its neighbors and leave its tenants to provide for themselves.

The Church   Intertwined with the manorial system was the Church. Its members were vassals to various lords, and therefore owed loyalty not only to the officials of the Church and the pope in Rome, but also to other lay leaders, as well. At the local level, the Church reinforced the feudal system by offering it instruction—including support of the code of chivalry—and charity, itself another form of insurance for the most humble of society. Through the Crusades and other events, the Church also remained involved with the final unit of the feudal system: the military.

Among the responsibilities of vassals to lords was the duty of defense. If a lord required military help, the vassal was sworn to respond. For the great lords who served even greater overlords and/or the king, the duty of defense meant more than appearing at a battle with a sword. These vassals owed their superiors forces, numbers of men, trained and fit and able to win a war. Kings, for example, asked tenants–in–chief for military support, and they in turn raised armies by calling on their pledged mesne–tenants. The result was private armies and career knights.

Knighthood   Perhaps no single figure represents the Middle Ages to the modern mind more than the knight. Some were landholders, and others accepted fiefs in other forms, such as money or similar gifts. All required their own support staffs for training and help. Boys who expected to become knights, often sons of knights themselves, began their military apprenticeship as young children sent to the courts of lords or kings. There the pages, or young students, learned about weaponry, hunting, falconry, dogs, and the code of chivalry. By puberty, knights in training became squires. Each served a knight and learned firsthand about warfare and courtly society. By 21, squires with sufficient skill, reputation, and wealth could become knights.

For these men, trained for more than a decade before even reaching knighthood, war was a lifetime occupation. As various knights—and beneath them, common soldiers—were loyal to specific lords, a balance of power often emerged among the highest level of counts and barons. When this balance failed, internal fighting broke out until the medieval arms race returned to equilibrium. The high number of knights and military men who relied on the patronage of lords and/or kings led to war by necessity: if the forces existed, then they would find someone to fight. The military manpower was too expensive and time–consuming to maintain simply to leave it inactive. Thus war, external and civil, as well as invasions and boundary disputes typified the feudal age.

All of the ingredients of the feudal system served to make society local, personal, and hierarchical. The manor, the smallest unit of feudal society, served key political and economic roles by providing justice, protection, administration, and a primitive form of insurance. The church and the military, bound to the feudal system as well, had their own forms of hierarchy between superiors and dependents. All of the relationships that built the feudal pyramid from its base to its point relied on two key ingredients to hold the contract together: self–interest, backed by the knowledge that both sides had to meet their obligations for each side to benefit; and honor, fueled by the values of the code of chivalry. These motivations did not always ensure that all interactions were ideal, but they did form the enduring backbone of feudalism for centuries.

Literature of the Feudal Era

Since feudalism was an evolved system, developed over centuries through local, decentralized, informal precedents, rather than an implemented system, in which leaders devised a plan and then set in place, major writings on feudalism did not appear before or even during the development of the system; instead, they appeared after feudalism was in widespread practice. Perhaps the most important writings were not the examinations of the feudal system and the celebrations of the code of chivalry, but the modest contracts between lords and vassals, the granting of benefits and similar transactions. One of the most lasting impacts of the feudal era is the concept of the contract.

Otherwise, feudalism did not have theorists as much as it had commentators, or thinkers who observed the system after its development and remarked upon it, practitioners, or those who used its rhetoric to further their own goals, and artists, or those who expressed the values and conflicts of feudalism through fiction, song, and other media. Perhaps one of the best writings to exemplify feudalism in practice is Bernard of Clairvaux's "Letter to Pope Eugenius III." Bernard of Clairvaux (1090–1153), or Saint Bernard, was a French mystic, orator, and leader of the Cistercian order of monks. He also was a political

figure who made many journeys for peacekeeping, charity, and reform. In approximately 1146, Bernard wrote to his friend Pope Eugenius III to encourage the Pope's faith and action in the Second Crusade and its goal to take Jerusalem under Christian control. In the letter, the feudal interrelationship of the Church and state is clear: Bernard wants the Pope to launch a military campaign and gather lay leaders behind its banner. The influence of chivalric thought is also evident—Bernard praises courage, criticizes cowardice, and underscores the values of faithfulness and spirituality:

> The news is not good, but is sad and grave. And sad for whom? Rather, for whom is it not sad! Only for the sons of wrath, who do not feel anger, nor are they saddened by sad events, but rejoice and exult in them. . . . I tell you, such a general and serious crisis is not an occasion to act tepidly nor timidly. I have read [in the book of] a certain wise man: 'He is not brave whose spirit does not rise in difficulty.' And I would add that a faithful person is even more faithful in disaster. The waters have risen to the soul of Christ, and touch the very pupil of his eye. Now, in this new suffering of our Lord Christ, we must draw the swords of the first Passion. . . . An extraordinary danger demands an extraordinary effort. The foundation is shaken, and imminent ruin follows unless resisted. I have written boldly, but truthfully for your sake. . . . But you know all of this, it is not for me to lead you to wisdom. I ask humbly, by the love you particularly owe me, not to abandon me to human caprice; but ask eagerly for divine counsel, as particularly incumbent upon you, and work diligently, so that as His will is done in heaven, so it will be on earth.

Bernard's writings, such as his influential letters to Pope Eugenius III embody the very soul of feudalism. Eugenius III and other officials listened to Bernard's advice. The Church appreciated Bernard's outspoken example as a leader of his day, and in 1170, only 17 years after his death, Bernard was canonized.

If Bernard's work represents the religious end of feudalistic writings, then the work of John of Salisbury represents the political theory of the period. John of Salisbury (1120?–1180) studied in France under some of the greatest minds of the era: Peter Abelard, William of Conches, and Thierry of Chartres, among others. He was the secretary to the Archbishop of Canterbury for years and Bishop of Chartres for the last four years of his life. John is best known for two works of political scholarship, both of which were influential among scholastic philosophers in his own day. *Metalogicus* (1159) painted a portrait of scholarly life, criticized educational practices, and explored the debates of teaching methods and theories. John's work marked him as a humanist, a thinker concerned with the betterment of humankind through reason and learning.

His second work, also completed in 1159, was *Policraticus: Of the Frivolities of Courtiers and the Footprints of Philosophers*. In this treatise on government John set out the criteria by which political systems should be judged. He used the familiar metaphor of the human body to show how all parts of the political body should work together in harmony and reciprocity, thus satisfying natural law, divine will, and the general good. *Policraticus*, arguably the first work of medieval political theory, strengthened the core of feudalism with its praise of balance, mutual obligation, and loyalty between superiors and their dependents:

None the less, in order to address generally each one and all, they are not to exceed the limits, namely, law, and are to concentrate on the public utility in all matters. For inferiors must serve superiors, who on the other hand ought to provide all necessary protection to their inferiors. For this reason, Plutarch says that what is to the advantage of the humbler people, that is, the multitude, is to be followed; for the fewer always submit to the more numerous. Therefore, magistrates were instituted for the reason that injuries might be averted and the republic itself might put shoes, as it were, on its workers. For when they are exposed to injuries it is as if the republic was barefoot; there can be nothing more ignominious for those who administer the magistracies. Indeed, an afflicted people is like proof and irrefutable demonstration of the ruler's gout. The health of the whole republic will only be secure and splendid if the superior members devote themselves to the inferiors and if the inferiors respond likewise to the legal rights of their superiors, so that each individual may be likened to a part of the others reciprocally . . .

Bernard of Clairvaux's letter and John of Salisbury's treatise, one a glimpse of feudal thought in action and the other a window into feudal thought in theory, represent the non–fiction writings of the era. The High Middle Ages, however, was known as a renaissance in poetry, music, and fiction. Perhaps the most long–lived contribution of the age is the birth of Arthurian literature. One of the earliest examples of King Arthur's exploits appeared in the tenth– or eleventh–century collection known as *The Black Book of Carmathen*. The author and exact date of the work is unknown, but the impact of it and its Arthurian contemporaries cannot be overestimated. Not only did the stories entertain, but they also instructed readers in the political tenets of feudalism and the corresponding values of chivalry.

In one poem, a dialogue between Arthur and a porter known as Glewlwyd Mighty–grip, Arthur introduces his men and, with them, the traits he prizes in them: fearlessness, wisdom, and faithfulness. His men have fulfilled their obligation to him by fighting for him and counseling him. In return, Arthur is looking after his duty toward them, reminding Glewlwyd that "a lord would protect them." Arthur is portrayed as a proper lord with worthy dependents who honor the feudal contract with their superior. The reciprocal relationship they share is personal and affectionate, and it encourages the chivalric virtues in them all. When readers thrilled to the adventures of the king and his knights, they also received instruction on the complex relationships of the feudal system.

[Glewlwyd:] Who comes with you? [Arthur:] The best men in the world. [Glewlwyd:] To my house you will not come unless you deliver them [Arthur:] I shall deliver them and you will see them. Wythnaint, Elei, and Sywyon, these three; Mabon son of Modron, servant of Uther Pendragon, Cystaint son of Banon, And Gwyn Godybrion; harsh were my servants in defending their rights. Manawydan son of Lyr, profound was his counsel. Manawyd carried off Shields pierced and battle–stained. And Mabon son of Mellt stained the grass with blood. And Anwas the Winged and Lluch of the Striking Hand, they were defending on the borders of Eidyn. A lord would protect them; my nephew would give them recompense.

Later in the Middle Ages the tone of works began to deviate from fictional and non–fictional positive, unapologetic views of feudalism. Books such as Brunetto Latini's *The Book of Treasure* (1266) and John Wyclif's *On the Duty of the King* (1379) and later works by Christine de Pisan and Machiavelli, among others, shifted the emphasis from chivalric virtues and reciprocal obligations among the people to focus on the power of the king. This shift ushered in a new era of nation–states with powerful monarchs and bring an end to the Middle Ages and its system of feudalism.

Bernard of Clairvaux, John of Salisbury, and *The Black Book of Carmathen* all illuminated some aspect of feudalism as a political system. One document, however, embodied feudalism more than any other: the Magna Carta, or The Great Charter of English Liberty Decreed by King John. John did not originate the idea of the charter; on the contrary, he signed it under compulsion from his barons and the Church in 1215. The impulse for the combined lay and religious demand for the compact rested squarely in feudal thought. The King, as the greatest lord in the country, still owed duties and responsibilities to his vassals. The barons and Church forced John, who extended his powers whenever possible, to recognize his obligations and to place himself under the same law as his subjects. The claims against John flowed directly from the notion of the feudal contract. John's signature not only reinstated the monarch's acceptance of his feudal relationships, but it also paved the way for the English and U.S. constitutions.

60. Moreover all the subjects of our realm, clergy as well as laity, shall, as far as pertains to them, observe, with regard to their vassals, all these aforesaid customs and liberties which we have decreed shall, as far as pertains to us, be observed in our realm with regard to our own.
. . .

63. Wherefore we will and firmly decree that the English church shall be free, and that the subjects of our realm shall have and hold all the aforesaid liberties, rights and concessions, duly and in peace, freely and quietly, fully and entirely, for themselves and their heirs, from us and our heirs, in all matters and in all places, forever, as has been said. Moreover it has been sworn, on our part as well as on the part of the barons, that all these above mentioned provisions shall be observed with good faith and without evil intent. The witnesses being the above mentioned and many others. Given through our hand, in the plain called Runnimede between Windsor and Stanes, on the fifteenth day of June, in the seventeenth year of our reign.

Even the Magna Carta, which captured a feudal moment in time while also anticipating later constitutional theory, could not halt the European evolution toward powerful monarchs ruling centralized nation–states. Even as John agreed to the demands of the barons and the Church, the days of the Middle Ages were numbered.

William the Conqueror. (The Library of Congress)

THEORY IN ACTION

Regardless of where it was found, feudalism in all of its forms shared certain characteristics. It was localized, not centralized; it was based on personal relationships; and it outlined hierarchies of people from superiors to subordinates. What this meant for the lands in which feudalism developed, however, differed according to the place and its past history.

One of the debates surrounding feudalism is the question of its true source: Roman organization as widely implemented by the Roman Empire, or Germanic traditions as found in the tribal systems of Germany? Perhaps the best answer to this is to accept both foundations as precursors to the feudal system. Without the vacuum of authority created by the dissolution of the Roman institutions, much of the West would not have needed the local hierarchies or personal relationships of feudalism. On the other hand, without the Germanic *comitatus* and the model of its operation, much of the West might not have evolved the practices of feudalism. The political theory and practice owed much to both sets of precursors.

Where feudalism evolved, however, determined what the system meant for each place. For example,

lands that once had been under the control of the Roman Empire such as France and England had experienced efficient, centralized, large–scale governance by a distant ruler. The fall of Rome and rise of feudalism meant a general decentralization of power, an entropy of authority. By contrast, other areas such as Germany and Russia had experienced very localized governance at the level of the small village or nomadic tribe. The rise of the feudal system with its hierarchies and contracts meant an evolution in the way people ordered themselves, a standardization of practices, even a growth in organized authority. What was a disintegration of government for some was actually an increase in government for others.

Even those areas with similar backgrounds experienced feudalism differently, according to regional influences. France and England, for instance, shared a past as part of the Roman Empire. For both, the loss of concentrated authority in Rome, and the infrastructure and information that came with it, meant a drastic change to a system less uniform, stable, and distant. But the feudalism that developed in each country was unique.

The French Experience

The French form of the feudal system is the one often taken as the model of true feudalism in practice. This is largely due to the fact that the French mon-

BIOGRAPHY:

William the Conqueror

William I of England was the illegitimate son of the Duke of Normandy and a tanner's daughter. After the death of his father in 1035, William became duke. The young boy had to fight off many challenges to his rule, but as he grew his resourcefulness and ambition became evident. He fought off French invasions and planned to expand his power to England, where his cousin Edward the Confessor was king. When Edward died and Harold, Earl of Wessex was crowned his successor, William received the blessing of the Pope and took his Norman army to England to challenge Harold. After the death of Harold in the Battle of Hastings in 1066, William named himself King of England.

The Norman Conquest under William had important repercussions for England. The King established separate ecclesiastical courts, brought foreign officials to replace some English ones, and conducted a survey known as the Domesday Book, which documented statistics about the country. The Anglo–Saxons in England rebelled but were unsuccessful in their attempts to overthrow their conquerors. William died in 1087 after being fatally wounded in a riding accident, and his son William II succeeded him in England (his son Robert succeeded him in Normandy).

William's reign affected feudalism in two ways. First, it placed another layer on top of the existing lord/vassal structure. William considered England his by right of conquest, and he distributed land in manors to his supporters and loyal subjects. These vassals of William in turn were lords to other vassals, and so on. Rather than evolving naturally and locally, William's redistribution represented the first—and, to some degree only—top down reordering of the feudal relationships by a king. Although this changed the names of some of the lords, though, this did not change the system itself or the way the superior/dependent partnership functioned.

The second way William influenced feudalism was by clarifying the nature of the system's pyramid; vassals were lords to men who were in turn vassals to greater lords, and as power increased, the numbers decreased. At the top of the pyramid of power stood the king. William established the precedent that loyalty to the king superseded all other feudal obligations to lesser lords or kingdoms. This suggested that power was far more centralized than it actually was, and it seemed to contradict the informal, decentralized, personal nature of feudal relationships. Though few kings in the following years were strong enough to exploit this development, William's clarification of the weight of subjects' loyalty to sovereigns sowed the first seeds of feudalism's demise and foresaw the later development of the great monarchies in the era of nation–states.

---

archs devised their power solely from the feudal pyramid, rather than sometimes using extra–feudal power to trump the feudal contract. One useful illustration is that of King Louis VI and his attempt to settle the problem between the Count of Auvergne and the Bishop of Clermont. The king believed the count was at fault in a dispute with the bishop. So, in 1126, Louis VI with his forces mounted an expedition against the Count of Auvergne.

Duke William VIII intervened, and stopped the potentially violent campaign against the count. The duke was a sworn vassal of Louis VI and was also the lord of the count, who was a sworn vassal to him. According to the feudal contract, William reminded his lord and his vassal, the king could not decide who was guilty and punish that party. Justice required a trial, and it was the duke's responsibility as the count's lord to provide it. The court of Auvergne was summoned, and the issue was decided by the feudal court procedure. Even the king was constrained by the due process of the feudal justice system. The fact that he was a king—and a foreign one at that—did not absolve him from the law.

Even foreign monarchs were held accountable under French feudalism. For generations, the kings of England held French lands that had been donated to them by French kings, for example. The infamous King John, King of England from 1199 to 1216, lost these lands because he had failed his duties as a vassal to the King of France. The fact that he was a ruler of another nation did not place him about the feudal contract in France.

BIOGRAPHY:
Ieyasu Tokugawa

The founder of the influential Tokugawa shogunate began as a vassal in Japan, a warrior and military leader. He helped Nobunaga and Hideyoshi unify Japan and received a healthy amount of land in return as a fief. He located the capital of his manor in Edo, later known as Tokyo. Through a combination of wealth and wise administration, Tokugawa became a powerful fiefholder, or *daimyo*. When Hideyoshi died and left a vacuum of power in Japan, the ambitious Tokugawa defeated rival barons in the Battle of Sekigahara (1600). His victory led him to become *shogun*, or military dictator, of the country.

As shogun, Tokugawa centralized and institutionalized a unique brand of feudalism. Among his decisions was the choice to make his former opponents hereditary vassals to his supporters. He also made attendance at court compulsory, encouraged international trade, and controlled the building of castles within Japan. He revived Confucianism as well, grafting the reverence for the family to concern for personal honor to further strengthen the ties of the feudal contract. His authority as a military leader with a loyal army to back his position trumped that of the emperor. After his death in 1616, the Tokugawa shogunate continued, as did the trend of power collecting in the hands of the wealthy and influential *daimyo* instead of the emperor. The *daimyo* remained the primary powerhouse behind Japanese feudalism for more than 250 years after Ieyasu Tokugawa.

English Feudalism

The English experience with feudalism was different. William the Conqueror's insistence that the feudal oath did not outweigh the loyalty a subject must feel for his sovereign set the stage for the ultimate trumping power of the monarchs over the standard feudal system. The Norman Conquest introduced the idea that all of the land belonged to the king, so even if land had been granted as a fief in several transactions, stepping down the feudal pyramid with each one, no one could claim the land was his alone, independent of the crown. William therefore insisted that all vassals holding fiefs take the Oath of Salisbury (1086), which meant they had to swear an oath of fealty to the king.

Henry I, King of England from 1100 to 1135, later insisted that all oaths of fealty include a reservation proclaiming loyalty to the king. The balance of power tipped from feudal courts to royal decisions, and the monarch's power grew. By the time of King John's reign (1199–1216), the monarch could afford his own army independent of those raised by lords from among their vassals. In a real sense, the conspiracy of the barons that led to the Magna Carta in 1215 was based on an assertion of feudal rights: the Magna Carta stated that the king was not above the law. Even the Magna Carta could not halt the consolidation of power in the sovereign, however. As the thirteenth century drew to a close, the monarchy's power eclipsed the balance provided by feudalism, and the system declined.

Feudal Germany

In still a third variation of feudalism, Germany's version was characterized by an emphasis on the role of princes. Feudalism evolved in Germany as it did elsewhere, but was reorganized and strengthened by Frederick I, Holy Roman Emperor from 1155 to 1190 and King of Germany from 1152 to 1190. In 1180, Henry the Lion, Duke of Saxony and Bavaria, failed to appear as required before the royal court, which was acting in its feudal capacity as the lord's court. This breach of Henry's duty as a vassal caused him to lose his imperial fiefs.

The powerful margraves and dukes who supported the King's pursuit of feudal due process against Henry received their reward when Frederick reorganized the state apparatus to more closely follow a feudal model. These aristocrats became princes of the empire, a new order of privileged lords whose vassals by law had to be of lesser class and rank. Although fiefs usually reverted to lords—and, in the case of the princes, to the king—upon the death of the vassal, these princes built a custom of inheritance among themselves that took increasingly more land out of the hands of the monarch. Thus Germany developed a powerful class of lords that checked the authority of the monarch and remained dedicated to many, if not all, feudal processes. The fiefs owned by the major feudal princes later became the modern German states such as Austria and Prussia.

Feudalism in Japan

Though England, France, and Germany experienced variations on the theme of feudalism, none was quite as different as the form that developed in Japan, if for no other reason than its longevity. The Japanese system evolved in the religious climate of Confucianism and Zen Buddhism, with an emphasis on the family and its honor. Beginning in the eighth century, the royal court could not afford to maintain all of the members of the Japanese imperial family in regal style. Some family members therefore obtained tax–free estates in lieu of court support. Territorial barons known as *daimyo* administered these lands. By the twelfth century, the *daimyo* had amassed power as great if not greater than the emperor. Eventually one would rise up to become *shogun*, a feudal military leader who served as the emperor's deputy and in effect ruled Japan. The rise of the shogunate system led to an institutionalized, imposed feudalism based around military leadership.

The Japanese civil wars of the fourteenth through sixteenth centuries did not dissolve feudal thought; after Ieyasu Tokugawa reunified Japan, the *daimyo* who had opposed him were made hereditary vassals to those who had supported him before 1600. The *daimyo* of both sides relied on the *samurai*, the parallel of European knights, to maintain military and civil administration on their lands. The *bushido*, like the code of chivalry in the West, developed to explain and express the values and virtues of the system. Though the Tokugawa shoguns tried to shift authority away from the *daimyo*, eventually those in Western Japan overthrew the shogunate in 1868 in what is known as the Meiji Restoration. The emperor then accepted the fiefs back from the barons and expanded his own authority. By 1871, the feudal privileges of the *daimyo* were no more. The last vestiges of feudal thought, however, survived with the practice of emperor worship until 1945.

ANALYSIS AND CRITICAL RESPONSE

Feudalism as a system had strengths and weaknesses. When weighing them, it is important to view feudalism in its historical context and in the abstract, as a political theory. These two different windows into feudalism provide useful means of assessing its positive and negative traits.

Benefits

In the historical view, feudalism had many benefits. First and foremost, it provided a form of order to fill the vacuum in the West created by the fall of the Roman Empire. Internal strife, civil wars, and territorial disputes might have been more frequent and more violent had the system of personal, binding relationships not connected the people of each region. Of course feudalism brought with it its own form of arms race in the West, and certainly included its own form of bloodshed, but the decentralized order it brought to the West was far better than the chaos that might have reigned.

The localized nature of the system also allowed a certain natural defense for the manor. As a nearly self–sufficient unit, the manor sustained those who lived on it; they could be cut off from contact with others due to the spread of fighting or disease and survive. In an era of sporadic hostilities and virulent plagues, the manor was a protective harbor for many individuals.

This order in the West developed a symbiotic relationship with the institution of the Church, relying on it for its infrastructure at times, competing with it for authority at other times, and sometimes even helping to preserve its own internal hierarchy. Such a relationship allowed groups such as the monks and nuns of the monastic orders to focus their energies on learning and education. Many of the classic works from antiquity survived through the work of monastics who translated and protected copies of the texts. Without these efforts, modern civilization would have lost much of the classical knowledge of the Greeks and Romans, among others.

The code of chivalry that grew up in support of and in harmony with the feudal system also spawned a cultural renaissance in the High Middle Ages. Monarchs such as Eleanor of Aquitaine were inspired by the values of courage, loyalty, and courtly love, and they supported artists and authors and poets who extolled chivalric virtues. Women authors and artists were published and celebrated, and new heroes of history and fiction became larger than life. The feudal era gave birth to the legends of King Arthur, among others, and left an indelible mark on the imagination of the West.

Feudalism therefore provided important opportunities for the literate elite. It also, however, provided new protection to the less educated. Although the lords still exercised great control—and, in the wrong hands, even tyranny—against the lowest individuals in the feudal hierarchy, the serfs who worked the land, these peasants enjoyed more rights protection under the feudal system than elsewhere. For example, the Roman system recognized human slavery and expected that some classes of people had little if any claim to certain basic living standards. The manorial system of feudalism, however, provided for courts to solve disputes and even a primitive form of insurance against crop failure, disease, and other disasters. Serfs had

MAJOR WRITINGS:

Feudalism in Fiction

With two Nebula awards and two Locus awards to her credit—not to mention more Hugo awards for novels than any author except the late Robert A. Heinlein—the celebrated Lois McMaster Bujold is one of the great literary success stories of the present day. She has broken new ground for women science fiction writers and, in the process, she has brought military science fiction and space opera new twenty–first century sensibilities and respectability.

Bujold first took up her pen in 1969 as an author of *Star Trek* fan fiction. She then fell in love with heroes of her own making. In 1985, Baen bought her first three novels set in the Vorkosigan universe, and a modern–day epic was born. Significantly, the award–winning Vorkosigan novels offer an acclaimed and lengthy examination of feudal society.

The Vorkosigan novels examine the planet of Barrayar. Though the culture of the planet reflects a Russo–Germanic society, the planet's feudalism in practice represents a more English model. This feudalism is a devolution of politics, an ad hoc system filling the void left by another way of life; Barrayar, suddenly cut off from its fellow planets, experienced a Dark Age much as England experienced great changes after the fall of Rome. Bujold's story lines explore the values of the code of chivalry, and the hierarchy of the feudal pyramid, in contrast to a twenty–first century model of a liberal democracy known as Beta Colony.

Although Bujold concludes that feudalism as a political system is primitive in many ways, especially in its militaristic and antifeminist tendencies, she also sees aspects to admire, including the emphasis on individual and family honor, and the reciprocal responsibilities binding lord to vassal. Through her series of novels—including *Shards of Honor* and *A Civil Campaign*—Bujold highlights her fascination with the personal justice of the feudal court. Many history texts deal with the specific context of the feudalism of the past, but Bujold's use of fiction to study feudalism offers a unique take on the subject.

responsibilities to their lords, but in return the lords also had certain duties toward the serfs. This system wasn't perfect, but it did represent an evolution in the notion of individual rights.

Weaknesses

Historically speaking, feudalism also had its negative traits, as well. Internally, it carried the seeds of its own destruction, in the West and elsewhere. The lords—or, depending on the place, the Church or princes or barons—became powerful fiefholders who in many circumstances altered the feudal rules to concentrate more wealth and power in their class. As the status of these groups grew, they threatened the authority of those above them. Monarchs responded by trying to shift authority back to their side and centralize power in themselves. This inherent instability in the feudal system disrupted the balance on which the feudal pyramid relied and eventually led to the rise of the nation–state and the powerful despots who ruled them.

Furthermore, the rise of the towns threatened the very fabric of feudalism. The manorial system, with its local economy of agriculture and manufacturing, led to the rise of the town, in which specialist artisans pursued their trade and eventually became financially independent. Like the manors themselves, these towns grew into partial self–sufficiency. With freedom, money, and accomplishment, the townspeople formed a new middle class that somehow did not fit in the traditional hierarchical pattern of the feudal pyramid. Were the townspeople lords or vassals? To whom did they owe duties and responsibilities? Of course most townspeople fell under the rule of a monarch, but this indicated a sovereign/subject relationship, not necessarily a lord/vassal one. The towns, in a sense, outgrew the feudal system and helped to enable the rise of the powerful monarchies.

Feudalism also had a weakness externally. The same decentralization that offered benefits at the time also meant that feudalistic lands were susceptible to attacks from the outside. With private armies attached to lords and their manors, and communication difficult and time–consuming, feudal lands faced extreme difficulties when trying to offer coordinated resistance to attackers. In Europe, invasions from the north, east, and south contributed to the fall of feudalism. The localism of the system made its lands easy to divide and conquer.

Of course, if feudalism is judged ahistorically, one of the most obvious criticisms it would face is that of its exclusive nature. With the exception of certain aspects of the code of chivalry, feudalism applied only to men. Women were treated as property, not as property holders. The equation of lord and vassal, superior and dependent, did not include women as a factor at all. In the context of history, however, this exclusivity is no more surprising than the class–consciousness that pervaded the system. In the Roman Empire and elsewhere, women often were treated with the same degree of political dismissal. It is worth note, however, that the feudal era did provide several stunning examples of women in positions of power and prestige, including rulers such as Eleanor of Aquitaine, authors such as Marie de France and Christine de Pisan, and even fictional characters of import such as Guinevere and Morgan of Arthurian romance—not necessarily flattering images of femininity, but certainly powerful ones. Moreover, the code of chivalry provided protection, if not equality, for women as long as their birth was somewhat noble. These small improvements notwithstanding, feudalism's strength did not lie in its inclusiveness.

Contract Theory

Apart from its historical context, feudalism also had strengths and weaknesses as a theory. Perhaps its greatest contribution is the formulation of contract theory. Feudal lords and vassals owed each other duties and responsibilities. Over time, these became understood, and either party had the right to make legal claims against the other if the compact was not followed. This principle remained in common law and not only governed individuals, but also extended to the compact theory of government—the idea that government is a contract between the governors and the governed—which made possible the evolved constitution of Great Britain and the written Constitution of the United States. Ironically enough for a system that for centuries lacked a formal, written political theory, feudalism influenced modern political and legal thought in a key and lasting manner.

Decentralization

Another aspect of feudalism that provided positive and negative points was the fact that the decentralized spontaneous order allowed hierarchies to exist due to the intense personal nature of the relationships involved. Vassals did not pledge allegiance to a symbol; they placed their hands in the hands of their lords and looked them in the eye. The appeals to loyalty, honor, and personal reputation needed to ensure that both sides met their obligations were much more likely to be motivating factors when those involved really knew each other. The system survived as long as it did due to this built–in personalized process.

Moreover, the decentralization of feudalism meant that each manor and its court could tailor social and legal traditions around the specific needs of the people involved. Regional preferences regarding behavior and religion survived because no general, external law applied to everyone across the continent. This informal, organic system streamlined processes and contributed to the self–sufficiency of the manors. Just as social and legal traditions were scattered, so were military personnel. The decentralization of armed forces meant that organized, devastating warfare was very difficult and expensive to undertake. The Crusades notwithstanding, this lack of unity meant that large–scale violence was less prevalent under the feudal system than it became under the great monarchies.

The competing legal systems and private armies of feudalism did make it difficult for nationalism to take hold across Europe. As the feudal era was in decline, monarchs faced the tremendous task of standardizing the law, consolidating the military, and constructing smooth lines of communication. The resulting nation–states gained many capabilities—coherent policy, exploration, diplomacy, etc.—but lost the personal relationships, tailored legal precedents, and, in some cases, individual liberty enjoyed under the feudal system. The rise of the great monarchs made widespread technological and scientific achievements possible, but it also made large–scale persecution and warfare equally viable. The increased stability of the nation–states was bought at the price of the freedom enjoyed under the more local and informal nature of feudalism.

As a theory, feudalism is difficult to isolate. What is the best image of feudalism? The manorial court? The Round Table? The *samurai*? Is it the provincialism of the French serfs or the extravagance of the German princes? The adaptiveness of feudalism, its ability to show different faces in different times and places, makes its study a unique challenge. This adaptiveness made it possible for feudalism to survive for more than 1,500 years.

TOPICS FOR FURTHER STUDY

- In what ways do the legends of King Arthur reinforce the principles of feudalism?

- Consider what the Norman Conquest meant for England. Did William the Conqueror help or hurt the cause of feudalism? Explain.

- Investigate the way of knights and samurai. How did the code of chivalry in Europe compare to the code of *bushido* in Japan?

• Could feudalism exist in a non–agricultural society? Why or why not?

BIBLIOGRAPHY

Sources

Barber, Richard, ed. *The Arthurian Legends: An Illustrated Anthology.* Rochester: The Boydell Press, 1979.

The Bayeux Tapestry. Available at http://www.hastings1066.com/.

Bernard of Clairvaux. "Letter to Pope Eugenius III." In Cary J. Nederman and Kate Langdon Forhan, eds. *Readings in Medieval Political Theory, 1100–1400.* Indianapolis: Hackett, 1993, 21–23.

Cavendish, Marshall, ed. *All About Knights.* London: Children's Books Limited, 1981.

Ganshof, F. L. *Feudalism.* 3rd English Ed. New York: Harper Torchbooks, 1964.

Daidoji, Yuzan. *Code of the Samurai: A Modern Translation of the Bushido Shoshinsu.* Charles E. Tuttle Co., 1999.

Hicks, Michael. *Bastard Feudalism.* New York: Longman, 1995.

Hoyt, Robert S. Hoyt. *Feudal Institutions: Cause or Consequence of Decentralization.* New York: Holt, Rinehart and Winston, 1961.

John of Salisbury. "*Metalogicon* and *Policraticus*." In Cary J. Nederman and Kate Langdon Forhan, eds. *Readings in Medieval Political Theory, 1100–1400.* Indianapolis: Hackett, 1993, 26–60.

Jupp, Kenneth. "European Feudalism from its Emergence Through Its Decline," *The American Journal of Economics and Sociology.* 59:5 (December 2000).

Leinwand, Gerald. *The Pageant of World History.* Englewood Cliffs, NJ: Prentice Hall, 1990.

Magna Carta. Available at http://www.7cs.com/Magna.html.

Marie de France. "The Fable Of A Man, His Belly, And His Limbs." In Cary J. Nederman and Kate Langdon Forhan, eds. *Readings in Medieval Political Theory, 1100–1400.* Indianapolis: Hackett, 1993, 24–25.

Miller, David, ed. *The Blackwell Encyclopedia of Political Thought.* Cambridge, Blackwell, 1991.

Nederman, Cary J. and Kate Langdon Forhan, eds. *Readings in Medieval Political Theory, 1100–1400.* Indianapolis: Hackett, 1993.

Reynolds, Susan. *Fiefs and Vassals: The Medieval Evidence Reinterpreted.* Oxford: Oxford University Press, 1994.

Reuter, Timothy, Chris Wickham, and Thomas N. Bisson. "Debate: The 'Feudal Revolution.'"*Past & Present.* 155 (May 1997).

Strayer, Joseph R. *Feudalism.* Reprint edition. Malabar, FL: Robert E. Krieger, 1987.

Wilhelm, James J. and Laila Zamuelis Gross. *The Romance of Arthur.* New York: Garland Publishing, Inc., 1984.

Further Readings

Barber, Richard. *The Knight and Chivalry.* Rochester: Boydell & Brewer, 1996. This book explores the code of chivalry and the unique position of the knight in the feudal order.

Brown, R. Allen. *The Normans and the Norman Conquest.* Rochester: Boydell & Brewer, 1994. This work examines the history and impact of one of the foundational events in the feudal era, the Norman Conquest.

Cantor, Norman, ed. *The Encyclopedia of the Middle Ages.* New York: Viking Press, 1999. This resource compiles information on the people, places, and events of the Middle Ages, including the major figures and ingredients of feudalism.

Geoffrey of Monmouth, *History of the Kings of Britain.* Reprint Edition. New York: Penguin, 1981. This book provided the legend supporting both the Arthurian tradition and the code of chivalry.

Totman, Conrad. *Tokugawa Ieyasu: Shogun.* Torrance, CA: Heian International Publishing, 1988. This work investigates the most important figure in Japanese feudalism.

SEE ALSO

Capitalism, Nationalism

Imperialism

OVERVIEW

Imperialism is a term used to describe the domination of one state over a number of others. In the early twenty–first century imperialism is generally thought to be a bad idea. After World War II ended in 1945—and increasingly during the late twentieth century—most people came to view imperialist policies as both morally reprehensible and as economically unsound.

During the Cold War both superpowers, the United States and the Soviet Union, were officially opposed to imperialism and generally tried to prevent other countries from pursuing such policies. This was partly because their two ideologies, communism in the Soviet Union and democratic capitalism in the U.S., were opposed to imperialism. They also had national interests that conflicted with those of the major European imperial powers. In addition, the many newly independent countries of the Third World opposed European imperialism, which they believed had been only recently bad for them.

But imperialism has not always been so unpopular. Indeed, many countries have openly and aggressively pursued imperialist expansion. Throughout much of human history there have been writers who have extolled imperial conquest, politicians that have designed policies to enable imperial rule, and peoples who have supported imperial designs.

WHO CONTROLS GOVERNMENT? Nation–state

HOW IS GOVERNMENT PUT INTO POWER? Conquest

WHAT ROLES DO THE PEOPLE HAVE? Provide military and labor services

WHO CONTROLS PRODUCTION OF GOODS? Nation–state

WHO CONTROLS DISTRIBUTION OF GOODS? Nation–state

MAJOR FIGURES Genghis Khan; Hernán Cortés

HISTORICAL EXAMPLE Mongol Empire, 1206–1368

CHRONOLOGY

c. 10,000 B.C.: The Neolithic revolution begins

c. 330 B.C.: Alexander the Great conquers much of the Middle East, North Africa, and India

221 B.C.: The Chinese Imperial state is founded

1071: Ottoman Turks defeat the Byzantine armies at Manzikert, making Asia Minor Turkish

1207: Genghis Khan begins the Mongol conquest of China

1521: Hernán Cortés defeats the Aztecs at Tenochtitlan (Mexico City) during the conquest of New Spain

1526: The Mogul Empire is created in India

1840: Great Britain defeats China in the Opium War and will dominate the world economy for fifty years

1878: Restoration of the Japanese Meiji begins seven decades of imperial expansion

c. 1880: European nations begin the "Scramble for Africa"

1918: Defeat in World War I signals the end of the Ottoman Empire

HISTORY

Historically, there have been many forms of imperialism. Indeed, arguably, the whole history of human civilization may be written as the rise and fall of consecutive imperial political powers. These started to occur after the *Neolithic* (or farming) revolution, which led humans to settle and create political units capable of organizing political, administrative, economic, and military power on a large scale. The first instances of these political enterprises occurred where fertile arable land, water, staple food crops, and suitable climate and geography intersected with the arrival of human beings emigrating, at first from Africa and increasing their numbers substantially.

The parts of the world which allowed the formation of the first substantial states were the Middle East (particularly along the Nile and Euphrates rivers), in the river valleys of north India, and in the coastal lands and large river valleys of China. Typically, an imperial order was preceded by a system of smaller states coexisting with one another in relations that varied from amicable trade and cultural intercourse to violent conflict and war. Such multi–state systems broke down when one of the participating states was able to accumulate sufficient power to overwhelm the others and replace a society of competing and cooperating states with imperial rule. This was the manner in which, for examples, the Egyptian, Persian, Roman, Chinese, Ottoman, and Aztec empires were formed.

The ancient imperial states of Rome and China were created at almost the same time by similar processes and sustained by broadly similar methods of military force and then administrative efficiency. On the other hand, empires based on the outstanding abilities of a singular individual—Alexander the Great, who, according to legend, wept when he had no more worlds to conquer; Attila the Hun, who defeated the Roman imperial forces; the Mogul empires, which were later even more extensive—were based almost solely on military conquest, and often did not long survive their creator's death.

The more recent cases of European imperialism are interesting for two reasons. First, attempts to displace the state system within Europe by an imperial domination of one state have failed since the collapse of the Roman Empire. The resulting constant competition helped create the expansionist tendencies of the European system as a whole. Secondly, the collection of European states expanded their own system throughout the world through a number of competing yet cooperating imperial orders, thereby developing the modern global state system.

Recent European–based imperial expansion is often treated as if it were the only instance of imperial subjugation by one political entity over another. This is an extremely ahistorical perspective. Competition within and between political structures, sometimes involving territorial expansion and imperial conquest, is part of the process of human evolution. The most recent forms have often—but not always—involved the subjugation of non–Europeans by European peoples. But this is more a reflection of the distribution of power in the modern era than it is of the European peoples having a more deeply developed imperial ambition than others.

Imperial expansion is as much an expression of power relations as it is of cultural intentions.

Ancient Imperialisms

The first three areas to be brought under intensive agricultural cultivation and thereby support large settled populations with stable political entities were in the Middle East, northern India, and China. In each area, competing states soon vied for supremacy and one emerged, for some time, as the dominant imperial power.

For several thousand years in the Middle East, the Egyptian state, ruled by Pharaohs and based on the alluvial soil and annual floods of the Nile Valley, was the dominant military force. It rested on a large population, mass infantry, advanced horse–utilizing military technology, and an agricultural output well organized by a sophisticated state administration. It successfully competed with other neighboring entities, particularly the Persian Empire, which was able to build a similar edifice on the basis of the Euphrates River.

In northern India, the two great rivers, the Ganges and the Indus, also supported state systems, which were from time to time to generate dominant powers. This process is described in *The Arthashastra* by Kautilya, a fourth–century Indian political philosopher often compared to the Italian philosopher Machiavelli, whose learned works were designed to assist a ruler in his dealings with rivals, his subjects, and other states. This system was to be later subjugated by the Moguls.

In east Asia, Chinese civilization also supported a period known in Chinese history as that of the Warring States. This came to an end in the third century B.C., when these diverse but culturally similar states were unified by Ch'in to create the Chinese imperial state.

In the Mediterranean world, Greek civilization also threw up a city–state system 2,500 years ago. Like contemporary China and India, and later Europe and Central America, the Greek world comprised a number of discrete sovereign authorities welded together by a common civilization. Wars between the Greek states were common. Indeed, the first study of international relations deals with one of the longest of the generalized wars between them. Thucydides' *History of The Peloponnesian Wars*, which describes a state system not unlike the modern one, marked by trade, diplomacy, competing national ambitions, internal disputes over power and policy, and war. These states coexisted in this form until they were overwhelmed by one of their number, when Alexander the Great of Macedon united them all by conquest in the fourth century B.C. He then went on to create, also by conquest, an empire which stretched from Greece to Egypt to India.

Alexander made architectural and civic improvements in vanquished cities, particularly those in or near Greece—probably because he felt the communities had lost too many Greek characteristics due to centuries of Persian rule. Yet he respected the customs and religion of all conquered territories, although this

was likely done more for political reasons than benevolence on his part. As Theodore Ayrault Dodge wrote in *Alexander*: "He thus made firm his hold on the territory he conquered, not only by the best measures for military occupation, but by fostering political good–will in the cities."

The Empire of Alexander the Great, however, had little firmer basis than his own ambition and military genius, and disintegrated shortly after his death into a few separate regimes. The region of the eastern Mediterranean then reverted to its more common condition of a number of competing state entities. This ended with the imposition of Roman imperial power during the centuries before the birth of Christ.

The Roman Empire

The Roman Empire was based on the Mediterranean coastal region with the water transport system at its core. It was created by conquests, which elevated Rome from one city–state among many, to the dominant imperial power. As Roman arms extended its power, so its techniques and material basis expanded. Initially, Roman power depended on a powerful infantry, but this was augmented by other military arts learned in the long process of conquering the Mediterranean seaboard from the Atlantic to the Persian Empire. The Romans were governed by an aristocratic, representative, and republican form of government. Their imperial expansion and then rule did not depend on the whims of one or indeed a generation of military conquerors. Only after the empire was stabilized did the Emperor replace the Senate.

The Mediterranean enabled Roman galleys to transport military power, food, and other supplies along internal lines of communication. Vines, olives, fish, pastoral animals, and wheat provided the staple foods. The Romans then added a system of roads, water supplies, and cities to this imperial economy. Roman legions could then both protect the frontier against barbarians and move quickly along internal lines of transportation to deal with rebellions. They used a very advanced and detailed administration based on a common law for all citizens of the empire, although slaves may have comprised one–half the population of the Italian peninsula at the peak of the empire. Although Rome was the principal beneficiary of this system, local *oligarchies* (government by a small faction of persons or families) were brought sufficiently within its orbit to provide it with the support base to maintain the empire for hundreds of years.

This empire was based initially on military conquest that extended it from England, through Germany, the Balkans, the Levant (countries on the east-

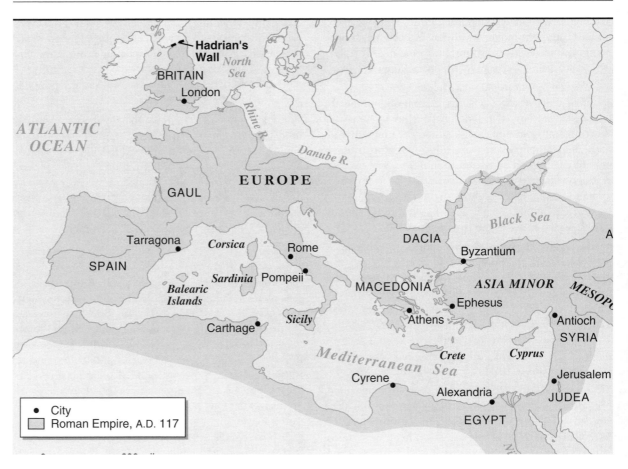

Map of the Roman Empire, circa 117 A.D. (Gale)

ern shores of the Mediterranean Sea), and Egypt—for long its granary—to the North African Atlantic seaboard and the rest of North Africa. Its economy was based on slavery, a labor force that was, during the early empire, supplemented by continuous conquest and enslavement of the defeated peoples. In its later and declining years, it was sustained by extensive use of increasingly murderous games, which may have consumed a quarter of imperial economic output by the third century, in order to keep the urban mobs docile politically by providing "bread and circuses."

The Western Roman Empire lasted for eight hundred years, and then was overrun by the barbarian tribes from the Eurasian steppes. The Eastern Empire, centered on Constantinople (now Istanbul, Turkey), lasted longer in various forms, being progressively eroded until 1453 when it was also overrun by a barbarian tribe, the Ottoman Turks.

Gibbon's famous argument says that the Roman Empire fell because the adoption of Christianity sapped the early ferocity of the Romans and they lost the abil-

ity to rule fairly but, more importantly, harshly when the moment required. But, in addition, the Roman technical and organizational military advantages were sapped by years of revealing them to their opponents; the sources of slave power eroded with the end of conquests and were difficult to replace; and the skills of the Romans' opponents improved. As an imperial system, the Romans also probably lacked the incentive and initiatives to implement technological change in a manner that might have enabled their infantry to withstand the continual erosion of their capacity to master the cavalry of the horsemen of the steppes. In addition, the Empire was beset with internal divisions that periodically sparked civil wars. During its decline this produced the two empires, with Byzantine Constantinople surviving into the fifteenth century.

Chinese Empires

The Chinese imperial state, formed during the Han Dynasty (206 B.C.–220 A.D.), lasted to the present era. China culture dates back to between 2,500 and 2,000 B.C. in what is now central China. Centuries of migration and development brought about a distinctive system of writing, philosophy, and political organization recognizable as Chinese civilization.

After the Warring States Period (475–221 B.C.) much of what became modern China was unified. In that year, the state of Ch'in, the most powerful of the Warring States, subjugated its rivals. The king of Ch'in consolidated his power, took the title of Emperor, and imposed Ch'in's centralized, non–hereditary bureaucratic system on his new empire.

The organizational and cultural continuity of the Middle Kingdom was then accompanied by cycles of rise and decline of imperial dynasties. Tyrannical dynasties were often followed by long periods of stability. Confucian thought concentrated on each person's place in society and harmony, rather than the rights of the individual: the scholar–officials had high social status and provided theories for maintaining social harmony, while the peasantry provided the food.

The alien peoples on the frontiers of Chinese civilization twice conquered China and established new dynasties, only to be absorbed into the system of culture and governance. In the thirteenth century, the Mongols from the northern steppes were the first alien people to conquer all of China. It came under alien rule for the second time in the seventeenth century, when Manchu conquerors came again from the north.

But for centuries, the only foreigners that Chinese rulers saw came from the less–developed societies along their borders. The Chinese believed they were the self–sufficient center of the universe, surrounded by inferior barbarian peoples. This view was not disturbed until the nineteenth century and China's confrontation with the West. China then assumed its relations with Europe would be conducted according to the tributary system that had evolved between the Emperor and the lesser states on China's borders, including Vietnam, Korea, and Thailand.

The imperial expansion of the Chinese state was undertaken by military expeditions pushing out the frontiers in the north and south. To defend against barbarians, the fortified walls built by the various warring states were connected to make the Great Wall. A number of public works projects were also undertaken to consolidate and strengthen imperial rule, requiring enormous levies of manpower, resources, and repressive measures. The imperial system initiated during the Ch'in dynasty set a pattern that was developed over the next two millennia.

Han Dynasty   During the Han Dynasty (206 B.C. to 220 A.D.) a civil service examination system was ini-

tiated and paper developed. The Han Dynasty also developed its military powers and expanded the empire westward as far as the Tarim Basin in modern Xinjiang, securing caravan traffic across the "silk route" to the Roman Empire. Chinese armies also invaded and annexed parts of Vietnam and Korea in the second century B.C. The Han court developed the "tributary system," under which non–Chinese states were allowed semi–autonomy in exchange for symbolic acceptance of Han overlordship. But in 220, the Han imperial dynasty collapsed into nearly four centuries of rule by warlords, although technological advances continued, including gunpowder and advances in medicine, astronomy, and cartography.

Ming Dynasty   The Ming Dynasty (1368–1644) was founded by a Chinese peasant and peaked during the first quarter of the fifteenth century. Chinese armies reconquered Annam and kept back the Mongols. A huge Chinese fleet sailed as far as the coast of Africa and many Asian nations sent tribute to the Chinese emperor. These Ming maritime expeditions stopped suddenly with the last voyage of the grand fleet in 1433. The great expense of large–scale maritime expeditions was abandoned for northern defenses against the Mongols. Conservative officials also believed naval expansion and commercial ventures were alien to Chinese ideas of government. The powerful Confucian bureaucracy wanted an agrarian–based society.

During the Ming Dynasty, with a population of 100 million and a prospering economy, arts, and political system, the Chinese believed that they had achieved the most complete civilization and that nothing foreign was needed. The Chinese entered a period described by Mark Elvin in *The Pattern of the Chinese Past* as high–level equilibrium, or stagnation.

Qing Dynasty   Nonetheless, in 1644, the Manchus took Beijing and established the last imperial dynasty, the Qing (1644–1911). Although the Manchus were not Han Chinese, they assimilated a great deal of Chinese culture during the conquest and retained many Ming institutions, including the civil service system. Confucian philosophy, emphasizing the obedience of subject to ruler, was enforced as the state ideology. The Manchus conquered Outer Mongolia and Central Asia to the Pamir Mountains, and established a protectorate over Tibet. Under Manchu rule the Chinese empire achieved its largest territorial extent and received tribute from many other states.

New threats to the integrity of the Chinese Empire then came by sea from the south as Europeans began arriving in the sixteenth century. The success of the Qing Dynasty in maintaining the old order proved to be a liability when the empire was confronted with growing challenges from seafaring Western powers. Centuries of peace and self–satisfaction had hardened the attitudes of the ruling elite and its power.

China proved unable to meet the new challenges, and the Qing Dynasty collapsed and ended the two–thousand–year–old system of dynastic imperial rule. It was already experiencing economic difficulties, as over 300 million Chinese had no industry or trade to absorb the labor supply. Scarcity of land led to widespread rural discontent and a breakdown in law and order, and revolts erupted in the early nineteenth century. Secret societies gained ground, combining anti–Manchu subversion with banditry. The European imperial powers pressed onto this weakened state.

Collapse of China's empire   First, in 1557, the Portuguese established a foothold at Macao from which they monopolized foreign trade at Canton. Soon after the Spanish arrived, followed by the British and the French. Trade between China and the West was carried on in the guise of tribute: foreigners were obliged to follow the elaborate, centuries–old ritual imposed on envoys from China's tributary states as the imperial court expected that the Europeans would be treated as cultural and political tributaries.

The first exception was Russia, which began seizing Chinese territory. The Treaty of Nerchinsk in 1689 with Russia established a border between Siberia and Manchuria (northeast China) along the Amur River. It was China's first bilateral agreement with a European power. In 1727, the Treaty of Kiakhta defined the remainder of the eastern Sino–Russian border. But other Western efforts to expand trade on equal terms were rebuffed, the official Chinese assumption being that the empire was not in need of foreign products. Despite this attitude, trade flourished, even though after 1760 all foreign trade was confined to Canton.

Then, in the 1840 Opium War, China was humiliated militarily by superior British weaponry and technology and faced territorial dismemberment. In 1911 the dynastic system of imperial China collapsed into civil war and was eventually replaced by communism in 1949. The communist historians then wrote their own history of China, built on a dogmatic Marxist model of progression from primitive communism to slavery, feudalism, capitalism, and finally, socialism. It conveniently ignored Chinese imperialism.

THEORY IN DEPTH

Imperialism is a practice that is designed to benefit the imperial power, and not those who are subjugated by it. It is most rapacious when the imperial power is a proponent of naked force and simple looting, as with Genghis Khan, and most benign when pursuing advantageous commercial exchange, like the U.S. Nonetheless, there may be collateral benefits to the subjugated power because more advanced techniques of production and even cultural practices are introduced to the weaker and subjugated society. This conception has been criticized by post–colonial theories, who argue that all societies are morally equal and none benefit from being conquered.

The pursuit of imperialism usually involves an imperial or metropolitan government of a substantial state that is well organized and has a coherent identity. This state is often distinguished by its military power which may arise from its having a large population or territory, being well organized for war, or having developed some military technology which gives it the capacity to win wars and extend its rule over other states. The people who rule this state then will need the ambition to use that power to extend their rule. Historically, most countries that acquire considerable power usually develop the ambition to use it. This is not always the case, however, and imperial China did not expand in the late–fifteenth century although it clearly had the naval power to do so. The state then uses its power to conquer other societies. Generally, it will have to pursue a general systemic policy of aggression and subjugation in order to qualify for the description "imperialist." A state which conquers one or two neighboring territories would usually be described as a merely regionally aggressive state. It then rules the conquered territory to its advantage by deploying skills other than sheer force to maintain its domination. This involves the establishment of administrative, trading, financial, and ideological systems which maintain imperial rule and ensures that it benefits the imperial country— since a loss–making colony is not worth maintaining. The conquering state often, and more commonly at least in the modern era, uses an ideology to disguise and justify its behavior. Occasionally this ideology—such as Islam or communism—may indeed be the driving force of the imperial impulse, but this situation rarely lasts long if the conquests are only maintained at a cost and for ideological gratification. In any case, such unprofitable imperial adventures run the risk of quickly generating imperial overstretch and subsequent contraction. Most imperial states are then eventually defeated by internal decay, resistance within the imperial domains, an inability to retain conquests earlier achieved, or by other imperial powers defeating them in the contest for resources.

Whether an imperial system survived its initial creation depended on the capacity of the ascendant imperial power to consolidate and maintain its rule against both internal revolt and external attack. The skills required for this task were quite different from the capacity to impose an imperial order in the first place. The administrator with bureaucratic procedures and records needed to replace the soldier.

The Imperialist System

The imperialist impulse and process generates several types of state, which may be recognized in the historical accounts so far given.

Many historians feel that at the core of the imperial project is an imperial power, run by people with ambition, determination, and a murderous taste for expansion. It also, importantly, needs the power to translate the ambition into practice. The experience generates an arrogant culture, which typically despises others and to some degree glorifies the violence, bloodshed, and mayhem which violent conquest requires. Individuals of ferocious character usually command.

The recipient of these ambitions is the colonial society, subjugated by force of arms and quiescent either before, during, or after the imposition of alien rule. Since its own national culture becomes subordinate it then, typically, in some measure becomes self–deprecating and values the culture of the imperial power, often more than its own. It is also usually less well developed, although this may be restricted to solely the military arts. And the wealth generated by the colony must not only be siphoned off to the imperial power, but that which remains organized and distributed by it.

Empires also create settler states, either the better to consolidate their rule and the exploitation that accompanies it, or for reasons of strategy in which the settler communities can be better relied on than those who are merely conquered. The Romans often settled their frontier provinces with retired soldiers; the Norman nobility was awarded portions of the conquered English realm; the Spanish settled South America, and the British North America and Australasia. The fate of these settler states is often problematic when the empire that aided them recedes. European–dominated states remain secure in the Americas; yet Russians remain stranded in the former republics of the Soviet state; while the settler–dominated state apparatuses in Southern Africa have yielded to indigenous political power.

Countries Based on the Imperialist System

The forms of the imperial state are almost too diverse to accept categorization; the impulse to empire lies deep in human nature. The ancient world offers many examples of talented megalomaniacs successfully pursuing imperial conquests—Alexander the Great or Genghis Kahn—only for these to be abandoned after the leader's death.

It also offers, in Rome, a long–surviving imperial system of rule based on sophisticated military organization, technology, order, and imperial law, but still dependent on suppression and slavery. Similarly, China developed through an integration of a civilization with an empire from about the second century B.C. that was to last until 1911, and arguably to the present day. Islam, as a religious empire, was based on conquest and then conversion to a religion and has also survived. The Ottomans took over the Levant and became dominant and Islamic, but still an empire based on foreign control, and eventually collapsed. The Aztecs, on the other hand, were very primitive in their system of subjugation and sacrifices and quickly collapsed, as did the Zulus when confronted by superior external power.

The modern world offers similar diversity. The Hapsburg Empire was founded in dynastic power yet expanded into a global system of bullion imperialism and military districts justified by Catholic doctrine. The British Empire was always commercial, but augmented by settlers, first in Wales, Scotland, and Ireland, and then in the far flung territories outside Europe. The Napoleonic Empire was one that started with a revolutionary imperialism that even appealed to the supreme intellect of Beethoven before descending into a more transparent French dictatorship. German imperialism and military conquest in both World War I and World War II was fueled by nationalist ambition to acquire resources in Eastern Europe. Japanese expansion and the creation of the Great East Asian Co–prosperity Sphere, with Japan and its Emperor at the head, was also clearly self–interested. Soviet imperialism, like Islamic imperialism, was inexplicable without reference to ideology and strategy. U.S. imperial ambitions have always been tied to free trade and commerce, foundations laid by the British in the Thirteen Colonies.

Imperialist states, then, have been governed by: Egyptian Pharaohs, noble Greeks, famous Roman authors, Chinese emperors, pagan cavalry, Islamic zealots, Turkish warlords, African chiefs, Amerindian princes, Spanish Catholic grandees, English Queens, Russian empresses, French revolutionaries, German Kaisers, American Republicans, and Russian communists. Few systems of rule fail to answer the imperial call if the opportunity arises.

Drawing of Genghis Khan.

THEORY IN ACTION

In the pre–modern world the pursuit of empire was a common aspiration. States were formed, related with one another and competed for imperial dominion. The size of the empires these states could create were dependent on: its initial military capabilities; the size of the imperial economy; the administrative structures they could devise and sustain; and continuing military power they could effectively deploy against hostile forces of both rebellion and invasion at point of threat. They usually required ambitious, ferocious and determined leadership. The modern era was to expand these capabilities, and so the size of the empires they supported.

The Mongol Empires

Genghis Khan (1162–1227) expressed his motives: "The greatest happiness is to vanquish your enemies, to chase them before you, to rob them of their wealth, to see those dear to them bathed in tears, to clasp to your bosom their wives and daughters."

Genghis was born Temujin in 1162 on the great Eurasian heartland steppes. In 1187 the Mongols made him their great leader and gave him the name Genghis Khan (universal ruler). But the Mongol shepherds and horse people were not then united into one political entity. Genghis soon defeated rival Mongol clans, and in 1206 he was declared Khan of Khans and king of "all people who lived in felt tents."

Expansion Genghis then concentrated his forces against other empires in order to expand his own. In 1207 he began the conquest of modern China, then divided into three separate empires: the Qin; Tangut to the north; and the Sung Empire in the south. The Mongols subdued the Tanguts in 1209 and then campaigned against the Qin Empire in 1211. Genghis continued his army's advance until 1215, when modern Beijing was conquered and most of the Qin Empire came under his control. In 1218 Genghis turned on the Kwarezm Empire—which encompassed modern Afghanistan, Iran, and Turkestan—and led a force of 90,000 men from the north and sent a general with 30,000 men to attack from the east. Genghis' army was victorious and a full–scale invasion of the Kwarezm Empire took place. The entire area was added to the Mongol Empire.

Genghis started his conquests with the advantage of a mass, highly skilled, extremely mobile cavalry force, which, although often outnumbered, overcame adverse numbers by maneuverability and ferocity. As with other imperialists, each victory taught Genghis new methods of warfare, which were used to make his forces stronger. With the Kwarezm Empire destroyed, an army of 20,000 was sent to Russia to seize more territory. In 1223, those Mongol warriors beat a Russian army of 80,000 and began the conquest of the Russian principalities. The Mongols fought their way through Russia and into Europe and destroyed entire cities in Hungary, Poland, and Russia.

These triumphs were arrested by the death of Genghis Khan, who died from internal injuries when he fell from his horse during a hunt in 1227. This sent the advancing armies back to create a new leader. Genghis had united the Mongols and created the largest empire ever built in the life of one man. "With Heaven's aid I have conquered for you a huge empire," Genghis told his sons before he died. "But my life was too short to achieve the conquest of the world. That is left for you."

The Empire was divided between Genghis' three sons: the Golden Horde in west Asia, including Russia; the Middle East Khanate; and the main area of the East Asia Khanate, including the Mongol homeland. Despite this, the Mongol Empire was still controlled by one man, Ogadai (1185–1241), who was officially elected Khan in 1229. Ogadai was a ruthless barbarian who set about expanding the Great Mongol Empire.

BIOGRAPHY:
Genghis Khan

According to legend, Genghis Khan came into the world in 1162 grasping a lump of clotted blood, a favorable omen for a future warrior. He was named Temujin by his father Yesugei, who was chieftan of a sizeable camp of various clans. While growing up, Temujin used his greatest assets—personal charisma and shrewdness—to climb the ranks of the various Mongol clans. He won a power struggle against a former ally and was proclaimed Genghis Khan (universal ruler) in 1187.

After becoming supreme ruler of the Mongols, Genghis Khan restructured the Mongolian tribes into a primarily military organization. The population was divided into military units of tens, hundreds, and thousands, with households and cattle to supply them.

This military reorganization of the now–unified Mongol state allowed Genghis Khan to conquer first neighboring states and then more distant empires. When outnumbered, the Mongols built man–sized puppets and lit hundreds of extra campfires on the steppes to confuse their enemy. Genghis took advantage of the enemy's size by forcing them to fight with their backs to a mountain; from that position, they had little choice but to retreat up the mountain's sides as the Khan's troops slaughtered them mercilessly. Another favorite trick of the Mongol forces was to advance upon their foe in "terrifying silence" and then burst into earsplitting shrieks as they charged. By 1227, Genghis had annexed the territory from western Russia to China.

The conquered populations were ruthlessly suppressed and then exploited. Many resisting cities were burned and destroyed; conquered people were subjected to heavy taxation and forced labor; and even if they surrendered, they had to pay heavy tribute. For most peoples, Genghis Kahn was a savage tyrant.

Genghis died of complications from falling off a horse in August of 1227. He was buried in northeast Mongolia, and it is said that forty beautiful maidens and forty horses were slaughtered at his grave. His legacy of brutal conquest remained alive. Under his son Ogodei, Khan of Khans, the Mongols brought to submission southeast Asia, Russia, and Eastern Europe, and reached within thirty miles of Vienna. Only the death of Ogodei in 1241 turned back the horde, which probably would have crushed Western Europe as easily as it had the rest of the world, and vastly altered the course of history.

Genghis Khan's cruelty is the stuff of legend, but the carnage he left in his wake was often a simple matter of expediency; it was easier to slaughter a city than to post valuable troops in order to keep it. And today, in the country of Mongolia, Genghis Khan is a legendary hero who is even credited with introducing democratic reforms. His vast empire is said to have allowed trade to flourish between different countries, encouraging continued trade along the famous Silk Road and forming additional trade routes throughout the vast Eurasian continent. It also linked Western and Eastern cultures, allowing them to exchange ideas and technology.

This view of Genghis Kahn is described in Paula Sabloff's book *Modern Mongolia: Reclaiming Genghis Khan*. In the same way, some Marxists extol that other great barbarian warrior, Attila the Hun, for having humbled the slave–owning empire of Rome. A savage conqueror can, thus, be readily made into a national hero. However, many modern historians feel that Genghis was probably no worse than any other conqueror of medieval times—he simply became the most infamous because he accomplished the most.

Genghis left orders to increase the size of the Mongol Empire, in particular by conquering China. It only took five years for the Mongol armies to complete this and the Chinese emperor was finally killed in 1234. The following year, the Mongols sent troops both east and west to capture the Asian lands lost after Genghis' death, to reoccupy the Korean peninsula, and to advance into Europe. One hundred and fifty

thousand Mongol troops attacked Europe in 1236 and captured many new territories. That same year, Korea was reoccupied and a rebellion there was crushed.

After the Mongol conquest of China there opened a vast international trade, and along the routes people exchanged ideas. A wealth of information flowed along with the goods. The Chinese people were not forced to adopt Mongol customs or religion, but there

Drawing of Kublai Khan. (*The Library of Congress*)

certainly were restrictions. People were not allowed to gather in public or own weapons of any kind. The Khans were probably weary of the sheer numbers of the Chinese. The conquered peoples did not like the occupation and its restrictions, but probably found ways to adjust and go on living as normal a life as possible. Many Chinese even served as low–ranking officials in the Mongol government.

The Mongol army conquered lands well into Europe between 1236 and 1242. The troops entered Russia and in 1237 attacked the city of Riazan, which became the first of many to fall to the Mongols. Riazan was offered the standard Mongols terms: surrender, and hand over one tenth of everything, including people, and pay constant tribute. Only then would the Mongols spare the city. The city refused and it was destroyed. Throughout 1237 and 1238 several Russian principalities were similarly conquered. One of the last cities in Russia to be conquered was Kiev, when it too fell to the Mongol catapults and poisoned arrows in 1240. The city was burned to ashes and most of the population slaughtered. The Mongol armies then moved on and between 1240 and 1241 seized many cities in Poland and Hungary, including the cities of Buda and Pest, which were all but destroyed. (These two cities would unite to become Budapest in 1872.) The Mongols then continued towards Vienna. During these battles, well over 220,000 Pol-

ish, Hungarian, and other soldiers were killed by the Mongols.

Breakdown of the Mongol empire In early 1242 the Mongols reached the outskirts of Vienna. But Ogadai had died a month earlier, and the Mongols retreated to their Russian territory to choose a new Khan. No Mongol invasion of Europe was to take place again, although the Mongols remained in control of Russia for the next 250 years.

In 1259 two men were declared Khan. The internal conflict that followed was a major turning point of the Mongol Empire. It was never united again after 1260. Kublai was proclaimed the only Khan in 1264, and moved the Mongol capital from central Mongolia to Beijing. He then spent most of his life in China, where he enjoyed the culture and felt more at home. There was a loss in communication and messages took longer to travel across the empire. As a consequence, many Mongols could not relate to China, and the coherence of the empire was lost. This left much of the empire to local self–rule and the empire Genghis Khan had created began to crumble.

Despite the internal breaking up of the Mongol Empire, Kublai continued to expand its territory, and in 1267 started to bring all of modern China within the Mongol Empire. This gave the Chinese a national territory that survives to this day. In 1274, Kublai decided to expand his empire beyond China and attacked the islands of Japan. But typhoon turned these campaigns into dismal failures.

Kublai died in 1294, leaving the legacy of a unified China. But by 1335 the Mongols were forced out of the Middle East, and revolution and attacks left much of the empire in pieces. Finally, in 1368 the Yuan Dynasty, started by Kublai in China, was overthrown by the Chinese and replaced with the Ming Dynasty, who drove out all remaining Mongol armies. The Mongol Empire had lasted from 1206, when Genghis was proclaimed Khan of Khans, until 1368. Thus, one of the largest empires ever created was destroyed in 162 years.

The impact of these Mongol empires was often arrested by the deaths of individual leaders and only sustained where the conquering military forces were able to assume ruling–class status within existing state structures—as occurred with the Manchu Dynasty in China. Generally their motivation was the ambition of ferocious leaders and loot for their followers.

The Turkish Ottoman Empire

The Turks emerged in the mid–sixth century as a nomad empire in the heart of Asia in what is now

Turkestan. The Turks then scattered over a vast area of the Russian steppes, speaking related dialects. From the ninth century, Turks began to enter the Arab Caliphate as slaves or adventurers serving as soldiers and so infiltrated the world of Islam. The Caliph Mu'-tasim (833–842) was the first Muslim ruler to surround himself with a Turkish guard. Turks rose to high rank—commanding armies, governing provinces, and sometimes ruling as independent princes. The disintegration of the Abbasid Empire and then the Samanid collapse at the end of the tenth century opened the Persian and Arab territories to Turkish nomad tribes.

Growth of the empire

In 956 the Seljuk Turks embraced Islam and soon after so did many other Western Turks. In the late–eleventh century the Seljuks entered West Asia and prolonged the life of the moribund caliphate for another two hundred years, took Asia Minor away from Christendom, and opened the path to the later Ottoman invasion of the Levant and Europe.

In 962 one of the Turkish officers, Alp–tagin, seized the town and fortress of Ghazna in what is now Afghanistan. The Kara–Khanids, another Turkish people, crossed the Jaxartes River and captured the city of Bukhara in western Asia in 999. Turks also made expeditions into India, then a mosaic of principalities with no strong state capable of resisting invaders. They looted Hindu shrines and destroyed idolatry in the name of Allah and his Prophet.

The Turks then drove towards the Byzantine frontiers and produced a social crisis in the Persian and Arab lands. The nomadic Turks raided estates, destroyed crops, robbed merchant caravans, and fought other nomads—such as Kurds and Bedouin Arabs—for the possession of wells and grazing lands. They began raiding Byzantine territory. Turkish armies pushed into the valleys of Armenia and Georgia, and into Anatolia. An invasion of Egypt was only abandoned at the news of an impending Byzantine counterstroke.

The Roman Emperor, Romanus Diogenes, tried to clear the Turks out of his dominions, but the Turks met him at Manzikert (in modern eastern Turkey) in 1071 and inflicted a catastrophic Byzantine defeat, making Asia Minor Turkish. This struck a fatal blow at Christian and imperial power in Anatolia. With the Byzantine army defeated, the Turks spread over the central plateau, first in pastoral settlements, then taking possession of towns and fortresses. The Byzantine Empire faced total ruin.

In 1453, the Turks conquered the Byzantine capital of Constantinople. Under Mehmed the Conqueror (1432–1481), the Ottomans rebuilt the devastated city. The Golden Age of the Ottoman Empire, 1481–1566, shortly ensued, under three sultans: Bayezid II (reigned 1481–1512), Selim I (reigned 1512–1520), and Suleiman I the Magnificent (reigned 1520–1566). Bayezid extended the empire in Europe, added outposts along the Black Sea, put down revolts in Asia Minor, and turned the Ottoman fleet into a major Mediterranean naval power. Selim first eliminated all competition by having his brothers, their sons, and all but one of his own sons killed. During his short reign the Ottomans moved into Syria, Mesopotamia (Iraq), Arabia, and Egypt. At Mecca, the chief shrine of Islam, he took the title of caliph, ruler of all Muslims. The growth of the empire was for some time an impediment to European trade, and led European states to seek routes *around* Africa to China and India, an inconvenience that helped lead to the discovery of the New World.

The empire in its prime

Sultan Suleiman the Magnificent brought the Ottoman Empire to its zenith and from 1520 until 1566 ruled the most powerful state in the world. He more than doubled Ottoman territory, expanding it throughout the Balkans and Hungary to the gates of Vienna, captured Belgrade (1521) and Rhodes (1522), broke the military power of Hungary, and in 1529 lay unsuccessful siege to Vienna. He also waged three campaigns against Persia. Algiers fell to his navy in 1529 and Tripoli (now Libya) in 1551. In 1570, his successor, Selim the Sot, invaded Cyprus, then under Venetian jurisdiction. The Ottomans sacked the capital, Nicosia, and massacred 30,000 of its Greek inhabitants.

One reason the Ottoman Empire was able to survive as long as it did was the way the conquerors treated the ordinary people of their ever&dash∈tending empire. This is perhaps best illustrated in the Balkans. The Turks often acted with extreme prejudice toward military or government officials, but the people were free to practice their own religion, and mixed marriages were permitted, if not openly encouraged. Nonetheless, the burden of financing the empire often fell upon the conquered peoples in the form of taxation.

Decline of the empire

The decline of the Ottoman Empire began in 1566. As Suleiman grew tired, his *viziers*, or prime ministers, took more authority. After his death the army gained control of the sultanate. This growing internal weakness was confronted by growing powers in the west. The nation–states of Europe emerged from the Middle Ages under strong monarchies and built armies and navies which were powerful enough to attack the decaying Ottoman Empire.

In 1571 the combined fleets of Venice, Spain, and the Papal States of Italy defeated the Turks at the great naval Battle of Lepanto, off the coast of Greece. Although the empire rebuilt its navy, the central government became weaker and large parts of the empire began to act independently with nominal loyalty to the sultan. The army was still strong enough, however, to prevent provincial rebels from asserting complete control. Indeed, new campaigns were undertaken, the Caucasus and Azerbaijan seized, and the empire expanded to the peak of its territorial extent.

Reforms undertaken by seventeenth–century sultans did little to prevent decay. Beginning in 1683 with the attack on Vienna, repulsed in 1688 by Eugene of Savoy, the Ottomans were at war with European enemies for forty–one years. In this, the empire lost much of its Balkan territory and possessions on the shores of the Black Sea. In addition, the Austrians and Russians began to intervene on behalf of the sultan's Christian subjects.

The weakness of the central government and its military decline led to increasing loss of control over the provinces. Local rulers carved out regions in which they ruled directly, regardless sultan in Istanbul. Local populations often preferred their rule to the corrupt administration of the distant capital. The notables formed their own armies and collected their own taxes, sending only nominal contributions to the imperial treasury.

Under Mahmud II (1785–1839) the empire further declined, despite reforms in the army, government, and education. Greece won independence in 1829. Control of North Africa passed to local notables and in Egypt Muhammad Ali (1769–1849) set the foundation of an independent kingdom. In 1853, Tsar Nicholas I (1796–1855) of Russia commented on the Ottoman Empire: "We have on our hands a sick man, a very sick man."

The Ottomans then developed strong ties with Germany, and fought on the Germans' side in World War I. Russia hoped to use the war to gain access to the Mediterranean and perhaps capture Constantinople, an aim frustrated by the Russian Revolution of 1917 and its withdrawal from the war. Nonetheless, the Ottoman Empire was defeated. The punitive post–war settlement outraged the Turkish nationalists. In 1922 the last sultan, Mehmed VI (1861–1926), fled after the sultanate was abolished. A new republican government emerged at Ankara, capital of the new Turkish non–imperial nation–state.

The Indian Mogul Empire

Indus Valley civilization flourished in northern India from 2600 B.C. to 2000 B.C. The Aryans who invaded India in 1500 B.C. from the northwest found an already advanced civilization. They introduced Sanskrit and the Vedic religion, a forerunner of Hinduism, to the area. Buddhism was founded in the 6th century B.C. and spread throughout northern India, most notably by the great king Asoka (269–232 B.C.), who also unified most of the Indian subcontinent for the first time. But thereafter India was divided into warring states.

In the sixteenth century, Muslim invaders conquered these states and founded the great Mogul empire, centered on Delhi, which lasted until 1857. Babar (1482–1530), a Turkish–Mongol prince from Afghanistan and the founder of the Mogul Empire, invaded India in 1526. His grandson, Akbar the Great (1542–1605), strengthened and consolidated this empire. He was the greatest of the Mogul emperors and under his 49–year reign, conquered all of northern India and Afghanistan, and extended his rule far south. The long reign of his great–grandson, Aurangzeb (1618–1707), represented both the greatest extent of the Mogul empire.

The Moguls were a Muslim elite who ruled over a Hindu majority. Akbar maintained his rule by Mogul military might and religious tolerance. For employment in government positions, talent and ambition took precedence over ethnicity and religious faith. Akbar also took a great interest in the arts, particularly architecture. But after Akbar's death—he may have been poisoned by Muslim government officials who were suspicious of his religious tolerance—the empire began to decline. This decline continued under Aurangzeb (1618–1707), who became emperor in 1658. Mogul control in south India came under increased pressure with revolts by the Hindu Maratha princes. To worsen matters, Aurangzeb lacked Akbar's religious tolerance, imposed special taxes on Hindus, destroyed their temples, and forced them to convert to Islam. Soon after Aurangzeb's death, the empire began to break up, enabling the British to step in.

The new emperor, Bahadur Shah I (reigned from 1707 to 1712), was unable to prevent Mogul decline and his efforts to collect taxes and to impose greater control over the Rajput states of Amber and Jodhpur were unsuccessful. His policies toward the Hindu Marathas were also a half–hearted mixture of conciliation and suppression: they were never defeated and resistance to Mogul rule persisted in the south. The provinces became increasing independent with the decline of Mogul central authority in the period between 1707 and 1761. This resurgence of regional identity accentuated both political and economic decentralization as Mogul military powers ebbed. The provinces, particularly Bengal, Bihar, and Avadh in northern India, became virtual independent kingdoms recognizing the Mogul Emperor in name only.

These provinces laid the foundations for the princely states under the British Raj. These princes relied on the support from their relatives, from the lesser nobility, and from the peasants. Their rule was very personalized, with followers swearing allegiance to the ruler alone and not to the state. As such, with the death of a prince, allegiances shifted and loyalty divided, making cooperation impossible. The princes were thus never strong enough to dominate any sizeable territories and the Mogul Empire shrank, although it lasted until 1858 in the face of growing European, particularly British, encroachments.

Vasco da Gama, the Portuguese explorer, first visited India in 1498, and for the next century the Portuguese had a virtual monopoly on European trade with the subcontinent. The English East India Company set up its first factory at Surat in western India in 1612 and expanded its influence by fighting the Indian rulers and the French, Dutch, and Portuguese traders simultaneously. Bombay was taken from the Portuguese and became the seat of English rule in 1687. The defeat of the French and Mogul armies by Lord Clive in 1757 laid the foundation of the British Empire in India. The East India Company continued to suppress native uprisings and extend British rule until 1858, when India was formally transferred to the British Crown following the Indian Mutiny in 1857–1858. British rule was enabled by the fall of the Mogul Empire and the subsequent division of India.

By the sixteenth century in Eurasia, the balance between the nomadic cavalry and the agrarian peoples had shifted irrevocably to the latter. They had a continuing advantage in numbers, supplemented by an increasingly well–organized infantry and further supplemented by firepower, artillery, fortifications, and better means of transport and mobility. These characteristics were to be consolidated by the peoples of Western Europe and, augmented by maritime technology, produce some of the mightiest and far–reaching imperial structures thus far devised. As they ventured outside Europe they encountered other imperial structures already constructed far from the Eurasian heartland.

The Aztecs

The Aztecs dominated northern Mexico in the early sixteenth century, at the time of the Spanish conquest led by Hernán Cortés (1485–1587). They originated from north Mexico as a small, nomadic, tribal people living on the margins of civilized Mesoamerica. In the twelfth and thirteenth centuries they settled in the central basin of Mexico, where small city–states fought one another in shifting alliances. The Aztecs consolidated on small islands in Lake Texcoco around Tenochtitlan (now Mexico City).

During the fifteenth century the Aztecs created an empire that was larger than any in the Americas except that of the Incas in Peru. It had a highly specialized and stratified society with an imperial administration and a trading network, as well as a tribute system, a sophisticated agricultural economy, and a developed, primitive religion. The annual round of rites and ceremonies in the cities involved human sacrifice. It was a flourishing, savage imperial system.

Aztecs had professional military officers but no professional army. Every boy was trained to fight and a vital part of everyday life for the Aztecs was warfare. A boy became a man by capturing his first prisoner. The Aztecs' courage and strength helped them build their empire and establish themselves as the fiercest of all the tribes in the Valley of Mexico. War was partly a ritual: a site was chosen and armies met in a battle that was usually short and ended with the surrender of the weaker side and the taking of prisoners.

The objective was to disable an opponent by striking his leg so he could be taken prisoner. Prisoners were the real war trophies, since they were used as sacrifices in religious festivals. The Aztecs and their enemies used spears, slings, and bows and arrows to fight at close range. Blades were chipped from obsidian (rock of volcanic glass) and mounted on weapons. A freshly made obsidian blade was as sharp as the Spaniards' steel swords, but soon lost its edge and was easily broken. The Spaniards used steel swords, guns, armor, and cannons. The Spaniards' purpose was military victory and then profit.

Cortés landed on the Yucatan Peninsula of Mexico in 1519, and the Aztecs greeted the Spaniards. The Spaniards set up camp and Moctezuma II, the Aztec ruler, sent gifts of gold to Cortés. The Spaniards burned their own ships and set off for Tenochtitlan with four hundred Spaniards, sixteen horses, and several cannons. Cortés persuaded many of the subject nations who were enemies of the Aztecs to join him. The Spaniards soon reached Lake Texcoco and with their native allies were invited to stay in one of the palaces by Moctezuma II. Fighting broke out, Cortés took Moctezuma II hostage and tried to control Tenochtitlan. The Spaniards led the final attack on Tenochtitlan with four hundred men and about 150,000 rebellious native allies. The Aztec capital was finally destroyed in 1521 and Mexico City was built on top of the ruins.

Herná Corté making a treaty with the Aztecs. *(Corbis Corporation)*

The Spanish introduced horses, cattle, sheep, and pigs to the American continent. They also brought fruits, sugar, and other grains, and took potatoes, tomatoes, beans, maize, and whatever bullion they could find (and it was vast) back to Europe. They divided the continent into military districts, which later became independent states.

The Incas

The Incas were the last great empire in South America. The civilization started around 1200 and lasted more than three hundred years—until the Spaniards arrived around 1530. At its peak the Inca Empire stretched from Ecuador to Chile, or almost 3,000 miles.

The Incas built an extensive irrigation system and grew many different kinds of staple crops, including the potato. They used animal manure and bird droppings, known as *guano*, as fertilizer. Those that lived in the desert lowlands grew tomatoes, tropical fruit, and cotton; the Incas that lived in the mountains grew potatoes. People at high elevations herded llama and alpaca, which supplied food and wool. The Incas also grew peppers, peanuts, avocados, and beans. Orchids were grown for medicine and people chewed cocoa leaves. The Incas built vast stone terraces on the mountainsides.

The capital of the Inca Empire, Cuzco, had a population of up to 300,000 people. They had a highly organized system of government, with the king as head and a High Council. The system had a structure of elected officials who governed and its territory was divided into administrative provinces. The people paid taxes, often through labor contributions.

The Incas had initially created this empire by conquering other tribes. The entire Inca Empire had a population of about ten million people. The Incas built a 10,000– to 20,000–mile road system, including pontoons and suspension bridges. But the Incas were also proficient craftsmen and administrators and organized their communications by mail from runner to runner who might cover 350 miles a day. In battle, they used spears and whips.

In 1532 Spaniards arrived and the Incas thought they were their gods, which diminished initial resistance. Many people quickly died from the diseases the Spanish brought from Europe. The Incas were then defeated in the field by the Spaniards' guns, against which they were no match. Their domain was then divided into areas of military administration under the Spanish Empire and provided considerable booty for the victorious Europeans.

The Zulu Empire

The Zulus are a tribe native to the KwaZuluNatal province of South Africa. Historically, the Zulus were a warrior nation and believed themselves to be descendants of the patriarch Zulu, the son of a chief in the Congo basin in central Africa. European apartheid–era textbooks taught that South Africa was virtually empty of human habitation when colonized by the Dutch in 1652. In truth, the Zulu people had begun to migrate towards their present location in Natal during the sixteenth century.

The crucial turning point in Zulu history occurred during the reign of Shaka (1787–1878), king of the Zulus from 1816 to 1828. Prior to his rule, the Zulus consisted of numerous clans or political entities that were culturally related but disorganized. Shaka is depicted as a mighty and fearsome warrior who united the clans into a single powerful tribe. He introduced a new system of military organization and revolutionized his army's weaponry and military tactics. He also introduced new battle formations and was a strict and brutal disciplinarian. Soldiers were required to remain celibate and violation of this was punishable by death. Shaka greatly increased the power of his tribe,

Shaka Zulu. (The Granger Collection, New York)

and conquered clans and tribes were incorporated into the Zulu nation. In eleven years he increased their number from 1,500 people to fifty thousand warriors alone.

From the time of Shaka, the Zulus fought many wars of defense to keep themselves from being dominated by the encroaching European powers and settlers. Before they succumbed to the British, Chief Bambatha led the final Zulu uprising in 1906. From then on the tribe that had once been master of much of the eastern coast and interior of South Africa, was subjected to an increasingly harsh series of racist laws in the state of South Africa that led to poverty and dis-

BIOGRAPHY:

King Shaka Zulu

King Shaka Senzangakhona laid the basis of the Zulu Empire in the early nineteenth century by protracted warfare and conquest. By use of force and often fear, Shaka gained control over a number of other Zulu clans and expanded his territory systematically. His warriors raided Zulu and then other villages and often burnt them down; captured or killed women and children; put young men into the army; and killed rival chiefs.

Shaka, born to a Zulu chief in 1787, joined the Zulu army and became its highest commander. He gained supremacy over the Zulu clans, enforcing his power with brutality. Zulu territory was then expanded by force, and Shaka created the most powerful kingdom in southern Africa through constant battle and ferocity. Shaka was assassinated by his half–brother in 1828.

The image created of him by contemporary Europeans was of a brutal savage, and during the colonial period white historians justified their control over the Zulus by using that image to condemn the independent African states they had conquered. Other African tribes also described Shaka as a ruthless tyrant and oppressor.

But for modern Zulus, Shaka is a national legend. He was a brave and inventive warrior who dominated local political opponents by ferocity and ruthlessness. He defeated other tribal chiefs to build a unified Zulu kingdom, with advanced centers of administration and regimental barracks and discipline. He recruited young men into the national army directly under his control. While he was undoubtedly a ruthless leader who used terror, he did imposed a whole new state superstructure over his kingdom which grew rich on cattle captured during almost constant military activity.

Shaka is revered every year at his gravesite by Zulu nationalists. They have revived him as a symbol of pre–European Zulu greatness. His is the more violent rewriting of history in a post–colonial mode.

empowerment. This was maintained until apartheid was abolished in South Africa in 1994.

European Modern Imperialism

Imperialism is now most popularly used to describe the expansion of Europe from the fifteenth to the twentieth century. This expansion was truly exceptional because it created worldwide imperial systems, which were often larger, more populous, and more diverse than preceding ones. But they were not exceptional in purpose or design.

The imperialism of Europe created the modern and contemporary world. It was based on: technological advantages which were progressively extended through a social system which encouraged scientific advances; the correspondingly superior military power of the European states; the more productive economies of the European peoples which their societies encouraged; the larger populations which, for a while, these processes generated in Europe; and the better organized political and administrative forms the states of Europe devised which enabled them to channel superior resources to expansion. At different times the Europeans excused and supported these activities by suitable ideologies including, at first, varieties of Christian doctrine and later by a Darwinian social and scientific outlook.

After the fall of the Roman Empire, Western Europe broke into a myriad of political organizations loosely described as "feudalism." While this political anarchy resolved itself into better order, the secular authority of the Holy Roman Empire and the spiritual authority of the Pope, operating through the Universal Church, were at least theoretically acknowledged. But during the Dark and Medieval Ages, from the time of Charlemagne (742) to the first voyage to America in 1492, Christendom was confined to Europe by the Mongols, Islam, the Ottoman Empire, and the Atlantic Ocean. The power of various European states ebbed and waned, often creating small imperial systems: the Holy Roman Empire, the Norman lands, and the Plantegenet English empire. But limited feudal, dynastic states were the norm.

The Christian Crusades were mounted into the Levant against Islam in the twelfth and thirteenth centuries, but repelled by the Arabs and the Ottomans. The Europeans then embarked on a period of quite brilliant expansion to the west and south, which took them to imperial mastery of much of the world. This was not driven by a more rapacious culture, or by a more avaricious economic system. What marked out the modern Europeans was their greater capacity, deriving from their better developed and more advanced economic, military, and political systems. This higher level of development was achieved by the combination of commercial capitalism and the intra–European competitive state system.

These processes generated an internal revolution in Europe. Each state adopted the most advanced system the other states produced which led to a continuing process of technological progress, which an empire, like China, found difficult to generate. Then in 1492, Columbus broke Europe out of its geographic confines by connecting it to the wider world into which European power penetrated for the next five centuries.

The Advance of European Imperial Power

European imperial power advanced into the world in phases. During the sixteenth century the two Iberian states created the initial structure of the Atlantic economy. Under the Papal Treaty of 1494, Spain and Portugal divided the world between them approximately at longitude 60 degrees (an imaginary line which would cut through modern–day Newfoundland, the western Atlantic, and Brazil), with Spain taking that to the west, Portugal that to the east.

Spain   Spain had recently evicted the Muslims and developed the finest infantry in Europe. After Cortés' conquests in Mexico in the early–sixteenth century, the Spanish used large and impressive galleons to transport booty from the New World back to the Old. When the Habsburg House of Austria joined that of Spain, it added artillery to its murderous armory. Its ferocious Catholicism, hardened by the fight with Islam and sharpened by the Inquisition, served as a fine imperial ideology to excuse the pursuit of riches and justify conquest. The diseases the Spaniards carried, often recently imported from Asia during the Plague, killed more Amerindians than the formidable steel weapons, cavalry, and religious zeal which they had never before encountered. Some estimates had their population falling from around fifty million down to two million.

The Spanish created an empire that stretched from contemporary California and Florida to Tierra del Fuego, the islands that make up the southern tip of South America. They then explored the Pacific Ocean, which became for three centuries a Spanish "lake" across which Spanish merchant fleets transported booty from the Philippines. During most of this time, Spain was governed by Hapsburgs as a part of one of the largest European dynastic domains.

Portugal   Portugal was smaller, but also better placed and less distracted by European ambitions. The

Papal deal had given it what became Brazil and the rest of the world to the east. Portuguese captains then undertook remarkable voyages which brought them to Africa and Asia on numerous and profitable voyages of discovery and enrichment. The Portuguese met Spanish power in Southeast Asia, at longitude 120 degrees, where Spain took the Philippines and Portugal Malacca and what became Timor. But Portugal was more limited in military power and was confined by size and then current technology to naval trading stations, and a chain of Portuguese ports circled the globe from Brazil to Japan.

For a time the crowns of Portugal and Spain were united by dynastic succession and the Habsburgs ruled the most extensive empire the world had known and on which the sun truly never set, embracing as it did territories in Europe, America, Africa, the Pacific, and Asia. But within two centuries it became exhausted by the efforts of defending it.

In Asia, European power was at first limited to trading stations (often fortified) established along the coast after 1511 and the early phase of the Age of Vasco da Gama. Portugal was restricted to trading stations in southern Africa, Goa, Malacca, Macao, Japan, the Spice Islands, and Timor. These fortifications often gave the Portuguese a capacity to intervene in local politics but not for the imposition of extensive imperial rule on a heavily populated continent. During the seventeenth century the Iberian states began to face rivals in their quest for world imperial dominion from the Protestant Netherlands and Britain and Catholic but nationalist France.

The Netherlands   In 1648 the Netherlands emerged from the Thirty Years War independent of the Habsburgs and became, arguably, the first liberal capitalist state, and soon set about using their naval power to acquire colonies in New York, Cape Town, and the East Indies. They did this in competition with the British, against whom they fought and lost several wars, relinquishing New York and Cape Town in the process. Nonetheless, they held onto colonies, including the Netherlands East Indies until 1949, and during those three centuries exploited them remorselessly and effectively, transferring great wealth to the small and wealthy European state.

Britain and France   The British began their imperial trajectory in the reign of Queen Elizabeth I (1533–1603), a late medieval warlord of immense capacities. England was consolidated as a state and successfully defended against the Spanish Armada in 1588. It then began the conquest of North America, where it established a series of colonial settlements. These became the thirteen colonies, profitable to the British as trading partners monopolized by British merchant marine.

The French also joined in the imperial conquest of North America by claiming the Hudson Valley corridor to the Great Lakes, and then moving into the Mississippi Valley with a view to joining Canada to New Orleans in the Gulf. This was an area immensely rich in timber, pelts, and fertile land for colonial settlement. Several wars between the British and French necessarily ensued, but were inconclusive before 1756.

The Seven Years War—the first genuinely world war—was fought between the British and French empires in 1756–1763, and waged for profitable imperial possessions in North America, the Caribbean, India, and east Asia. This war ended in a British victory and the French were evicted from Canada—and from India. The thirteen British colonies now had little need for British protection and declared their independence in 1776, which led to war.

The resulting United States of America now became the first serious version of the modern settler colonial state, liberal in government but imperial towards other territory despite its anti–imperial ideology. It set about acquiring more territory owned by others in a series of purchases (Louisiana and Alaska), seizures (Texas), and colonizations that pushed the frontier to the Pacific coast. The combination of resource rich territory and industrious population made the U.S. an outstanding example of the benefits to be derived from imperial expansion and settlement.

The British had temporarily ended the ambitions of the French outside Europe, but they re–directed their attentions. After the revolution of 1789, the French created an empire in Europe under the direction of the military genius, Emperor Napoleon Bonaparte. He revolutionized the map of Europe through a series of military campaigns that saw him effectively undefeated in the field from 1798 to 1813. This made France the imperial ruler of the richest continent on earth, but unable to expand outside it after the defeat of the French fleet by Britain's Lord Nelson at Trafalgar in 1805. The French control of Europe was then ended by their defeat in Russia in 1812–1813, in Spain in 1814, at the Battle of the Nations in 1814, and finally and decisively, by the Duke of Wellington overwhelming Napoleon's forces at Waterloo in 1815. Napoleonic rule, however, greatly enriched France.

The British were now the masters of the world outside Europe. They undertook the first attempt to create a global commercial system in place of discrete imperial aggrandizements. With mastery of the world's oceans after 1805, a small but capable and mobile army, a rapidly industrializing economy soon producing nearly forty percent of world output, and with a financial system based in London, the British now attempted to open the world to free trade and commerce. Between 1815 and 1870 the British used their power not to enlarge their already extensive colonies, but to open the world to commerce. After 1870 a number of other states emerged as rival powers and undertook imperial expansion designed to take territories into their own exclusive zones in traditional imperialist fashion. These included a revived France under Napoleon III, a newly unified Germany led by Otto von Bismarck, the post–Civil War United States, and, in east Asia, the Russians and the Japanese.

Asia's experience   During this process Asia was opened to European power. At first, this involved exposing reluctant states to commerce, a procedure started by the British in the 1840 Opium War with decaying imperial China, and extended by the U.S. in Japan in 1853. But as the European states became more powerful, the trading stations around the coast of Asia were not sufficient to provide access to the increasing quantities of raw materials and foodstuffs and larger markets that the Europeans believed Asia potentially presented. The Europeans undertook the conquest of Asia proper.

The Russians spread across the great Eurasian steppe and its large population and military technology, including gunpowder, took its toll. Under a series of aggressive rulers, including Peter the Great and Catherine the Great, they seized territory from the nomadic tribes and then the Chinese state from the seventeenth to the twentieth century and expanded as far as Alaska, which they later sold to the U.S. In the nineteenth century they annexed a number of mostly Muslim republics in Central Asia.

In the 1870s the French began the conquest of the Indochina states of Vietnam, Cambodia, and Laos. The Japanese, newly modernized and understanding the benefits of colonial expansion, defeated China in 1895 and Russia in 1905 and constructed an empire in east Asia that was to continue to expand until 1943. The United States seized the Philippines from Spain in the war of 1898. And by the 1870s even the British had returned to imperial expansion and, in quick succession, expanded their direct rule across the whole of India, Burma, the states of Malaya, and the north Borneo colonies. The Dutch also accelerated their conquest of the entire East Indies.

The Europeans then began carving up China. The Middle Kingdom was unable to resist the attacks of the imperial powers by the late nineteenth century. Russia seized territory to the north; and Japan to the east. The British, Germans, and French established spheres of influence with "Treaty Ports" and extra–territorial rights. And finally, when patriotic Chinese resisted, the U.S. organized a joint force to put down the Boxer Rebellion. In 1911, the dynastic state finally collapsed, to be replaced in theory by a republic, but in fact by a civil war which did not end until 1949.

Africa   At the same time, the Europeans completed their conquest of Africa. Africa was first integrated into the Atlantic economy by the provision of slaves. Slavery had existed in Africa since pre–Roman times and had been maintained by the Arabs. Slave–based plantation economies were well known to the Mediterranean world and were introduced to the Canary Islands. Slavery was then brought to America. The American natives often did not serve this function well and African slaves were imported. During the three centuries of the slave trade, tens of millions of Africans were transported to the Americas and their use was integral to the establishment of imperial economies for the production of sugar, then cotton.

The Portuguese consolidated their hold on Mozambique, Angola, and Guinea–Bissau. The Spanish retained Spanish Sahara. The French established a Second Empire, adjacent to France, in North Africa as far south as the Equator. Late in the century, the British pursued a railway and corridor from the Cape to Cairo and acquired a string of possessions from the South African colonies to Egypt. The late–coming Germans took some colonial remains in South West Africa, Tanganyika, and German Somalia. The rush was so indecent that the Congress of Berlin was convened in 1884–1885 to provide order to the onslaught and draw some clear boundaries. Even then, Italy later joined the scramble and acquired Libya in 1909 and Ethiopia, indecently late, in 1935. By that time no independent states existed in Africa, although most powers were having trouble making a profit from African colonies except where precious metals were found. Even then, as in South Africa, the British found the European Boer settlers a problem to contend with in war.

Decline of Imperial Systems

This competitive expansion of the European–based empires, contributed to the tensions that led to war in 1914, but the real causes were in Europe. Nonetheless, the defeat of the Central Powers led to them losing their imperial systems. In Europe, this created modern national states in the place of the German and Austro–Hungarian dynastic creations.

But losing a war is not necessarily the only way to lose an empire. For a good example of the problems that widespread colonization can cause, one need look no further than Great Britain. Near the end of the nineteenth century, Britain was the most powerful nation on earth. Their empire extended to all parts of the world. But the difficult war fought against the Boers hurt British prestige. Decades later, victory in World War I had nearly bankrupted the country. It became harder and harder to justify spending money on strange lands thousands of miles away from home. Moreover, Indian troops had fought for Britain on the assumption that they would be granted independence, which did not happen. The Indian people grew agitated, and feelings of betrayal and nationalism surged. A generation later, Britain tapped all of her resources once again to win World War II. The people were weary of talk about the glory of empire, and wanted the government to concentrate on the needs of its citizens at home. "Conquering these new areas cost money, as did setting up the governments to run them," wrote William W. Lace in *The British Empire: The End of Colonialism*. By 1945, Britain no longer had the money or the will for imperialism. Britain's prize for winning both world wars would be the loss of its empire and the loss of its status as the most powerful nation on earth.

The defeat of the Ottoman Empire in World War I led to the creation of a modern Turkish national state and a re–division of the Middle East. Persia (Iran) also became a nation–state. Under the League of Nations system of mandates, the British got Palestine, Trans–Jordan, Iraq, and Gulf states, and the Saudi Arabian regime came under British protection. These were added to the neighboring Egypt and the Sudan to control the route to India. The French got Syria and the Lebanon with its large Christian community dating from the Crusaders. These moves were in part designed to give the Europeans access to oil reserves rapidly emerging as the world's most valuable commodity.

Defeated in 1918, Germany was reorganized for military expansion under Adolf Hitler from 1933 to 1939. It then pursued the same imperial aims once more under the Nazi regime from 1939 to 1945. This involved German imperial domination of Europe from France to the Urals to the benefit of the German state and people. This was briefly achieved by aggressive war in the early 1940s.

The Soviet Union

But the last great European empire was that of the revolutionary Soviet regime led by Vladimir Lenin, which replaced tsarist rule in Russia. The Soviet

Union's imperial system was created in three layers. After 1917 Lenin took over most of the Russian imperial state, crushing secessionist nationalist movements after the Bolsheviks seized Moscow and St. Petersburg, particularly in Ukraine and Georgia but also in Central Asia. In a deal with Hitler in 1939 the Soviets then annexed territory in Eastern Europe, including the states of Lithuania, Latvia, and Estonia, as well as much of Poland. After 1945 they directly annexed the rest of Poland and also established puppet, semi–colonial regimes in East Germany, Hungary, Czechoslovakia, Bulgaria, and Rumania. This was the inner colonial territory. Then in the 1970s, during the retreat of U.S. power, they were able to acquire client regimes in Indo China, Cuba, several African states, and parts of the Middle East.

But this empire was not profitable to the Soviet state. Indeed, by the 1980s it was a severe drain on its resources. The cost of this imperial system was greatly increased by the policies of the Soviet leader from 1964 to 1982, Leonard Brezhnev. Maintenance of the satellite states took up one–quarter of the Soviet economy by 1980. This cost included large subsidies to communist Cuba, North Korea and Vietnam, cheap energy sales to the east European puppet regimes, and grants and aid to the many Third World regimes that had come under Soviet patronage. In addition, the Soviets maintained a defense budget to compete with the U.S.–but with an economy perhaps ten percent as large. In the late 1980s, this whole imperial edifice, created with great ideological zeal and at considerable material cost, was dismantled by the reformer Mikhail Gorbachev.

ANALYSIS AND CRITICAL RESPONSE

The last phase in the expansion of the imperial power of the European states after 1870 was so spectacular that it sparked a major controversy about the reasons for it. A number of explanations were offered at that time, and subsequently by historians.

The most obvious was that they conquered other countries because they had the power to do so. This theory of "the pursuit of power" was advanced by Hans J. Morgenthau in his textbook on international relations, *Politics Among Nations: The Struggle for Power and Peace*. This pursuit of power had been common behavior by states since the Neolithic revolution. The disparity in power between the Europeans and others was for long so great that it made imperial conquest very cheap. The "lust for power" inherent in the state, particularly its military forces, pro-

vided a culture within which conquest could be justified by the security and strategic interests of the state. Even if conquest was distant, annexation could be justified in terms of denying resources to rival states. Democrat critics often pointed to the aristocratic nature of the ruling classes of nineteenth and early twentieth century European states and the believed predilection for war, chivalry and battle endemic to that class. This was, however, a difficult argument to later adduce for non–aristocratic states like the U.S. or Australia.

Other authors produced culture–based arguments. Some of these were centered on the culture of Christendom in Europe, which, it believed, had some responsibility to civilize primitive cultures and bring them within the bounds of Christian civilization. This rarely, however, looks more than a *ex post facto* justification for state policy undertaken for more practical and usually profitable reasons. It is unlikely that Cortés, for example, was more inspired by the conversion of souls than by the pursuit of booty. Other writers, less charitably again, believed that the arms manufactures drove states to expand their ambitions in order to fill profitable arms production contracts. This, again, proved more difficult to demonstrate than assert.

Capitalism

More commonly blamed, particularly in the late nineteenth and early twentieth century, was the European system of production itself, now known as capitalism. Among such critics were both liberals, like John Hobson in his book *Imperialism: A Study* and marxists, like Vladimir Lenin in his polemic *Imperialism: The Highest Stage of Capitalism*.

Hobson, an opponent of the British pursuit of the Boer War, wrote in 1900 against the European settler states in southern Africa. He argued that the capitalist countries of Europe were by the end of the nineteenth century dominated politically by the owners of capital. These capitalists could not find sufficient profitable outlets for their investments. As a result, they successfully urged the governments to pursue overseas and colonial expansion so that they could invest safely in these new colonies and make a profit. In the Boer War British capital was after the rich opportunities offered by gold and diamond mining in the Boer republics. To deal with this problem, Hobson argued, income should be redistributed to the poor in Britain, so that capitalists would be able to find profitable outlets and markets at home.

Lenin published his pamphlet in 1917 as part of his general program of seeking the revolutionary overthrow of the Russian Tsarist regime. He wanted to link the First World War to capitalism in order to garner support from the numerous Russian opponents of the war for his revolutionary cause. Taking much of his argument from Hobson, he said that under "monopoly capitalism" the states of Europe were driven by large financial cartels pushing each country to seek imperial conquest in order to gain profitable investment opportunities. In the process of competing for these colonies, they had gone to war with each other. The only way to stop that war was to overthrow capitalism.

These arguments were ill–founded. Most investments from the capitalist countries did not go to their colonies but to other independent and wealthy capitalist states. Imperialism and war had existed as part of the human political condition since the Neolithic revolution. The First World War had its origins almost entirely in European politics. And when Lenin did replace tsarism with a revolutionary state it proved to be among the most expansionary and war–like in the world.

Benefits of Imperialism

A common view is that one positive aspect of imperialism is that new ideas and superior technologies are introduced into the conquered lands. Some feel, however, that this is an arrogant, Eurocentric viewpoint, that any positive qualities of colonialism are far outweighed by the disease, slavery, suspicion, ill feelings, and oppression often brought to new lands. Yet more than a few historians do point to specific positive qualities of imperialism, all while acknowledging the negative. As William Prescott wrote of the Aztecs in his 1837 work *Conquest of Mexico*:

> How can a nation where human sacrifices prevail, and especially combined with cannibalism, further the march of civilization? The influence of the Aztecs introduced their gloomy superstition into lands before unacquainted with it, or where, at least, it was not established in any great strength.

Prescott did not feel that this alone justified the Spanish conquest and acknowledges the atrocities that occurred during battle, but also stated that not every result was bad for humanity, and that Cortés and his soldiers were, in many ways, simply a product of their time. In addition, it should be remembered that the destruction of the Aztec Empire may not have been possible without the surrounding Native American tribes who allied themselves with the Spaniards.

The Mongol conquest of China is often linked with the opening of a massive trade route that spread ideas and discoveries to groups of people who had before not even known of each other's existence. This

certainly was a positive aspect. The Mongol occupation also probably helped to strengthen Chinese ethnic pride. However, it is unlikely that the Chinese benefited more, in the long run, from Mongol control than from earlier native rule.

For most of human history, philosophers have accepted that imperial expansion and conquest are a necessary part of organized political societies and their interaction with one another. In classical Greece, the martial skills and dispositions were cultivated alongside those of the intellect to produce a rounded citizen. Pericles' speech over the Athenian dead in Thucydides makes a virtue of dying for democratic Athens. Alexander the Great was raised in the imperial tradition and ranks high among Greek heroes for pursuing conquest by force throughout his short life. The Romans made heroes of their conquerors and Julius Caesar's *The Conquest of Gaul* may be read as propaganda advertising his qualifications for even higher office. This tradition continued into Christian Europe. Indeed, the greatest of the Renaissance political philosophers, Machiavelli, devotes considerable space to advising *The Prince* on how to deal with a conquered province.

Imperial behavior applied equally to states of differing ideological hues: the Islamic Ottoman Turks; the Christian Charles V and Philip II, dynastic rulers of the extensive Hapsburg dominions; the Bourbon absolutist monarchy in France; commercial and liberal Britain; Revolutionary France under the Directorate and Napoleon, both in pursuit of the conquest of Europe; Napoleon III and the new French empire in Africa; Kaiser Wilhelm and the Nazis in pursuit of German military imperialism into eastern Europe; Teddy Roosevelt and the "New Imperialism" of republican America; and the egalitarian settlers of Australia and New Zealand in their pursuit of the domination of the southwest Pacific.

In this pursuit of imperial expansion, societies had many and diverse proponents. Charles Darwin's account of *The Evolution of the Species*, with its implied doctrine of the survival of the fittest species, was readily turned into "Social Darwinism" in justification for the conquest of the socially backward by the technologically advanced. Marx argued that European colonialism of stagnant Asia would prod what he called the "Asiatic Mode of Production" out of its lethargy and into the world of capitalist progress.

Critics

Again, this is not to say that the imperialist impulse has lacked critics. Throughout history, the commercial and agricultural classes may have preferred what the Enlightenment philosopher, Immanuel Kant, extolled as *Perpetual Peace*. Kant argued that a society of rational republican states would be peaceable. But other impulses beat in the human heart and the expansionist ambitions of a Genghis Khan or Catherine the Great would offer periodic reminder of the aphorism: "If you seek peace, prepare for war." Nonetheless, the final period of European expansion coincided with the evolution of liberal and representative governments whose spokesmen had more interest in commercial and cultural exchange than imperial conquest. From them, evolved the contemporary critics of imperialism who dominate Western considerations of the phenomenon in the early twenty–first century.

Liberals have decried imperial expansion since Richard Cobden and his biographer, John Hobson, in *International Man* criticized European colonialism in the nineteenth century. In this, they merely followed American liberal and anti–imperial sentiment that originated in the American Revolutionary War. Ignoring its own record of colonial expansion, the U.S. then embarked on Great Power status in 1917 with a full–blown, anti–imperial ideology. During the second part of the twentieth century American power was then deployed successfully to dismantle the European colonial structures. In this pursuit, it was motivated partly by liberal ideology and partly by a desire to access the closed markets and other commercial opportunities of the colonial empires, as David Mosler and Bob Catley described in their book, *Global America: Imposing Liberalism on a Recalcitrant World*. The Marxist school has, since Lenin's 1917 polemic, persistently criticized what it claims to be the uniquely capitalist form of imperialism. Among its recent proponents has been Harry Magdoff in *The Age of Imperialism*. Its force has been, understandably, diminished by the long period of expansion undertaken by the Soviet state, only to be followed by its collapse. The unworkability of Soviet economics as an alternative to market forms has contributed to the demise of the Marxist school.

For a period in the 1970s, the Marxist school was supplanted by "Dependency Theory," of whom Andre Gunder Frank, who wrote *On Capitalist Underdevelopment* in 1975, was the best–known author. This theory held that during the era of colonialism the Europeans had created dependent economies in the Third World which, because of their structural dependence on the world market, would always remain poor and underdeveloped. This argument was taken up by many Third World intellectuals and regimes but was progressively abandoned by the 1990s. This was because its adherents had created such murderous regimes whenever they had come to power, notably in Pol Pot's

Khmer Republic; because many Third World states adopting liberal and market economics did indeed develop; and because its postulates were increasingly seen as excuses by incompetent Third World regimes for their own failures.

The Current Status of Imperialism

Contemporary critics of imperialism tend to be more cultural in form. They often derive their argument from people like Franz Fanon, a black Francophone who depicted Third World citizens as *The Wretched of the Earth*, subjugated by rapacious Europeans, whose very psychology could not survive healthily in its suborned condition without a violent resistance. Mahatma Ghandi pursued a pacifist form of this argument in his support for traditional Indian cultural modes. The Arab American Edward Said, in *Orientalism*, developed a similar perspective deriving from the Israeli–Palestinian dispute. This position, often termed "post–colonial theory," argues that the non–European world is persistently misrepresented and demonized by Western politicians and intellectuals, thereby justifying the political domination over it, which Europeans pursue. This argument ignores the waves of imperial expansion and contraction—many of them by non–Europeans—that have gone into the making of the modern world. It is, nonetheless, widely felt in parts of the Third World.

Yet the European empires did retreat. The European retreat from the Americas started with the American Declaration of Independence in 1776. It was then extended during the Napoleonic Wars when most Spanish colonies in the Americas declared their independence at the behest of Simon Bolivar and with the encouragement of the British and protection of the British fleet. The emancipation of the Americas then proceeded through the nineteenth century with slave revolts in Haiti, secession in Brazil, and agreed self–government in Canada.

After the First World War, the Ottoman Empire was dismantled by the Europeans. The British and French assumed League of Nations mandates in the region, but those states, including Egypt, Israel, Jordan, Iraq, Kuwait, Israel and Palestine, quickly acquired their independence. As U.S. power replaced that of the European colonialists by the 1970s, so the structure of power in the region assumed classical geopolitical new dimensions, together with some new attempts at imperial expansion, including the abortive Iraqi annexation of Kuwait in 1991.

The emancipation of Asia began with the dismantling of the German Empire after defeat in 1918. Australia, New Zealand and Japan got mandated territories in the process. Then in 1945 the Japanese Empire was also emancipated. In 1946, the U.S. granted independence to the Philippines. Two years later the British began their evacuation of Asia with the independence of the Indian Raj into four major successor states. In 1957 and 1963 the British left their southeast Asian possessions, most of them forming the Federation of Malaysia, and finally, in 1997, Hong Kong. China asserted its sovereignty under a communist regime in 1949, the same year in which the Dutch were evicted from Indonesia by a combination of nationalist war and U.S. diplomatic pressure. In 1956 the French left Indo China, after waging an unsuccessful war to maintain their colonial possessions. European imperialism in Asia was largely finished.

The Europeans' exit from Africa was similarly rapid. Italy lost its colonies after its defeat in 1943. The French tried to maintain their empire but desisted after their defeat in the Algerian Civil War in 1958. The British, as in Asia, were keener de–colonizers and started the process in Ghana in 1957. It was then extended—albeit not without difficulty—throughout their African possessions in Nigeria, Kenya, Tanzania, the short–lived Central African Federation, Uganda, and Zimbabwe/Rhodesia. In 1960, Belgium left the Congo. The Portuguese hung on their ancient colonies in Angola, Guinea–Bissau, and Mozambique until a 1974 anti–colonial military coup in Lisbon. In South Africa and South West Africa/Namibia the apartheid regimes ended in 1994. Africa had gone back to the Africans.

The Pacific Ocean territories were, by and large, the last to be emancipated. New Zealand left Samoa in 1962 and the British vacated Fiji in 1970. The Australians granted independence to Papua/New Guinea in 1975 and the British quickly thereafter vacated Melanesia. But the French still retain New Caledonia and Tahiti and the U.S. American Samoa. But these remained among the few exceptions to the generalization that the Europeans had, with the exception of the settler states, vacated their imperial conquests in the wider world.

Why did imperialist Europe retreat? Most of this retreat occurred at a time when the dominant powers of the international system, the U.S. and the Soviet Union, were opposed to the kind of classic imperialism which the Europeans practiced. These superpowers supported anti–colonial movements against European power and put considerable pressure on the imperial powers to retreat.

The colonized people also became more difficult to rule as the ideas and techniques, particularly weaponry, spread more widely among them. Local and traditional rulers of colonial territories believed they could as well govern their people as Europeans. As these processes occurred, so the cost of governing colonies rose.

At the same time the anti–colonial ideas so deeply rooted in the socialists and liberal political movement in Europe spread among the increasingly enfranchised lower classes, so the willingness to bear the rising financial and casualty costs of imposing imperial rule fell. In Britain, for example, the first seriously anti–imperialist government was the Labour government of 1945 to 1951. The French abandoned Indo China when the electorate rejected the cost after the defeat at Dien Bien Phu in 1954.

By 1960 it had become clear to most European regimes that it was actually less profitable, if not unprofitable, to be imperialist. This realization dawned on the Soviets in the 1980s. Some imperial states then preserved the policy for other reasons: the political pressure of settlers (Britain); archaic calculations by military or fascist regimes (Portugal); or a geo–strategic calculation, for example, to have somewhere to test nuclear weapons (France).

At the beginning of the twenty–first century it is most commonly believed that the appropriate and most desirable form of political organization is the nation state. This idea was first forcefully pursued by liberals like the U.S. President Woodrow Wilson (1856–1924) in his Fourteen Points of 1917. It has been taken up by the Charter of the United Nations that enshrines this doctrine.

Why Has There Been No Total World Empire?

Until the modern era, the level of technology would not support a global empire. The Habsburgs possessed a globe–encompassing domain, but probably ruled no more subjects than contemporary China and found it impossible to sustain. The British were supreme for perhaps thirty years, but even then had trouble in the Crimean War of 1854 to 1856. Today, the United States is the only remaining superpower, but is still vulnerable, as evidenced by the attack on the World Trade Center in New York City on September 11, 2001.

No power has been able to imperialize the modern state system, although a succession have tried, as Paul Kennedy described in 1987 in *Rise and Fall of the Great Powers*: the Habsburgs, Bourbon France, Pitt's England, Napoleonic France, nineteenth–century Britain, Germany under the Kaiser and the Nazis, the Soviets, and now, arguably, the United States. This is because of the operation of countervailing tendencies. The operation of the Balance of Power leads other countries to unite against the aspiring dominator. Powers that are too ambitious, find themselves exposed to "Imperial Overstretch." The tendency for "combined and uneven development," leads other states to match eventually the innovations of the most powerful. And the technology for making global dominance a serious possibility is not yet available.

Conclusion

Imperialism usually starts with military conquest; it then uses this opportunity to install an administration or government, which organizes a transfer of resources from the colony to the metropolitan state. At the simplest level, this may be achieved by looting, as with Genghis Khan, or with bullion transfer, as with the Habsburgs, or with tribute to the Chinese empire. The more sophisticated means are systemic, like Rome or Britain, and involve colonies and colonial administrations who are made to trade profitably only within the empire. This may be expanded by investments in appropriate commodities like mines, plantations, or factories. Settlements may be used to get suitable labor to extract wealth, as in the Thirteen Colonies, in Australia or New Zealand, or in South Africa. If empire is not profitable, by the exchange of goods or by resource transfer, it will be sooner or later abandoned.

But the search for a single motive for imperialism may be fruitless. It stems from well springs deep in the human personality, and from impulses deeply buried in political societies.

TOPICS FOR FURTHER STUDY

- Was Gibbon's description of the Roman Empire reasonable?

- Why did the Chinese state outlast the Roman Empire, despite Rome's superior military advantage over its conquered territories?

- Was Islamic imperialism during the *caliphates* purely motivated by religious ideology?

BIBLIOGRAPHY

Sources

Blacker, Irwin R., ed. *Prescott's Histories: The Rise and Decline of the Spanish Empire.* New York: Viking Press, 1963.

Ebrey, Patricia Buckley. *The Cambridge Illustrated History of China.* London: Cambridge University Press, 1996.

De Hartog, Leo. *Genghis Khan: Conqueror of the World.* Leo De Hartog, 1999.

Kennedy, Paul. *Rise and Fall of the Great Powers,*. New York: Random House, 1987.

Lace, William W. *The British Empire: The End of Colonialism.* San Diego: Lucent Books, 2000.

Mosler, David, and Bob Catley. *Global America: Imposing Liberalism on a Recalcitrant World,* Praeger, 2000.

Further Readings

Elvin, Mark. *Pattern of the Chinese Past,* Stanford University Press, 1973. An interpretation of Chinese history which emphasizes the high–level of Chinese achievement by the sixteenth century.

Gibbon, Edward. *The Decline and Fall of the Roman Empire,* Knopf, 1993. A classic history of the expansion and collapse of the Roman Empire, which attributes its failure to the adoption of the Christian religion.

Kennedy, Paul. *Rise and Fall of the Great Powers,* 1987. A description of the manner in which different states have tried to dominate the European international system since 1500, and an explanation for the failure of each from the Austrian Hapsburgs to the Soviet communists.

Machiavelli, Niccolo. *The Prince,* Knopf, 1992. This book is an attempt by a former Italian government official to provide advice to any aspiring imperial ruler, or Prince, about how to gain and then keep political power.

Morgenthau, Hans J. *Politics Among Nations: The Struggle for Power and Peace,* McGraw–Hill, 1985. This is the classic modern statement of how nations become involved in the struggle with one another for power, influence, and empire—no matter what ideology they espouse.

SEE ALSO

Capitalism, Marxism

Liberalism

OVERVIEW

Liberalism is not a precise ideology. It does not have clear system of beliefs or a set of texts to which its adherents must subscribe. It is rather a set of attitudes, including particularly an emphasis on the recognition of the rights of the individual and tolerance, which permits considerable diversity of views among liberals. It can be described but not prescribed.

Liberalism is a term that was first used in England the early nineteenth century. It is now used in much of the world to indicate a political system characterized by freedom of association, the rule of law, and the rejection of arbitrary authority. Liberalism also provides for individual freedom, equality before the law, possession of private property, clear constitutional limits on governmental power, and representative and democratic political decision making. Many of the richest societies are liberal—including the major Anglophone countries of the United States, Britain, Canada, Australia, and New Zealand—and, with some qualifications, most of the countries of the European Union.

The term "liberal" has a somewhat different usage in the U.S. to most of Europe and elsewhere in the English–speaking world. In the U.S., liberal is often used in a way that elsewhere would mean leftist, or one who supports the expansion of the power of the state or government. In Europe, this is reserved for the terms socialist, social democrat, or leftist, and liberal there usually means some one who does not support the expansion or use of the power of the state in political or economic affairs.

WHO CONTROLS GOVERNMENT? Individuals supported by the people

HOW IS GOVERNMENT PUT INTO POWER? Popular vote of the majority

WHAT ROLES DO THE PEOPLE HAVE? Vote; Bring about social change

WHO CONTROLS PRODUCTION OF GOODS? Private citizens

WHO CONTROLS DISTRIBUTION OF GOODS? Private citizens

MAJOR FIGURES John Stuart Mill; William Gladstone

HISTORICAL EXAMPLE Great Britain, 1870–1900

CHRONOLOGY

1670: Benedict de Spinoza's *A Theological-Political Treatise* is published

1688: The Glorious Revolution occurs in England

1748: Baron de Montesquieu's *The Spirit of the Laws* is published

1779: Jeremy Bentham's *Introduction to the Principles of Morals and Legislation* is published

1786–1788: The Constitutional Convention is held in the newly created United States of America

1868: William Ewart Gladstone becomes the Liberal Party Prime Minister of Great Britain

1869: John Stuart Mill's *On Library* and *The Subjection of Women* are published

1962: Milton and Rose D. Friedman's *Capitalism and Freedom* is published

1971: John Rawl's *A Theory of Justice* is published

1992: Democrat Bill Clinton is elected President of the United States

Liberalism can be understood as a political tradition that has varied in different countries. In England, the birthplace of liberalism, the liberal tradition in politics has centred on individual rights, religious toleration, government by consent, and personal and economic freedom. In France, liberalism has been more closely associated with secularism and democracy. In the U.S., liberals often combines a commitment to personal liberty with an antipathy to capitalism, while liberals in Australia tend to be much more sympathetic to capitalism, but often less enthusiastic about the state defending civil liberties.

HISTORY

Liberalism is a doctrine that emerged from the European Enlightenment of the eighteenth century. It became particularly strong in England, but also in the U.S., France, and later, other Anglophone societies like Australia. In each of these countries it assumed slightly different forms.

The major philosophers of liberalism belong to a number of groups of theorists. The first includes several theorists of the seventeenth and eighteenth centuries who preceded liberalism proper but who anticipated its doctrines. These were followed by the political and economic theorists of classical liberalism in the mid–nineteenth century. Later, other liberal theorists modified those doctrines of the classical liberals and are often called "social liberals." There also emerged in the twentieth century defenders of classical liberalism including, in the economic sphere, the "Austrian School."

A History of Liberal Theory: The Precursors of Liberalism

Until the seventeenth century, most European political philosophy was chiefly set in theological terms. One of its principal concerns was the achievement of God's will on earth and the protection of the Christian religion.

The Enlightenment was an intellectual movement during the eighteenth century which believed humans had the ability to discern truth without appeal to religious doctrine. This marked: the beginning of scientific history; the need to justify doctrine by reason; freedom is necessary to advance progress; historical criticism as necessary to determine the historical legacy; the need for critical philosophy; and the use of ethics as separate and independent from the authority of religion and theology. It also entailed a suspicion of all truth claiming to be grounded in some kind of authority other than reason, like tradition or divine revelation.

In his *Critique of Pure Reason* (1781) the leading German Enlightenment philosopher Immanuel Kant (1724–1804) asserted all that can be known, is things as they are experienced. Other Philosophers attempted to know God as he is in himself by reasoning up to Him. This was, according to Kant, a vain attempt. God could not be experienced by man. Kant did not entertain the possibility that God could break into the realm of history and reveal himself.

But Kant was not an atheist. He postulated the existence of God, but denied the possibility of any cognitive knowledge of him. It was man's conscience that testified of God's existence, and He was to be known through the realm of morality. Kant published another work, *Religion Within the Limits of Reason Alone* (1793), which set forth his conception that religion could be reduced to the sphere of morality. For Kant, this meant living by the categorical imperative—which he summarized in two maxims: "Act only on that maxim whereby thou canst at the same time will that it should become a universal law"; and "Act as if the maxim of thy action were to become by thy will a universal law of nature."

In other words, every action of humanity should be regulated in such a way that it would be morally profitable for humanity if were elevated to the status of law.

The Federalist Debates and the U.S. Constitution

In terms of political philosophy, the defining moment of the seventeenth century was the English Revolution. The two revolutions at the end of the eighteenth century, in America and then in France, established substantial monuments to the intellectual debates about constitutionality. The Thirteen Colonies in America revolted against the English Crown and enforced their Declaration of Independence (1776) in a revolutionary war. There then ensued debate among and between the former colonies about what system of government should prevail. This was resolved at the Constitutional Convention in Philadelphia, 1786–1787, in favor of the Federalists.

What form of government best suited a commercial civilization in the New World? Somewhat ironically, the British Constitution figured largely in discussion of that issue because the Americans appreciated that the British, whatever their other failings, had made most progress in that respect. The interpretation Baron de Montesquieu (1689–1755) and the founding fathers of the American state placed on the English Constitution, was that the separation of powers limited the power of the state and should be adopted as a principle of American government. The next great debate concerned which interests could be represented, and this was progressively resolved in favor of universal franchise in the New World, and then in the other liberal states.

Montesquieu has been called "the godfather" of the American constitution. In eighty–five *Federalist Papers*, 1787–1788, Montesquieu's temper and spirit is omnipresent and is often cited by anti–Federalists and Federalists alike. The anti–Federalists contended that Montesquieu had argued that a republic which extended over too large a territory would come unstuck. The Federalists, led by Alexander Hamilton (1757–1804) and James Madison (1751–1836), responded by arguing that Montesquieu had seen that the way to overcome this was to establish a confederation of republics. They also cited Montesquieu that representation should be proportional to the size of the population.

Madison said that Montesquieu "has the merit of displaying and recommending" the doctrine of the sep-

aration of powers "most effectually to the attention of mankind," but also that politics is about the institutional balancing of social forces. That very approach to the problem of politics explains the extremely different character of *The Federalist Papers* from the Declaration of Independence. The Declaration, penned by Thomas Jefferson (1743–1826), is a general statement about rights and love of freedom. Jefferson's politics was essentially driven by a republican conception of honor, by a deep faith not only in man, but in revolutionary action itself, by a mistrust of commercial society, by a desire to preserve an agrarian economy, and by an essentially populist distrust of institutions. Despite this, he nonetheless kept slaves.

The concerns of Hamilton in *The Federalist Papers* were different and governed by the desire to create peace and commercial prosperity, to provide a strong industrial base for America and thus to make her a strong military power, to provide institutions which could mediate conflict by providing a balance between local and national interests. He was as practical as Jefferson was romantic, and was as afraid of democratic abuses as of monarchical abuses. Hamilton's republicanism was not borne out of a belief in high minded ideals, but out of the reality of the American situation. Ultimately Jefferson's charge that Hamilton was a monarchist amounted to Hamilton's seeing the need for a head of state to have executive powers, which were not reducible to the powers of the legislature. Hamilton was a follower of Montesquieu, but not of the British monarchy.

The delegates to the Constitutional Convention, of course, had a restricted conception of the scope of proper interests, being themselves almost exclusively slave–owning southerners or wealthy northern merchants. The constitution they created was not primarily intended to be democratic and it restricted the franchise to property–owning males, thereby excluding women, the working classes and the slaves from the political community. But nonetheless they did embody in the new Republic's political system the notion that legitimate interests would conflict and needed a process of resolution.

The solution of the Federalists was not one which guaranteed immediate liberties for dominated social groups. It was, however, one which was able to provide a compromise between the strongest interests of the day, by taking the strongest interests in the New World vying for political power and forging a new political system. This would provide: a strong defensive capacity; a strong central government, able for the most part to provide commercial and political stability for a vibrant industrial society; and a form of government in which local interests still had strong representation, and in which more people than ever in history had freedom.

This solution, then, did not lay in a political elimination of the diversity that sprang from the dispersal of interests, talents, desires, and sentiments, but of realizing that a large distribution of interests would, in general, counteract the danger of factionalism itself. "Extend the sphere, and you take in a greater variety of parties and interests; you make it less probable that a majority of the whole will have a common motive to invade the rights of other citizens." Or break the society "into so many parts, interests and classes of citizens that the rights of individuals, or of the minority, will be in little danger from interested combinations of the majority."

This argument was also a way of defending the Federalists program of a confederate republic. For a confederate republic would also aid this process of dispersion by adding another geographical layer to the interests that would be formed at either a local or state level. Thus linkages of interests could be formed between social groups, which constituted a minority in some states while being a majority in others. Further, alliances of social interests cutting along geographical lines would tend to protect minority groups. At the same time, interests based upon geographical factors might take on greater relevance at one time, while at another time, social factors which were operating nationally may dominate. The great value of Confederalism, then, was that the polymorphic nature of factionalism would aid the minority.

But while the Federalists argued that the large territory of America combined with "the multiplicity of interests" made it highly unlikely that a majority would pursue a common and unjust cause, that was only true with respect to those peoples included in the franchise. The lack of franchise would mean that those people without political representation—particularly indigenous Americans and slaves, and to a lesser extent women—could be endangered by a system in which they were just one interest among many, but lacked political rights. Thus it took almost eighty years and a war before the ambition articulated in the Jefferson Virginian Ordinance, that slavery be abolished, was realized. And the diversity of interests would not help the indigenous American as the railways moved West and the expansion of the frontier meant that Indians were driven off to reservations and treaties were routinely broken.

But the Federalists saw that there were numerous ways in which power could be congealed to the detriment of other interests. The majority could suppress or rob the minority if they exercised legislative power. There was also simply the danger, recognized by Montesquieu, that the legislature would see any restraints upon its power as restrictive, as merely the resistance of vested minority interests. Because of the danger this created for the whole, the Federalists constantly emphasized the higher priorities that must guide the national government. But at the same time, the states serve as a useful buffer against the legislature's tendency to over–extend. The Federalists thus found that the solution to balancing powers within the government had already been solved by Montesquieu and created a liberal if not wholly democratic constitution.

Alexis de Tocqueville and the American Example

A visiting Frenchman later found much to admire in the political system which the American Federalists had created, but also cause for concern. After visiting the U.S. in the early 1830s, Alexis de Tocqueville (1805–1859) returned to France and wrote *Democracy in America*:

> Let us not turn to America in order to slavishly copy the institutions she has fashioned for herself, but in order that we may better understand what suits us; let us look there for instruction rather than models; let us adopt the principles rather than the details of her laws...

While Montesquieu had looked to Britain and urged the French monarchy to change its ways; Tocqueville urged republican France to follow America's lead. Tocqueville looks to the New World for the most advanced constitutional arrangement.

In an 1848 speech to the French Chamber of Deputies, he warned that France rested on a volcano and that the working classes would overthrow the "foundations" upon which society rested unless property were distributed on more equally. But Tocqueville believed that social processes and change eventually resulted in political development and urged the extension of representation within a liberal state to encompass the enfranchisement of the working, non–propertied classes as was occurring in America. In the main, the U.S. had successfully combined individual freedoms with egalitarian social conditions. The two exceptions, for Tocqueville, were African and indigenous Americans. Women, on other hand, had a different situation and "although the American woman never leaves her domestic sphere and is in some respects very dependent within it, nowhere does she enjoy higher station."

With the African and Native Americans, things were very different. "In one blow oppression has deprived the descendants of the Africans of almost all the privileges of humanity. The United States Negro has lost even the memory of his homeland; he no longer understands the language his fathers spoke..." This oppression was compounded by slavery. Native Americans had not been slaves, but they lived on "the edge of freedom." Their life had been destroyed through the dispossession of their lands; their adoption of new tastes such as firearms, iron, brandy, and cloth, and the dwindling of wild game.

The progress that had developed in America, combining liberty and equality had, then, come at a terrible price for Blacks and Native Americans. Tocqueville saw the paradox that what is good and progressive is not good and progressive in all respects. America had opened up a future for the world, but had done so by robbing the Indians of their lands and enslaving African Americans. Slavery was also an economic liability.

But, in the main, America had managed a blend of the pursuit of private interests and public freedom. This blend did not mean that the American political institutions were perfect. But what mattered for Tocqueville was the overall liberty and well being for most of the inhabitants, based upon the core principle running through American society: each person is the best judge of his interests. In government, administration and in private life, this way of looking at things inculcated a dynamic, responsible, daring, and energetic spirit.

Unlike Karl Marx (1818–1883) and Jean–Jacques Rousseau (1712–1778), Tocqueville does not see inequality, as such, as a problem. It was only a problem if it was static, continually rewarded the idle rather than the industrious, and if it blocked the energies of the population. Tocqueville's approach to inequality was pragmatic: it brings with it certain characteristics and incentives, but there is nothing valuable about it as such.

In America, says Tocqueville, the principle of the sovereignty of the people existed from the beginning of the colonies, even though "the colonies were still bound to the motherland." While voting rights were restricted to certain classes of property holders, the democratic ethos was rife in the provincial assemblies. Thus when America revolted against the British, "the dogma of the sovereignty of the people came out from the township and took possession of the government; every class enlisted in its cause." Even those classes which had most to lose from the expansion of democracy, were swept along with it in the revolution. It was, then, that bonding of classes against a common external enemy, combined with an ethos that had been introduced at the moment of colonization that made the establishment of American democracy so smooth.

At the time different states had various property qualifications for voting. But Tocqueville saw that the trend was toward eliminating restrictions and expanding the franchise. Democracy was an infectious political form suggesting that there is something intrinsically desirable about it for the majority of people. But that does not mean that it is a perfect form of government, or even the most adequate form of government for achieving a range of outcomes. Tocqueville saw that the egalitarian ethos of a democratic society carried a leveling tendency, but the leveling effect is seen by Tocqueville as eliminating the worst of the extremities which plague other regimes.

For Tocqueville, the most important negative in the trade–off between aristocratic and democratic societies consisted in the diminution of glorious achievements which tended to come when a society is placed in service to the ambitions, tastes, and talents of a group who see their talents, tastes, virtues, and actions as the *raison d'être* of society. But the most significant gain is the energy that gets unleashed through mass participation in political affairs.

Democracy does not provide a people with the most skilful of governments, but it does what the most skilful government often cannot do: it spreads throughout the social body a restless activity, and energy not found elsewhere, which, however little favored by circumstances, can do wonders. This is liberal doctrine.

Tocqueville, like the Federalists, feared the tyranny of the majority and believed that it was inevitable that the power of the majority would dominate. Tocqueville takes care not to say that American democracy is tyrannical, rather that there is no inherent political check against it. One problem was the instability of laws and public administration. Laws would be far more likely to be rapidly introduced and just as rapidly dropped, as some new idea took the public's attention. The reformists' energy was great in the United States, but projects were frequently left unfinished. A more insidious feature of the power of the majority, according to Tocqueville, was the power over thought. Whereas, says Tocqueville, in monarchies, the monarch is not able to compel moral authority, this is precisely the ground that the majority tries to occupy.

Tocqueville's assessment of the inevitability of democracy, then, was matched by a cautious appreciation of the values of democratic society. The precarious balance achieved in America between liberty and equality was praised by Tocqueville. But he also grasped the tension that existed between them. America was fortunate in having the cultural roots which sustained this balance. Tocqueville knew that those

Friedrich A. Hayek. (The Library of Congress)

roots were different from other countries, including France, which he saw were destined to go down the pathway of democracy. Thus there was a deep sense of foreboding that democracy would not be as smoothly established in the old world as in the new world, that there the pull toward equality could easily tip the balance toward an egalitarian despotism, as occurred under fascism.

The same dilemma was being grappled with in England. John Stuart Mill (1806–1873), who reviewed *Democracy in America*, praised it as the first philosophical book on democracy as it manifested itself in modern society. Mill was to evolve as the most important single advocate of applying the doctrines of liberalism, many of them already practiced in America, to Europe.

The Social Liberals

One of the most influential of the new liberals was the English academic Thomas Hill Green (1836–1882). Green did not, like Marx, propose a social revolution, but he did believe that a free society would only emerge if the state played a directing role in changing the social circumstances of men and women. In arguing for this, Green reformulated the most fundamental idea of liberalism, liberty itself. As he wrote in *Liberal Legislation and Freedom of Contract* in 1861:

We shall probably all agree that freedom, rightly understood, is the greatest of all blessings; that its attainment is the true end of all our efforts as citizens. But when we thus speak of freedom.... we do not mean merely freedom from restraint or compulsion. We do not mean a freedom that can be enjoyed by one man or one set of men at the cost of a loss of freedom to others.

Green's position was expressed in the language of liberalism. Liberalism had arisen in opposition to the propertied classes being above the commercial class, not primarily in opposition to the classes beneath it. Although the commercial class had not wanted to spread political power to those who could soak its own wealth, the language forged in opposition to the aristocracy was the language of universality, right, equality, progress, as well as freedom. Freedom was only one of the variables in the political rhetoric that the emergent middle class had used in its political struggle. The rising working classes did not need another language in order to make its claims.

Green's philosophical conception of freedom, then, was not contrary to the ideas already embedded in liberalism, in spite of carrying a freight that many liberals viewed as contrary to the kind of society they wanted to build based on private initiative free from paternal directions.

Furthermore, what also gave Green credibility was his emphasis upon the delivery of improved living standards. The core argument of liberal political economists had never simply been that freedom was good for the wealthy, but that in a liberal society wealth would be most speedily generated and more people would benefit than under any alternative economic system. It found its economic expression most famously in Adam Smith's "invisible hand," and was in Green's time transforming the subject of economic inquiry by replacing political economy into neo–classical economics. Green did not dispute the central tenets of this liberal political economy. The liberal tradition had provided a new benchmark for measuring the value of political arrangements: progressively advancing prosperity.

Closely related to this was the connection that had been established within the liberal tradition, between the value ascribed to property and the value ascribed to capacities or personal properties. Locke's defense of private property rested upon the fact that a claim had been established through labor. In other words, private property was the expression, as Kant and then Hegel pointed out more clearly than Locke himself, of an action and an act of will. Madison had also spoken of "the diversity of faculties of men, from which the rights of property originate." The "first object of

BIOGRAPHY:

Friedrich A. Hayek

As the expansion of the state occurred, some liberal economic theorists warned that this would entail the destruction of liberal political economy on which the prosperity of modern society depended. The most influential of these philosophers were known as the "Austrian School", and one of its most important members was Friedrich August von Hayek.

Friedrich A. Hayek was born in Vienna and studied at the University of Vienna, sitting in on von Mises' classes. Hayek wrote on *Monetary Theory and the Trade Cycle* in 1929, which analyzed the effects of credit expansion on the capital structure of an economy. After emigrating to Great Britain in the early 1930s, Hayek became a British citizen in 1938. He lectured at the Fabian Socialist Centre and the London School of Economics (LSE), and his lectures were published in a second book on the *Austrian Theory of the Trade Cycle, Prices and Production* (1931). He was appointed Professor at the University of London as the LSE passed out of the Fabians' control.

In London he argued with Keynes, and the Hayek–Keynes debate was one of the most important debates in monetary economics in the twentieth century. In his *The End of Laissez Faire (1926)*, Keynes presented his interventionist pleas in the language of classical liberalism. As a result, Keynes was heralded as the "savior of capitalism," rather than an advocate of inflation and government intervention.

Although Hayek was publicly defeated, he became involved in another grand debate in economic policy on socialist economic calculation. Hayek's essays on the problems of "market socialism," developed by Oskar Lange and Abba Lerner when answering Mises and Hayek, were collected and later appeared in *Individualism and Economic Order* (1948). But again, Hayek appeared to lose the technical economic debate with the Keynesians concerning the causes of business cycles and, in view of the rising tide of socialism, his general philosophical perspective was increasingly labeled as a primitive version of liberalism.

Hayek, however, persisted. The problems of socialism he saw beginning to emerge in Britain led him to write *The Road to Serfdom* (1944). If socialism required the replacement of the market with a central plan, then, Hayek pointed out, an institution must be established to be responsible for formulating this plan. To implement the plan and to control the flow of resources, the state would have to exercise broad power in economic affairs. But in a socialist society, the state would have no market prices to serve as guides. It would have no means of knowing which production possibilities were economically rational. Further, those who would rise to the top in a socialistic regime would be those who liked exercising discretionary power and making unpleasant decisions. These people would run the system to their own personal advantage and destroy the freedom of society on which liberal economic prosperity depended.

Hayek at first achieved fame when young, but as the socialists gained popularity, the intellectual and political world moved away from his ideas. Nonetheless, he lived long enough to see his position recognized. Both Keynesians and socialists were eventually reduced by events, and Hayek became a key figure in the late twentieth century revival of liberalism.

He won his 1974 Nobel Prize in Economics, but also wrote about government intervention, economic calculation under socialism, and development of social structures. Although Hayek championed classic liberal economic policies of the late–nineteenth century, he also came to influence conservative politicians like Ronald Reagan and Margaret Thatcher. Hayek was awarded the Medal of Freedom in 1991 by U.S. President George Bush, and died the next year in Freibury, Germany.

government," he said, "was the protection of these faculties." With Mill the defense of liberty had for all its warnings about paternalistic government not primarily been an argument about protecting private property, but an argument about how personal capacities and energies would best flourish.

Thus the path has already been established within the liberal tradition for Green to emphasize that the job of the state is to equip its populace with the necessary skills for the exercise and development of their capacities. A state which fails to do this, thus becomes complicit in tyranny and the unfair preservation of privilege, in much the same way as the pre–liberal state had been complicit in the preservation of privilege for the select few. Private property, then, is justifiable only to the extent that it does not serve as a barrier to members of a particular social group developing their faculties. Green says because property is, "only justifiable as the free exercise of the social capabilities of all, there can be no true right to property of a kind which debars one class of men from such free exercise altogether." For social liberal theorists like Green, "the people" must mean all of those who are capable of exercising their rights and who have not acted in such a manner that they may be legitimately deprived of them. But having the capacity to exercise their rights means that barriers to them must be removed.

In addition, the argument that the state should not intervene in a non–criminal contract freely entered into may seem to be a strong argument to the social liberal position. But as Green well knew, the liberal tradition had explicitly rejected the idea of voluntary entering into slavery. Rights were inalienable. Green, thus beginning from the invalidity of a contract of slavery, goes onto argue that "no contract is valid in which human persons, willingly or unwillingly, are dealt with as commodities, because such contracts of necessity defeat the end for which alone society enforces contracts at all." Humans as rational beings should never be treated as means, because they are ends in themselves.

Green justified increasing state intervention, but did not see himself as a proponent of illiberal ideas. Protective labor legislation, public health and public education were justifiable, because they raise the well–being of those members of the population who otherwise would not be able to exercise their freedom or contribute to the public good.

The philosophy articulated by Green was built upon the synthesis of the liberal ideas of private power, the republican concern with the public good, and the egalitarian spirit of Rousseau. But it was also built in response to the social and political changes taking place in Britain. Late nineteenth century liberalism had become a doctrine as suspicious of the minority wealthy bourgeoisie, as seventeenth– and eighteenth–century liberalism had been of the aristocracy. The liberal politician Joseph Chamberlain (1836–1914) said in 1885 that "the great evil with which we have to deal is the excessive inequality in the distribution of riches."

Liberal theorists in the twentieth century, with a few exceptions, continued further down the path of seeing the task of the state as providing the conditions for social justice. Invariably that meant restraining the liberty of the wealthy. The best known exceptions to this were mainly economists, such as Ludwig von Mises (1881–1973) and Friedrich von Hayek (1899–1992). The Mises–Hayek Theory of the trade cycle—which Hayek formulated with the brilliant economist Ludwig von Mises—argued a "cluster of errors" characterizes the cycle. Excessive credit expansion occurs artificially lowering of interest rates that misleads businessmen who are led to engage in ventures that would otherwise have been unprofitable. This false signal produces poor coordination of production and consumption in society. This at first produces a "boom," and then, later, a "bust," as production adjusts to the real, and lower, pattern of savings and consumption in the economy. The intervention of government makes recessions worse.

Among philosophers the libertarian Robert Nozick also stands out. More typically, Leonard Hobhouse (1864–1929) in his classic twentieth–century defense *Liberalism, 1911*, said what all liberals had accepted, that "liberty itself only rests upon constraint." He argued that "the function of the state is to override individual coercion" in order to maintain social justice and such rights as "the right to work" and the right to a living wage. Wealth and property were therefore treated as social goods.

THEORY IN DEPTH

Benedict de Spinoza

In seventeenth–century Holland, Benedict de Spinoza (1632–1677) became first modern philosopher to overtly defend political democracy. Spinoza's philosophical starting point was the need to make a radical separation between theological scripture and philosophy: each one must be allowed to function without subordination to the other. This was a major problem for Spinoza and a central subject of his in *A Theological–Political Treatise* (1670). Spinoza's political problem was largely, though not exclusively, centred around the problem of freedom of speech.

Spinoza saw himself as a philosophical scientist, and realized the issue of free speech could be a matter of personal survival. He knew that while he was safe in the commercial republic of Holland, because of the perceived dangerousness of his philosophy he was not at liberty to live in various other parts of Europe.

Spinoza believed that nature was governed by scientific laws. Spinoza's understanding of all natural beings was premised on the simple idea that they are what they do. Nature is what it does, and what it does is its right. As he succinctly put it: "Whatsoever an individual does by the laws of its nature it has a sovereign right to do." Thus Spinoza made a heretical equation that was to make his name a byword for infamy: the power of nature and the power of God are the same power.

The virtue of democracy, to Spinoza, was that it will create the strongest possible power. For the sovereign will be the people as a whole. Thus the act of transference is a mutual act of transference whereby the citizens are the body politic; they are not merely subjects, but they are reconstituted in their role as sovereign legislators. Interestingly, the very thing which most other democratic theorists fear, the excessive power of the people, is what Spinoza endorses when he defines a democracy as: "a society which wields all its power as a whole. The sovereign power is not restrained by any laws, but everyone is bound to obey it in all things; such is the state of things when men either tacitly or expressly handed over to it all their power of self–defense, or in other words, all their right."

In this respect Spinoza endorses a radical form of democracy, because a democracy is least likely to ignore the pubic good, for it is its own good. A democracy is, in terms of Spinoza's philosophy, dedicated to compromising between the different powers that can come into collision.

A democracy simply provides an opportunity for all the adult male sovereign powers to provide laws that enable them to pursue their interests in so far as that is feasible. Spinoza specifically excludes slaves, criminals, children, wards of the state, and women from exercising political power. Spinoza's defense of democracy rests on a thoroughly realist foundation:

> The object of government is not to change men from rational beings into beasts or puppets, but to enable them to develop their minds and bodies in security, and to employ their reason unshackled; neither showing hatred, anger, or deceit, nor watched by the eyes of jealousy and injustice. In fact, the true aim of government is liberty.

This was the first overt expression of the key philosophical doctrine of political liberalism.

In a democracy, freedom of opinion is vital for the people to discuss the advantages and disadvantages of any piece of legislation, thus enabling it to overturn old laws if their disadvantages outweigh their benefits. While, then, Spinoza indicates that no ruler is acting in his best interest if he suppresses free speech, in a democracy such a suppression would be most contrary to the best interests of the sovereign body itself.

While Spinoza was the first philosopher to provide an elaborate defense of modern democracy, he also provides a few of the hallowed conceptions usually associated with the great documents of liberal democracy. But Spinoza's conception of rights and powers also deeply contradicts the notion of natural rights that is ingrained in the constitutional tradition and incorporated in such documents as the American Declaration of Independence and the French Declaration of the Rights of Man. The first modern political theorist who can be credited with providing a liberal as well as a democratic account of state theory was John Locke.

John Locke

The Englishman, John Locke, is generally regarded as being the first liberal thinker, although the term itself did not gain common currency until over a hundred years after his death. Previously, great political theorists had equated human nature with rapaciousness, only constrained by fear and force; Locke saw human nature as civil, reasonable, tolerant, and industrious, with its distribution of talents and opportunities being essentially equal.

Locke wrote *Two Treatises of Government* (published in 1690) in the context of the Glorious Revolution—which placed the House of Orange on the English throne—and the English Bill of Rights. For Locke, as long as one is not struggling to survive, there is a natural tendency to realize the advantage that comes from mutual respect of the rights of all to preserve their life, liberty, health, limbs, and goods. Locke does preserve a distinction between natural right and natural law, the latter of which is distinguished by its enforceability. But the legitimacy of that power derives from the right that everyone has to preserve their own basic rights. No one has the right to invade the rights of others, and "every one has the right to punish the transgressors of that Law (of nature) to such a Degree, as may hinder its Violation."

Locke's state of nature, with its original natural rights and fundamental human civility, crowned the parliamentary revolution by cementing the fiction that natural rights did indeed precede the formation of the state. And he does so by transforming the particular issue of the English nearly liberal transformation of the seventeenth century into a universal political theory. He adopted a virtual silence on the particular historical controversy, while providing a general theory in *An Essay Concerning Human Understanding* (written from 1671, published in 1689), which was derived from his experience.

The *ahistoricism* of his theory meant that it could be appealed to anywhere at anytime, and would later be transposed with great success as a defense for founding new institutions in America. But the disciple of Locke can also argue as if the institutional balances which were the product of over four hundred years of intense and often bloody struggles in England can simply be imposed on societies that have no organic dispositions toward liberal democracy. Locke does not present the state of nature as if it were built upon the English experience; rather, it is the experience of reason itself. Where respect for liberty prevails, he seemed to believe, so would prosperity.

For Locke, the danger to peace was not the grasping natures of men pursuing their own interests, but the rapacious behavior of the monarch and his contempt for natural rights. This forced men to move from the calm state of nature to the state of war to protect their property and their rights. The lesson of the civil war, for Locke, was not the need to defend the absolute power of the monarchical sovereign. Rather, the lesson was that the Stuart monarchy had lost, and it had to pass down its stolen powers if the institution were to continue at all.

For Locke the cause of the conflict was the violation of those very liberties which Locke saw as natural and widely held. The people who fought against the thieving monarchs—including himself, of course—had only acted to protect what was reasonably and rightfully theirs. Further, it was through their natural respect for the rights and reasons of each other that the wealth, which the monarch sought to extract through taxes, was theirs in the first place. A king does not generate prosperity: industry, cooperation, and exchange do that. Locke argued that the nature of production and the way its bounties should be distributed is plain to anyone who sets their mind to it.

The exercise of freedom and reason and its industrious deployment is thus, for Locke, the natural disposition of man. The role of government is not to change this disposition, but merely to assist its facility and development by providing for a neutral judge when disputes occur.

Locke grounded his theory of government upon reason, but this was not the purpose of government. As Locke put it: "Government has no other end but the preservation of Property," by which he means "Lives, Liberties and Estates." Locke does not criticize private property. But at the same time, he saw that private property was a corollary of social evolution. Locke does not in any way seek to make philosophers into kings, for the government must represent what the majority of the people desire. Although, Locke does assume that what will bind the majority is the protection of their own liberty.

Locke does not worry about the majority then robbing from the rich, since the suggestion in *The Two Treatises of Government* is that the majority is meant to include only landed property holders. There is ambiguity since "property" in Locke can mean wealth and even capacity as well as land and he does not go into any detail about who is to have the franchise. But it is reasonable to assume that Locke, like so many liberal theorists even into the nineteenth century, did not automatically equate political and civic rights. Likewise, given that the general thrust of the *The Two Treatises of Government* is so in harmony with the English parliamentary model and the tenor of the "Bill of Rights," it is also reasonable to assume that Locke believed that the criteria for representation in the parliament was, to a large extent, already sufficiently refined. In his lifetime this was very narrow. On the other hand, the justification of "political and civil society," for Locke, rests upon the consent of "All Men," "Mankind" and "the People." He also points out the need to have "fair and equal" representation and to make sure that electorates are not numerically distorted.

Probably, Locke did not trouble himself with the dangers of a democracy allowing the poor to take the property of the rich because he did not believe the poor would acquire political power. By so grounding the theory of government on the right of private property, Locke may have hoped that whoever constitutes the governing body would be aware of the sacrosanct nature of this right. His political solution to the preservation of the right of property is that there can be no taxation without the support of the majority, and the government has no right to deprive people of their property. Indeed, if it attempts to do so, then the people have a right to rebel.

Locke's theory of government does not solve all the problems of a democracy. But it does clearly set forth the doctrine of government as essentially a representative body of the people's rights and interests. In Locke, the political theory of the liberal–democratic state finds an eloquent and refined defense. But there is one crucial problem: how to justify curtailing the will of the majority if it makes unjust claims by intruding on the rights of a minority, or single person. Locke's theory of the state was built around the need to defend a right, the right to property.

Charles Secondat, Baron de Montesquieu

The French aristocrat, Charles Secondat, Baron de Montesquieu, was the first great theorist to raise the question of the social character and degree of social evolution of a people when exploring how government could expresses the interests of its people. His profound importance also rests on his making the connection between the commercial base of a society and its institutions of government, and the doctrine of the separation of powers.

In his *Spirit of the Laws* (1748) he says that what constitutes good governance will depend upon the "humor and disposition of the people in whose favor it is established." While Locke had relied upon natural reason to safeguard natural rights and limit government, for Montesquieu, reason was always filtered through the complex layers which constitute a particular nation.

But before Montesquieu delves into the geographical, historical, and sociological dimensions of the different "spirits" of the nations and laws that he examines, he dissects the different forms of government and the principal spirit which differentiates the monarchy, from the republic, from the aristocratic and from the despotic. Montesquieu's seemingly neutral observations about the different spirits and different laws has a specific political purpose. This can be gleaned from the opening of *The Spirit of the Laws* where Montesquieu urges caution on reformers, appealing to the general public to appreciate the complexity of a nation and its government. He encourages "every man to love his prince; his country, his laws." Aware of the energies of the rising commercial class—especially in England—he argued that reform would best achieve its goal in France if gradual and in conformity with the general character and habits of the country.

Any attempt at a radical leap from the human imagination to the actual political and social reality will not succeed. One model society provided Montesquieu with the benchmark he most esteemed: the most politically civilized country of the period, increasingly liberal England. The argument of *The Spirit of the Laws* was that France should follow England's lead. For it was England that was the most prosperous, most free, most tolerant nation, and had the most advanced form of government.

England had achieved a blend of the monarchical, aristocratic, and republican virtues through the evolution of its constitutional system and through long periods of struggle, compromise and institutional devolution. Montesquieu believed England's institutions combined the republican virtues of equality and consistency in the rule of law, with the aristocratic virtue of moderation, and the monarchical virtues of ambition and honor. But because of the power of the House of Commons, republican virtues will dominate. In France, on the other hand, there was a dangerous gap between social and political power, and the centralization of po-

Charles Secondat, Baron de Montesquieu.
(The Library of Congress)

litical power in the monarch only contributed to retarding the general prosperity of the nation.

Montesquieu's deep appreciation of the political trade–offs brought about by social conflict underpinned his major contribution to political theory. Montesquieu provided an understanding of constitutionality based upon the separation of powers that was to be integral to the American liberal democracy.

Montesquieu transformed what looked like a description of the English constitution, into an argument for making the British model of government the benchmark for judging other models. Montesquieu's English model may work in other parts of the globe provided that the ethos of the people is effected by the experiences of trade and commerce. Montesquieu believed that there was a strong correlation between the spirit of liberty and trade.

What Montesquieu esteemed, was a real entity, which has a real history. If people want liberty, religious tolerance, and prosperity then they should follow the English model. English political experience may have created the series of lucky accidents that gave birth to the model, but others may be able to learn from those accidents. Montesquieu knew that disregard for liberty could occur under any system of government and that republics were not immune from this.

Liberty was defended by Montesquieu in his doctrine of the "separation of powers." Montesquieu's argument for a mixed constitution evolved because he thought deeply about the links between the social and the political, and about the benefits that would flow from necessary compromises. He was a social scientist in an era when science and rationality achieved unprecedented acclaim—during the Enlightenment.

Jean-Jacques Rousseau

A leading French critic of the *ancien regime*, Jean–Jacques Rousseau (1712–1778) was an idealist democrat whose major contribution was locating the source of constitutionality in "the general will." In him the possibility of the separation of liberal from democratic theory emerges. The French Revolution's *Declaration of the Rights of Man and of the Citizen* (1789) paid tribute to Rousseau: "The law is the expression of the general will. All citizens have the right to concur in prison or through the representatives in its formation. It must be the same for all whether it protects or punishes. All citizens, being equal before it."

But although Rousseau's genius located the general will, the cost for this great insight was that the political reality of different, often competing interests is avoided. Politics was reduced to the morality of a single moral principle which enabled its adherent to dismiss as illegitimate the entire historical experience of nations which contained competing interests. Civilization had been built on false and pernicious foundations—private property and self–interest. With Rousseau begins in earnest the disastrous attempt to use political means to attain a vague form of social freedom which is supposed to be in tune with both human nature and our moral conscience, based on a common will.

The Rousseauian political agenda was then built around exchanging tangible partial liberties for general intangible ones. In place of the private happiness that comes from pursuing one's own interests, which liberals came to support, one should, for Rousseau, take one's place within the community's pursuit of the general will. Rousseau's appeal derived from nostalgic and idyllic sentiments, which he expresses so forcefully. But Rousseau turns these sentiments into a mood of great despair: "Man is born free, and everywhere he is in chains."

Rousseau endorsed a politics in which the sovereignty of the people has no restraint. The use of the general will totally politicizes community experience. The purpose of the community becomes political existence itself, a far cry from Locke's notion of politics as a necessary means for our own ends. This endorsed collective totalitarianism from the Terror to Stalin. In the "general will," Rousseau helped create that formulation of democracy, which eventually could give it a fascist, communistic and wholly illiberal character.

The Philosophy and Theory of Classical Liberalism

In the year of the Declaration of Independence, 1776, Adam Smith (1723–1790) published *An Inquiry into the Nature and Causes of the Wealth of Nations*, and founded the science of political economy. Its basic doctrine was that human labor is the only source of a nation's wealth. Smith advocated (and observed) the division of labor in the productive process, stressed the importance of individual enterprise and argued the benefits of free trade between countries. The true wealth of a nation, he held, lay not in the possession of gold but in the achievement of abundance. He warned against unnecessary intervention by the state in this process. In these conclusions, he was in part recommending the path which Britain was already undertaking, as it embarked, during his lifetime, on the world's first industrial revolution.

He is also commonly associated with the notion of the "invisible hand" which, operating through the self–interest of each individual and untrammeled by state regulation, would produce the general welfare of economic growth, development and prosperity.

Smith argued that wherever government went beyond protecting personal liberty and property it inhibited economic development. He saw in many places poverty attributable to state interference and believed the only sources of wealth and prosperity were industry and the natural powers of production of men. He concluded what was required was to leave economics to itself, since there was harmony between individual and public interests, and that the natural pursuit of economic interests would produce the greatest prosperity. Smith included in political economy not only trade, exchange and production but also political institutions and laws.

Smith appears to point to unrestricted liberty as the best principle of political economy. But he speaks also of "the natural effort of every individual to better his own condition, when suffered to exert itself with freedom and security," as the cause of national wealth and prosperity.

As the British state emerged in 1815 as the most powerful in the world, so Smith and the theories of liberal political economy which he had founded, were deployed to reform its political and economic structures. By the 1830s those who had become known at first as radicals, like Richard Cobden (1804–1865), and then later the more establishment Liberals under Prime Minister William Gladstone (1809–1898), pursued the idea of the *laissez–faire* state. The liberal economic regime, suggested by Smith, had not only become the model which Britain provided for the world, but a design to which it aspired.

Jeremy Bentham

The ancien regime in France had led to revolution, popular democracy, mob rule, and then military expansion under the Napoleon. England emerged victorious in 1815 as a wealthy, industrial and powerful country with an aristocratic system of government. Agitation for liberalization and democratization quickly emerged with the peace. Several prominent philosophers were influential in spreading the ideas which were to underpin the resulting creation of mid–nineteenth century, liberal England.

If Smith developed the idea that economic prosperity depended on the pursuit of self–interest and the operation of the "invisible hand," it was left to others to divine the purpose of the state. Jeremy Bentham published anonymously, also in 1776, *A Fragment on Government*, in which he formulated his celebrated utilitarian principle, "the greatest happiness of the greatest number." By it exclusively he would judge the value of juridical, political, social, ethical, and religious systems and institutions. In 1779 Bentham's chief work, *Introduction to the Principles of Morals and Legislation*, appeared.

After 1815, Bentham's writings and ideas became widely influential. In England, his ideas of political reform were taken up by the leaders of emerging radical liberalism. Bentham attacked the Established Church and applied the utilitarian test to religion. In ethics, Bentham maintained happiness was the sole end of conduct and reduced moral obligation to the sanction inherent in the pleasant or painful results of action. The spread of his ideas contributed to Catholic Emancipation in 1829 and the parliamentary reform Act of 1832 extending the franchise to the middle class.

Bentham was also the founder of the concept of "utility" in economics, defining it as private happiness, the modern economic usage. He associated man's pursuit of happiness as a matter of the incentives provided by the balancing of pain and pleasure, prices and wages. The reforms Bentham pursued were directed towards good government, abundance, security and equality. He followed Adam Smith as part of the search for abundance, but advocated a state which provided guaranteed employment, minimum wages

Jeremy Bentham.

and a variety of social benefits. Much of his influence on ideas and legislation was through a circle of pupils and disciples, amongst whom were many economists, including David Ricardo (1772–1823) and John Stuart Mill.

John Stuart Mill

Like Tocqueville, Mill witnessed a social and political transformation that was without any historical parallel: the synthesis of the continuing triumph of liberal principles and the industrial revolution, with the expanding social power and political mobilization of the lower classes. Like Tocqueville, Mill also saw that the modern liberal democratic state could not adequately be described as having a mixed constitution. Ultimately, in any state there was one sovereign power, and in a democratic state it must be the people. Whereas Montesquieu saw the monarchy and House of Lords as still representing considerable social power, Mill no longer saw this as necessary. The burning issues of the day, for Mill, were how exactly the will of the people was to be constituted, and then how it was to be channeled for the greatest political good.

The question of what constituted the greatest good, for Mill, was addressed in the most important defense of liberal principles since Locke. In that work, *On Liberty* (1869), Mill focused upon what Toc-

BIOGRAPHY:

John Stuart Mill

John Stuart Mill was the eldest son of James Mill, friend and disciple of Jeremy Bentham, and was taught Greek, Latin, mathematics, philosophy, and economics intensively from a very early age by his father in London. Young John did not go to school or associate with other boys of his age. Mill gave a vivid and moving account of his life, and especially of his peculiar education, in the *Autobiography*, posthumously published in 1873, that he wrote toward the end of his life.

Mill's father then got him a comfortable job at the India Office where he worked for thirty–five years while producing an enormous published output. As a result, despite an extremely cloistered life, he became one of the most influential of Victorian liberal thinkers, on philosophy, economics and politics. In the 1830s he edited the *London and Westminster Review*, a radical liberal quarterly journal.

At first, like his father, Mills was a utilitarian. Then, after a severe mental crisis in 1826–1827, he became more romantic and wrote about poetry and its importance. He was, shortly thereafter, influenced by his wife, Harriet Taylor, who co–authored extensively with him before and after the death of her first husband. John and Harriet were married in 1851. Mills then moved towards humanism and idealism.

He also, later on, became somewhat sympathetic to socialism. He was a strong advocate of women's rights, including the franchise, and supported proportional representation, labor unions, and farm co–operatives. But principally, he was a defender of individ-ual liberty against the interference of both society and state.

Mills was a Liberal member of parliament for Westminster from 1865 to 1868, where he advocated women's suffrage, the interests of the laboring classes, and land reform in Ireland. However, he made little impact on the Parliament.

As a philosopher, Mill was technically competent, but no pathbreaker. His *System of Logic* (1843) argued that scientific method could apply to social as well as purely natural phenomena. It is now little read.

Mill is better known for *Principles of Political Economy* (1848), but this has also slipped closer into obscurity. He is often included in histories of economic thought as a minor disciple of Adam Smith or a lesser contemporary of David Ricardo. Nonetheless, some of his observations about the environment may deserve revival.

In politics, his essay "On Liberty" (1859) aroused controversy at the time and may now be read as a defense of the individual against middle–class conformity, a common viewpoint among intellectuals today. He argued that the state should only interfere with the conduct of individuals when so doing would prevent a greater harm to others. His *Considerations on Representative Government* (1861) contains numerous interesting and practical suggestions for political reform, many now implemented in different countries. His *Utilitarianism* (1861) is a classic defense of that view, but it is not now so widely regarded. *The Subjection of Women* (1869) now looks enormously prescient.

---

queville had seen as the greatest single benefit that democracy had conferred upon the social character of America, a prodigious energy. For Mill, the primary purpose of politics is to unleash the energies of the species. Liberty takes on supreme importance for Mill because it energizes those who act in accordance with it. Liberty, then, is not simply an end in itself, as it is for Kant. Liberty is valuable because it is useful.

Intrinsic to the development of liberty, for Mill, is the expression of one's wants and the willingness to involve oneself in the interests of the nation. Unless one does this, one's liberty will inevitably be curbed by circumstances that are imposed by interests that have emerged from another group. Mill does not believe that politics is just about the expression of self–interest, partly because he sees the very concept of "self–interest" as unclear. Further, unless a group participates in the decisions which concern it, it is not developing the energies required for its own growth.

Mill saw that two major social groups had been thus far deprived of participation in popular government: the laboring class and women. For the laboring class, there was a major social transformation taking place that could create serious social problems. There was serious danger of class conflict if the state became beholden to one of the two major disputing interest groups: the wealthy classes and the laboring classes. Ideally, it would be best if these classes were to hold "about an equal number of votes in the Parliament." Mill adopted the scheme of proportional representation developed by Thomas Hare, wherein people choose between parties in a geographic location in a particular constituency and for a series of candidates from all over the country. Once a candidate has a sufficient number of votes, or quota, to be elected, the remainder for him go to second candidate until he gets a quota, and so on to the third and subsequent candidates until the places are exhausted. Mill believed that this approach would guarantee diversity of representation, and indeed variations of this system have been successfully utilized in Australia.

The second proposal that Mill had for moderating against the danger of self–interest submerging the national interest, was the provision of education for all classes. Mill believed that education was indispensable for the viability of popular government. If one could not read, write, or do simple arithmetic then one is incapable, for Mill, of participating in the political process. He even suggested that voters should be asked to a copy a sentence out of a book and do a simple math exercise. The key to good government, for Mill, lay in combining energy and intelligence. He even proposed that voters who had achieved a certain level of education be granted more votes, and that a second chamber be created on a *meritocratic* basis (selected by intellect).

Mill invoked the principle of no representation without financial contribution. Bankrupts and those who are dependent upon charity or state welfare for their livelihood should be excluded from the suffrage. Those who introduce new taxation, suggested Mill, must also feel the effect of it. Mill well knew that public goods come at a price and that one group may be happy for another group to pay the bill, just as one generation may want the successor generation to pick up the tab for its enjoyments.

Mill is an important figure in history because his large body of wide ranging works were persuasively, logically, and factually argued; because he made a synthesis of the various strands of pre–liberal thought into a more coherent modern form of liberalism; and because he stated the case for a liberal democracy just as that kind of society was, for the first time, coming into existence in Britain and the United States.

Liberals and Women's Rights

One group for whom the franchise was becoming an issue were women. Greek philosopher Plato (428–348 B.C.) thought women capable of having a

John Stuart Mill.

political input and argued that women should be included in the guardian class. Aristotle, however, had defended the more traditional view of women as incapable of making any contribution to political life. This view was pretty much the standard philosophical view of women in the Middle Ages, although Descartes had to a minor extent broken with this tradition. But generally, even the more radical democratic spirits did not desire political power for women—Spinoza rejected the idea and while Locke vigorously argued against paternalism, within the family he believed that it was natural that the male should rule, and by implication political power should fall to him. Even Rousseau, while working for the removal of man's chains, had in Emily sought to ensure that women's role remained divorced from politics.

The exceptions were Marie Jean Condorcet (1743–1794), Jeremy Bentham, and the woman usually credited as the first to write a sustained treatise for the emancipation of women, Mary Wolstonecraft (1759–1797).

Condorcet in "On Granting Civil Rights to Women" (1790), compared the situations of Blacks and women, attacked their maltreatment and the institutional discrimination that they had to endure. He insisted that reason was universal, and that women could not be denied their rightful status as rational beings. Condorcet argued in *Five Memoirs of Education*

that women should be educated just as men are, an issue that Daniel Defoe had raised almost a hundred
years earlier, and the historian, Catherine Macaulay,
also advocated in her *Letters on Education* (1790).
Condorcet's argument for women having civil rights
was consistent in its advocacy that such rights should
also be accompanied by political rights, provided the
property qualifications for the vote were also met.

Jeremy Bentham was also an advocate for
women's rights. In an unpublished manuscript of 1789
he objected to equating women with infants and the
insane for the purpose of excluding them from the
vote. In a number of published works, including *Cat-
echism of a Parliamentary Reform* (1809), the *Radical Reform Bill* (1819), and the *Constitutional Code*,
he argued for extending educational and political opportunities to women.

In *Vindication of the Rights of Woman* (1795),
Mary Wolstonecraft emphasized the absurd contradiction between Rousseau's conception of rights,
which she largely accepted, and the subordinate role
of women, which he advocated. For Wolstonecraft,
the inferior economic, political and moral circumstance of woman was the result of socialization not
her nature. For her, the transformation of women's
role was largely a matter of education. Women needed
to acquire new skills so that they would possess the
necessary virtues for independence and participation
in public life.

Mill's views   When Mill wrote his *The Subjection of
Women*, the idea of gender emancipation was already
current. There also existed a movement for the female
suffrage, although it was nowhere near as strong as
the trade union movement and the push for political
power then being made by the working class. But, for
Mill, the circumstance of the denial of women's rights
was not equivalent to other situations. The circumstance of women was different from any other social
group and this largely explained the complicity by
women in their own lack of political power. Further,
Mill believes, the nature of women has been more
thoroughly distorted through their relationships than
any other social group, including slaves. The duties of
women, Mill says, have been stretched beyond that of
slaves: "no slave is a slave to same lengths and in so
full a sense as a wife is. Hardly any slave, except one
immediately attached to his master's person, is a slave
at all hours and minutes of the day." Even a slave is
not under obligation as a wife to sleep with a master
who degrades and tortures her.

But a growing number of women were by then
demanding political representation. It was understandable, for Mill, that this movement was not supported by huge numbers, in light of the power relations between the sexes. He added that, "It is a political law of nature that those who are under any power
of ancient origin, never begin by complaining of the
power itself, but only of its oppressive exercise. There
is never any want of women who complain of ill usage by their husbands." For Mill, the value of liberty
is bound up with the unleashing of energies and talents. Mill's plea for the emancipation of women is
made within the context of a general theory of liberty
and political representation, the theory of liberalism.

Mill saw the enfranchisement of the laboring
classes and of women as indicative of the general
progress of humanity in its political institutions. He
also believed that such a change in the balance of political expression would have a generally benign effect on the social circumstance of the groups represented as well as the society as a whole. Closely
related, was his belief that human progress was generated through discontent with the existing order. Each
new group who had been through the process of demanding their liberty and articulating their moral dis-
contents were entering into the creative task that lay
before the species: its collective intellectual, moral and
material improvement. The spirit of liberty was, for
Mill, a restless one, but its very restlessness was indicative of the energizing character of human freedom.

Mill sat between those liberals who wanted to expand the powers of the state to help achieve greater
liberty for the disadvantaged, and those who saw that
any such attempt would drag liberalism into the sphere
of socialism, and that the emphasis upon social equality would have harmful effects for individual liberty
and social prosperity. Both groups saw Mill's form of
liberalism as unsatisfactory: the former because Mill
did not provide enough for the state to play a more di-
rective role in opening up the conditions of liberty;
the latter because Mill was veering too close to paternalism, straying too far from his belief in the importance of the energies of the individual. This is a
central dilemma for modern liberals.

The achievement of the franchise for the working
classes and women meant that for the first time in human history all interests had been accepted as, in principle, having a legitimate right to representation in the
politics of the state. Because this was a new situation
it took some time for it to become clear what form
this mass representation would assume. Since this political transformation took place almost everywhere in
the advanced states at about the same time as the mat-
uration of the process of industrialization, the two
combined to take the form of a social democratic pro-

gram that shared common features in the different states. The risk entailed for advanced liberal states now became not that the interests of the masses would be ignored, but that their excessive pursuit could destroy the march of progress altogether as the state encroached excessively on the domains of civil society.

John Rawls

In the philosophical sphere the egalitarian project of the social liberals only achieved its full expression when the social democratic movement itself was mature, and arguably past its apogee, in the form of the American John Rawls' (1921–), A *Theory of Justice* (1971).

By that time Rawls made the claim that justice is to society what truth is to knowledge. Writing at the high water mark of social democratic political power, Rawls established links between justice as fairness and between the basic liberal rights and freedoms. He argued for the right to vote, freedom of conscience and the press, the rule of law, fair and equal opportunity, and the principle of the greatest benefit to the least–advanced member of a society in what seemed to be a mere restatement of the basic stock of liberalism. He also said the policy makers of the state should pursue such policies blindly. Paradoxically, this came at a time when liberal economists argued that such a conception of social justice, when translated into increasing economic demands upon the state to deliver real resources, was playing a major role in causing stagflation and thus in restraining national prosperity.

The idea of the original position is perhaps the most lasting contribution of John Rawls to theories about social justice. The original position is a hypothetical situation in which rational calculators, acting as agents or trustees for the interests of concrete individuals, are pictured as choosing those principles of social relations under which their principals would do best. Their choices are subject to certain constraints, however, and it is these constraints which embody the specifically moral elements of original position argumentation. Crudely, the rational calculators do not know facts about their principals, which would be morally irrelevant to the choice of principles of justice. This restriction on their reasoning is embodied, picturesquely, in Rawls' so–called veil of ignorance, which obstructs information, for instance, about principals' age, sex, and religious beliefs. Once this information about principals is unavailable to their agents, the plurality of interested parties disappears, and the problem of choice is rendered determinate.

British Prime Minister William Ewart Gladstone.

THEORY IN ACTION

Gladstone and the Liberal Party in Britain

William Ewart Gladstone became the Liberal Party Prime Minister of Great Britain in 1868. At that time, there was much unrest in among the Irish people over their role in the commonwealth. The Act of Union in 1801 had religiously bound Ireland to the Protestant Church of England, a fact that caused tension among Irish Roman Catholics for generations.

Gladstone introduced and passed the Disestablishment Act in 1869, which repealed the Act of Union and allowed the Irish the freedom to support whichever church they chose. Gladstone also introduced a land act in 1870 which provided compensation for Irish tenants who were evicted by English landlords without cause.

Gladstone's ministry enacted a host of measures which, as he put it, opened the windows of opportunity for Englishmen. These measures included the Education Act of 1870, the opening of all branches of the civil service except the foreign service to competitive examination in 1870, the abolition of purchase of commissions in the army by royal warrant and the opening of the universities to non–members of the Church of England in 1871, and the secret ballot act of 1872.

The same degree of support was not given to all these measures by Gladstone, but the fact simply serves to illustrate his view of the role of prime minister, which was to act as mediator between factions in the cabinet and reconcile differences where possible.

Gladstone's approach to foreign affairs was also established in his first ministry, which came into office shortly after the end of the U.S. Civil War. As a member of Parliament, Gladstone had caused some hostility in America by supporting the South in the Civil War. The North had strenuously objected when ironclads (warships with sides of armored metal plates) manufactured in Britain were delivered to the Confederates, and after the war there was a need to reestablish normal relations between the two countries. The Treaty of Washington in 1871 agreed to the U.S. request that claims for damages be submitted to arbitration. This act went a long way toward easing any tension between the two nations. Britain's destiny may well have turned out to be a very different one had it lost the United States as its most powerful ally.

An unsuccessful attempt to pass a temperance bill that came close to an act of prohibition—and trouble over the continuing Irish question—hurt Gladstone in the election of 1874, and he was defeated. However, he was reelected in 1880, and soon introduced his first Home Rule bill for Ireland, which was defeated in Parliament by thirty votes. Gladstone continued his support for the bill, and when the Liberals returned to office after the election of 1892, he introduced a second Home Rule bill the following year. The measure passed Parliament's House of Commons but was defeated in the House of Lords. Gladstone retired the following year.

Gladstone's terms as Prime Minister saw many changes come to Great Britain. The army regulation bill shifted control of the armed forces from the monarchy to Parliament; indeed, the prestige of Parliament rose during his tenure. For the first time, all schools were evaluated by the government, standards in education soared, and more people had access to government positions. However, British imperialism reached its notorious high point—the "Scramble for Africa"—during the Gladstone era.

Social Liberalism and Social Democracy

As the franchise extended in liberal societies, so the powers and functions of the state were expanded. Partly as a result of socialist agitation, the power of illiberal political factions was used to undermine the classical liberal state.

During the early part of the twentieth century, all the developed states experienced the rise of such so-cial democratic movements. They combined a number of characteristics that sprang from the achievement of the more or less universal franchise at about the same time in industrial societies. The result was a transfer of demands from the political sphere concerning representation in the deliberations of the state, to arguments about the purposes for which the state should be used. The more common form of the expression of social democracy was a democratic electoral coalition pursuing social and economic rights to augment the political gains already won for the masses. Social democratic parties began achieving Parliamentary representation by the 1890s and thereafter social democrats began to seriously influence political agendas everywhere. The line between social liberals and social democrats became very difficult to discern.

Social democracy has few outstanding theoreticians. In the political sphere the most developed were in Britain, where the Fabian Socialists argued for more state ownership of the economy, higher taxes, and more welfare benefits by using an elected Labour government to legislate for an extension of the egalitarian principle from the political to the economic and social sphere. In Germany, similar arguments were evolved by the previously Marxist Social Democratic Party led by Karl Kautsky and Eduard Bernstein. In the economic realm, the dominant social democratic theoretician was John Maynard Keynes (1883–1946) who gave theoretical legitimacy to the political aspirations of the social democratic political philosophers and politicians.

Liberalism and Christianity

From the Enlightenment, reconciling the growth of secular liberalism with the continuation of Christian religious doctrine also became an important issue for theology. Eighteenth century romanticism did this by stressing the intuitive and synthetic nature of human reason in which truth was gained by grasping the whole rather than by an abstract analysis of the parts. This was a reaction to the critical rationalism of the eighteenth century. Influential here was Friederich Daniel Ernst Schleiermacher (1768–1834), a founder of modern or liberal theology. He accepted the validity of the Enlightenment criticism of dogmatic Christianity, and saw religious belief as subjective. Theological statements no longer were perceived as describing objective reality, but: "Christian doctrines are accounts of the Christian religious affections set forth in speech."

Other liberal theologians, like Albrect Ritschl (1822–1889), saw religion in terms of personal morality. He argued in *Justification and Reconciliation*, that "Christianity is the monotheistic, completely spiritual and ethical religion, which, on the basis of the life of its Founder as redeeming and establishing the kingdom of God, consists in the freedom of the children of God...the intention of which is the moral organization of mankind." Religious truth could not be verified and existence of God could not be rationally demonstrated.

These views led quickly to the academic study of comparative religions. Christianity was no longer seen as unique and as knowledge of the wider world and other cultures and religions became available, the Bible was studied in its cultural setting. All religions were seen as being intellectually similar and, possibly, valid.

The social gospel movement then tried to apply Christianity to industrial societies and enlist the new working class. The American Walter Rauschenbusch, wrote in *A Theology of the Social Gospel* that, "The social gospel seeks to bring men under repentance for their collective sins and to create a more sensitive and more modern conscience." The task of the church was working to end human suffering and establish social justice. In the late nineteenth century even papal declarations talked about justice for labor. Liberalism made Christian authority wholly subjective, based on individual spiritual experience. Ultimate authority was not to be found in the Bible or Church, but increasingly in reason and conscience.

Modernism was used to describe a similar movement within the Catholic Church. In the U.S. the term was applied to radical liberal theology in the early decades of the twentieth century. By the 1930s many other denominations were also affected. The implication was that Christianity had to be "modernized" in every age in order to remain socially and rationally relevant.

In liberal societies, religion tended to decline and become more secular in outlook.

The Neo–liberal Revolution in the 1980s

Milton Friedman (1912–) is an intellectual descendant of the Austrian School, the best known of all "Monetarist economists" and won a Nobel Prize in economics in 1976. He was born in New York in 1912 and after working at Columbia University (and for the government), he became Professor of Economics at Chicago University. He did his best–known work there, surrounded by other Monetarists, also often termed the "Chicago school."

In the 1970s, the social democratic state, which had been steadily encroaching on the liberal economy

throughout the developed world, created, with other developments, the crisis of "stagflation." In this, it experienced a devaluation of the currency and a cessation of economic growth more or less simultaneously. In this critical context, the ideas of classical liberal political economy were revived in the intellectual sphere and implemented by a series of liberal politicians operating through the agencies of the powerful liberal states which they governed.

This neo–liberal counter–revolution in the realm of economic ideas is most closely associated with Friedman. Although prolific, his best known popular work was, with Rose D. Friedman, *Capitalism and Freedom* (1962). He was already an advocate of market economics and paying closer attention to the growth of the money supply, when the crisis of stagflation occurred in the mid–1970s. He then proved to be an able media performer and had an impact far beyond the academy, as his Nobel Prize attested.

Friedman argued that Keynesian demand management techniques had gone too far in distorting the market and had choked economic growth; that the growth of the money supply had generated inflation; and that the increased size of the state had become a political burden on developed countries. He advocated reducing state intervention in the economy, controlling the growth of the money supply and de–politicizing the economy. This message had an impact in all developed countries, but more in some than others. It was essentially the message of classical liberal political economy.

The Political Liberal Revival

Friedman's ideas first began to take hold among policy makers in the years 1974–1975 when the developed countries experienced both stagnation and inflation. But the first major politician to take liberal ideas seriously, and not merely as a short–term solution to the stagflation crisis, was Margaret Thatcher, Prime Minister of Britain from 1979–1990.

Britain had developed an extensive welfare state and state owned sector of the economy in the hay day of social democracy, 1945–1975. It also had one of the worst records of economic growth of developed countries. In the mid 1970s, under a Labour government, it encountered a severe crisis of stagflation. The opposition Conservative Party at first espoused similar policies under its centrist leader, Edward Heath. Margaret Thatcher then replaced him and won the 1979 election on a radical liberal/monetarist platform. During the next decade she reduced the state sector, cut the welfare state and reined in the money supply.

The result was a radically re–structured British economy and society along more liberal lines.

The pain involved in this transition was considerable, but under pressure to relent, Thatcher famously insisted, "This Lady is not for turning." Britain emerged as one of Europe's stronger economies in the 1990s and the next Labour government, elected in 1997, did not reverse the liberal reforms.

As the Cold War and communism ended in 1991, this liberal impetus was sustained in the U.S. by Bill Clinton, U.S. President 1993–2001, who, although a Democrat, led the international economy into a period of globalization. As David Mosler and Bob Catley describe in *Global America: Imposing Liberalism on a Recalcitrant World*, this represented the apogee of liberal sentiment and a new attempt to recreate a global political economy along the lines attempted by liberal England in the mid–nineteenth century.

Clinton was elected on a reforming and welfare expanding policy and only swung away from social democracy after a considerable electoral defeat in the 1994 mid–term Congressional elections. Thereafter, he eschewed expanding the state sector and, rather, set about creating a free trading global economy in which American prosperity could be built on the strength of its industry. By the time of his second term he was dissolving the automatic entitlement to welfare, which had been established for Americans after the New Deal, and was concentrating on the strengthening of a global world order of liberalism.

During this period, world trade expanded rapidly, global production levels also increased, income levels for U.S. citizens were enhanced and the number of liberal democratic states increased. From being an advocate of social democratic reform, Clinton became the heir of the liberal tradition and its courier into the twenty–first century.

ANALYSIS AND CRITICAL RESPONSE

Liberals accord liberty primacy as a political value, and liberals have typically maintained, with Locke, that humans are naturally in "a State of perfect Freedom to order their Actions." Restrictions on liberty must be thoroughly justified, hence John Rawls' first principle of justice: "Each person is to have an equal right to the most extensive total system of equal basic liberties compatible with a similar system for all."

Liberals disagree, however, about the concept of liberty. Sir Isaiah Berlin (1909–1997) arguably the twentieth century's most eminent liberal, advocated in *Four Essays on Liberty* (1969) for a "negative conception of liberty." For Berlin the liberal state's commitment to protecting liberty is, essentially, the job of ensuring that citizens do not coerce each other without compelling justification. Other liberals emphasize positive freedom and want a larger role for the liberal state.

At the start of the twenty–first century this revolved around the "political correctness" debate. Is it permissible to restrict the freedom of speech of some citizens in order to impose the definition of freedom espoused by others? The classical liberal would surely respond in the negative.

Liberalism, Property, and the Market

For classical liberals, liberty and private property are related, but "social" liberalism challenges this close connection between personal liberty and a private property based market order. Modern social liberals, especially in the U.S., believe that far from being "the guardian of every other right," as James Ely argued in *The Guardian of Every Other Right: A Constitutional History of Property Rights* (1992), property rights generate an inequality. This theme is central to contemporary American liberalism, which combines strong endorsement of civil and personal liberties with little enthusiasm for private ownership.

There are several states which function effectively at the onset of the twenty–first century that are based on the principles of liberalism. The two most prominent examples are the U.S. and the United Kingdom, particularly after both undertook extensive liberal reforms in the 1980s. The U.S. has only about thirty percent of the economy going through the state sector and maintains an open economy and strict separation of political powers. Britain has reduced the state share of the economy and privatized most of the state owned enterprises that the Labour Party had previously brought into public ownership. After a similar process of liberal reform in the 1980s, which has been sustained under the Liberal led government, Australia may be regarded as a successful liberal society with a constitution drawn from both London and Washington.

France and most European Union states may be better regarded as social democratic societies because their state sectors are over forty percent of their total economy, a proportion which most liberals would regard as excessive. New Zealand also falls into this category.

There are number of other states which have some of the attributes of liberalism but do not function well. Legally and formally, Russia has a liberal constitution and economy, but in fact it functions as an oligarchy, both politically and economically. Japan has a liberal political constitution, but has been ruled since 1950 effectively by one governing coalition except for 1993–1994. Also, its state has considerable control over its economy and this has contributed to the condition of economic stagnation which has prevailed since 1990.

Liberalism's Influence and Critics

Liberalism is unique in that while it may not have ever been truly implemented as a political system in any country, it has influenced many political systems in many different eras. It is much more than coincidence that on the timeline between the absolute kings and queens of the seventeenth century and the representative governments of today sit a large number of brilliant liberal thinkers who called for the limiting the power of the monarchy. Moreover, it was liberal ideas that toned down the evils of imperialism by calling for the teachings of Christianity and an end to the slave trade. And although Mill's views on the rights of women fell short of equality, they were nonetheless far ahead of their time, and inspired many who carried on the fight for women's suffrage. Nineteenth–century liberals instituted reforms in education and sought to improve working conditions. Some historians even feel that liberalism had a profound effect on the arts and culture by their very doctrine of challenging traditional themes. Liberals moved away from war and religion to a more peaceful, secular world view.

That is not to say that liberalism does not have its critics. Socialists and communists criticize liberals for defending capitalism. Democrats generally support liberalism, but are wary of the limitations it places on the power of government. Social democrats and supporters of Keynes believe liberalism places too much confidence in market economics. Statist economic developers think liberalism cannot deliver rapid economic growth. Fascists believe liberalism is too soft a belief with which to defend the civilized order. Post–modernists believe liberalism to be the doctrines of "dead white males." And conservative critics have argued that the historical stability of liberal societies is based on a pre–liberal sense of shared identity amongst their members; liberalism only works in already well–ordered societies.

Liberalism is a set of beliefs about society, politics, and economics that developed, uniquely, in the most–developed countries of the world by the late–eighteenth and nineteenth centuries. It has proven to be successful in the wealthy English–speaking countries and has provided a foundation for their continuing prosperity and liberty.

Nonetheless, it has proven difficult to transplant to other societies and its critics claim that liberalism only functions effectively in societies that have nurtured liberties and energies consistent with liberal principles for several generations. Not all nations may be ready for liberalism; those that are believe it is the most advanced way to run a country.

TOPICS FOR FURTHER STUDY

- Why was Rousseau's idea of the "general will" illiberal?
- Examine the attempts Gladstone made to settle the "Irish Question" and the effects of those policies.
- Explain Hayek's criticism of socialism and how it pertains to liberalism.

BIBLIOGRAPHY

Sources

Catley, Bob A. and Wayne Christaudo. *This Great Beast: Progress and the Modern State.* London: Avebury, 1997.

Commire, Anne, ed. *Historic World Leaders.* Detroit: Gale Research, 1994.

Freeden, Michael. *The New Liberalism: An Ideology of Social Reform.* Oxford: Clarendon Press, 1978.

Gilbert, Felix, gen. ed. *The Norton History of Modern Europe.* New York: W.W. Norton and Co., 1971.

Harris, Paul and John Morrow, eds. *Lectures on the Principles of Political Obligation and Other Essays.* Cambridge: Cambridge University Press, 1986.

Hayek, F.A. *New Studies in Philosophy, Politics, Economics and the History of Ideas,*, 1993. London: Routledge and Kegan Paul, 1978.

Mosler, David, and Bob Catley. *Global America: Imposing Liberalism on a Recalcitrant World,* Praeger, 2000.

Smith, Rogers M. "Unfinished Liberalism," in *Social Research.* Fall, 1994 (vol. 61, no. 3).

Further Readings

Benn, Stanley I. *A Theory of Freedom,* Cambridge University Press, 1988. A powerful statement of the case for using the state to create positive liberty.

Cranston, Maurice. *The Encyclopedia of Philosophy,* Paul Edwards, ed., Macmillan and the Free Press, 1967. Cranston's essay "Liberalism" is a classic statement of the history and evolution of liberal doctrines.

Green, Thomas Hill. *Lectures on the Principles of Political Obligation and Other Essays,* Paul Harris and John Morrow, eds., Cambridge University Press, 1986. Green's 1895 essay is the original statement of the social liberal position of the need for a liberal state to provide positive freedoms for its citizens.

Hayek, F.A. *New Studies in Philosophy, Politics, Economics and the History of Ideas,* Routledge and Kegan Paul, 1978. Hayek's essay "Liberalism" is a re–statement of classic liberal doctrine in the late–twentieth century context when liberalism was re–emerging as a dominant doctrine in the developed countries.

Mill, John Stuart *On Liberty and Other Essays,* John Gray, ed., Oxford University Press, 1991. This collection of 1859 essays contains many of the key statements by the most influential English liberal theorist of the nineteenth century.

SEE ALSO

Capitalism, Conservatism, Federalism

Libertarianism

OVERVIEW

Despite the obstacles of many centuries, national boundaries, and terminology confusion, the tradition known since the 1950s as libertarianism forms a coherent legacy from its founding by fathers John Locke and Adam Smith in the sixteenth and seventeenth centuries through its organization as a U.S. political party in 1971 and beyond. This individualist political theory has spawned classic works, inspired revolutions, fueled activist movements, and earned Nobel Prizes. Its history has included a rise and decline, and the end of the twentieth century revealed a reemergence for this long-lived tradition. Individual rights, property, constitutionalism, and universalism form the heart of libertarianism.

WHO CONTROLS GOVERNMENT? Restricted officials

HOW IS GOVERNMENT PUT INTO POWER? Group dissatisfied with previous powers

WHAT ROLES DO THE PEOPLE HAVE? Enjoy rights while not infringing on others

WHO CONTROLS PRODUCTION OF GOODS? Private individuals

WHO CONTROLS DISTRIBUTION OF GOODS? Private individuals

MAJOR FIGURES Ayn Rand; Russell Means

HISTORICAL EXAMPLE Austrian School of Economics

HISTORY

It is not unusual for the term libertarianism to bring blank stares from theorists and politicians alike; one joke suggests that a libertarian is what you get when you cross a libertine with a librarian. Although the term libertarianism is rather new, the political theory it represents—at different times also called liberalism or classical liberalism, among various other things—can be traced back to classical thought. An intellectual child of the West, libertarianism gained supporters and lost momentum in its long history, only to enjoy a new popularity around the globe at the end

CHRONOLOGY

1690: John Locke's *Two Treatises of Civil Government* is published.

1776: *The Wealth of Nations* by Adam Smith is published.

1871: Carl Menger founds the Austrian School of Economics.

1943: Ayn Rand introduces the Objectivist Movement with the publication of *The Fountainhead*.

1944: Friedrich Hayek's *Road to Serfdom* is published.

1962: *Calculus of Consent* by James Buchanan and Gordon Tullock is published.

1971: The U.S. Libertarian Party is organized.

---

of the twentieth century and the beginning of the twenty–first. The broad principles of libertarianism allowed the tradition to grow, evolve, and adapt to new political and technological realities across the planet and centuries.

The first seeds of libertarian thought appeared in ancient Greece and Rome. For example, the Greek Sophists embraced the idea of equality among individuals; some went so far as to criticize the prevailing belief in natural slavery. The Athenian Pericles (c. 495–429 B.C.) praised the Greek polis and its system of equality under the law in his famous *Funeral Oration*. Friedrich Hayek (1899–1992), noted Austrian economist, Nobel Laureate, and libertarian, recognized the Roman statesman Cicero (106–43 BC) as the most influential precursor to libertarianism due to his defense of the concept of natural law. After antiquity, the influence of monotheism—the belief in one god for all—through Judaism and, later, Islam and Christianity reinforced the idea of one central law to which all people are held accountable.

The development of Christianity, in particular, brought new dimensions to proto–libertarian thought. After the Christian church split between East and West (1054), both sides offered important ideas to the young political theory. The Eastern church fathers from the Alexandrine School and beyond contem-

plated the perfectibility of humanity as a theological question. This added the issue of human flourishing and self–betterment to the political dialogue, which anticipated later German contributions to libertarian theory. In the West, especially in the Middle Ages, church leaders preserved the classics in general and studied economics and political science in particular. Different orders and communities developed specialties. For example, the Spanish School of Salamanca combined the study of Greek, Islamic, and Christian philosophy to develop a theory of market prices that informed later economic arguments borne of the Scottish Enlightenment. The second split of Christianity, that of the Reformation (begun in 1517), led to a similar dual influence on libertarianism. Catholic thought continued to explore natural law theory while Protestantism, with its "priesthood of the believer" doctrine, introduced a more potent individualism to the political landscape.

Political changes also added ingredients to the tradition. The rise of absolutism in Europe challenged the political, economic, and social freedom of the people. Opponents of powerful kings in England developed the myth of the ancient constitution—a notion of an ideal contract formed over time between ruler and ruled, government and governed, and solidified by the Anglo–Saxons before the Norman invasion of 1066—to justify their claims to individual rights and their conviction that monarchs were not above the law. As early as the English Civil War (1642–1651), political groups such as the Levellers wanted to take the ancient constitution concept a step further and develop a written constitution to mirror the idealized political compact between the people and their state. Perhaps the best example of proto–libertarian thought was Leveller John Overton's 1746 work *An Arrow Against All Tyrants*, which articulated a theory of individualism, property, and limited government in order to call for a written constitution.

John Locke

Though clear precursors to libertarianism had existed for centuries, the theory itself awaited a systematic, definitive treatment. John Locke (1632–1704) provided this careful and comprehensive discussion and therefore became known as one of the fathers of libertarianism. In groundbreaking works such as *A Letter Concerning Toleration* (1689), *Two Treatises of Civil Government* (1690), *Some Considerations of the Consequences of the Lowering of Interest, Raising the Value of Money* (1692), and *A Vindication of the Reasonableness of Christianity* (1695), the English Locke made three important contributions to libertarian theory.

John Locke. (The Library of Congress)

BIOGRAPHY:
John Locke

John Locke was born in 1632, the son of a Puritan country lawyer of Wrighton. He taught Greek and rhetoric at Oxford while completing his studies in medicine and science. His interests turned to moral and political theory thanks to his father's enthusiasm for the parliamentary cause during the English Civil War and the influences of his colleagues—specifically, his friendship with Lord Ashley and his relationship with Robert Boyle through the Royal Society. Locke held minor official positions until the Duke of York took the English throne in 1683, which forced Locke to flee to Holland. Locke returned to his homeland after the Glorious Revolution to widespread popularity, new positions, and favor in the eyes of William and Mary. He published numerous works of political theory and philosophy in many languages. His most influential books include *A Letter Concerning Toleration* (1689), *Two Treatises of Civil Government* (1690), *Some Considerations of the Consequences of the Lowering of Interest, Raising the Value of Money* (1692), and *A Vindication of the Reasonableness of Christianity* (1695).

Locke's greatest contribution to political theory was his systematic exploration of the concepts that compose libertarianism; his was the first such comprehensive treatment of the tradition. For example, he explored the ideas of natural law, private property, and toleration, and he examined the nature of the social contract, the implicit agreement binding the government to the governed. He argued that all individual rights ultimately draw justification from self–ownership, through which a person's thoughts, beliefs, possessions, and labors are his or her own. His defense of life, liberty, and property—and the right of revolution for citizens whose government fails to protect these rights—influenced revolts such as the American and French Revolutions, documents such as the American Declaration of Independence, and even activism such as the U.S. Civil Rights Movement. By illuminating the values and issues of individualism, Locke provided the framework for an ongoing dialogue and earned the title of father of libertarianism.

First, he examined the nature of individual rights. He argued that individuals were not bound to obey governmental laws that ignored their rights and therefore contradicted natural law. Second, Locke articulated a positive view of human nature that challenged the prevailing view of humans as incapable of peaceful coexistence without intrusive state interference. Third, he explained the idea that governments derived legitimacy from the consent of the governed. The compact, or agreement, between the state and its citizens placed duties on both; if the government failed to meet its responsibilities and breached the contract, citizens, according to Locke, possessed the right to revolt. Last, Locke argued that liberty was dependent on private property. A state that protected private property ensured the freedom of its citizens. Locke defined property as an act of creation—mixing labor with land grew crops, which therefore were property—and thus expanded the term to include political ideas, religious beliefs, and even an individual's self. Locke's contribution to political theory in general and libertarianism in particular cannot be overstated.

The Scottish Enlightenment

The first movement of libertarianism took place on the heels of Locke's foundational work, and this time it originated in Scotland. The Scottish Enlightenment (1714–1817) began with the 1714 publication of

BIOGRAPHY:
Adam Smith

Adam Smith's father died before his son and name-sake was born in Scotland in 1723. The junior Adam Smith studied at the University of Glasgow, where he was influenced greatly by Professor Francis Hutcheson. Hutcheson introduced Smith to the realm of moral philosophy, which included natural religion, morals, jurisprudence, and government. Smith longed to discover a natural law to explain human action in the same way that Isaac Newton articulated laws for the natural world. His first work, 1759's *The Theory of Moral Sentiments*, suggested that people are motivated by the need for approbation. Individuals, Smith argued, know what society expects of them thanks to internal "impartial spectators," mechanisms that remind people of the approval and/or disapproval of others.

This effort, at once psychological, sociological, and anthropological, was followed by the 1776 tome *An Inquiry into the Nature and Causes of the Wealth of Nations*, which added economics to the list of Smith's achievements. In this work, Smith identified the division of labor as the key to increased production, and therefore wealth. He defined the ingredients of price as rent, wages, and profit—an insight that became a standard fact of elementary economic understanding. Smith's most famous contribution, however, was the metaphor of the invisible hand to describe the spontaneous order of free markets and the natural harmony of interests they produce.

Smith's gift lay in synthesizing large amounts of detailed information into a useful, interdisciplinary analysis and translating his understanding to language many people could understand. He believed that liberty could focus self–interest into socially beneficial activity, and his works communicated his message successfully. His writings were translated into many languages during his lifetime and they remain classics; his scientific approach to issues of freedom complemented the theoretical views of Locke and made Smith the second father of libertarianism.

Bernard Mandeville's *Enquiry into the Origin of Moral Virtue, or The Fable of the Bees*. This controversial book suggested self–interest, not morality, fueled the actions of individuals; it also marked a shift from interest in political theory to more expansive attention on economic and philosophical matters with regard to individual liberty. Adam Ferguson (1723–1816), David Hume (1711–1776), and Henry Homes, or Lord Kames, continued the movement with contributions in history, political science, philosophy, and economics. Perhaps the most noteworthy member of the Scottish Enlightenment also became known as the second father—the co–parent with John Locke—of libertarianism: Adam Smith (1723–1790). Smith did for moral philosophy and economics what Locke had done for political theory. In his most famous work, the 1776 *An Inquiry into the Nature and Causes of the Wealth of Nations*, Smith drew a portrait of societies in which people acted out of self–love, and yet the unplanned, uncoordinated market, or "invisible hand," coordinated their decisions and provided for the common good. His vision of the harmony of interests created by free trade made Smith not only the foremost economist of his era and the father of capitalism, but was also one of the lasting visionaries of libertarianism.

Other Western Influences

If libertarianism proper first came together as a coherent theory in England and Scotland thanks in part to the atmosphere of order, stability, and individualism provided by Whig leadership after the Glorious Revolution, then it blossomed in France, where its ideas rebelled against the more feudalistic French institutions of state and church. The first wave came in the form of the French Enlightenment (1717–1778). Key philosophers such as Voltaire, Baron de Montesquieu (1689–1755), and Marquis de Condorcet (1743–1794) challenged the intolerance and arbitrariness of established authorities and called for rational inquiry, free speech, and greater individual liberty. The French Enlightenment, then, was essentially a libertarian affair. The products of its greatest minds became some of the foundational literature of libertarian thought. A later, second movement, the French Physiocratic movement (1759–1776), was to economics what the French Enlightenment was to philosophy. Leaders such as Françoise Quesnay (1694–1774) and Jacques Turgot (1727–1781) argued against the traditional policy of mercantilism, which included the hoarding of precious metals as well as planned industry and protectionism, in favor of free trade, open markets, and limitations to government involvement in the economy. Put in practice, many of the French philosophers' and physiocrats' ideas—

BIOGRAPHY:

Frederic Bastiat

If Adam Smith learned how to reach a broader audience with his ideas about free markets, then Frederic Bastiat made an art of it. Bastiat was born in Mugron, France in 1801. Deeply opposed to the protectionism practiced on behalf of some industries by the French state, Bastiat wrote to limit government intervention in the economy. He founded the Associations for Free Trade in 1846. The organization's journal *Le Libre-Change* , or *Free Trade*, became a vehicle for Bastiat's views. His most popular work, however, formed part of the 1845 book, titled in English *Sophisms of Protection*. In his "Candlemakers' Petition," Bastiat effectively parodied the rationale behind protectionism by presenting a fictional petition to the state: candlemakers asked for protection against the sun, explaining that candlemaking and related industries would profit greatly if the sun were eliminated as a competitor in providing light to the world. The ridiculousness of the petition underscored Bastiat's critique of governmental interruption of markets on behalf of special interests and became a staple of economics texts for over a century thereafter.

Bastiat used metaphors to capture the imagination and opinion of his reading audience. In his essay "What is Seen and What is Not Seen," he used the image of a boy breaking a window to explain opportunity cost—money spent on one thing costs the opportunity for that money to be spent on something else—and challenged the prevailing view that war and other acts of destruction actually benefited the economy.

> Have you ever been witness to the fury of that solid citizen, James Goodfellow, when his incorrigible son has happened to break a pane of glass? If you have been present at this spectacle, certainly you must also have observed that the onlookers...seem with one accord to offer the unfortunate owner the selfsame...'Everybody has to make a living. What would become of the glaziers if no one ever broke a window?'

Now, this formula of condolence contains a whole theory that it is a good idea for us to expose...in this very simple case, since it is exactly the same as that which, unfortunately, underlies most of our economic institutions.

Suppose that it will cost six francs to repair the damage. If you mean that the accident gives six francs' worth of encouragement to the aforesaid industry, I agree...The glazier will come, do his job, receive six francs, congratulate himself, and bless in his heart the careless child. *This is what is seen.*

But if, by way of deduction, you conclude, as happens only too often, that it is good to break windows, that it helps to circulate money, that it results in encouraging industry in general, I am obliged to cry out: That will never do! Your theory stops at *what is seen*. It does not take account of *what is not seen.*

It is not seen that, since our citizen has spent six francs for one thing, he will not be able to spend them for another. *It is not seen* that if he had not had a windowpane to replace, he would have replaced, for example, his worn-out shoes or added another book to his library. In brief, he would have put his six francs to some use or other for which he will not now have them....

From which, by generalizing, we arrive at this unexpected conclusion: 'Society loses the value of objects unnecessarily destroyed'...'Destruction is not profitable.'

Toward the end of his life, Bastiat opposed the rise of socialism and communism, which he saw to be inextricably linked with protectionism. His position won him seats in the Constituent Assembly and Legislative Assembly of 1849. He died shortly thereafter, hailed by the famous economic theorist Joseph Schumpeter as "the most brilliant economic journalist who ever lived." Bastiat's gift for metaphor allowed him to draw persuasive and enduring illustrations of libertarian economy theory and reach a new audience with the ideas of free markets.

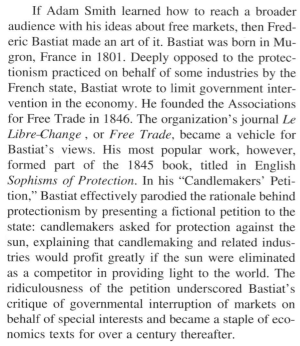

pro–individual, anti–state—led directly to the French Revolution.

One of the characteristics of the rise of libertarian thought was the fact that the ideas evolved in different nations almost simultaneously, and different strains and traditions informed and influenced others. This was the case with the Democratic–Republicans

(1776–1820) in the English Colonies–turned–United States; much of the theory embraced by Thomas Jefferson (1743–1826), father of the Declaration of Independence, and James Madison (1751–1836), father of the U.S. Constitution, with regard to individual rights, natural law, and the social contract came from the British libertarian tradition. In turn, the U.S. interpre-

MAJOR WRITINGS:

Social Statics

If John Locke and Adam Smith represented the mainstream foundation of libertarianism, then Herbert Spencer illustrated one of its peripheries. Spencer's works revealed his search for a broad, holistic, scientific pattern to explain social phenomena; this contrasted with some other libertarian theorists' belief that human action was too complex to be categorized or planned. Nonetheless, Spencer made one contribution that did find its way to the mainstream of libertarian theory: his law of equal freedom. This law proposed that, morally, every person should be free to do as he or she wills, provided that he or she does not infringe on anyone else's freedom to do the same. In his 1850 *Social Statics*, Spencer's logical means of following each argument to its ultimate conclusion led him to argue that, under the law of equal freedom, individuals have the right to ignore the state:

> As a corollary to the proposition that all institutions must be subordinated to the law of equal freedom, we cannot choose but admit the right of the citizen to adopt a condition of voluntary outlawry. If every man has freedom of any other man, then he is free to drop connection with the state—to relinquish its protection and to refuse paying toward its support. It is self–evident that in so behaving he in no way trenches upon the liberty of others, for his position is a passive one, and while passive he cannot become an aggressor. It is equally self–evident that he cannot be compelled to continue one of a polit-

ical corporation without a breach of the moral law, seeing that citizenship involves payment of taxes; and the taking away of a man's property against his will is an infringement of his rights. Government being simply an agent employed in common by a number of individuals to secure to them certain advantages, the very nature of the connection implies that it is for each to say whether he will employ such an agent or not. If any one of them determines to ignore this mutual–safety confederation, nothing can be said except that he loses all claim to its good offices and exposes himself to the danger of mal-treatment—a thing he is quite at liberty to do if he likes. He cannot be coerced into political combination without a breach of the law of equal freedom; he can withdraw from it without committing any such breach, and he has therefore a right to withdraw....

> Nay, indeed, have we not seen that government is essentially immoral? Is it not the offspring of evil, bearing about it all the marks of its parentage? Does it not exist because crime exists? Is it not strong—or, as we say, despotic—when crime is great? Is there not more liberty—that is, less government—as crime diminishes? And must not government cease when crime ceases, for very lack of objects on which to perform its function? Not only does magisterial power exist *because* of evil, but it exists *by* evil. Violence is employed to maintain it, and all violence involves criminality. Soldiers, policemen, and jailers; swords, batons, and fetters are instruments for inflicting pain; and all inflection of pain is in the abstract wrong...Wherefore, legislative authority can never be ethical—must always be conventional merely.

tation of the right of revolution and the experience of constitution building influenced the French libertarian tradition. Writers such as Thomas Paine (1737–1809) and leaders such as the Marquis de Lafayette (1757–1834) divided their time between the continents to participate in both the American and French Revolutions. The anti–authoritarian individualism of the revolutionary age made it one of the high impact points of libertarianism; the theory quite literally changed the face of nations and the lives of millions.

Over the next century, different individuals pushed the Western consensus on political theory, much of which was libertarian, to further conclusions. Brits William Godwin (1756–1836) and Mary Wol-

stonecraft (1759–1797) introduced new ideas about self–perfectibility and feminism. Their political works also influenced art through their daughter, Mary Shelley of *Frankenstein* fame, and the Romantic poets in her circle. Another couple, the French Germaine de Stael (1766–1817) and Benjamin Constant (1767–1830) provided libertarian critiques of the French Revolution's successes and failures. Wilhelm von Humboldt (1767–1835) produced a Germanic, Romantic notion of self–cultivation and liberty. Economists such as the French Jean Baptiste Say (1767–1832) and the English David Ricardo (1772–1823) brought new scientific tools to bear on the legacy of the Scottish Enlightenment and French

Physiocrats. French theologian Felicite Robert de Lamennais (1782–1854) linked the idea of freedom of religion with the goal of state decentralization. The French Frederic Bastiat (1801–1850) took this a step further with journalistic writing in favor of the *laissez–faire* economics pioneered by Adam Smith.

The libertarian approach also influenced the humanities, as scholars such as the British Herbert Spencer (1820–1903) and American William Graham Sumner (1840–1910) applied the tools of science to anthropology and history in search of broad patterns of human behavior. The visibility of renowned thinkers such as Alexis de Tocqueville (1805–1859) and John Stuart Mill (1806–1873) brought even further attention and validity to the tradition. American Elizabeth Cady Stanton (1815–1902) articulated an activist libertarian feminism and organized the first U.S. bid for women's suffrage. The international, interdependent work of such minds proved the importance and popularity of libertarian ideas during the nineteenth century.

Others experimented with putting these ideas into practice. For example, the Manchester School (1835–1859) in England organized in support of libertarian ideas such as free trade, or *laissez–faire* economics, international markets, and pacifism, and in opposition to outdated rules such as the medieval Corn Laws that granted government monopolies to certain producers and protected others from competition. Led by Richard Cobden, the movement succeeded in repealing laws and propelling advocates into national office. In the United States, the Transcendentalist Movement (1835–1882) took the views of Godwin, Condorcet, and Humboldt on human perfectibility and employed them in writings, speeches, and even experimental utopian communities. The passive resistance plan of Henry David Thoreau, which influenced modern world leaders from Gandhi to Martin Luther King, Jr., was but one lasting contribution of the Transcendentalists.

After centuries of proto–libertarian Western thought, libertarianism coalesced around the figures of John Locke and Adam Smith and went on to achieve prominence in the nineteenth century. A number of historical events conspired to make the time ripe for libertarian thought. European culture allowed scholars, philosophers, authors, and activists the opportunity to travel, compare notes, test assumptions, and communicate effectively. This exchange of information ensured that economic or political authoritarianism in the form of protectionism or absolutism could no longer confine citizens, since they readily could compare their lots with those across the border. It also meant that new ideas could have ripple effects across

MAJOR WRITINGS
Two Treatises of Civil Government

Two Treatises of Civil Government appeared in 1690. In the *Second Treatise*, Locke posed the question: if individuals naturally are free, why should they ever choose to cede some of their natural rights to government? The answer, Locke argued, was that the state was necessary to protect property and liberty. Where protection ended, he continued, so did the legitimate authority of government:

123. If man in the state of nature be so free, as has been said; if he be absolute lord of his own person and possessions, equal to the greatest, and subject to nobody, why will he part with his freedom? Why will he give up this empire, and subject himself to the domination and control of any other power? To which 'tis obvious to answer, that though in the state of nature he hath such a right, yet the enjoyment of it is very uncertain, and constantly exposed to the invasion of others. For all being kings as much as he, every man his equal, and the greater part no strict observers of equity and justice, the enjoyment of the property he has in this state is very unsafe, very insecure. This makes him willing to quit this condition, which however free, is full of fears and continual dangers: and 'tis not without reason, that he seeks out, and is willing to join in society with others who are already united, or have a mind to unite for the mutual preservation of their lives, liberties and estates, which I call by the general name, property.

124. The great and chief end therefore, of men's uniting into commonwealths, and putting themselves under government, is the preservation of their property. To which in the state of nature there are many things wanting....

131. But though men when they enter into society, give up the equality, liberty, and executive power they had in the state of nature, into the hands of the society, to be so far disposed of by the legislative, as the good of the society shall require; yet it being only with an intention in everyone the better to preserve himself his liberty and property; (for no rational creature can be supposed to change his condition with an intention to be worse) the power of the society, or legislative constituted by them, can never be supposed to extend further than the common good....

Rose Wilder Lane, author and advocate of libertarianism. (AP/World Wide Photos)

BIOGRAPHY:
Ayn Rand

Many of the most prominent libertarian theorists made their marks through specialized scholarship or political office. Ayn Rand, however, chose to communicate her individualistic beliefs through works of fiction and popular philosophy. The results left her a bestselling author and a one–woman intellectual movement. Born in St. Petersburg, Russia, Rand emigrated to the United States after the Bolshevik Revolution, where she was haunted by her experience with communist totalitarianism in Russia and her frustration toward the West's drift toward socialism. Her first novel, *We the Living*, appeared in 1936, but her breakthrough work came in 1943 with *The Fountainhead*. She followed its tremendous success with non–fiction such as *Capitalism: The Unknown Ideal* (1946) and *The Virtue of Selfishness* (1964) and fiction such as *Anthem* (1853) and *Atlas Shrugged* (1957). From 1961 to 1976, she also published *The Objectivist Newsletter* (renamed *The Ayn Rand Letter* in 1971) to support her views further.

In all of her works, Rand promoted the philosophy she called objectivism, a subset of traditional libertarianism. Objectivism, according to Rand, meant that individual effort and ability served as the sole source of genuine achievement; all individuals' highest moral end was their own happiness, and any notion of a group threatened all people as individual rights–bearers. She believed that altruism and sacrifice for the so–called "common good" was a vice that rewarded non–producers and penalized creative entrepreneurs. *Laissez–faire* economic systems and limited states, she argued, created the best atmosphere for the exercise of talent and pursuit of happiness. Her fictional characters—creative individuals who escaped society to follow their own ends—became live through various film adaptations, and her books sold by the millions. In 1991, nine years after her death and fifteen after her newsletter ended publication, a Gallop Survey ranking the most influential literature in the United States found the fiction of Ayn Rand to be second in national influence, surpassed only by *The Bible*.

national boundaries; the American and French Revolutions are good examples of this interplay between countries. Older policies such as mercantilism also failed during this period, leaving a vacuum for new approaches that libertarian ideas filled. In the dual realms of ideas and action, libertarianism found success in the nineteenth century.

Decline and Return

Many of the conditions in the West that led to the rise of libertarianism in theory and practice changed at the turn of the century, however. Rapid industrialization created new economic problems; ethnic pride and nationalism destroyed international trade and the flow of information; communism and Nazism not only increased the size and scope of government within nations, but also forced other countries to expand their states to meet the challenge of world war; depression left citizens dependent on entitlements rather than jealous of their individual rights. By the dawn of the twentieth century, libertarian thinkers offered quiet critique of a mainstream that had left their ideas behind. Two economic movements, the Austrian School (1877–present) and Chicago School (1927–present), formed to oppose the trend of centralized economic planning, but their voices remained on the periphery of the Western debate about political theory.

The tide turned once again in favor of libertarianism in the middle of the twentieth century, however. The experience of world war, depression, and totalitarianism suggested that the short–term solutions of centralized planning, government intervention, and collectivism had not only failed to offer viable solutions, but also had created other problems in terms of everything from economic inefficiencies to political stalemates to human rights abuses. The simultaneous publication of four influential and contrasting works in 1943 and 1944—the Russian Ayn Rand's philosophical novel *The Fountainhead*, the American Rose Wilder Lane's political manifesto *The Discovery of Freedom*, the American Isabel Patterson's journalistic commentary *God of the Machine*, and the Austrian Friedrich Hayek's economic analysis *The Road to Serfdom*—heralded the return of libertarianism as, if not a mainstream consensus, at least a credible voice of opposition. In 1944, Friedrich Hayek's *The Road to Serfdom* helped to usher in the reemergence of libertarianism on the Western, and eventually world, stage; it remains the most well known work of libertarianism's most long–lived movement, the Austrian School of Economics. In this work, Hayek warned that centralized economic planning by its very nature would lead to totalitarianism in whatever nation it was practiced.

The *laissez–faire* economic approaches of the Austrian and Chicago schools gained ground among scholars, and Ayn Rand's individualistic Objectivist Movement (1943–1976) appealed to a popular audience, as well. By 1971, a third political party, the Libertarian Party, had formed in the United States with a platform supporting free markets, civil liberties, non–intervention, peace, and free trade.

No single success illustrated the reemergence of libertarianism better than the Public Choice School of Economics (1969–present). Founded after the 1962 publication of *The Calculus of Consent* by James Buchanan (1919–) and Gordon Tullock (1922–), the movement analyzed public policy from a market angle. Accordingly, they viewed politics as exchange, and asserted that politicians, lobbyists, bureaucrats, and others involved in policymaking acted with the same self–interest that motivates other actors in the private sector. This idea led to a myriad of methodological innovations in economics, political science, and public policy studies, and supported libertarian conclusions about the limitation of state power. This approach held important implications for analyzing government and policy, and by the twenty–first century had inspired everything from the New Economic History methodology to the burgeoning field of free market environmentalism, with influences felt as far

and wide as the United States, India, China, and the former Soviet bloc. Buchanan cemented his legacy by cofounding (1969) and for a time directing the Center for the Study of Public Choice. His work with the libertarian–inspired public choice theory earned him a Nobel Prize in Economics in 1986.

The new millennium opened with a record number of libertarian organizations and institutions worldwide devoted to political, economic, historical, and philosophical inquiry. In 2000, a Rasmussen Research poll revealed that 16 percent of U.S. citizens were ideologically libertarian; in the same year, the Libertarian Party's candidates for the U.S. House of Representatives won 11.9 percent of the vote, which set a record for votes received for any third party in the nation's history. The tradition born in antiquity and raised in the Enlightenment found new life in the Information Age.

THEORY IN DEPTH

Defining Libertarianism

A tradition as long–lived and diverse as that of libertarianism often suffers problems of definition. In fact, many who embraced or embrace libertarianism would disagree even about the name of the political theory. Until Leonard Read, founder of the Foundation for Economic Education, began to call himself a libertarian in the 1950s, no one had applied the term to the tradition. Before that, depending on the time and place, libertarians might have self–identified as individualists, voluntaryists, whigs, radical republicans, democratic–republicans, free thinkers, or liberals; moreover, proponents of individual movements within the libertarian framework often adopted the labels of the subset—from the Levellers and the Transcendentalists to the Austrian economists and objectivists— rather than the larger title. To complicate things further, there remains a strong urge from many within the libertarian community to disassociate with the frequently misunderstood term "libertarianism" and use the name "classical liberalism" instead.

Considering the complexity of the terminology issue, it is not surprising that those who try to define the tradition do so in somewhat different ways. For example, E. K. Bramsted, co–editor of the monumental anthology *Western Liberalism: A History in Documents from Locke to Croce* (1978), asserted that libertarianism champions 1) the rights of individuals, with careful attention to the more endangered rights of minorities, 2) the right of property in particular, 3) the government's obligation to protect property, 4)

MAJOR WRITINGS:

An Inquiry into the Nature and Causes of the Wealth of Nations

Eighty–six years after Locke explained the purpose of government, the second father of libertarianism, Adam Smith, explained the nature of markets in *An Inquiry into the Nature and Causes of the Wealth of Nations* (1776). According to Smith, free markets coordinated individual self–love and, through the division of labor, allowed for a harmony of interests to exist. Thus the butcher, brewer, and baker each had products for sale to Smith:

> This division of labour, from which so many advantages are derived, is not originally the effect of any human wisdom, which foresees and intends that general opulence to which it gives occasion. It is the necessary, though very slow and gradual, consequence of a certain propensity in human nature which has in view no such expensive utility; the propensity to truck, barter, and exchange one thing for another....
>
> In civilized society [man] stands at all times in need of the co–operation and assistance of great multitudes, while his whole life is scarce sufficient to gain the friendship of a few persons. In almost every other race of animals each individual, when it is grown up to maturity,

is entirely independent, and in its natural state has occasion for the assistance of no other living creature. But man has almost constant occasion for the help of his brethren, and it is in vain for him to expect it from their benevolence only. He will be more likely to prevail if he can interest their self–love in his favour, and shew them that it is for their own advantage to do for him what he requires of them. Whoever offers to another a bargain of any kind, proposes to do this. Give me that which I want, and you shall have this which you want, is the meaning of every such offer; and it is in this manner that we obtain from one another the far greater part of those good offices which we stand in need of. It is not from the benevolence of the butcher, the brewer, or the baker, that we expect our dinner, but from their regard to their own interest. We address ourselves, not to their humanity but to their self–love, and never talk to them of our own necessities but of their advantages. Nobody but a beggar chuses to depend chiefly on the benevolence of his fellow–citizens. Even a beggar does not depend upon it entirely. The charity of well–disposed people, indeed, supplies him with the whole fund of his subsistence. But though this principle ultimately provides him with all the necessaries of life which he has occasion for, it neither does nor can provide him with them as he has occasion for them. The greater part of his occasional wants are supplied in the same manner as those of other people, by treaty, by barter, and by purchase.

---

limited constitutional government, and 5) a belief in social progress. John Gray broadened this description in *Liberalism* (1986) to include philosophies that demonstrate 1) individualism, 2) egalitarianism, and 3) universalism. In *Liberalism Old and New* (1991), J. G. Merquior argued that the theories of 1) human rights, 2) constitutionalism, and 3) classical economics—in other words, free market positions such as that taken by Adam Smith—compose libertarian thought. David Boaz noted six ingredients for libertarianism in *The Libertarian Reader* (1997): 1) skepticism about power, 2) the dignity of the individual, 3) individual rights, 4) spontaneous order, 5) free markets, and 6) peace.

Although scholars have differed in the individual lists they have used to describe libertarianism, much consensus exists about the "big ideas" undergirding the tradition as a whole. First, libertarians

place an ethical emphasis on individuals as rights–bearers prior to the existence of any state, community, or society. This means that people have rights by virtue of the fact that they are people; no government grants these rights, and thus no government can take them away. Second, the libertarian tradition supports the right of property, and this, taken to its economic conclusion, leads to support of a free market system. From Adam Smith's invisible hand to Friedrich Hayek's spontaneous order, libertarian economists have described how the decentralized, private mechanism of the market creates the best outcomes for self–interested individuals as well as economies. Third, libertarians over the centuries have desired a limited constitutional government to protect individuals not only from other individuals, but also from the expansion of the state itself. Last, libertarianism proposes that these values—individu-

BIOGRAPHY:

Friedrich A. Hayek

Born in Vienna, Austria in 1899, Friedrich August von Hayek studied law, psychology, and economics at the University of Vienna, where he earned his Ph.D. in 1923. He studied at New York University the following year and then returned to Austria to study with the eminent economist Ludwig von Mises. Mises was the most visible member of the Austrian School of Economics, which Carl Menger founded in 1871, and which became the longest–lived movement in libertarianism. Hayek's prominence soon rose to challenge and even surpass that of Mises. From 1931 to 1950, Hayek served as the Took Professor of Economic Science and Statistics at the University of London. In 1947, he organized the Mount Pelerin Society, an ongoing international organization that met to discuss the principles and preservation of libertarianism. In 1950, Hayek became a Professor of Social and Moral Science at the University of Chicago; in 1962, he relocated to the University of Freiburg in Germany, where he taught economics until his retirement. Hayek became the first libertarian theorist to receive a Nobel Prize in 1974, when he received the honor for his work in Austrian economics.

During his long and productive career Hayek published many books and articles. He began with *Monetary Theory and the Trade Cycle* (1929) and *The Pure Theory of Capital* (1941), but gained greatest attention with his 1944 *The Road to Serfdom*, in which he argued that socialism inevitably leads to totalitarianism. In his 1952 *Counter–Revolution of Science*, he asserted that human unpredictability makes it impossible to apply the methodology of physical science to social studies, and he followed with ideas about the legal frameworks needed to maintain a free society in *The Constitution of Liberty* (1960) and *Law, Legislation and Liberty* (three volumes in 1973, 1976, and 1979). His last publication, *The Fatal Conceit*, appeared in 1988. Throughout his career, Hayek supported the view that the spontaneous order of the market remained the most efficient information system available to humanity; state intervention in the economy, he said, only creates misleading signals that lead to misallocation. Hayek's work through publications, universities, and the Mount Pelerin Society made him the most recognizable member of the Austrian School of Economics, and one of the most celebrated representatives of libertarianism.

---

alism, property, limited government—work for all people in all times; they are global and ahistorical. Other, more specific policies follow from these ideas: nonviolence, in order to preserve life and maintain free trade; nonaggression, in deference to individual rights. Specific political platforms and activism campaigns springboard from these broader ideals.

What It Is Not

Though the ingredients of libertarianism appear to be very general, they do exclude certain thinkers commonly linked with Enlightenment or rights–based theory. Failure to embrace all of these values, however, does point to a very fundamental difference with the minds that compose the historical libertarianism. Two diverse cases of philosophers associated with but not belonging to the tradition serve as case studies. First, the British theorist Jeremy Bentham (1748–1832) and

his fellow utilitarians supported certain individual rights and *laissez–faire* economics, as long as they produced the greatest happiness for the greatest number of people. Libertarian ends—rights and free markets—therefore served as convenient means to these thinkers, but the eventual ends they sought betrayed an intellectual collectivism incompatible with libertarianism's individualism. "The why" in this case matters as much as "the what." On the other hand, French philosopher Jean–Jacques Rousseau (1712–1778), who perhaps is known best for his theory of the social contract—an idea at first blush in harmony with libertarianism's emphasis on constitutional government—believed in an almost mystic notion of "the general will." The abstract nature of this idea created a power elite to interpret and impose this will, by force if necessary. The coercion and unaccountability connected to the implementation of Rousseau's model put him and his theory outside of the libertarian framework.

Differences Within the Movement

Beyond the key ideas of libertarian mentioned above, two parallel concepts survive throughout the history of the tradition. One rests on a negative view of human nature, accepting that all people are fallen and incapable of perfection. It follows from this perspective that power must be limited because, otherwise, some corrupt individuals could do even more harm than others. The second view maintains that all people inherently are good and perfectible. It follows from this position that power must be limited in order to allow humans to explore their potentials and evolve toward a more ideal order of self–government. In addition to these two philosophical positions remain the historical and religious contexts of thinkers and their times; libertarianism's heritage includes arguments made from Protestant (John Locke), Catholic (Felicite Robert de Lamennais), and atheist (Ayn Rand) assumptions, among others.

Defining a tradition labeled with ever-changing names, derived from multiple centuries, and developed in different countries poses a challenge; indeed, if most of the luminaries of the tradition were brought back and questioned about libertarianism, they doubtless would not understand the question. Nevertheless, most would understand and adhere to the ideal of non-coercion and, in one form or another, its related facets: individualism, property, constitutionalism, and universalism. These values often lead libertarians to the same conclusions about the role of government (limited to the protection of rights, if government is needed at all), the role of the people (enjoy their rights while not infringing on others' rights), and the control of distribution and production (all privatized and directed by the free market).

Due to its close relationship with the Enlightenment—or, perhaps more properly, Enlightenments—libertarianism benefited from the era's remarkable communication and interdependence, at least in the West. Just as the fire of revolution swept Europe and America, each igniting another, often sharing leaders and literature in the process, libertarian theory gained from the dialogue of thinkers and ideas borne of a variety of homelands and backgrounds. Any single attempt to chronicle the past of libertarianism must by its very nature fall short of doing justice to the richness and complexity of the individuals and movements within it. National differences did leave their mark, however. Three distinct flavors coexist and often blend in libertarian political theory.

Historically, British, French, and German contributions to libertarianism each provided a variation on the theory's theme. The British offered a realistic tradition of law. John Locke's work built on the foundation of the ancient constitution ideal; Adam Smith's approach to markets carried a scientific thirst for patterns. Mechanisms of the social contract and the corresponding right of revolution evolved from this British sensibility. The French dialogue added a rationalistic tradition of humanism. Whereas many of the greatest British minds used scholarly works as vehicles for their messages, many of the most accomplished French philosophers used the novel or the play. English revolt remained preoccupied with the letter of the law, while French revolt also focused on symbolic speech and national pageantry as key vehicles for political statement. At the heart of the French Revolution, and libertarian thinkers, such as the Marquis de Condorcet, lay a faith in the progressive evolution of humanity. British thought often remained rooted in Protestant realism, but French intellectuals often embraced a more agnostic or atheistic sensibility with reason as a secular god.

Beyond the realistic British tradition of law and the rational French tradition of humanism rested the organic German tradition of individualism. More than its counterparts, this strain of libertarianism came from an aesthetic viewpoint. Though the Austrian School's understanding of spontaneous order was colored by a German sensibility, the best example of this individualism remains Wilhelm von Humboldt. Humboldt's *The Limits of State Action*, published posthumously in 1851, proposed that the individual's highest purpose was *bildung*, or self-cultivation. In order to meet his or her potential, according to Humboldt, each person must possess freedom and a variety of experiences. The state, then, should act only as a "nightwatchman" by reacting to trespasses but not interfering proactively. Humboldt's belief in the cultivation of the self and the potential of human flourishing typified the Romantic German strain of libertarianism.

The three varieties of the libertarian tradition evolved in their own historical, political, and social contexts. In his 1986 work *Liberalism*, John Gray characterized these views as competing yet complementary definitions of liberty, with Britain representing independence, France self–rule, and Germany self–realization. All three remain inextricably woven into the fabric of the tradition, at times blending in the thought of a given movement or individual, at other times diverging into separate patterns across years and miles.

THEORY IN ACTION

No single thinker better illustrates the intersection of British, French, and German flavors of libertarianism than John Stuart Mill (1806–1873). The son of James Mill, a utilitarian philosopher and the author of the first English textbook of economics, John Stuart Mill was heavily influenced by the "greatest happiness for the greatest number" calculus of his father's utilitarian thought. He also studied extensively on his own, reading Greek and Latin classics as well as free market economists such as Adam Smith and David Ricardo. His intensive scholarly pursuits, added to the tensions he found between individualism and utilitarianism, led him to suffer a nervous breakdown in his early twenties. After recovering he undertook the private task of developing a more libertarian utilitarianism to resolve the problems he observed.

Mill's most celebrated writings—*On Liberty* (1861), *Considerations on Representative Government* (1861), and *Utilitarianism* (1863)—represented a crossroads of British, French, and German strains of thought. Mill drew upon the English libertarian tradition by warning against the tyranny of opinion that silences voices in the dialogue of ideas and calling for a kind of intellectual toleration of others' views. Mill called forth the French tradition of self–rule to propose an ethical sphere of privacy for each individual, a space that the state and the majority cannot touch. Neither toleration nor privacy sat easily with the traditional utilitarian plan to impose the system producing the most good for the most people.

Most significantly, Mill revised the standard "greatest happiness for the greatest number" equation that formed the bedrock of utilitarianism; to do this, he relied on the German tradition in general and Humboldt's aesthetic individualism in particular. With Humboldt's exhortation to pursue self–cultivation in mind, Mill altered the equation to include the quality of happiness as well as the quantity in judging utility, with those higher pleasures of self–realization ranking highest in quality. Mill's attempt to reform and repair utilitarianism led him to fuse the diverse strains of libertarian thought. Tensions remained—When could privacy be invaded? Who judged the quality of happiness?—and eventually led him to a pessimistic view of society and its options. Nonetheless, he continued to believe that individuals made the best decisions concerning themselves and the general welfare when acting alone or in voluntary associations—in other words, without governmental interference. The three forms of libertarian thought, at times competing with each other and at times complementing each other, united in Mill's work and continue to remain joined in the libertarian tradition.

After Mill, international movements such as the Austrian School and Chicago School in economics, the Objectivist movement in philosophy, and the Pub-

lic Choice School in economics and public policy have put libertarian ideas into practice through their scholarship, theory, fiction, and policy analysis. All four of these movements remain active with formal institutions and continued publication in the twenty–first century.

Others, however, looked to put libertarian ideas into practice through less scholarly, more political means. In the United States, for example, some self–proclaimed libertarians sought and won office through the tradition two–party system. Perhaps the most obvious example is self–proclaimed libertarian Ron Paul (1935–), the long–time Republican Congressman from Texas, whose voting record reflects the position of many libertarian activists on a variety of national issues.

Despite the success of some Republicans, Democrats, and Independents of libertarian persuasion who sought public office in the United States, others believed that the political theory required its own party in order to offer a separate message and alternative values to the nation's public. On December 11, 1971, a small gathering in the Colorado home of activist David Nolan became the first meeting of the Libertarian Party. The party soon made history. In 1972, the party's first national convention nominated University of Southern California Professor of Philosophy John Hospers (1918–) for its presidential candidate. Tonie Nathan (1928–) received the party's nomination for vice president; she then became the first woman in U.S. history to receive a vote from the Electoral College.

The party gained new political ground, it seemed, with each major election. By 1976, Libertarian presidential and vice presidential candidates Roger MacBride and David Bergland achieved ballot status in thirty–two states and received over 170,000 votes. In 1978, Ed Clark (1926–) ran as a Libertarian party member in the race for Governor of California and received five percent of the vote; in the same year, Alaska's Dick Randolph became the first Libertarian elected to a state legislature.

The Libertarian party truly gained widespread national attention for the first time in 1979, when it earned permanent ballot status in California after over 80,000 voters registered as Libertarians. The next year, Libertarian presidential and vice presidential candidates Ed Clark and David Koch appeared on the ballot in all fifty states, the District of Columbia, and Guam. For the first time, national advertisements ran to introduce U.S. voters to the Libertarian Party and its platform. The Clark/Koch ticket received almost one million votes in the election.

BIOGRAPHY:

Russell Means

Libertarianism has influenced not only scholarship, policy, and art, but it also has contributed to activist movements. Few public figures represent this side of the libertarian tradition as well as Russell Means. Means was born an Oglala/Lakota on the Pine Ridge Indian Reservation near the U.S. Black Hills. In the 1960s he began to work for Native American self–determination and individual rights. He became the first national director of the American Indian Movement, a group organized to promote American Indian sovereignty and protest rights abuses, and worked for over a decade with the United Nations. His concern for individual liberty and the limitation of government power led him to embrace libertarianism publicly. In 1988, Means ran for the nomination of the Libertarian Party as candidate for U.S. President.

Russell Means mastered several media in the interest of sharing his libertarian message. He starred in several commercial films including *Last of the Mohicans* (1991) and *Pocahontas* (1995), produced albums of political protest music, and penned his autobiography, *Where White Men Fear To Tread* (1995). He remains best known as an orator and activist who thrives on symbolic speech—he stormed Mount Rushmore, occupied Plymouth Rock, and led a seventy–one day takeover of Alcatraz to gain attention for his cause. By tapping into Native American individualism and bringing his heritage to bear on the Libertarian Party, Means underscored the fact that the libertarian tradition can apply to more than just the white mainstream.

Russell Means, standing in front of a statue of a Native American. (AP/World Wide Photos)

By 1982, Libertarians had achieved political visibility at the state level. For example, Louisiana candidate for governor James Agnew earned twenty–three percent of the vote, while Alaska gubernatorial candidate Dick Randolph took fifteen percent and Arizona gubernatorial candidate Sam Steiger won five percent. Two years later, the David Bergland/Jim Lewis ticket brought the Libertarian party into third place—a Libertarian first—for the White House. Also in 1984, Alaska elected its third Libertarian state legislator. Eleven other Libertarians won local offices across the nation. By 1986, over two hundred Libertarian candidates across the United States received a total of 2.9 million votes.

Republican U.S. Congressman Ron Paul left his party to run for president as a Libertarian in 1988. Over 430,000 million citizens voted for him and his running mate, Andre Marrou, giving the Libertarian party almost twice the votes of any other third party. Though Paul later returned to the Republican party, he never renounced his libertarian perspective. Approximately two million voters cast ballots for Libertarian candidates in 1990; that number nearly doubled in 1992, counting only state and federal races. The twenty–three Libertarian candidates for U.S. Senate won over one million votes, making the 1992 vote total the highest for a third party since 1914. Once again, the Libertarian presidential ticket remained on the ballots of all fifty states as well as those of Washington, D.C. and Guam.

The party broke more U.S. national records in 1996, when it became the first third party in the country's history to earn ballot status in all fifty states in two presidential elections in a row. Presidential nominee Harry Browne earned almost 500,000 votes, while nearly eight hundred state and federal Libertarian candidates won a total of 5.4 million votes. Public intellectuals and celebrities such as African–American civil rights leader Roy Innis (1934–) and talk radio personality Art Bell (1945–) publically embraced the party and its platform, as well, adding to the visibility of the party.

In the year 2000, Libertarian candidates for the U.S. House of Representatives alone took 1.6 million votes, yet another national record for any U.S. third party. The year 2000 was also the first time in eight decades that a third party had contested a majority of the seats in the U.S. congress. In fact, 1,430 Libertarian candidates ran in the 2000 election, a number more than twice that of all other third party candidates together. In 2001, more than three hundred Libertarians held elective office, which is more than double the number of all other third–party officials combined. The numbers reveal the Libertarian party to be the largest, most long–lived, and most successful third party in the United States.

The Libertarian party platform achieved a certain stability across the years. The party's principles echo those of the theory on which it is based: liberty, individual rights, and the ability to pursue one's goals peacefully, without governmental interference. The Libertarian party platform has applied these principles to support a limited government designed to protect individual rights, a state with little or no involvement in the social or economic spheres of individuals' lives or on the international stage beyond the establishment and protection of free trade. Many of the party's positions might sound familiar either to Republicans—lower taxation, privatization of government agencies, and school choice—or to Democrats—pro–choice regarding abortion, anti–censorship regarding the First Amendment, and equal rights for gay and lesbian couples.

Other positions seem more unusual; for example, the Libertarian party supports the legalization of drug use and prostitution, as well as the right to die. Some who identify with libertarian political theory choose to remain aloof from the party because it tends to follow ideas to their consistent conclusions, even if the resulting policy seems extreme or idealistic. These libertarians prefer to work for small changes from within the major two parties, believing that incremental accomplishments will in the long run add up to more than great changes that never found implementation. Even at the party level, libertarianism remains caught in the chasm between how things are and what is feasible, and how things could be and what is ideal.

Libertarianism has found adherents across the globe, as well, particularly through movements such as the Austrian School of Economics that unify the work of economists the world over who share the same convictions. The consistent growth and accomplishment of the U.S. Libertarian party, however, despite its controversy among some libertarians, is one of the success stories of the twentieth century.

ANALYSIS AND CRITICAL RESPONSE

Over the centuries, and especially in its time of decline in the early twentieth century, libertarianism faced criticism from some theorists and laypersons alike; even in its reemergence in the late twentieth and early twenty–first century, the theory never commanded a majority of adherents the Western mainstream. As one would expect, some critiques of the tradition reflect more insight than others.

Critiques

Libertinism   A common and easily answered challenge to the tradition is the concern that libertarianism, in effect, is little more than libertinism in sophisticated trappings; in other words, the theory uses the rhetoric of philosophy to justify the worst excesses and self–indulgences of sensual license. Liberty for individual choice, these critics argue, is little more than permission to feed every appetite—be it drugs, obscenity, promiscuity, or other "vices"—without accountability to a higher law.

Libertarians respond to this concern in two ways. First, if people are free to make decisions concerning their lives, they are as free to choose not to do something as they are to do it. No one forces people to make "wrong" choices. For example, alcohol and tobacco are legal in the United States, yet many U.S. citizens choose not to drink or smoke. No one is forced to do so; moreover, in the libertarian framework, individual decision–makers would be responsible for the consequences of their actions, good or bad—this accountability is the direct opposite of libertinism's license. Second, libertarianism does not deny the call of a higher law: it simply proposes that governments should not necessarily coerce individuals to follow it. Many libertarian thinkers also published and spoke in order to practice moral persuasion, to convince individuals that their view of the good was the one to adopt. Religious, community, and other voluntary associations would be free to pursue their idea of the right way to live and try to persuade others to follow their example. They would not, however, have access to the monopolistic power of the state to enforce their conception of the virtuous life on others. In short, libertarians explain that individualism is not an excuse for vice; instead, it is a call for noncoercion.

Individualism leading to atomism A second critique with a similar appeal to morality suggests that libertarianism's focus on individualism leads to atomism. In other words, individuals lose all sense of community and instead lead isolated, empty lives driven by nothing but selfishness. Once again, the libertarian answer is twofold. First, defenders would say, individual choice means just that: individuals might choose to value empty materialism and self–involvement, but individuals might also choose to connect to other individuals in meaningful and enriching ways. No particular outcome follows just because people are not coerced into leading the same kind of lifestyle.

An even more compelling response, however, is that critics use a primitive and two–dimensional understanding of community when they seek centralized planning and forced membership, or believe some ideal form of community somehow existed before the individuals who composed it. Life and its relationships, the argument continues, are too complex to be built by coercion. Individuals who enjoy the liberty to be creative and innovative in the ways they relate to one another create true communities spontaneously. Individualism is not the death of community, libertarians explain—in fact, it is often the recipe for more unexpected, diverse, and fulfilling communities than those previously imagined.

Liberty vs. stability Critics also claim that libertarianism overestimates the value people place on liberty as opposed to other options such as stability, equality, or virtue. Is it better to be free, or secure? Or equal? Or good? The libertarian response is rather simple: in the framework of individual rights, people could choose to value any measure of the good they wish. They are not forced to be free. If, for example, they wish to follow a certain code of virtue, form communities with those of like minds, and try to encourage others to do the same, they may. The only limitation is that they may not harness the authority of the state to enforce their value on everyone else. Of course, one might argue that this response still maintains liberty as the primary value.

Market failure Beyond moral concerns rest economic ones. A trio of economic critiques of libertarianism draws responses of variable usefulness. First, some opponents believe that libertarianism's emphasis on free markets ignores the so–called "market failure" problem of externalities, or spillover effects, which occur when people uninvolved in an exchange are harmed or benefited by that exchange. These effects might be desirable or unwanted. For example, universal educa-

tion produces a positive externality; even if an individual does not have a child to be educated, he or she reaps the benefit of living in a society where laws and elections are determined by an educated citizenry. In an extreme libertarian framework, public education might not exist. Pollution exemplifies a negative externality with dispersed effect. Everyone might be hurt a small amount by air pollution, but costs are too high for any one individual, for instance, to sue every industry in the nation for damages. The result is that everyone suffers a very small amount from pollution, but no one does anything about it.

Libertarians admit that the problem of externalities exists in a completely free market situation. They respond that these small effects—if there were large, concentrated effects on any one person, damages could be sought through legal means—are a price of living in a free society, in the same way that the cost of free speech is that we must tolerate some indecent speech in the process. Furthermore, the argument continues, the cost of eliminating externalities by government means would exceed the cost of living with the externalities due to the government failures of efficiency. Some libertarians admit that there might be a role for government in correcting the externality problem, however. These theorists stress that solutions must strive to mirror the market through choice and competition as much as possible. School vouchers, allowing parents choice and allowing schools to compete, or housing vouchers, allowing low–income families to seek their best options for homes, for example, would be a preferable initiative than public schools or government housing projects.

Stratification of wealth A second problem with markets, critics claim, is that they promote stratification of wealth—or, to use a catchphrase, "the rich get richer and the poor get poorer." The libertarian response contains two parts. First, the argument goes, the stratification of a pure market system would not be as extreme as it is in mixed systems like that in the United States that include government regulation and interference in the economy; stratification is more the product of rent-seeking, or using power and influence to lobby for government protectionism and favoritism, than of profit-seeking. Even so, the libertarian reasoning continues, it would be better for some people to live in relative poverty created by stratification than for everyone to live in absolute poverty due to the inherent miscalculations of planned economies as seen, for example, in the former Soviet Union. As with the issue of externalities, the libertarian position seems in part to be one of taking the lesser of two evils.

Role of corporations   A third economic criticism of libertarianism is that the tradition's focus on free markets is naïve, for it overlooks the fact that other institutions besides the government—such as, for example, corporations—also represent centralized power over individuals. Some libertarians counter that corporations have reached their current strength in part due to the state. Governments are lobbied by corporations and in turn give them legal and financial special treatment; moreover, the regulatory boards set up by governments to oversee corporate behavior often are co–opted by insiders who lobby for positions of power—in effect, the watchers are watching themselves. Other libertarians counter that the tradition's support of decentralization would lead not to undoing markets to solve this problem, but rather to redoing the corporate structure that has evolved over the last century. The classic retort to this critique, however, is that corporations, though powerful, cannot do what governments do. Only states hold the monopoly on coercion.

Enforcement   The most successful argument against libertarianism is the question of enforcement. Who makes everyone play by the rules in the absence of coercion? Peace and free trade might work well as long as all nations agree to be peaceful traders, but what happens when one nation attacks another? How can the rogue nation be made to "play fair," except by coercion, perhaps even violence? Libertarians differ on their response to this question. Though many support a noninterventionist foreign policy, they also maintain the right of a nation to defend itself. The question remains, however, at what point does self–defense begin? May a country strike preemptively at a potential threat, or must it wait until it suffers harm? This question also applies to internal matters within communities.

At day's end, the value of libertarianism remains tied to our understanding of the human condition. Are individuals capable of the demands of a libertarian world?

Criticisms aside, the libertarian tradition has much to recommend it: a long and varied past, a tradition of toleration and diversity, and broad principles that leave it open to adaptation and innovation. As a political movement, the theory has consistency on its side. In the United States, for example, the Democratic Party calls for freedom in the social sphere but government regulation in the economic one, and the Republican Party calls for freedom in the economic sphere but government regulation in the social one. The Libertarian Party continues to add members thanks to its consistent view of governmental nonin-terference in either sphere of life. As a theory, libertarianism has reaped impressive fruits, including multiple, productive movements and methodologies, and more than one Nobel Prize. Perhaps most importantly, the by–products of the libertarian theory speak for themselves. For example, the tradition's emphasis on individual rights helped to create a number of movements—abolitionism, feminism, and civil rights among them—that offer the theory impressive character references. One thing is certain: with centuries under its belt and a reemergence to welcome the new millennium, libertarianism remains a living and relevant political theory.

TOPICS FOR FURTHER STUDY

- Consider the issue of an involuntary military draft. In what different ways might a libertarian criticize this policy?

- Read the political platforms of the two major political parties in the United States. Which of the two might be more likely to integrate libertarian ideas into its policy agendas? Why?

- If a libertarian were able to create his or her ideal libertarian society, what would it look like? Could it function effectively? Why or why not?

BIBLIOGRAPHY

Sources

Barry, Norman. *On Classical Liberalism and Libertarianism.* New York: St. Martin's, 1987.

Bergland, David. *Libertarianism in One Lesson.* 6th Edition. Costa Mesa, CA: Orpheus Publications, 1993.

Boaz, David, ed. *The Libertarian Reader.* New York: The Free Press, 1997.

Boaz, David. *Libertarianism: A Primer.* New York: The Free Press, 1997.

Bramstead, E. K. and K, J. Melhuish, ed. *Western Liberalism: A History in Documents from Locke to Croce.* London: Longman, 1978.

Buchanan, James and Gordon Tullock. *The Calculus of Consent: Logical Foundations of Constitutional Democracy.* Ann Arbor: The University of Michigan Press, 1962.

Gray, John. *Liberalism.* Minneapolis: University of Minnesota Press, 1986.

The Libertarian Party. Available at http://lp.org.

Merquior, J. G. *Liberalism Old and New.* Boston: Twayne Publishers, 1991.

Narveson, Jan. *The Libertarian Idea*. Philadelphia: Temple University Press, 1989.

Rand, Ayn. *For The New Intellectual*. New York: Signet, 1961.

Sturgis, Amy H. "The Rise, Decline, and Reemergence of Classical Liberalism." *Great Thinkers in Classical Liberalism: The LockeSmith Review, Volume I*. Amy H. Sturgis, Nathan D. Griffith, Melissa English, Joshua B. Johnson, and Kevin D. Weimer, eds. Nashville: The LockeSmith Institute, 1994: 20–56.

Further Readings

Anderson, Terry L. and Donald R. Leal. *Free Market Environmentalism*. Revised Edition. New York: St. Martin's, 2001. This book explores one of the most timely issues considered by the Public Choice School.

Friedman, Milton and Rose. *Free to Choose*. New York: Harcourt Brace Jovanovich, 1980. This is an introductory work by two of the more popular modern libertarian writers.

Hazlitt, Henry. *Economics in One Lesson*. 2nd Edition. New Rochelle, NY: Arlington House: 1985. This work serves as an introduction to libertarian economic theory.

Humane Studies Review. http://www.humanestudiesreview.org. This is the site for a decades–old international, interdisciplinary journal of libertarian studies.

Libertarian Party. http://www.lp.org. This is the official site of the Libertarian Party in the United States.

Machan, Tibor, and Douglas B. Rasmussen. *Liberty for the 21st Century*. Lanham, MD: Rowan and Littlefield, 1995. This is a helpful compilation of modern libertarian works.

SEE ALSO

Capitalism, Conservatism, Liberalism

Marxism

OVERVIEW

Marxist theory was developed in the 1800s by Karl Marx and Friedrich Engels. The Marxist ideology includes a philosophy of man, a political and economic program, and a theory of history. Marx's ideas were changed and altered after his death to suit the needs of those subscribing to them, and were changed further to accommodate communism as practiced by Vladimir Lenin in the Soviet Union in the beginning of the twentieth century. The hybrid created by Lenin is commonly called Marxism–Leninism, communism, or socialism, depending on the source. Marxism is a special brand of communism, specific to the time of Karl Marx. It was instrumental in forming the ideology of modern communism as well.

Marx's philosophy of man is that humanity is defined by its ability to meet its needs. It does this by laboring on natural materials. Man does this labor for the species as well as for himself. Marx explained that all human creations, including houses, governments, food, and art, combine to create the human world which is made from the productivity of man. He argued that the entire species should benefit from this production, rather than just the producers, as in capitalism.

Marx and Engels wrote and published *The Communist Manifesto* in 1848. It explains the class struggles and the historical problem between the exploiters and the exploited. Their ideas were novel in that they felt history was fueled by the changes in means of production, where other historians had written only of battles, treaties, inventions, and discoveries.

CHRONOLOGY

1818: Karl Marx is born.

1848: Marx and Engels complete *The Communist Manifesto*.

1867: The first edition of Karl Marx's *Das Kapital* is published

1883: Karl Marx dies.

1889: The Second International is founded.

1902: Lenin publishes *What Is to Be Done?*

1917: Bolsheviks, led by Lenin, gain control in Russia.

1919: Founding of the Third International.

1922: Stalin becomes the Communist Party's general secretary.

1924: Lenin dies; Stalin takes control of Russia.

Karl Marx.

The Marxist doctrine was refined and changed, especially after Marx's death. Engels changed the revolutionary propaganda into a more peaceful patience and a quiet confidence of the evolutionary victory of a classless society. Under Vladimir Lenin, Marxism became more removed from the proletariat. According to Lenin, the workers could not organize their own revolt and needed leaders to plan and lead the revolution. Lenin also felt that revolution could and should occur in non–industrialized and non–capitalist nations. Lenin's version of Marxism is commonly referred to as Marxism–Leninism. Joseph Stalin further altered Marxism to such a degree that it could barely even be called Marxism. His version, more so than Lenin's, effectively destroyed the equality and freedom that Marxism was designed to promote.

HISTORY

Socialist and Utopian Beginnings

Socialism was labeled as such in the 1820s and has since been used by Karl Marx (1818–1883) and other philosophers to describe ways to organize society. Marxism stems from socialist and communist ideas, though Marxism itself didn't exist until the middle of the nineteenth century.

Socialists do not agree with capitalism, and believe competition between individuals breeds inequality. Cooperation is a better system to socialists, and a shared ownership of the forces of production and distribution will guarantee equality. Socialists feel that each member of society should have the same materials. Socialism does not necessarily dictate shared government, however, though some socialists are democrats.

Karl Marx was a socialist who molded some of his ideas from the ancient Greek philosopher Plato (428–348 B.C.). Plato wanted to begin a republic free of strife. He did not subscribe to democracy but rather felt that his republic should be run by "philosopher–kings," trained individuals who made the rules for everyone else to obey. Plato felt that the personal interests of the population would not necessarily be helpful for the common good but would inhibit the decision–making process. People's desires would block their judgment. Plato put community above all else.

Another socialist thinker was English statesman and author Sir Thomas More (1478–1535). He transferred the Greek word "utopia" to English to describe an island with an ideal society. The secret of the utopia's success was socialism. All the wealth was shared, and poverty and crime did not exist. Rulers

BIOGRAPHY:
Karl Marx

Karl Marx was born May 5, 1818, in the Rhine province of Prussia (Germany). He was the oldest living son in a family of nine children. Both of his parents were Jewish but a year before Karl was born his father converted to the Evangelical Established Church. Young Karl was baptized when he was 6, though he was influenced more by the radical ideas of the Enlightenment than by religion. He was discriminated against because of his Jewish heritage, which may have begun his distaste for social inequality.

At the University of Berlin in 1836, Marx was introduced to George Hegel's teachings and he began his association with the Young Hegelians. Hegel's doctrines explained that when there were two ideas or desires in conflict, they would meet and form a third option better suited to both. The Young Hegelians moved toward atheism and political action and the Prussian government began to drive them from the universities.

After graduating in 1841, Marx began to contribute regularly to a newspaper in Cologne the following year. When he was the editor, the newspaper was suspended by the government soon after for its revolutionary ideas. In 1843 Marx married the daughter of a family friend, Jenny von Westphalen, and they moved to Paris. While there Marx began to associate with communist societies. He wrote *The German–French Yearbooks*, which did not prove very successful but created an alliance with Friedrich Engels which continued until Marx's death. Marx was expelled from France and he and Engels went to Brussels in 1845. The two men collaborated closely after that.

The Communist League was formed in 1847 and Marx and Engels were asked to write its doctrine. A year later when it was completed, the League adopted it as their manifesto. *The Communist Manifesto* has become one of the most important documents written about economic theory and social history. It explains that history is a series of struggles between the classes. It rejects social utopias and philosophical socialism centered around alienation. The Manifesto dictates 10 steps to communism, including progressive income tax and the abolition of inheritance.

In 1848 Marx was indicted for his writings and for advocating the nonpayment of taxes. He was acquitted, but banished from Paris. Marx went to London in 1849 and remained there for the rest of his life. He was frustrated by his failures on mainland Europe and rejoined the Communist League in London. He spent from 1850 to 1864 living in extreme poverty—Engels was supporting him financially—and relative seclusion. Several of his children died and his wife suffered breakdowns. The Marx family lived on scant means as Marx continued to write his theories.

In 1864, the International Working Men's Association was founded. Marx wrote *Das Kapital*, which became the bible for the International. He was sought out to be a leader and organized various parties and ideas. The International flourished and intervened in union disputes.

After the Franco–German War in 1870, Marx slowly lost control of the International and it was disbanded in 1876. Marx's energies waned and he experienced prolonged bouts of depression. He was still consulted on political matters but stayed largely removed. His wife died in 1881 and his eldest daughter in 1883. He died the following year.

Marx's most famous work, *Das Kapital*, became known as the "Bible of the working class" by the International Working Men's Association. *The Communist Manifesto* had similar weight as well, and despite Marx's poverty and struggle, he had an enormous impact on the world. Despite the apparent failure of his theories, Marx's writings remain some of the most influential ideas in human history.

---

were elected and there was freedom of belief. Farming, which More considered the least–favored work, was divided amongst everyone.

Two hundred years after More, Jean–Jacques Rousseau (1712–1788) created another idea of a perfect society in his works on political theory, most notably *The Social Contract*. He felt that people were naturally good, and that society's inequality drove evil into people. He agreed with More and Plato that community was the answer.

The French Revolution, in conjunction with the Industrial Revolution at the end of the eighteenth century and the beginning of the nineteenth century, had profound effects on political thinking. Europe's monarchy was brushed away and the privileges enjoyed by the clergy were invalidated. Liberty swept the land and equality became the battle cry. The populace realized that they had the power to alter the reality with which they were so unhappy. Though the Industrial Revolution was slow, it was unstoppable. Though the standard of living went up and there was more material to go around and less work needed to create it, work days for factory workers were seemingly endless and the conditions horrendous. Women and children worked for low wages and were easier to control than men. They often worked sixteen–hour shifts. Towns became crowded as people looked for work in the factories. Their needs, housing, and sanitation were ignored. Slums sprouted up everywhere. It was this poverty and dissatisfaction that made people begin to think that capitalism was not the best economic and political option.

Charles Fourier (1772–1837) felt that men were generally good and could therefore be organized into utopian societies. He envisioned communal units of 1,500 people per unit. The people would live in buildings called *phalansteries*, which he described in great detail. He also explained how the groups would relate to each other. Work would only be done a few hours per day, and children, who Fourier said enjoyed getting dirty, would do the unappetizing work that adults shunned. Fourier's ideas influenced many socialist communities.

Another important socialist and utopian advocate was Robert Owen (1771–1858). Shocked by the working conditions in Britain (and himself the co–owner of a large spinning mill in Scotland), he began to form ideas of his own. In his mill, the work day was only 10 hours long. Children went to school instead of to work in the factories and his workers lived in houses and had sanitation and gardens. Owen still made money, despite his fair treatment of his workers. He began New Harmony, Indiana, as a utopian community but, like the other utopias, it didn't last long—only from 1824 to 1828.

Marxist Developments

Marx's ideas on socialism were so convincing that they spawned their own term: Marxism. Marx's version of socialism not only explained the evolution of society but also examined the reasons for conflict within society. Marx grew up in Germany and was strongly influenced by his father and by his neighbor, Ludwig von Westphalen, an important political figure. Marx studied philosophy at the University of Berlin and joined the Young Hegelians, a group interested in the ideas of German philosopher George

Wilhelm Friedrich Hegel (1770–1831). The group was radical and revolutionary and, because of Marx's affiliation with them and his political activity, he was unable to get a job in academia when he received his doctorate in 1841.

He turned to journalism to make his living and edited *The Rhine Newspaper (Rheinische Zeitung)*, until the newspaper was shut down five months later for its liberal content. Marx and his wife moved to France where, in the midst of the revolution ideology, Marx developed his theories. Marx met Friedrich Engels (1820–1895) in Paris. Marx had many novel ideas but was less adept than Engels at explaining them in print. Engels had discovered England's working class at his family's factory in Manchester in 1842. He was already a communist and began his relationship with Karl Marx two years later in 1844. The two men wrote *The Holy Family* and *The German Ideology*.

Marx's writings were controversial. He wrote a great deal about the ills of his homeland and, in 1845, Germany convinced France to expel him. Marx moved to Brussels, Belgium. Engels went with him and the two joined a group called the Communist League. In 1847 the League asked them to create a statement about its beliefs, and Marx and Engels wrote *The Communist Manifesto*. The Manifesto got little immediate attention because of the Revolutions throughout Europe in 1848. Marx and Engels finally got to experience the revolution about which they'd been writing. When the French government fell, Marx went to Cologne, Germany, and became the editor of *The New Rhine Newspaper (Neue Rheinische Zeitung)*. He was in Cologne when the workers rose up in Paris. Marx supported them enthusiastically in his newspaper, but after three days of fighting the workers were defeated. Marx was arrested in Cologne. During his trial, he made a speech about the conditions in Europe and, to the surprise of many, he was acquitted. Unable to jail him, the Prussian government expelled him again. The Marxes moved to London where they spent the remainder of their years.

Marx continued to write and was supported by Engels, who went to take over the management of his father's Manchester cotton firm factory. Engels also contributed to Marx's writing of *Das Kapital*, his critique of capitalism—the economic data and technical information comes from Engels. Engels also completed the second and third editions of *Das Kapital* after Marx's death in 1883.

Marxist Decline and Revival

At that time, the industrial nations of Western Europe were in the middle of enormous social, economic,

MAJOR WRITINGS:

Das Kapital

Marx's *Das Kapital*, first published in 1867, took him more than a quarter of a century to complete. It is an analysis of the free market economic system—the text is filled with comprehensive economic equations and hypothetical situations of workers in factories or on plantations. Marx felt that the capitalistic system created more and more wealth but was unable to use it wisely or spread it out equally. The flaws in the system exploited the masses, he said, and would continue to do so until the workers' frustrations reached the breaking point. Marx frequently breaks out of the technical prose to lash out at what he sees as inequities in the capitalistic system or his theories on economic history:

> One thing, however, is clear—nature does not produce on the one side owners of money or commodities, and on the other men possessing nothing but their own labour–power. This relation has no natural basis, neither is its social basis one that is common to all historical periods. It is clearly the result of a past historical development, the product of many economical revolutions, of the extinction of a whole series of older forms of social production. (Chapter VI).

> Capital is dead labour, that vampire–like, only lives by sucking living labour, and lives the more, the more labour it sucks. The time during which the labourer works is the time during which the capitalist consumes the labour–power he has purchased of him.

> If the labourer consumes his disposable time for himself, he robs the capitalist.

> The capitalist then takes his stand on the law of the exchange of commodities. He, like all other buyers, seeks to get the greatest possible benefit out of the use–value of his commodity. Suddenly the voice of the labourer, which had been stifled in the storm and stress of the process of production, rises. (Chapter X, Section 1).

> In modern agriculture, as in the urban industries, the increased productiveness and quantity of labour set in motion are bought at the cost of laying waste and consuming by disease labour–power itself. Moreover, all progress in capitalistic agriculture is a progress in the art, not only of robbing the labourer, but of robbing the soil; all progress in increasing the fertility of the soil for a given time, is a progress towards ruining the lasting sources of that fertility. The more a country starts its development on the foundation of modern industry, like the United States, for example, the more rapid is this process of destruction. Capitalist production, therefore, develops technology, and the combining together of various processes into a social whole, only by sapping the original sources of all wealth—the soil and the labourer. (Chapter XV, Section 10).

---

and political change. The quality of education rose and population stabilized. Child labor began was discouraged, and the Western European countries began to look for colonies to further bolster their prosperity. This "imperialism" was in the name of trade and resources. Britain, France, and Germany claimed colonies in Africa, the Near East, and Asia.

This colonialization raised worker dissatisfaction. Not only did citizens have to fight in the colonial wars, but foreign investment meant that factories would be built abroad and that there would be no new jobs at home. At the same time, conditions had improved because of the capitalist systems. France, Germany, and England were becoming increasingly democratic, and labor unions formed in France by 1884. By 1900, there were 2 million union members in England, 850,000 in Germany, and 250,000 in France. Political parties represented the working class in all three countries.

Socialism wasn't dead, however. The German Social Democratic Party, a Marxist party, was formed in 1875. Marx hadn't supported its ideology, which included state–controlled education. Marx had complained that the party's platform didn't look at the future. Socialist legislators were elected in Germany, however, despite the problems with the party.

Meanwhile, in England, the Labor Party had formed and had elected members to parliament. In Germany chancellor Otto von Bismarck (1815–1898) was trying to quiet the socialists by giving in to some of their demands. Social legislation was also passed in France and England and conditions in the factories improved.

Vladimir Lenin, addressing a crowd of supporters in 1917. (Archive Photos, Inc.)

In the beginning of the twentieth century, England passed social insurance policies providing old age, sickness, and accident insurance. There was also a minimum wage law and unemployment insurance. If Marx had still been alive, he might have seen these successes as cause to alter his ideology. As things stood, Western Europe was moving away from revolutionary Marxism and concentrating on long–term reform. English Fabian Socialism (socialism based on slow change rather than revolution) overtook Marxism in its popularity because of its adherence to gradual social reform. There was skepticism surrounding Marxism, and after Engels' death in 1895 there was no one left to defend its creation with equal authority.

The German Experience

In Germany, the Marxist Social Democratic party kept growing. The socialists there were dedicated to Marxism but they had trouble relating Marxist ideas to the already improving conditions under capitalism. Marxists split into two groups, the Orthodox Marxists and the Revisionists.

Karl Kautsky (1854–1938) was a leader of the Orthodox Marxists. He edited the *New Times (Neue Zeit)*, a publication of the German Social Democratic party. He agreed with Marx's economic arguments and centered on the problems with the lives of the working class. He felt that class struggle was evident because

of the impossibility of an agreement between the proletariat and the bourgeoisie. He ignored the idea of revolution, however, and argued that the working class could gain control peacefully.

Eduard Bernstein (1850–1932) wanted to update Marxism to address the improved conditions of the working class. He was a founder of Revisionism and he led the party in its abolition of the call for revolution. Bernstein claimed that the crisis inherent in capitalistic systems would become less frequent as capitalism developed and industry consolidated.

The Orthodox Marxists argued that the proletariat would revolt. They thought the workers would take control of the government, rather than overthrow it as Marx had dictated. They used peaceful methods to explain Marxism to the bourgeoisie to meet some of their goals. The Revisionists argued that Marxism was outdated. Both parties condemned violence and even the Orthodox Marxists were a muted version of what was envisioned by Karl Marx.

World War I brought more challenges to Marxism. A radical wing of the German Social Democratic party criticized the democracy used by the Orthodox and the Revisionist parties. Rosa Luxemburg (1870–1919) was unhappy with what the parties had done to Marxism. Luxemburg changed Marx's ideas, stretching them to include a theory of imperialism. She looked at the European colonialization from an economic standpoint and argued that colonialization was necessary for capitalistic countries to increase their markets. Without new markets they could not progress and if they could not progress, they would not reach socialism. She felt that when the available markets had been saturated, capitalism would collapse and socialism would sweep up the debris.

Luxemburg believed in Marxism's class struggle theory. She fought for revolution and encouraged workers to strike and stifle whatever they could as practice for the final revolution that would overturn capitalism forever.

The defenders of Marxism were a loose selection of socialist groups that convened in congresses every three years. Marxism had been one of the competing socialist doctrines of the First International and the most respected during the Second International in 1889. The International reaffirmed the Marxist's doctrines of class struggle and revolution. When World War I broke out in 1914, the socialist sector splintered and Marxism's influence declined in Western Europe. At the same time, however, the Marxist Vladimir Lenin (1870–1924) was leading a revolt in Russia.

Marxism in Russia

Marx had dismissed Russia as being too backward to deal with, much as he had dismissed the peasants as being too backward to take control. In 1917 Tsar Nicholas II was ousted and a Provisional Government was put in his place. Soon after that, the Bolsheviks and Marxist-Leninists took over the government. Lenin began to mold Marxism to his methods. He kept Marx's ideas of revolution and, for the first time, began to implement Marxist ideology.

Lenin had to bend Marxism quite a bit to fit it into Russia. Lenin understood that in Russia the working class was too small to revolt on its own. He gathered the support of the peasantry by turning the land over to the peasants and was rewarded with their support. He talked about common interests and he altered the nature of Marxist revolution. While Marx had felt that revolution would be spontaneous, Lenin felt that the workers only wanted to improve their working conditions and their wages and that this was not enough to create a revolution. He felt that they needed to be led by revolutionaries who would take control, and he felt that the proletariat would not be equipped to handle the power if they got it on their own through revolution.

Marx had described a proletariat dictatorship as a government directly created after revolution with the purpose of bringing in a communist society. Lenin called his beliefs Marxism and considered himself a Marxist despite his alterations. Lenin felt that a party–controlled government was essential to success and, once in power, he suppressed opposition and silenced objectors in the name of achieving socialism. Instead of the freedom and creativity that Marxism predicted, Lenin's reality was a repression and lack of equality that was only exaggerated by his successor, Joseph Stalin (1879–1953). Russia under Stalin could no longer be referred to as Marxist; communism, or more specifically, a harsh form later named Stalinism, took its place.

THEORY IN DEPTH

Marxism is a political theory and a means of achieving that theory. Karl Marx developed Marxism in the nineteenth century. He was unhappy with capitalism and felt a need for a new order. He drew his ideas from studies of industrial revolutions, from the ideas of the German philosopher George Hegel, from the European Enlightenment, and from a commitment to social equality and justice. Marxism is centered around the idea of social change and revolution to overthrow the capitalistic injustices heaped upon the common man. It covers three areas: philosophy, history, and economics.

Philosophy

Philosophically, Marxism studies the human mind. It examines the method by which man defines himself and how he decides what is real and what is not. Marx felt that ideas and practices were never fixed but were rather in a state of constant evolution based upon the surroundings at the time. He agreed with his early mentor, Hegel, who felt that change came through two opposing forces which struck each other and through their contact created a third entity. Hegel called this the "synthesis." The two opposing forces which created the synthesis were the "thesis" and the "antithesis." In time, the synthesis becomes a thesis with its own antithesis and, through a collision, creates another synthesis.

Though Hegel's notion of continual change gave Marx a framework, Marx wasn't fully satisfied with it. Hegel felt that change resulted from "world spirit," and that this spirit developed freedom. Marx felt that such vague notions made no sense. He believed that people controlled their own future. He rejected the idea that the spiritual world held importance and wanted to bring things back to earth. He applied Hegel's spiritual metaphors to the physical world, which he found much more practical, viable, and believable.

Marx also declared that philosophy had to become real. It was not enough to observe and comment on the world—one must try to change it and to make it better. Marx thought that knowledge centered around an analysis of ideas and that, without taking the next step to action, things became stymied. He looked at each problem in relation to others and then related them in turn to economic and political realities.

Marx's philosophy on the causes of revolution was unlike most prominent thinkers of his time. In the nineteenth century, major historical events such as revolution were usually explained in terms of great and dynamic leaders or religious figures. Marx sought to explain revolution in economic terms. He stated that when technological improvements are made in society, the power structure impedes that technology from being used in the best way. In the case of capitalism, Marx thought that its rules of private property ownership would stand in the way of the developing technology that was greatly increasing the production of goods and services.

This theory did have a historical precedent—during the Middle Ages, when technological progress in society was a leading factor in the demise of feudalism and the birth of capitalism. Centuries later, the advancements of the Industrial Revolution would lead, according to Marx, to the only possible outcome: the destruction of capitalism by violent revolution. As *Today's Isms* states: "Marx could find no instance in history in which a major social and economic system freely abdicated to its successor. On the assumption that the future will resemble the past, the communists, as the *Communist Manifesto* says, 'openly declare that their ends can be attained only by the forcible overthrow of all existing social conditions.' This is a crucial tenet of Marxism–Leninism, and one that clearly distinguishes it from democracy."

History

Marxism also examines history. It explains that history is a series of conflicts and arrangements of social arenas. Labor helps to define the social groups. The way in which people labor with the tools available and the groups in which they operate are what defines the different sections of history. Marx labels five historical chapters in the way labor is conducted: the slave state, feudalism, capitalism, socialism, and finally, Marxism. He argues that capitalism exploits the workers in the same way that the slave state does and, for this reason, cannot last. The inequalities of capitalism will lead to revolution to equalize resources. Socialism will ensue, and after the wrinkles are ironed out of socialism, Marxism will replace it.

Marx felt that history could only be explained in terms of what people had done in, and to, the material world. The pattern was the same as Hegel's thesis, antithesis, and synthesis. Continual conflict created new items to create new conflict, and so on.

Marx also said that every society had a "superstructure." This structure was comprised of the religious beliefs, laws and customs, and the political institutions and ideas. The superstructure protected the upper classes more than the lower. Religion, for example, would teach the poor that it was a virtue to live in poverty and to concentrate on the afterlife rather than on the life being lived at the moment. The poor would therefore not have a good reason to object to their condition, given the explanation of its worth.

Marx talked at length about this class struggle and the barriers it created. He felt that change was inevitable, and that the lower class would eventually reach a breaking point at which they would revolt to improve their condition.

It was this sort of class struggle, according to Marx, that would bring societal change. Mankind has traveled through history this way, from the phases of slavery to feudalism to capitalism. When farming took over hunting and gathering, a more distinct superstructure was necessary. When feudalism followed slavery, serfs with their increased freedom created a new class, the bourgeoisie. Eventually, this group overthrew the feudal lords and capitalism swept in.

Economics

Marxism's main focus is economics. Marx's program for man begins with satisfying one's needs. Men need to satisfy certain needs such as food and shelter. Their means of achieving this are a struggle with nature. Hunting and building disturb nature. Through this disruption, man finds himself human because of his own labor. At the same time, he appreciates his mastery of nature. Born in nature, man becomes human, ironically, by fighting nature. Marx contends that all of history is the struggle between man and nature through his labor. Man is self–sufficient and free only when he manipulates the nature that created him.

Capitalism, Marx believed, stole freedom. Marx dissects capitalism to explain its inadequacies. A laborer is paid for the work he does, for example, but is paid an amount to allow him to support his family rather than an amount based on the profit he has given his employer. The laborer is separated, alienated, from his product. This destroys his freedom. The capitalists profit enormously, according to Marx, while the workers make a subsistence living regardless of the worth of their creations. Workers are not paid according to their value, and this injustice will lead to dissatisfaction and the collapse of capitalism. Since there is a lack of freedom, capitalism is not a viable long–term option.

The workers are a class of their own, the proletariat, while the owners of production are a higher class, the capitalists. There is middle class, the bourgeoisie, who don't labor in the same way as the proletariat but rather organize the labor and work from offices to direct and manage the factories. Marxism dictates that the struggle between the capitalists and the proletariat will end in socialism. Socialism will be the synthesis of the thesis and antithesis of the proletariat and the capitalist.

The most important thing about any society, Marx said, is the way in which it provides for itself. Its economic means, for example, could include hunting and gathering or factories and grocery stores. Marx called these methods a society's *modes of production*. The modes of production could be very simple or infinitely complicated, depending on the society. The *means of production* were the tools the society used to satisfy its needs, such as knives and spears or machinery and computers.

The *relations of production* were the owners of the means of production. The capitalists, the village chiefs, the monarchs, or the elders could be the relations of production. The relations of production were either owned by society as a whole or were privately owned by individuals. Marx felt that private property allowed inequality and provided a way to create different classes—a small upper–class that had almost everything and a large lower class with virtually nothing to sustain itself.

Marxism identifies "alienation" as a central problem with capitalism. Since labor isn't directly related to its value, it is alienated labor. The worker is also alienated from himself because he is selling his labor and has become a commodity. He is further alienated by specialization. His task becomes so minute that he can perform it very quickly which speeds up production, but his expertise is so limited that he is virtually useless. Adam Smith (1723–1790), the "father of capitalism," argued that such specialization, though marvelous for capitalists, rendered the worker worthless in any real measure. The worker is then alienated from his humanness. It is this alienation, in addition to exploitation of the workers by the capitalists, which form the contradictions that will disband capitalism.

Marx goes on to say that private property becomes a principal means of alienating oneself. It is this private ownership that separates one from the collective and creates individual existences separate from the whole.

The economic alienation is coupled with a political alienation. The capitalistic society of the bourgeoisie is separated into economics and politics. Marx viewed the political arena as the vessel for separating the classes and for allowing one class to dominate the next.

The market Marx analyzed the market system in depth in his *Das Kapital*. He studied the economy wholly rather than in parts. His ideas center on the belief that economic value comes directly from human labor. Marx felt that capitalism would develop to include more and more contradictions. The inequality of the laborer's pay versus the capitalist's profit was the first contradiction. In addition, technology invites trouble. A machine will allow a capitalist to produce more at a lower cost, but competition keeps him from realizing more gain. He must keep up with the latest machinery to remain competitive, which means transferring money once designated for workers and applying them to technology instead. As a result, his rate of profit declines.

The market will also be shaken by crisis periodically. This instability creates increasing poverty, as people are not able to keep up with the fluctuating market. The separation of the proletariat and the capitalists increases and the classes are even more distinct. The monetary assets are controlled by fewer and fewer people and what remains is shared by more and more.

Class struggle Marx also explains how the worker's position will lead to revolution. One thing the working class will gain is knowledge about group activity. The factory workers learn to work cooperatively and will eventually see that they can channel this cooperative effort into a movement to better their condition. This is what Marx calls *class consciousness*. The realization of one's condition will lead to a greater understanding and, in turn, to conflict between the classes. Pressures build and the workers begin to demand change.

Marx spoke at great length about this class struggle, which is the focal point of his social evolution. When man is conscious of his alienation, he will move toward revolution. This will be the beginning of communism. There are two forms of revolution for Marx. The first is a standard uprising of the proletariat after having been exploited past their breaking point. The second type of revolution is more permanent—a provisional merger between proletariat and bourgeoisie rebelling, together, against capitalism. Later on, when there is a proletariat majority to the coalition, power

BIOGRAPHY:

Friedrich Engels

Friedrich Engels was born on November 28, 1820, in the Rhine province of Prussia (Germany). He was a friend and colleague of Karl Marx and the co–author of the *Communist Manifesto*, which became the bible of the Communist Party.

Engels grew up in a liberal family of Protestants loyal to Prussia. His father owned a textile factory in Bremen and expected Engels to be a part of the family business. Because of this, Engels led a double life.

When Engels was 18 he began work with his father. During working hours, Engels was an apprentice and an athlete. He also studied language. After hours, however, he read revolutionary works and became interested in the Young Hegelians, leftists following the ideas of the philosopher George Hegel, who asserted that progress and change come from opposing views that, when they clash, form a new ideology. The Young Hegelians were trying to accelerate the process by denouncing all things they found oppressive.

In 1841, Engels returned to Bremen and enlisted in an artillery regiment in Berlin. He frequented university lectures, though he wasn't enrolled, and the articles he'd written got him accepted into the Young Hegelian group of "The Free." After he finished his service a year later, Engels met Moses Hess. It was Hess who sparked his interest in communism, explaining that the consequence of the Hegelian idea was communism.

In 1842 Engels went to Manchester, England, to help with his father's partnership in a cotton plant. He continued to live his double life, writing communist articles after hours and meeting radical personalities.

Engels laid out an early form of scientific socialism in two articles he wrote for the "German–French Yearbooks." He found contradictions in liberal economics and felt that private property ownership created a chasm between the rich and the poor. By then Engels had begun to collaborate with Karl Marx, whom he'd met in France. Their first joint work was *The German Ideology*, which denounced those who didn't support revolution. Marx had formed a notion, which Engels endorsed, of history which ended, necessarily, in communism.

The Communist League held its first congress in 1847. At the second congress, Marx and Engels drafted the communist principles to which the League would subscribe. This *Communist Manifesto* became the bible to the Communist League.

Though Marx was the central creator of Marxism, Engels was his specialist on questions of the military, international affairs, science, nationality, and economics. It was Engels who sold *Das Kapital* with his review of the book. When Marx died in 1883, Engels became the central Marxist figure. He finished volumes two and three of *Das Kapital* from Marx's notes and manuscripts.

Engels developed cancer and died at the age of 75 in 1895 in London, England. With Marx, he helped to create Marxism and to shape the communist views that would later be used (and abused) by Vladimir Lenin and Joseph Stalin in Soviet Russia.

---

is transferred completely to the proletariat. It was this revolution that would bring capitalism to an end and allow socialism and, finally, Marxism, to take its place. After the establishment of a Marxist economy, class structure would disappear from society.

Engels' View

Friedrich Engels, Marx's friend and the co–author of *The Communist Manifesto*, added his comments to Marx's capitalism critique. Engels felt that man's mentality could be its own prison. Ideologies allowed people to understand themselves and where they fit into the puzzle. These ideas masked the true picture, their exploitation. Ideologically, for example, the capitalist will give the workers the impression that he is working in their best interest. The workers will feel that, though they are paid small sums, they are appreciated and cared for. But in reality, the capitalist will simply be spouting words to boost morale and encourage loyalty, so that he can continue to get as much labor from his workers as possible, and for the lowest price. According to Engels, workers focus on the ways in which they are *not* exploited rather than on all the ways in which they are.

In addition to the Marxism drawn out by Mark and Engels, there is Soviet Marxism. It is debatable as to whether or not the version of Marxism practiced by Vladimir Lenin in Russia was still true Marxism or whether it was so distorted that it became something else entirely.

THEORY IN ACTION

When Marx and Engels died at the end of the nineteenth century, Marxism's evolution was inherited by the revolutionaries of the next generation. In Western Europe at that time, conditions improved for factory workers. Economic prosperity meant improved living standards across the board. Workers formed unions and were able to negotiate better working conditions and earnings. Many European countries were becoming more democratic, moving away from Marxism, and were prospering.

In Western Europe the people felt satisfied and, rather than jeopardizing what they'd gained by having a revolution, they worked to gradually improve their conditions. Marxism fizzled into smaller groups of intellectuals who, in order to gain any support at all, stressed reform in place of revolution.

When the Second International was formed as the latest communist entity, it was an international organization of socialist parties. Its members slowly lost their revolutionary spirit in favor of long–term reform. Democratic socialist writer Eduard Bernstein said that capitalism was making life better, not worse. He pointed out that violent struggles between the classes was not the best way to create change. Capitalism would gradually evolve into socialism, he said. His ideas were called *revisionism* and were considered an updated version of Marxism. The Second International went along with his ideas.

While Marxism was shrinking away in Western Europe, it was spreading into Russia and gaining momentum. Much of Russia's population was poor. The majority were peasants who had been liberated from serfdom and slavery by Tsar Alexander II (1818–1881) in 1861 but who lived in the same conditions they had before their freedom. Though Russia was also going through an industrial revolution, it was far behind Europe. To make matters worse, the tsar had almost complete power over his people. There was a huge class difference between the minute elite and the uneducated mass peasant population. The groups didn't interact at all. Ironically, most of the revolutionaries were from the elite class and knew little of the life of the people for whom they were concerned.

Das Kapital was translated into Russian in the 1870s (ironically, the tsarist censors didn't think it would be read because of its difficult style). The first Russian Marxist group, The Liberation of Labor, was formed in 1883. The Russian Marxists were a small minority and the majority of the socialists didn't subscribe to Marx's call for world revolution.

Marxism Under Lenin

Vladimir Lenin was born in 1870. He grew up in a middle class family and had a happy childhood. During his adolescence, however, two significant things happened that helped lead him down the road to professional revolutionary. When Lenin was 16 his father, a schoolteacher, died of a stroke; the following year his brother was hanged for being involved in a revolutionary plot to kill the tsar.

Lenin was expelled from the university he was attending for participated in a student protest. Studying from home he learned about revolutionary leaders and read *Das Kapital*. Lenin became one of the most important leaders of Russian Marxism and spent the next 17 years helping the communists gather momentum. He became a Marxist in the 1890s, taking some of his ideas from Marxism and combining them with Russian revolutionary tradition. His version of Marxism is commonly known as Leninism or Marxism–Leninism.

Lenin's ideas Lenin did not agree with Marx's assumption that a society must pass through capitalism before it reaches socialism. Lenin desperately wanted socialism. He did not want to wait for Russia to go through capitalism—he wanted change to happen quickly, so he organized a political party. In keeping with Russian socialist tradition, Lenin distrusted the masses. The masses, at the time, wanted the Marxist party to be modeled after the German Social Democratic Party. Lenin, however, felt that the party workers would be happy with minor changes and would ignore the need for revolution. They would not reach "revolutionary consciousness," Lenin said. He organized his ideas in a pamphlet published in 1902 called *What Is to Be Done?* named in honor of a book written by Nicholas Chernyshevsky (1828–1889), a Russian revolutionary.

Lenin felt that a group of professional revolutionaries should be in control of the revolution. This group would make the decisions instead of the proletariat. Decisions would be made by the leaders, the central committee. Policy could be debated but when a decision was reached, it was to be followed. In addition, Lenin's party was to be kept secret to avoid censorship by the government.

This party model was also taken from Chernyshevsky's book. Many of the Marxists in Russia did not agree with Lenin's party ideas and thought that the central committee would become a dictatorship. This argument led to a split in the Russian Social Democratic Party the next year. The two sections were called the Bolsheviks (the majority) led by Lenin, and the Mensheviks (the minority). Leon Trotsky (1879–1940), a young revolutionary who grew to enormous power in the party, criticized Lenin's ideas. He said that Lenin's party would substitute itself for the proletariat, the central committee would substitute itself for the party, and the dictator who took control would substitute himself for the central committee. Many years later, Trotsky ignored his own words and became a Bolshevik, helping to bring them to power.

Lenin also changed another aspect of Marxism. Marxist analysis predicted that the first countries to overthrow their governments and their capitalistic economies would be the most economically advanced, by definition of having to first evolve through capitalism. That meant that Western Europe would have to do it first, given its relative economic success. Lenin didn't see any evidence of revolutionary ideology in the West and therefore couldn't accept Marx's prediction. Lenin argued that when Marx wrote *Das Kapital*, capitalism had not yet become worldwide. Since Marx's death, capitalism had swept the planet and had led to exploitation of Asia and Africa. Lenin called this exploitation "imperialism." He said that imperialism had good points and bad points. One bad point was that the socialist revolution would be put off in the capitalist countries because they were able to boost the living conditions of their proletariat from the goods they'd exploited from Africa and Asia. One good point was that the capitalist–imperialist system had an Achilles' heel. Russia's capitalism was much less steady and could, therefore, be the first to collapse— a direct reversal of Marxist theory. This revolution would then spread in reverse order from Marx's theory, going from the lesser advanced countries to the more advanced.

Lenin felt that his revolutionaries should use any means necessary to overthrow capitalist Russia. Before the Bolsheviks seized control in 1917, Lenin endorsed extortion, fraud, robbery, and other crimes. After he came to power he seemed willing to do anything to keep it. This belief allowed him to commit heinous acts of cruelty to try to create a society that would put an end to such cruelty forever.

Revolution in 1905 Until 1904, the Marxist leaders and Russian revolutionaries remained in exile and were unable to unseat the tsar. In 1904, Russia went to war with Japan. The tsar, Nicholas II, thought it would be easy to defeat the Japanese, but the war proved to be disastrous. Conditions worsened in Russia. There was a revolution in 1905, which began with peaceful demonstrations but ended in massacre by the tsar's troops. As the revolution spread to the Russian capital of Moscow, Lenin returned to Russia from Europe to lead the Bolsheviks, and Leon Trotsky led a strike against the government.

After the failed revolt, Lenin was forced into exile from 1907 until 1917 and, from a distance, struggled to keep the Bolsheviks united. To this end he organized the Bolshevik Party Conference in Prague in 1912, which officially separated the Mensheviks from the Bolsheviks.

Through their experiences, the Bolsheviks and the Mensheviks learned separate lessons. The Mensheviks decided that the proletariat was too small for a revolution and that capitalism had to mature before the proletariat would be in the majority. The Bolsheviks felt that waiting for capitalism to mature was a waste of time. Lenin looked for ways to increase the proletariat's numbers. He decided to try to ally the peasantry with the proletariat. The peasantry wouldn't hold any decision–making power, but their numbers alone would be useful. Lenin decided that he could win the peasants by giving them a few of their demands. Karl Marx had argued that the peasants were a warped class, but Lenin needed them for his program to have enough support for an uprising to succeed.

Although the 1905 revolution failed, Nicholas II was pressured to make changes. He created a constitution and made some steps toward ensuring the people had civil rights, at least on paper. Russia had its first parliament, the *Duma*. The Duma had limited power that catered to the upper class but was a step toward democracy. The government also tried to raise the peasantry's standard of living, improve the army, create opportunities for education, and bolster the industrial revolution. However, despite the changes, the majority of the population remained very poor and the upper classes were displeased with the weak nature of the reforms.

Changes in Russia World War I began in 1914. Russia, France, and England fought against Austria–Hungary and Germany. From the onset of the fighting, Russia suffered crippling defeats. The national pride the country felt when the troops first marched off to war quickly faded. Marches and riots swept the country. Workers and soldiers turned against the tsar, and Nicholas II was forced out in March 1917. The 300–year–old Romanov Dynasty was thrown away, and a Provisional Government composed of leaders of the Duma and noblemen was swept into place.

BIOGRAPHY:

Vladimir Lenin

Vladimir Lenin was born April 10, 1870, in Simbirsk, Russia. The founder of the Russian Communist Party, also known as the Bolsheviks, he altered Marxism and formed his own brand of political theory which is commonly called Marxism–Leninism or Leninism.

Lenin was the third of six well–educated children. He was academically successful at a young age and graduated first in his class in high school. Very adept in Greek and Latin, he seemed to be on the road to becoming a professional academic. When he was 16, however, he began to rebel. Along with his siblings, he joined the revolutionary movement to improve the political and civil rights of Russia's citizens.

Lenin's father died after having been threatened by the government while Lenin was still an adolescent. Soon after his father's death, his older brother was hanged for associating with a terrorist group. These two events may have cemented Lenin's feelings against the government and paved the way for his future success as a revolutionary.

In 1887 Lenin enrolled in Kazan University to study law and Marxism. He became a Marxist in 1889 and passed his law examinations in 1891. He was a practicing lawyer from 1892 to 1893 who served peasants and artisans, helping the poor rather than the rich. He developed a hatred for the legal system's tendency to favor the wealthy and, in turn, he began to hate lawyers.

Lenin moved to St. Petersburg in 1893 and began to broaden his Marxist associations while working as a public defender. He was sent to meet Russian exiles in 1895. When he returned, he and his Marxist comrades created the Union for the Struggle for the Liberation of the Working Class to unify the Marxist factions. The Union supported the working class, strikes, helped with their education and published information on Marxism. Lenin was thrown in jail for 15 months and afterward was sent to Siberia in exile.

Upon his return to Russia in 1900, Lenin began to build support for his ideas. Marxists were a small minority and to create a revolution that would overthrow the government, Lenin needed to have a majority. Many Russians supported the Populists, who believed that Russia was in the midst of capitalism and that it needed to remain capitalistic to reach its perfection until everyone had reached a high economic level at which point socialism would naturally ensue.

Lenin disagreed, arguing that even if land was divided and properties shared it would not be socialism but rather would be a different type of capitalism. Lenin felt that Marxism was the only way to socialism. He wrote *What is to be Done?* in 1902, outlining the problems with capitalism and the virtues of socialism.

By 1921 Lenin had crushed all opposition parties arguing that they did not support the Soviet cause. Many of the peasants and members of the working class had become disenchanted with Lenin's government. The party became overrun with incompetence and even the agency responsible for promoting organization, run by Joseph Stalin, was very inefficient. In 1922, Stalin became the general secretary of the party and consolidated his power. Lenin was frustrated that Russia was so far from his portrait of Socialism in his *State and Revolution*. He fell ill that spring and never fully recovered. Lenin continued to have episodes of sickness and, though he still wrote socialist propaganda, he never returned to the leadership position. He dictated a series of articles called the "Testament" centering on his fears of instability of the government with dominating people such as Trotsky and Stalin. He died of his third stroke on January 21, 1924. British Prime Minister Winston Churchill later wrote that the Russian people's worst misfortune was Lenin's birth; their next worst, Lenin's death.

The Provisional Government planned to create a democracy like those in the West. They wanted to promote capitalism and reform instead of revolution. The government enacted laws expanding civil rights and shortening the work day to eight hours. They freed political prisoners and planned for a national election. But it wasn't enough.

Russia was still in the war, and the Provisional Government's popularity cascaded downward. Lenin returned to Russia from exile in Europe the same year, arriving in Petrograd (formerly St. Petersburg) on April 16, 1917. Lenin was determined to overthrow the Provisional Government believing he was the only one who could lead Russia into socialism. He denounced this government as imperialistic despite its claims of democracy.

The Bolsheviks revolt By the autumn of 1917, the Bolsheviks were the majority party and Lenin decided to make his move. Though many of his supporters wanted the Provisional Government replaced by a coalition of the major parties, Lenin convinced them that a dictatorship of one party would be better. Trotsky helped Lenin to win support and, in October, Lenin's central committee voted to overthrow the government.

The Bolshevik militia, called the Red Guards, deposed the Provisional Government in the first week of November 1917, by seizing important areas in Petrograd and arresting the ministers of the Provisional Government. The takeover was easy and smooth, and much of Russia missed it entirely. In a day, with a relatively small death toll of several hundred, the Russian democratic experiment had ended. The world's first attempt at Marxism had begun, with Lenin at its helm.

The Bolsheviks initially controlled only Petrograd and the surrounding countryside, but Lenin wanted more. He did two things to increase his popularity and control. He gave Russia's farmland to the peasants to win their support, and he began negotiations to end the war. The Treaty of Brest–Litovsk, signed by Germany in 1918, gave Russia freedom from the war in exchange for territory—territory, Lenin knew, Russia would get back someday.

The next step for the Bolsheviks was to exterminate their rivals. Lenin met opposition when he fought to make Bolshevik control over the government absolute. He finally allowed a tiny minority party to have a small voice, but after a few months even that was quashed and control became entirely Bolshevik.

Newspapers that were not socialist were shut down and Lenin's secret police, the *Cheka*, infiltrated the population and eliminated opposition to their leadership. In 1918 the Bolsheviks got rid of the Constituent Assembly which had been elected the year before.

Lenin's repression of opposition led to civil war. The fighting lasted until 1920. Virtually everyone who was not Bolshevik, or The Reds, was fighting against them. The Whites, or anti–Bolsheviks, were supported by Britain, the United States, and France.

By using savage and bloody tactics, the Bolsheviks eventually won the civil war. They created the first concentration camps in history to house their political prisoners. The Cheka crushed worker strikes and stole food from anyone who had it, forcing peasants to give up their grain.

The Bolsheviks seized food, controlled the factories, forbid trade, forced labor, and crushed dissension. These policies killed the Russian economy but supplied the Red Army with food and supplies which was, in Lenin's view, crucial.

When the civil war ended, the Bolsheviks' power was shaky. The economy had been flattened, riots and strikes flooded the cities, and a massive famine killed 5 million people from 1921 to 1922. In response, the Bolsheviks met for their Tenth Party Congress to discuss how to bolster the economy and the Bolshevik's popularity. Lenin suggested an end to the *war communism* that had confiscated provisions from the peasants. He created the New Economic Policy, designed feed his starving country. It allowed farmers to sell their goods while paying the government a percentage of their profits in tax. Peasants who had lost their incentive to grow crops began to replant. After two years, the country began to feed itself again.

Trouble within the party Many of the Bolsheviks were frustrated by this provision, however, because it stank of capitalism. The *war communism*, which confiscated goods from the peasants and distributed them among the troops, had been a step toward socialism, and had already failed.

The New Economic Policy created another problem. According to Marxism, in order to achieve socialism the industrial revolution had to continue until it reached modernity. The economic policy didn't have the resources for this, however, and the industries controlled by the state were too inefficient to amass the profits needed to invest in technology, nor could the taxes be raised without killing the incentives for peasants to produce food. Moreover, Lenin believed the New Economic Policy would relieve the peasants' fears and ease the transition to communism.

The Bolsheviks were also in the midst of a political struggle. During the civil war the opposition to the Reds had been violently silenced leading to resentment and dissatisfaction with the Bolsheviks. At the Tenth Party Congress that accepted Lenin's New Economic Policy, the leaders of the Congress created the post of general secretary to organize the party's regime, giving the post to Joseph (Dzhugashvili) Stalin.

Lenin had not expected party corruption, as it was not in keeping with Marxism. However, the party was overrun with it during the 1920s and officials used their power to satisfy personal whims. Lenin was very worried that Stalin was involved in this corruption. Stalin used his title to acquire power and Lenin decided that Stalin should be replaced. Before he could advocate his position, however, Lenin suffered the first of his three strokes. He was confined to his bed for a year and died of his third stroke in 1924.

After Lenin died, his version of Marxism became called Leninism or Marxism–Leninism. Lenin had warped many of the ideas of Marxism to rationalize revolution in Russia and his dictatorship. His version was very different from that of Marx and Engels, and even more distant from the moderate reform sector of Marxism that had swept through Western Europe.

ANALYSIS AND CRITICAL RESPONSE

As with so many other political systems, Marxism in practice didn't work exactly as it did in theory. Marx and Engels assumed that corruption wouldn't be a problem under communism and that the negative vices and traits that caused such corruption were spawned from the inequality and dissatisfaction of capitalism. Since Marxism would provide for all, there would be no dissatisfaction and, therefore, no reason for criminal activity. Perhaps it is impossible to say if this would be the case, as a true Marxist state has never really been reached.

There has not been a Marxist success without simultaneous abuses by those in power. Marx's ideas have been called idealistic. It is utopian, to use Marx's own word, to believe that a society can exist without a class struggle of some kind. It was unrealistic to expect that work would be done voluntarily, crime would not exist, political and religious differences would be forgotten, and everyone would live happily. One of Marxism's major failings is placing so much emphasis on economic matters while downplaying—almost dismissing—factors such as religion and ethnic pride. For example, in today's Middle East, if all economic problems were suddenly solved, it's difficult to imagine that all other problems would go away, too

Many of the details of Marxism didn't blend with one another. Marx's moral disagreement with capitalism and particularly his studies which showed communism was unavoidable don't seem to hold up when measured against modern history—Japan, Germany, and the United States have had thriving capitalist economies for decades; and yet, at the dawn of the twenty–first century, a Marxist revolution in any of the three seems almost inconceivable. Marx's contention that capitalism had to first mature to its fullest state before the inevitable communist revolution was

also disproven in the reverse—Russia hardly had a thriving capitalist economy when the Bolsheviks took over in 1917.

Moreover, Marx's views on the causes of imperialism were also at odds with events that occurred long after his death. *Today's Isms* states: "Communist imperialism cannot be explained in Marxian economic terms, according to which imperialism is the last phase of an advanced capitalist economy with an abundance of capital that it seeks to invest in less developed areas." Indeed, modern–day Germany and Japan are two examples of capitalist governments that don't seem to have any imperical ambitions, while the cash–strapped Soviet Union of the mid–twentieth century aggressively set up communist satellite states all over Eastern Europe. Of course, by the mid–twentieth century Stalin had so twisted communist theory that Marx himself likely would've been disappointed if he had seen what the first country to base itself on his ideas had become. The truly ironic thing is if Marx had been around in the 1930s to express those disappointments in Stalin's Russia, he probably would've found himself exiled to Siberia—or worse.

Marx also believed that, after the communist revolution, the class structure of society would disappear. But that was not the case in Soviet Russia. Indeed, the proletariat fell even further behind the small class of quasi–intellectual government officials who—in the name of the state—controlled the means of production. In fact, it has been the advanced capitalist economies that showed a change for the better. Of the twentieth–century capitalist societies, Eugene O. Porter writes in *Fallacies of Karl Marx*: "The middle–class is not disappearing, but increasing, as a result of the greatly expanding educational system which produces professional men and women—doctors, lawyers, teachers, etc., most of whom are property owners and therefore of the petty bourgeoisie as defined by Marx."

Marx and Engels claimed that, scientifically, socialism was the only way history could end. They called this theory "scientific" socialism and considered it much more sound than the idealistic dreams of the utopians. Engels, after Marx's death, hinted that their theories may need modification, given that socialism had yet to ensue.

After Vladimir Lenin came to control Russia in 1917, his version of Marxism became known as Marxism–Leninism. He altered many of Marx's ideas to rationalize his seizure of power and the atrocities committed by his Bolshevik party. He justified the ends by the means and was willing to do anything to force socialism onto tsarist Russia.

Friedrich Engels.

Lenin added to Marxism the idea that a new party had to be created to control the working class. He also added the idea of Marxist revolution in one country instead of the worldwide revolution that Marx had predicted. Lenin sought control rather than leadership. His dictatorship became more severe when he encountered opposition that could force him from power. He felt compelled to silence it, and did.

The Bolsheviks changed their name to the Communist Party in 1918 to distinguish their revolutionary selves from the moderate Marxists in Western Europe. The Communist International, set up by the Bolsheviks in 1919, was separate from the Second International's organization of socialist parties. Lenin wanted only revolutionary socialism and so created the Communist International to allow for a split.

Marxism–Leninism, signified socialist ideology in tandem with mass murder. Lenin voiced some comments on Marxism that shed light on some of the causes of its struggle in Russia. In his 1923 speech, "Better Fewer, But Better," Lenin spoke about some of the areas in which his Marxism had strayed from the vision recorded by Karl Marx.

Lenin's speech, by title and content, included the idea that rule was better controlled by a small, competent minority than by the masses. This was a direct split from Marx's contention that the revolutionary

party would succeed because of its control by the masses, or the proletariat (the working class.) Lenin's statement, "We must follow the rule: Better fewer, but better," was a switch from the Marxist ideals he planned to follow.

Lenin also felt that it was important to progress slowly and that change that was forced quickly would eventually ring false. His simultaneous need to be able to defend his country from aggressors was an obstacle, however. The two desires could not find a way to coexist. Lenin stated: "We must show sound scepticism (sic) for too rapid progress . . . we must remember that we should not stint time on building it, and that it will take many many years." At the same time, Lenin felt: "What interests us is . . . the tactics which we, the Russian Communist Party . . . should pursue to prevent the West–European counter–revolutionary states from crushing us."

Lenin's own claims are that to reach a Marxist world, progress could not be rushed, yet at the same time it was imperative to have a powerful country to protect Marxist ideals. Though Lenin said that ". . . we shall be able to keep going not on the level of a small peasant country, not on the level of universal limitation, but on a level steadily advancing to large–scale machine industry," he wanted these conflicting goals to happen simultaneously. These plans could have led to their own failure.

Marxism was designed to be a road to equality and freedom. Society would be fair and repressive methods would be unnecessary. The Marxist reality in Russia was very different from the ideology it claimed to follow. The state did not whither into nothing but rather grew until it virtually destroyed everything else. The state controlled everything—industry, agriculture, education, art, and the media. Travel was only allowed with permission and the state spied on its citizens so that it could bury dissension.

There is some debate as to why the quest for Marxism created such blood bath in Russia. Marx believed that checks and balances, as found in the Constitution of the United States, were unnecessary. He felt that the evils of the world would disappear when equality took over because it was the poverty and need caused by capitalism that created the evils to begin with. The Russian experiment of Marxism was a failure. The freedom and equality that Marxism was created to promote were ignored. Crime flourished at the highest level: It did not melt away as Marx had predicted. Marxist theorist Rosa Luxemburg (1871–1919), commented on the problems of freedom when she said, "Freedom only for the supporters of the government, only for the members of one party—however numerous they may be—is no freedom at all. Freedom is always and exclusively freedom for the one who thinks differently." In Soviet Russia, the ones who thought differently were quite often killed, which may help to explain why freedom was so thoroughly lacking and why, despite good intentions at the onset, Soviet Russia endured such violence in the name of so–called equality.

TOPICS FOR FURTHER STUDY

- Does the evolution of Marxism end with Marx's death? With Engels' death? Can Marxists in the twentieth century alter the meaning of Marxism and still call it Marxism, or is Marxism necessarily the philosophy set down by Karl Marx?

- Is Marxism fatally flawed in its assumption that crime will not exist with equality, or is it simply that the world has never really seen equality and thus crime has never had a chance to snuff itself out?

- Although Marxism failed in Soviet Russia, could it succeed elsewhere?

BIBLIOGRAPHY

Sources

Ebenstein, Alan, William Ebenstein, and Edwin Fogelman. *Today's Isms,* Upper Saddle River, NJ: Prentice Hall.

Feinberg, Barbara Silberdick. *Marx and Marxism,* New York: Franklin Watts, 1985.

Klages, Mary. "Marxism and Ideology," University of Colorado, Boulder, 1997.

Kort, Michael G. *Marxism In Power—The Rise and Fall of a Doctrine,* Connecticut: The Millbrook Press, 1993.

Laidler, Harry W. *History of Socialism,* New York: Thomas Y. Crowell Company, 1968.

Martin, Joseph. *A Guide to Marxism,* New York: St. Martin's Press, 1980.

Marx, Karl and Engels, Friedrich. *The Communist Manifesto,* New York: Verso, 1998.

Porter, Eugene O. *Fallacies of Karl Marx,* Texas Western College at El Paso, 1962.

Service, Robert *A History of Twentieth–Century Russia,* Cambridge: Harvard University Press, 1998.

Volkov, G.N., ed. *The Basics of Marxist–Leninist Theory,* Moscow: Progress Publishers, 1982.

Further Readings

Dunayevskaya. *Marxism and Freedom: From 1776 Until Today,* Humanity Books, 2000. Traces the history of Marxist Socialism and explains why its opposition to freedom led to its demise.

Marx, Karl and Friedrich Engels. *The Manifesto of the Communist Party,* 1848. This call to arms to the workers was written by Marx and Engels in the middle of a revolutionary upheaval throughout Europe.

Pelinka, Anton. *Social Democratic Parties in Europe,* New York: Praeger Publishers, Inc., 1983. Provides more information on the political background which influenced Karl Marx.

Volkov, G.N., ed. *The Basics of Marxist–Leninist Theory,* Moscow: Progress Publishers, 1982. Describes Marxist-Leninist theory and its relationship to capitalism.

SEE ALSO

Capitalism, Communism, Socialism, Utopianism

Nationalism

OVERVIEW

Nationalism is sometimes labeled a political phenomenon or ideology that is not truly a theory. Some political activists and scholars see nationalism not as something to be theorized about but merely as a strong, sentimental feeling about one's own country, a patriotic fervor directed toward advancing the "national interest." Others view nationalism as the driving philosophy behind social movements that can both infect and inspire (depending on one's viewpoint) large numbers of people living in the same geographical region to attack other groups or countries for the anticipated benefit of one's interests. Still others see nationalism as a phenomenon that can be appropriately conceptualized and described, analyzed, and explained in theoretical terms. The variety of perspectives on nationalism—whether, for example, nationalism simply exemplifies overzealous feelings for one's country or is rightfully placed within the scope of political theories—has fluctuated over time. At certain periods in history, no one talked about "nationalism" *per se*, although the concept of "nations" appeared during European Middle Ages, if not earlier. Nationalist movements seem not to have occurred before the eighteenth or early nineteenth century. Beginning with the fall of the French Emperor Napoleon in the early 1800s and the expansion of European imperialism across Africa and Asia in the late nineteenth century, nationalism increasingly appeared as a phenomenon whereby those seeking independence from imperial powers claimed rights to self–determination and gathered support for their national liberation movements.

WHO CONTROLS GOVERNMENT? State officials

HOW IS GOVERNMENT PUT INTO POWER? Crisis situation

WHAT ROLES DO THE PEOPLE HAVE? Support the nation

WHO CONTROLS PRODUCTION OF GOODS? Owners of capital

WHO CONTROLS DISTRIBUTION OF GOODS? Owners of capital

MAJOR FIGURES Ernest Renan; Johann Gottfried Herder

HISTORICAL EXAMPLE Republic of Turkey, 1923–present

CHRONOLOGY

c. 1142: Dekanawidah establishes the *Haudenosaunee (Iroquois)* confederacy of five Native American nations.

1320: Growing nationalism among the Scots and warfare with England results in the Scots' Declaration of Arbroath.

1800: German theologian Johann Gottfried Herder publishes his *Outline of a Philosophy of a History of Man.*

1806–1807: German philosopher Johann Gottlieb Fichte delivers his lectures, "Addresses to the German Nation."

1882: Ernest Renan lectures on *"Qu'est-ce qu'une nation?"* ("What is a nation?").

1914–1918: World War I devastates Europe.

1939–1945: World War II ravages Europe, North Africa, East Asia, and Southeast Asia.

1944: Hans Kohn publishes *The Idea of Nationalism: A Study of Its Origins and Background.*

1950s—1960s: National liberation movements in many African colonies of European imperial powers produce a rapid succession of newly independent African states.

1981: Anthony D. Smith publishes *The Ethnic Revival in the Modern World.*

1983: Ernest Gellner publishes *Nations and Nationalism.*

In the late twentieth century, particularly after the demise of the Soviet Union in 1991, the study of nationalism became a well–developed field, crossing the disciplinary boundaries of political science, sociology, anthropology, international relations, and history. Theories of nationalism can be divided into roughly two major categories: *ethnic nationalism*, based on concepts of shared ethnic identity, and *civic nationalism*, based on shared appreciation and respect for key political values.

Other theorists, including scholars from the developing world, have viewed the theoretical construc-

tion of national identities and of nationalism as something far more complex than can be adequately summarized into two categories. Similarly, differences of opinion are to be found as to whether nationalism is a modern phenomenon, appearing only when societies shifted from feudalism to capitalism and began to form independent states, or whether nationalism has existed for centuries, if not millennia, as the natural expression of people's deepest sense of their cultural and ancestral roots. By the late twentieth century, many assumptions typical of the earlier theoretical approaches to nationalism were challenged by the rise of movements throughout the world advocating ethnic separatism and irredentism ("consolidationist" movements, in the words of Deborah Larson of the University of California at Los Angeles, as cited by Kristen Williams in *Despite Nationalist Conflicts*). The growing demands of indigenous peoples for political and cultural self–determination and the increasing heterogeneity of populations in multicultural societies in much of the developed world also are challenging traditional notions of nationalist theory at the start of the new millennium.

HISTORY

Nationalism, as a field of study, is fraught with controversial interpretations, including disagreement over when nationalist thinking and nationalist movements first appeared. The historical review presented here of the development of nationalism in theory and in practice thus should be read with an awareness of this lack of consensus among scholars as to the exact nature of nationalism, the causes for its arising in particular societies and periods of history, and the best way it should be theorized.

Beginnings

That said, it is worth noting that early examples of the concept of the nation can be found in both the European and the non–European world, together with rather precise political formulations of how nations should function and work together. For example, at some point between the eleventh century and the early sixteenth century (estimates of the exact date range from 1142 to 1450), *Dekanawidah*, known as The Peacemaker, emerged from the Native American nation of the Hurons in the Great Lakes region to establish the *Haudenosaunee* (pronounced "ho–dee-no–sho–nee," known by the French as the *Iroquois*), a political confederation of five (later, six) Native American nations living in the northeastern region of what would later be the United States of America.

Across the Atlantic, at about the same time, the system of feudal states and monarchical rule established during the European Middle Ages gradually was reshaped as commerce grew, urban areas developed, and the Renaissance introduced new concepts of the position of man (and woman) within European society. Among the earliest European groups to build a national identity were the Scots, who between 1296 and 1328 fought King Edward I (1239–1307) and the English in the Scottish Wars of Independence. Prepared on April 6, 1320, the Declaration of Arbroath, the Scottish nation's formal declaration of independence from England, was drawn up at the Monastery of Arbroath in Scotland and sealed by 38 Scottish lords. Addressed to the Pope, the Declaration spoke of the Scottish nation and urged the Pope to disregard the English claim on Scotland, which the Pope subsequently did.

On October 24, 1648, the Treaty of Westphalia was signed between the King of France, the Holy Roman Emperor, and their allies, ending the Thirty Years' War between Catholics and Protestants in Europe and marking new boundaries for European states. For the most part, however, a genuine sense of national identity had yet to develop among the peoples living in each of these European states. Although religious influence on political affairs would continue to shape history, governments would now be based more on a secular rather than religious rule. In 1690, a half–century after the Treaty of Westphalia, English physician John Locke (1632–1704) published his "Second Treatise on Government," further developing English philosopher Thomas Hobbes' (1588–1679) "social contract theory" to identify civil government as resting on the consent of the governed. Locke's writings are now seen by many as having sparked the "Age of Enlightenment" in Europe—a period in history when the rights of individuals were enumerated and exalted and the concept of government based on the will of the people took hold. Interest in democratic self–governance and political self–determination grew among European and American philosophers and ordinary citizens alike.

Transformations

France, one of the most powerful European countries at the time, underwent profound political changes in 1789. On July 14 an angry mob stormed the Bastille Prison in Paris, sparking the French Revolution with the goal of achieving "Liberty, Equality, and Fraternity" for all citizens living in France. The growth of a "bourgeois" middle class had led to demands by commoners for a greater say in their governance, which up to then had been controlled mainly by the

Johann Gottfried Herder.

clergy and the nobility. October 16, 1793 saw the execution by guillotine of Queen Marie Antoinette and King Louis XIV of France, ending royal rule in France and paving the way for an attempt at democratic rule. However, the repression and violence visited upon those unwilling to subscribe to the new method of government was so enormous that the country fell back into disarray under the "Reign of Terror" of the Jacobins, who wished to instill an excessive degree of control and order on French society and to eliminate all who they deemed enemies. A decade later, Napoleon Bonaparte, a general in the French army, led the French people on an expansive campaign to conquer Europe.

Witnessing the transformation of European states away from monarchical rule, German theologian Johann Gottfried Herder (1744–1803) published his *Outline of a Philosophy of a History of Man*, a set of theories developed by Herder between 1774 and 1781, which detailed his views on the proper identity of nations and on the growth of nationalism. In this document and others he wrote over the next two decades, Herder promoted the idea that true nations are comprised of persons who share a common ancestry and linguistic heritage, along with common cultural and religious traits. His idea of "romantic nationalism" was one of the earliest theoretical portraits of nationalism as stemming from the desires of language

BIOGRAPHY:

Johann Gottfried Herder

Johann Gottfried Herder was born on August 25, 1744, in Mohrungen, East Prussia, a Central European state with a population largely Germanic in ancestry. Herder began his formal academic studies in the field of medicine but later switched to theology. Listening to lectures of the famous philosopher Emanuel Kant during his studies from 1762–64, Herder became particularly interested in Kant's geography lectures on the relationships among "meteorological, physical, and human factors." Through his studies with Kant, Herder also came to know the writings of French philosopher Jean–Jacques Rousseau and the English empirical philosophers. In 1764 Herder moved to Riga in the Russian Empire, where he preached and taught for five years. In 1767 Herder was ordained a minister, served in two churches in Riga, and taught in the Cathedral School there. Increasingly well known and respected as a writer, Herder published his first book, *Uber die neuere deutsche Litteratur. Fragmente (Excerpts from Recent German Literature)* at age twenty–three.

In 1769 Herder moved to France, keeping a diary of his voyage by sea, which was published after his death and revealed his hopes of becoming a world–famous writer and a significant political actor. Herder apparently wished to reform the Russian education system and to devise a new constitution for Russia.

After arriving in France, Herder increasingly saw himself as German and felt depressed by the decay of French political and social life in the decades preceding the French Revolution. In 1770 Herder was invited to tutor the son of the Prince of Holstein back in Prussia and to travel with his young student to Italy.

Disenchanted by life in the French capital and attracted by this new offer, Herder quickly left Paris and moved to Eutin, Holstein's capital city, in March 1770 to begin tutoring. On the way to Italy with the prince's son, Herder stopped in Hamburg and Darmstadt, where he met the woman he later would marry, Caroline Flachsland. However, apparently feeling humiliated by how he was treated as a tutor, Herder quit his job after reaching Strasbourg with the prince's son in July 1770. There, Herder sought treatment at the Strasbourg Faculty of Medicine for an eye problem that had afflicted him since childhood. While in Strasbourg, Herder started up a lifelong friendship with the German poet Goethe, leading to his eventual move to Weimar, where Goethe was minister of the court of Duke Karl August. In 1776, Goethe convinced the Duke to make Herder Superintendent of Schools, Chief Pastor, and Court Preacher. Herder came to Weimar, where he spent a quarter of a century, dying there on December 18, 1803.

---

communities to shape their own destinies and to create their own territorial states.

Johann Gottfried Herder

Johann Gottfried Herder was one of the earliest of the European writers on nationalism. His principal works include *A Treatise upon the Origin of Language* (1772) and *Outline of a Philosophy of the History of Man* (1784–91). Herder's concept of nationalism focused on the cultural side of nation formation, with ethnicity figuring much more significantly in the development of nationhood than the more "civic" aspects featured by later theorists. In *Herder's Social and Political Thought: From Enlightenment to Nationalism*, F.M. Barnard described Herder's life and the development of his nationalist vision, noting that Herder's conception of nationalism emerged during the German Romantic period that began in the eighteenth century. At that time, the idea of a German national identity

grew in popularity across the feudal states that eventually would be united as the German Confederation of 1815 and later, in 1871, as the German Empire.

Despite his personal charisma and ability to attract others to take part in stimulating intellectual discussions and correspondence with him, Herder became increasingly isolated in his work and views and dissatisfied with life as he aged. Nonetheless, he reportedly was a keen observer of his surroundings and enjoyed being of service to others. Herder's discontent with the social and political life of his times had much to do with the lack of democratic practices in eighteenth century German society. Concerned with social justice, Herder objected to the exclusionary nature of German hereditary politics, nobility, and feudal structures, to the arbitrariness of political tyrants, and to the continual warfare of nations that sought to dominate each other. He was especially opposed to slavery and colonialism.

Religiously taught and inspired, Herder drew from the Bible, secular humanist principles, and the humanitarian writings and philosophy of the Renaissance and the European Enlightenment periods in developing his theory of nationalism. He found the Hebrew people particularly interesting, for he viewed them, according to Barnard, as the "oldest example of a *Volk* [people] with a developed national consciousness and of an 'organic' community in which socio–political organization grew naturally out of the socioeconomic functions of its members." This concept of "*Volk*" was key to Herder's understanding of nationalism. The character of a *Volk*, in Herder's mind, was shaped in particular by language, which brought people together into a community and allowed them to express their innermost spiritual qualities in a natural way. Herder saw language and ethnicity as needing to correspond to a political, territorial state. Consequently, mixtures of ethnic communities living in the same territorial region would not form as vital or cohesive a state as a single language community would.

In some ways, Herder's conception of nationalism overlaps with "civic nationalism." He believed that self–government and the choice of individuals to be governed by a state were essential. However, in his theory of "linguistic nationalism," Herder assumed that when a state coincided with an ethnic community, legislation would not need to be coercive, since laws would flow naturally from the social awareness of the *Volk*. While he valued the creation of individual states, each corresponding to a specific *Volk*, Herder also viewed the respect of different peoples for each other and for international cooperation as extremely important. Thus, the right of one particular ethnic community to self–determination could be exercised only if self–governance did not prevent another *Volk* from governing themselves. Rather than advocating a formal world government structure, however, Herder believed international cooperation could best be achieved through looser associations of nations where mutual interests would be advanced by peaceful cooperation.

Historical events in Europe just after Herder's death created new boundaries for major European states and inspired further thought among political philosophers on the nature of the nation and the phenomenon of nationalism. Between 1806 and 1807, the French army under the leadership of Napoleon defeated Prussia. During these same years German philosopher Johann Gottlieb Fichte (1762–1814) delivered a series of lectures, "Addresses to the German Nation," advancing the idea that common "civic" values are the basis for nations; that is, a liberal citizenry

is fundamentally based on shared respect for individual freedoms and liberties and that government is created of, by, and for those governed. Having grown ever more dictatorial and autocratic, Napoleon's rule eventually came to an end. Crowning himself Emperor of France, Napoleon eventually met his downfall at the Battle of Waterloo in Belgium in 1815, where the Prussian army halted Napoleon's murderous, self–annihilating campaign. In the same year, the German Confederation was formed, linking thirty–nine German feudal states (thirty–five monarchies and four free cities), a significant step toward the unification of Germany to take place in 1871 under King Wilhelm I (1797–1898).

Throughout the nineteenth century, dramatic political changes continued to occur in Europe, sparked by the growing number, size, and economic importance of capitalist industries and the appearance of a solid middle class. Political and economic discontent grew at mid–century, especially among the lower-level aristocrats and the *bourgeoisie*—the newly appearing middle class consisting largely of businessman and businesswomen—who saw their interests inadequately represented in the governing structures of Europe. In 1848 economic problems, discontent by the middle class over their lack of opportunity for political participation, and growing nationalist movements led to revolutionary attempts to establish a new political order. To a substantial measure, the growing influence of Karl Marx (1818–1883) and Friedrich Engels' (1820–1895) writings on socialism and communism as alternatives to capitalism inspired political insurgencies and economic riots in many European cities that year. Though the revolts failed to establish more liberal, socialist governments, nationalist movements gained momentum throughout Europe from the tumultuous events of that year.

Building Nations

Following the French expulsion of Austrians from power in Northern Italy by 1859 and the uniting of southern Italian city–states under the leadership of Giuseppe Garibaldi (1807–1882), Italy became a single kingdom in 1861 under Victor Emmanuel II (1820–1878), acclaimed by popular vote. Ten years after Italy was united, King Wilhelm I was crowned emperor of the new German Empire, at the conclusion of the Franco–Prussian War. The unification of Prussia and the thirty–nine German states and cities of the German Confederation culminated the campaign to unify Germany into a single state by the military conquests of Otto von Bismarck, chancellor of Prussia. Nation building in Europe was at a high point. A decade later, on March 11, 1882, French philosopher

Ernest Renan (1823–1892) lectured on *"Qu'est–ce qu'une nation?"* ("What is a nation?") at the Sorbonne, Paris' premier university. His lecture, published in Paris by Calmann–Levy later that year, explored questions of the essence of national identity and national unification movements and marked out new theoretical territory in developing a civic conception of nationalism.

Around this time, concepts of national identity became ever more exclusive, with the criteria for supposed membership in national groups growing increasingly specific and focused on culture and "race." The growth of anti–Semitism in France and Germany during the late 1870s reflected growing popular sentiment toward what it meant to be a member of a nation, this time in a cultural and racial sense. In terms of political party activity, nationalism was becoming an increasingly dangerous phenomenon by the 1890s, especially for those deemed unworthy of inclusion as members of the nation. The growth of anti–immigrant parties such as the "Know–Nothing Party" in the United States and the Dreyfus Affair of the 1890s in France—a case of anti–Semitic action directed against Captain Alfred Dreyfus (1859–1935), a French general staff officer who was convicted of treason despite insubstantial evidence—marked the dangerous turn nationalism was taking in both Europe and America.

For the African continent, the most significant event of the nineteenth century arguably was the 1884–85 Conference of Berlin, involving the heads of several European states, among them France, Germany, Belgium, Portugal, and Spain. At this series of meetings, the participating European countries established their "rights" to stake out colonial claims and extend their political and economic control in Africa. Only Liberia, colonized by freed American and Caribbean slaves beginning in 1822 and made independent in 1847, and Ethiopia, historically an independent kingdom (except under Mussolini's Italian occupation from 1936 to 1941), escaped the ravages of the European imperialists in the decades that followed the Berlin Conference. What came to be known as the "Scramble for Africa" had begun, with dire consequences for the indigenous nations across the African continent, from the Arab Maghreb in the north to the Cape of Good Hope in the south.

At the close of the nineteenth century, an international conference in Europe offered the promise of a future world where national sovereignty would be better respected and nations would cooperate in peace. In 1899 this First International Peace Conference was held in the Belgium city of The Hague to establish the fundamentals of multilateral diplomacy and light the way for a future world federation of nations working

collectively toward peace and security. Although the principal goals of the Hague Peace Conference of 1899 and the Hague Conference of 1907—including goals for disarmament—have not yet been realized a century later, the Hague Conference represented a new step forward in seeking the means to settle differences without violence, putting forth a greater respect for the rights of all.

World War

Unfortunately, the resolve to create a more peaceable means to settling disputes did not prevent the outbreak of a massive war in Europe a few years later. From 1914 to 1918 the First World War raged across Europe. Engendered by nationalistic claims to territory in the Balkan Mountains region of southeastern Europe, the war entangled Europe's major states in what came to be the bloodiest war in history. Toward the close of the war, President Woodrow Wilson of the United States gave his "Fourteen Points" speech before a Joint Session of the U.S. Congress on January 8, 1918, outlining his recommended program to resolve the problems associated with the First World War and to prevent future outbreaks of violence among nation–states. As his fourteenth point, Wilson recommended the following: "A general association of nations must be formed under specific covenants for the purpose of affording mutual guarantees of political independence and territorial integrity to great and small states alike."

Although the cease–fire, or Armistice, of November 11, 1918 ended World War I, the peace agreement formally concluding the First World War was the treaty signed at the Palace of Versailles just outside of Paris on June 28, 1919. While the Treaty of Versailles reinforced Wilson's plan to create the League of Nations headquartered in Geneva, Switzerland, it simultaneously laid the groundwork for future wars. By requiring the German state to pay costly war reparations, the Treaty of Versailles virtually guaranteed that Germany would face severe economic problems in the years to come. The war reparations and consequent downslide in the German economy, further undermined by the Wall Street stock market crash 1929, fostered sufficient discontent among the German people that the charismatic political actor Adolf Hitler managed to take the reins of power in Germany. Capitalizing on the desire of the German people to rekindle their national pride and to carve out a significant place for themselves in Europe and the world, Hitler's popularity in Germany grew rapidly during the difficult times of the 1920s and early 1930s. The attention given by the German National Socialist Party ("Nazi" Party) to Germany's economic troubles, coupled with rising racist sentiment and the growth of nationalist ideology and rhetoric, appears to have made Hitler's extremist party more successful in gathering public and electoral support than other extremist parties of that time. Although his popularity had begun to decline when he was named German Chancellor by President Hindenburg of Germany on January 30, 1933—a move largely the result of political infighting—his promotion to Chancellor placed him in a political position where he could wreak increasing havoc on the peoples of Germany and the rest of Europe.

Between 1939 and 1945 the Second World War devastated Europe and the Asian Pacific region as ultra–nationalist leaders sought to enlarge their political jurisdiction and create societies that matched their plans for advancing their own peculiar perspectives on what best constitutes a nation. The 1930s saw the build–up of Hitler's genocidal campaign by the Nazis, a disastrous attempt to rebuild the German nation by exterminating those Hitler and his cohorts considered "non–Aryan" and consequently "racially inferior": essentially, all who were non–white, non–Protestant, and non–German—specifically, minorities such as Jews, Roma (Gypsies), homosexuals, Roman Catholics, and the mentally and physically disabled—were targeted. Even before Hitler's sudden rise to power, Italian military commander Benito Mussolini had begun his fascistic campaign to heighten Italy's position in Europe, and his own position as well. As Hitler's popularity in grew and Germany built itself into a state to be reckoned with, Mussolini struck out on his own nationalist, murderous campaign across Italy, the Balkans, and North Africa, based on the ideology that the Italian state could reclaim the former glory of the Roman Empire. Japanese Emperor Hirohito (1901–1989) did likewise with his genocidal treatment of the peoples of China, Korea, and other countries in Southeast and East Asia as he sought to increase the power of the Japanese state.

The United Nations   Before the Second World War had fully ended, a new international organization of sovereign states, the United Nations (UN), was founded in hopes of preventing future wars by encouraging cooperative efforts of nation–states acting together to foster peace and development through a system of collective security. An event of lasting international importance was the conference held in October 1945 in San Francisco, involving the political leaders of the five principal states of the Allied Alliance that had fought in World War II—the United States, France, Britain, the Soviet Union, and China. The leaders of these states gathered to write a charter

for a new international organization, one that despite its shortcomings would be vastly more effective than the failed League of Nations. Whereas the League had lacked the power to enforce its members' decisions and could not stop the rise of Hitler or the other Axis leaders, the UN was designed to provide measures by which states could reinforce directives to nations failing to comply with standards of international law and behavior. Additionally, the new UN ideally would promote peaceful economic and social development in all parts of the world, for the benefit of all.

It is worth noting here that one problematic aspect of the United Nations has to do with its composition as a collective body of *states* rather than of individual *nations*, nationalities, or peoples. Most of the member states of the UN actually comprise a mixture of nations—for example, Great Britain's population includes not only the English but also the Scottish, Welsh, and Irish minorities along with members of many other nations who voluntarily immigrated or were brought to Britain's shores. Other nationalities such as the Kurds, the Palestinians, and the Basques lack their own nation–states as well as UN representation. These stateless peoples have been at a decided disadvantage in international arenas like the UN, a problem many hope eventually will be overcome as more nations are granted their own territorial states and as international recognition and representation are granted to at least some stateless peoples, including the indigenous nations often called "First Nations" or the "Fourth World."

The Cold War   Despite the good intentions of those who created the United Nations, the "Cold War" that was waged between the United States and its democratic allies and the Soviet Union and its communist allies from the late 1940s until the break–up of the Soviet Union in 1991 all but prevented the UN from achieving many of its goals for several decades. Pitting democratically governed states whose economies were primarily capitalist or mixed (socialist blended with capitalist) against totalitarian, communist states, the Cold War monopolized the political attention and the military and economic resources of much of the developed world for over four decades. Since the weapons of mass destruction developed in the arms race between the Soviet Union and the United States included myriad nuclear missiles and other highly destructive arms, direct warfare could not be conducted between these two superpowers. Instead, many proxy (substitute) wars came to be waged between "Western bloc" colonies (developing nation–states influenced and financed by the United States) and those of the "Eastern bloc," influenced and financed by the Soviet Union. These wars entailed the deaths and maiming of countless civilians and combatants in the very parts of the world that suffered most from poverty, malnutrition, poor health, and underdevelopment.

Third World Independence

During the Cold War period, however, not all political events in what came to be known as the "Third World" (less–industrialized, less economically developed regions) were unwelcome by their peoples. Beginning in the early 1950s and extending through the 1960s, numerous African nations achieved their independence from the European imperial powers that had colonized them and had deprived them of their rights, their land, and their economic resources. Nationalist independence movements in many African colonies developed momentum as one after another of Europe's former colonies liberated themselves from their former rulers. In a relatively quick succession of declarations of independence, the newly established African states typically agreed to set their territorial boundaries along the lines of those established arbitrarily by the European imperialists during the Scramble for Africa. This meant, however, that many tribal and ethnic groups came to be divided across two or more countries, despite their common heritage and culture. The implications of the construction of national boundaries by the Europeans in the nineteenth century and of the subsequent legal reinforcement of these boundaries upon independence in the 1950s and 1960s were that in many countries, interethnic warfare would be waged toward the end of the twentieth century as ethnic groups sought to establish their authority to govern themselves and improve their economic and social lot.

In both Africa and Europe a substantial rise in internal strife within states appeared toward the close of the twentieth century. From 1981 through the early 1990s, popular democratic uprisings took place in Eastern Europe and brought the end of communist rule. The Polish Solidarity (*Solidarnosza*) movement, started in 1981 among striking shipyard workers in the Polish city of Gdansk on the Baltic Sea, climaxed with the electoral victory of President Lech Walesa (1943–) in 1990 and the inauguration of a democratically elected parliament. The execution of communist dictator Nicolas Ceausescu of Romania and his wife in October of 1989 marked the culmination of dramatic public protests against Ceausescu's autocratic rule and the triumph of the Romanian people, among the most impoverished in Europe during the years of communist rule. Perhaps most exhilarating for both Western and Eastern observers was the November 1989 fall of the Berlin Wall that had divided

East and West Berlin since 1961, culminating in the reunification of East Germany with West Germany in 1990. The democratization of other countries in Eastern Europe and the declarations of independence of many of the republics of the former USSR after its break–up in August 1991 similarly astounded the world at large. Many of these popular movements were stimulated not only by the desire to end autocratic communist rule but also by growing national movements that have sought to reclaim the ethnic and national identities of the people of Europe and Asia submerged under communism.

Problematic Nationalism

Not all nationalist movements in Europe in the post–Cold War period have been positive, however. In the southeast region of Europe, for example, violent warfare in Bosnia and Croatia in the early 1990s, spurred on by attacks from Bosnian Serbs supported by the Serbian Army of Yugoslavia, led to the first genocide in Europe since World War II, followed a few years later by genocidal war in Kosovo and revenge killings in Serbia. By creating a federated country in the Balkans—Yugoslavia—from previously separate states along the Adriatic Sea, the 1919 Treaty of Versailles had brought a mixture of ethnic and religious groups together into one federated nation–state that would survive the years of communist rule, only to crumble disastrously into brutal interethnic warfare and genocide in the early 1990s when communist control in Eastern and Southeastern Europe dissolved. Manipulated by unscrupulous political leaders wishing to hold onto power at all costs despite the end of communist rule, the peoples of the former socialist Yugoslavia witnessed and became victims of some of the worst interethnic fighting and atrocities of the twentieth century.

Political developments in other parts of Southeast Asia, South Asia, and Latin America in the post–World War II period have similarly represented the interplay of various forces, including autocratic repression as well as democratic, nationalist movements whose participants have aimed to express or reassert their ethnic identities and claims for civil governance by attaching their demands to a national state. Not all efforts have succeeded in realizing self–determination, but many nationalist leaders and activists have established themselves as viable political actors and forces to be reckoned with on the international stage. Increasingly during the 1990s and into the early twenty–first century, as an after–effect of the end of the competition between the United States and the Soviet Union for allies and influence, local conflicts have escalated into wide–ranging interethnic violence that has been difficult to control.

These "low–intensity" wars have killed and injured countless people, and conflict resolution efforts have been only minimally successful at quelling their violence. Not only have interethnic conflicts taken place in the developing world, but also in countries such as Northern Ireland and Cyprus, plagued with what sometimes appear to be never–ending conflicts (often labeled "intractable") between ethnic and national groups. In many cases, the problems have centered on competing claims for the assertion of political authority at the state level by numerous stateless nations such as the Basque minority in Spain and the Palestinians in the Middle East.

Other nationalist challenges are perhaps less violent but more long–standing and equally hard to resolve—for example, the struggle of indigenous peoples worldwide to secure their own territory and resources in the face of a dominant ethnic group that controls state governance. The case of the Saami of northern Scandinavia and the Kola Peninsula of Russia is one such case where the level of direct violence in the late twentieth century was relatively low compared to the violence experienced by ethnic and religious groups contending for power in such places as Sri Lanka, Kashmir, and the Philippines. As with many Native American groups, the problems faced by the Saami and other indigenous minority nations stem from a state authority's imposing its will through internal colonization and the negation of previous treaties and formal agreements—or at least from the perception by stateless peoples that this is taking place. In such cases no clear arbiter other than, perhaps, the United Nations or the International Court of Justice (the World Court) in The Hague exists to decide how such claims should be settled. Furthermore, what Norwegian peace theorist Johann Galtung has termed "structural" violence—violence indirectly wrought by oppressive social, political, and economic structures and discriminatory practices—afflicts indigenous communities worldwide but is particularly hard to correct since the violence is occurring at the systemic level.

THEORY IN DEPTH

Definitions of 'Nation'?

Crucial to the concept of "nationalism" is the definition of "nation" and its distinction from the notion of "state." To begin with, a "state" in a political sense can be defined as a politically governed territory with distinct boundaries, having the sovereign authority to control its own domestic affairs and to represent the interests of its polity (i.e., those living within and governed by the political authority of the state) in deliberations and interactions with other states. The concept of the polity as a collection of persons sharing specific political values (such as the preservation of individual freedoms and liberties or the notion that all individuals in the polity should have the right to make political decisions together) or certain common characteristics (for example, language ties or a common cultural heritage) does not really come into play in the strict definition of a state. In contrast, the idea of the "nation-state" brings together the belief that territorial boundaries, political authority, and the composition of the population inhabiting the territory somehow should coincide, theoretically with the population all belonging to the same homogeneous nation. Few nation–states actually fit this strict definition, since nearly all states in the twenty–first century are composed of a multiplicity of peoples from many national groups.

In defining the nation, scholars have produced both culturally and civic–oriented definitions, although some, such as Anthony D. Smith, have attempted to combine elements of both. To Smith, a nation is a group of people who share the same geographical territory as well as certain common elements of history, culture, economy, and law.

In his 1882 lecture, "*Qu'est–ce qu'une nation?*" ("What is a nation?"), Frenchman Ernest Renan described a nation as

> a large–scale solidarity, constituted by the feeling of the sacrifices that one has made in the past and of those that one is prepared to make in the future. It presupposes a past; it is summarized, however, in the present by a tangible fact, namely, consent, the clearly expressed desire to continue a common life. A nation's existence is, if you will pardon the metaphor, a daily plebiscite, just as an individual's existence is a perpetual affirmation of life.

Benedict Anderson, in *Imagined Communities: Reflections on the Origin and Spread of Nationalism*, defines a nation as "an imagined political community—and imagined as both inherently limited and sovereign." Anderson is one of the key theorists of "constructed nationalism," where nationalism is viewed as a socially constructed idea meant to serve the interests and needs of the members of a nation and those participating in nationalist movements. Presenting the view that nations are "imagined communities" created in the minds of those who live in them, Anderson's book represents a departure from the views of the "primordialists" who considered nationalism an outgrowth of an innate human need for ethnic community.

Definitions of "Nationalism":

Theories of nationalism range from explanations focusing on the why and wherefore of the formation of social movements that take on a nationalist tone to attempts to explain the basis of the concept of "nation" and campaigns to promote a nationalist agenda. Whether the motivation to identify with a "nation" is a biologically based, "primordial" given, characteristic of all populations, whether it is something cultivated by political philosophers and activists seeking to promote specific agendas under the guise of ethnic identity, or whether it is something in between continues to be hotly debated. Many theorists look at nationalism as having existed only from the seventeenth or eighteenth century onward and as having its origins in Western European philosophical thought. Others view nationalism as a phenomenon with a more ancient history and interpret the drives to create great empires among the peoples of antiquity as synonymous with attempts in recent times to forge nation–states aligned to the ethnic identity or political values of the inhabitants.

Most Western–trained scholars view nationalism as a modern phenomenon, but some continue to insist that nations and nationalism originated much further back in time. Disagreement also persists as to whether the desire to establish territorial states coinciding with national groups is biologically determined or is shaped by political actors. The "primordialists"—those who see the quest for ethnic identity and solidarity as rooted physically in the human animal—see ethnicity as related to the official announcement of the species and the preservation of one's own community, however defined. In contrast, many "modernization theorists" tend to believe that the impetus for nationhood and the development of distinct national identities are integrally connected to the rise of capitalism and the end of political empires and monarchies that began with the period of the European Enlightenment in the seventeenth century. Other modernizationists view ethnic identity formation and the growth of nationalism as phenomena of the post–Napoleon era, beginning only in the early nineteenth century.

Civic nationalism and ethnic nationalism
From the mid–twentieth century on, if not earlier, many scholars of nationalism came to view the range of differences in theoretical approaches to nationalism in a fairly dichotomous (i.e., two–category) way, distinguishing between "ethnic nationalist" and "civic nationalist" approaches. Michel Seymour, Jocelyne Couture, and Kai Nelson summarized the main differences between these two conceptualizations of nationalism in the introduction to their edited volume, *Rethinking Nationalism*. Aligned with the views of Ernest Renan, civic nationalists believe "that a nation is a voluntary association of individuals." A good example would be the French Revolution. The ethnic nationalist's approach is "based upon language, culture, and tradition, and thus appeals to more or less objective features of our social lives." Nationalism in Germany during German Romanticism is ethnic nationalism, as are Johann Gottfried Herder's views.

However, as the authors further note, "A careful reader of Renan and Herder will protest that this is an oversimplification of their views, for both authors integrate objective and subjective features in their characterization of the nation." Consequently, theories of nationalism cannot accurately be categorized into two distinct groups, since the features of certain theoretical formulations of nationalism labeled "ethnic" may well overlap with aspects of a mainly "civic" nationalism.

Like Johann Gottlieb Fichte (1762–1814), but contrasting with Johann Gottfried Herder—two of nationalism's early theorists who wrote at the start of the nineteenth century—Renan viewed nations as resulting from political efforts to define a physical space for democratic governance by those who share similar civic values such as the preservation and promotion of individual rights, freedoms, and liberties. Cultural, linguistic, and ethnic identities do not predetermine national movements, Renan claimed. Instead, it is the political action of those who seek to unify a people based on a notion of shared experience and destiny.

Renan's famous lecture at the Sorbonne University in Paris in 1882, *"Qu'est–ce qu'une nation?"* ("What is a nation?"), raised questions about the origins of nations and the nature of their identity. After briefly examining the history of a number of nations, empires, and dynasties, Renan concluded,

> Forgetting, I would even go so far as to say historical error, is a crucial factor in the creation of a nation, which is why progress in historical studies often constitutes a danger for [the principle of] nationality. Indeed, historical enquiry brings to light deeds of violence which took place at the origin of all political formations, even of those whose consequences have been altogether beneficial.

To Renan, nation building requires "that all individuals have many things in common, and also that they have forgotten many things."

Renan saw nations as a relatively modern phenomenon, "brought about by a series of convergent facts."

MAJOR WRITINGS:

"Qu'est–ce qu'une nation?"

Ernest Renan's lecture, *"Qu'est–ce qu'une nation?"* ("What is a nation?"), delivered at the Sorbonne University in Paris in 1882, examined basic issues touching upon nations and nationalism. Exploring the various circumstances through which nations have been formed, Renan developed his civic conception of nationalism. He concluded that common racial or ethnic characteristics do not necessarily produce separate nations. Renan maintained that "there is no pure race and . . . to make politics depend upon ethnographic analysis is to surrender it to a chimera. The noblest countries, England, France, and Italy, are those where the blood is the most mixed. . . . We touch here on one of those problems in regard to which it is of the utmost importance that we equip ourselves with clear ideas and ward off misconceptions." Instead, Renan determined that a nation is built on historical events that have produced a common legacy for a group of people who share in the present the desire to bind themselves together as one. In his words, Renan asserted, "A nation is a soul, a spiritual principle. Two things, which in truth are but one, constitute this soul or spiritual principle. One lies in the past, one in the present. One is the possession in common of a rich legacy of memories; the other is present–day consent, the desire to live together, the will to perpetuate the value of the heritage that one has received in an undivided form. . . . To have common glories in the past and to have a common will in the present; to have per-

formed great deeds together, to wish to perform still more—these are the essential conditions for being a people." Renan concluded that a shared past and a continuing sense of wanting to live together in the present are the most–critical factors in the building of nations.

In his views of what constitutes a nation, Renan opposed Herder and subsequent philosophers who claimed that ethnicity, language, and culture have more to do with nation–building than do liberal democratic principles. Renan observed that during the French Revolution, Europeans believed that the political institutions appropriate for governing "small, independent cities, such as Sparta and Rome," could be used effectively in larger nations—a serious misconception, to his mind. Renan found even more problematic the late–nineteenth century tendency to confuse race "with nation and a sovereignty analogous to that of really existing peoples is attributed to ethnographic or, rather, linguistic groups." Taking a historical outlook on the construction of nations, Renan commented, "Since the fall of the Roman Empire or, rather, since the disintegration of Charlemagne's empire, western Europe has seemed to us to be divided into nations, some of which, in certain epochs, have sought to wield a hegemony over the others, without ever enjoying any lasting success." He discovered such nations to be a relatively recent phenomenon, not found in the great empires of the past such as the Persian Empire, the empire of Alexander the Great, China, or Egypt.

Sometimes unity has been effected by a dynasty, as was the case in France; sometimes it has been brought about by the direct will of provinces, as was the case with Holland, Switzerland, and Belgium; sometimes it has been the work of a general consciousness, belatedly victorious over the caprices of feudalism, as was the case in Italy and Germany.

In other words, a variety of events can lead to a nation's emerging on the historical scene. Nonetheless, according to Renan, the determining factors in the creation of nations are not race, religion, culture, or language, as these may unite a people but do not oblige

persons to act together. As Renan said, "A community of interest is assuredly a powerful bond between men. Do interests, however, suffice to make a nation? I do not think so. Community of interest brings about trade agreements, but nationality has a sentimental side to it; it is both soul and body at once . . ." Renan admitted that geography, too, influences the formation of nations, although it, too, is not a determining factor. In the end, Renan concluded, "A nation is a spiritual principle, the outcome of the profound complications of history; it is a spiritual family not a group determined by the shape of the earth."

In *Nationalism and the State*, John Breuilly, too, identified nationalism as a modern phenomenon. Additionally, Breuilly sees nationalism as an evanescent phenomenon: appearing and then disappearing after serving its function. Instead of arising as a naturally occurring feature of nations defined as persons sharing a common culture, nationalism, according to Breuilly, is a politically pragmatic phenomenon: having accomplished its end, it then disappears.

Worth noting here is Michael Billig's concept of "banal nationalism," which he discusses in his book by the same name. Billig identifies patriotism as a banal, or everyday, form of nationalism, a pervasive phenomenon in nation–states that can quickly be kindled up into what Billig terms "hot nationalism." This form of fervent, ultra–patriotic feeling—evident in the heated displays of patriotism by many Americans in response to the September 11, 2001 catastrophes—can sometimes produce significant, often harmful results such as the granting of excessive powers to a chief executive, the suspension of constitutional rights, and xenophobic attacks against those perceived to belong to "terrorist" religions or nationalities.

THEORY IN ACTION

In "The Promise, the Peril," a special report appearing in the December 17, 2001, issue of *Newsweek* magazine, Marcus Mabry and his colleagues asked a critical question pertinent to scholars of nationalism: "How do you build a nation?" The authors suggest that Europeans and Americans accomplished nation building by "subjugation and might" during the days of imperialism. And they conclude that, since the end of the Cold War, the task of nation–building increasingly has been taken on by the United Nations. Clearly, the business of constructing a nation depends on contextual historical factors that vary significantly from case to case and over time. What worked to build a nation–state in eighteenth century Europe is not necessarily what works in the twenty–first century, particularly where nation–states were already constituted but were subsequently torn apart by ethnic violence, civil strife, or international warfare, only to be shaped again.

Nationalist theories range widely in scope and content, despite the certain amount of agreement that exists among scholars of nationalism as to what constitutes a "nation" and how a "nationalist" social movement can be identified and described. In many ways, nationalism would have assumed far less importance had there been no European colonization of

Africa, Latin America, and Asia. It was to the liberation struggles that appeared in response to the oppressive nature of European imperial control that theories of nationalism took on special importance, starting especially in the late nineteenth century. Nonetheless, the specific context of oppression may be less important to the creation of national movements than the reality of oppression itself. Without the appearance of national movements to liberate oppressed peoples, whether as an outgrowth of the development of liberal thought amidst autocratic rule in Europe in the late 1600s and early 1700s, in response to industrialization, or in relation to campaigns in Africa in the 1950s and 1960s to throw off the shackles of European control, theories of nationalism hardly would have flourished or become as finely nuanced as they had by the early twenty–first century.

As to whether nationalist theories are necessary to inspire oppressed peoples to work for their own liberation, the debate continues. Some theorists maintain that nationalist campaigns—that is, nationalism in action—cannot occur without there first being intellectuals who envision the possibilities of creating a new national identity and new political structures to match (essentially, a "top–down" stage in the process), followed by the cultivation of these ideas among the masses, then the emergence of capable political actors who can lead their people to press for recognition of their nationalist demands ("bottom–up," or grassroots, stage). Whatever the case, it is obvious that virtually no nation–state in the world today could have been formed or would have achieved independence without some measure of motivated, concerted action on the part of historical actors seeking to secure an environment where their own national group could play a significant political role.

The Haudenosaunee

The *Haudenosaunee*, or Six–Nations Confederacy, known to the French as the *Iroquois* (a name resembling a common greeting used by Native Americans in the confederacy), overlaps the northeastern part of the United States. The case of the *Haudenosaunee* exemplifies the fact that Native American and other indigenous political systems can be based on a concept of nationhood differing somewhat from more Western European–based concepts of a nation.

Some scholars may doubt that Native American nations are true identity nations in the actual sense of the word. Among the *Haudenosaunee*, however, the concept of "nation" as an identity group clearly exists and has for centuries. Closely related to the spiritual history of the people belonging to each of the Six Nations, *Haudenosaunee* national identity implies membership in both a constituent nation (for example, the Mohawks) and in a confederation of distinct but integrally connected nations.

The identity of each of the Six Nations was shaped by historical events that took place perhaps some one to two thousand years ago, if not longer. These events were originally recorded in *wampum*—sacred messages in beaded code created from black and white beads of shell—although most *wampum* was destroyed by the European colonizers of North America. Some of the earliest tales of the *Haudenosaunee* concern the origins of the confederacy that would later shape the course of American history not only through treaties, peaceable agreements, and battles between the indigenous nations and the European settlers, but also through the influence of the *Haudenosaunee* constitution and practices on the American Articles of Confederation and, to perhaps a lesser extent, on the U.S. Constitution.

Apparently responding to dissension and continual fighting among the five Native American nations of the Senecas, Cayugas, Onondagas, Oneidas, and Mohawks, The Peacemaker, also known as *Dekanawidah*—a member of the Huron nation from the North American Great Lakes region—met with the Five Nations' leaders somewhere between 1000 A.D. and 1450 A.D. He provided the confederate chiefs with a model for governance through a new constitution known as the Great Law of Peace (Great Binding Law or *Gayanashagowa*). According to the Great Law, each nation of the *Haudenosaunee* was to play an integral role in the affairs of the confederacy, which would be governed by the chiefs and the clan mothers through direct—that is, participatory—democracy, meeting regularly in clan councils and in councils of the entire league, or confederacy. The original political association thus formed consisted of five Native American nations, with the Tuscarora Nation joining the confederacy as the sixth nation in the early 1700s. Planting a Tree of Great Peace in the Onondaga Nation, centrally located among the other four nations, The Peacemaker designated the Onondaga Nation the "Keepers of the Fire," the council fire around which the nations' chiefs would meet to discuss affairs of mutual interest and determine domestic and international action.

In the *Haudenosaunee* confederacy, women as well as men have figured highly in political decision making. Each of the clans making up the Five (later, Six) Nations is guided by a woman, the clan mother, who is entrusted with monitoring the political decisions of those sitting in council and who can depose any leader deemed to be acting not in accordance with the Great Law of Peace. Additionally, *Haudenosaunee* clan mothers have the responsibility to deliberate in their own councils, governing structures parallel to the chiefs' councils, and to grant citizenship in the confederacy to other Native Americans through clan adoption. For example, the Wyandots of Ohio and the Delawares (the *Lenni Lenapes*) were adopted into the *Haudenosaunee* by this method. Furthermore, the clan mother of the Onondaga Nation has played a central role in the affairs of the *Haudenosaunee*. In the early twenty–first century, Clan Mother Audrey Shenandoah presides over the *Haudenosaunee*.

Effects of the outside world Despite the long tradition of deliberations and direct democracy practiced by the *Haudenosaunee*, the political integrity of Native America has been severely challenged by the presence of European Americans on native soil and by interference from the United States government and state governments in indigenous affairs. By the late twentieth century the majority of Native American tribes and nations were facing severe economic and social problems such as extremely high unemployment, alcoholism, inadequate health care, poorly equipped schools, and a lack of political autonomy, all this despite the numerous treaties they had signed over the centuries with the various states of the U.S. and the federal government. Nearly all of these problems stemmed from the policies of "internal colonialism" conducted against Native Americans by the United States government and by state governments as well. Systematically stripped of the rights to their own natural resources on Native American land and lacking an adequate economic base from which to operate and raise revenue, Native Americans have suffered severe discrimination and the dispossession of their land and resources.

In consequence, numerous casinos run by Native Americans on their reservations or lands sprang up at the close of the twentieth century and the start of the new millennium as an alternative means of generating revenue for the indigenous nations. Among the *Haudenosaunee* as with certain others in Native America, in 2001 internal debates raged over the appropriateness of building and operating gambling casinos on Indian land. These "Indian casinos" are sometimes seen as a panacea, or cure–all, to the economic troubles of Native America. For instance, Foxwoods Resort and Casino, operated by the Mashantucket Pequot Tribal Nation on their own sovereign territory within the state of Connecticut, is filled with slot machines and other games of chance and features well–known performers and athletes. Foxwoods has proven so lucrative that casino proceeds easily covered the construction of a Museum and Research Center that opened in 1998 on Mashantucket Pequot land.

Another case in point: the Oneida Nation, one of the Six Nations of the *Haudenosaunee*, grappled in 2001 not only with the question of whether its Turning Stone Casino in Verona, New York, was worth keeping and replicating but also with serious internal dissension. The controversy was brought on primarily by concern among many Oneidas that their traditional ways are being jeopardized and their political autonomy from the State of New York is being undermined by Turning Stone. New York State authorities increasingly have tried regulating gambling casinos on Native American land, despite prior agreements that the *Haudenosaunee* could operate their own economic concerns without state interference such as taxation and regulation. Disagreement over whether relying on casinos as a means of building greater economic wealth for the indigenous peoples of North America is a healthy course to pursue extends far beyond the *Haudenosaunee*. Numerous other Native American nations and tribes in the United States and Canada are facing similar debates and problems with the handling of casinos, some involving instances of corruption and murder sparked by conflicts over the rightful ownership and operation of these enterprises.

As some people—including many Native Americans—see it, then, casinos may be flourishing at the moral, spiritual, and cultural expense of the very people they are meant to serve. Additionally, the casinos are viewed as a potentially dangerously one–sided way of generating income. Should a particular casino fail to attract sufficient clients, few other economic alternatives may be available to sustain newly created projects and the ongoing economic and social needs of Native Americans. Gambling addiction, added to the already prevalent problem of alcoholism among many Native American groups, also is seen as an inherent problem with this method of raising revenue, a serious hazard whose potential to further destroy the health and integrity of Native American nations is substantial.

Included within the debate over the validity of gambling casinos on Native American land is the critical issue of whether indigenous peoples are best served by assimilating, or blending in, with the cultural majority population in whose midst they live, whether they should maintain an existence separate from and parallel to the surrounding majority, or whether indigenous peoples profit most by considering themselves as simultaneously belonging to two societies—the indigenous and the non–native—that is, citizens of both the majority society and of their own indigenous nations, or as some in Canada have termed

it, "citizens–plus." The special challenge for indigenous minorities, as for the larger, encompassing state, is to discern where multiple cultures and identities fit "in the political and social order of the nation state" and how a sense of alienation can be avoided when not all belong to the dominant culture.

National identity Based on differing conceptions of what it means to be an American, contentious disputes have arisen over obligations to the various governments that seek to both nurture and control indigenous nations. The *Haudenosaunee* consider themselves to be a sovereign, independent people living in the midst of non–indigenous citizens of the United States. As such, the *Haudenosaunee* issue and carry their own *Haudenosaunee* passports that, though unrecognized by the United States government, are viewed as legitimate national documents by certain other Western nations, including Switzerland. Seeking representation at the level of the United Nations at the turn of the millennium consequently was one objective of the *Haudenosaunee* who attended the Millennium Summit of worldwide religious traditions held at United Nations headquarters in New York in August 2000.

Similarly, the efforts of the *Haudenosaunee* to right environmental wrongs in New York State have been recognized internationally, including at the UN, where in July 1995 the UN Environment Programme hosted a day–long session to consider *Haudenosaunee* concerns about the pollution of Native American lands in New York State. However, the claims and desires of the Six Nations have often conflicted with the assumptions and practices of the United States government, and the ultimate outcome of the *Haudenosaunee* quest for recognition as a sovereign nation and for UN membership was uncertain at the close of 2001. Possessing dual or triple national identities—for example, simultaneously belonging to the Onondaga Nation and the *Haudenosaunee* while at the same time being a citizen of the United States—has raised significant challenges and posed problems and contradictions not easily resolved.

Although many of the *Haudenosaunee*'s recent experiences have been far more positive than the casinos controversies imply, the nature of national identity among America's indigenous peoples has been radically affected in recent years by shifts in community fortunes associated with gambling revenues. Since the basis of economic livelihood by necessity shapes culture, the identity of indigenous nations in America has been changing as the economies have changed. National identity, as scholars such as Anthony D. Smith have noted, is not a fixed entity but can change and mutate over time, sometimes in pos-

Mustafa Kemal Atatürk (center), heading for the celebration of the ninth anniversary of the Republic of Turkey. (AP/World Wide Photos)

itive directions, sometimes in ways harmful to the group. As the casino dilemmas reveal, long–standing conflicts between Native American nations and the United States over issues of sovereignty, land rights, and rights to economic resources are far from being settled and in fact have become more complicated over time.

Atatürk and the Modernization of Turkey

In the early years of the twentieth century, Turkey was governed by the Ottoman Dynasty, formed during the expansion of control by the Ottoman *caliph* (leader of Islam) some six hundred years earlier. Straddling Europe and Asia, Turkey was still a primarily agrarian country, a composite of ethnic groups as varied as the Ottoman Turks and the nomadic Kurds, a stateless people living in several countries. Having emerged as a military hero among Turks in 1915 while the rest of Europe was embroiled in World War I, Mustafa Kemal (1881–1938) led the Turkish liberation struggle beginning in 1919 against Ottoman rule, a campaign that culminated in independence for the Republic of Turkey in 1923.

Born to Ali Riza, his father—a customs official who later became a merchant but died while Mustafa was still a child—and to Zubeyde, his mother, who single–handedly raised Mustafa and his sister after his father's death, Mustafa grew up in the former Ottoman city of Salonica, now a city in Greece. Enrolled at first in a traditional religious school then educated in a modern school, and afterwards in a military high school, Mustafa Riza was given the name Kemal— "perfection"—by one of this high school teachers in honor of his high scholastic achievement. After graduating from the War Academy in 1905, Mustafa Kemal and his compatriots fought and successfully deposed the Ottoman sultan in 1908, the beginning of an illustrious military career for the future president of Turkey.

After the Republic of Turkey was proclaimed, with Mustafa Kemal as its first president, Mustafa proceeded to implement widespread reforms throughout the various sectors of the Turkish government and society. During his fifteen–year reign as president, Mustafa—who was renamed "Atatürk" ("Father of the Turks") in 1934 by the Turkish Parliament when legislation was passed requiring everyone to adopt a surname—managed to modernize Turkey more quickly than had ever been done in any other state. Reforming the political, social, legal, economic, and cultural sectors of Turkey, Atatürk secularized the government and the education system, granted women equal rights

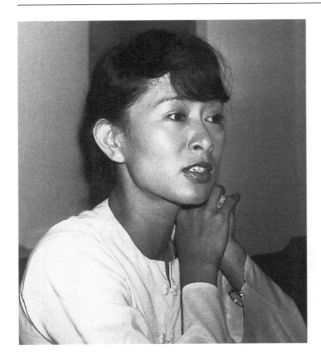

Aung San Suu Kyi. (Corbis-Bettmann)

with men (including full political rights), converted the Arabic script–based alphabet used in Turkey to a new Turkish alphabet based on Latin script, shifted Turkish dress from traditional Middle Eastern garb to Western–style clothes, and promoted the arts, sciences, agriculture, and industry.

A charismatic leader, Atatürk exemplified the type of leadership around which a new national identity could be formed and for which a nation could be mobilized to achieve remarkable conquests in such fields as health, education, and diplomacy in a very short time. Recognized by the League of Nations for his commitment to world peace, Turkey's first president led the way for Turkey to be invited to join the League in 1932. And by encouraging his people to reshape their national identity in more modern directions, Mustafa Kemal Atatürk facilitated Turkey's transformation into a society which by century's end would be preparing itself for entry into the European Union.

Aung San Suu Kyi and the Democratization of Burma

Northwest of Thailand and Laos and tucked in just south of India and China, the country of Burma (renamed "Myanmar" by the military government that captured state power in 1988) is a country with a long history of efforts toward democratization. Colonized

by the British, Burma achieved independence in 1947. Just before the transition to independence was to take place, however, a bloody military coup toppled those who rightfully should have assumed power—most prominently Burma's national hero, Aung San, who had assisted the Allies in their fight against the Japanese in World War II. Aung San would have become Burma's first president had he and most of his prospective cabinet not been assassinated by a jealous general bent on seeking this position for himself. Just two years earlier, Aung San's daughter, Aung San Suu Kyi, had been born.

Though she does not recall much about her father since he died when she was only two years old, Aung San Suu Kyi reports having been inspired by her father's reputation and image. A formidable Burmese leader in her own right, Suu takes after her father in her charismatic ability to draw supporters to the cause of human rights and democracy in Burma, despite—or perhaps in part, because of—her status as a prisoner of conscience. Suu was placed under house arrest in 1989 by the military *junta* who took over after the previous national leader, Ne Win, resigned in July 1988.

Educated in England at Oxford University, Suu had returned to Burma in 1988 to care for her dying mother. Apparently unwittingly, she arrived at just the right time to organize a democratization campaign among Burmese anxious to see an end to fifty years of military rule. Beloved by her supporters, encouraged by the international human rights community, and assisted by Burmese grassroots activists, Suu has pursued a non–violent campaign of resistance to Burma's military rulers and has worked to build a democratic future for Burma where democratic political participation will finally be possible.

The political strategy followed by Suu and her fellow members of the National League for Democracy, the party she quickly founded in 1988, has been one of non–accommodation to the demands of the *junta*—the State Law and Order Restoration Committee (SLORC)—coupled with persistent encouragement for non–violent protests and the promotion of democracy and human rights. In 1989 Suu was placed under house arrest by the military *junta*, who feared the growing success of her democracy movement and Suu's increasing popularity as an active political force. While under house arrest, Suu and her party won the national election of 1990. Although Suu rightfully should have assumed the presidency of Burma after her election, this was blocked by the military *junta*. In 1995, Suu was released from her house arrest. Matters intensified when a pro–democracy uprising at the University of Yangon was crushed by the military in 1998. Additionally, Suu's sentence was reimposed in September 2000, when Suu was accused of leaving Rangoon to participate in a political event.

The winner of the 1991 Nobel Peace Prize, Aung San Suu Kyi was honored and the cause of democracy in Burma was promoted by the Nobel Laureates attending the annual Peace Prize ceremonies in Oslo, Norway in the fall of 2001 and the special ceremonies commemorating one hundred years of the Prize. Recognizing Suu's achievements with a special letter of support directed toward Burmese military leader Than Swe, the Nobel laureates in early December 2001 requested the Burmese government to release Suu from house arrest and to negotiate with her for democratic reforms. In October 2000 Suu began secret, UN–facilitated talks with the Burmese military *junta* to secure the release of other political prisoners, and within one year about two hundred prisoners were released. Aung San Suu Kyi reportedly is optimistic that her talks with the *junta* will lead to progress for the Burmese people. As she stated in a videotaped message released in the year 2000, "We are absolutely confident that democracy will come to Burma." Suu's campaign to build a solidaristic union of Burmese citizens committed to the values of democracy, human rights, and non–violence appears to be gradually paying off.

Flooding Nubia, Submerging a Nation

The ancient African nation of Nubia, situated along the Nile River in what is now southern Egypt and the northern part of the Sudan, is a five–thousand–year–old civilization whose relics from the past include exquisite rock carvings, temples, monuments, painted tombs, and buildings of stone. Once the rival of ancient Egypt, Nubia conquered Egypt around 700 B.C. The Nubian kingdom continued to flourish several centuries into the Christian era, its black kings continuing to rule from their capital city of Meroe. Although most Westerners seem to know little about Nubia, this African archaeological treasure boasted more pyramids in the Sudan than Egypt had. Furthermore, the oldest city yet discovered in Africa is one being excavated in Nubia at the turn of the new millennium.

By the early twentieth century, however, the Nubian nation was threatened with cultural extinction. As Egyptian engineers sought solutions to the problem of severe water shortages in Egypt due to population growth along the Nile and the need for greater sources of water for agricultural cultivation, a plan was devised to dam the Nile and create a reservoir of water. Damming the Nile River at Aswan, the Egyptian government completed the first Aswan Dam in 1902 and heightened it twice in the three decades that followed. Again in the early 1960s, a second Aswan Dam was built, again flooding the Nubian national homeland. When much of their land was flooded as the dam was built and the Nile was redirected, thousands of Nubians were forced to relocate to Cairo or to Khartoum, the Sudanese capital. Lower Nubia was submerged, along with many monuments from antiquity not saved by the United Nations Educational, Scientific and Cultural Organization (UNESCO) salvaging campaign prior to the flooding.

The displaced Nubians have traveled to Cairo and Khartoum and farther, reaching the United States and Europe in their quests for new homes after Lower Nubia was flooded. Among those forced to migrate was Hamza El Din, born in Troshka, Nubia (Sudan) in 1929. Trained as an electrical engineer in Cairo, where he had moved when Nubians began to migrate, El Din took up the *oud*, a stringed wooden instrument—the Arabic predecessor of the European lute—after graduating from the university. Formally shifting his career to music, El Din studied in Italy and later returned to Nubia, traveling by donkey to collect traditional Nubian folk songs. El Din invented a unique blending of Nubian rhythms and sounds with Arabic and contemporary music, harmonizing musical elements across cultures.

Visiting the United States in 1964, El Din participated in the Newport Folk Festival and his career in music took off. He began recording his original combinations of Nubian–Arabic music. Using music as his vehicle to achieve recognition for the plight of the Nubian nation, its forced migration, and the tragic disappearance of the Nubian landscape, El Din has performed throughout the world and recorded several albums of his Nubian–Arabic musical synthesis. The first Nubian musician to become known in the West, El Din has been vocal about the tragedies suffered by the Nubian nation and the damage to the natural environment and ancient cultural treasures of Nubia.

In 1998 the Sudanese Minister of Irrigation and Water Resources, Sharif al–Tuhami, announced the Sudanese state's plans to construct three new hydroelectric dams on the Nile. One of these, the Hamdab High Dam, would be located in Nubia at Merowe at a cost of up to 1.5 billion dollars. El Din in 2001 was continuing to play an active role in the shaping of international consciousness surrounding Nubia and the ancient land's destiny. Alerting the world of the Sudanese government's plans to replicate the efforts of the Egyptians by constructing additional dams along the Nile that would completely flood Nubia, including the few remaining ancient treasures of the Nubian

Numerous attempts at peace between Israel and Palestine have been made, often facilitated by the United States. Here, U.S. President Bill Clinton (center) watches as Palestinian Yasser Arafat (right) and Israeli Yitzhak Rabin shake hands after signing the 1993 Oslo Peace Accords. (Archive Photos, Inc.)

nation, El Din in 2001 continued to perform concerts in America, his homeland since 1968, and to participate in lectures concerning the land of Nubia and his music. Lacking state power, the Nubian nation is obliged to bring its concerns to the international community in hopes of securing assistance and support in its quest to save the last remaining traces of this ancient land from obliteration. The states of Egypt and Sudan literally have turned a deaf ear to the pleadings of Hamza El Din and others intent on preserving the ancient Nubian culture and carrying the Nubian nation's rich heritage into the twenty–first century.

Creating Israel, Denying Palestine?

Authorized by UN Resolution 181 of 1947, the State of Israel was created out of territory belonging to what had been known for a quarter century as the British mandate for Palestine, an area placed under British control by the Council of the League of Nations in September of 1922. Near the end of World War I, the British had issued a statement of support for a Jewish state in Palestine through the Balfour Declaration. The Declaration of November 2, 1917, issued as a letter written by Arthur James Lord Balfour, British Foreign Secretary at the time, to the British Lord Rothschild, was a formal declaration of sympa-

thy on the part of the British king and cabinet with the Zionist Federation, whose goal was the creation of an Israeli state in the Middle East. Although it remains somewhat unclear as to why Britain issued this declaration, speculation has it that Britain wished to win the support of Jews for the ongoing war effort in Europe.

With the founding of the State of Israel in 1948, a move sanctioned by UN General Assembly Resolution 181 of November 29, 1947, some 780,000 Palestinians lost their homes and were forced to migrate out of Palestine, as their villages were destroyed. Over the next fifty years the Palestinians would become the largest stateless dispersed population in the world, with some 3.7 million Palestinians officially registered with the UN at the turn of the new millennium, including the descendents of the original Palestinian refugees, and countless more Palestinians internally displaced—that is, living near their original homes but unable to return. About one–quarter of the 1.3 million Palestinian citizens living in Israel by 2001 were internally displaced persons. Treated by the Jewish state as second–class citizens, the Palestinians lacked full participatory rights in the political structures of Israel and were subject to discrimination in employment, housing, and other sectors of their daily lives.

Although the Jewish people, too, had been denied a homeland for centuries following their expulsion from the heart of the Middle East, the creation of the State of Israel after World War II without the simultaneous creation of a State of Palestine was viewed by many—both Palestinians and non–Palestinians—as a disastrous course of action. While in 1947 the Palestinians had the right to accept a separate state for themselves, based on UN Resolution 181, they rejected this offer, hoping to secure a more favorable solution. For the next fifty–plus years, the Middle East would be embroiled in religious and ethnic conflict, heating up at times into active wars or simmering at a lower but still deadly temperature. Since the 1980s low–intensity warfare taking the form of the *Intifadah* waged mostly by Palestinian boys and youths and more virulent attacks on Israel by extremist groups such as Hamas, coupled with the intense aggression of the Israeli military, have produced a seething, seemingly never–ending conflict that has been extremely difficult to contain, let alone resolve.

At the turn of the millennium the continuous actions of extremist Jewish settlers intent on informally expanding the State of Israel by building Jewish homes on Palestinian territory (despite international prohibitions against such further encroachments on Palestinian land) have provoked additional violence on both sides and further complicated attempts to gradually cede territory to the Palestinians so they, too, may have their own state. Weaknesses in the creation and performance of the self–governing Palestinian Authority, the reluctance of Israel to fully withdraw from the Palestinian West Bank and Gaza Strip, the slow pace of diplomatic negotiations, and the lack of sufficient international pressure on both Israel and the Palestinian Authority to end the cycle of violence and establish greater security in the region have made it unlikely that full peace will be realized in this troubled region anytime soon.

International agreements and peacemaking efforts notwithstanding, the Palestinian–Israeli conflict over the right to establish a secure Israeli state, the right of Palestinians to return to the land of their or their ancestors' birth and to claim their own state, and the right for both Jews and Arabs, let alone Christians, to live in and govern Jerusalem, regarded as an especially holy city by Muslims, Jews, and Christians alike, has proven to be one of the thorniest international conflicts in modern history. Key problems associated with this entangled conflict have revolved around the inconsistent recognition of Palestinians and Jews as distinct nations deserving full territorial and political rights, including control of a state. When stateless peoples like the Palestinians and (formerly)

the Jews contest claims over the same piece of territory, arguing from historical memory that each merits a stake in the territorial pie, if not the whole pie, then a peaceable, just outcome will be very difficult to achieve. Exemplifying the problems inherent in conflicting claims to national territory and the right to a sovereign state, the Palestinian–Israeli conflict will not be easily resolved in the near future, despite the number of scholars who have theorized about national identity–building and the construction of the nation.

Ghana

Kwame Nkrumah (1909–1972), known by many as the "Father of African Nationalism," became the first president of the independent West African nation of Ghana in 1960. He shared his esteemed title with the American black socialist leader Marcus Garvey, who reportedly inspired much of Nkrumah's thinking on the need for black–led independence movements in Africa and the African diaspora. Nkrumah wished to see the Gold Coast (as Ghana was called while governed by the British) independent and ruled by Africans themselves. Ghana achieved internal self–rule in 1951 and in March 1957, became the first sub–Saharan African state to step out from under the yoke of European imperialism. (On December 24, 1951, Libya became the first North African state to attain independence—and like Ghana, from British rule.)

Nkrumah's early life Born in 1929 among the Akan people in the village of Nkroful in Nzimaland, the far southwestern area of the Gold Coast, Kwame Nkrumah trained for his first career as a teacher at the Prince of Wales College in Achimoto, just north of Accra. Inspired by the school's Vice Principal, Dr. Kwagyir Aggrey, who had trained in America as an educator, Nkrumah grew convinced that the best means to improve the conditions of Africans' lives was through education. Working to inspire his own students to develop their academic potential, Nkrumah began a number of literary clubs and academic societies for his students and became increasingly interested in discussing the political affairs of Africans with his colleagues at the Catholic school at Axim in Nzemaland, where he served as headmaster. The failure of indigenous Africans in the Gold Coast in 1934 to successfully oppose a British Sedition Bill aimed at stopping the anti–colonial press, coupled with the growing resistance of African cocoa farmers to British exploitation of their industry, led Nkrumah to seek training in the disciplines that would allow him to contribute to the Gold Coast's liberation campaign.

Kwame Nkrumah.

Moving to the United States in 1935, Nkrumah earned a Bachelor of Science degree in economics and sociology from Lincoln University in Philadelphia in 1939 and a Bachelor of Theology degree from Lincoln Theological Seminary in 1942. He also received a Master of Science degree in education plus a Master of Philosophy degree in 1945 from the University of Pennsylvania, where he completed significant work toward a doctorate in philosophy. Later in 1945, Nkrumah moved to London, where he soon began participating in twice–weekly discussion sessions at the home of Dr. Hastings Kamuzu Banda, an African also educated in America. Among the other attendees at these sessions were a raft of future African leaders, including Jomo Kenyatta (c. 1894–1978), Julius Nyerere (1922–1999), Kojo Botsio, and Harry Nkumbula. In London, Nkrumah also attended lectures at the London School of Economics and Political Science on politics and socialism, helped organize the West African national Secretariat, and began the Pan–African Movement, serving as Joint Secretary to the Fifth Pan–African Congress in Manchester, England, in late 1945. Building relationships with members of the British Parliament who were sympathetic to the cause of African liberationists and to socialism, Nkrumah laid the groundwork for his future political career, contributing articles to periodicals advocating independence for African colonies and collaborating with George Padmore, a West Indian socialist writer and activist who also opposed colonial rule.

Formation of Ghana   By the late 1940s Nkrumah and his compatriots were ready to challenge British control of the Gold Coast, a country rich in minerals and cocoa farms and ripe for revolution. Nkrumah believed, however, that an effective revolution could be waged only if the economic needs of the citizens of Ghana were appropriately addressed. His campaign to liberate the Gold Coast from British rule thus included advocating a form of socialist governance, a policy of "African Socialism," whereby the state would own key industries and develop the national infrastructure along with social welfare programs to serve the needs of ordinary people. Nkrumah returned to his homeland in 1949 and founded the Convention People's Party (CPP) with the goal of achieving immediate national independence. He was imprisoned for several months in 1950, having encouraged his fellow countrymen to participate in illegal strikes. After the Gold Coast was granted internal self–rule in 1951, Nkrumah served as prime minister from 1952 to 1957. When Ghana became a fully independent country in 1957, Nkrumah continued to serve as prime minister until 1960, when he became the country's first president.

Although Nkrumah was initially welcomed as Ghana's first president after independence, mismanagement and corruption under his rule led eventually to a tightening of power by Nkrumah and to very unwelcome restrictions on freedom of expression and freedom of association within the country. Courting support from the Soviet Union, Nkrumah took Ghana in increasingly socialist and authoritarian directions. In 1964 Nkrumah made Ghana a one–party state, led by his own CPP. His increasingly dictatorial style coupled with his failure to deliver on the economic and social benefits he had promised Ghanaians led to Nkrumah's loss of power in a bloodless coup while he was visiting China in 1966. Nkrumah returned to West Africa to live in exile in Guinea until his death in 1972, serving as a co–head of state for Ghana during that time. One year after his death, Nkrumah's reputation as one of the great political leaders of the period of African independence was restored.

Nkrumah believed that only a pan–African union of solidarity could ensure Africans true financial, social, and political independence and security. For this reason, Nkrumah led the way for the formation of the Organization of African Unity (OAU) in 1963, founded in Addis Ababa, Ethiopia after a conference involving thirteen African states and nineteen African colonies soon to become independent. Greatly respected and admired by many of his fellow Ghanaians and by countless other Africans, Nkrumah sought to achieve economic self–sufficiency for the newly independent African nation–states through cooperative understanding and the creation of a genuine brotherhood of nations across Africa. Although his dream to unite Africans through a pan–African union was not realized in his day, Nkrumah's contributions to the liberation movements that transformed Africa in the wake of World War II were arguably unparalleled. The twenty–first century may yet see a rejuvenation of interest in the pan–Africanism Nkrumah envisioned as common solutions are sought for such problems as interethnic violence, poverty, HIV/AIDS and other epidemics, and the lack of adequate infrastructure marking the sub–Saharan region. A newer, more–inclusive concept of nationhood encompassing the wide range of ethnic communities living in African states—inspired by Nkrumah's past efforts and achievements and by the more–recent accomplishments of his fellow Ghanaian, UN Secretary–General Kofi Annan—may in fact be part of the solution to the challenges facing this important region of the world.

ANALYSIS AND CRITICAL RESPONSE

Despite the reticence of some theorists to admit that nationalism is an appropriate subject for theoretical study, plenty of evidence exists—and scholarly arguments as well—that indicate national identity, nation–building, and nationalism are all suitable topics for theoretical analysis. Yael Tamir argued in his article, "Theoretical Difficulties in the Study of Nationalism," that theories of nationalism are necessary for several reasons. In order for a respectful discourse to take place on nationalism and national movements and in order for the members of different nations to be able to appreciate and respect the differences in their concepts of national identity, the world needs theories of nationalism. This becomes especially evident when we examine some of the challenges presented by nationalism and the adherents of particular conceptualizations of what it means to be a nation.

As noted in the *Macmillan Encyclopedia 2001*, "While it was hoped that nationalism would make for peace, in practice it has often resulted in xenophobia, rivalry, oppression of ethnic minorities, and war." Unfortunately, nationalism in both theory and action has produced both negative as well as positive conceptualizations and realities for countless individuals and groups throughout the world. In part, this is due to the nature of nationalist claims, which tend to be exclusionary. Additionally, early nationalist theories may have failed to account for or to predict the rise in ultra–nationalist movements and violent sentiments that would appear on the world scene as national fervor developed to a heightened pitch or overzealous or misguided political leaders took the stage to direct domestic and international affairs in ways Herder, Fichte, and Renan perhaps never anticipated.

Shortcomings

Some scholars see the tendency to divide theories of nationalism into "ethnic" versus "civic" categories as a serious problem, claiming that this dichotomous depiction is inaccurate and lacks thoroughness. Others note that in discussing the "civic" nature of certain theories of nationalism, "civic" has erroneously been seen as synonymous with "liberal democratic." While some scholars have argued that Hitler's racist campaign to rebuild German national identity cannot properly be labeled "nationalist" because of Hitler's sharp departure from democratic values, others point out that Hitler nonetheless did construct a view of national identity around a particular conception of nationhood—however distasteful and deadly that conception proved to be. Not all shared political values reflect liberal democratic notions.

Additionally, nationalism in many ways presumes certain conditions that perhaps no longer fit the reality of social and political life in the late–twentieth and early–twenty–first centuries, both in the developed world and in economically developing regions. For example, questions concerning the possible irrelevance, inapplicability, or imperfect agreement of nationalism to multicultural societies are being considered by a number of theorists in the new millennium. Third–World scholars, too, have found fault with nationalist theories' tendency to overemphasize the perspective of Western scholars and to downplay the differences in national development that have occurred in developing regions. The Indian concept of nation has been attuned to the importance of both spiritual and material aspects, according to Partha Chatterjee and a concept of Indian cultural identity allegedly developed before Indians attempted to cast off English dominance and political control. However, many Western scholars have tended to view liberation movements in the developing world and the simultaneous development of national identities among colonized peoples purely as reactions to imperial control, not as independently constructed movements.

Several scholars also have remarked upon the somewhat questionable relevance of many nationalist theories in the late twentieth and early twenty–first centuries to the needs and interests of indigenous and stateless nations. Seeking to broaden definitions of the nation and interpretations of national movements and claims, these scholars have remarked on the tendency of many theorists of nationalism to focus on the typical course of development followed by Western nations, while ignoring the differential paths of Fourth–World and stateless nations. To construct their own national identities and negotiate relationships with those who colonized them and set their territorial boundaries, generally without their consent, indigenous and developing nations deserve appropriate theoretical analyses that illuminate the specific conditions of their existence and development and the alternative notions of national identity that distinguish them from the dominant cultural majority.

Gender Politics

Gender politics and their relation to national identity–building and nationalist movements also has been a neglected area of scholarship in this field. Although concepts of the nation have typically stemmed from notions of a *patrie* (fatherland) and its associated heritage, theorists of nationalism generally have failed to adequately question whether the conceptualization of a nation has a particularly male thrust. Few theorists have taken up the question of whether and how gender relations come into play in the creation of national identities and the waging of nationalist campaigns. Whereas women and men have both played key roles in pursuing the course of their nations' development throughout the world, assuming indirect as well as direct roles in forging national identities and laying claims to state power, very few twentieth century writers in the field of nationalism have addressed how gender relates to nationalism.

As Ernest Renan remarked toward the close of his 1882 lecture at the Sorbonne, "Man is a slave neither of his race nor his language, nor of his religion, nor of the course of rivers nor of the direction taken by mountain chains. A large aggregate of men, healthy in mind and warm of heart, creates the kind of moral conscience which we call a nation." Presumably, Renan also meant to include women in this discussion, although he neglected to say this directly. The implication is that men rather than women have built nations—a rather indefensible claim, considering the number of women over the centuries who have sacrificed sons, husbands, brothers, and friends to the violence involved in most nation–building efforts and the number of women who themselves have assumed key roles as political activists, social reformers, and educators of the members of new nations.

TOPICS FOR FURTHER STUDY

- What is the relationship between ethnic identity and nationalism?

- According to international law, to what extent are indigenous minorities, immigrants, and national minority groups permitted to rightfully advance claims of self–determination? Do some groups deserve their own territorial state more than others? Would the world be a more peaceful place if every nationalist movement were granted its own territorial space and the possibility of self–governance?

- To what extent did the American reaction to the September 11, 2001, terrorist attacks on the World Trade Center and the Pentagon represent ultranationalist fervor stemming from what Michael Billig terms "banal nationalism"?

BIBLIOGRAPHY

Sources

Africa News Service. "Sudan Plans to Build Three New Hydroelectric Dams across the Nile." September 8, 1998. News article published initially in Addis Tribune, September 4, 1998. Available at http://www.vitrade.com/sudan_risk/Egypt/980908_3_hydroelectric_dams_built.htm, December 17, 2001.

Agyeman, Opoku. *Nkrumah's Ghana and East Africa: Pan–Africanism and African Interstate Relations*. London: Associated University Presses, Inc., 1992.

Ataturk.com. "Mustafa Kemal Atatürk, 1881–1938." Accessed 11/15/01 at http://www.ataturk.com/index2.html.

Barnard, F.M. *Herder's Social and Political Thought: From Enlightenment to Nationalism*. Oxford: Clarendon Press, 1965.

BBC News. "The Balfour Declaration." BBC News, November 1, 2001. Available at http://news.bbc.co.uk/hi/english/uk/newsid_1632000/1632259.stm, December 17, 2001.

BBC News. "Peace greats urge Suu Kyi release." BBC News, December 8, 2001. Available at http://news.bbc.co.uk/hi/english/world/asia–pacific/newsid_1699000/1699384.stm, December 9, 2001.

Breuilly, John. *Nationalism and the State*, 2nd ed. Chicago: University of Chicago Press, copyright 1982, 1985, 1993; published by University of Chicago Press in 1994.

Brody, Donal. "Kwame Nkrumah The Early Years 1909–1947." Great EpicsTM Newsletter, Vol. 1 No. 7, October 1997. Great Epics Books, 2001. Available at http://www.greatepicbooks.com/epics/october97.html, December 4, 2001.

Brown, David. *Contemporary Nationalism: Civic, ethnocultural and multicultural politics*. London: Routledge, 2000.

Callison, James P. and University of Oklahoma Law Center. "The Iroquois Constitution." Available at http://www.law.ou.edu/hist/iroquois.html, December 2, 2001.

Chen, David W. and Charlie LeDuff. "Bad Blood in Battle Over Casinos; Issue Divides Tribes and Families as Expansion Looms." *The New York Times,* October 28, 2001.

dassk.com. "Welcome to Daw Aung San Suu Kyi's pages." Available at http://www.dassk.com/dawsuu.htm, November 15, 2001.

ebooks.whsmithonline.co.uk. "Nkrumah, Kwame (1909–1972)." From *The Hutchinson Family Encyclopedia.* Helicon Publishing Ltd, 2000. Available at http://ebooks.whsmithonline.co.uk/ENCYCLOPEDIA/53/M0002453.htm, December 4, 2001.

Eley, Geoff and Ronald Grigor Suny, eds. *Becoming National: A Reader.* New York: Oxford University Press, 1996.

Gates, Henry Louis, Jr. "Into Africa: Black Kingdoms of the Nile." Available at http://www.bbc.co.uk/history/africa/africa3.shtml, December 17, 2001.

Gellner, Ernest. *Nationalism.* New York: New York University Press, 1997.

George–Kanentiio, Doug. "Iroquois at the UN." (Originally published in *Akwesasne Notes New Series,* Fall 1995, Vol. 1 Nos. 3–4.) Available at http://www.ratical.org/many_worlds/6Nations/IroquoisAtUN.html, November 15, 2001.

Gittings, Bruce M. "The Declaration of Arbroath." Available at http://www.geo.ed.ac.uk/home/scotland/arbroath.html, December 17, 2001.

Greenfeld, Liah. "Is Nationalism Legitimate? A Sociological Perspective on a Philosophical Question." In *Rethinking Nationalism,* Canadian Journal of Philosophy Supplementary Vol. 22, eds. Jocelyne Couture, Kai Nielsen, and Michel Seymour (Calgary, Alberta, Canada: Canadian Journal of Philosophy, copyright 1996; first published 1998).

Hamideh, Abbas on behalf of Al–Awda/Palestine Right To Return Coalition. "Palestinian refugees' right to return should be acknowledged by Israel." OP–ED article. *The Journal News* (Westchester County, NY), December 10, 2001.

Haudenosaunee Confederacy. Available at http://www.snenatrons.org.

Ivison, Duncan, Paul Patton and Will Sanders, eds. *Political Theory and the Rights of Indigenous Peoples.* Cambridge: Cambridge University Press, 2000.

Jagan, Larry. "Signs of hope for Aung San Suu Kyi." BBC News, December 9, 2001. Available at http://news.bbc.co.uk/hi/english/world/asia–pacific/newsid_1699000/1699780.stm.

Jocelyne Couture, Kai Nielsen, and Michel Seymour, eds. *Rethinking Nationalism.* Canadian Journal of Philosophy Supplementary Vol. 22. Calgary, Alberta, Canada: Canadian Journal of Philosophy, copyright 1996, first published 1998.

Johansen, Bruce Elliott and Barbara Alice Mann, eds. *Encyclopedia of the Haudenosaunee (Iroquois Confederacy).* Westport, CT: Greenwood Press, 2000.

Kandogan, Eser. "Mustafa Kemal Atatürk." Available at http://www.cs.umd.edu/users/kandogan/FTA/Ataturk/ataturk.html, November 15, 2001.

Kelsey Museum of Archaeology, University of Michigan at Ann Arbor. "The Building of the First Aswan Dam and the Inundation of Lower Nubia: Images from the Collections of the Kelsey Museum." Available at http://www.umich.edu/kelseydb/Exhibits/AncientNubia/PhotoIntro.html, December 10, 2001.

Kelsey Museum of Archaeology, University of Michigan at Ann Arbor. "Ancient Nubia: Egypt's Rival in Africa." Press Release. Available at http://www.umich.edu/kelseydb/Exhibits/AncientNubia/AncientNubiaPressRelease.html, December 10, 2001.

Kyi, Aung San Suu, ed. and with an introduction by Michael Aris, foreword by V. Havel. *Freedom from Fear and Other Writings.* New York: Penguin Books, 1991.

Mabry, Marcus, Michael Meyer, Lara Santoro, Tom Masland, and Joe Cochrane. "The Promise, the Peril: Special Report." In *Newsweek,* December 17, 2001.

McClintock, Anne. "'No Longer in a Future Heaven': Nationalism, Gender, and Race." In *Becoming National: A Reader,* eds. Geoff Eley and Ronald Grigor Suny (New York: Oxford University Press, 1996).

Macmillan Encyclopedia 2001. London: Market House Books Ltd, 2000.

Ministry of Foreign Affairs, Government of Israel. "The Mandate for Palestine: July 24, 1922." Available at http://www.mfa.gov.il/mfa/go.asp?MFAH00pr0, December 17, 2001.

Oneida Nation. Available at http://www.oneidasfordemocracy.org.

Oxford English Reference Dictionary, The. Oxford: Oxford University Press, 1996.

Poole, Ross. "National Identity, Multiculturalism, and Aboriginal Rights: An Australian Perspective." In *Rethinking Nationalism,* Canadian Journal of Philosophy Supplementary Vol. 22, eds. Jocelyne Couture, Kai Nielsen, and Michel Seymour (Calgary, Alberta, Canada: Canadian Journal of Philosophy, copyright 1996; first published 1998).

Prager, Carol A. L. "Barbarous Nationalism and the Liberal International Order: Reflections on the 'Is,' the 'Ought,' and the 'Can.'" In *Rethinking Nationalism,* Canadian Journal of Philosophy Supplementary Vol. 22, eds. Jocelyne Couture, Kai Nielsen, and Michel Seymour (Calgary, Alberta, Canada: Canadian Journal of Philosophy, copyright 1996; first published 1998).

Renan, Ernest. "What Is a Nation?" In *Becoming National: A Reader,* eds. Geoff Eley and Ronald Grigor Suny (New York: Oxford University Press, 1996).

Rosenberg, Dan. "Hamza El Din." Available at http://www.afropop.org/explore/artist_info/ID/336/Hamza%20El%20Din/, December 10, 2001.

Seymour, Michel with Jocelyne Couture and Kai Nielsen. "Introduction: Questioning the Ethnic/Civic Dichotomy." In *Rethinking Nationalism,* Canadian Journal of Philosophy Supplementary Vol. 22, eds. Jocelyne Couture, Kai Nielsen, and Michel Seymour (Calgary, Alberta, Canada: Canadian Journal of Philosophy, copyright 1996; first published 1998).

Shenandoah, Audrey. Haudenosaunee Delegation at the United Nations, Millennium World Peace Summit (August 28–30, 2000), Address by Audrey Shenandoah, Clan Mother, Onondaga Nation. Available at http://www.peace4turtleisland.org/pages/haudenosauneedelegation2000.htm, November 15, 2001.

Simpson, Audra. "Paths Toward a Mohawk Nation: Narratives of Citizenship and Nationhood in Kahnawake." In *Political Theory and the Rights of Indigenous Peoples*, eds. Duncan Ivison, Paul Patton, and Will Sanders. Cambridge: Cambridge University Press, 2000.

Smith, Anthony D. "The Origins of Nations." In *Becoming National: A Reader*, eds. Geoff Eley and Ronald Grigor Suny (New York: Oxford University Press, 1996).

Tamir, Yael. "Theoretical Difficulties in the Study of Nationalism." In *Rethinking Nationalism*, Canadian Journal of Philosophy Supplementary Vol. 22, eds. Jocelyne Couture, Kai Nielsen, and Michel Seymour (Calgary, Alberta, Canada: Canadian Journal of Philosophy, copyright 1996; first published 1998).

Williams, Kristen P. *Despite Nationalist Conflicts: Theory and Practice of Maintaining World Peace*. Westport, CT: Praeger Publishers, 2001.

Wilson, Woodrow. "Fourteen Points" speech before the Joint Session of the U.S. Congress, January 8, 1918. Available at http://www.lib.byu.edu/rdh/wwi/1918/14points.html, December 10, 2001.

www.ratical.org. "The Six Nations: Oldest Living Participatory Democracy on Earth." Available at http://www.ratical.org/many_worlds/6Nations/index.html, November 15, 2001.

Yahoo.com. "Hamza El Din–Biography." Available at http://musicfinder.yahoo.com/, December 17, 2001.

Zuelow, Eric G.E. E–mail conversations with Barbara Lakeberg Dridi, October—December 2001.

Zuelow, Eric G.E. "The Nationalism Project." Available at http://www.nationalismproject.org/, October 28, 2001.

Further Readings

BBC World Service. "The Nation State." Available at http://www.bbc.co.uk/worldservice/africa/features/storyofafrica/14chapters4.shtml. Focusing on the development of independent nation–states in Africa after World War II, this site identifies some of the key African leaders of the anti–colonial liberation movements and includes audio clips of historic speeches.

Braveheart This film depicts the development of Scottish identity and of nationalism among the Scots in the early 1300s, including the War of Independence from England and the Scottish Declaration of Arbroath of 1320.

Encyclopedia of Nationalism, Volumes 1 and 2. Editor–in–Chief, Alexander Motyl. San Diego, CA: Academic Press, 2000. This encyclopedia contains a range of theoretical articles and case studies pertaining to nationalism, covering all regions of the globe.

Kanatiiosh. "Welcome to Peace 4 Turtle Island." Copyright 2001. Available at http://www.peace4turtleisland.org/. Excellent collection of pages related to *Haudenosaunee* (*Iroquois* Confederacy) contemporary affairs and history, including links to books about the *Haudenosaunee*.

Zuelow, Eric G.E. "The Nationalism Project." Available at http://www.nationalismproject.org/. This site contains a wealth of resources and information related to the theoretical and practical study of nationalism.

SEE ALSO

Federalism, Imperialism

Pacifism

OVERVIEW

Although the goal of almost every political system or theory is peace, many thinkers and politicians regard pacifism as an unrealistic strategy for achieving that end. International peace, they argue, can only be attained by a combination of hard–headed diplomacy and military preparedness. Domestic peace, they claim, will only be achieved with a strong police force and a tough court system. Pacifism, say many thinkers, belongs not in the domain of politics but in the realm of religious ideology. At best, pacifists are seen as hopeless idealists or as otherworldly dreamers. Thus, pacifism is recognized in standard political philosophy by its rejection.

Very often, pacifism is equated with passiveness, even though there is no linguistic link between the two words. Therefore, the application of pacifism, or anything approaching pacifism, is regarded as disastrous. Mention the word "pacifism" and Neville Chamberlain's (1869–1940) failed effort to appease Adolf Hitler (1889–1945) at Munich is recalled and condemned as an example of what happens when real world leaders move too far in the direction of pacifism. Ironically, even some pacifists agree that pacifism has little practical value. They present the concept as a religious principle or a political ideal to be followed regardless of practical consequences.

Many modern–day pacifists see the world quite differently. They insist that peace, stability, and justice can only be attained by linking means and ends.

WHO CONTROLS GOVERNMENT? Officials supported by the people

HOW IS GOVERNMENT PUT INTO POWER? Peaceful removal of unjust regime

WHAT ROLES DO THE PEOPLE HAVE? Protest peacefully unjust laws or actions

WHO CONTROLS PRODUCTION OF GOODS? The people

WHO CONTROLS DISTRIBUTION OF GOODS? The people

MAJOR FIGURES Mohandas Gandhi; Martin Luther King Jr.

HISTORICAL EXAMPLE U.S. civil rights movement in 1960s

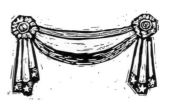

CHRONOLOGY

700-600 B.C.: Isaiah begins to envision a kingdom based not on military might but on peace and humility.

c. 563-483 B.C.: Siddhartha, who became known as the Buddha, is said to have discovered the path to Truth.

c. 30 A.D.: Jesus of Nazareth is executed by the Romans.

395: Augustine is made Bishop of Hippo.

1647: George Fox begins the Society of Friends or Quakers.

1828: Leo Tolstoy develops a strong pacifistic critique of the evils of oppressive power and violence.

1948: Mohandas Gandhi is assassinated.

1950s: Martin Luther King, Jr. uses the principles of pacifism to gain civil rights for African Americans.

1960s: Gene Sharp develops the model of Civilian Based Defense.

1968: Martin Luther King, Jr. is assassinated.

1994: Aung San Su Kyi is placed under house arrest for using nonviolent Buddhist principles to challenge the non–democratic government of Burma.

1994: The new South African constitution contains provisions for a Truth and Reconciliation Commission.

Thus, the way to achieve peace is to do peace. Pacifism holds that war and violence are circuitous paths to peace at best and dead ends at worst. Today, after a century that witnessed trench warfare, the atomic bomb, the Holocaust, and genocide, there is a renewed willingness to consider the merits of pacifism as a practical political theory with applications for the real world. Pacifism, its supporters content, can combine both peace and power. Pacifists note that some of the great political gains of the twentieth century resulted from nonviolence. The independence of India, the civil rights victories in America, and the liberation of Eastern Europe from the Soviet Union came through nonviolent means. The leaders of those movements used nonviolent techniques to exert great pressure on unjust political and social systems. For those leaders and their followers, nonviolence was a strategy for bringing about change that in former times would have been sought through violent revolution.

While at the international level, most people still consider force to be the most reliable means of protecting national interests and preserving the peace, pacifist theorists have started to offer credible alternatives. Nuclear pacifism, international law, and civilian–based defense are three ideas that reject conventional strategies for maintaining order at the global level. Nonviolent methods of national defense, say pacifists, save lives, are more democratic, cost less, may work better, and are environmentally friendly. When looking at ways of keeping order within a nation, pacifists suggest new and nonviolent ways of dealing with criminals, handling ethnic disputes, and managing community conflict. Not only do pacifists recommend their nonviolent strategies as cheaper and less painful, they also argue that nonviolence can be more effective.

HISTORY

Pacifism as a theory began with religious rather than with explicitly political thinkers. In India, Jainism (sixth century B.C.) and Buddhism (third century B.C.) stressed strict self–mortification and purification that rejected the passions that led one away from God, Truth, or Enlightenment. Of all the human passions, violence was regarded as the most dangerous. The eighth–century B.C. prophets of Ancient Israel and, later, Jesus in the first century, proclaimed a pacifism rooted in the idea that all people are children of one God, in the concept of divine mercy, and in the belief that love could transform enemies. Later, in the seventh century, the prophet Mohammed (570–632) preached a religion that prohibited violence and exploitation within the community of faith (Islam) and against taking innocent lives in any situation.

Although the first Christians were probably non–violent, by 180 A.D. a few Christians served in the Roman army. With the conversion of Emperor Constantine I (288–337) to Christianity in 312 A.D., pacifism declined in importance. In fact, once Christians were in the majority and Christianity became the official state religion, Christians came to believe that they had a duty to defend both the faith and the empire with force. Augustine, Bishop of Hippo

(354–430), advocated the use of force against the heretical Donatists. On a philosophical level, in his book *The City of God,* Augustine argued that inner motives were more important than external behavior. In his view, Christians could wield the sword so long as their hearts were fixed on God's Kingdom rather than on self–promotion and self–protection.

Pacifism in the Medieval World

In the medieval world, the ideal of pacifism was all but abandoned by Christians and Muslims. Inquisitions, crusades, and jihads were sanctioned as examples of obedience to God. The brave knight or the warrior–martyr were honored as God's most obedient servants. Pacifism continued to exist as an ideal, but only in marginalized form. Monks, holy men, and priests might be expected to live a life of pacifism, but anyone holding a position of responsibility within the state was expected to exercise force against heretics, ordinary criminals, and external enemies. When, in the late Middle Ages and early part of the Reformation, radical Christians such as the Waldensians or Anabaptists called on Christians to reject any type of violence, they were hunted down, tortured, and executed. Their pacifism was regarded as a grave danger to a society that did not distinguish between loyalty to the church and obedience to the state. In the seventeenth century, when followers of George Fox (1624–1691), founder of the Society of Friends, called on the faithful to reject the use of violence, they were reviled and persecuted.

The early modern era continued to reject the concept of pacifism. In the turbulent years marked by religious wars and succession struggles, pacifism seemed wildly irrelevant, even dangerous and immoral. As authoritarian rulers in Europe brought order and built nations, military might was regarded as a fundamental element of every successful state. When authoritarianism gave way to democracy at the end of the 1700s, violent revolution was seen as the liberating tool of the masses.

Events in the world of politics were paralleled by developments in the intellectual world. Generally, pacifistic ideas were not considered seriously by political thinkers. They regarded pacifism as an unrealistic concept that had little application in the real world. The best way to prevent violence, they argued, was to exercise violence against those who posed a threat. Nevertheless, even within the ancient world, there were some restrictions on violence. Babylonian, Hebraic, and Roman law outlined guidelines that required fair treatment of lawbreakers and placed limits on the conduct of warfare. Concepts such as "an eye for an eye" prevented violence from spinning into an escalating cycle of vengeance and retaliation. Much of this thinking about limits was codified in the "Just War Theory" supported by the Church. Underpinning these laws and guidelines was the common sense concept of fairness and the realization that violence must be monopolized by the state if it was to be contained within manageable proportions. In practice, that meant that revenge and unlimited retaliation were controlled by placing them in the hands of recognized governments exercising force in a dispassionate and predictable manner. In practice, that also meant that revolution against a government, however unjust, was generally not sanctioned.

Pacifism into the Twentieth Century

With the Enlightenment and the subsequent emergence of nineteenth–century liberalism, political idealists began contemplating a world in which human beings would rise above the barbaric and outmoded practices of warfare. The future, they believed, belonged to wise pacifists. Heartened by the great progress they observed in the scientific and technical worlds, these thinkers assumed that improvements in the political and moral realms were equally possible. In their view, advancements in the area of international law and international organizations would replace the need to resolve conflicts with violence. In spite of powerful contrary evidence such as the American Civil War, colonialism, and World War I, this hope was sustained. Optimism about the ability to end war and resolve conflict peacefully reached a high point in the 1920s. Treaties to limit or ban the use of weapons and the founding of the League of Nations suggested that humans could exchange the brutality of armed combat for the civilized procedures of the courtroom and international government. The dream of a world federation uniting all nations and people of the world did not seem like an unrealistic vision. Nevertheless, the prospects that pacifism would become an acceptable political ideology vanished as liberalism crumbled under the onslaught of twentieth–century human tragedy.

The 1920s ended with a debilitating global recession that called into question the ability of humans to manage the economy. Furthermore, racism and imperialism, previously regarded as positive or, at least, acceptable values, began to be regarded as evil and dysfunctional. Italian dictator Benito Mussolini's (1883–1945) invasion of Ethiopia, Japan's advances into Manchuria and southeast Asia, Hitler's incursion into Poland, the Holocaust, the Allied forces' carpet bombing of German cities, and the American use of the atomic bomb all shattered the last vestiges of liberal pacifism. On the other side of the ideological

Anti-war protesters holding a peaceful demonstration against the Vietnam War at United Nations Plaza.
(AP/Wide World Photos)

spectrum, evidence from the Soviet Union suggested that a communist revolution to create a worker's utopia had degenerated into a police state. Clearly, education, idealism, discussion, and goodwill would not be enough to solve the deep–seated social, economic, and political problems of the world. In the darkest days of World War II, some began to doubt that the humane ideals of liberalism and democracy were robust enough to counter the militaristic machinations of nazism, fascism, and bolshevism.

By the mid–1930s, leading Western pacifists were abandoning their earlier optimism. The American Reinhold Niebuhr (1892–1971), formerly a prominent pacifist, denounced political pacifism as dangerous and religious pacifism as morally irresponsible and spiritually self–righteous. The superlative evils of totalitarianism could only be countered with the lesser evil of force being exercised by nations and individuals who reluctantly but courageously recognized their obligation to challenge tyranny.

Nevertheless, by the time the twentieth century drew to a close, it was evident that pacifism had made great progress. In Asia, Mohandas K. Gandhi (1869–1948) had employed nonviolence to gain independence for India in 1947. Then, in the 1950s and 1960s, Martin Luther King, Jr. (1929–1968), used

nonviolent methods to make significant inroads into racial segregation in the United States. In part, King succeeded because "White America" feared King's more radical counterparts such as militant black leader Malcolm X (1925–1965). However, it is clear that King's nonviolence, which he credited to Gandhi and to Jesus, was the key factor in transforming race relations in America. By 1960, most of the African continent had broken loose from European colonialism. The leading figure in this movement, Kwame Nkrumah (1909–1972) of Ghana, was a firm believer in Gandhi's technique of nonviolence. Motivated by practical political considerations, Nkrumah recognized that nonviolent protest was more effective against the colonial masters than violent confrontation. While violent protests would be put down quickly, nonviolent action would be much more difficult to deal with because of political and moral constraints on the British.

The Vietnam War

Nonviolent protest was also used in Europe and North America to challenge and change the prevailing political agenda. In the United States, nonviolent activists forced the Lyndon Johnson (1908–1973) and Richard Nixon (1913–1994) administrations to end the Vietnam War. The activists regarded the war as an extension of French colonial activities in Southeast Asia. While some protesters such as Daniel (1921–) and Philip (1923–) Berrigan, both Catholic priests, were motivated by religious conviction, others such as Students for a Democratic Society (SDS) operated on the basis of moral or political belief. Nonviolent protests included refusing to register for the draft, holding sit–ins and teach–ins on university campuses, fleeing the country to take refuge in Canada, withholding taxes designated for military operations, breaking into draft board offices, and entering military sites to attack weapons of mass destruction in a symbolic fashion. The Berrigan brothers were at the forefront of those resorting to dramatic acts of prophetic protest and civil disobedience against a political system they considered anti–human. In Vietnam itself, devout Buddhist pacifists such as Thich Nhat Hanh worked to alleviate the suffering of victims on both sides of the conflict. Many Buddhists were killed by both the communists and anti–communists who wanted people to take sides instead of identifying with the displaced and dying of both political camps.

Following the Vietnam War, pacifist activists continued their protests while shifting their focus. Now, they challenged the enormous build–up of nuclear weapons in the world. Groups such as Greenpeace called attention to environmental degradation, which they labeled "ecocide." Pacifists criticized the way powerful northern hemisphere nations oppressed people of the third world. Pacifists also opposed the use of the death penalty in countries such as the United States. Often they challenged laws and customs limiting the rights and privileges of minorities, women, and homosexuals. Paradoxically, these same activists generally did not oppose abortion, saying that support for the rights of women to control their own bodies took precedence over the very weak rights of the unborn. Ironically, the strongest opponents of abortion were often vigorous supporters of a strong national defense and of the death penalty.

The Counterculture

While a number of pacifists were committed to a counterculture vision and to counterculture protests, others operated within mainstream religious or political institutions. In Europe, the Green Party, with a pacifistic agenda that included a call for social justice, the rejection of nuclear weapons, and respect for the environment, was able to gain enough support to become a serious opposition group. In the United States, churches and civic groups were successful in getting some courts to incorporate alternative approaches to civil and criminal justice and in pressing Congress and the Executive to give more attention to the environ-

ment, human rights, third world development, and nuclear issues. In response to pacifistic concerns, both the State Department and the Defense Department attempted to explain military operations such as the invasions of Granada, Panama, and Kuwait in "Just War" terms. In Japan, strong pacifist sentiments limited the size, scope, and strategies of the Japanese military and resisted deploying or storing nuclear weapons on Japanese soil.

Pacifism and the Fall of Communism

In the 1980s, the political and military hold of the Soviet Union crumbled. Many military strategists insist that the Soviet Union fell because it was unable to withstand the relentless military competition from the West. But, other analysts credit the peaceful protests of the Eastern Europeans for the demise of the Soviet Empire. Starting with Polish labor leader Lech Walensa's (1943–) nonviolent Solidarity Movement, Eastern Europeans threw off Soviet rule. While the Soviets would have responded with crushing force to any violent uprising, they were less certain about how to deal with peaceful citizen protests. In the end, the Soviet Empire was defeated, not by the heavy long–range missiles of the United States, but by the millions of ordinary citizens who engaged in nonviolent protest against their Communist governments. Even in China, where an authoritarian remained in power at the end of the twentieth century, the greatest challenge to the regime came from a peaceful protest at Tiananmen Square in 1989. Symbolic and nonviolent challenges such as the Goddess of Democracy erected by students and the actions of a single unarmed man who managed to stop a tank riveted the attention of the world and forced the central government to reevaluate its policies. The nonviolent strategies of the Tiananmen protesters probably were more effective against the authoritarian regime than any armed confrontation would have been. In Myanmar (formerly Burma), political leader Aung San Suu Kyi (1945–) resorted to nonviolent hunger strikes to challenge the authoritarian government that ruled her nation. Although still not successful at the end of the twentieth century, she won a Nobel Prize for her nonviolent strategy. Another Nobel Peace Prize went to South African Archbishop Desmond Tutu (1931–) for his efforts to bring about a peaceful end to the Apartheid regime. Drawing on his African heritage and his Christian principles, Tutu had consistently advocated confession, forgiveness, restitution, and reconciliation as the best way to deal with injustice.

As the twentieth century drew to a close, the value of nonviolence as a political strategy was recognized by a number of governments that incorporated certain

MAJOR WRITINGS:
Deuteronomy

Deuteronomy 20:5–8: When you go to war. . .the officers shall say to the army: "Has anyone built a new house and not dedicated it? Let him go home, or he may die in battle and someone else may dedicate it. Has anyone planted a vineyard and not begun to enjoy it? Let him go home, or else he may die in battle and someone else enjoy it. Has anyone become pledged to a woman and not married her? Let him go home or he may die in battle and someone else marry her. Then the officers shall add, "Is any man afraid or faint–hearted? Let him go home.

The principles of Deuteronomy are that the enjoyment of life takes precedence over the pursuit of war, that people should not be compelled to fight, and that the tactics of war must be limited.

---

nonviolent strategies into their national policy. Several Scandinavian countries developed plans to use nonviolence as a method to deter and resist invasion. And, in the United States, Congress funded the U.S. Institute of Peace, whose mission was to study and promote non–lethal methods of conflict resolution. In part, the motivation for establishing the Institute was to assuage critics of traditional hard–line diplomatic and military strategies and, in part, the motivation was a revival of the old tradition of progressive liberalism. However, the main motivation was the desire to find cheaper, more durable, and less destructive methods of dealing with conflict. To achieve that end, the Institute was willing to consider strategies advocated by pacifists.

THEORY IN DEPTH

Pacifists who rely on religious teachings for support must deal with the obvious contradictions contained in their religious traditions. Christians, Muslims, and Jews must come to terms with the fact that the Old Testament and the Qur'an sanction holy war and jihad, thus validating violence as a cultic activity and religious obligation. Hindus must acknowledge that the Ghagavad Gita regards war as a duty. Jainists

and Buddhists must deal with the fact that their pacifism is intertwined with a strong rejection of worldly passions and desires in a way that is sometimes offensive to modern people. Furhter, proponents of African Traditional Religion recognize that their gods often are mobilized to support battles against enemies.

The Old Testament

The Old Testament, a foundational document for Jews, Christians, and Muslims, sometimes supports the concept of using violence so long as it is contained within the structures of the state. But, pacifists remind modern readers that the early Hebrews and their neighbors practiced a tribal religion in which the gods fought for their people. The total destruction of enemy tribes was the norm and at the end of every skirmish, no matter how minor, boasting warriors claimed to have annihilated hundreds and thousands of their opponents. Later, Hebrew monotheism challenged that xenophobic tribal view. Stories of battles, handed down through oral tradition, were reshaped to downplay the role of human warriors. Thus, the Exodus is said to have occurred without even one Hebrew killing an Egyptian. In fact, the human hero of the battle was Moses whose primary activity was to hold up his staff while the divine hero, God, destroyed the Egyptian army. Years later, the hero Gideon defeated the Midianite army after sending the vast majority of his warriors home. According to the Book of Judges, the explanation for Gideon's bizarre strategy was to prevent Israel from claiming victory instead of recognizing the power of God. At the watershed battle of Jericho, the Hebrews limited their activity to rituals such as blowing trumpets and shouting as they marched around the heavily fortified city. When walls of that previously invincible city fell, human warriors could take no credit. In his final speech, Israel's greatest warrior of all, Joshua, retold the story of the conquest of the land. Joshua reminded the people that God, not they themselves, had won the battles.

As Hebrew law and theology were codified in writing sometime after the tenth century B.C., the militaristic tenor of earlier thought was challenged even more. Deuteronomy, Israel's law book, outlined rules for the conduct of war and explained the provisions for excusing men from military service. Anyone who had been engaged to be married, built a house, or planted a vineyard was exempt. Deuteronomy even released men who feared going into battle. Furthermore, the book required that combatants not destroy fruit trees even if such destruction would lead to victory.

Israel's prophets and writers of the Psalms (songs), developed a strong theology of nonviolence and a vision of God's faithful kingdom. In fallen temporal society, the worship of idols, the use of magic and sorcerers, the exploitation of the poor, a reliance on foreign military alliances, and the use of horses and chariots were all condemned as undermining faith in a single–minded and singular God. In the eighth century B.C., the prophet Hosea explicitly linked militarism and injustice when he said, "You have plowed iniquity, you have reaped injustice, you have eaten the fruit of lies because you trusted in your chariots" (Hosea 10:13). When envisioning God's triumphal final kingdom, a symbolic way of explaining the goal of creation, the prophets presented a portrait of peace and justice; the seventh–century prophet Isaiah described an idyllic time when even predation in the animal kingdom would cease (Isaiah 65). More concretely, in the sixth century B.C., the preacher Zechariah described the Messiah, God's anointed servant/king, as victorious in humility and peace.

The Teachings of Jesus

The life and teachings of Jesus of Nazareth (c. 4 B.C.–c. 29 A.D.) were strongly supportive of pacifism. Jesus specifically called on his followers to show love to their enemies, to turn the other cheek when attacked, and to practice mercy and forgiveness. Jesus supported his teachings by grounding them in the very nature of God. Thus, he linked nonviolent love to the most fundamental reality of the universe. Christian pacifists such as John Howard Yoder (no relation to the author of this essay) note that Jesus' message was all the more remarkable because he lived in an occupied country that had a long history of violent political confrontation. When Jesus proclaimed himself God's Messiah (anointed king) he was identifying himself with the temporal liberation of the nation of Israel. The clarity of that message was obvious to his Jewish contemporaries. His disciples looked forward to a political victory. Almost to the end of Jesus' life, James and John expected to sit on thrones when he achieved victory. And at least one, and perhaps as many as four, of his twelve disciples belonged to a radical and violent revolutionary group called the Zealots. While the actions of several disciples are all we have to suggest that they were adherents of that group, the name of one, Simon the Zealot, established the point beyond doubt. Jesus' messianic claim was obvious to the Romans who executed him for sedition. On his cross, they placed the inscription "King of the Jews."

While conventional wisdom and theology expected a warrior messiah, Jesus reinterpreted that vi-

Jesus Christ preaching the Sermon on the Mount.
(Archive Photos, Inc.)

sion. The Kingdom he promoted would be based on principles of compassion, generosity, and forgiveness. Thus, he would rule over a community held together by love and humility rather than violence and power. In perhaps the most dramatic demonstration of this vision, he made his triumphal entry into Jerusalem riding on a lowly donkey, an animal of the common people and a beast of toil, not on a horse, a symbol of military might and royal prestige. In modern times, his action would be equivalent to participating in a state parade riding in a used car instead of standing in an attack tank or an armored limousine.

Pacifism and Muslim Thought

Muslim thought, although less explicitly peaceful than Christian doctrine, can be used to support some elements of a pacifistic philosophy. Muslim theology begins with the unequivocal affirmation in the one God, Allah, who created an orderly universe. The duty of both humans and nature is to surrender or submit (Islam) to Allah. As God's agents on earth, humans have an obligation to live in obedience. God, who is merciful, gives humans the capacity to follow his will and create a just and orderly society. While not condemning state force, the Qur'an denounces tribalism and economic exploitation. Since there is only one God who created all people, there can be only one hu-

BIOGRAPHY:
Lala 'Aziza

The Islamic commitment to peace was exemplified by Lala 'Aziza, "Our Lady of Goodness," a devout Moroccan Muslim who lived in the mid–1300s. A teacher and doer of good works, she was highly renowned as a peacemaker. Not only did she mediate conflicts between opposing tribal groups, she challenged a powerful governor/general who was determined to conquer her region. Walking out alone to meet the warring general, she risked her life to speak of God's demands for justice and to explain the sin of hurting God's creation. Convinced by Lala 'Aziza's religious arguments, the general retreated, leaving her town untouched and untaxed. After her death, 'Aziza's tomb became famous as a place of refuge and reconciliation. Since then, no bloodshed or any type of violence has been permitted at the site and the attendants offer protection to anyone seeking refuge from attack or capture.

---

man race. In the faithful Islamic community, all stand before God in equality. All who submit to God are brothers and sisters. In the Mosque, when men and women are at prayer, there is no distinction based on wealth, race, class, or family standing. All pray directly to God. No one needs an intercessor whose special knowledge, authority, or stature sets him or her apart and above.

Pacifism in Asia

In Asia, Jain Dharma, an Indian religion generally known as Jainism, has been one of the most important sources of pacifism. Jainism attributes its origins to a series of heroic victors (Jinas). The last and greatest of these heroes, Var–dhamana, supposedly lived in the sixth or fifth century B.C. Renouncing great wealth for self–mortification, he is said to have died of starvation after fasting in order to free himself from this life. Jains hold that karma, the accumulated good and evil humans have done, binds people to an endless cycle of birth, death, and rebirth. Through complete asceticism, best exemplified in *ahimsa* or complete nonviolence, the soul is released and self is

extinguished. The strictest adherents of Jainism go to great lengths to take no life, even the lowest forms. They wear veils to avoid inhaling and killing insects, and they eat only foods such as milk, fruit, and nuts that can be consumed without destroying the life of the donor organism. Jains avoid violence in any form because violence is the most powerful way to accumulate negative karma and be attached more firmly to this life. In fact, negative karma may do more than require that one remains trapped in the cycle of life, death, and rebirth; it may lead the self into an even lower stage in the following life.

Hinduism contains many concepts similar to those in Jainism. Also originating in India, but somewhat later, many of its concepts are contained in the *Bhagavad Gita*. Through pure thoughts and actions, Hindus seek to be released from the cycle of existence. Renouncing all selfish desires, Hindus avoid both pleasure and pain, sensations that bind one to self and to this world. Although neither Jainism nor Hinduism insist that their followers practice pacifism at a governmental level, both religions had an important influence on the thinking of Mohandas Gandhi, the most famous pacifist of the twentieth century.

Buddhism Buddhism is another powerful Asian voice that has sometimes been used in support of pacifism. According to tradition, Buddhism began with Siddhartha (c. 563–483 B.C.), a wealthy young man born into a family of warriors in northeast India. After having married and fathered a son, Siddhathra renounced the comforts of his home to search for the peace of Nirvana, an escape from the pain of repeated existence. He was disappointed to find that extreme asceticism including self–punishment did not help him achieve his goal. Instead, he discovered that quiet contemplation involving concentration and focused meditation enabled him to grasp the truth. Thus, he became the Enlightened One or the Buddha. For the remainder of his life, he taught his followers the Four Noble Truths that lead to truth or enlightenment. Rather than being a negative religion or philosophy that renounces this life, Buddhism is a positive thought system promising that human beings can attain both moral understanding and moral improvement. The first of the Four Noble Truths recognizes the universal reality of suffering. At a social level, this can be interpreted as a call on people to empathize with the pain and deprivation of the less fortunate. The second Noble Truth identifies craving, lust, and desire as the cause of suffering. This teaches people that selfishness and ambition lie at the root of evil and misfortune. The third Noble Truth states that suffering and pain can be ended, but only if people turn away from efforts to dominate, accumulate, and seek only their own pleasure. Finally, the fourth Noble Truth outlines the concrete steps one must take to achieve enlightenment. Among these steps are admonitions against ill–will, cruelty, harsh language, lying, sexual exploitation, theft, or killing. Although most often applied at an individual level, many Buddhists have used these admonitions to provide guidance for political leaders. In modern times, individuals such as the Dalai Lama (the title of the leader of Tibetan Buddhism) and Thich Nhat Hanh (1926–) have relied on Buddhist thought to construct a pacifist philosophy for political conduct. What is consistent in the ideas of all Buddhists is the strong emphasis on inner qualities and a correct moral attitude, and there is less attention to political strategies or techniques. A good and wise leader will do the good. A leader lacking deep inner moral grounding, no matter how skilled and shrewd that person may be, cannot be trusted to govern peacefully.

While religion has provided the foundation for many pacifists, logic and reason have been the guides for other advocates of nonviolence. The Greek and Roman Stoics developed theories calling for extreme self–control that enabled people to rise above human passion and pain. Keenly aware of the multi–ethnic nature of human society, the Stoics called for a community that accepted all people, no matter what their origin, as having equal worth and dignity. Such values contributed to the development of pacifist theories and practices based on the inherent rationality and equal value of all human beings.

Best known as a Christian thinker, Augustine Bishop of Hippo (354–430) mainly drew on classical logic and on Roman legal concepts to develop his theories regarding peace. As a Neo–Platonist, Augustine believed the universe was constructed in a manner so that every element seeks rest in its natural place. Augustine held that peace, in a static, orderly form, was an intrinsic quality of all existence. Even robbers and warriors, he wrote, long for peace. Turning to the world of politics, Augustine promoted the Just War Theory, a concept outlined earlier by the Roman Stoic Cicero (106–43 B.C.).

Just War Theory

Although not a doctrine of pacifism, the Just War Theory does place important limits on the conduct of war. As developed later by the Catholic Church and accepted by Protestant thinkers, the doctrine requires that combatants act only under the authority of a legitimate rule (Just Authority). Thus, rebellion or revolutionary violence is prohibited. The Just War Theory also insists that warfare is never legitimate unless there is an actual, not just a potential, threat (Just

Sculpture of Buddha. (Corbis Corporation)

Cause). Furthermore, the theory holds that the belligerents must not expand their goals once war begins (for example, not shift the intent from defense to conquest) and that the central aim of any war should be a peaceful resolution and a restoration of harmonious relations (Just Intention). These three principles (just authority, just cause, and just intention) are generally classified under the category of *jus ad bellum*, or law before war. Warfare, once it begins, must adhere to rules know as *jus in bello*, or law during war. These guidelines, also known as Just Means, are intended to protect non–combatants and their property, to prohibit inhumane methods of combat, and to outlaw a dis-

Henry David Thoreau. (The Library of Congress)

proportionate response to an injury. Along with the Peace of God, a medieval injunction similar to Just Means, and the Truce of God, a medieval regulation restricting the days when war could be conducted, the Just War Theory attempted to sharply limit the conduct of war. While all of these ideas were associated with the Church, they were in fact based on principles of reason and logic first proposed by the Romans.

Reformers

From the Middle Ages until modern times, pacifism has been relegated to more marginal religious movements and utopian thinkers. Authorities both in the dominant Catholic and Protestant Churches and in the emerging nation states all assumed that the use of force and violence were essential for the maintenance of social order. Reformers such as Martin Luther (1748–1826) and John Calvin (1509–1564) held that since God had created human society and the state, God expected Christians to participate in the military. In France and England, Catholic and Anglican thinkers supported similar ideas. Only groups such as the Anabaptists and the Society of Friends called on individuals and governments to renounce the use of force. In contrast to Catholic and mainline Protestant thinkers, they saw the fourth–century conversion of Constantine and the establishment of Christianity as the official state religion as the fall of the faith. In the view of paci-

fists such as the Anabaptists, there was no way to reconcile New Testament teachings with the sword of the political kingdom. The Anabaptists insisted that fidelity to the peaceful example of Jesus was the central tenet of Christianity. Thus, people and individuals using violence stood outside God's will. Even the use of force against invading armies or against heretics, regarded at that time as traitors to the state, was not legitimate. The Society of Friends, or Quakers, who focused on the idea that God indwells all human beings, regarded war and violence as a violation of the high value of people regardless of race, nationality, gender, or station in life. In colonial America, William Penn (1644–1718) attempted to implement Quaker ideals in his newly founded Pennsylvania.

Secular proposals for national or world systems based on the principles of pacifism emerged during the Enlightenment. One of the most persuasive and carefully developed was contained in the writings of the German philosopher Immanuel Kant (1724–1804). In his book *Perpetual Peace,* published in 1795, Kant argued that no state had a right to invade or acquire another state. Unlike property that could be exchanged in the market, a state is a society of free human beings that no one has a right to rule or dispose. Kant held that standing armies would eventually be abolished. Linking militarism with authoritarianism, Kant said that a free and democratic society would not consent to war that was costly both in its implementation and aftermath. What free people, he asked, would willingly accept losing their lives and property for the sake of fighting? Although Kant recognized that pacifism was not likely to be accepted soon, he believed that the unifying power of global commerce guaranteed the eventual establishment of perpetual peace.

Henry David Thoreau

The American transcendentalist Henry David Thoreau (1817–1862) based his argument for pacifism on his devotion to radical democracy and on his faith in the innate ability of all humans to know the truth. Thoreau stands as a champion of the idea that the claims of the state can never take precedence over the moral authority of individual conscience. The state, therefore, had no right to use force to compel or control. In his essay "Civil Disobedience" Thoreau argued that states tend to be oppressive and parasitic. War, in his time the American invasion of Mexico, and official support for slavery proved to Thoreau that the government was unable to act in a virtuous manner. As a result, Thoreau insisted that people cannot turn over their moral responsibility to others. According to Thoreau, the individual must always follow his or her conscience, even if that means disobeying the law. Not only should moral persons refuse to participate in military action, they should even withhold financial support for governments engaged in an aggressive war. Thoreau himself spent a brief time in jail for refusing to pay his war tax. Responding to charges that disobedience to the state recklessly undermined social stability, Thoreau said that nonviolent protest causes no harm to others since there is no bloodshed. Nor is there any real danger to the state, which will easily continue its business even if thousands refuse to pay their war taxes as a matter of conscience. When told to voice his protest through the ballot box rather than through illegal acts, Thoreau replied that going through the proper channels took too long. We need to vote with our entire lives, he said, not just with a strip of paper. Thoreau's actions and writings were influential for later pacifists such as Tolstoy and Gandhi who used peaceful civil disobedience against an immoral or unjust state.

Leo Tolstoy

While Thoreau joined pacifism with democracy, Leo Tolstoy (1828–1910) combined pacifism with anarchy. Born into a wealthy family, Tolstoy entered the military and served in the Crimean War. Deeply disillusioned with war, he left the army to begin a career in writing. An intense Christian, he pondered the tension between the demands of the Gospel and the reality of an oppressive hierarchical order kept in place by the Russian government and the Russian Orthodox Church. Several times he wrote letters to the Czar asking him to forgive assassins and to lessen state repression. Increasingly, Tolstoy regarded any form of organized power, whether church, state, or economic, as contradictory to peace and the well–being of the people. Eventually, Tolstoy became an absolute pacifist.

Although he claimed to base his pacifism on his complete obedience to God, Tolstoy had much in common Thoreau. Like Thoreau, he believed each individual possessed a deep intuitive awareness of the truth. This awareness was contained in traditions handed down from generation to generation, in human reason, and in the deepest emotions of the heart. These tell us that all violence, whether the brutal violence of war or the everyday institutional violence of the state, is wrong. Violence, in Tolstoy's view, was closely linked to greed and self–interest. He believed every human being was tempted by those instincts that were most deeply and dangerously embedded in large–scale institutions such as government and the state church.

Tolstoy rejected any appeal to pragmatism. Saying that human beings cannot see the larger design of history, he admonished people never to suspend God's law of nonviolence, even to protect the innocent. Tol-

BIOGRAPHY:
Mohandas Gandhi

A mediocre student and a poor public speaker, Mohandas Gandhi was unable to find a job in India after completing a law degree in England. Reluctantly, he moved to South Africa where he found work with an Indian law firm serving Asian clients. In South Africa, where he lived from 1891 to 1914, Gandhi developed his views and strategies about nonviolent social and political change. In South Africa he became a gifted political activist.

Soon after his arrival in South Africa, Gandhi was thrown off of a train because he refused to sit anywhere but in first class. As a result of this event, Gandhi determined that he would never again accept injustice and that he would always defend his dignity. During his long stay in Africa, he organized the Asian community to resist government attempts to deprive Asians of the vote, to force them to carry a passbook, and to delegitimize traditional Indian marriages. Although not always successful in his efforts, Gandhi gained a wide reputation as a political activist, and he perfected the theories that enabled him to win freedom for India. Gandhi returned to India in 1914, but he did not become actively involved in politics until 1919 when he led a protest against the Rowlatt Bills, which permitted imprisonment without trial. From that time until India became a state in 1947, Gandhi led the struggle for Indian independence by using nonviolent techniques such as protest marches, hunger strikes, and boycotts.

In the end, Gandhi's ideals and strategies succeeded. Not only was he able to mobilize millions to his cause, he was able to pressure or persuade the British to grant independence to India. In the months following independence, Gandhi turned his attention to healing the rift between the Muslim and Hindu communities of the Asian sub–continent. He was bitterly disappointed that independence for India resulted in the formation of two separate and antagonistic states, India and Pakistan. On January 30, 1948, he was assassinated by a Hindu fanatic opposed to Gandhi's work for reconciliation.

stoy criticized people who relied on wildly hypothetical and unlikely scenarios in order to justify more mundane state or personal violence. He challenged the common argument that violence was necessary to defend the weakest members of society. Tolstoy responded to the age–old question about what to do if a criminal threatened to kill or molest an innocent child and if the only way to stop the criminal seemed to be deadly force. Tolstoy argued that there are always other options to lethal force. One might plead with the assailant. One might place oneself between the criminal and the victim. Or, one might pray for divine intervention. In any case, Tolstoy said that the situation was so exceptional that it could not be generalized to defend the use of state violence. It was hypocritical, he said, to use the example of an innocent child to justify protecting national borders, killing smugglers, and using violence against someone stealing fruit.

In the end, Tolstoy's pacifism was based on his understanding of human worth and weakness. While reason and emotions can serve as a guide for behavior, Tolstoy rejected their use to justify the exercise of force against other human beings. Even if logic suggests that violence is necessary, Tolstoy asserted that human limitations prevent people from understanding the larger picture that only God can know. Comparing people to bricklayers who have been given their specific task but not the larger blueprint, Tolstoy said humans can never presume to be knowledgeable or moral enough to play the role of God and take the life of another human being. Looking beyond Tolstoy's theistic language, we are left with his central argument that no human being stands large enough to deprive another of their life or liberty.

Gandhi

In the twentieth century, Tolstoy's most influential admirer was Mohandas K. Gandhi. Drawing on Jainism, Hinduism, and lessons from Christianity, Gandhi used these religious and philosophical concepts to build powerful political movements. Faced with the challenges of racism, colonialism, class conflict, economic exploitation, and violence, he used pacifism as the basis for victories against the segregationist policies of South Africa and the imperial rule of Great Britain. With Gandhi, for the first time in history, pacifism moved from the periphery of political thought, where it often had been regarded as a curiosity or as an unrealistic ideal, to the center stage of political action.

Gandhi's central concepts The two main elements underlying Gandhi's theory and practice were concepts he developed and tested in South Africa. The first, *ahimsa*, is the doctrine of complete nonviolence he learned from his Hindu–Jainist mother. Gandhi believed that while violence (*himsa*) protects the external, *ahimsa* protects the soul, the eternal, and the values that last. In Gandhi's view, *ahimsa* can be observed in the evolution of the human species. Looking at history, he saw humans progressing from cannibalism to hunting, thus from eating other humans to eating animals. Then people turned to settled farming and the consumption of grains and vegetables. Eventually they began living in towns and cities. At each stage, Gandhi noted, *himsa* decreased and *ahimsa* increased. This progression, he argued, was the only alternative to the extinction of all but a ferocious few. Gandhi observed that the greatest thinkers and prophets throughout history taught *ahimsa*. None, he said, advocated *himsa*. Harmony, truth, brotherhood, and justice are all expressions of *ahimsa* and are attributes that distinguish humans from animals. While *ahimsa* is an intrinsic part of human nature, Gandhi did not believe it was easily exercised. Just as people must train for war, they must also train for nonviolence. Such training must cultivate the capacity for sacrifice and the ability to overcome fear. Gandhi held that the act of confronting an opponent with *ahimsa*—especially when this confrontation led to suffering on the part of the person practicing *ahimsa*—would transform the opponent. *Ahimsa*, he said, has the ability to change an enemy's heart and open an inner understanding. Only then can an adversary begin to change his or her mind. While *ahimsa* required great inner courage, it did not rely on physical strength and could be exercised even by children, women, and the elderly. Now, change could be in the hands of ordinary people, not just highly armed and destructive soldiers.

Gandhi's second central concept was *satyagraha* (soul force or firmness in truth). Although influenced by the concept of suffering love as exemplified by Jesus and taught by Tolstoy, Gandhi mainly drew on Hindu concepts of self–purification in developing this idea, which he first articulated while in South Africa. He believed that by holding fast to the truth, one would be able to convert an adversary. Yet, for Gandhi, *satyagraha* was primarily a spiritual exercise, not a political strategy. An integral element of *satyagraha* was extreme self–restraint. For Gandhi personally, this meant denouncing sex, luxury, rich foods, fine clothes, and comfortable beds so that he could devote all of his energies to a single task. *Satyagraha*, however, was not a passive or negative concept. The high degree of self–restraint allowed the practitioner of *satyagraha* never to waver from the truth. Thus, Gandhi refused to cooperate with unjust laws, officials, or governments because cooperation would have meant giving in to evil. When his own followers became unruly and rioted, Gandhi withdrew support for their cause and fasted until the people turned away from their violence.

Like Thoreau and Tolstoy, Gandhi believed in the innate goodness of all human beings. He was confident that truth would prevail in the end. By adhering faithfully to the truth and always rejecting violence, he thought he could touch the goodness in his adversaries. He believed that once the truth was known, the perpetrators of injustice would be sorry for their conduct. Consistent with this perspective, Gandhi always refused to take advantage of an opponent's weakness. When the British were preoccupied with the Boer War and involved in World War I, Gandhi suspended his efforts to exert pressure. In fact, he mobilized an ambulance corps to assist his oppressor. He hoped those efforts would lead the British to respond with equal magnanimity and kindness.

Gandhi's pacifism In spite of his reputation as a man of peace, Gandhi was not a complete pacifist. True, Gandhi held that war always was inconsistent with *ahimsa* and that war was an unmitigated evil. Furthermore, as a man who refused to prosecute an opponent in court, he said that he would not participate in war. Yet, Gandhi recognized that life brings conflicting duties. He said that an individual who benefits from government must at times extend assistance in defending that government from military attack. He stated that anyone who did not believe in *ahimsa* or merely wanted to avoid combat out of fear should be obligated to participate in military service. But, while Gandhi held open the possibility of defending a nation with force, he was consistent in his conviction that internal social and political change should only be pursued though pacifistic means.

Gandhi's nonviolent positive direct action represented a major step forward in the theory and practice of pacifism. No longer was nonviolence seen as a passive concept emphasizing withdrawal or non–participation. No longer was nonviolence a mere theological, philosophical, social, or political critique. With Gandhi, nonviolence became a powerful strategy to transform individuals, communities, societies, nations, and even imperial systems. The ideas and tactics of Mohandas Gandhi, a man who became known as Mohatama (Great Soul), have been used to bring civil rights to people of color in America, freedom for colonized and oppressed people in Africa, political rights for Eastern Europeans formerly controlled by Communist systems, and relief for citizens of the Philippines and Indonesia where dictatorship previously had

Gandhi. (AP/Wide World Photos)

reigned. In each case, the transformation took place with minimal loss of human life, damage to property, or disruption of the fundamental social fabric. Even in places such as Tiananmen Square in China where nonviolent protests did not succeed, the subsequent government response was less destructive than if the protesters had engaged in an armed uprising. Finally, at the end of the twentieth century, as theorists such as Gene Sharp began to consider nonviolent alternatives to military systems, they turned to Gandhi's example.

Martin Luther King Jr. In the United States, Martin Luther King Jr. combined the teachings of Gandhi with those of the Old Testament prophets and Jesus to articulate a pacifist theory of political and social change. Thrust into the civil rights struggle in Montgomery, Alabama, King preached nonviolence as a means of obtaining equal rights for African Americans. Toward the end of his life, a life cut short by an assassin's bullet, he turned his attention to economic injustices and to the evils of the Vietnam War.

The son of an eloquent Atlanta preacher, King excelled in school and went on to pursue a Ph.D. in theology at Boston University. In Boston, he met and married Coretta Scott, who introduced him to the writings of Mohandas Gandhi. Also in Boston, he embraced a more liberal, socially active understanding of the Gospel. From that foundation, he developed a phi-

Dr. Martin Luther King, Jr. speaks to supporters at a rally. (The New York Amsterdam News)

losophy that called for radical social change but that renounced all use of violence.

In reading the Bible, King saw God as a redeemer of the poor and oppressed. Christians, he concluded, had an obligation to follow the example of the Good Samaritan who risked his life and offered his wealth in behalf of an enemy in distress. Christians also were called to follow the example of Jesus, who showed love and compassion for enemies. Martin Luther King Jr. believed in the redemptive power of suffering. Referring to the mistreatment of the African–American people, King compared their travails to the agony of Christ. African–Americans, he said, understood suffering in a way that more privileged Americans did not. Their history of suffering gave them a moral stamina and credibility that would enable them to triumph in the end. Like Gandhi, King believed that suffering had a powerful impact on an adversary who could be transformed by seeing the example of someone accepting suffering and turning the other cheek. Both Gandhi and King shared an optimism about the possibility that evil men and women could change their attitudes and ways when confronted with the truth, especially when the truth is presented by someone willing to accept pain without retaliating.

In spite of his emphasis on suffering, King always displayed an aggressiveness, shrewdness, and politi-

cal savvy that distinguished him from many of his more cautious African–American colleagues. Black people, he said, must be both tender hearted and tough minded. They must be as peaceful as doves, but as shrewd as foxes. Other African–American leaders such as Booker T. Washington (1856–1915) had attempted to make economic and social progress through strategies of respectful deference, cautious appeals, and hard work intended to prove the worth of black people. King called on his followers to confront racial discrimination by refusing to participate in unjust systems. If segregationist America forced blacks to sit at the back of the buses and to give up their seats for whites, then King called on black people not to ride the buses at all. If public facilities such as restaurants refused to allow blacks equal access to service, King helped organize sit–ins that served as a nonviolent demand for equal treatment. If blacks faced rejection or discrimination at the polls, King promoted voting rights campaigns to educate and register them. Police, politicians, business owners, ordinary citizens, and even church leaders in the American South responded with anger and violence. King spent time in jail, received many threatening letters and telephone calls, was under frequent police surveillance, had his house bombed, and lived under constant fear of assassination. He was even criticized by many liberal Americans who viewed King's methods as dangerously confrontational. Some of these people said that King should be held responsible whenever conservative whites in the segregated South responded to his movement with violence.

Although King promoted a confrontive form of advocacy, along with the Southern Christian Leadership Council and the National Association for the Advancement of Colored People (NAACP), he always insisted that people should respond to violence with nonviolence. Rigorous preparation sessions in which trainers hurled insults and spat in the faces of volunteers helped prepare the marchers, protesters, and demonstrators for what they faced as they sought to bring change to America.

King's views on Vietnam In the mid–1960s, King increasingly turned his attention to issues of poverty, both black and white, and to what he considered to be the injustices of the Vietnam War. He said the rights to vote or to have equal access to public transportation should not be claimed as victories so long as people are "smothering in an airtight cage of poverty in the midst of an affluent society." The Vietnam War, he asserted, inflicted double pain on people of color. First, the war itself was racist because a predominantly white and wealthy nation attempted to suppress a poor Asian nation. Second, the American government drafted a disproportionate number of its own poor and black people to fight and die on the front lines of the war. King's shift in focus from his previous emphasis on civil rights deeply angered President Lyndon Johnson, who felt he had done more for black people than any other president since Abraham Lincoln. In Johnson's view, King was an ungrateful menace to the American national interest.

Martin Luther King Jr's critique of the Vietnam War continued a long tradition of religious and political opposition to military preparation and military action. Much of the opposition, whether religious or secular, was articulated in a negative manner. Pacifist opponents to the military pointed out the immorality, flaws, and dangers of the military without suggesting any alternative system for national defense. In the mid–1900s, the American Protestant pacifist A.J. Muste, a prominent member of the Fellowship of Reconciliation (FOR), linked totalitarianism and depersonalization to militarism and war. Muste argued that conscription represented a form of conformity or paralysis that takes away the ability of citizens to choose for themselves, resist evil, or maintain their self–respect. Because conscription is an indispensable tool of governments preparing for war, Muste called on pacifists to refuse any form of the draft, even when the govern-

MAJOR WRITINGS:
Letter from a Birmingham Jail.

You may well ask: "Why direct action? Why sit–ins, marches, and so forth?...Frankly, I have yet to engage in a direct–action campaign that was "well–timed" in the view of those who have not suffered unduly from the disease of segregation.

Martin Luther King Jr. went to Birmingham in 1963 to help the Southern Christian Leadership Council (SCLC) stage protests in their communities. There King met his nemesis, Police Commissioner Eugune "Bull" Connor, a man who had made a reputation for himself by intimidating blacks. Staging a boycott that Easter, during one of the busiest shopping seasons of the year, King and the SCLC targeted downtown department stores. Connor arrested the demonstrators, including King and placed him in solitary confinement. It was here that King wrote his famous letter.

In his *Letter from a Birmingham Jail*, King clearly explained that nonviolent direct–action involved confrontation intended to create tension. Thus, for King, nonviolence could be exercised in the form of calculated pressure designed to force an opponent to respond. Although such confrontation was an integral part of Gandhi's work, King expressed the idea much more openly. Furthermore, in the letter written in response to criticisms from white clergy, King acknowledged that the "pent–up resentments and latent frustrations" of Black people had to find a channel for release. Nonviolent protest, he argued, was far more healthy and creative than violence.

ment allowed pacifists to engage in alternative service activities such as hospital or overseas development work. Muste argued that resistance to conscription would be the first step toward a more peaceful and brotherly world. His vision for a peaceful world was based on the hope that ordinary citizens would refuse to give their minds and bodies to the service of war. Eventually, that refusal would force policy makers to find alternative means to achieve their goals. Underlying Muste's thought, and the thought of most mid–twentieth century pacifists, was the idea that militaristic political leaders or ideologies were the root cause of war. War would cease if only moral people could be persuaded to resist the efforts of those leaders to mobilize the resources of their nations for combat.

Pacifism and the Nuclear Buildup

In the 1970s and 1980s, the attention of anti–war activists was focused on the massive buildup of nuclear weapons in the United States and the Soviet Union. Strategic thinking in both countries was based on the concept of mutually assured destruction (MAD), a theory codified in the SALT I and SALT II treaties (Strategic Arms Limitation Treaties). Employing a triad of delivery systems—airplanes, submarines, and land–based missiles—the United States and the Soviet Union had the capacity to annihilate their counterparts with less than thirty minutes warning. Both had the ability to continue the attacks for days and even months through the use of nuclear–powered submarines that could lurk under the ocean for long periods of time before surfacing to launch missiles with nuclear warheads. SALT I and SALT II placed limits on the number of delivery systems but did not actually reduce the numbers of weapons. Furthermore, the treaties banned the use of any form of anti–ballistic missiles (ABMs) that might have defended against incoming missiles. Since the technology for ABMs was not close to being developed, and likely could not be developed (certainly not to the point of being effective against massive numbers of incoming missiles), the ban on AMBs was simply a ratification of reality. However, it underscored the point that peace was being maintained by the mutual realization that any first strike would inevitably lead to massive retaliation resulting in the total destruction of cities, infrastructure, and industry. By the 1980s, scientists began to realize that even a "moderate" number of nuclear launches would stir up so much dust and debris that the world's temperature would drop below the levels needed to sustain plant and animal life. Thus, even an unanswered attack would destroy both the intended target and the attacker.

Some critics of prevailing nuclear doctrine drew on the concepts of the Just War Theory. Prominent among these were Catholic thinkers whose views were expressed in Pope John XXIII's 1963 encyclical letter *Pacem in terris* (Peace on Earth). In 1983, *The Pastoral of the U.S. Bishops on War and Peace* provided an even more pointed criticism of national defense systems relying on nuclear weapons. Secular opponents of nuclear weapons also appealed to the Just War Theory. They held that the disproportional and indiscriminate nature of nuclear weapons made nuclear war incompatible with the Just War concept. Anti–nuclear critics relied on other theories as well.

Betty Reardon

Betty Reardon, feminist, futurist, and advocate of a world governance system based on the use of law rather than threat, outlined her anti–nuclear views in her 1985 book *Sexism and the War System*. Reardon linked the existing military system with authoritarian patriarchy. She argued that a very small number of elite men, mainly from western industrialized nations, saw coercive force as the most efficient way to maintain control over the world's people and resources. Employing hard, emotionless logic, they concluded that using the threat of nuclear weapons was the most effective way to achieve their goals in the northern hemisphere. In the poor countries of the southern hemisphere, the western elite ruled through local allies—dictators, generals, and large landowners—who were rewarded for their support of the hierarchical world system. Reardon observed that the heavily militarized world system diverted trillions of dollars from more productive enterprises. In Reardon's view, the growing global poverty that affected women and children especially was a direct result of excessive military expenditures.

Reardon held that warfare and militarization were based on "negative masculine values," and she saw a connection between the opposition to nuclear weapons and the feminist movement. She contrasted the destructive intentions of war with the constructive inclinations of the environmental movement, campaigns for social justice, and calls for economic equity. She believed that while men often saw power, bravery, and force as the way to maintain social order, women tended to focus on more nurturing, affirming, and cooperative values and actions. She suggested that the existing emphasis on military might strengthen non–democratic and non–participatory forms of government.

Reardon also argued that real change would not take place through a strict logical analysis of military systems. Change would come only when people adopted a new inner attitude toward life that incorporated both male and female modes of thinking. Instead of concentrating on the "rational" promotion of self–interest and rights (values of separation), women think of connections and relationships (values of community). According to a feminist perspective, training for citizenship and political leadership should teach people to nurture and sustain life, not just to exert power and use force. By placing more emphasis on forgiveness and reconciliation, again traditionally more feminine inclinations, Reardon said human society would become more tolerant and less aggressive.

Although Betty Reardon's pacifism was notable for its feminist content, her thought has much in common with most thinkers who developed anti–militarist and anti–nuclear theories. All of those people saw themselves as protesting scientific and technical systems that had the power to cause death on a hitherto unimaginable scale. All of these people challenged doctrines that nuclear strategists saw as unassailably logical. And, all of these people rejected the notion that planning for death was a safe or moral way to preserve life.

Aung San Suu Kyi

In the Far East, Buddhist philosophy has provided the underlying inspiration for important pacifist thinkers and activists. In Myanmar (formerly known as Burma) Aung San Suu Kyi, a long–time advocate of democracy and human rights, drew on the moral imperatives of her Buddhist faith as she confronted an authoritarian government. For Suu Kyi, Buddhism imparted an uncompromising sense of duty and a certain vision of right and wrong. Those gave her a moral confidence that sustained her through hunger strikes, house arrest, imprisonment, and civil disobedience campaigns. At every step of the way, she emphasized the importance of always relying on nonviolence. Furthermore, she believed that political leaders could act with integrity and nonviolence. She said that Buddhism calls on leaders to strive for a very high level of moral enlightenment or perfection. In her view, the problem with modern politics has little to do with a lack of managerial competency on the part of government officials. Rather, bad government is caused by the unwillingness of leaders to cultivate good moral character.

According to Suu Kyi, Buddhism's political vision posits an original state of purity and perfection from which people fell. The role of political leaders is to restore peace and justice. The *dhamma* (life task) of a ruler is to be true to virtue, justice, and the law. Among the Ten Duties of a political leader are liberality, morality, self–sacrifice, kindness, non–anger, nonviolence, forbearance, and non–opposition to the will of the people. Morality is further defined as avoiding not just theft, adultery, falsehood, and indulgence, but also avoiding the destruction of life. Forbearance is the quality that enables rulers to stand above the personal feelings of enmity and ill–will that lead to anger and violence. A forbearing leader will conquer ill–will with loving kindness and will respond to wickedness with virtue. For Suu Kyi, Buddhism requires that each human being be treated as a person of infinite worth. Like Buddha, every person has the potential to realize the truth. Because of this potential, rulers have a duty to treat every human being as some-

one of value and also to seek the truth that will enable them (the rulers) to govern in a nonviolent manner.

The Dalai Lama

Another prominent Asian leader incorporating the principles of Buddhism and pacifism into a political philosophy is the Dalai Lama XIV, Tenzin Gyatso (1935–), the leader of the Tibetan people. When China invaded Tibet, the Dalai Lama attempted to negotiate with the Chinese government. When it became clear that China would not relinquish control over Tibet, he escaped to India where he established a Tibetan government in exile. Throughout his life, the Dalai Lama has insisted that Tibet be free and that freedom should be won through nonviolence. In accordance with his Buddhist vision, he has outlined the way a government should be managed. The most important concern of any government, he said, must be mercy. Not only should a government attend to the happiness of every citizen, it should instill in citizens a sense of responsibility for every living thing, including animals and plants.

Truth, genuine democracy, and nonviolence must be used as guidelines for governance. The Dalai Lama also insists that government must protect the freedom of religion. No government, group, or individual can use violence to impose religious conformity, and traditional customs must be protected. Thus, minority and indigenous cultures should never be suppressed either through direct violence or more subtle forms of coercion or persuasion. Consistent with his other views, the Dalai Lama says nonviolence must respect the right of free speech and expression. The Dalai Lama has proposed making Tibet a sanctuary of human and environmental peace in the heart of Asia. For this vision and for his nonviolent struggle for Tibet's liberation, he was awarded the Nobel Peace Prize in 1989.

Pacifism in Africa

One should not imagine that America, Europe, and Asia are the only continents where pacifistic ideas and practices have emerged. In Africa, many myths, legends, and proverbs admonish people and leaders to live peacefully. One remarkable example is a legend from the Kingdom of Buganda, a region located in modern–day Uganda. In the 1870s, Uganda was ruled by a despotic monarch who controlled his people through a highly structured administration and through violence. Reputedly, he would test out a new gun by going into the main thoroughfare and shooting an innocent passerby. The king's power was supported by Buganda's national story, the tale of Kintu, a mythological first king, first farmer, first father, and first human being. According to the narrative, Kintu was a stern ruler who punished subordinates for any form of disobedience. In fact, the official Kintu story attributed the end of paradise to disobedience. Angered at human disobedience, Kintu departed, taking with him the bounty of his original kingdom. According to tradition, Buganda's first kings were Kintu's legitimate heirs. Supposedly, these men devoted a great deal of time trying to find their departed father. Their hope was to restore the glories of his Garden of Eden–like kingdom. Accounts of their lives described them as quick to use harsh violence to maintain their power and control their kingdom. Thus, the national story affirmed the importance of violence as an integral element in any strong political system.

Rewriting the myth In the 1870s, an individual or group of individuals rewrote the national myth to condemn violence and to portray Kintu, the father of the country, as a man who loved peace and abhorred violence. The new story stressed that Kintu had a great aversion to any bloodshed, not just of humans but also of animals. Specifically, Kintu was described as being strongly opposed to capital punishment. In the new version of the story, paradise ended not because of disobedience to Kintu, but because his sons became exceedingly violent. This suggested that violence lies at the heart of human suffering. As the story went on to describe the lives of the Ganda kings, it focused on one king who was said to have found Kintu. While out hunting, the king came across a magnificent court–like setting. There, at the center and dressed in white, was a very peaceful Kintu. Tragically, the king was never able to converse with Kintu because, in a fit of rage, the king killed a disobedient subordinate. Instantly, Kintu vanished and no one in Buganda has ever encountered him again.

Of course the point of the revised story was that the fall of the Ganda kingdom, and of humankind in general, was linked to violence. Furthermore, the inability of people to recapture the bounty and glory of that mythological past was presented as a direct consequence of violence, especially the violence of political leaders. Because it was told during the reign of one of Buganda's most brutal monarchs, it is clear that the revised tale was presented as a pointed critique of violence.

THEORY IN ACTION

No state in history has adopted pacifism as its governing philosophy. Even most pacifists do not ex-

pect that the theory ever will be fully implemented. Nevertheless, a number of governments have adapted components of pacifist theory or have borrowed ideas advanced by pacifists. Pacifistic concepts have also been applied, sometimes without a great deal of conscious attention to theory, by people resisting oppressive governments. While much of traditional pacifist thought has been relatively theoretical and has been offered more as a critique or a vision than as a serious plan for real world politics, in the later half of the twentieth century, a number of people have developed proposals for how nations might defend themselves through nonviolence. On the domestic level, pacifism sometimes has influenced the way the judicial system operates, and pacifist principles have been used to deal with community and regional disputes. Pacifists have also offered suggestions about how diplomatic practices might be improved through the use nonviolent principles.

Gene Sharp and Nonviolence

Political theorist Gene Sharp has advanced a theory of how modern nation–states might use nonviolence as an effective method of national defense. Sharp has developed a strategy of civilian–based defense (CBD) that he believes is more effective, more efficient, and more democratic than current defense plans. According to Sharp, conventional defense systems are marred by a number of fundamental problems and contradictions. First, they are enormously expensive, costing the world trillions of dollars annually. Second, Sharp points out that they are generally incompatible with democracy. The hierarchical, secretive, and authoritarian nature of modern military systems comes into conflict with a democracy that values equality, openness, and citizen participation. In many countries of the world, military dictators are the greatest enemies of democracy. Third, modern military systems do not actually protect their people. Whenever such systems actually have been used, the result for people and property has been enormous devastation. Now that a number of nations rely on nuclear weapons for their defense, the use of such weapons would not result in protection but instead result in annihilation. Fourth, defense systems based on the military are so inherently destabilizing that they lead to insecurity rather than security. Because modern weapons can easily be used for offense, an opponent has no way of knowing if a weapon such as a missile is defensive or offensive. As a result, that opponent may order a preemptive attack to avoid being the target of a first strike. Sharp says weapons that invite attack are as much a danger to their owners as they are to their intended targets. As a result of these basic flaws, Sharp argues that nations must develop alternative defense strategies.

Sharp accepts the proposition that any effective defense system depends on the ability and willingness to exercise power. He also agrees that defensive power must be able to combat a military invasion. But, Sharp believes that effective combat can rely on the shrewd use of completely nonviolent forms of power. Sharp's nonviolence does not require a religious or ethical commitment to pacifism. In fact, he rejects the idea that his theories are pacifistic. Nevertheless, because he advocates a nonviolent form of defense, his proposals commonly are cited by pacifists. Sharp's ideas are based on the notion that through the nonviolent power of protest, non–cooperation, and intervention, well–trained civilians can repulse an invasion or resist a tyrant.

Sharp believes that through disciplined and carefully designed programs of nonviolence, nations can defend themselves by relying on civilians rather than on military personnel. He notes that even without planning or a coherent strategy, Eastern European nations threw off the Soviet Empire. Presumably, with more planning and training, countries could be even more successful. In part, citizen–based confrontation works because it disorients an oppressor. When faced with violent resistance, a tyrant or invader actually gains strength and resolve. But, when faced with carefully orchestrated noncompliance on the part of unarmed civilians, the tyrant or invader is unsure of how to respond. While ordinary soldiers react with bravery or ferocity when attacked by opposing armies, they may loose their will to fight when they are directed to attack nonviolent protesters.

Steps for nonviolent defense Sharp says that for nonviolent defense to be truly effective, strategists must put as much effort into its planning and training as they would into conventional military preparation. Effective CBD, he says, involves three distinct steps that require increasingly more discipline, preparation, and commitment. The first step, protest, is the most simple and can involve masses of people. Through marches, picketing, vigils, handing out protest literature, humorous pranks directed against officials, renouncing any honors bestowed by an opponent, holding public protest meetings, or emigrating, people express their disapproval of an illegitimate government. This may undermine the confidence of a tyrannical regime and encourage other citizens to identify with the protesters.

Sharp's second step is nonviolent non–cooperation, which makes it difficult for an oppressor to carry on the day–to–day activities of governing. CBD activists may engage in strikes or boycotts, they may refuse to come to work, they may work slowly and inefficiently, they may resist paying taxes, or they may stop buying products associated with an oppressive regime.

The third step, nonviolent intervention, is designed to throw sand in the machinery of government and of the economy. For example, an invading army may find that road signs have been changed, that the trains or planes "inadvertently" have been rerouted, and that massive numbers of disabled automobiles have formed tangled traffic jams blocking critical bottlenecks. The activities linked to step three require more planning, courage, and discipline.

Sharp acknowledges that CBD activists may face reprisals involving torture and death, but he notes that conventional soldiers always risk danger. Like ordinary soldiers, combatants using CBD should be prepared to pay a high price for their efforts. In fact, Sharp asserts that CBD has more in common with traditional military struggle than with pacifistic concepts such as conciliation and agitation. Unlike Gandhi or King, Sharp has little interest in touching the conscience or changing the heart of his opponent.

The future of CBD Although CBD has not been adopted completely by any government, its supporters recommend it as a viable real–world policy. They suggest that CBD is still in its infancy and will evolve into a much more attractive alternative. In time, nations might incorporate CBD as one part of their defense policy and, even further into the future, they might rely on it entirely. The countries most likely to turn to CBD would be smaller nations with little prospect of withstanding powerful adversaries through the use of conventional methods. CBD provides them with a means of resistance that would be equally effective and far less destructive to their homelands. Several Scandinavian countries have given serious consideration to incorporating elements of Sharp's thinking into their defense strategies. Although not claiming to follow the guidelines of CBD, teams of Christian peacemakers have applied similar principles in the Middle East and Latin America. Recruited as a kind of army of peace, men and women have volunteered to stand between warring parties in places like Israel, Palestine, and El Salvador. Willing to accept the same risk as armed combatants, their goal is to stand in visible protest to the violence that is destroying homes and lives.

War and Healing

Around the world, political, social, and ethnic conflict has weakened or destroyed communities and nations. In response to the deep pain resulting from injustices that often rise to the level of war crimes or crimes against humanity, pacifists have offered solutions they believe will aid in stopping the cycle of revenge and retaliation that often accompanies such conflict. Pacifists also hope nonviolent efforts at reconciliation will begin to heal the debilitating psychological wounds that trouble former child soldiers, victims of brutality, and even participants in politically motivated criminal behavior. While these healers would not necessarily claim to be pacifists in every part of their life, they employ theories and techniques that are pacifistic by their nature. Many of these concepts and methods have been developed by pacifists such as Mennonites, Quakers, or other religiously motivated individuals. Often attached to churches, nongovernmental organizations (NGOs), or the United Nations, pacifist peacemakers respond to the social and psychological residues of past hurt. They focus on uncovering the truth, they encourage perpetrators of crimes to acknowledge their activities, they urge the victims to express their deep pain, and they seek to help all parties move beyond the past. Frequently, the language of these peacemakers includes religious terms such as shalom, justice, repentance, forgiveness, and reconciliation. In spite of their close links to religion, the goal of these peacemakers is to restore society so that normal politics and government can resume.

In Cambodia, peacemaking teams attempted to help citizens deal with the horrors of the Pol Pot (1925–1998) era. In Central and South America, they assisted victims who had experienced the torture, unlawful imprisonment, loss of family and property, and terror designed to silence and intimidate political enemies. Peacemakers have also worked with the soldiers and officials responsible for those acts of violence. At times, such people are encouraged to confess their actions. At times, peacemakers help everyone recognize that the men and women who inflicted violence were themselves victims and pawns of larger forces. In the Balkans, where ethnic conflict reached the level of war crimes, peacemakers have attempted to mend the torn fabric of society. In Northern Ireland and Palestine, peacemaking teams have tried to reconcile bitterly divided communities.

Nonviolent Efforts in Africa

Some of the best–known efforts at reconciliation and peacemaking have taken place in Africa. In Liberia, Sierra Leone, Angola, and Mozambique,

peacemakers have attempted to rehabilitate former child soldiers. In Sudan, Kenya, and Somalia, they have worked both with high–level political leaders and warring ethnic communities. And in Rwanda, where the 1994 genocide killed nearly one million people, peacemakers have tried to deal with the intense and explosive pain resulting from the fact that most of the killings were carried out by former friends or neighbors who used clubs and machetes.

The TRC   In South Africa, peacemaking and reconciliation were incorporated into the 1994 national constitution. At the urging of Anglican Archbishop Desmond Tutu, the men and women who wrote the constitution included a provision that created a Truth and Reconciliation Commission (TRC). The task of the Commission was to help the nation deal with the violence and injustice of the apartheid era. During the apartheid years, both the security forces of the White South African government and the militant activists of the resistance movements committed acts of torture and terror. Fearful that a never–ending round of reprisals would cripple the new nonracial government and deeply polarize South African society, the nation's leaders decided to establish the TRC. For a number of years in the 1990s, TRC members traveled around the county listening to stories of injustice and loss. The TRC also heard the confessions of perpetrators of injustice and loss. While a compensation commission determined a monetary payment that served as restitution, the real goal of the TRC was simply to allow both sides to tell their stories. For those who had suffered, just being able to describe what had happened and perhaps to learn the truth about lost loved ones was far more important than the meager cash compensation. For those who had committed atrocities, the liberating act of confession was more important than the amnesty they received from prosecution and future punishment.

The TRC represented a radical departure from conventional views about justice that are based on the principle of retribution. While some criticized the TRC for allowing the guilty to escape with seemingly little cost, others predicted that telling the truth would lead to private acts of revenge. In the end, neither of those fears proved true. The individual acts of contrition and truth–telling led to genuine experiences of forgiveness. Former enemies were able to accept the past and move forward to a more hopeful future. Indeed, the national mythology became a mythology of reconciliation. Instead of telling stories of bravery in combat, people recounted tales of meeting former enemies, sharing meals, and becoming friends. To a large extent, the model established by President Nelson

Mandela (1918–) encouraged such developments. For example, Mandela invited all former residents, both guards and inmates, of Robben Island to a gathering at the Executive Mansion in Cape Town. Mandela's strong commitment to champion forgiveness rather than revenge did much to heal the deep wounds caused by years of violence.

VORP in the U.S. and Canada

Another example of pacifistic principles being used at the domestic political level are the Victim Offender Reconciliation Programs (VORP) that have emerged in the United States and Canada. While traditional criminal justice is based on the concept of inflicting pain on the criminal, VORP is designed to rehabilitate by appealing to the criminal's conscience and by restoring relationships. Traditional criminal justice operates in an atmosphere of antagonism and separation. Victims and perpetrators do not interact except through the highly structured and ritualized court system where communication is monopolized by disinterested professionals. In general, the offended party is the government whose laws have been broken rather than the victim whose person or property has been violated. Consistent with that principle, the penalties (jail time or fines) are paid to the state and not to the one who has suffered loss. Too often, the results are bitterness and anger for both the victim and the criminal, prison (which can further brutalize the criminal), and a very high rate of recidivism (relapse into criminal behavior). Furthermore, the victim may not receive any compensation and has no guarantee that he or she will ever hear the perpetrator explain his or her actions.

VORP, most frequently used for juveniles or first–time offenders with the greatest chance for rehabilitation, is based on a much different approach. Working closely with the regular court structure, the VORP coordinator contacts both the criminal and the victim to see if they would be open to participating in the program. Then the coordinator talks to both parties to learn their stories and arrange for a joint meeting. In that meeting, as the victim tells the story of what happened, the criminal is obligated to put a human face on the target of the crime. Now, the abstract "rich person" becomes a real individual who struggles to pay a mortgage, buy clothes for his or her children, and make ends meet with a payroll. The "distant person" becomes a human being who suffered deep trauma from the robbery, vandalism, or physical attack. The victim can also gain a new perspective. Now, instead of faceless thug, he or she confronts a person who is beginning to accept responsibility and express remorse.

Benefits of VORP   At the joint meeting, the parties agree on a method of compensation that takes the victim's loss into account. Rather than a fine to the court, the criminal agrees to restore the victim's property, pay for any bodily injuries, or engage in some type of work that would be satisfying to the victim. The goal of this strategy is not to let criminals off the hook with an easy remedy, but to engage them in some kind of constructive response that enables them to understand the consequences of their activities and to feel that they have done something positive to repair the damage. The VORP coordinator monitors not just the meetings, but the process of restitution. While not always successful, VORP has been shown to work significantly better than jail sentences. And in cases where the victims and offenders will continue to live in the same community, there is a sense of security for the victim that does not exist when a still resentful criminal is released from prison or has paid a fine.

VORP originally began as a response to nonviolent crimes, but some of its principles have been applied to very serious felonies such as murder and rape. In such cases there is no effort to avoid the normal court system or reduce a prison sentence. Rather, there is an attempt to work with criminals while they are in jail. In jail, they are placed in direct contact with victims, although perhaps not their own, who describe the loss, pain, and humiliation they suffered. Often, for the very first time, a criminal begins to realize that victims were not faceless non–entities. Perhaps for the first time, the criminal can begin to feel remorse and desire change. Because virtually all criminals are eventually sent back into society, this process is a very important step towards making that reentry successful.

ANALYSIS AND CRITICAL RESPONSE

One of the most challenging problems for pacifists is the question raised by Reinhold Niebuhr (1892–1971), a theologian, political thinker, and a former pacifist. A liberal social progressive, Niebuhr once served as president of the Fellowship of Reconciliation, America's most prominent pacifist organization. During the 1920s, he believed peace was reasonable and that people were perfectible. He thought that with more education and enlightenment, people would improve to the point where war and injustice would become obsolete. But, with the Great Depression and the rise of totalitarian systems in both Germany and Russia, he reassessed his earlier position. Rejecting liberal optimism, Niebuhr argued that sin, not a lack of education or a fair legal system, was the major reason why evil persisted.

In Niebuhr's view, sin was the unwillingness of human beings to accept their own nature. On the one hand, people were driven by deep–seated natural emotions such as the desire for power or for survival. People were also entrenched in economic and social systems that could not easily be changed. Niebuhr believed these drives and systems affected all humans. On the other hand, Niebuhr noted that people were able to contemplate ideals. They had the power to imagine and strive toward perfection. In Niebuhr's view, the natural drives and systems had to be kept in balance with the imagined ideals. Neither side of the equation should be embraced without restraint. According to Niebuhr, evil was the attempt to ignore the ideals by giving oneself entirely to the drives of nature or trying to escape the limits of nature by clinging only to ideals. The Nazis, he believed, had chosen to abandon themselves exclusively to the drives of nature. But pacifists, he charged, had forsaken the ambiguities of the real world to seek refuge in the world of ideals. According to Niebuhr, that path was evidence of the sin of pride, and it allowed great evil to succeed. What was needed, Niebuhr argued, was for good people to remain in the real world and to choose the most practical option, even if that meant accepting the lesser of two evils. In Niebuhr's view, the commandment to love one's neighbor sometimes required a person or nation to take up arms. Absolute pacifism, he said, was ineffective against terrible evils such as Nazism and it refused to accept the responsibilities of living in the real world.

For many critics of pacifism, and even for many pacifists, Niebuhr's logic seemed irrefutable. Not only did he provide strong reproof of overly optimistic liberalism, he offered a powerful criticism of excessively idealistic pacifism. Furthermore, Niebuhr seemed to give advice that could be used by people holding positions of responsibility in government. Because Niebuhr asked policy–makers to choose the lesser of two evils, his writings offered improvement even if they did not promise perfection. For their part, pacifists calling for people to "turn the other cheek" seemed to have nothing practical to say to chief executives, diplomats, and people in the military.

What is the response of pacifists to thinkers such as Niebuhr who see pacifism as an appealing, but hopelessly unrealistic ideal? Specifically, do pacifists have any answer to the problem of World War II, a problem that was so troublesome for Niebuhr and millions of other thoughtful people? Although their views have not found their way into mainstream textbooks, pacifists claim they have a response to people like Niebuhr.

Pacifist Views of World War II

Pacifist historians remind people that the popular view of World War II is often a very selective version filtered through the eyes of Hollywood or one–sided nationalistic accounts. In those versions, the Allies are portrayed as innocent victims of aggressive German and Japanese surprise attacks. There is no hint of any Allied responsibility. In fact, the Allies' only failure was said to have been an unwillingness to confront evil sooner. Chamberlain's debacle at Munich is regarded as a clear lesson that more, not less, force must be applied to potential conflicts. Furthermore, according to popular opinion, the battles of World War II were fought by tough, strong, young men from Germany, Japan, the United States, Britain, France, and Russia. There is no suggestion that most of the casualties were innocent civilians. Finally, defenders of the war argue that World War II was fought not only to save democracy, but also to rescue Jews being destroyed in the Holocaust. There is no reference to anti–Semitism in America or in the European democracies. And there is little reference to the fact that the Allies also intentionally killed many unarmed men, women, and children.

Real aims of the war In looking at the causes of World War II, pacifists remind people that World War II was actually a continuation of World War I, and they recall that World War I was caused by the reckless arms buildup that took place in the early years of the twentieth century. Although European nations only wanted to intimidate their neighbors, not start a war, the situation got out of hand and Europe stumbled into war in 1914. The punitive and unjust "peace" that France and Britain imposed by the Treaty of Versailles left Germany humiliated and economically devastated. That "peace" created a perfect climate for the rise of Hitler who found a group to blame—the Jews—and who promised to restore Germany's glory. A pacifist would place much of the responsibility for World War II on the excessive militarism that led up to World War I and to the harsh peace forced on Germany in 1919.

Some pacifists argue that the Allies did not enter World War II to save Jews. Anti–Semitism was widespread in Europe and America. In fact, many people in countries such as France, Belgium, and England supported Hitler's anti–Jewish rhetoric. At a time when Hitler still allowed Jews to emigrate from Germany, the United States turned away a ship loaded with Jews seeking asylum. Eventually, the ship returned to Germany where many of its occupants eventually suffered extermination. These anti–Semitic attitudes and actions, both in Europe and America, signaled to Hitler that the rest of the world condoned, perhaps even admired, what he was doing in Germany.

As for the war with Japan, some pacifist historians contend that in 1941 the Japanese Prime Minister Konoye (1891–1945) was eager to negotiate with the United States and that he would have been willing to reverse Japanese expansionism in the Pacific. But, he wanted to do so in a gradual manner that would not result in a loss of face for Japan or the Emperor. The Prime Minister, who feared assassination at the hands of hard–line militarists if the talks became public, pled for secrecy. However, after a spirited internal debate, the U.S. government took a hard line and issued a public call asking the Japanese to back down. As a result, Konoye resigned and the far more aggressive Hideki Tojo (1884–1948) was installed as Japan's leader. At that point, planning for Pearl Harbor pushed ahead and led to the confrontation that neither nation really wanted.

Looking at Germany's war in Eastern Europe, pacifists note that only fifty years earlier other European powers also had engaged in campaigns of conquest and colonization. The territories taken in those actions remained under European control in the 1930s. Thus, Germany saw eastward expansion simply as a replay of what England, France, and Belgium had done in Africa and Asia. Therefore, in the view of pacifist historians, it was hypocritical for the Allies to condemn Germany for its attempts to colonize Eastern Europe and Russia.

The Holocaust Pacifists readily agree that the Holocaust was an unmitigated evil. However, they point out that most of the Jews who were rescued during World War II were not saved by Allied armies, but by the nonviolent actions of civilians who sheltered Jews and/or smuggled them out of Nazi– or Fascist–controlled territory. According to some reports, 80 percent of all Jews saved in France were rescued in that manner. In Italy, the numbers were 90 percent, in Belgium about 50 percent, and in Denmark almost 100 percent of the Jews who escaped extermination were saved by civilians. To say that Jews were rescued by heroic Allied armies is a misrepresentation of history.

Pacifists note that the idea of targeting innocent civilians for extermination was an idea first implemented by Winston Churchill (1874–1965), not by Adolf Hitler (1889–1945). Until 1940, bombing raids on both sides had been conducted against industrial or military targets. Civilian casualties, even when heavy, were generally accidental side effects of attacks against such facilities. But, in 1940, Churchill began the deliberate bombing of German cities. Bomber commanders were ordered to drop their bombs into the very hearts of German cities, not at industrial or military targets. Churchill believed that such raids

would weaken the support of German civilians for Hitler. Even after D–Day on June 6, 1944, when it became increasingly clear that the war was ending, the bombing of civilians continued. One of the targets of these bombing raids was Dresden, a city with no military significance. In all, between 600,000 and 800,000 German civilians were killed in the actions against urban settlements. Ironically, such bombing served to strengthen support for Hitler and, thus, actually may have prolonged the war.

The atomic bomb In August, 1945, the Americans dropped atomic bombs on Hiroshima and Nagasaki. The bombs killed more than 200,000 civilians and injured almost an equal number of people. By August 1945, no significant military targets still remained in Japan. Furthermore, the Japanese navy had been destroyed, and the Japanese army had been cut off from the mainland. Pacifist historians contend that since the bombings were designed to destroy civilians and not military installations, they were not much different from the Holocaust. Both the Germans and the Allies were willing to sacrifice innocent civilians for political or military gains. The only difference, pacifists argue, is that the Germans brought the people to the ovens while the Allies dropped the ovens on the people.

As for the argument that the atomic bomb was needed to convince the Japanese to surrender, historians point out that the Japanese government had already made overtures through Russia that it wanted peace. In July 1945, former Prime Minister Konoye flew to Moscow to negotiate for peace. His only condition was that Japan not be occupied and that the Emperor not be dethroned. Thus, an offer of surrender was on the table before the bomb was dropped. Even after the bomb fell on Hiroshima and Nagasaki, the Japanese did not surrender until they received assurances that the Emperor would remain on his throne.

Pacifism and the Future

Gene Sharp's proposals for CBD, the use of nonviolent methods for dealing with political and ethnic conflict, and the VORP programs are three examples of how nonviolence theory has influenced or could influence real world politics. No political theory is ever implemented in its pure form. That is true of communism, democracy, and monarchy. All functional modern political ideologies began as distant and incomplete visions in the minds of thinkers and activists who were considered impractical idealists. In the view of many pacifists, what today seems impossible will one day become accepted convention. Less than 1,000 years ago, many people would not have been able to conceive of a well–ordered world without the protection of holy wars or human sacrifice. Less than 200 years ago, many responsible people were convinced that society could not function if slaves were freed or if people other than propertied males participated in politics. As recently as the 1940s, few people would have dreamed that both Japan and Germany could become staunchly democratic and pro–American nations. Clearly, these examples prove that profound change is possible. Pacifists believe, at least hope, that in the future their views will be incorporated into the constitutions and policies of most nations around the world.

TOPICS FOR FURTHER STUDY

- Must pacifism like Thoreau's come into conflict with government policy or even come into conflict with the very existence of the state?
- What pacifistic themes are there in Tolstoy's novels?
- Study one of Gandhi's many nonviolence campaigns in South Africa or India. What made them effective?
- Examine newspapers and periodicals of the 1930s and 1940s. Was Gandhi viewed as a hero in the West at that time? Also, what did Americans think of Martin Luther King Jr. and his activities in the 1960s?
- In today's textbooks, are pacifists or pacifistic ideas and actions given any credit for helping to end slavery, for challenging segregation, or for strengthening democracy? Internationally, are they given any credit for helping to end the power of the Soviet Union over Eastern Europe?

BIBLIOGRAPHY

Sources

Aung San, Suu Kyi. *Freedom From Fear and Other Writings.* London: Penguin, 1991.

Gandhi, Mohandas. *All Men are Brothers.* New York: Continuum, 1980.

The Holy Bible, New International Version. Colorado Springs, Colorado: International Bible Society, 1984.

King, Martin Luther Jr. *Why We Can't Wait.* New York: Harper & Row, 1991.

Nhat Hanh, Thich. *Being Peace.* Berkeley, CA: Parallax Press, 1987.

Reardon, Betty. *Sexism and the War System.* Syracuse, NY: Syracuse University Press, 1985.

Yoder, John H. *The Politics of Jesus.* Grand Rapids, MI: Eerdmans, 1972.

Zehr, Howard, J. *Changing Lenses: A New Focus for Crime and Justice.* Scottdale, PA: Herald Press, 1990.

Further Readings

Ackerman, Peter, and Christopher Kruegler. *Strategic Nonviolent Conflict: The Dynamics of People Power in the Twentieth Century.* Westport, CT: Praeger, 1994. Explanation of how nonviolent civilian actions have succeeded in modern times.

Barash, David P. *Approaches to Peace, A Reader in Peace Studies.* New York: Oxford University Press, 2000. An excellent anthology containing a wide variety of essential texts on nonviolence.

Hawkley, Louise, and Juhnke, James, eds. *Nonviolent America, History Through the Eyes of Peace.* Newton, KS: Mennonite Press, 1983. A study of pacifism in America and a description of how nonviolent actions have been overlooked in the writing of American history.

Krog, Antjie. *Country of My Skull: Guilt, Sorrow, and the Limits to Freedom in the New South Africa.* New York: Random House, 1998. A vivid and moving account of testimony heard by the Truth and Reconciliation Commission.

Sharp, Gene. *Making Europe Unconquerable: The Potential of Civilian–based Deterrence and Defense.* Cambridge: Ballinger, 1985. An explanation of how Sharp's theory could be used to build an effective defense for European nations.

SEE ALSO

Imperialism, Socialism, Utopianism,

Patron–Client Systems

Patron–client systems are organized by people of power, both men and women, who build and keep the loyalty of people of more humble position. Both patrons and clients regard the link between them as a personal attachment similar to the bond of affection holding members of a family or kin group together. However, unlike families, where the linkage is regarded as permanent and often is taken for granted, a patron–client relationship must be renewed constantly and renegotiated continuously. Throughout history, clients have provided the work, income, popular acclaim, votes, political allegiance, and military support that patrons need to maintain power and position. For their part, clients have gained protection, access to resources or information, group identity, and opportunities for advancement. Although no modern government would claim to operate according to the principles of patron–clientage, many nations throughout the world are guided by the logic of patron–client transactions. No government escapes the influence of patron–client considerations.

The strength, prominence, and persistence of patron–client arrangements suggest that, along with democracy and authoritarianism, patron–client systems represent a generic form of the way human beings organize their society and govern. Most people think of the modern world as being dominated either by liberal democratic or authoritarian systems. Liberal democracies are characterized by personal liberty and citizen participation. In a liberal democracy,

WHO CONTROLS GOVERNMENT? Wealthy officials

HOW IS GOVERNMENT PUT INTO POWER? Overthrow or fall of previous regime

WHAT ROLES DO THE PEOPLE HAVE? Obey leader

WHO CONTROLS PRODUCTION OF GOODS? Government and wealthy businesspeople

WHO CONTROLS DISTRIBUTION OF GOODS? Government and wealthy businesspeople

MAJOR FIGURES Pope Adrian IV; Juan Perón

HISTORICAL EXAMPLE Zaire, 1965–1997

CHRONOLOGY

1000 B.C.: Patron–client systems are the most common way to organize government.

348 B.C.: Greek philosopher Plato dies.

496 A.D.: The Fall of Rome.

1154–1159: Adrian IV reigns as Pope.

1513: Machiavelli writes *The Prince*.

1715: King Louis XIV of France dies.

1882: The U.S. Congress passes the Pendleton Act.

1946–1955: Juan Perón presides over a vast patronage system in Argentina.

1971: John Rawls publishes *A Theory of Justice*.

2000: Vicente Fox is elected as president of Mexico.

principles such as freedom of assembly and movement, the right to hold property, the right to act without observation in one's home, and the right to fair trials offer basic protections for all citizens. In addition, liberal democracies are marked by the unrestricted flow of information, multiple political parties, and free and fair elections that allow citizens to select their leaders. Authoritarian systems are characterized by clear lines of command and control emanating from the top. In authoritarian societies, an individual or small group of people direct political and perhaps economic affairs according to what they think is best. Obedience, order, and efficiency are the goals of authoritarianism, while liberal democracies seek to maximize freedom, a vigorous flow of ideas, and political equality.

In reality, in spite of the claims of their governments, many people in the modern world do not live in either democratic or authoritarian systems. Instead, they live in patron–client systems that operate with an entirely different logic. Patron–client systems focus on holding leaders and followers together through a regular exchange of personal favors, support, and protection. Unlike democracies, patron–client systems do not insist on elections, division of power, and the legal protection of individual or corporate rights. Unlike the subjects of authoritarian regimes, people living in patron–client systems make no ultimate concession of obedience to the state or a dominant leader. While both authoritarian and democratic governments generally conduct their affairs within the framework of codified legal structures and pre–set budgets, patron–client systems are not as constrained in their behavior. In patron–client systems an individual's main preoccupation is building personalized attachments either to powerful superiors or to supportive inferiors. Every arrangement, benefit, penalty, law, and appointment is negotiable. Everything can be purchased and everything can change.

HISTORY

Patron–client systems are among the oldest political forms in the world. Before humans developed self–conscious political systems, people organized themselves around leaders of hunting and gathering bands that were generally composed of people related by blood or marriage. Ideally, the head of the band would have been the father or the oldest male relative. Because such leaders probably acted more as patriarchs, facilitators, and guides, and because society would have been relatively undifferentiated and unstratified, such leaders should not be considered political leaders. Rather, they were simply hereditary heads of families or informal heads of very small communities.

However, as society became more complex, as wealth became more pronounced, and as defense became more challenging, men, and at times women, emerged as leaders and defenders of families or regions. In many parts of the world, archeologists have discovered very early burial sites in which a small minority of the people were interred with symbols of wealth and political power. Presumably, those people were seen as big people, leaders charged with defending and guiding the community. People generally would have used the language of kinship to describe such leaders who would have been regarded as fathers or senior kin. But, in fact, the patron's entourage was composed of people with varying degrees of genetic attachment and many people were connected to their patrons by bonds of choice rather than blood. This was the beginning of politics.

Ancient Patron–Client Systems

Patron–client systems were very common in ancient times. In the Old Testament, the entire Book of Judges is devoted to describing a patron–client system that functioned between 1200 and 1000 B.C. Although great monarchies dominated Egypt and the Tigris–Euphrates Valley, the area now known as Palestine,

Israel, Jordan, and Lebanon was ruled by warrior leaders who remained in power by standing up against neighboring big men and by nurturing the loyalty of their people. The Greek epic poet Homer's *Odyssey* makes it clear that a remarkably similar political landscape existed in the lands bordering the north shores the Mediterranean Sea.

According to the Book of Judges, the times were turbulent as warrior–chiefs (patrons) mobilized followers (clients) to defend against, attack, and plunder their neighbors. A chief who was successful both in providing a secure defense and in taking booty from surrounding peoples was able to stay in office. From the stories in Judges, it is possible to identify the qualities required for a patron to gain and keep power. Military prowess was a requisite virtue. An ability to defend one's own people, skill in plundering people of other ethnic groups, a willingness to act cruelly and treacherously against rivals and enemies, and an exceptional strategic competence were regarded as key attributes of leadership. While generous and protective toward supporters, patrons killed or extracted labor and material wealth from their enemies. Successful leaders were not bound by ordinary rules of law, but they resorted to trickery and cunning to gain and retain power. The ability to provide material rewards was essential in gaining the support of followers. Often such wealth came from the spoils of battle. "A girl or two for each man," highly embroidered cloth, ornaments from camels, and golden earrings are some of the rewards that the Book of Judges says was distributed to clients. In addition, patron rulers in the Book of Judges gave their daughters to loyal and successful warriors. As bearers of children and workers, women were regarded as economic assets as much as companions or lovers.

A patron's power was not measured only in terms of military force or the ability to distribute wealth. Dispute resolution may have been the main way patrons built up a following. For example, in the Book of Judges, the judge Deborah held court under a tree where people came for litigation. Presumably, their appearance was voluntary and was motivated by Deborah's reputation as an effective mediator. Another source of a patron's power was dispensing blessings and curses. This may seem inconsequential to modern secular readers, but in pre–modern times such blessings and curses were regarded as highly effective. Both, it was believed, could determine the destiny of an individual or group. In addition, great patrons were thought to be endowed with supernatural powers, such as the extraordinary strength of Samson, an Israelite judge.

A patron's image   Not only the actions, but the public image of the patron was critically important. A big man or woman (patron) cultivated a persona of strength, generosity, shrewdness, ruthlessness, decisiveness, and courage. Praise singers glorified great patrons as evidenced by the Song of Deborah, one of the most ancient texts of the Old Testament. According to the song, before Deborah came as a defender, villages had been insecure and roads had been abandoned due to the insecurity that gripped the land (Judges 5). Other judge–patrons were lauded for their ability to slaughter enemies. Although exaggerated, the words of praise singers show what people valued in a patron leader. Predictably, one of the greatest dangers for a patron was to be regarded as weak; thus, a common taunt was to charge that a male leader was so inconsequential that he could be killed or subdued even by a female.

One judge–patron, Abimelech, illustrates the severity of being known as weak. Abimelech's father was Jerub–Baal (also known as Gideon), one of the greatest warrior–patrons of ancient Israel. Living in the eleventh century B.C., Jerub–Baal accumulated many wives and concubines by whom he fathered more than 70 sons, but the large political following he built up during his life fell apart when he died. Abimelech, whose mother was a concubine from the town of Shechem, then mobilized his mother's relatives who gave him money to "hire reckless adventurers." With their support, he murdered all of his brothers except the youngest, Jotham, who escaped. In an accusatory speech to the people of Shechem, Jotham likened Abimelech to a dangerous thorn bush that offered refuge to friends and devastation to foes. Jotham's prophecy proved to be accurate. Furious when the people of Shechem defied him by ambushing and robbing travelers (presumably their defiance was not sharing the loot), Abimelech laid siege against the city, killed its people, and destroyed its fortifications. According to the story, about 1,000 people died when Abimelech set fire to the strong tower where they had taken refuge. From Shechem, Abimelech went to punish another group of disobedient people living in the city of Thebez. Again he stormed the tower where all the people had fled, but as Abimelech prepared to set the tower ablaze, a woman dropped a millstone on his head, severely wounding him. Concerned about his reputation as a great warrior, Abimelech ordered his armor–bearer to end his life with a sword so that people would not remember him as the man killed by a mere woman (Judges 8 and 9).

Greece   The political landscape described by Homer's *Odyssey*, written around 850 B.C., is similar

Odysseus, hero of Homer's Odyssey. *(Corbis Corporation)*

to that of the Book of Judges. Crafty heroes, not systems, dominate human affairs. In Homer's Greece, numerous petty kings ruled small groups of clients. Ordinary people were protected best not by bureaucrats or laws, but by the strength and shrewdness of a patron who could deal with a constant succession of novel and formidable challenges. On one level, Homer's tale of Odysseus was the chronicle of a hero's struggle against supernatural or superhuman foes and dangers. But, on another level, the story admonished listeners to trust their fate to an honorable and wily champion who would bring them safely through life's journey. This is consistent with one of the central realities of patron–client systems: patrons are great men and women whose personal charisma, cunning, and strength enable them to emerge as leaders and defenders.

Another central feature of the ancient Greek was the importance of boundless generosity. A good patron was lavish in his display and distribution of wealth. Modern Americans would describe this practice as "pork barrel politics." The central symbol of such generosity was the feast. For example, at the very beginning of the *Odyssey* before Odysseus returned home, his house was filled with men who not only were courting his wife (a woman everyone presumed must now be a widow) but also who were enjoying

daily feasts at the expense of Odysseus' son Telemakhos. Telemakhos complained about the constant economic drain caused by men who gathered at his house slaughtering the cattle, sheep, and goats; drinking the best wine; and squandering the family's wealth. However, both Telemakhos and the many clients recognized that the political preeminence of Odysseus' house was dependent upon a constant distribution of food and drink. At one point, one of the young men benefiting from the feasting told Telmakhos directly that he could never hope to become king if he failed to entertain the scores of supporters. The nature of the political bargain was made clear by the young man's words: Telemakhos could not succeed his father if he refused to satisfy the material wants of his clients. Discontent meant that the clients would abandon the house and shift their loyalty and support to a more generous political patron.

The emergence of democracies, tyrannies, monarchies, and empires with their insistence for routinized systems of administration, predictable patterns of taxation and distribution, reliable methods of transferring power, and standardized legal procedures eventually superceded patron–clientage in the ancient world. In Greece, Athens adapted democracy while Sparta developed a highly structured state–centered authoritarianism. Both in Athens and Sparta, institutions and laws replaced the rule of individuals. Although patron–clientage continued to exist in many of the Greek city states, the system was no longer celebrated. This change was reflected in the philosophical writings of the day. For example, both Socrates (c. 469–c. 399 B.C.) and Plato (428–348 B.C.) condemned the characters in Homer's *Odyssey* as immoral and unworthy of respect. According to Plato, good rulers were utterly selfless in their thinking and austere in their life.

Rome One should not imagine, however, that patron–client practices ceased to exist in an increasingly institutionalized ancient world. Within the Roman Empire, a polity famed for its efficient bureaucracy and systemic legal code, patron–clientage remained a prominent feature of political life. Successful generals such as Julius Caesar (102–44 B.C.) were able to gain control of Rome by winning the support of their soldiers who benefited from the loot collected in war and by winning the favor of the ordinary people through conspicuous displays of generosity that included extravagant feasts and public entertainment. Successful Roman leaders also depended on the backing of political clients who hoped to advance by means of the money and influence of powerful patrons. With the fall of the Roman Empire in 476 A.D., political control moved east to Constantinople, the capital of Byzantium. Palace intrigue, ever–shifting alliances built on the dispensing of rewards or punishments, and the personalized exercise of power were hallmarks of Byzantine politics. In fact, the word Byzantine has come to mean intrigue and unfathomable complexity in the political realm. In any case, Byzantium was a classic example of patron–client politics. Although modern observers tend to criticize the Byzantine system as unworkable and unethical, Byzantium outlasted Rome by almost exactly 1,000 years.

The Middle Ages to the Twentieth Century

In Western Europe, Rome's political successor was a patron–client system rather than the citizen–centered democracy practiced by the Greeks or the bureaucratic authoritarianism exercised by the Romans. Feudalism, a system that persisted to some degree until the French Revolution, was essentially a highly developed form of patron–clientage. Working within systems of ever–changing and highly personalized alliances, clients and patrons gave and sought contributions and spoils, obedience and loyalty, and deference and security. In the sometimes turbulent world of the Middle Ages (when people could not rely on city–states, empires, or nations for security) people could count on personalized relationships for support and protection. Such relationships could be established

more quickly and firmly (essential in a time when old institutions were crumbling) than monarchies or democracies, which often took centuries or millenniums to mature.

The monarchies that eventually emerged to create the modern nation–state system in Europe incorporated many of the principles of the patron–client system. Italian statesman and political theorist Niccolò Machiavelli's (1469–1527) *The Prince* outlined the methods used by rulers to build and retain a loyal group of clients. Although needing to maintain the appearance of following laws and ethical standards, Machiavelli argued that a successful ruler should be flexible, wily, and willing to punish or reward. Machiavelli did warn patrons of the pitfalls of excessive generosity; nevertheless, he recognized the importance of distributing largesse in order to build up a base of supporters. Monarchs such as Louis XIV of France and Elizabeth I of England were skilled practitioners of many of Machiavelli's principles.

The modern era In modern times, patron–client systems have lost the official respect of most politicians and theorists. In Great Britain, patron–client politics were curtailed in the mid–nineteenth century. In 1853, Chancellor of the Exchequer William Gladstone (1809–1898) requested that officials serving in India be selected on the basis of an open, competitive examination rather than through family or political connections. In addition, within Parliament itself, patronage came under fire. Between 1847 and 1866, about 100 newly elected members of Parliament (MPs) were unseated because of electoral corruption. In the United States, patron–clientage, known as the "spoils system" (to the victor go the spoils), reached its high point immediately after the Civil War. The administrations of Ulysses S. Grant (1822–1885) and Rutherford B. Hayes (1822–1893) were among the most notorious for dispensing favors—political and financial—to party loyalists who used their positions in Congress, in tax collection agencies, in custom houses, in city halls, and in departments such as the Post Office and Interior to amass fortunes and to build solid networks of supporters and sub–clients. In return, both great and small beneficiaries were required to make contributions to the party treasury and to use their offices and influence to promote the election and advancement of members of their party. So powerful was the patron–client system that the real movers and shakers of nineteenth–century American politics were often semi–obscure political bosses operating in "smoke–filled rooms." The actions of these men were not subject to public scrutiny and many of them did not even hold elected office. Only after a disappointed patronage seeker shot and killed newly elected President James A. Garfield (1831–1881) did the United States pass legislation designed to put an end to patronage. The Pendleton Act (the Civil Service Reform Bill of 1883) mandated that government appointments be made on the basis of open and competitive examinations and that office holders could not be required to make monetary contributions to their party. Although at the time of its passage the Pendleton Act covered only 12 percent of federal government positions, throughout the years the number of positions protected by civil service rules increased. Later, in 1939 the Hatch Act was written to prohibit both federal and state government employees from active involvement in partisan politics. In spite of these efforts, patron–client politics continue to function in America at the local, state, and federal levels.

In other nations of the world, patron–client procedures influence, even dominate, political dealings. Although technically a democracy, Japan has long functioned as a patron–client system. In Latin America, patronage networks, not democratic or even authoritarian principles, guide politics in many countries. In China, the rules of patronage compete with the doctrines of the Communist Party. The same was true in the Soviet Union under communism. Following the fall of communism, Russia has been governed as much through patronage as through either authoritarianism or democracy.

The Salampasu   The most prominent patron–client arrangements in modern times are in Africa. Before colonialism disrupted the normal flow of traditional African politics, most people in Africa organized their political affairs according to the principles of patron–client relations. One example would be that of the Salampasu people of the Congo. Although the Salampasu rejected the idea of organizing themselves into a centralized state—states can be both expensive and oppressive for citizens—they developed highly structured forms of political organization. The most prominent feature on the Salampasu political landscape was the big man or patron. Big men competed with each other to attract groups of young men as their followers. By joining a big man's group, the young men received training and experience as hunters and warriors. They also stood to benefit from the spoils of battles waged by the big men; among the most important rewards given by a big man was access to women. Because the big man's wealth and power enabled him to obtain numerous women, technically regarded as his wives, he alone could give or withhold permission to sleep with and eventually marry such women. By working and fighting for a big man, young

men could obtain enough wealth to "purchase" a wife whose children and labor would now be theirs and not the big man's. Because women and children were centrally important for farm work and food preparation, a Salampasu man's wealth and status were determined by his ability to obtain wives and have children.

The task of the Salampasu big man was very challenging. He needed to maintain the appearance of strength, generosity, and fairness. People had to fear his power to punish effectively, depend on his capacity to reward generously, and trust his ability to resolve disputes equitably. These were the essential ingredients in the glue that held his community together. While clients needed a patron, a patron required clients. Without a strong group of clients or followers, a leader would be defeated in battle. Without the wealth he accumulated through his office and through the work of his children and wives, he would be unable to reward his followers and attract new clients. Without the political skill and cunning needed to please and calm his ambitious and contentious band of clients, his entire village could disintegrate.

Although the Salampasu people never developed a centralized state, in many other parts of Africa, powerful and ambitious big men were able to establish institutions of government that continued beyond the patron's death. While some chiefdoms contained only several thousand inhabitants, others became so large and powerful that they could properly be called kingdoms. But, in virtually every case, the polities operated as patron–client systems. Office holders were collectors of tribute and dispensers of largesse. Generally, such transactions were counted as gifts. For example, an office–seeker or local chief would visit a more powerful central chief and offer "gifts" such as meat, dried fish, cloth, live animals, metal, or women. Gift-giving was particularly active during times of political transition. People hoping to obtain an office would bring gifts to key decision–makers or to people who could give access to such policy makers. The individual bringing the largest gift had the best chance of gaining an appointment. The person or persons receiving the gifts might encourage greater gift–giving by telling each candidate that the choice would be made soon, that they were the most likely choice, and that their chances would be enhanced by an even more generous gift. Of course, the decision–maker could continue this only for so long. Eventually, he or she had to make a selection but, even then, the flow of gifts did not necessarily come to a halt. Now, each loser could be told that the individual who won the position would not likely remain for long and that they, the loser, would certainly be the next choice so long as they retained the favor of the top political players.

Another source of tribute revenue came through legal procedures. People involved in court cases were often required to pay a fee. While some of this was to be given as restitution to the aggrieved party, a major portion went directly to the chief who was hearing and deciding the case. When people approached a chief to receive a legal ruling, they frequently came bearing gifts of tribute. People in the Western world consider gifts given in return for a political appointment or to obtain a favorable ruling in court as bribery. For people operating according to the rules of a patron–client system, such gifts are indications of seriousness and support. Someone able to mobilize substantial tribute is a person willing to make a real commitment to the cause. A person able to offer large amounts of money has the support and confidence of those who know him or her best. In addition to their value as measures of personal resolve and peer solidarity, such gifts might be considered user fees that pay for the costs of operating a government.

Tribute Someone who obtained a political office by offering tribute could then use that position to generate even more wealth. For example, someone appointed as a lower level chief, judge, tax collector, or ferry–crossing operator could then gather fees and tributes on an ongoing basis. Such an appointee would be expected to share a standard percentage with the patron who had made the appointment. Every office holder, except for the supreme chief, was both a patron and a client. Every person with the power to make a decision, offer access to a higher official, or provide important information had the right to collect tribute. In that sense, political offices became a source of ongoing revenue. Permission was not granted or advancement permitted because of merit or a legitimate claim. Rather, permission and advancement came when the proper amount of tribute had been paid and the proper degree of respect and deference had been offered.

While people of lesser rank often gave tribute to people with more power and status, leaders at the top gave gifts as demonstrations of their power and generosity. At times, such gift–giving was dramatic and lavish. In the nineteenth–century slave trading kingdom of Dahomey, which dominated the territory now known as Benin, the king gave gifts in a spectacular manner. Each year, when officials (the king's clients) gathered at the capital, a large replica of a sailing ship was pulled into the main square. From the ship, the king's servants threw out expensive trade goods to the assembled crowds. Such displays were tangible demonstrations that the king was the supreme patron whose strength, courage, and wisdom enabled him to

dispense largesse to the entire nation. At these same ceremonies, the king executed slaves as a way to give gifts of tribute to the ancestors and gods who stood above even him.

When African countries became independent, many of them around 1960, most people involved in the transition assumed that the new leaders would establish liberal democratic regimes. Those that did not, it was thought, would pursue the path of communism and Marxism. In spite of these hopes and expectations, by the end of the twentieth century it had become clear that virtually every African country followed the rules of patron–clientism instead of either democracy or communism. Parliaments, elections, budgets, regularized administrative procedures, and official legal codes were all routinely subverted in order to accommodate the values of the patron–client system. Large portions of most African budgets were managed in a way that conformed to the logic of patronage. For example, African heads of state routinely announced that they were giving massive "personal" gifts to schools, churches, communities, individuals, and organizations. If the national football teams won an important international tournament, the president might choose to give each player a personal gift such as a car, house, or money. Or, a communication from the president's office might tell people that a city's electricity has been restored because the president generously had donated oil to fuel the municipal generators. Similarly, jailed journalists released from detention were said to have gained their freedom because of the magnanimity of the head of state, not because the constitution or the law protected their right to freedom of the press.

Modern Africa

The current–day preoccupation with honoring African heads of state is further evidence of the patron–client system in operation. As chief patron of the nation, the chief executive's picture hangs in every business, is imprinted on every piece of currency, and appears first on the evening television news. When the president travels around the capital, he is transported in an extensive motorcade that includes elaborately costumed motorcycle riders, numerous armed vehicles, many black curtained limousines, several chase vehicles, and the automobiles of various ministers and government officials. For important occasions, such as the return from a trip abroad, the President is greeted at the airport by the entire cabinet; prominent church, educational, and business leaders; cultural dancers; a sometimes reluctant foreign diplomatic corps; and the press. School children may be marshaled to stand along the road and "spontaneously" cheer the returned leader whose dealings or negotiations abroad are described in a laudatory fashion by the state–owned media.

The fact that so many officials and citizens of African countries accept these patterns as normal suggests that the practices should not be seen as immoral aberrations; rather, they should be seen as competing methods of conducting politics. Although Western politicians, journalists, and bankers condemn the African patron–client system as illegal and wrong, the system's robust persistence shows that many Africans disagree. To some extent, modern Africans are torn between two worlds. On the one hand, most African states claim to be democratic, and most African legal codes condemn the practices of patronage. On the other hand, both leaders and followers engage in patron–client politics. Many would consider a leader who refuses to dispense patronage as mean or stingy, and many would regard ordinary people who avoid participating in the patronage system as naïve or weak.

THEORY IN DEPTH

In spite of their ancient pedigree and their extensive distribution even in modern times, patron–client systems are orphans in the world of political theory. When Francis Fukuyama (1952–) wrote his 1992 essay *The End of History and the Last Man*, he argued that only one political system, democracy, had retained its legitimacy and attractiveness at the end of the twentieth century. He noted that fascism and nazism have long been discredited and that the fall of the Soviet Union effectively ended the prospects of communism persisting as a viable system. Fukuyama did not even mention patron–client governments. For Fukuyama, patron–clientism does not exist or is inconsequential. Fukuyama's views reflect the perspective of the political science community. Unlike other philosophies or systems such as democracy, socialism, communism, or even anarchism, the patron–client system has no supporters, advocates, or theorists. Textbooks about comparative politics generally divide the world's political systems into democratic or authoritarian arrangements. Such books give scant attention to patron–client systems. Democracies are categorized as parliamentary or presidential, while authoritarian governments are described as totalitarian, communist, fascist, theocratic, or monarchical. Books on comparative politics often assume that governments not fitting easily into one of those two groupings eventually will evolve to become either democratic or authoritarian. Or, it is thought, a few unstable systems, such as Nigeria's, may continue to vacillate between the two. Implicitly, or even explicitly, such comparative politics books suggest that every nation eventually must choose between democracy and authoritarianism. Other comparative politics books sidestep the matter by placing governments that are neither democratic nor authoritarian into a non–political category. A large number of countries in Africa, Latin America, or Asia are not seen as responsive enough to be democratic or efficient enough to be authoritarian. These countries are then lumped into classifications that are more economic, social, chronological, or geographical than political. These states are often referred to as poor countries, developing nations (not modern), third–world countries, or southern–hemisphere countries. They are not labeled as patron–client regimes, which would place them in a formal political category.

When modern political scientists discuss patron–client systems, they do so in a negative or dismissive manner. Governments strongly influenced by the principles of patron–clientage are regarded as archaic, inefficient, corrupt, and even criminal. Often, patron–client systems are described as systems on the path to collapse. Nevertheless, their resilience, adaptability, extensive distribution, and weed–like ability to spring up almost instantly in a political void are all characteristics that make such systems worthy topics for description and study. In spite of powerful efforts to eradicate patron–client systems, their ability to persist suggests remarkable durability and success.

Criticism of the patron–client system did not begin just with modern political theory. In the Old Testament Book of I Samuel, the people began to complain about the system of judges or patrons. Soon after 1000 B.C., people asserted that their patrons, the judges, were unable to maintain law and order or provide effective defense against invaders. Furthermore, critics expressed their displeasure by saying that their system was obsolete. Neighboring peoples were being ruled by kings. Monarchy was a more prestigious method of governance, and the Hebrew people did not want to be left behind.

In Greece, people came to the similar conclusion that patron–client structures were antiquated and inadequate. Plato expressed this most pointedly when he rejected both Homer and Homer's heroes. For Plato, the practice of politics was to be above economic and personal considerations. Plato recommended that rulers live with only the barest of material possessions. A good ruler, he said, is someone who owns little or nothing. Plato tried hard to prevent personal loyalty and regard for kinship from affecting political decisions. In order to avoid any conflict of interest between the personal and the public, Plato recommended that top political leaders live in a strict communist setting in which they own nothing and share everything. He even went so far as to suggest that leaders share a community of husbands and wives so that the bonds of marriage would not compromise a ruler's impartiality and his or her ability to make judgments that were in the best interest of the entire community. Plato challenged the very heart of the patron–client system that celebrates personal loyalty and gives far more weight to relationships than to abstract and impersonal rules or procedures.

Pope Adrian IV

In the Middle Ages, patron–clientage was celebrated. Perhaps the best medieval defense of the patron–client system was made by Pope Adrian IV (1100–1159) who led the Catholic Church in the twelfth century. Adrian's views were recorded by his friend and critic, the political thinker John of Salisbury (1115–1180). In the twelfth century, both religious and secular institutions were organized according to the principles of patron–client systems. People at the top collected revenue by taxation, by rendering favorable legal judgments, by assisting people seeking appointments to offices, and by confiscating land or money. This wealth was used to support a lavish lifestyle and to gain the support of followers who were loyal so long as they continued to benefit from gifts, appointments, and opportunities to extract wealth from others. Anyone wanting to win a court case, gain a church or state office, or obtain shelter from being preyed upon by more powerful people sought the protection of a reliable patron. Of course, there was a price to pay for that protection.

Adrian's analysis and defense of the patron–client system came in response to a series of pointed criticisms raised by John of Salisbury. Questioning the very heart of the patron–client system, John asked how patrons could justify the enormous flow of resources into the hands of the political elite. Prudent and cautious, John said he was not speaking for himself but for the many people who regarded the practice of exchanging money for favors and offices as oppressive and immoral. John then listed a host of problems within the Church of Rome. Because the Church in the twelfth century functioned like a secular state, John's critique would have been equally applicable to the patron–client governments that existed in the rest of Europe. In fact, with its army, extensive network of taxation, court system, and vast administrative structure, the Church had a patron–client type of government that surpassed that of many regions and territories ruled by medieval princes.

John of Salisbury's message John began by accusing the Vatican of having become an oppressive stepmother rather than a caring mother. The leaders in Rome, he charged, were vainglorious and proud lovers of money who lived in extravagant luxury. To maintain their opulent life in Rome, they extorted gifts and payments from subordinates throughout Europe. Furthermore, church judges did not decide cases on the basis of justice; rather, they bartered justice for a price. John noted that the only way to get any action from the church bureaucracy was to pay a bribe. In addition, he pointed out that church leaders stirred up strife among people of lesser power and influence in order to keep them from uniting and forcing meaningful change at the highest levels. Even the top leaders could not keep harmony among themselves. In their competition for power, position, and money, they preyed upon each other and their gains were short-lived. The Pope himself, John said sadly, was seen by many people as the worst offender of all. His avarice and duplicity had become an intolerable burden upon the faithful. The Church had become, John of Salisbury asserted, a wanderer in a trackless wilderness. The Church had strayed from the true way and had given itself over to duplicity and avarice. Where, John asked, was humility, self-restraint, and honesty?

Looking beyond the accusatory tone of John of Salisbury's message, it is clear that he was describing an actively functioning patron–client system. Maintaining the flow of tributes (church taxes, bequests, offerings, bribes, and rents) into the coffers, or treasury, of Rome, the great bishoprics, and the powerful monastic orders was the main preoccupation of the church hierarchy. This money was used to support a lavish lifestyle and to provide political and military security for the top leaders. Although the ordinary people groaned under the weight of oppression, they were unable to unite against prominent leaders who used their money and influence to divide and weaken any potential opposition. In such a system, personal attachments and loyalties— not fair laws and courts, rational budgets, or predictable administrative procedures— determined how decisions were made and carried out. Decisions about church jobs and court cases were made on the basis of payment, not competence or justice. Leaders were far more concerned about building up strong groups of clients than they were with holding to principles and laws.

The Pope's response In his response, Pope Adrian IV offered both an explanation and a defense of the patron–client system as it operated in the Middle Ages. A practical politician and administrator, Pope Adrian answered John of Salisbury by using an analogy in

MAJOR WRITINGS:

Adrian IV

Once upon a time all the members of the body conspired against the stomach, as against that which by its greediness devoured utterly the labors of all the rest. The eye is never sated with seeing, the ear with hearing, the hands go on laboring, the feet become callous from walking, and the tongue itself alternates advantageously between speech and silence. In fine, all the members provide watchfully for the common advantage of all; and in the midst of such care and toil on the part of all, only the stomach is idle, yet it alone devours and consumes all the fruits of their manifold labors. . .[In response, the other parts of the body] swore to abstain from work and starve the idle public enemy. . .[By the third day] almost all commenced to be faint. . .the eyes were found to be dim, the foot failed to sustain the weight of the body, the arms were numb, and the tongue. . .[could not speak]. Accordingly all took refuge in the counsel of the heart and after deliberation there, it became plain that these ills were all due to that which had before been denounced as the public enemy. Because the tribute which they paid it was cut off, like a public rationer it withdrew the sustenance of all. . . .And so. . .persuaded by reason, they filled the stomach, the members were revived, and the peace was restored. And so the stomach was acquitted, which although it is voracious and greedy of that which does not belong to it, yet seeks not for itself but for the others who cannot be nourished if it is empty. And so it is. . .in the body of the commonwealth, wherein, though the magistrates are most grasping, yet they accumulate not so much for themselves as for the others. . . .For the stomach in the body and the prince in the commonwealth

perform the same office. . . .Do not therefore seek to measure our oppressiveness or that of temporal princes, but attend rather to the common utility of all.

Pope Adrian IV admitted that rulers could be "voracious and greedy," but he suggested such grasping was done for the common good. The rapaciousness of leaders was necessary to ensure that the state would have sufficient resources in order to operate and in order to ensure that resources were distributed generously to the people. Adrian saw the greed of the patron as essential to the health of the larger political structure. Implicit in Adrian's argument is the notion that only a wealthy patron could be counted on as a reliable source of nourishment for the body politic. A poor king, pope, or prince would be unable to be generous to the people. A humble and impoverished leader could not "attend. . .to the common utility of all." Adrian's observations about the patron–client system reflect a frankness and honesty that some political leaders try to obscure. Adrian freely admitted that there is a high cost associated with government. To quote a modern cliché, he was simply saying "there is no free lunch." He also acknowledged the fact that for a political system to function satisfactorily, the system must control substantial amounts of resources. He seems to say that the effective state must be greedy. For patronage to flow from the hands of the leader, tribute must flow into the leader's treasury.

which he compared church and state government to the human body. In using this image, Adrian was drawing on an old tradition. Classical Greek and Roman political thinkers had often compared the political community to the body. But, while philosophers such as Plato and Aristotle had always equated political leadership with the head or the brain, the seat of decision–making and thought, Adrian said the leaders should be compared to the stomach instead. Adrian told a fanciful story about how the other parts of the body once became critical of the stomach because it only consumed while they all did the work. They noted that while the eyes did the seeing, the ears the hearing, the feet the walking, and the tongue the talking,

the stomach was idle. Yet, it consumed everything. From the perspective of the other body parts, it seemed that the stomach's only action was to eat what came to the body through their efforts. As a result, those parts of the body decided to go on strike against the stomach. No longer, they agreed, would they put anything into the lazy stomach. The result, said Adrian, was nearly fatal because all the parts became too weak to function. After giving the matter some thought, they realized their plight had come about because of what they had done to their supposed idle enemy. They finally realized that the stomach was the most essential organ of the body for it served as a supplier for all the other parts. If the stomach went hungry, all went hungry. Newly enlightened, the other body parts then decided to "fill the stomach." The result was the restoration of all the parts and the return of peace. The stomach, asserted Adrian, should not be regarded as evil. The stomach was not eating just for itself, but for the entire body.

Pope Adrian's point was that the patronage in a political system should be respected and accepted, not condemned. Instead of begrudging the lavish rewards obtained by high church or political leaders, people should recognize the essential nature of their leaders' work. Explicitly comparing the food entering the stomach to tribute demanded by temporal princes, Adrian reminded John of Salisbury that without very large inflows of wealth into the political system, nothing could flow back to government functionaries or to the people themselves. Like a paymaster in the army, a king, pope, or prince could distribute goods and services in the commonwealth only so long as resources were coming in constantly.

The Middle Ages

At the popular level, medieval ideas of government were even more supportive of patron–client concepts. The medieval lord or knight was portrayed as the beneficent embodiment of the big man, the central figure in a patron–client system. As can be seen in medieval mythology such as the stories of King Arthur, the big man was regarded as a defender of the peace who slew supernatural foes such as dragons and protected the people against temporal foes such as robbers and enemy warriors. The big man was also a defender of truth and morality. While Arthur's knights searched for the Holy Grail, a symbolic way of saying that they sought the restoration of divine grace and perfection on earth, other medieval big men struggled to destroy Muslims and Turks, people thought to epitomize aggressive forms of chaos and evil. Finally, the big man was regarded as an individual of great strength, courage, and piety. Social order and good government did not come because of structured and institutionalized bureaucracies or systems. Rather, they depended upon the personal qualities and character of a big man at the center. Such leaders had more in common with the ancient heroes like Deborah or Odysseus than with modern monarchs or tyrants.

The Middle Ages marked both the high point of patron–client political systems and the beginning of modern authoritarian monarchies that can be seen as institutionalized and centralized adaptations of patron–client arrangements. Therefore, the medieval period was marked by thinkers making an intellectual transition to monarchy. The great medieval theologian and political thinker Thomas Aquinas (1225–1274) saw patron–clientage as consistent with the very nature of the universe God had created. First, like the ancient Greeks, Aquinas observed that human beings, and even many animals, were intended to live in groups. Second, Aquinas believed that just as the universe required a divine creator and guide, the human community needed a political guide or head. Although Aquinas was speaking of monarchies, he noted that kings bore a certain resemblance to the father (*pater* or patron) of a household. Thus, Aquinas continued to think of the monarchy in terms of patron–client concepts. Very suspicious of democracy, he insisted that the best political system would be organized around a father–like figure. But, rejecting tyranny, he insisted that political rule must aim at the common good of the multitude rather than the private good of the ruler. The ruler, said Aquinas, must function as a shepherd whose task is too feed the flocks. Unlike Adrian IV, Aquinas was not willing to justify the most crass elements of the patron–client system. While Adrian defended the greedy patron, Aquinas said "woe to the shepherds that feed themselves," and he condemned the tyrant who "seeks his own benefit." Nevertheless, Aquinas did not reject the concept of a patron–client type of government. He only insisted that the sheep as well as the shepherd should be fed.

It is evident that for both Pope Adrian and Aquinas, the image of "eating" was central to the patron–client system. But, this concept was most fully developed in African political thought. In traditional Africa, political ideology was recorded not in books or letters, but in myths and legends passed down from one generation to another through oral recitation. By telling stories, many of them entirely imaginary, African people expressed their opinions about what worked, what was moral, and what had always existed. Often their deepest political and social values were articulated by describing a man or woman who supposedly was the original human being, the first settler in the land, the founding chief, or the initial farmer or hunter. That person and his or her actions were regarded as normative for all times. What they did was seen as ideal and a model for successive generations.

The Legend of Kuaba

Legendary stories of political origins in Africa describe a patron–client system. The Kanyok people who live in the Congo tell one story about an original settler-chief named Kuaba. (The term *kuaba* means "to distribute"). According to the tale, Kuaba was a great hunter who came to a land where people did not know how to hunt. He killed a large animal and distributed the meat to the grateful locals. As a result, the local people made Kuaba (the distributor) their chief, and his descendants have continued to rule the area. Clearly, Kuaba is a big man in a patron–client system. Had he lived in modern America, his name would not have been "Kuaba" but instead would have been "Pork Barrel." Furthermore, "Pork Barrel" would have been regarded as a title of honor, not of scorn. Other Kanyok stories affirm the central importance of patron–clientage to politics. Many stories talk of chiefs who fell from power because they became drunk and failed to hold a feast or distribute food. These stories should not be taken literally any more than the American cliché "he threw his hat into the ring" should be understood as a statement about headgear. The accusation of drunkenness was another way of saying a chief was inept or weak. The failure to hold a feast was a symbol for not sustaining the practice of redistribution, which was essential to the entire patron–client system. Kings and chiefs did not lose their office because they refused to follow the law, because they were dishonest, because they made unpopular appointments, or because they did not protect human rights. Rather, they fell from power because they were unable to redistribute political spoils to their supporters. As a result, their followers drifted away and transferred their allegiance to another chief or contender for office. The true test of a system was not whether it was law–abiding, democratic, or efficient in terms of achieving goals. The true test was its success in satisfying the people through the practice of pork barrel politics.

While in much of Africa patron–client values have remained the ideal even in modern times, in Western society patron–clientage has given way to more supposedly rational forms of politics and economics. In *The Prince*, Machiavelli rejected the idea of generous material liberality, the lynchpin of patron–clientage. Machiavelli noted that a ruler who spent his or her own resources on building up a base of supporters would eventually run out of wealth and lose the ability to retain people's loyalty. A ruler who spent the resources of others would need to tax or plunder his subjects to obtain the means to maintain the patronage system. Such a policy would result in resentment and hostility leading to disloyalty and even revolt. Better, Machiavelli argued, to be seen as a miser than as rapacious.

Rousseau and Beyond

Later Western political thinkers unanimously agreed that the capricious and materialistic aspects of the patron–client system were both inefficient and immoral. Swiss–French philosopher Jean–Jacques Rousseau (1712–1778) is but one example of such thinkers. To some extent, twentieth–century governments, whether democratic or authoritarian, follow in the wake of Rousseau. Like virtually all other modern thinkers, Rousseau vests complete authority in the state. While one may argue about whether he was a precursor of democracy or totalitarianism, it is clear that he left no place for individual challenges to the sovereignty of government. A legitimate government expressed the "general will" that superceded all expressions of parochial interests. There was no place for selfishness in Rousseau's state. The rule of law, not the rule of individual patrons, was the only guarantee of human freedom.

In any case, with Rousseau and almost all thinkers since his time, political philosophers assumed that equality and impartiality were essential for a well–functioning government. One person–one vote, secret ballots, impartiality before the bar of justice, and equal access to all government services are key components of political systems that reject the principles of patron–clientage. Modern governments, whether democratic or authoritarian, claim to be fair, impersonal, and predictable. Systems not heroes, budgets not bribes, and courts not connections are supposed to govern political affairs in the modern state.

The thinker who did the most to challenge the moral and philosophical underpinnings of patron–client practices was Jeremy Bentham (1748–1832). A child prodigy, Bentham developed the intellectual foundations of modern utilitarianism. In his *Introduction to the Principles of Morals and Legislation* (1789), Bentham argued that the only legitimate basis for judging any political action was to measure the pleasure or pain that action produced. Reason tells us, he said, that no one can justify actions that result in more pain than pleasure. Even painful endeavors such as war or punishment of criminals are carried out in the expectation of reducing pain and increasing pleasure in the long run. Central to Bentham's thought was the idea that pleasure and pain needed to be judged according to how extensively they were experienced. While criminal activity might conceivably bring pleasure to one individual, the sum total of the pain experienced by the many victims would far exceed the sum total of the pleasure experienced by the criminal. While a bribe might benefit both the giver and the taker, their gains would be more than offset by the totality of losses to society as a whole. Bentham's reasoning led him to reject political actions or systems that rewarded individuals at the expense of the larger group. Predictably, he opposed all patron–client arrangements. One of Bentham's central ideas was that all political appointments should be based on merit and that merit must be ascertained through open and competitive examinations. More than any other thinker, Jeremy Bentham has been credited with having affected the direction of modern British domestic politics. Many of his followers were elected to Parliament, where they put his principles into law. In the 1800s, Britain adapted a public health system, a national education system, open competition for civil service jobs, and more rational methods of organizing government departments. All of these reforms resulted in more equitable government systems that provided higher levels of service to every citizen regardless of social standing or personal connections. Now, people had a right to government assistance simply because they were English citizens, not because they managed to attach themselves to a powerful patron. Now, individuals were appointed to positions of leadership because of competence and intelligence rather than because of their family or wealth. While actual practices often fell short of these ideals, nineteenth–century England did make important progress in moving away from a patron–client system.

John Rawls

John Rawls (1921–), who speaks of the importance of a "veil of ignorance," built an entire theory of justice on principles that challenge the deepest inclinations of people operating patron–client systems. His theory proposes that a person's wealth or status should have no bearing on governmental policy. To make this happen, Rawls argues that every decision–maker should act as though he or she has no knowledge of whether they would benefit or lose from their decision, no knowledge of their social standing or economic position, and no knowledge of their strengths or weaknesses. Any expectation of personal gain or advantage should be put aside when public affairs are at stake. Thus, taxes should be assessed with the complete fairness and objectivity that could come only if the decision–maker could not know how he or she would be affected. Thus, legal penalties, zoning decisions, or constitutional changes should always be put into place by people acting as though they have no inkling of the consequences for themselves. In contrast to Rawls' veil of ignorance, a patron–client system is based on the premise that every political decision is made in order to give special advantage to favored individuals.

Bentham and Rawls are but two of many modern political thinkers struggling with the issue of objectivity and fairness. For these thinkers, a concern for absolute even–handedness and impartiality represents one of the most critical tests of any good government policy. A second set of tests measures efficiency. Can a given policy or action be implemented with the lowest possible cost and effort for the greatest possible

MAJOR WRITINGS:
A Theory of Justice

The principles of justice are chosen behind a veil of ignorance. This ensures that no one is advantaged or disadvantaged. . .by the outcome of natural chance or the contingency of social circumstances. Since all are similarly situated and no one is able to design principles to favor his particular condition, the principles of justice are the result of a fair agreement or bargain.

For John Rawls in *A Theory of Justice*, every law, political decision, or governmental structure should be enacted or put into place without even the slightest accommodation to a person's wealth, connections, or status.

result? Political philosophers such as Rawls and Bentham are the ideological voices of modern government. Whether democratic or authoritarian, all modern governments have gained, or claim to have gained, a monopoly over the values and resources that had once been controlled by successful patrons for unequal distribution to their clients. Modern bureaucracies regularize everything so that favoritism is both difficult and illegal. Long–range budgets make it hard for political leaders to use government resources to cultivate privileged constituencies. Civil service examinations prevent leaders from making non–merit appointments to their favorites. The hope is that these measures will bring high levels of efficiency and fairness. All of the resources of the state will be used for the greatest common good and happiness. Nothing will be diverted for the private pleasure and power of a privileged elite supported by a cadre of followers purchased through political spoils. Most apologists for modern government regard patron–client systems as dangerous and immoral enemies that must be eliminated.

Goran Hyden

Goran Hyden, an academic who has also worked with development agencies in Africa, advances a more sympathetic analysis of patron–client systems. Labeling patron–client systems as "economies of affection," Hyden notes that in many countries of the world, people make economic and political decisions with the expectation of solidifying personal relationships rather than with the hope of material profit. People who manage to acquire surplus resources invest their wealth in other people, not in impersonal operations. Thus, a man or woman with extra money will give the money either as a gift to a patron or a loan to a client. They are less likely to put the money in a bank or even plow it back into their own private business. Hyden argues that people investing in the "economy of affection" do so quite rationally. For many people, the most reasonable option is entrusting the wealth with a patron or client in hopes of reaping future favors or assistance. By accepting the gift, a patron obligates himself or herself to provide future protection, partiality, and aid. By taking a loan, a client enters into a relationship of personal and financial liability. Banks may collapse and businesses are risky. Investing money in patrons or clients who are friends and relatives is regarded as more secure. Just as people with material wealth invest in the economy of affection, people with political resources or needs do so as well. Someone with the power to appoint, to offer a contract, or to make a legal decision will do so in a way that strengthens a personal bond. Instead of offering an official job to a person who has no personal link to the giver, it is more logical to offer the job to someone who would need to and who would be able to return a favor.

THEORY IN ACTION

At the beginning of the twenty–first century, patron–client systems had no philosophical advocates nor were they embodied in any formal constitutional or legal structures. From the perspective of political theory or constitutional law, patron–client systems do not exist except as aberrations and illegalities. Nevertheless, when looking at how governments actually function, patron–client systems continue as active members of the modern political community.

Many governments in Asia follow the principles of patron–clientage. For example, the Suharto family of Indonesia and the Marcos family of the Philippines amassed enormous fortunes and great political power through a system of awarding favors to themselves and richly rewarding their political cronies. Although both countries held elections, people voted along the lines of patronage blocs. Both countries contained some of the marks of authoritarian systems, but bureaucrats, party officials, and regional constituencies acted according to the rules of patron–clientage; they followed presidential orders only if they believed they could extract substantial personal or group rewards by

doing so. Additionally, people in those countries organized themselves into political parties, even though personal loyalty was far more important than ideologies or political principles. Both countries also had carefully crafted legal systems, but court cases were decided on the basis of friendship and client support rather than on judicial merit.

Decidedly more democratic than either Indonesia or the Philippines, India has also been ruled by a patron dynasty. In India, the Nehru family (Motilal Nehru, Motilal's son Jawaharlal, Jawaharlal's daughter Indira Gandhi, and Indira's sons Rajiv and Sanjay) controlled a patronage network associated with the dominant Congress Party. Protection for Indian businesses, subsidies for workers and farmers, and bureaucratic jobs for party loyalists were important elements of patronage dispensed by the Congress Party and the Nehru dynasty. As in Indonesia and the Philippines, high–ranking people benefited personally from special financial arrangements that grew out of their political influence.

Japan

Japan offers an important example of the tension between the theoretical ideal of democracy and the day–to–day reality of patron–clientage. The Japanese constitution, written after World War II by the American occupation authorities, is highly democratic. However, the actual operations of the Japanese political system are conducted as much according to the rules of a patron–client system as they are according to the principles of liberal democracy. This is especially evident in the operations of the Liberal Democratic Party (LDP), Japan's dominant political party. The LDP name suggests both that it is liberal (open, free, and innovative) and democratic (a bottom–up organization giving great voice to the people). For almost all of the post World War II period, Japanese politics have been dominated by the Liberal Democratic Party. Although founded in 1955 to prevent the emergence of a socialist government, the party is not organized around a political ideology. Rather, the party is made up of groups of party factions whose main goal is to attract faithful clients and to obtain and distribute the spoils of patronage. The leaders of the factions stay in power by rewarding their supporters and making alliances with other faction leaders. No faction leader has a political platform or agenda that is much different from the platform or agendas of other leaders. The key qualification for becoming a faction leader is demonstrated success in accessing funds for the faction. Such funds might come from the central party treasury or from arrangements, often secret, with big business.

The LDP Ambitious party members make their way up through the ranks of the party, not by staking out a clear ideological position or even by appealing directly to the voters. Rather, they advance by attaching themselves (as clients) to powerful factions or faction leaders (patrons). A junior politician who is successful in gaining the support of a strong political patron can count on party sponsorship during a campaign. This sponsorship brings him or her money, assistance in organizing, and aid with publicity. The top faction leaders or patrons who extend this help then can count on the backing of their client colleagues when making a bid for a cabinet position or even for the posts of prime minister or LDP president. To a very large extent, the LDP is devoid of ideology or a clearly articulated political agenda. As a result, internal debates within the party do not deal with ideological differences but with personal loyalty and the distribution of political spoils. Personal popularity or great oratorical skills are not important ingredients for political advancement in the Japanese patron–client arrangement.

Because political advancement depends on successfully manipulating the patron system, Japanese politics tends to be dominated by older politicians who have had time to build up a base of clients. As a result, when a faction leader dies, another senior leader takes over and attempts to hold the faction together by using the same patron–client practices. These senior members of the LDP are involved in deals, intrigues, and maneuvers designed to maximize their power and influence. Money and promises are the main resources they use in a quest that is for personal political gain rather than for the public good. In a patron–client system, people with political power use their position or influence to dispense favors, open doors, or help others circumvent rules. In return, they receive money, loyalty, and support. Both in the 1970s and 1980s, Japanese prime ministers and other high officials were implicated in scandals involving bribes, expensive gifts, and stock. By accepting money from large corporations such as the Lockheed Corporation or Recruit Company, those politicians gained resources that they could use to maintain their hold over lower level politicians (clients) in their factions.

In its internal operations, the LDP functions as a network of political patrons and clients. Since the time of its founding in 1955, the LDP has protected its primary client base of business and farmers. Farmers are heavily subsidized and protected, while businesses are shielded from competition from abroad. In return, both groups have provided unwavering loyalty to party bosses. Even after Prime Minister Kakuei Tanaka (1918–1993) was convicted of taking bribes in 1983,

his faction remained dominant because he was a master of patronage and protection. Tanaka's group lost out to another faction only after he suffered a debilitating stroke.

Perhaps because patron–client structures are so pervasive internally, Japanese politicians accept an international political arrangement that is essentially patron–client in nature. After suffering defeat in World War II, Japan switched from being America's enemy to becoming one of America's friends. To a large extent, the relationship was a patron–client association. Not only did the United States act as demilitarized Japan's main protector, the United States also served as Japan's main export market. As Japan's patron, the United States provided both military and economic security. In return, Japan as client offered friendship, loyalty, and deference.

The family To a large extent, the patron–client system that dominates Japanese politics reflects the type of arrangements the Japanese use in their families. Traditional Japanese families look to a patriarch, an individual sometimes referred to as the "main pole," for leadership, protection, and guidance. In a family, personal attachment is far more significant than rules or abstract formulas. The family is governed by bonds of affection and trust. People within the family are given preference over people outside the family; no one would think it unfair or unethical if a family member received special treatment that gave him or her an advantage over non–family members. People find their personal security in the partiality offered to them in a family. An individual is protected, assisted, and honored because he or she is in the family. In Japan, the same kind of logic prevails within the larger political world. What outsiders see as corruption and chicanery is regarded by people in Japan as faithfulness or even patriotism. They find nothing wrong with awarding government contracts to political supporters, and they are willing to pay higher prices for products in order to protect Japanese businesses. Until the recession that plagued Japan throughout much of the 1990s, few Japanese people questioned the cozy patron–client relationships that dominated politics or that bound politics and business.

Argentina

Argentina and Mexico provide examples of how patron–client systems have long dominated politics in Latin America. Juan Perón (1895–1974) and Eva (Evita) Perón (1919–1952) exemplified all the characteristics of successful patrons, including gift–giving and an image of being larger than life.

BIOGRAPHY:

Juan Perón

Born in 1895, Juan Perón rose from a middle–class background to become the charismatic, strong man ruler of Argentina. A military officer, he participated in a coup that unseated President Ramon Castillo in 1943. In the new government, Perón became director of the National Department of Labor. Perón took advantage of this position to build up a strong client base among the workers called *descamisados* (those without shirts) by winning for them benefits such as better wages, social security, and housing subsidies. By 1944, Perón was able to use this power base to oust the president and install a friendly general in office. Although Perón's rivals managed to have him arrested in 1945, Perón's worker client base mobilized by the thousands to protest his detention. About this time, Perón married the enormously popular actress Maria Eva Duarte. Known as Evita, she is the woman recalled in the Broadway production and the Hollywood movie. Evita strengthened her husband's standing among the working masses and, in 1946, Juan Perón was officially elected president.

The Peróns maintained their power though typical patron–client type activities. First, Juan Perón provided generous economic rewards for his most important client supporters. When he first came into office, the Argentine economy was flush with revenues the nation had earned during World War II when it exported food. Perón was able to draw on budgetary surpluses to reduce the length of the work week, institute paid vacations, and offer retirement benefits to the workers. In addition, through a publicly supported charitable foundation, Evita dispensed about ten million dollars annually to the poor. People were led to believe that government–sponsored welfare came to them because of Eva Perón's personal concern about their lives. Second, both Juan and Eva Perón cultivated their images as people who were larger than life, perhaps even semi–divine. Statues were erected in conspicuous locations, children were indoctrinated about the virtues of the Peróns, and many public places

were named in their honor. State propaganda encouraged people to regard Perón as powerful and magnanimous; he was presented as the patron from which all good things flowed. Eva Perón, who rose from very humble origins, was adored by Argentina's poor as having been one of them. She was seen as a type of goddess and mother figure who loved and protected the disadvantaged. Although calculating and manipulative, she succeeded in maintaining a public persona of charm, generosity, and compassion. People in Argentina regarded Eva as a woman who had a sincere concern for their well being. As the "softer side" of Perón's regime, Eva kept many citizens from recognizing the exploitative aspect of the vast patronage machine that kept Perón in power. When she died of cancer in 1952, Perón and the nation mourned her as a saint.

Perón's regime began to fall apart after Eva's death, partially because his popularity waned without his wife. Also, his extravagant spending had placed severe strains on the economy. Perón could no longer afford the largesse that had held together his client network. As a result, people turned against him and, in 1955, a military revolt forced him to resign and flee into exile.

But, Perón was not finished. The governments that followed Perón proved to be ineffective. Over the years, Perón's reputation as a generous patron actually increased. Although the Perónist political party was outlawed, the number of people supporting Perón actually increased. Typical of leaders operating in a patronage system, Perón presented himself as non–ideological, and he drew support both from the extreme right and the extreme left. Both groups regarded him as a potential savior. Unable to obliterate Perón's memory, in 1972 the government allowed him to return. At first he operated behind the scenes, but in 1973 he ran for the presidency and was elected by a landslide. Perón never had time to demonstrate his ability to operate his rebuilt patron–client system because he died in July of 1974.

Mexico

Mexico has also been governed according to the principles of patron–clientage. Until the election of Vicente Fox in 2000, throughout most of the twentieth century, Mexico was ruled by the Institutional Revolutionary Party (PRI). PRI has claimed to be revolutionary, radical, Marxist, democratic, and nationalistic. None of these labels are entirely appropriate; Mexico could have been more accurately described as a patron–client system.

As in Japan, much of the patronage in Mexico has been exercised through a dominant political party. Until the year 2000, elections in Mexico did not reflect the principles of open democracy, even though the country had always claimed to hold competitive, multi–party elections. Throughout most of Mexican history, elections have not been authentic contests in which the ruling party risked losing its power. In fact, PRI's dominance had been so great that the party sometimes secretly subsidized moderate opposition parties to maintain a façade of democracy, to make sure that the opposition remained moderate (feared biting the hand that fed it), and to weaken support for potentially more radical critical voices. In addition to supporting a non–threatening opposition, PRI leaders have actually disqualified some of their own candidates for parliament in order to make way for cooperative opposition leaders. In this way, even opposition parties benefited from the spoils of patronage.

In Mexico, the key figure in the patronage network has been the president, who traditionally served for one six–year term. As both head of the party and head of the government, the president was responsible for thousands of political appointments, which in turn provided numerous individuals with access to lucrative rewards. Party loyalists received positions in the cabinet, the bureaucracy, public corporations, and nationalized industries. Other faithful individuals were tapped to serve as regional governors. Historically, such people have benefited by an unwritten law that allowed them to participate in and overlook a certain level of corruption and/or political favoritism leading to personal enrichment.

Mexican society was structured into corporate associations that long have organized clients into manageable groups. For example, workers, farmers, professional people, businesses, and government employees were grouped together in associations that were expected to represent the interests of their constituents. In principle, that means the leaders of these groups could have an adversarial relationship with the government. In reality, the leaders of these groups were political clients approved by the PRI or the pres-

ident. Such leaders do not count success in terms of legislation or regulations that benefit their constituents, especially if such benefits come at the expense of the ruling elite; rather, they measure success in terms of the personal benefits they themselves receive. For example, government–approved labor leaders receive substantial personal benefits in return for making sure that labor unions do not become overly critical of government, that they do not go on strike, or that they do not make wage demands that could harm big business.

In the past, patronage flowed not just to friends of the regime, but also to potential opponents. University graduates, men and women who may have been radical critics of the government and the party during their years in school, were appointed to important government positions or were given contracts to serve as highly paid consultants. Such co–opted individuals soon softened their criticism; however, opponents who refused to take advantage of the spoils they were offered found themselves in great difficulty, such as being put in jail. But, if they repented and expressed their loyalty to the system, they sometimes moved directly from jail to high–level jobs in the government.

Propaganda and payoffs Another important element of the Mexican patron–client system has been the skillful use of propaganda and indoctrination. Through the press, educational institutions, and party rallies, people are told that they benefit greatly from the generous patronage of the PRI. For example, during presidential campaigns, the PRI candidate would visit every region of the country dispensing gifts and political favors. Several times in history, the government nationalized foreign corporations or seized and redistributed land to the poor. These acts were portrayed as having provided substantial payoffs to ordinary people who were expected to vote loyally for the party. Although in actuality, well–placed individuals or organizations tended to be the ultimate beneficiaries of such nationalization and redistribution, the media and the government were successful in convincing people otherwise. Since the government sold newsprint paper to favored newspapers at highly subsidized prices, it could also punish or threaten to punish uncooperative editors and publishers. Furthermore, the government was not afraid to use violence and intimidation against students, politicians, or labor leaders who expressed opposition or discontent.

While many people have criticized the Mexican political system as corrupt and inefficient, the actual record has been quite positive. First, the Mexican patron–client system has proved to be extremely stable

Mobutu Sese Suko, president of Zaire from 1965–1997. (The Library of Congress)

during most of the twentieth century. Mexico's presidents have all served their full six–year terms. None have been ousted by a coup, and none have attempted to remain in power beyond their elected tenure. Second, Mexico's military has been firmly under civilian control and makes no attempt to influence policy. Third, Mexico has experienced strong economic growth in the post–World War II period. Associated with this growth has been a substantial increase in personal income and a massive transformation of the population from rural to urban. Fourth, Mexico has managed to provide a reasonable level of social and educational services to a rapidly growing population. By the end of the twentieth century, Mexico had greatly reduced illiteracy. Finally, although not democratic itself, Mexico's patron–client system provided the foundation for a transition to genuine democracy. Prior to the election of Vicente Fox (1942–), President Ernesto Zedillo (1951–), although an active participant in the patronage system, used his power and influence over the PRI to insist that the 2000 elections be free and fair. As a result, Vicente Fox of the opposition National Action Party (PAN) won the presidential election. While Mexico may continue to operate according to the logic of patron–clientage, the highest patrons will be subject to voter approval.

Africa

Of all the continents in the world, Africa has the most persistent and powerful patron–client political systems. Liberian Presidents William Tubman (held office from 1944 to 1971), William Tolbert (in office from 1971 to 1980), Samuel Doe (1980 to 1989) and Charles Taylor (elected in 1997) are examples of how chief executives function as chief patrons. These men used the resources of the state to channel funds and favors to loyal supporters. All relied on symbolic displays of largesse to show the people that they were generous patrons. At least one time, Doe reputedly drove around Monrovia tossing out $20 bills to people on the streets. All four presidents would attend important functions at schools, churches, neighborhoods, and villages where they "personally" donated large sums of money to grateful constituents. Like previous Liberian presidents, they maintained enormous farms clearly visible from busy roads. Critics of the presidents charge that the purpose of the farms—private operations heavily subsidized by public funds—was to satisfy the personal greed of the chief executives. However, since it would have been easier to pocket the state funds directly rather than channeling them through an agricultural enterprise, the true purpose of the farms was more complex. The farms were started as a high profile way of telling the Liberian population that as the country's chief farmer, the president was the country's chief provider. As important, but lesser patrons, government ministers also maintained farms, albeit on a somewhat more modest scale. In addition to portraying themselves as generous providers, Liberian presidents cultivated an image of power and strength that included cruelty and capriciousness. Like a strong father, the patron president either rewarded or punished depending upon the client's degree of loyalty. The patron president's image was carefully manipulated by the state–controlled media that presented him as strong and magnanimous. Media images of power, wealth, generosity, and harshness reinforced the perspective that all rewards and punishments ultimately originated from the nation's chief patron who had both the resources and the will to reward and punish.

Zaire Generally seen as the champion of patron–clientage, President Mobutu Sese Seko (1930–1997) of Zaire presided over a vast patronage system that lasted from 1965 until 1997. Ruling through the army and his political party, Mobutu presented himself as the father of the nation, the founder of the political party, the head of state, and the dispenser of all benefits. Although he began his rule as a typical patron, not all that different from presidents such as those who ruled Liberia, by the end of his tenure, virtually 90 percent of all state resources were channeled through his hands. Revenues from giant state–owned or state–controlled mining companies went directly into his personal accounts. While some of the money was used to support an ostentatious lifestyle, much of it was redistributed to political clients within the government or party. At the top of the client heap were the *Grosses Legumes* (roughly translated as big enchiladas or big shots) who gained enormous wealth in return for their loyalty and protection. These *Grosses Legumes* built patronage networks of supporters who received kickbacks, lucrative positions on boards of directors, or opportunities to siphon off money from state controlled banks or corporations. As a result, Zaire's economy spiraled downward into virtually a complete collapse. By the end of his life, Mobutu's only preoccupation was maintaining the support of his key clients. Since the economic system was no longer able to supply him with enough resources to pay off his clients, Mobutu simply turned his clients loose to plunder at will. These men and women were allowed to run illegal diamond mining and smuggling operations, to launder money and transport drugs for international criminals, and to extort money from the remaining businesses and travelers in the country. As a staunch ally (client) of the United States and France, Mobutu benefited from foreign aid, especially during the cold war. Instead of being used for development—for example improving roads, hospitals, or schools—the money from foreign aid was rerouted to maintain the patron–client system.

In the end, Mobutu's patronage system collapsed because the beneficiaries were unable or unwilling to make a positive contribution to the economic life of the nation. Because both patrons and clients acted as parasites on the nation's economy, the economy suffered. Many businesses, forced to make payments to predatory political patrons, either operated with very narrow profit margins or became bankrupt. Some businesses withdrew into a shadowy underground world where the line between legal and illegal activities became blurred. In the end, some of Zaire's most successful businesses were connected to international criminal transactions that became central pillars of Zaire's economy by the 1990s.

Kenya Another example from Africa is the government of Kenya. In 1998 terrorists bombed the U.S. Embassies in Nairobi, killing about 200 people. Local TV and radio coverage of the event illustrated the importance of the patron–client system for Kenyans. Instead of focusing primarily on the number of dead and injured, the government's progress in tracking down the terrorists, or the physical damage to downtown Nairobi, official media devoted the majority of their attention to stories praising President Daniel Arap Moi (1924–). The media described Moi visiting the injured in hospitals, Moi promising to donate funds to assist families of the bereaved, Moi encouraging rescue workers, and Moi vowing not to rest until the "perpetrators were brought to book." While the TV and radio did report on the dead and injured, on the destruction, and on the investigation, the main character in every story was the president. Some Kenyans and American observers saw this as a crass example of how Moi used a monumental tragedy for personal political advantage. But, many Kenyans were extremely grateful for the news coverage—it showed that in times of great adversity, the person at the very top of government took a personal interest in those who suffered. It also demonstrated that the patron was in charge and would work tirelessly for his people. At a time when the entire nation was in shock and mourning, the president responded to his clients' deepest political concerns.

Parastatals In most countries of the world where patron–client arrangements dominate politics, parastatal companies are critically important components of the system. A parastatal business is state–owned and managed, although it produces goods and services that would come from the private sector in a free–market economy. In countries such as the United States, the post office operates as a parastatal. But, in patron–client counties, energy, manufacturing, tourism, banking, telecommunications, and even agriculture might be dominated all or in part by parastatals. Because the state is either the sole or majority share–holder, the board of directors and the top management personnel are appointed by the government. As a result, such appointments often are made on the basis of ethnic, political, or personal loyalty rather than on the basis of competence or experience. Because the appointments are regarded as rewards, the patrons (those who make the appointments) expect the clients (those who are appointed) to continue expressing their fidelity by channeling money back to the patrons. This might be in the form of direct payments or it might be in the form of sweetheart contracts with companies owned by the patron. Also, because the appointments are seen as rewards, there is little effort on the part of the patron to insist on either competency or integrity on the part of the client. In turn, people appointed to high positions in parastatals function as patrons to friends and family members who receive jobs, below–market prices, or non–competitive contracts.

Often, parastatals are used by high government officials to strengthen their support among the citizenry. For example, a parastatal mill and bakery might produce bread at very low prices. Since, as the corporate owner, the government will underwrite any financial loss, the mill and bakery managers are not concerned if low prices take away any potential profits. Their main concern is pleasing their political and economic patrons at the top of government. For their part, the powerful political patrons running the government hope that low bread prices will win them favor in the hearts of the masses. Again, since operating losses are covered by government revenues and do not come out of the politicians' own pockets, the high–positioned patrons are not concerned about profitability or efficiency. In the end, an important economic enterprise, in this example a mill and bakery, have been captured by the patron–client system. Patron–client loyalty, rather than sound economic practices, becomes the guiding managerial concerns.

ANALYSIS AND CRITICAL RESPONSE

Today, patron–client systems are universally condemned by political theorists. Joel Migdal's classic book *Strong Societies and Weak States* has outlined a number of the problems that plague patronage systems. It is tempting to see the patron–client system as a calculated effort on the part of the political elite to maintain itself in power by purchasing the loyalty of its immediate entourage and of the masses of the people. Migdal, however, suggests that the leaders in a patron–client structure are actually captives of a web of never–ending obligations that originate from below. To maintain his or her system of clients, a leader must constantly reward these clients because dissatisfied followers will shift their loyalty to a more generous benefactor. In order to stay in power, a patron president must provide top officials with a steady stream of favors or opportunities to make money. Those officials, in turn, must do the same for their immediate subordinates. The main goal of people in the system becomes survival, not policy implementation. In fact, the politics of survival often undermines policy. For example, a government budget may allocate funds for much needed roads, roads whose construction would improve the economy and advance government priorities. However, in order to keep the loyalty of high officials or political bosses, a president might be obligated to overlook massive fraud that diverts money designated for transportation into the pockets of his "supporters." For their part,

the "supporters" need the money to satisfy the expectations of their own clients. Migdal also notes that in a patron–client system, the patron at the top must constantly be alert to the possibility that a political competitor might build up a more robust network of clients and make a bid to unseat the patron. To avoid that danger, a head of state will engage in something Migdal calls the "big shuffle." With the big shuffle, a leader periodically rotates top officials in order to prevent them from building a firm base of client support. For example, a president may dismiss an entire cabinet and then reappoint all or most of the members to new posts. Thus, a former minister of transportation might become minister of finance. While this process results in great inefficiencies, it undermines a minister's efforts to establish a clique of supporters within his or her own ministry. Similarly, in order to dilute the power of a potential rival, a president might create a duplicate agency or department. This has the added advantage of creating an entirely new group of loyal clients. The disadvantage, of course, is inefficiency and confusion.

Advantages

Although most political analysts denounce patron–client systems, their pervasiveness and persistence suggests that they may offer benefits that must be acknowledged. First, patron–client systems are adaptable and flexible. Like weeds in a newly defoliated landscape, patron–client systems spring up to provide some sort of government where previously there was none. Nobles in the Middle Ages, warlords in collapsed modern states, and strongmen in the struggling regimes of the former Soviet Union all attempt to impose order, no matter how exploitative or corruptible, upon societies where formal government has ceased to function. In time, these nobles, warlords, and strongmen may succeed in establishing legitimate governments. Most of the monarchies of the world began from the seeds of patron–clientage. At a more mundane level, patron–clientage can step into a vacuum formal governments are unable to fill. For example, in the 1980s, the government of Nigeria expelled tens of thousands of guest workers because the Nigerian oil boom had faltered. These workers were forced to return to poor neighboring countries that had no formal resources or infrastructure to cope with a vast influx of unemployed people seeking housing and food. To the surprise of West African governments and international relief agencies, there was no crisis. The reason was that these thousands of people were able to access immediate help from patrons in their local communities. Coming home, they reattached themselves to a patron–client system that provided them with lodging, food, and other resources.

Second, patron—client systems have proved to be remarkably stable. Their endurance over many thousands of years and in all regions of the world is proof that they can work. A key reason for their stability is that they offer rewards for the patrons at the top and benefits for the clients at the bottom. The elite gain prestige, authority, and economic dividends. Their client subordinates receive security, a direct and personal link to someone with power, and economic assistance in times of need. This relationship, which benefits both parties, is maintained mainly through a series of voluntary exchanges. The fact that all parties believe they profit from the arrangement accounts for the system's persistence.

Compatibility

Third, patron—client systems are compatible with the customs of many traditional societies. Most traditional societies value hierarchy and respect. Elders, people with wealth, and individuals with power are elevated above ordinary people. The patron—client system affirms that hierarchical arrangement. In traditional societies, people at the bottom and people at the top are linked together through personalized relationships of reciprocity. Humble people offer support and deference, while more exalted people provide physical and economic security. The exchange is not abstract and impersonal. Rather, it is an exchange between people who consider themselves as friends. The patron—client system operates in that manner. Furthermore, in traditional society, people at the top can bend the rules or make exceptions to help those of lesser stature. People are treated as individuals. Rather than being controlled or limited by abstract budgets, uncaring bureaucracies, or inflexible laws, people in a patron—client system are part of a political structure that is responsive and relational. Individuals and groups within a patron—client network can turn to a person who has the wealth, standing, and power to assist them. People who retain many traditional values may prefer a political system featuring a strong and reliable patron. For them, such a patron seems to be the best protection against the disorientation of modernization, the uncertainties of the global economy, the capriciousness of the weather, and the insecurity and harshness of poverty.

Fourth, patron—client systems offer a type of accountability and service that many regard as effective. For one thing, the responsible person is always clearly identifiable and accessible. With a patron—client system, everyone knows who is in charge and who can provide help. When machine politics dominated big American cities, an out—of—work individual could go into an alderman's office and be given cash on the spot. The alderman also might use his connections to find a job for the petitioner. In Chicago, during the Richard J. Daley (1902–1976) era, construction contracts (many of them directly funded by government) provided work for thousands of city residents. For other people without the skill or strength to build highways, bridges, or skyscrapers, state and local government offered them work as elevator operators, doormen, security personnel, clerks, receptionists, janitors, and park workers. As part of the patron—client exchange, these workers were expected to kick back part of their paychecks as "voluntary donations" to the party machine. This money was then used to finance the political campaigns of elected officials. Another American example was the William Marcy Tweed era (1823–1878). Boss Tweed, as he was known, gained power in the New York City Democratic party, controlling party nominations and party patronage. He became a state senator in 1868, which extended his influence into state politics. Votes were openly bought and other dishonest vote—getting methods were employed. Through the control of New York City expenditures that defrauded the city to the extent of at least $30 million, he and his main supporters profited extravagantly. While today we see such things as corruption, many ordinary people regarded the system as their most secure form of protection.

Give and Take

In a study of post—Perón Argentina, sociologist Javier Auyero looks at the patron—client system from the perspective of those at the bottom of the socio—economic ladder. Rather than seeing themselves as being exploited by the people at the top, they regard themselves as beneficiaries of a system that helps them solve problems, links them to resources, and provides them with security. Although Juan Perón died in 1974, his political party continues to have strong support among Argentina's poor. Many political scientists denounce the Perónist party as an organization crassly seeking to buy votes through helping people gain access to government resources and services to which people should be entitled by virtue of being citizens. Critics say the Perónists take advantage of the government social services agencies that distribute free food to the poor. Because the Perónists (acting as patrons) control the locations where food is distributed, their impoverished clients consider the food as a gift from patrons. Because the government welfare bureaucracy is too complicated for most people to understand, the assistance provided by the local Perónist officials is seen as a generous favor. By monopolizing information and resources, these local political patrons who dispense knowledge or things to the people come to be regarded as protectors and saviors. While academic critics take a negative view of this arrangement, the poor people living in Argentina's slums have a much different perspective of their patrons. To the poor, the patrons are friends who care about their welfare. The patrons are seen as people who listen to the people's needs, who toil and sacrifice to help people meet those needs, and who are always available to assist. In the eyes of the poor, the patrons truly care about the people. Furthermore, the low–level local patrons have connections linking them to more powerful figures in the party or government. Normally, those people would be too busy or distant to be of any use to the very poor. But, through the efforts of local patrons (who are the clients of the more distant politicians), poor people can sometimes benefit from what goes on at the higher levels of society. Especially during election time, a low–level patron may be able to gain the ear of an important politician who might provide extra milk, field trips for poor school children, or even a government job.

Auyero also suggests that the local political patrons also see themselves as helpers, not as exploiters. They think of themselves as people with access to a larger network of individuals and organizations that have the resources to assist those at the very bottom of the socio–economic ladder. Without the help of the local patron, the poor would never be able to be connected to that assistance. The local patrons see themselves as channels and problem–solvers. They see nothing wrong with receiving favors in return for their services. From the poor, they gain respect and admiration, and from the people higher up in the system they get political promotions or a cut of the resources that are distributed to the poor. Local patrons who do a good job are able to build up a solid client base that enables them to mobilize supporters for political rallies and to deliver votes during elections. Such patrons may themselves be able to run for office and advance even higher in the system.

The fact that so many people in the modern world continue to cling to the patron–client system proves that it is a robust political arrangement. Highly educated leaders and citizens, people who are well informed about both democracy and authoritarianism, continue to choose patron–client systems over their supposedly more effective modern counterparts. People do not retain patron–client structures because they are unaware of alternatives. They keep the system because they believe it offers them more security and the greater rewards than other political systems.

TOPICS FOR FURTHER STUDY

- In the book of Samuel in the Old Testament, why did the Hebrew people want to exchange the patron–client system for a monarchy?

- Heroic figures in both the Old Testament and in Ancient Greek legend engaged in activities most modern people would consider cruel or devious. Yet, writers and storytellers in ancient times praised such individuals. Why would people want patrons who acted in such a manner?

- What are the characteristics people want in a patron?

- How effective was Juan Perón as a political leader who met the real needs of his people?

- In what way do American politicians, for example members of Congress, act as patrons for their constituents? How much attention do successful politicians devote to solving constituent problems with bureaucratic agencies such as Social Security?

- What were the advantages of machine politics in large American cities? For example, why did New Yorkers support someone such as Boss Tweed?

- Are African political leaders who engage in patronage acting immorally or unwisely?

BIBLIOGRAPHY

Sources

Auyero, Javier. *Poor People's Politics: Peronist Survival Networks and the Legacy of Evita.* Durham, NC: Duke University Press, 2001.

Bentham, Jeremy. *An Introduction to the Principles of Morals and Legislation*, J.H. Burns and H.L. A. Hard, eds. Oxford: Oxford University Press, 1996.

Homer. *The Odyssey.* New York: Anchor, 1963.

John of Salisbury. *The Statesman's Book*, in William Ebenstein and Alan Ebenstein, *Great Political Thinkers, Plato to the Present.* New York: Harcourt College Publishers, 2000.

The Holy Bible, New International Version. Colorado Springs: International Bible Society, 1984.

Rawls, John. *A Theory of Justice.* Cambridge, MA: Harvard University Press, 1999.

Yoder, John C. *The Kanyok of Zaire: A Political and Ideological History to 1895.* Cambridge: Cambridge University Press, 1992.

Further Readings

Bayart, Jean–Francois. *The State in Africa: the Politics of the Belly.* London: Longman, 1993. Bayart regards the patron–client system as a greedy predator or societies attempting to build democracies.

Ike, Nobutaka. *Japanese Politics: Patron–client Democracy*. New York: Knopf, 1972. Ike describes the way patron–client arrangements have influenced the practice of democracy in Japan.

Migdal, Joel S. *Strong Societies and Weak States, State–Society Relations and State Capabilities in the Third World*. Princeton, NJ: Princeton University Press, 1988. Study of how patron–client social values overwhelm "rational" state political systems.

Pye, Lucian W. *The Spirit of Chinese Politics*. Cambridge, MA: Harvard University Press, 1992. One of the world's leading experts on political culture, Pye examines the underlying social values that guide Chinese politics.

Royko, Mike. *Boss: Richard J. Daley of Chicago*. New York: Dutton, 1988. Royko, a popular Chicago columnist, first published the book in 1971 when Daley was still mayor. The book is an acclaimed inside account of how a patron–client system really worked in a big American city.

SEE ALSO

Communism, Populism, Republicanism, Socialism

Populism

OVERVIEW

Populism's personalities have manifested themselves differently at various times: as an agrarian phenomenon backlash to industrialism, as a nationalistic phenomenon bypassing the existing power structures, and as a political phenomenon rebelling against the elite. At its heart, populism is a reaction against change. It tends to come from the lower and working classes, the so–called "common men," against technological, intellectual, and political innovation. The populist impulse tries to preserve a way of life and a distrust outsiders, including the power elites who rule and make decisions and the immigrants and foreigners who compete against the populists in the marketplace. As populism began as a reaction against industrialism, it primarily is a product of the nineteenth, twentieth, and twenty–first centuries.

WHO CONTROLS GOVERNMENT? Elected officials

HOW IS GOVERNMENT PUT INTO POWER? Elected by popular vote

WHAT ROLES DO THE PEOPLE HAVE? Pressure big business if unfair or unethical

WHO CONTROLS PRODUCTION OF GOODS? The people

WHO CONTROLS DISTRIBUTION OF GOODS? The people

MAJOR FIGURES William Jennings Bryan; George Wallace

HISTORICAL EXAMPLE OF GOVERNMENT People's Party in U.S South in the 1890s

HISTORY

It is not unusual to hear candidates, platforms, and even political parties described as populist by pundits and analysts. The word seems to mean different things to different people, or everything to everyone. Populism in its varied forms has appeared across the world, but perhaps no nation has provided a better illustration of the varieties and patterns of the political theory than the United States.

CHRONOLOGY

1829: Andrew Jackson becomes president of the United States.

1857: In England, Aleksandr Herzen begins the newspaper Kolokol and with it the first free Russian press abroad.

1869: The Knights of Labor are founded in the United States.

1881: Members of the People's Will terrorist society assassinate Tsar Alexander II.

1891: Delegates representing voter alliances, farm organizations, and reform groups meet in Cincinnati and discuss the formation of a Populist Party, also called the People's Party.

1896: William Jennings Bryan delivers his "Cross of Gold" speech and is nominated as the presidential candidate of the Democratic and Populist parties.

1946: Juan Perón is elected president of Argentina.

1950: Senator Joseph McCarthy starts the Red Scare by announcing that communists have infiltrated the U.S. State Department.

1968: George Wallace runs for U.S. president as the candidate of the American Independent Party.

1979: Jerry Falwell founds the Moral Majority.

1992: Ross Perot runs for U.S. president as an independent candidate.

The seed of populist thought began with the War of Independence and its promise that the people could liberate their government from the hands of elites far away and take control of it themselves. The egalitarian spirit of the Declaration of Independence—"all men are created equal"—and the empowerment of the U.S. Constitution—"We the people"—reinforced this promise. Two visions informed this impulse. First, the experience of the Protestant Reformation in Europe and the subsequent Great Awakenings in North America fostered belief in a personal God who could be reached by individuals without the mediation of a religious hierarchy. This religious change also social-

ized people to expect breaks with old churches and the establishment of new ones, emotional rhetoric, vivid oratory, and communal meetings. In other words, people learned to question authority, break with tradition, and gather to enjoy intense community building.

Another building block of what became populism was the message of the Great Enlightenment, the idea that individuals could be reasonable and rational—and that the past and the people in it often were not. The permission to think for one's self, and to criticize the traditions that came before, including the systems of government and privilege, fed into the populist mentality. Many revolutionary writers such as Thomas Paine, who supported the War of Independence, drew from the rationalist religion of the Enlightenment when appealing to the masses to rise up against England.

Thomas Jefferson, U.S. President from 1801 to 1809, served as a kind of proto–populist figure. Though not a true democrat in the sense that he didn't support direct decision making by all citizens for all affairs of state, Jefferson did present a striking change from his predecessors, George Washington and John Adams. Both behaved more like kings than commoners. Jefferson, on the other hand, downplayed ceremony, wore bedroom slippers to official meetings, and delighted in undermining the mystique surrounding public office. His heart, too, was with those he called "yeoman farmers," the individuals who worked small subsistence farms, who supported themselves by their labor, and who guarded their rights with zeal. Jefferson believed these agrarians were the key to the survival and stability of the nation, and in this sense anticipated the foundations of populism.

Perhaps the first true populist leader in the United States was Andrew Jackson (1767–1845), president from 1829 to 1837. A war hero and frontiersman, Jackson ran on a "let the people rule" platform that appealed to the masses—who in turn stormed the White House after his inauguration to eat and drink and celebrate the election of one of their own. Jackson thanked his supporters by putting them into office, creating a new precedent called the "spoils system," in which a leader dispensed appointments to loyal followers upon election.

The U.S. entered into a period of uncontrolled inflation, agitated by wild speculation in Western lands. In July of 1836, Jackson sought to stem the tide by issuing by issuing Specie Circular, which declared that the federal government would only accept hard money for the purchase of public lands. The edict simply added to the difficulties of sound banks, helping to precipitate the Panic of 1837.

BIOGRAPHY:

Andrew Jackson

Andrew Jackson is remembered as the first great populist leader of the United States. Common people identified with him and what he represented. His legend played into the mainstream's vision of a man of the people. He was twice a war hero. At the age of 13 he fought in the War of Independence and was captured by the British. After the revolution he became a frontiersman in Tennessee, where he often was fighting and dueling. He built a reputation as a plainspoken and able attorney, and then became a war hero a second time in the War of 1812. "Old Hickory," as he was called, led his troops to a remarkable victory against the British at the Battle of New Orleans.

Jackson approached his goal of the presidency differently than his predecessors. Before Jackson, candidates did not believe they should appear to want the position. They strove for disinterestedness. George Washington had started the tradition of acting like the Roman citizen Cincinnatus who, according to history, left his plow reluctantly when called to public service and returned to it when his duty was done. Washington and those who followed him allowed friends and supporters to pass good words along about their can-

didacies, but did their best to seem as if they preferred to be at their plow rather than in the president's chair. Jackson changed this tradition. He willingly showed his desire for the position. He campaigned for himself and played to his legend whenever possible. Rather than appealing to the elites with quiet statesmanship, he played to the masses with assurances that he was one of them and he wanted to let the people rule.

The fact that he was irreverent, rowdy, western, loud, assertive, and clearly a Washington outsider endeared Jackson to the people. After his election in 1828, citizens from across the nation went to the inaugural celebration in Washington, D.C. After the swearing–in ceremony, the people stormed the White House eating, drinking, dancing, singing, and celebrating their victory—and damaging a costly amount of furnishings in the process. Jackson fulfilled many of their expectations, dismantling privilege and championing the interests of labor and small agriculture. The momentum of his election, reelection, and the subsequent age of the common man spawned reform movements including abolitionism and women's suffrage that outlived his administrations but served as his most important legacy.

Jackson was also known for his policy of Indian removal. Believing that the massive transfer of Native Americans beyond the Mississippi River was ultimately the most human policy, he signed over ninety resettlement treaties with various tribes. Thousands of Indians found themselves forced to migrate along a "Trail of Tears."

In May of 1830, Jackson vetoed appropriations for the Maysville Road, a major artery stretching from Maysville, Kentucky, to Lexington. In his message, he denied that internal improvements were a federal responsibility. Yet, by the time he left the presidency, he had authorized more federal funds for such activity than all of his predecessors combined, and was especially enthusiastic when they were sponsored by loyal democrats.

Jackson attacked those he saw as elites living off of the work of the common people and called for equality of opportunity and access for everyone. Labor unions, abolitionism, and suffrage and temperance campaigns blossomed as local grassroots reforms

gained momentum. Later, Abraham Lincoln, president from 1861 until his assassination in 1865, and his image—to many whites, the everyman who grew up without privilege in a small log cabin in the woods, and to many blacks, the great emancipator and champion of the disenfranchised—built upon the image of Jackson and further burned populism into the mind of Americans.

Farmers' Demands

For the first century of its existence, the United States was primarily an agricultural nation. As the nineteenth century drew to a close, however, new economic realities meant that the traditional farming interest and the new labor interest were warily watching the growing industrial economy. Independent political groups with populist goals began to appear: the Patrons of Husbandry in 1867, the Knights of Labor in 1869, the Greenback Party in 1876, the New York Farmers' Alliance and Texas Farmers' Alliance in 1877, the Farmers' Alliance in 1877, the Northern

Andrew Jackson, seventh president of the United States. (The Library of Congress)

Farmers' Alliance in 1880, the Colored Farmers' Alliance in 1886, the Southern Farmers' Alliance in 1887, and the National Farmers' Alliance and Industrial Union in 1889. These groups called for railroad regulation and tax reform. After the Panic of 1873, which caused agricultural prices to plummet, many populists blamed the government's currency policy and the bankers and industrialists they believed determined it. As a result, they added another demand to their list: the unlimited coinage of silver.

The groups discovered that they could not get the attention of the Democratic and Republican parties while acting as separate entities. When neither major party made a commitment to the silver question in their 1892 presidential conventions, a third convention was held at Omaha to combine the different interests and create the Populist Party. Its goal was to take the Democratic Party's place as the second–most popular party in the nation. The platform it adopted called for specific economic policies: the free coinage of silver, a graduated income tax, plentiful paper money, the end of national banks, government ownership of all transportation and communication, eight–hour workdays, pensions, and a revision of the law of contracts. Members' anti–immigrant position manifested itself in a call for new immigration rules and laws forbidding the ownership of property by non–citizens. The platform also supported the direct election of U.S. senators. With its partnership of western and southern farmers and eastern industrial workers, the Populist Party nominated James B. Weaver as its candidate for the presidency. Though he polled more than one million votes, he lost to Grover Cleveland (1837–1908).

In the next presidential election, the Democratic Party borrowed the Populists' main tenet by adopting the issue of free silver coinage and nominating the eloquent William Jennings Bryan for its presidential candidate. Most populists voted with the Democratic Party instead of their own. However, the numbers still were not enough to defeat the Republican Party and its candidate, William McKinley (1843–1901). The 1896 defeat drove a further wedge between the urban and rural members of the populist coalition, and the Populist Party disintegrated. Some of its platform issues such as the direct election of senators came to pass despite the short–lived nature of the party organization.

New Concerns

The twentieth century brought several different incarnations of the populist persuasion. The first two decades primarily belonged to labor, especially as represented by the American Federation of Labor and its co–founder and president until 1924, Samuel Gompers (1850–1924). The main goals of labor were higher wages, shorter hours, and greater freedom. Labor found friends in the new breed of anti–corporate journalists who fed on scandal, such as William Randolph Hearst (1863–1951), as well as investigative journalists known as "muckrakers" who examined business in search of questionable practices to expose. Many reform laws were passed and standards introduced. After Gompers' death, the end of World War II, and the economic boom that followed, however, the labor movement lost ground.

The next wave of grassroots political action appeared as temperance societies. Although various groups had existed for decades to fight the ills of alcohol and drunkenness, a growing consensus among rural, religious, business, and women's groups gained attention through the well–organized Anti–Saloon League and Prohibition Party. After World War I, mass enthusiasm for prohibition swelled and the Eighteenth Amendment to the U.S. Constitution made the manufacture, transportation, and sale of alcoholic beverages illegal. Rather than creating a sober society, though, the law created a generation of outlaws dedicated to bootlegging, smuggling, and organized crime. In 1933, the Twenty–first Amendment repealed prohibition.

BIOGRAPHY:

George Wallace

George Wallace personified the intersection between the rural and religious wings of populism in the mid–twentieth century. Trained as an attorney, Wallace was active in the Alabama Democratic party. He served in the state assembly from 1947 to 1953 and on the bench as a district court judge from 1953 to 1959. He ran for governor of the state in 1962, avowing states' rights, the common worker, the Christian family, and an anti–Washington attitude. He believed in segregation and promised to keep Alabama schools segregated despite federal orders to integrate them. He won the gubernatorial election and soon was put to the test; in 1963, two black students tried to enroll at the University of Alabama. Wallace blocked their path and relented only when President John F. Kennedy took control of the Alabama National Guard and threatened to use it against him.

Wallace's wife, Lurleen Burns Wallace, succeeded him as governor as Wallace launched a presidential campaign—although no sensible person ever questioned who really ran things in Alabama. George Wallace received the nomination of the American Independent Party, a populist coalition of Southerners, Northern labor, Christian fundamentalists, and others wary of the Washington elite. The 1968 party platform of the American Independent Party is an excellent example of populist politics in action. Although Wallace lost the election, he was reelected governor

of Alabama in 1970. In 1972, he entered the Democratic presidential primaries, but his campaign all–but ended when an assassination attempt left him paralyzed below the waist.

Despite his disability, Wallace served as Alabama's governor again from 1975 to 1979 and from 1983 until his retirement in 1987. Wallace's position on a number of issues drew criticism from across the nation, especially from intellectuals and the upper and middle classes, but Wallace was extremely popular with Alabama workers of all races. His position on segregation, for example, whether on the level of maintaining a familiar, agrarian–based lifestyle or on the level of rebelling against a distant ruling elite, captured a populist moment in time for the United States.

Late in his life, Wallace apologized for his segregationist views and policies of the past, and sought forgiveness from the people he had so hurt and offended. Moreover, he said his views against integration in the 1960s were about taking a stand against the federal government's interference into the affairs of Alabama, not about racism. Whether Wallace was truly repentant only he knew for sure. However, a number of former adversaries decided to break bread with him. In 1995, on the thirtieth anniversary of the Selma march, members of the Southern Christian Leadership Conference welcomed George Wallace at a ceremony at the Alabama state capitol.

The next face of populism didn't come from the Democratic Party on the left, but from the Republican Party on the right. Just as agriculture and labor and temperance had judged that their communities, values, and way of life had been under attack by elites, so, too, in the post–World War II era, did the conservative mainstream believe their Christian, capitalistic society was under attack from within by the forces of communism. Perhaps the most famous anti–communist crusader was Senator Joseph McCarthy (1908–1957). In 1950, he announced that communists had infiltrated the U.S. State Department. The resulting "Red Scare" led to congressional hearings to root out so–called subversives; investigators ruined others' careers even when un–American activity could not be proven. Eventually the Senate censored McCarthy for his behavior and the press exposed many of his unsubstantiated

claims, but by then the seeds of anti–communist, nationalist populism had been planted among Americans. This conservative wing of populism reemerged in the 1960s behind the figure of George Wallace (1919–1998).

Anti–Washington Populism

Wallace, who became governor of Alabama in 1963, was an avowed states' rights supporter and segregationist. He blocked the doors of the University of Alabama in 1963 when two black students tried to attend classes. His rhetoric blamed the Washington establishment for imposing views on the American South—and, in some cases, North, especially Northern labor—with which they did not agree; he tied issues of race, religion, and anti–communist nationalism together to present an image of a way of life threatened by so–called liberal politics. In 1968, he ran for president as the candidate of the American Independent party, the platform for which read like a populist primer–the campaign's slogan was "Send Them a Message!" "Them," no doubt, was the Washington (and northeastern) elite. Wallace won five southern states and 46 electoral votes.

In 1972, Wallace entered the Democratic presidential race, but his candidacy was virtually destroyed by an assassination attempt that left him paralyzed below the waist. He returned to serve Alabama as governor from 1983 to 1987. Wallace remains one of the most–controversial political figures of the twentieth century, but variations of his anti–Washington fervor can be found in both the writings of the People's Party of the 1890s and in politicians campaigning for office in the twenty–first century. In *The Politics of Rage*, Dan T. Carter calls Wallace "the most influential loser in twentieth–century American politics."

The coalition of conservatives that followed McCarthy and his plea for the people to retake Washington survived into the 1980s as the Religious Right, with political–spiritual leaders such as Jerry Falwell and Pat Robertson. This grassroots movement relied on churches and other institutions outside of the traditional party structure to gather and maintain support for family values, strong defense, a government legislating in the social realm but unobtrusive in the economic sphere. This populist group feared big business less than big government and big interest groups such as those revolving around gender, race, and the environment. The coalition tended to be Republican but also drew from the southern wing of the Democratic Party—such as those who had supported Wallace—and propelled Ronald Reagan to the presidency from 1981 to 1989.

Perot and Buchanan

The xenophobia of the earlier labor movement reemerged in the 1990s with a backlash against free trade. Ross Perot (1930–) formed a short–lived following with a mix of labor, religious right, and independent voters. His nationalist rhetoric played to the McCarthyist patriots, but his concerns about immigration and protectionism referred back to the Populist Party of Weaver and the Democratic Party that had absorbed it. His Reform party placed candidates in high positions such as the governor of Minnesota, but soon platform issues such as the national debt were adopted by the major parties and the purpose behind the separate party seemed to vanish.

Like Perot, Pat Buchanan also fought to create a successful coalition around concerns about immigra-

tion and democracy in the 1990s, but found that the Wallace–like rhetoric that gained supporters in the 1960s did not do so thirty years later. Backlash against the Electoral College system after the disputed presidential election of 2000 offered yet another reflection of the beliefs of the Populist Party and its concern about direct democracy.

American populism began the twenty–first century as a mixture of labor and immigration concerns on the left and religious and family values concerns on the right. The September 11, 2001, destruction of the twin towers of the World Trade Center in New York City and the attack on the Pentagon in Washington, D.C., created a groundswell of grassroots nationalism that transcended party. At is core, however, rested deep anxieties about immigration, economy, and values—worries that the common people were under attack, that a new definition of modernity displaced the mainstream, that a way of life was endangered by a sinister few. In short, the initial reaction of a nation in crisis revealed a populist mind set.

THEORY IN DEPTH

Several core beliefs form the foundation of populism. First, the theory embraces rule by the people. In practice, this translates as democracy—not its close relative, republicanism, in which representatives of the people rule, because these representatives might act for their own interests instead of the interests of the people. Decisions should come from the people themselves, according to populist theory. This has translated into revolt against monarchs, as in Russia, and support for new leaders who bypass traditional power structures, as in Latin America. In the United States, the populist impulse for democracy has shown itself in the desire to elect U.S. senators directly and to abolish the Electoral College system.

A second core concept of populism is that of the minority elite and majority imperiled. In every form of populism, supporters have believed that the decision–making authority of the state rested with an elite who was out of touch with the mainstream—privileged monarchs, entrenched oligarchies, even the "Washington insiders." In many cases, populists have painted these elite not as unfortunately uninformed, but as willfully ignorant of the plight of the common people, unaware because the members of the elite are busy pursuing their own interests; not surprisingly, these interests seem, at least in populist rhetoric, to be contradictory to the interests of the mainstream.

A third basis for populist theory is the idea of the good and legitimate political action as one that springs from the bottom up rather than from the top down. The grassroots nature of populist movements worldwide springs from this conviction. In the village, on the street, from the union, within the church: these are the places from which political action flows, not only because these venues are near and convenient, but also because they should be the birthplace of citizens' participation. In this sense, the personal is political; the living room is the nation on a much smaller scale.

Reaction, then Action

Despite the fact that populism as a theory contains several core concepts, painting the theory in an abstract manner is difficult. At its heart, populism is not about central principles and consistent assumptions; in effect, populists do not adopt a system of thought and then behave accordingly. Populism is about reaction, not action, and as such, it has evolved gradually. James Weaver reacted against wealthy interests and the assault on the farmer; Juan Perón in Argentina reacted against the oligarchy and the assault on labor; Jerry Falwell reacted against secularization and the perceived assault on family values. All believed they were standing up for the common people, the backbone of their nations, the quiet majority that had been exploited and endangered by the powerful elite.

At its most narrow and shallow, populism is a desire to displace a system with one that can offer more for its constituents—hence the rise of dictators who buy the people's affection with money, policy, or inspiring rhetoric. The people might not even be getting a regime that gives them a greater voice in the process; it might be enough that the new elite went through the motions of appealing to the masses—in fact, it might be enough that the new elite is just different than the old one. The impetus here need not be one of high political theory. Instead, it might simply be the knee–jerk instinct of a given people at a particular time.

More bound in time and place is the agrarian instinct of populism, the inevitable backlash against industrialism—or, in the case of the 1990s and supporters of Ross Perot, industrialism's backlash against the information age. Regardless, it is the expression of anxiety about change and what the new world would mean for the economic and political lifestyle of the people it left behind. It is about a people feeling displaced by new national or world realities, people struggling not to be forgotten. A feeling of entitlement accompanies this world view; if the people are the government, then the government should pay to preserve the people's lifestyle. The Populist Party's platform, for example, included a list of things the government could do to institutionalize and reward the party members' way of life. In a sense, those populists were trying to mold the apparatus of the state to meet their self–interest, the same thing they claimed their political rivals had done.

For example, the Populist Party called for measures to protect agricultural interests and labor concerns. This included an increase in circulated currency via the unlimited coinage of silver, a graduated income tax that would require the wealthier to pay more and the poorer to pay less, government ownership and regulation of the railroads, economic protectionism to benefit those in agriculture, and the direct election of U.S. senators, for example. They supported other measures, too, designed to strengthen political democracy—they did, after all, believe their views were held by a majority of U.S. citizens—and give farmers comparative economic power with business and industry leaders.

Different scholars have viewed this movement in various ways across the years. Some in the early twentieth century viewed populists as the forerunners to another, albeit more urban, reform movement known as progressivism. Economic historians played into the "frontier thesis" first articulated by Frederick Jackson Turner and viewed populism as an answer to the frontier desire for economic inclusion and attention, with "frontier" applying both to the geographic location of the populists as well as their figurative positions within the economy and society. Later scholars of ideology found the populists to be less on the frontier than behind the times, motivated by irrational fears and a combination of knee–jerk racism, sexism, and anti–Semitism, and class envy as they bemoaned a process—industrialism—that could not be undone. Some intellectuals in the 1960s reacted against this interpretation and argued that populists represented the underprivileged and challenged not industrialism but capitalism. Recent historians have looked less at the economic policies of the populists and more at their social and cultural impacts and their call for democracy as a lifestyle as well as a system. Needless to say, the legacy of the agrarian populists in the United States remains a contested and controversial subject for scholars and students alike.

The most theoretical and abstract of the strains of populism is the desire for inclusion, for involvement, for greater participation and less control by the elite. The call for direct democracy in the ideal world, or at least increasingly democratic institutions of government in the real world, follows from this point. Even in so–called democracies, the efficiency of republicanism remains in tension with the values of democracy.

A political cartoon of William Jennings Bryan giving the Cross of Gold speech. (Corbis Corporation)

As a grassroots campaign, populism is less of a political theory than a political reaction. Its various faces reflect core ideas, but also illustrate variations in how they are applied, from Abraham Lincoln to Nazi leader Adolph Hitler.

The Cross of Gold Speech

Since populism often appears as a popular, grassroots movement carried by emotional orations and symbolic acts, no systematic literature of populism exists. Even the publications of populist leaders have targeted mass readership, and so seem more like propaganda than political theory. Three significant forms of populist expression remain the speech, the party platform, and the editorial.

When William Jennings Bryan addressed the Democratic Nation Convention in Chicago on July 9, 1896, his speech so impressed the crowd that he received two parties' presidential nomination, that of the Democratic and Populist parties. Bryan addressed the issue of free coinage of silver, a policy that would have helped in the short–term farmers and others hurt by deflation, and criticized those who wanted the government to stay with the gold standard for currency— Eastern bankers and Washington insiders, according to the populists. Bryan was not an economist, and did not even pretend to understand the issue from a fiscal point of view. In true populist form, he stated, "The people of Nebraska are for free silver and I am for free silver. I will look up the arguments later."

When he spoke, Bryan touched on every populist theme: the War of Independence, Christianity, and the underdog common man. Excerpts from his speech prove the skill and populist nature of his address:

Mr. Chairman and Gentlemen of the Convention: I would be presumptuous, indeed, to present myself against the distinguished gentlemen to whom you have listened if this were a mere measuring of abilities; but this is not a contest between persons. The humblest citizen in all the land, when clad in the armor of a righteous cause, is stronger than all the hosts of error. I come to speak to you in defense of a cause as holy as the cause of liberty— the cause of humanity. . . . Mr. Carlisle said in 1878 that this was a struggle between 'the idle holders of idle capital' and 'the struggling masses, who produce the wealth and pay the taxes of the country;' and, my friends, the question we are to decide is: Upon which side will the Democratic party fight; upon the side of 'the idle holders of idle capital' or upon the side of 'the struggling masses?' That is the question which the party must answer first, and then it must be answered by each individual hereafter. The sympathies of the Democratic party, as shown by the platform, are on the side of the struggling masses who have ever been the foundation of the Democratic party. There are two ideas of government. There are those who believe that, if you will only legislate to make the well–to–do prosperous, their prosperity will leak through on those below. The Democratic idea, however, has been that if you legislate to make the masses prosperous, their prosperity will find its way up through every class which rests upon them. You come to us and tell us that the great cities are in favor of the gold standard; we reply that the great cities rest upon our broad and fertile prairies. Burn down your cities and leave our farms, and your cities will spring up again as if by magic; but destroy our farms and the grass will grow in the streets of every city in the country. My friends, we declare that this nation is able to legislate for its own people on every question, without waiting for the aid or consent of any other nation on earth; and upon that issue we expect to carry every State in the Union. I shall not slander the inhabitants of the fair State of Massachusetts nor the inhabitants of the State of New York by saying that, when they are confronted with the proposition, they will declare that this nation is not able to attend to its own business. It is the issue of 1776 over again. Our ancestors, when but three millions in number, had the courage to declare their political independence of every other nation; shall we, their descendants, when we have grown to seventy millions, declare that we are less independent than our forefathers? No, my friends, that will never be the verdict of our people. Therefore, we care not upon what lines the battle is fought. If they say bimetallism is good, but that we cannot have it until other nations help us, we reply that, instead of having a gold standard because England has, we will restore bimetallism, and then let England have bimetallism because the United States has it. If they dare to come out in the open field and defend the gold standard as a good thing, we will fight them to the uttermost. Having behind us the producing masses of this nation and the world, supported by the commercial interests, the laboring interests, and the toilers everywhere, we will answer their demand for a gold standard by saying to them: You shall not press down upon the brow of labor this crown of thorns, you shall not crucify mankind upon a cross of gold.

Not once did Bryan mention Black American farmers or their role in the future of the party or the country.

Despite the backing of two parties, William Jennings Bryan could not win the presidency. Decades later, George Wallace, 1968 presidential candidate of the populist American Independent Party, also faced defeat in election to the White House. The 1968 platform for the American Independent Party, like Bryan's "Cross of Gold" speech, hit on traditional populist themes such as labor, nationalism, and Christianity. The platform's preamble reflects this well. It specifically called for an education program "assisted but not controlled by the federal government," peace at home and abroad (meaning an end to the Vietnam War and thus an end to the growing anti–war movement), and controlling government spending. Wallace's anti–Washington rhetoric can be heard by many of today's politicans as they campaign for office.

Like George Wallace, Richard Viguerie, author of such books as *The New Right: We're Ready to Lead* and *The Establishment vs. The People*, came at populism from the conservative Republican side. His article represents the third major kind of populist work, the editorial. In the October 19, 1984, issue of *National Review*, Viguerie penned "A Populist, and Proud of It." Excerpts from this work show that the primary message of American populism changed little in a century:

> Populists stand in opposition to the elitists who believe that people are not smart enough to manage their own affairs and that, therefore, the government should select intelligent, qualified persons to run society—"intelligence" and "qualifications" being measured by the degree to which a person conforms to an establishment stereotype. . . . The People's (or Populist) Party of the 1890s was not, after all, the band of racists and socialists that some writers have described. In some cases they advocated socialist measures, to break up the concentration of power in the hands of the establishment. But it did so because the establishment had first used the power of government to enrich itself at the expense of farmers and workers.

THEORY IN ACTION

Populism's many forms—as a backlash to industrialism, as nationalism bypassing the power struc-

tures, and as a drive against the elite—are evident in the examples of Russia, Latin America, and the United States.

Populism developed into the dominant radical impulse in Russia in the nineteenth century. The revolutionary writer and leader Aleksandr Herzen (1812–1870) fueled the movement. In the historical agrarianism of Russia he saw the key to the nation's future. He believed that the traditional peasant communes of rural Russia could serve as the model for a cooperative commonwealth that, through its abolition of private property and emphasis on the common good, could skip the capitalist growing pains exhibited by Great Britain and the United States and move directly to socialism. His idealization of the peasantry, appeal to "go to the people," and encouragement of rebellion influenced many of the students and intellectuals of the early to mid–nineteenth century.

Russia

In 1861, Tsar Alexander II (1818–1881) freed the serfs in one of his many reforms. The freeing of the serfs—a symbolic crescendo that really didn't change the peasants' lives all that much—along with the wake of revolutionary thought from the west enticed the Russian youth, and a populist movement grew. Thousands of Russian students tried to get the peasants in the rural areas to join them in a call for more reforms, but the peasants generally didn't follow the *intelligentsia* call for revolution. The leaders of the movement grew frustrated, and their actions grew more and more violent. There were frequent assassination attempts against the tsar.

By the 1870s, most populists had grown disillusioned with the idea that the people would rise up and take control of the government; instead, these revolutionaries decided they would have to topple the government first and then give it to the people. The goal was the same, but the strategy for achieving it had changed. The anarchist revolutionary Mikhail Bakunin, whose writings and activism inspired Spanish laborers to band with the syndicalist movement and fight in the Spanish Civil War, played to a different audience in his native Russia: disillusioned, alienated intellectuals. With Bakunin's work as an inspiration, small groups of mostly student revolutionaries turned to terrorism to attack the tsar and the monarchical system in general.

One of the fruits of this movement was the secret society Land and Liberty, which was formed in 1876. Their efforts to promote a mass uprising resulted in their expulsion from the countryside. The most violent wing of the group formed the People's Will in 1879.

BIOGRAPHY:
Aleksandr Herzen

Aleksandr Herzen, revolutionary and writer, is remembered as the father of Russian populism. In 1834, the government transferred his post as a civil servant to the outer provinces of Russia as punishment for belonging to an unorthodox political circle that advocated the state ownership of production. Herzen's *de facto* exile gave him a new appreciation of the agrarian lifestyle and planted the seeds for his later idealization of the peasantry of the countryside. He returned to Moscow six years later and then left Russia for good.

Herzen traveled to Paris and supported the Revolution of 1848 there. He then moved to Great Britain to establish the first free Russian press abroad, including the Russian–banned but nonetheless widely disseminated newspaper *Kolokol*, which was published from 1857 to 1862. He also published a number of standalone works such as *Who Is To Blame?* (1847), a novel about disillusionment with Russia, *From the Other Shore* (1855), a critique of contemporary European revolutions, and the four–volume *My Past and Thoughts* (1855), a history of Russia and retrospective of revolutions.

Though a Westernizer for years, Herzen continued to think back on his time in Russia and on the process of industrialization that he witnessed in Western Europe, with its urbanization and mechanization. By the late 1840s, Herzen began to argue that Russia might be able to skip the stage of industrialization altogether by modifying the traditional peasant commune to become a series of socialist villages held together by a confederation. His message about learning from the common people and adapting their agricultural lifestyle as an alternative to the systems of Western Europe launched the Russian populist movement.

In 1881, members of this terrorist society finally succeeded in assassinating Tsar Alexander II. Other populists opposed such violent tactics. Rather than seek change immediately, they placed their hopes in gradually winning public support, which they sought with propaganda and education. Even though terrorist activities represented only one part of the populist impulse in Russia, interest in the theory began to wane. Moreover, when Tsar Alexander III (1845–1894) took over, he repealed many of his father's reforms. The spirit of the movement—from both ends—was over, and Russia slipped back to a complete totalitarian state.

Georgy Plekhanov, a former member of Land and Liberty who embraced populism but denounced violence, formed the League for the Emancipation of Labor in 1883. His views began to change as he read Karl Marx and began to work with fellow radicals such as Vladimir Lenin. Soon he doubted that the agricultural ideal of the peasant commune would be possible without allowing capitalism and industrialism to progress first. Plekhanov left populism behind and became the father of Russian Marxism. After the Russian Revolution of 1917, the country faced a communist, not populist, future and the agrarian village was replaced with urban factories.

Russia's experience with populism fell into the category of an agrarian phenomenon rebelling against industrialization. The elite *intelligentsia* idealized the lives of country peasants and sought to bypass the turmoil of industrialism by creating a network of loosely confederated communes dedicated to working on the land. The movement failed for two reasons: first, the violence used by the fringe–group terrorists backfired and turned the mainstream away from their message. Second, populism became sidelined by the momentum of Marxism, which had seduced populist leaders and the mainstream imagination.

Latin America

Populism also has appeared as a nationalistic phenomenon bypassing the power structure of a given country, which is what happened in Latin America. The first country to experience this form of populism was Argentina. Juan Perón first gained power as a member of the military regime that seized control of Argentina in 1943. Perón nursed a fierce ambition and an abiding interest in social policy. He courted the labor class by a combination of clever advances: he criticized the former ruling oligarchy and foreign imperialists, playing on old resentments; he offered wage increases, pensions, and benefits; he preached social justice and national strength; and he praised Argentine industrial and military power. When he ran for president in 1946, Perón won easily. Together he and his remarkable actress wife, Eva, or Evita, who became even more popular than her husband, continued to cultivate a base of support among laborers. Perón's rise to power marked a revolutionary period in Argentine history and sparked similar patterns in other Latin American countries.

For example, Rómolo Betancourt and his comrades led Acción Democrática, the mainstream political party in postdictatorial Venezuela. In the footsteps of Perón in Argentina, they promised substantial benefits to members of the labor and middle classes in return for support of reform and a generally capitalistic system. Juscelino Kubitschek, the president of Brazil, had a similar story in the 1950s and 1960s; though not strictly populist in philosophy, he did harness the successful populist strategy of Perón and Betancourt to gain a following from the bottom up and rise to power. A variation on this theme appeared after World War II with the rise of Christian Democratic parties, which drew their platforms for social reform from Roman Catholic teachings. These popularly based groups first achieved power in Chile with the presidency of Eduardo Frei (served from 1964–1970) and then followed in Venezuela and El Salvador.

The United States

The United States' experience with populism predated those in Russia and Latin America and exhibited a split personality. On the one hand, the United States had its own version of agrarian backlash like that of Russia. On the other hand, American populism also was a political phenomenon of rebellion against the elite. The agrarian experience took shape with the advent of the People's Party in the 1890s. This grassroots movement responded to the economic complaints of southern and western farmers as the nation's economy changed in response to the Industrial Revolution.

People's Party   As the American population slowly spread west in the nineteenth century, railroads went with them. An increasing number of people lived in rural areas, the number of farms exploded—at the start of the Civil War in 1861 there were two million farms in the United States; by the end of the century that number had tripled. The farmers needed the railroads to ship their crops to the big cities.

Farmers usually had to borrow money from banks to pay for equipment or railroad transportation of their products. However, the bankers or railroad executives could charge whatever prices they desired. According to Howard Zinn in *A People's History of the United States*, in the late 1800s a farmer "had to pay a bushel of corn in freight costs for each bushel he shipped." In addition, farmers' profits were going steadily downward. Some farmers rented their land—some historians estimate that 90 percent of Southern farmers

Juan Perón. (The Library of Congress)

rented their land. Many lost their farms and had to become laborers on another farmer's land. Then *that* farmer would lose his job, and there would be two looking for work. And so on and so on.

In 1877, a group of farmers in Texas formed the Farmers Alliance. Nine years later, a group of Black farmers in Texas formed the Colored Farmers Alliance. That same year, members of the Farmers Alliance met in Cleburne, Texas, and produced a document known as the Cleburne Demands. They called for the government to regulate railroad costs and increase the money supply by allowing silver—instead of only gold—to be used as legal tender. Many farmers thought a huge part of the problem was a shortage of the money supply, making it even harder to get the shrinking number of dollars that were out there. The farmers began to work together to buy equipment and supplies in groups, thus at lower costs.

The movement spread like wildfire among farmers in the South and Midwest—some estimates have the Farmers Alliance numbers at almost half a million members by 1890. And it was in 1890 that the Populist Party formed. Many of its newest members were from the Farmers Alliance. The Populists actively sought the Black vote. Many local chapters of the Party were interracial, with debates among black and white farmers, although many aspects of segregation did find their way into the meetings.

In 1892, the Populists (or People's Party) nominated James Weaver for president. Democrat Grover Cleveland won the election.

The populists demanded that the government intervene in the economy to help small producers. In 1896, William Jennings Bryan, a Democrat, ran for the presidency on a populist platform and lost. His defeat signaled that the end was near for the agrarian populist movement in the United States. Indeed, the Colored Farmers Alliance was against the idea of giving up the populists' independent movement to ally themselves with the Democrats, but the rest of the People's Party did not listen.

The Twentieth Century The political phenomenon of rebellion against the elite in the United States has appeared and reappeared several times. The grassroots movement that propelled Andrew Jackson into the White House from 1829 to 1837 used the rhetoric of electing "one of the people" to rally support; the same was true for the election of Washington outsider Jimmy Carter in 1976. The rise of the Moral Majority in the 1980s with its call for a return to family values, the presidential candidacy of Ross Perot in 1992 and the subsequent creation of the Reform Party, and the popular reaction against the Electoral College after the disputed presidential election of 2000 all represent populist drives to eliminate the barriers between state power and the people. At its best, this movement fueled activism and reform; a classic example of this was the growth of suffrage, temperance, and abolitionist groups, among others, in the wake of Jacksonianism. At its worst, the harnessing of popular energy led to something close to mass hysteria; the extremes to which the anti–communism of the McCarthyism movement reached in the 1950s reflected this problem.

The examples of how populism has differed illustrate several aspects of the political theory. First, a nation's phase of development affects the nature of populism. The United States and Russia at the end of the nineteenth century were primarily agricultural countries experiencing early industrialism with its corresponding urbanization, mechanization, and specialization. This becomes important when looking at the Third World at the end of the twentieth and beginning of the twenty–first century, since Third World nations reached the same position the United States and Russia reached a century earlier. The history of populism provides a clue to what kind of activism and impulses to expect in the Third World.

Second, the experience of Latin America reflects the opportunities for leaders—not always benevolent ones—to appeal to the people, sidestep regimes, and play upon popular convictions as positive as national pride and personal self–respect and as negative as class hatred and virulent xenophobia. For these leaders to be successful, hostilities and resentments must exist within the labor and middle classes, and the existing regime must be stagnant, or at least apparently uninvolved with the issues concerning the non–elite. Although this face of populism has toppled ruling parties without bloodshed, it also has powered movements as destructive as the rise of Adolph Hitler and German Nazism in the twentieth century.

The last face of populism, political reaction against the elite, seems to be a normal force of change in many nations, often achieved peacefully. In the United States, for example, this need for popular involvement often is seen in small but meaningful ways, such as in the use of referendum, or voting on legislation passed by representative assemblies; popular initiative, through which regular citizens can bypass the legislature and offer legislation for voters to decide on in a referendum; and recall, which allows voters to demand an early election if unsatisfied with their representatives.

ANALYSIS AND CRITICAL RESPONSE

Populism as a political theory and movement defies simple categorization due to the number of faces it has worn. The specific form populism takes changes depending on which elite and/or government it is reacting against. Even so, the impulse for the common person to have direct say in the government without the rule of the elite can be analyzed in the context of its history.

The most obvious problem with populism is its name. The term "populist" has been stretched to encompass so many ideas it is almost meaningless. Richard A. Viguerie agreed that the term was not ideal when he wrote in his 1984 article "A Populist, and Proud Of It": "If there is a better word than 'populist' to describe the people I'm referring to, I will gladly use it. In 1982 my magazine, *Conservative Digest*, ran a contest to find a better word, and there were six hundred entries, but nobody came up with anything better than 'populist.' So I guess we're stuck with it."

Different Meanings

Populism refers to movements and activism concerned with small–scale agricultural life in the face of modernism, but it also refers to pro–industrial leaders who sidestep the power structure to woo the support of labor; therefore, India's Mahatma Ghandi and Argentina's Juan Perón can be called populists. Populism refers to the ways in which a ruler evokes the nationalism and xenophobia of a people to rally them around large causes, and yet it also refers to the ways in which a leader empathizes with the most unassuming background of people and values equality; therefore, Italy's Benito Mussolini and the United States' Abraham Lincoln might be said to be populists. If all four can be populists, is the word too abstract, too loose, too all–encompassing to have meaning? Aside from the lack of specificity of the term, other analytical points can be raised. Certainly empowering the people can be a positive thing; populism, after all, provided a springboard for abolitionism and feminism, among other things. Criticisms of populism, however, also exist.

One interpretation of populism is that it is a more recent manifestation of a long pattern of opposition in human societies: those at the center versus those at the periphery. The center of power, of course, has changed often in terms of philosophy and location. For several centuries before the advent of populism, this duality was the "crown and town" opposition; those at court got to know the monarch and draw closer to power and influence, while those in the towns lived far away from the kings and queens and not only had little power and influence, but also lived a different lifestyle in a different economic and political atmosphere than the one at court. In the case of U.S. populism, then, the crown might be the banks of New York City or the government buildings of Washington, D. C., while the town might be the farm in Georgia, the factory in Detroit, or the church in Missouri.

Another interpretation of populism views agrarian populism as the true embodiment of the political theory. In this approach, populists formed a democratic movement that provided the last and most articulate critique of corporate capitalism before the realities of the industrial age ended the agrarian lifestyle, and thus the only real alternative to commercial culture, permanently. This view suggests populists had the insight to realize that corporate capitalism did not promise or provide wealth for everyone; the populists themselves were proof that the new economy could hurt as well as reward.

This interpretation credits the populists with more foresight than could have been possible, however—the development of the economy in Russia and the United States, for example, was not inevitable. In fact, Russia and the United States as illustrations prove how differently the development might have evolved. To call the populists prophets of corporate capitalism, then, when corporate capitalism did not yet exist fully,

BIOGRAPHY:
H. Ross Perot

H. Ross Perot, a U.S. business and political leader, is best known as the founder and first presidential candidate of the populist Reform party. After service in the military, Perot began his career as a salesman for IBM. In 1962 he created one of the nation's first computer data service companies, Electronic Data Systems, or EDS. He sold EDS to General Motors in 1984 but retained an interest in EDS; after vocal criticism of GM's management, he sold his remaining interest in 1986 for $700 million. In 1988, he founded Perot Systems Corp., another computer service company.

Perot's political activism began during the Iran hostage crisis in 1979. When two of his employees were held in an Iranian prison, Perot paid for a rescue operation that liberated them. In 1992 he ran for the presidency as an independent candidate. His criticism of the size of the national debt brought him a grassroots following and nearly one–fifth of the popular vote. After the election, he became a vocal critic of the North American Free Trade Agreement, which promoted more open trade between the United States, Canada, and Mexico. His wariness of Washington insiders, praise of the common people, concern for labor, and distrust of foreign competition and immigration placed him squarely within the populist tradition.

In 1995 Perot created a national political party called the Reform Party. He ran as the party's candidate for president in 1996 but garnered fewer votes than in 1992. The Reform Party eventually outgrew its creator and gained new prominence in the late 1990s with the election of candidate Jesse Ventura as Governor of Minnesota. Perot's affect on the nation as an outsider critic of Washington politics, a rallying flag for grassroots activism, and creator of a significant alternative to the Republican and Democratic parties made Perot a key political figure in 1990s.

is using hindsight unfairly. Moreover, the claim that corporate capitalism did not benefit the populist seems strained, since the populists did not really take part in that economy. They were not corporate capitalists. In

Ross Perot on election night in Dallas, 1992. (Getty Images)

a sense, they were apart in their own agrarian economy, and their failure to join the growing new one—and not the new one itself—caused part of their plight.

The most compelling and least flattering interpretation of populism is that it was and is a reactionary force that maintained a backward–looking stance by means of a conspiratorial view of history. This view has three components. First, populism could not exist on its own in power; it does not set forth distinct principles, but rather moves in opposition to other things. It does not act; it reacts. Second, populists have tended to be at the end of social and economic trends, trying to preserve—and, in some senses, institutionalize—ways of life that no longer apply easily to the technology and demands of the time. Perhaps the most disturbing of the components is the third: the conspiratorial view of history. To have the "us" of populism, the oppressed, requires the "them" of populism, the oppressors. "The man" always put and puts the "little guy" down. The Populist Party, or People's Party, platform of 1892 put it this way: "A vast conspiracy against mankind has been organized on two continents, and it is rapidly taking possession of the world." American agrarians believed the eastern bankers had conspired with the Washington elite to disenfranchise the farmers. Likewise, the U.S. anti–communists believed that the U.S. State Department was full of communists planning to subvert

American family values. The worst–case scenario of this kind of thinking results in xenophobia—it is the fault of foreigners—or racism, sexism, and, in the case of Germany's Nazism, anti–Semitism. Blaming groups often leads more to hate and scapegoatism than productive strategies for growth.

Populism in Oz

The U.S. agrarian experience with populism not only changed the political landscape of the nation, but some say it also produced an enduring achievement in American literature: Frank L. Baum's *The Wonderful Wizard of Oz*, first published in 1900 after the peak of the agrarian populist movement, offered an entrancing children's story that doubled as an allegory of the American populist drama. The theory was first advanced by Henry M. Littlefield in his 1964 article "The Wizard of Oz: Parable on Populism" from *American Quarterly*. More than a few historians and critics have echoed Littlefield's findings.

The symbolism of the story centered around the key issue of the populist platform: free silver. The story of Oz—the word "Oz" itself a play on the abbreviation for ounce, the standard measure of precious metals—included the clashing images of the yellow brick road, a symbol of the gold standard on which the economy was based, and magic silver shoes (which were changed to ruby slippers for the movie because the producers felt that color looked better against the yellow road), which spoke to the desire by populists for free coinage of silver. Just as Dorothy found the road to be restrictive, but the shoes to be the answer to her needs, populists hoped the addition of elastic and abundant silver to the economy would limit the power of bankers and help the common people to preserve—or, in Dorothy's case, return—home.

If Dorothy served as a symbol of the United States, unknowing and innocent, held in the sway of gold without realizing the true liberating power of silver, then her companions also reflected other actors in the story of populism. The Cowardly Lion, for example, roared loudly but did little; in the same way, the great orator William Jennings Bryan made stirring speeches but failed to win the presidency despite repeated attempts. Perhaps the Tin Man represented the overworked and underpaid eastern workers, dehumanized and self–destructive regardless of how hard they worked, while the Scarecrow symbolized the Midwestern farmers facing drought and ruin, and in the Emerald City, or Washington, D.C., *The Wonderful Wizard of Oz* took the place of the U.S. president. Some critics see the Wicked Witches of the East and West as banker bosses and railroad barons, as well; after all, the book often returns to the theme of a people dominated and enslaved by powerful tyrants, whether they be the Munchkins trapped by the Wicked Witch of the East or the flying monkeys abused by the Wicked Witch of the West.

The Wizard of Oz became an American classic as a book, a play, and a motion picture, most notably as the 1939 Judy Garland film. At its core, however, it presented not a celebration but rather a sympathetic critique of the rise and fall of American populism. The farmer, the laborer, the politician—the U.S. public—in the novel traveled to the nation's capital to request that their wishes be fulfilled, but each of the wishes were somehow oversimplified or self–delusional. The Scarecrow really had a brain, for he was clever and shrewd, if somewhat unpolished; likewise, the Tin Man and the Lion already had a heart and courage, respectively, even if they did not know how to capitalize on their assets. Dorothy could have returned home at any time—she, too, possessed the means to help herself throughout the novel. More important still, the U.S. President ended up to be an everyman with no special powers to remake the world with magic.

At the end of the novel, silver had lost its magic as the shoes disappeared, agricultural interests reclaimed Washington as the Scarecrow ruled the Emerald City, industrialism pushed west with the Tin Man,

and the Cowardly Lion remained a player in the woods, just as Bryan remained active though never in charge. The newly freed Munchkins and flying monkeys had to negotiate their own way in this new reality. The naïveté of the characters' wishes gave way to the more complex reality of the changing world; the simplicity of their desires proved to be distractions rather than real reflections of their needs. In short, Baum appreciated the problems the populists raised, but found the solutions they offered to be naïve and overly elementary. The populists, he implied, often were their own worst enemies. In order to meet the challenges of a changing nation, they had to help themselves; in their doing so, Baum suggested, the movement known as agrarian populism all but disintegrated.

Of course, there are plenty of historians who may not wholeheartedly agree with Littlefield's analyis. William R. Leach offered another interpretation of *Oz*—as a celebration of the American big city. There are likely plenty of readers who believe it is simply a wonderful tale of fantasy. At any rate, it does offer a different and very interesting way to study the dynamics of Populism in the late–nineteenth century.

TOPICS FOR FURTHER STUDY

- Investigate and compare: in what ways were nineteenth–century Russian and American populism similar?

- Why was Eva Perón such a successful populist symbol?

- In what ways did the Populist party, or People's party, of the nineteenth century compare to the American Independent party of the twentieth century?

BIBLIOGRAPHY

Sources

Cayton, Andrew, Elisabeth Israels Perry, and Allan M. Winkler. *America: Pathways to the Present.* Needham, Massachusetts: Prentice Hall, 1995.

Clanton, Gene. *Populism: The Humane Preference in America, 1890–1900.* Boston: Twayne, 1991.

Holmes, William F., ed. *American Populism.* Lexington, MA: D.C. Heath and Company, 1994.

Johnston, Joseph F., Jr. "Conservative Populism: A Dead End." *National Review.* (October 19, 1984): 38–42.

Kazin, Michael. *The Populist Persuasion: An American History.* New York: HarperCollins, 1995.

Miller, David, ed. *The Blackwell Encyclopedia of Political Thought*. Cambridge, Blackwell, 1991.

Peffer, William A. *Populism, Its Rise and Fall*. Peter H. Argersinger, ed. Lawrence: University Press of Kansas, 1992.

Turner, James. "Understanding the Populists," *The Journal of American History*. 67:2 (September 1980): 354–373.

Viguerie, Richard A. "A Populist, and Proud Of It." *National Review*. (October 19, 1984): 42–44.

Wallbank, T. Walter and Arnold Shrier. *Living World History*. Glenview, IL: Scott, Foresman and Company, 1990.

Further Readings

Baum, L. Frank. *The Annotated Wizard of Oz: A Centennial Edition*. Michael Patrick Hearn, ed. New York: W. W. Norton & Co., 2000. This work explores The Wizard of Oz and helps to reveal it as an extended metaphor of the story of populism.

Goodwyn, Lawrence. *The Populist Moment: A Short History of the Agrarian Revolt in America*. Oxford: Oxford University Press, 1978. This book recounts the history of the farmers' movement and its relationship to populism.

Hahn, Steven. *The Roots of Southern Populism: Yeoman Farmers and the Transformation of the Virginia Upcountry, 1850–1890*. Reprint edition. Oxford: Oxford University Press, 1985. This book describes the early intellectual roots of populism in the United States.

Remini, Robert Vincent. *Andrew Jackson*. Baltimore: Johns Hopkins University Press, 1998. This biography focuses on the populist president Andrew Jackson and his influence on U.S. politics.

Taggert, Paul. *Populism*. Philadelphia: Open University Press, 2000. This general overview provides a theoretical look at populism as an idea.

Republicanism

OVERVIEW

Republicanism is familiar because it pervades political speech. Americans, for example, have long pledged allegiance not only to their flag but also to "the republic for which it stands." But republicanism is also elusive because there is no consensus among scholars or citizens as to exactly what a republic is. No wonder. Republican government has been practiced in a wide variety of times and places, including ancient Athens, Sparta, Rome, Renaissance Florence, and modern America. Similarly, republican political theory has been expounded by a wide variety of thinkers and statesmen, including Aristotle (384–322 B.C.) in ancient Greece, Niccolò Machiavelli (1469–1527) in sixteenth–century Italy, and Alexander Hamilton (1755–1804), James Madison (1751–1836), and John Jay (1745–1829) in eighteenth–century America. Though republicanism has meant many different things, a republic can be usefully defined as a government of citizens, rather than subjects, who share in directing their own affairs. This definition, though broad, has some important implications. Being governed by a king requires little virtue; the laws, backed by the threat of force, keep subjects in check. Governing oneself, in contrast, requires considerable virtue. Where citizens themselves have a hand in the laws and in the use of force, they must remember their duties and check themselves. For this reason, republicanism requires virtue. Virtue, however, understood as the capacity and willingness to restrain or sacrifice oneself for the common good, does not come easily.

WHO CONTROLS GOVERNMENT? Elected officials, majority of power in state leaders

HOW IS GOVERNMENT PUT INTO POWER? Popular vote of the majority

WHAT ROLES DO THE PEOPLE HAVE? Vote; serve the state in a crisis

WHO CONTROLS PRODUCTION OF GOODS? The owners of capital

WHO CONTROLS DISTRIBUTION OF GOODS? The owners of capital

MAJOR FIGURES Niccolò Machiavelli; John Jay

HISTORICAL EXAMPLE Ancient Sparta

CHRONOLOGY

1100–800 B.C.: The Greek *polis* takes shape

499–479 B.C.: Greek republics defeat monarchical Persia in the "Persian Wars"

509 B.C.: According to tradition, the year the Roman Republic is established

338 B.C.: Conquest of Greece by Philip of Macedon effectively puts an end to the independence of the Greek republics.

31 B.C.: Though the forms of republican politics remain, the rise to power of Octavian, later to be known as Augustus, effectively puts an end to the Roman Republic.

11th century A.D.: Rise of medieval town, seedbeds of republican revival, especially in Italy.

1531–1532: Publication of *The Prince* and *Discourses*, both authored by Niccolò Machiavelli, founder of modern republicanism.

1640–1660: Puritan Revolution in England.

1688: Glorious Revolution in England.

1775–1783: American Revolution.

1787–1788: Publication of the *Federalist Papers*, written by Alexander Hamilton, John Jay, and James Madison in defense of the proposed Constitution of the United States, which had been adopted by the Federal Convention in Philadelphia in 1787.

Therefore, republican politics is, to borrow political theorist Michael Sandel's phrase, a "formative politics" that uses public moral education and other means to form virtuous citizens.

HISTORY

The history of republics and republicanism begins in ancient Greece, whose very geography, featuring fertile plains separated by mountains, seemed to lend itself to small, independent, and distinctive political communities. The *polis* (*poleis* plural), as the Greeks called the kind of community in question, began to take shape between 1100 and 800 B.C. During that period, the nobles, an exclusive group of leading families, wrested political power from the kings. Thereafter, men who acquired wealth and importance through commerce rather than noble birth demanded and gained a share of political power. In addition, military change widened the circle of citizenship. Between 700 and 600 B.C., infantry warfare began its development into the military tactic of choice in Greece. The equipment necessary for the infantry warrior, or *hoplite*, was much less expensive than that required for the chariot or cavalry warrior. Consequently, a broader (though still limited) section of the population came to contribute heavily to warfare and to be in a position to demand a political role. The controversy over whether citizenship and political power should belong to the multitude, as in a democracy, or the few, as in an oligarchy, often led to violence and contributed heavily to wars within and between *poleis* throughout classical Greek history. The controversy would continue to divide republican leaders, citizens, and theorists long after the *polis* had disappeared.

The polis

Many *poleis* had fewer than 5,000 citizens, fewer than modern-day Harvard University has undergraduates. Only three *poleis* had more than 20,000 citizens. Even the adult male citizen population of Athens in the late fifth century B.C., which was immense by Greek standards, did not exceed 45,000, far fewer people, for example, than the 57,545 who turn up for a sold-out New York Yankees game. The smallness of the Greek *polis* meant its citizens could live together with an intensity and immediacy that citizens of modern states can imagine only with difficulty. To envision life as a citizen in Athens, for example, one must envision knowing one's fellow citizens and being known by them. One must envision participating in politics not by voting for representatives but by attending the Assembly personally and deliberating with one's fellow citizens about the most important public matters, such as whether to go to war or sue for peace, or whether or not to punish a general. One must imagine participating in the administration of justice, not only by serving frequently on juries, which consisted not of twelve but between 101 and 1,000 citizens, but also by serving as one's own prosecutor or defense attorney. One must imagine seeing the plays of great tragedians and comic writers not in a darkened theater with a few friends and many anonymous strangers but in the open air, as part of a public festival. Athens was by no means atypical.

Nonetheless, the tiny and consequently fragile *polis*, threatened with destruction by external enemies or civil war, did not exist merely to offer its citizens the opportunity to participate politically. It was a community of fighters that required extraordinary devotion and unity. Where citizens were the army, and wars frequent, communities had to be bound as soldiers are. To accomplish this task, legislators and statesmen appealed not only to the reason and interest of citizens but above all to tradition, to myths of common ancestry, and to the gods of the *polis*. While all the Greeks worshipped the Olympian gods such as Zeus and Hera, each *polis* had its own mode of worship and its own local gods. In the Greek world, patriotism was, as historian Paul Rahe put it in *Republics: Ancient and Modern,* "a religion of blood and soil." The need of the *polis* for solidarity and a set of beliefs to support it in the face of danger helps explain why even in Athens, renowned for its liberality, Socrates (c. 470–399 B.C.), arguably the founder of Western philosophy, could be prosecuted and put to death for impiety and corrupting the young.

Aristotle

Though the all–encompassing character of *polis* life was borne of necessity, the Greeks also considered the *polis* superior to other forms of association. Aristotle (384–322 B.C.) observed in the *Politics* that although the *polis* came into being "for the sake of mere life," it existed "for the sake of a good life." Aristotle knew human associations could be larger than the *polis*. Familiar with empires, he knew such associations were not necessarily as closely knit and demanding as was the *polis*. He rejected associations in which people united merely for the sake of mutual defense and economic exchange. Real politics, he wrote, could not take place in such associations and human beings could not achieve perfection in them, for, according to Aristotle's most famous claim, "man is by nature a political animal." By this, Aristotle meant that humans uniquely can reason, speak, and deliberate together about the just and the unjust, about the good and the bad. One could be fully human and exercise the virtues proper to human beings only in the *polis*, in which citizens participated accordingly. Aristotle, however, also realized political drawbacks and limits and, in particular, sought to temper the harshness that made the *polis* often inhospitable not only to philosophers but also to prudent statesmen.

Cost to the Public

The Greek citizen's devotion to public life came at a great cost. The Greek world depended on slave labor, which contributed significantly to the leisure

Engraving of Aristotle. (The Library of Congress)

citizens enjoyed to practice politics. In some *poleis*, including Athens, slaves were a large percentage of the total population. They were usually non–Greeks purchased, kidnapped, or acquired in war. Some slaves were very well educated. Some were allowed to start businesses and could hope to buy personal freedom, if not citizenship. Many were well treated, though those who worked in the mines at Athens, for example, suffered terribly. In any case, none enjoyed what was essential to a human life from the Greek standpoint—a share in the political community. That involuntary servitude existed in the heartland of republican freedom would always trouble admirers of the *polis*. As eighteenth century political philosopher Jean–Jacques Rousseau (1712–1778) observed in *The Social Contract*, the demands of Greek political life seemed to entail that "the Citizen [could] be perfectly free only if the slave [was] utterly enslaved."

In the early fifth century B.C., the Greeks, led by Athens and Sparta, won a series of stunning victories in a long war against the Persian empire. These victories were seen as confirming the superiority of political freedom to despotism. Nonetheless, it was not long before the Athenians and Spartans led separate coalitions in the destructive Peloponnesian War (431–404 B.C.), which pitted Greek against Greek, and led both to the defeat of Athens and to incessant political turmoil and bloodshed in Greece. In the

BIOGRAPHY:

Aristotle

Aristotle was born in 384 B.C. in Stagira, a town in Northern Greece. In 367 B.C., he came to Athens, then the Greek cultural center, to further his education. There, he joined the Academy of Plato and came to be a close Plato associate until the latter's death in 347 B.C. Later, tradition has it, Aristotle was personal tutor to King Philip II of Macedon's son Alexander, who would come to be known as Alexander the Great. In 335 B.C., he returned to Athens and founded his own school, the Lyceum. Though he enjoyed the favor of the Macedonian governor of Greece for some time, he had to flee Athens in 323 B.C. when, following the death of Alexander the Great, Athens launched a war to rid itself of Macedonian dominance. Aristotle died in exile in 322 B.C.

The Lyceum was devoted to nearly every area of knowledge, and Aristotle's range was similarly vast. His works span biology, physics, logic, metaphysics, psychology, poetry, rhetoric, ethics, and politics. The *Politics*, a treatise on *polis* life, was his most important contribution to republican political theory. In fact, it contains the first full articulation of republican political theory. While Aristotle was hardly uncritical of the *polis*, it is nonetheless fair to regard him as the intellectual father of republicanism.

Despite Aristotle's immense authority in the Middle Ages, the *Politics* took a very long time to gain influence. It did, however, directly influence the revival of republican thought in Renaissance Italy, and still enjoyed a wide readership in mid–18th century. Aristotle's political influence was gradually eroded by the emergence of modern republicanism, beginning with Machiavelli, which self–consciously broke from the Aristotelian tradition. Aristotle remains, nonetheless, important to thinkers wishing to modify or supplement modern republicanism.

---

fourth century B.C., Greek political life was to be, as H. D. F. Kitto put it in *The Greeks*, "confusing, wearisome, and depressing." In 338 B.C., Philip II of Macedon (382–336 B.C.) conquered Greece. Under his successor, Alexander the Great (356–323 B.C.), the Greek

polis did not altogether disappear, but its period of great power and independence had ended.

Ancient Rome

The next significant republican model was the Roman Republic. Established around 509 B.C., it had barely begun to fulfill its imperial destiny when Greece fell to Philip. Only in 396 B.C. did Rome make its first important conquest, the neighboring *polity* of Veii. But by 44 B.C., thirteen years before the Republic, in effect, gave way to one–man rule, Rome's possessions stretched from Spain to Syria. There were many similarities between Greek and Roman political institutions, and the Greek example may well have inspired republicanism in ancient Italy. But Rome, far more than any Greek *polis*, was a republican empire. Had the Persian wars proved that free political communities could turn back despotic aggression, the Roman Republic proved such communities could aspire to dominate the world. It also raised the question of how long a republic bent on expansion could remain republican.

Rome's innovation was to offer full or partial citizenship to allies and defeated enemies. By doing so, it could greatly increase its resources and manpower. The meaning of republican citizenship, however, had to change. In the tiny Greek *polis*, citizenship could mean direct participation in political decision making. But in the Roman Republic, where a citizen might live nowhere near Rome itself, citizenship for most would be merely the possession of a certain legal status and the advantages that went with it.

One important reason for the demise of the Republic was its need for soldiers to defend its acquisitions and to conquer new ones. Toward the end of the second century B.C., Rome abandoned the practice of requiring its soldiers to own a certain minimum amount of property and to equip themselves with arms. They were thereby enabled to draw on the landless and poor, who hoped to make a living from soldiery and were consequently more willing than others to fight long campaigns far from home. At the same time, these more or less professional soldiers had little stake in the existing political order, and their hopes for land grants and bonuses rested on their general's patronage. After this change, Rome careened from internal crisis to internal crisis, threatened by its own generals, whose troops were more loyal to them than to the political authorities. By 31 B.C., though republican forms would be retained for some time, rule had effectively fallen into the hands of one man, Octavian, soon to be known as Augustus. The Roman Republic had become the Roman Empire. For a long time after, republicans would worry that a professional military posed an unacceptable danger to freedom.

The Medieval City

More than a century passed before a republican revival began in earnest. Toward the middle of the 11th century A.D., the medieval city began to develop as trade increased. Some towns, in effect, could set up independent governments. They developed most fully in Italy, where, most notably in Florence and Venice, the medieval city was the site of not only new economic activity but also new republican politics. One can speak, as historian Peter Riesenberg does in *Citizenship in the Western Tradition*, of the development in Italy of a "new civic consciousness" in the twelfth and thirteenth centuries and of a gradual revival of "secular patriotism." The medieval Italian city used festivals, songs, and schools to foster in citizens the sense that the *patria*, the fatherland, was the highest loyalty, higher, at least at times, than their families, or even the Church. It drew on antiquity, especially the Roman Republic, for inspirational examples of the active life of self–sacrificing public service. In the fifteenth and early sixteenth century, as republican practice declined in Italy, republican theorizing and writing peaked in an intellectual, literary, and political movement, centered in Florence, that has come to be called civic humanism. Civic humanist writers drew on ancient history and political theory to defend republicanism. At the same time, for at least two reasons, the medieval city could hardly be regarded as a full–fledged revival of the old republican idea.

First, medieval Italian city life was emphatically commercial. The exercise of political rights, whatever moral value, had to be weighed against the cost, in time away from doing business, of attending public assemblies, or serving in office. The merchants and artisans who populated the cities were typically more concerned with the commercial benefits and protections of citizenship than with decidedly less tangible pleasures Aristotle promised to political participants. Eventually, citizenship itself became more associated with material benefits.

Christianity

Second, and more importantly, the medieval world was Christian, which meant it could not easily accept the republican ideal in good conscience. The medieval citizen was expected to be loyal first to his city, but the medieval Christian wanted to be loyal first to God. The medieval citizen was expected to embrace the active life, but the medieval Christian was expected to embrace, at least in part, the ideal of contemplation, prayer, and withdrawal from world affairs. The medieval citizen was expected to regard his fellow citizens as friends and the citizens of rival cities as strangers or enemies, but the medieval Christian was expected to regard all men as brothers. Thus, the would–be devoted republican citizen was tempted "from below" by the ideal of the merchant and "from above" by the ideal of the monk.

Niccolò Machiavelli (1469–1527) made the implicit opposition between Christianity and republicanism explicit and sided with the latter. In his view, Christianity, with its emphasis on submission, resignation, humility, and mercy, had softened men and turned their attention from worldly politics. Political leaders were fanatics and fools. By aiming for excessively high–minded virtues, Christianity had distracted human beings from seizing what they could reasonably expect to have: security, prosperity, and perhaps even lasting glory. In his *Discourses*, Machiavelli sings the praises of the expansionist Roman republic and, while criticizing it, suggests it did not go far enough in its single–minded and heartless devotion to acquisition and glory. In a way, Machiavelli treats ancient republicanism in the opposite of Aristotle, for while Aristotle seeks to soften that republicanism and make room for philosophy, Machiavelli seeks to harden it and subordinate peaceful virtues to the pursuit of victory. Machiavelli, the first to articulate a modern republicanism that decisively broke from Christian and classical models, was to have many followers.

That is not to say, however, that republicanism is simply anti–Christian. In Florence, not long before Machiavelli wrote, Girolamo Savonarola (1452–1498) had briefly attempted to turn Florence into a Christian republic. Prophets had long invested events in earthly cities with divine significance. Savonarola merely added to that tradition in understanding the restoration of Florentine republicanism, which had lapsed, as a spiritual renewal and in understanding the city of Florence as destined to purify Christianity and prepare the way for the city of God. Republicanism, which rejected human kingship, could be understood to assert that Christ alone was king. Savonarola's project failed, and he was hanged and burned as a heretic. But religious thinkers and believers, especially Protestants, would be pivotal to republicanism, above all in the establishment of republican government in England and America. Republicans in those countries would have to confront the problem that by the middle of the sixteenth century had all but destroyed republican life in Europe, the seeming helplessness of small republics in the face of large, centralized, monarchical states.

Revival

For the moment, however, republicanism had settled down for one of its long sleeps. While the Netherlands and Switzerland were exceptions, the rule in the sixteenth and much of the seventeenth century was the consolidation of monarchical power, which centralized bureaucracies supported and professional standing armies defended. Only in seventeenth–century England did republicanism decisively awaken in the Puritan Revolution (1640–1660) and the Glorious Revolution (1688), which ended with the vindication of the sovereignty of Parliament, the most representative and democratic part of the English government, and the reduction of the king's power. Almost a century later, England's American colonies, persuaded that the mother country had abandoned republican principles, fought and won the American Revolution (1775–83). In the debate over the Constitution of 1787, both the Federalists, who defended it, and the Anti–Federalists, who attacked it, looked mostly to the same standard. As the *Federalist Papers*, the most celebrated defense of the American Constitution, insist, the "general form and aspect of the government [must] be strictly republican," for "no other form would be reconcilable with the genius of the people of America" or "with the fundamental principles of the Revolution." Yet by republicanism, the authors of the *Federalist Papers*, Alexander Hamilton (1757–1804), James Madison, and John Jay did not mean what the Romans, or even the Florentines, meant. Though they chose the pseudonym Publius, the name of a Roman Republic hero, to underscore their allegiance to the republican tradition, they also called the new Constitution an "experiment" and warned their readers against a "blind veneration for antiquity."

The new republicanism, conceived in England but brought to term in the United States, contained elements of the old, but added to them a powerful political theory, liberalism, contained in the writings of, among others, John Locke (1632–1704) and the Baron de Montesquieu (1689–1755). Liberal republicanism follows Machiavelli in seeking to found politics not on high–minded virtues, but on more solid ground. For the liberal, the end of politics is not the promotion of virtue but the protection of rights. Virtue remains necessary, but human reason is capable of devising a new political science and new institutions that will narrow the gap between self–interest and the common good, so that the importance of virtue and the harshness of the virtue required for political success are both diminished.

While the statesman is by no means disparaged, liberals do not see the political life as the only full human life, nor do they view the public square as the primary theater of virtue. Industry, commerce, and the "pursuit of happiness" acquire a new respectability, made possible partly by less of a need of the modern liberal for the extreme self–sacrificing virtue de-

manded in the ancient *polis*. Also, the smallness conducive to intense patriotism and direct public participation was not required by the new liberal republicanism, which enabled the large territorial republic to enter the world stage for the first time and ultimately to compete with the great monarchical states. Nonetheless, the large republic had its controversies in the United States, and the Anti–Federalists doubted that even the limited virtues required to sustain the new republic could be maintained in a nation as large as the United States, governed by a powerful and always potentially tyrannical central government. The Anti–Federalists lost, but their doubts carried to future republican generations.

Rousseau was arguably the greatest critic of the new liberal republicanism. In his works, including the *Discourse on the Origin and the Foundations of Inequality Among Men* and the *Social Contract*, he attacked the emerging modern world and the theorists who helped coax it into being for, among other things, destroying virtue, promoting inequality, and falling far short of democracy. He compared the emerging modern, civilized man unfavorably to Spartans and Romans, on the one hand, and primitives and rustics on the other. While Rousseau himself had almost no hope for radical reform, his thought helped inspire demands to modify or abandon the liberal republican model, which were heard in, among many other places, the more radical French and Russian revolutions that came after the American one. Although liberal republicanism of a sort would come to dominate the world by the end of the twentieth century, it would never altogether escape criticism, nor did it altogether avoid giving in to at least some demands.

THEORY IN DEPTH

The Essentials of Republicanism

The political theory of republicanism holds that the best government involves citizens, rather than subjects, where citizens share in directing their own affairs. It was first developed and expounded in ancient Greece, most completely by Aristotle (384–322 B.C.) in his work, the *Politics*. Niccolò Machiavelli (1469–1527), who criticized and self–consciously broke with the old republican tradition, founded a new, modern republicanism. This new republicanism, modified and made more receptive to individual freedom by Machiavelli's successors, found enduring expression in the *Federalist Papers*. Alexander Hamilton (1757–1804), John Jay (1745–1829), and James Madison (1751–1836) wrote this collection of essays in 1787–1788 to defend the proposed Constitution of the United States. Modern republicanism has pervaded the United States and Western Europe, and is influential worldwide. While ancient, or classical, and modern, or liberal, republicanism differ in most respects, they share the conviction of self–government as the only worthwhile political arrangement.

Classical Republicanism

The Greek *polis* gave birth to republicanism, and Aristotle first fully articulated a republican political theory. Republicanism, however, was so profoundly transformed by Niccolò Machiavelli and the successors, such as John Locke and Baron de Montesquieu, who tamed his harsh teaching, that it is useful to distinguish between classical and liberal republicanism.

Classical republicanism starts from the premise that man is by nature a political animal. Human nature finds its fulfillment only in *polis* life, in which citizens deliberate about justice and the common good and rule themselves on the basis of such deliberation. *Polis* life, however, is extremely fragile. The *polis* must be small enough that citizens can assemble together, but must somehow defend itself against larger neighbors. Moreover, the *polis* may often be agitated for, as the *Federalist Papers* state, when matters of great national importance are discussed, a "torrent of angry and malignant passions will be let loose." In the *polis*, such matters, which affect vital interests and deep beliefs, are debated openly and often, and constantly threaten to tear it apart. Finally, the *polis* imposes unusual demands and responsibility on its citizens, who are expected to rule themselves by participating. For all these reasons, cultivating solidarity and a self–sacrificing virtue is among the first concerns of classical republican political theory.

Private life   Because it puts politics first, and because it asks so much of its citizens, classical republicanism tends to devalue private life. Indeed, the word "idiot" derives from a term the Greeks applied to a person who preferred private to public life. For the classical republican, politics is not a necessary evil one suffers in order to protect and advance private interests. On the contrary, private interest and even individual freedom are subordinate to the public interest and to the political freedom citizens can exercise only in common. The *polis*, Aristotle wrote, "is prior to the individual." The classical republican likes to devalue privacy because public engagement really is, for most humans, superior to any private pursuit. The classical republican frowns upon privacy because, as political theorist and Michigan State University professor Steven Kautz said in *Liberalism and Community*, "re-

publican virtue does not arise spontaneously in the souls of human beings" but "must be forced into being by a political community that restrains the private interests and appetites of individuals," which threaten to undermine devotion to the *polis*. For both these reasons, as Paul Rahe pointed out, the Greek may have had certain legal privileges as a citizen, but "as a human being, [he] possessed no rights against the commonwealth." Classical republicans see individuals not endowed by nature or God with rights beyond community reach. Moreover, the devaluing of private life extended to the family, as the following famous tale suggests. A Spartan mother had five sons in the army, which was engaged in battle. A slave arrived, and she asked him for news of the fight. He told her that her five sons had been killed. She responded, "Did I ask you that?" When he told her the Spartans had won the battle, she ran to the temple to give thanks to the gods.

Classical republicanism, for several reasons, also tends to devalue commerce and trade. First, politics, for the classical republican, is simply a noble pursuit. Man is a political, not an economic animal. What Aristotle calls the art of acquisition is necessary, for the *polis* cannot exist without material goods, nor can the citizen have the leisure to participate public affairs without a certain amount of wealth. But to devote oneself wholeheartedly to this art is to mistake the means for the end. Partly for this reason the Greeks tended to frown upon those engaged in commercial pursuits, even in *poleis* where commerce was viewed as necessary.

Commerce   Second, commerce produces inequalities, as some accumulate wealth and others fail. The classical republican, however, does not worry about economic inequality, because it is unfair. Rather, he worries that extreme economic inequality may have dire political consequences. Economic inequality threatens solidarity and, when extreme, results in a city divided along the lines of wealth. How will citizens see themselves as one people when one group prospers greatly while the other suffers greatly? One is almost certain to find instead, as Aristotle observed, "a state of envy on the one side and of contempt on the other," not one united city but, in all but name, two enemy cities sharing space. Economic inequality is also dangerous because the poor depend upon the rich, who can use their economic advantage to secure unchallenged political supremacy. Finally, as long as politics is a struggle between rich and poor, one has neither a genuinely political life—for one group exercises tyrannical authority over the other—nor stability, because there is always a group with everything to gain by toppling the status quo. Ancient theorists and legislators, realizing such dangers, proposed and often enacted laws regulating the market, and the purchase and inheritance of land, among other things, with a view to ameliorating the conflict between rich and poor. To take the sting out of the economic inequality that remained, most *poleis* had sumptuary laws to forbid conspicuous displays of wealth. Many had customs and even laws to insure that the rich applied some of their wealth to public works, or entertainment, or to serve other public needs.

Third, commerce promotes individualism and selfishness. It threatens to substitute the bottom line for the common good and personal wealth for the commonwealth. Whereas the citizen views fellow citizens as friends and even brothers, the merchant must view them as potential sources of profit. Whereas the citizen is tied to fellow citizens by shared convictions and attachments, merchants are bound to those with whom they deal by shared interest and by contracts. Whereas the citizen must exhibit a spirit of generous self–sacrifice, the merchant must take care not to give without getting in return. The merchant's values, from the classical citizenship perspective, are indifferent or even harmful. Moreover, the merchant, whose wealth is portable, is not attached to the *polis* as, for example, is the farmer, whose life is rooted in the soil of his homeland.

Fourth, commerce, when it extends to other *poleis*, opens citizens to foreign ideas and threatens unity of opinion. The Piraeus, the port of Athens, was known for its openness to innovation. Indeed, Plato (428–348 A.D.) sets his most famous dialogue, the *Republic*, in the Piraeus where, he tells us, a novel religious festival, devoted to a goddess new to Athens, is to take place. The ancients understood, Rahe said, the connection between economic and philosophic and political speculation, that "commerce in goods inevitably gives rise to a commerce in ideas." Once one opens oneself to foreign goods, one risks opening oneself to foreign gods. For this reason, Aristotle proposes that while a *polis* should engage in commerce, it should also enact "legislation which states and defines those who may or may, or may not, have dealings with one another."

New ideas   It may surprise that classical republicanism so concerns itself with shutting out new ideas. Classical republican theory, in fact, devalues not only commerce but innovation altogether. In one section of his *Politics*, Aristotle attacks what would seem to most a harmless and perhaps useful proposal, that "honors should be conferred on those responsible for any invention of benefit to the city." Aristotle, however, worries less about a society that embraces a single new

invention than one embracing the spirit of invention too enthusiastically. For to the classical republican, the spirit of invention is a threat to the law, obedience to which is secured not by pure reason but above all by custom, habit, and belief. From this perspective, to subject the laws to constant scrutiny and revision is reckless because it weakens them without cause. One must always weigh the benefits of innovation, even when good, against the danger of undermining laws and of unsettling the convictions upon which the force of law in general depends.

More broadly, the classical republic, because it demands so much virtue and solidarity, must be more cautious about admitting new ideas. Classical republicans believed no more than modern political theorists believe that human beings naturally sacrifice their own good for the public good, that they are naturally willing to die for each other, or that they spontaneously develop the ties of affection that citizens of a *polis* share. The works of classical political philosophy are filled with examples of the patriotic myths, among other things, that legislators must devise to bind a people. Because classical political theorists and legislators understood the difficulties of transforming humans into citizens, and how fragile the final product would be, they were cautious about exposing citizens to novel theories that might undermine their hard–won devotion.

The difficulty and importance of transforming human beings into citizens ready to meet their extensive obligations to the *polis* explains another facet of classical republican political theory, its overwhelming emphasis on education. Shaping the character of citizens was the first concern of ancient law. Education was directed toward developing citizen virtues as much as skills. It involved parents and tutors, and primarily by means of art and music. Among the most shocking features of Plato's *Republic* for the modern reader are both the minute attention this work on politics pays to the content and even the rhythm of poetry and the policy of censorship it proposes for the best city. Ancient theorists and legislators were mindful of beautiful art and music being more likely than rational speech to move people, especially the young. Therefore they paid attention to what dramas citizens heard, the festivals they attended, and even the buildings and statues they saw.

Religion   Religion, too, is an educational component for the classical republican. In fact, the poetry to which Plato pays so much attention in the *Republic* is about the gods, and the content he proposes to revise and regulate concerns their character and actions. It would hardly do to take such care about so many of the things that bring human beings together or pull them apart and then neglect their beliefs about the divine and the relevant rewards and punishments. Though the ordinary Greek was pious, Plato was not the only ancient classical thinker to suggest that founders and statesmen should modify and even invent stories about the gods to shape their native countrymen or persuade them to accept a law or policy. While perhaps few Greeks or Romans went that far, the less radical view of *polis* concerns with the religious beliefs of citizens was more common.

When he compared life in the classical republic to that in a monastery, Montesquieu spoke for liberal republicanism. He did not mean it as a compliment. Classical republicanism and traditional Christianity had, for liberal republicans, a common defect. Both tended to foster inhumanity and fanaticism in asking their adherents to devote themselves single–mindedly to a set of beliefs. The result in the classical case was the constant warfare that characterized *polis* life and, in the Christian case, the violent wars of religion that plagued Christendom.

While classical republicanism aimed too high, it expected too little. Classical republicans had not grasped that the judicious use of natural and political science could accrue peace and prosperity, and greatly relieve human suffering. According to liberal republicanism, it was possible to devise economic and political institutions that could make use of self–interest, which classical republicanism had so harshly suppressed, to serve the common good.

Liberal Republicanism

Liberal republicanism denies that humans are simply or primarily political. Instead, it insists on the dignity as human beings as laboring animals, who tame and transform the natural world. Whereas the classical republican finds human dignity above all in the capacity to reason about justice and the common good, the liberal republican finds at least as much to praise in turning barren wilderness into a comfortable home, conquering disease, and alleviating poverty. Liberal republicans see commercial activity as a means for self–interested individuals to better their own wealth, and that of others. According to this outlook, the classical citizen was, in many ways, an idle troublemaker, forever engaged in controversy in the public square. Liberal republicanism, therefore, views politics as an arena for passionate and dangerous quarrels about justice. Instead, politics is primarily a means of protecting and even enhancing the private and, on the whole, modest and pacific pursuits of industrious citizens. As political theorist Thomas Pangle explained in *The Spirit of Modern Republicanism*, "the

Italian philosopher Niccolò Machiavelli.
(Corbis Corporation)

American Framers," who embody the spirit Pangle described, "tend to honor political participation somewhat less as an end and considerably more as a means to the protection of . . . personal rights." In fact, the diminished prestige of political participation means participation through representatives is preferable to direct participation.

Differences Plainly, liberal republicanism exacts far less of its citizens than does classical republicanism. It consequently depends less on virtue and, far from devaluing commerce and innovation, is able to

BIOGRAPHY:

Niccolò Machiavelli

Niccolò Machiavelli was born in Florence, then an independent city, on May 3, 1569. His father, Bernardo, was a lawyer and, like many Florentines, admired classical learning. He made sure Niccolò received an extensive classical education. At the time such an education could open the door to political office, and in 1498, at age 29, Machiavelli was appointed head of the second chancery of the Florentine Republic and, shortly thereafter, Secretary to the Ten of War. As the latter, he took part in diplomatic missions and observed the affairs of the powerful up close. His public career ended abruptly in 1512, when the Republic collapsed and the Medici family was restored to power in Florence. Machiavelli, suspected of conspiracy against that family, was arrested in 1513 and tortured before being released and compelled to retreat to his country home, south of Florence. There, he turned his attention to the works that secured his fame. He died in 1527.

Machiavelli's best–known book is *The Prince*, whose main subject is not the republic but rule of one man. It is infamous for recommending fraud and murder and, more generally, for its open acknowledgment that to rule successfully one must cast aside conven-

tional morality and "learn to be able not to be good." Machiavelli, however, also wrote the *Discourses*, a book that appears to favor republics and secured his reputation as a republican political theorist. In adopting the same ruthlessly realistic stance as *The Prince* does, however, the *Discourses* are a deliberate departure from the republicanism of Machiavelli's predecessors. They aimed to and succeeded in establishing a new republicanism.

Machiavelli founded modern republicanism. It followed him in consciously lowering its sights and seeking not to perfect human beings through political activity, but to place the low but dependable passions of imperfect human beings, like the love of wealth, in the service of achievable goals, such as prosperity. While successors such as Montesquieu and Locke would seek to tame Machiavelli's teaching and found a liberal republicanism that was less militaristic and more hospitable toward human freedom, and while there was considerable disagreement among Machiavelli's successors about the shape of republican life, modern republicanism would never altogether abandon the perspective of its hard–headed founder.

---

embrace both with enthusiasm. For these reasons, it almost seems misleading to apply the same term, republicanism, to both classical and modern politics. However, liberal republicanism, though a truly radical break from classical republicanism, has more in common with its predecessor than it first seems.

Most importantly, liberal republicans agree with classical republicans that tyranny is an insult to human nature. While the authors of the *Federalist Papers* criticized the ancients for emphasizing direct political participation too much, they nonetheless agreed with the classical republicans that any defensible politics had to rest on "the capacity of mankind for self–government." They thought it important to vindicate human nature by demonstrating that it was possible for a society to establish "good government from reflection and choice." In holding this opinion, which characterizes liberal republicanism, they arguably exceeded the republican hopes of the ancients, who, after all, made so much of the need in politics, and especially in political foundings, to deceive the people. They were, as Pangle observed, "far from neglecting the dignity of man as citizen," even as they guarded the dignity of private man.

Further, while liberal republicanism needs virtue much less than its classical counterpart, it does not altogether neglect it, either. Returning to the *Federalist Papers*, we learn that for republican government to exist, there must be "sufficient virtue" in the people and its leaders. Undoubtedly, liberal republicanism drastically reduces the amount of self–restraint and self–sacrifice that self–government requires, but "republican government," still, presupposes more "than any other form" of government those "qualities of human nature which justify a certain portion of esteem and confidence," or trust. We learn that the most important restraint on the House of Representatives is "the vigilant and manly spirit which actuates the people of America." Unquestionably, vigilance in defense of one's own liberty, supported so strongly by self–

interest, counters human nature far less than the virtue practiced by the classical citizen. But it does not arise spontaneously, either, and requires considerable effort. Even the modern republic demands that citizens be responsible, however indirectly, for governing themselves, and therefore demands more virtue than other forms of government.

Not surprisingly then, liberal republican theorists and statesmen concerned themselves with education. However, the character of the virtues to be taught has important implications for the character of the education required. "Liberal virtues," Steven Kautz maintained, "are reasonable virtues." However much courage and capacity for self–restraint vigilance in defense of one's own freedom may require, it is fairly easy to make a case for it. It is hard to be vigilant but easier to be convinced that it is in one's own long–term interest to be so. In contrast, it is extremely hard both to practice the virtue the classical *polis* requires and to be convinced that it is reasonable and in one's own interest. Because liberal republicanism depends on reasonable virtues, liberal republican education need not aim at transformation; it does not have to convert a self–interested human being into a self–negating citizen. It can aim, instead, at enlightenment, at persuading someone with a narrow or short–sighted understanding of his or her interests, or a poor understanding of how to protect them, to take a more expansive view. That is not to say that liberal republicans can afford to dispense with the kinds of poetic and religious appeals upon which classical republicans rely so much. Liberal republican citizens, too, must commit great sacrifices, and no dry argument will move most, if any, human beings to die on the battlefield. Even in peacetime, liberal virtues being reasonable does not mean citizens must be reasonable all the time. Nonetheless, it is accurate to say that liberal republican theorists, because they are so much less ambitious in what they expect education to accomplish, are much more confident than classical republican theorists that citizens can be enlightened.

THEORY IN ACTION

The United States is the most prominent and influential example of the modern liberal republic. It is difficult, however, to understand the United States without understanding that its founders thought they had learned much from the previous experience of humanity in republican government. Republican theory and had been found so wanting that, as the *Federal-* *ist Papers* sharply assert, had modern republicanism not improved on ancient republicanism, "the enlightened friends of liberty would have been obliged to abandon the cause of that species of government as indefensible." To understand republicanism in practice, then, we begin with the ancient example of Sparta, that Greek city which, by implementing the classical republican idea in the most extreme manner, provided students of republicanism with a vivid portrait of that idea in action.

Sparta

Sparta was an extreme but revealing example of the classical republic. The Spartans had many foreign enemies and were, in addition, vastly outnumbered by the *helots*, conquered peoples whom they compelled to work their land. Internal and external threats pushed Sparta to emphasize, even more so than the other classical republics, solidarity over privacy; Sparta, therefore, was as much a military as a political unit.

Boys were removed from their homes and from the guidance of their parents at age seven. They joined a group of boys their own age and began the physical and mental training necessary to fight and persuade them to devote themselves completely to the common good. They would welcome death in battle as the highest honor. Those who successfully completed the rigorous education then joined a "common mess," a group of men who lived, ate, and fought together as a unit. While a Spartan was expected to marry before the age of 45, he did not live in his own home until he reached that age. Such regulations indicate the extent to which Spartans insisted that individuals submit to the demands of the *polis*. Perhaps the most striking instance is this: in Sparta, babies judged too weak or deformed to be useful citizen–soldiers were killed.

Sparta, perhaps more than any other classical republic, worried about the dangers commerce posed to solidarity. The Spartan citizen was simply forbidden to engage in commerce and could not own silver or gold. Spartan currency was, by design, difficult to transport and use. The Spartans devised several ways to ease economic inequality and its social tensions. The *polis* granted its citizens equal shares of public land and helots to work it. As some land was still privately owned, the gap between rich and poor remained, but it was relatively narrow. Rich and poor received the same tough education and dined on the same fare in the common messes. As in other classical republics, the rich were restricted in using their wealth and could not flaunt it. The wealthy, in fact, were expected to make at least some of their property available for the use of other citizens.

Isolation The Spartans shared, too, the classical republic's resistance to foreign ideas. In this, as in other matters, the Spartans took the classical idea to an extreme conclusion. Spartan citizens could not travel abroad without the permission of the authorities, and such travel was generally forbidden. Similarly foreigners were not allowed into Sparta without permission and were only admitted with compelling reason. Plutarch (c. 45–c.120 A.D.), writing of the legendary, and perhaps imaginary, Spartan lawgiver, Lycurgus, explains the reason for this prohibition: "With strange people, strange words must be admitted; these novelties produce novelties in thought." For similar reasons, Sparta exercised censorship over poetry and music in the *polis*. One Spartan magistrate is said to have cut off two of the nine strings of a musical instrument, worrying that an extravagance in music could have led to parallel behavior.

In a classical world known for citizen education, Sparta stands out, and stood out even at the time, for how it transformed humans into hardened, loyal citizens. From the time the seven year old left his home, he was trained, with the help of music, poetry, religion, and even dance, to think of himself, as Paul Rahe said, "not as an individual, not as a member of a particular household, but as a part of the community." His body was hardened through physical training that became increasingly grueling as he aged. Because a soldier was expected to be crafty as well as courageous and strong, the Spartan young had to steal to supplement their skimpy meals. If caught, they were whipped, not to discourage their stealing but to encourage them to improve at it. The Spartan's ingenuity was further tested in the "period of concealment," an important rite of passage in which the young man, about 20 years old, spent a year outside the community, living off his own strength and cunning. At each stage of their rigorous training, the youths were examined; to "graduate" was to have completed the transformation from soft, selfish human being to hardened, self–sacrificing, warrior–citizen.

For all that, the Spartans understood that perfect solidarity was impossible, even by their own intense, far–reaching education. In any *polity*, especially one in which citizens are trained early to be spirited, there is bound to be a struggle. The rich will want to establish an oligarchy. The poor will want to establish a democracy. The well–born or noble will want to establish an aristocracy. The most prominent of these may wish to establish a monarchy. Even in such a community as Sparta, managing these different factions was necessary to avoid civil war. The Spartan strategy was to accommodate in part the most important elements, so that all would have a stake in preserving the *polity*. The Spartans over time devised what was known as a mixed regime. The elements were so well–mixed that the Greeks hardly knew whether to call Sparta a monarchy, aristocracy, oligarchy, or democracy.

In parts Sparta was in part a monarchy because it had two kings. Kingship was hereditary and each king held office for life. Leading Spartan forces into battle, their power in the field was nearly absolute. They appointed officers, executed cowards, conducted religious sacrifices, and raised money and new troops. In a society often at war, these powers were important; by no means, however, were they the only power the kings had. Their power over adoptions and their leading role in arranging marriages for heiresses whose fathers had not found them husbands meant that they could help or hinder a family in its efforts to transfer and amass wealth through inheritance. Because they had privileged access to certain funds, such as the spoils taken from the enemy in battle, the kings could benefit their friends and harm their enemies economically. In a society which strangled commerce and in which the roads to fortune were few, such powers enabled the kings to wield formidable political influence. The kings were so powerful that the Spartans thought it necessary to have two of them, each watching over the other.

Sparta was in part a democracy because it had a popular assembly, consisting of all Spartan citizens that, within limits set by other bodies and officials, voted on the most important matters. In light of the aforementioned limits, however, Sparta arguably had a more important claim to democracy: it filled essentially by lot its most powerful office aside from the kingship, that of *ephor*. The Greeks viewed elections as an aristocratic device, since its aim was to insure that the best, an "elect," serve. The lot, on the other hand, was a democratic device because it meant any citizen could be selected, as in a lottery, to hold office. The five *ephors* served only one year and were subject to review and perhaps punishment at the end of that year, but while in power they were in many ways, as a group, the kings' equals. The *ephors* were so powerful that to some observers, a board of tyrannical dictators appeared to rule Sparta. At home, they enforced the sumptuary laws and kept watch over the all–important educational system. They alone could fine the kings for misconduct and even put them on trial for capital crimes. This was only the most impressive of their broad judicial powers. Legislatively, the *ephors* were empowered to summon the Assembly and Council of Elders. With the Council of Elders, they set the agenda for the Assembly. Finally, they exercised great authority in foreign affairs by, among other things, determining when Spartans could travel abroad and when strangers could visit Sparta, receiving embassies, negotiating with other *poleis*, and calling up the army when necessary.

Finally, Sparta was in part an aristocracy because of its Council of Elders. This council consisted of thirty members, including the two kings. The other twenty–eight, all above age sixty, were elected, Rahe explained, "from the priestly caste that seems to have constituted the city's ancient aristocracy" and were "always men of experience and proven worth." With the *ephors*, they set the Assembly's agenda and could nullify Assembly decisions that overstepped that agenda. With the *ephors*, they formed a jury for capital cases. This council of older men not only addressed the claim of the wisest and best to rule but also insured the wealthy that their interests would be represented to at least some extent in the *polity*. For the council—old, conservative, exclusive, and wealthy—was little inclined to support innovative laws to further narrowed the gap between rich and poor.

Sparta eventually collapsed. Always vulnerable because of its large and often rebellious *helot* population, it never recovered from its defeat to the city of Thebes in 379 B.C. Perhaps Sparta was destined to fail because it demanded so much of its populace. One such indication is that Spartans, renowned for their discipline at home, were also reputed for slackness and corruption when abroad. Even within Sparta, the laws against possessing gold and silver were widely ignored. Sparta, however, did not perish without leaving examples of virtue and military heroism that dazzled her contemporaries and fascinated even those who broke from the classical model.

The United States

Old forms of republicanism, classical and Christian both, contributed to the American founding, and the precise contributions of classical, Protestant, and modern elements in early American political thought is debated. Nonetheless, critics of classical republicanism unquestionably played a pivotal role in founding the United States. The authors of the *Federalist Papers*, thinking Sparta "little better than a well–regulated camp," sought to found a distinctly modern republic, free of the defects of the old republicanism. They saw republicanism as needlessly harsh and unmindful of private dignity. Its solution to political conflict was worse than the problem itself, for it destroyed liberty. Moreover, the classical republican insistence on direct political participation, impassioned citizens settling the most controversial matters in the public square, made political conflict insoluble in any case. "It is impossi-

ble," Alexander Hamilton says in the *Federalist*, "to read the history of the petty republics of Greece and Italy without feeling sensations of horror and disgust at the distractions with which they were continually agitated." The task of the American Constitution framers was to solve, with the help of advances in the "science of politics," the problems of classical republicanism, so that a new republic, respectful of private liberty and well–shielded from dangerous political conflict, could vindicate the capacity of human beings to live free. The United States set out to put into practice the theory of liberal republicanism.

In the liberal republic, government exists not to make citizens virtuous but to protect their private pursuits. When the United States declared its independence in 1776, it declared itself, in effect, a liberal republic, since the Declaration of Independence says both that men "are endowed by their Creator with certain unalienable rights" and that "Governments are instituted among men" to "secure these rights." In the new republic, even the creator, or "Nature's God" offers freedoms rather than commandments to human beings. This view of the divine diverges not only from classical republicanism, whose gods were called to transform human beings into virtuous citizens, but also from Christian republicanism, which even when respectful to political freedom did not understand rights to rank so much higher than duties in God's eyes. The United States took up the new principles championed by Edmund Locke and others and enshrined them in the first of its founding documents.

The* Federalist *debates The *Federalist Papers* authors argued that the new idea of liberty upheld by the Declaration could not be maintained without a new political science. "The science of politics [had] received great improvement" in modern times. "The efficacy of various principles" that the ancients did not know in full, if at all, was "now well understood." The 1781 Articles of Confederation, the first national constitution, had failed to take full advantage of those principles. But the 1787 Constitution that the *Federalist Papers* defended and which, with some amendment, has remained the law of the land in the United States, did take advantage of them in attempting to build a legal and institutional framework within which the new republicanism could prove superior.

Representation is among the most important principles of the new political science. Its purpose, according to the *Federalist*, is "to refine and enlarge the public views by passing them through the medium of a chosen body of citizens." So in the United States, citizens have a say in federal lawmaking not directly and in the public square, but indirectly, through the

MAJOR WRITINGS:

The Federalist Papers

The *Federalist Papers* are a collection of eighty–five essays in defense of the United States Constitution of 1787. Such a defense was a pressing necessity when the essays were written in 1787 and 1788, for the states had yet to approve the Constitution, and approval was by no means certain. Alexander Hamilton, a member of the convention that drafted the Constitution, and who would later be America's first Secretary of the Treasury, suggested a complete defense of the Constitution that would not only lay out the case for it but also respond to all important objections. He recruited John Jay, who would later be the first Chief Justice of the Supreme Court, and James Madison, who would become the fourth President of the United States, to write essays for the project. The three wrote under the pseudonym Publius, invoking the name of an ancient republican hero. The papers were published in newspapers in New York, Hamilton's and Jay's home state, and some were published in newspapers in a few of the other states. The *Federalist Papers* were also printed as a collection in two volumes.

The papers sought to prove that the individual states needed unification, that the Articles of Confederation, the first national constitution, could not bind the union, and that only such an energetic government as the Constitution would establish was up to that job. They sought to prove that the Constitution was genuinely republican and the only hope for republicanism. They described and argued in favor of the Con-

stitution's provisions for the presidency, the House and Senate, and the federal judiciary, including the Supreme Court. Perhaps most importantly, the authors of the *Federalist Papers* self–consciously stood for a new republicanism founded on a new science of politics. They were well aware that the Constitution was novel and sought to inspire the American people to pursue an extraordinary and almost unprecedented political experiment.

> The first question that offers itself is whether the general form and aspect of the government be strictly republican. It is evident that no other form would be reconcilable with the genius of the people of America: with the fundamental principles of the Revolution: or with that honorable determination which animates every votary of freedom to rest all our political experiments on the capacity of mankind for self–government. If the plan of the convention, therefore, be found to depart from the republican character, its advocates must abandon it as no longer defensible" (Federalist#39).

While the direct influence of the *Federalist Papers* is difficult to measure, unquestionably it served as a kind of debater's handbook for the Constitution's supporters. But the collection's influence is still more far–reaching, for Thomas Jefferson was not alone in regarding it as "the best commentary on the principles of government which ever was written." Scholars and lawyers still read the *Federalist*, thinking it contains valuable insights into what the constitutional framers meant and how the Constitution should be interpreted. It is still read, too, alongside such works as Plato's *Republic* and John Locke's *Two Treatises of Government*.

---

legislators they elect to serve in the Senate and House of Representatives. Classical republican theorists had resorted to harsh measures and delicate devices to calm the dangers that arose when citizens participated actively and directly in affairs of state. The American founders held that republican government is in no way compromised when the will of the citizenry is filtered through representatives, and indeed demands it. In the United States, a member of the House of Representatives, among other things, must be at least twenty–five years of age, must win an election and, once elected,

serves for two years. The first two requirements are designed to produce a body wiser than the general population and more capable of perceiving the common good. The privilege of serving for two years is designed to produce a body that can at least distance itself from the passions of the moment and view a "big picture" where others tend to address short–term needs. The Senate, with its six–year terms and its requirement that members be at least age thirty, is still more elite and removed from temporary shifts in popular opinion than the House.

The constitutional framers, however, did not count on the goodness of representatives to solve the problem of public disorder and division for, as the *Federalist* acknowledges, representatives may be, despite the best of precautions, "men of factious tempers, of local prejudices, or of sinister designs." Consequently, the new republic depended on another principle of the new political science, which the *Federalist* calls "enlargement of the orbit" of republican government, or the application of republicanism to a large, populous territory. It is difficult to overestimate the novelty of this strategy, at which opponents of the Constitution scoffed. Classical republican theory had held that republican government was appropriate only for small territories with small populations, for the solidarity republicanism required could not be achieved in large, diverse nations. The constitutional framers turned what seemed to be a tremendous disadvantage, the projected size of the Union, into an advantage. The new republic would deal with the threat of political division not by imposing uniformity of opinion and interest but by multiplying differences of opinion and interest, thereby weakening the influence of any single, narrow, partisan view. In a small *polity*, rich and poor may divide the population, and the poor may unite to eliminate property rights. In a large *polity*, there may be farming, industrial, immigrant, and native poor, and manufacturing, agricultural, technological, Southern, and Northern rich. In such a diverse *polity* with so many fault lines, it is difficult to gather a majority to oppress a minority, and majorities are at least unlikely to reflect narrow partisan interests. Enlargement of the orbit breaks the strength of partisanship not by suppressing the interests and passions of individuals and groups, but by channeling such interests and passions so that, even without intending it, they tend toward the common good. In this way, the United States puts into practice a liberal republican theory, that self–interest can be made to serve the common good more certainly and effectively than virtue itself.

Separation of powers   If representation and enlargement of the orbit of republican government tame political division, there remains the problem of tyranny. A government powerful enough to exert real influence over a large nation may more easily than most be used by an ambitious individual or group to rob the people of their freedoms. To frustrate would–be tyrants, the United States relies on another principle of the new science of politics, namely, separation of powers. The concept is this: to divide the power of governing among different departments or branches in such a way that one branch cannot exercise absolute power.

If one wanted to prevent a cannon from being fired in haste, someone might give one person the power to load the cannon, another the power to aim the cannon, and a third the power to fire it. Powers would then have defined and distributed powers so that one is ineffectual without the other and therefore difficult to abuse. Similarly the United States Constitution divides the power of governing among a legislative, executive, and judicial branch, in order to prevent tyranny. The power to make laws is ineffectual if one cannot enforce them, and the power to enforce the laws is ineffectual if one can neither decide which laws to enforce nor be sure that judges will accept one's interpretation of the law. The powers of the legislators in Congress, the executive in the White House, and the justices of the Supreme Court are legally defined in such a way that they are difficult to use tyrannically.

But, as the Federalists explain, "power is of an encroaching nature" and legal barriers may be insufficient to prevent ambitious public officials from seizing power. An ambitious president, for example, may effectively law by issuing executive orders or regulations; ambitious Supreme Court Justices may infringe on the authority of the other branches by reinterpreting the Constitution so broadly as to force revolutionary change in the nation's laws. However elegant a legal doctrine separation of powers may be, it fails, in the view of the Constitution's framers, to take into account human psychology, above all the lust for power. For that reason, the Constitution depends on yet another remedy offered by the new science, namely, checks and balances. As the *Federalist* famously states, one must give "to those who administer each department the necessary constitutional means and personal motives to resist encroachments of the others. . . .Ambition must be made to counteract ambition." For example, the president's power to veto the laws the House and Senate passes is technically speaking a violation of separation of powers, since it gives a legislative power to the head of the executive branch. But such a power is necessary if the president, the one most personally interested in maintaining the executive power against legislative attempts to seize parts of it, can resist the legislature. It is true that the veto and other checks and balances are as much legal mechanisms subject to failure as the separation of powers. But the authors of the *Federalist* thought that formal laws that the most interested parties could immediately use would prevent tyranny better than formal laws that could only be enforced by appealing to judges who, because their interests and ambition are less directly involved, might be lukewarm to legislative and executive privileges.

John Jay. (AP/Worldwide Photos)

Checks and balances The new principle of checks and balances is another way for the Constitution to put liberal republican theory into practice by, in the words of the *Federalist*, "supplying, by opposite and rival interests, the defect of better motives," so that "the private interest of every individual may be a sentinel over the public rights." Nonetheless, the American founders did not think it possible to do without a certain kind of virtue or a certain kind of civil education. James Madison was perhaps most active but hardly alone in working for what might be called the "constitutionalization" of the American people, that is, the education of American citizens who would know and revere the Constitution and the Bill of Rights added

in 1791. Only such citizens could be expected to be vigilant in defending their own liberties.

Of course, the adoption of the Bill of Rights does not end the story of republicanism in the United States, though the Constitution has rarely been amended since. Here is a very small sample of the changes: the development of political parties; the direct popular election of Senators, who were at first chosen by their state legislatures; the expansion in size and power of the federal government relative to the state governments; the expansion of the role of the Supreme Court in public policy. As long as the Constitution still counts for something in American politics, Americans will continue to debate the merits and dangers of each variance from the plan of the nation's founders and whether that plan was essentially good or fundamentally flawed. Similarly, although the United States is among the mightiest and wealthiest republics ever, its backers and detractors will continue to debate whether what was once called an "experiment" has succeeded at maintaining freedom.

ANALYSIS AND CRITICAL RESPONSE

Liberal republicanism entirely succeeded in supplanting classical republicanism and, for that reason, this section will focus on it. It has been some time since anyone has called for a return to the smallness, simplicity, and harshness of *polis* life. Nonetheless, liberal republicanism, measured by the big picture, remains an experiment. Few doubt that its willingness to channel rather than suppress individual self–interest and its openness to commerce and innovation has generated in many parts of the world a prosperity of which people had once only dreamed. Few doubt that its decision to depend less on virtue than on a new political science and the institutions and mechanisms it could devise has been at least a qualified success at achieving political stability and at fending off would–be tyrants. Nonetheless, liberal republicanism has been under constant attack by critics for its individualism and its faith in commerce, reason, and innovation.

Here is one criticism: liberal republicanism, if left to its own devices, leads to moral decline. After all, it unleashes innovation against custom and tradition, and self–interest against duty. The Declaration of Independence, which reveals much about liberal republicanism, looks up to "Nature and Nature's God," a God who speaks to human beings of what they have a right to do rather than of what they are commanded to do. The moral laxity of liberal republicanism may have been hidden early on when religion, custom, and tradition still captivated people. But that new philosophy's inability to inspire citizens manifests in high crime rates, drug use, family breakdown, and other social ills found in advanced liberal societies. All societies, even liberal ones, depend to some degree on citizen restraint. The question some critics of liberal republicanism raise is: does its deliberate strengthening of individualism and the spirit of reason and innovation come at the expense of the only means societies have of fostering self–restraint? To put it another way: does liberal republicanism undermine even the very limited moral virtue it, itself, requires?

Liberal republicanism may also cause political virtue to decline. Liberal citizens must, at the very least, remain vigilant. But it isn't at all obvious that citizens, liberated to enjoy and seek pleasure and profit, will scrutinize their government. Jean–Jacques Rousseau said in *The Social Contract* that "as soon as someone says about affairs of State *What do I care?* the State has to be considered lost." Critics of liberal republicanism argue that it tends to produce many such citizens. The liberal citizen may well not bother to know who their government officials are, let alone monitor them.

Rousseau feared that government officials soon discover they have more in common with each other than with the people they are supposed to serve. According to this argument, the government has an interest—whether in increasing its own power, or in profiting from office, or in getting reelected—that differs from the common interest, and prudent people should expect it to act on that interest when it can. It will enact pay increases at midnight; it will bury self–serving deeds in a thousand pages of legislation; it will make controversial announcements on Friday afternoons, when extensive media coverage or attention from constituents is unlikely. It can expect that, if some enterprising journalist uncovers a swindle and gets his or her story printed in the middle pages of a serious newspaper, very few hardworking and busy citizens will read it, let alone concern themselves with it. To make matters more difficult, the argument continues, governments tend to act this way out of collective self–interest, not individual immorality. To replace one corrupt elected official with another who seems less corrupt is unlikely to solve the problem. Instead, citizens must actively concern themselves with politics and with what their public servants are doing. This, however, the argument concludes, is precisely where liberal republican citizens fall short.

Size of the state Even were citizens to concern themselves more with what their public officials do, they might soon find that the size and complexity of mod-

ern states makes vigilance difficult. The United States government, for example, has at least some responsibility for not only law enforcement and security but, among many other things, health, education, transportation, communications, the arts and humanities, small business development, social security, scientific research, and the mail. To serve these functions, the United States government includes not only the president, Congress, and the Supreme Court but a vast and complex set of administrative agencies, employing, as of 1997, 2,787,137 workers. The government not only sometimes seems too large to control but also too demanding of expert knowledge. Citizens find themselves in a world in which the economic well–being of millions may hinge on whether or not the Federal Reserve Board, which oversees the U.S. banking system, chooses to push interest rates down a fraction of a point. Yet most citizens are far from understanding how such decisions are and should be made. It is difficult to understand what citizen vigilance means in such a world. No wonder that, as Michael Sandel reports in *Democracy's Discontent*, "Americans do not believe they have much say in how they are governed." Liberal republicanism can hardly be blamed for modern complexities, nor can it be simply blamed for the growth of the federal government's power. Nonetheless, liberal republicanism promised that energetic and free government was possible over an extended territory and complex society. It remains to be seen whether the development of liberal republicanism will prove this promise true.

Liberal republicanism may undermine not only political engagement in particular but also engagement in civil life more broadly. Alexis de Tocqueville, who visited America in the nineteenth century, was greatly impressed by its civil associations. Americans, he observes in *Democracy in America*, "use associations . . .to found seminaries, to build inns, to raise churches, to distribute books." In de Tocqueville's view, modern democracy tends to isolate individuals and concentrate the whole of their attention on their private affairs, narrowly understood. Civil associations were one means by which he saw Americans pursuing common goals in common. Yet associations were not easily maintained in an individualistic age, and Tocqueville feared individuals would finally reject associations. Then, impotent alone to achieve the goals once pursued through associations, they would call on government to manage the affairs they once managed together. Government would become an "immense tutelary power" that, without formally depriving citizens of their freedoms, offers to take care of every detail of life for them and gradually reduces them to a "herd of timid and industrious animals." Tocqueville called this possibility "administrative despotism." In *Bowling Alone: The Collapse and Revival of American Community*, Robert Putnam argues that meaningful participation in civil associations has declined in the United States. While he himself does not conclude that administrative despotism has arrived, his data has offered some ammunition to those who believe that it is here or on its way.

Unhappy citizens? There is still one more charge to add to the critical indictment of liberal republicanism and the individualism it promotes: they make people unhappy. "Communitarian" critics of liberal republicanism argue that it has detached individuals from communities. But communities provide a feeling of belonging. As Robert Bellah and his fellow authors concluded on the basis of their study of middle–class American life, "it would seem that [the] quest for purely private fulfillment is illusory: it often ends in emptiness instead."

The liberal republican is not defenseless against these criticisms. For one thing, liberal republicanism, while it may have emphasized education less than classical republicanism, never relied on untaught self–interest. The liberal republican may agree with individualism having gone too far without conceding that liberal republican theory must be changed or even abandoned, for that theory already warns that to be effective, self–interest must be not only properly channeled but liberal citizens must properly understand it. Moreover, the liberal republican may agree that the size and complexity of government makes citizen vigilance very difficult without conceding that liberal republicanism is responsible for an increase in the authority or centralization of governments. The liberal republican teaching that government was instituted among men to secure rights is a teaching of limited government. Finally, the liberal republican may agree that his or her creed often produces lonely individuals, but that standing alone affirms human dignity. In making this defense, the liberal may circumvent the charges but in any case it raises the question: do the dangers of individualism mean liberal republicanism must be abandoned or modified, or do they mean, instead, that the first principles of liberal republicanism need to be recovered?

Economics

Critics of liberal republicanism point not only to its emphasis on the individual but also to its willingness to indulge and even celebrate trade and industry. First, citizens whose main activity is pursuing profit and comfort tend to be soft. Commercial societies, as Paul Rahe pointed out, often have "little sympathy for the soldier's calling," and its members, "able to live the better part of. . .life in peace and in comfort," are "in no way inured to the loss of life and to the shedding of blood." Boosters of liberal republicanism may point to the military successes of liberal societies, especially the dramatic victory of the Allied forces in World War II. Such successes seem to dispute the argument that liberal societies are soft. Boosters may point, too, to the superiority in military technology of liberal republican societies, in which hindrances to innovation are few. As Rahe noted, however, liberal societies had great difficulty defeating Hitler, they could easily have lost the war, and their soldiers, despite the worthiness of the cause, were often unwilling or unable to fight. Moreover, even if liberal societies turn out courageous soldiers, they may be held back by a citizenry that is skittish about casualties, fears being drafted, and does not want its business interrupted under any but the most immediately threatening circumstances. The question of the military fitness of liberal commercial societies may still be open.

Second, to dignify commerce is also to justify the economic inequalities that result from commerce, as economic competition produces winners and losers. Yet these inequalities may be unjust. For one thing, success or failure in the marketplace may bear little or no relation to worth, at least as worth is commonly understood. An entertainer whose contribution to society is cracking jokes may make twenty times as much money as a police officer, whose contribution to society is risking his or her life to save others. Not only the basis but also the mere size of inequalities in commercial societies give critics ammunition. Rousseau states the case powerfully: "it is manifestly against the Law of Nature, however defined, that. . .a handful of people abound in superfluities while the starving multitude lacks in necessities." While liberal commercial societies can point to middle–class multitudes that are not starving as proof that Rousseau and others have it wrong, they have never been altogether able to silence their critics. Such critics insist Rousseau may have overstated the extent of the problem but not its fundamental character, that liberal republican societies leave some astoundingly rich and others virtually without hope. In reply, defenders of liberal society argue that whatever the degree of injustice and suffering found, it is more than matched by the degree of injustice and suffering found in illiberal societies, for government officials are worse at distributing wealth than markets are and curtail people's liberty in the bargain.

Economic inequality may be not only unjust but also politically dangerous. Michael Sandel has warned of the "civic consequences of economic inequality."

In particular, as the gap between the rich and the rest widens, unity decreases. The well–off flee the public schools for private ones, city parks for private clubs, city services for private security and private garbage collection. They grow disinclined to pay taxes for services they do not use. The poor and lower middle class, trapped in inferior schools and poorly served neighborhoods, grow increasingly resentful. Both groups feel little stake in a society or government that they have abandoned or that has abandoned them. Amid this class tension, liberal societies cannot muster the energy and resources for great accomplishments, or even the wherewithal for such ordinary accomplishments as keeping the streets clean and the schools safe. Sandel and many other critics pointed to a gap between rich and poor that only deepened in the 1980s and 1990s and that has, in their view, already begun to erode even the limited sense of national community liberal societies need to prosper.

Large corporations In addition, the critics argue, just as the concentration of political power in a big government causes citizens to feel and actually be powerless, so, too, does the concentration of wealth in large corporations. People largely unknown and unaccountable to the public determine in corporate boardrooms whether thousands of employees will live in comfort or suffer. The concentration of economic power threatens to leave citizens powerless in another way. By making large contributions to political campaigns, corporations may be able to influence public servants and to pass legislation and regulations that favor them, at the expense of citizens who can afford neither to make large contributions nor to hire lobbyists and lawyers. The rise of multinational corporations has further complicated matters. Even if citizens can persuade their governments to try to protect wages and livelihoods, corporations could simply move their plants and jobs overseas to countries that better serve their interests. The relative inability of even their big governments to help them contributes to the anxiety of liberal republican citizens who fear that they are "losing control of the forces that [govern] their lives." Such citizens, even if capable of exercising self–government effectively, would likely be too demoralized to even try.

The liberal republican is not defenseless against these attacks, either. The overall tendency of a free commercial society, the liberal republican argues, is not to concentrate economic power but to distribute power to a variety of centers that include but are not limited to large businesses. Moreover, while the political and economic power of such businesses may be potent, business is not a single interest that always acts in unison, but a multiplicity of interests often at odds politically and economically. This competition, along with regulations designed to promote competition and discourage conspiracies among businesses to fix wages and prices, at least diminishes the threat that the influence of large corporations will destroy meaningful self–government. Moreover, while world economic growth means money and jobs move easily from nation to nation and that the ability of governments directly to protect the jobs of its citizens is limited, defenders of liberal republicanism argue that citizens in societies open to innovation can best benefit from economic globalization. They argue that nations need more rather than less liberal republicanism, more rather than less restrictions to commerce and innovation.

Critics

Nonetheless, the question remains whether liberal republicanism has unleashed forces beyond its control. Critics on the left lament the dangers commerce and innovation pose to the environment when scientists and entrepreneurs fail to take a long view of the effects of their activities. Critics on the right lament the dangers commerce and innovation pose to humanity itself when scientists and entrepreneurs, for example, do not stop short at human cloning or manipulating genes for profit. Critics of both political persuasions fear liberal republicans have put excessive faith in the ability of reason to check itself and to control its technologies. But few critics wish to relinquish the benefits of progress, and many acknowledge that liberal republicanism has been an enormous success at producing such benefits. For that reason critics of liberal republicanism must grasp the following question: how does one secure the goods liberal republicanism offers without supposing that reason, suitably educated and guided by experience, can be expected to supply solutions to the problems that accompany those goods?

At least some of the criticisms of liberal republicanism draw on classical republican theory. Michael Sandel, for example, understood his project as reviving a republicanism that the triumph of its liberal elements have all but ruined. Sandel's concerns about the political effects of economic inequality, the importance of political community, and the freedom that consists not in the mere absence of external restraint but in self–government, hearken to a republican tradition that, in his view, sporadically drew from Aristotle's Greece to at least nineteenth–century America. Yet, as Sandel readily acknowledges, the old republican tradition was coercive, because it used government power to compel individuals to meet the demands of the *polity*, and exclusive because it distinguished so sharply between insiders and outsiders, where slaves and women were in important ways part of the latter group. Sandel hopes to restore elements of the classical republican ideal while avoiding its tendency toward coercion and exclusion. Yet, as Steven Kautz points out, critics such as Sandel seem to be caught between their real commitment to liberal republicanism and their disappointment in it, which is manifested in their worries about the decay of robust communities, the decline of intense and widespread political participation, and the effects of economic inequality. Kautz's observation raises this question about modern republicanism: are individualism and inequality accidental components of the republican freedom even critics of liberal republicanism seem to cherish, or are they, for good or for ill, the unavoidable accompaniments of freedom?

TOPICS FOR FURTHER STUDY

- The Federalists, who defended the Constitution, typically called themselves republicans. But they were not the only ones. The Anti–Federalists, who opposed the Constitution, also typically called themselves republicans. What were their arguments? In what ways did their understanding of republicanism differ from the Federalist understanding, and why did they think the Constitution threatened republicanism?

- Both classical and modern republicanism depend to some extent on education to produce citizens capable of meeting the responsibilities of republican life. How and to what extent have the public schools been instruments of citizen education, and how so today?

- Both classical and modern republicanism depend to some extent on citizens knowing about and engaging in politics. What does the evidence suggest about the political knowledge and activity of American citizens nowadays, and is it a good or bad sign for American republicanism? What policy measures, if any, can and should be taken to increase the political knowledge and activity of American citizens?

- In the ancient Greek world, Sparta's great rival was Athens and each *polis* was known then and has been known since for representing contrasting ways of life. How was Athens similar to Sparta, and how was it different? What does the comparison teach us about classical republicanism?

BIBLIOGRAPHY

Sources

Aristotle. *Politics*. Translated by Ernest Barker. Oxford: Oxford University Press, 1998.

Bellah, Robert N. et. al. *Habits of the Heart: Individualism and Commitment in American Life*. Updated Edition. Berkeley, CA: University of California Press, 1996.

Hamilton, Alexander, John Jay, and James Madison. *The Federalist Papers*. Edited by Isaac Kramnick. London: Penguin Books, 1987.

Kautz, Steven. *Liberalism and Community*. Ithaca, NY: Cornell University Press, 1995.

Kitto, H.D.F. *The Greeks*. Middlesex: Penguin Books, 1957.

Machiavelli, Niccolò. *The Prince*. Translated by Harvey C. Mansfield. Second Edition. Chicago: University of Chicago Press, 1998.

Montesquieu. *The Spirit of the Laws*. Edited and Translated by Anne M. Cohler, Basia Carolyn Miller, and Harold Samuel Stone. Cambridge: Cambridge University Press, 1989.

Pangle, Thomas L. *The Spirit of Modern Republicanism: The Moral Vision of the American Founders and the Philosophy of Locke*. Chicago: The University of Chicago Press, 1988.

Plato. *The Republic*. Translated by Allan Bloom. Second Edition. New York: Basic Books, 199.

Plutarch. *Lives of the Noble Grecians and Romans*. 2 vols. Translated by John Dryden. Revised by Arthur Hugh Clough. New York: Random House, 2001.

Putnam, Robert D. *Bowling Alone: The Collapse and Revival of American Community*. New York: Simon & Schuster, 2000.

Rahe, Paul. *Republics Ancient and Modern*. Chapel Hill: University of North Carolina Press, 1992.

Riesenberg, Peter. *Citizenship in the Western Tradition: Plato to Rousseau*. Chapel Hill: University of North Carolina Press, 1992.

Rousseau, Jean–Jacques. *The Discourses and other early political writings*. Edited and Translated by Victor Gourevitch. Cambridge: University of Cambridge Press, 1997.

Rousseau, Jean–Jacques. *The Social Contract and other later political writings*. Edited and Translated by Victor Gourevitch. Cambridge: University of Cambridge Press, 1997.

Sandel, Michael J. *Democracy's Discontent: America in Search of a Public Philosophy*. Cambridge, MA: Harvard University Press, 1996.

Tocqueville, Alexis de. *Democracy in America*. Translated and Edited by Harvey C. Mansfield and Delba Winthrop. Chicago: The University of Chicago Press, 2000.

Further Readings

Bloom, Allan, ed.. *Confronting the Constitution*. Washington D.C.: The AEI Press, 1990. This collection contains valuable essays on the intellectual and historical foundations of American liberal republicanism and on various attacks on those foundations.

Everdell, William R. *The End of Kings: A History of Republics and Republicans*. Second Edition. Chicago: The University of Chicago Press, 2000. Everdell gives a useful overview of the history of republicanismn.

Kagan, Donald. *Pericles of Athens and the Birth of Democracy*. New York: Simon & Schuster, 1991. While its interpretation of the classical republic differs in some ways from the one offered in this article, this history, which focuses on Athens and one of its greatest statesmen, Pericles, is a very useful window into Greek republican politics.

Skinner, Quentin. *Machiavelli*. New York: Hill and Wang, 1981. This concise introduction to the thought of Niccolò Machiavelli, though its understanding of Machiavelli differs in important ways from the one presented here, should be consulted for its views on Machiavelli's place in the republican tradition.

SEE ALSO

Capitalism, Conservatism, Federalism

Socialism

WHO CONTROLS GOVERNMENT? Society

HOW IS GOVERNMENT PUT INTO POWER? Revolution or evolution of other theories

WHAT ROLES DO THE PEOPLE HAVE? Share capital and means of production

WHO CONTROLS PRODUCTION OF GOODS? Society

WHO CONTROLS DISTRIBUTION OF GOODS? Society

MAJOR FIGURES Pierre–Joseph Proudhon; Julius Nyerere

HISTORICAL EXAMPLE Tanzania, 1964–1985

OVERVIEW

Socialism is a much used and abused term, which spans the political spectrum from the Right (the National Socialists of Hitler's Germany) to the Left (Stalin's communists in the Union of Soviet Socialist Republics). It has also described a great variety of regimes that have acquired and used the term for their own purposes, stretching from the poor African socialist states and Arab and Asian military dictatorships, to the wealthy social democracies of Western Europe and Australia and New Zealand.

Generally, we may take the term to describe those doctrines which seek to increase the power of society and the state to determine political, social, and economic processes, as against traditional mechanisms and institutions favored by conservatives, and individuals and the market as advocated by liberals. In common usage, the dividing line between socialism and communism is not always clear or sharp, but may be taken to be between those socialists who subscribe to the basic doctrines of Karl Marx, and those socialists who do not.

Within the boundaries of policy and ideology just described, there are still wide varieties of forms of socialism. There are also a considerable number of philosophers, political practices, and state policies embraced by the doctrine. As with so many modern political philosophies, however, in order to uncover their origins we must look to the emergence of socialist thought in modern Europe.

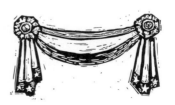

CHRONOLOGY

1516: Sir Thomas More's *Utopia* is published

1755: The Frenchman Morelly offers his view of a socialist Utopia in *Code of Nature*

1825: Claude Henri Saint–Simon calls for an easing between social divisions in *The New Christianity: Dialogues Between a Conservative and an Innovator*

1840: Pierre–Joseph Proudhon rails against private land ownership in *What is Property?*

1848: Karl Marx and Friedrich Engels publish *The Communist Manifesto*

1880s: Sydney Webb and Beatrice Potter Webb help form the English Fabian Socialists

1936: John Maynard Keynes publishes *General Theory of Employment, Interest and Money*

1945–1975: The welfare state evolves in the developed countries

1948–1975: Third World countries adopt socialist model regimes

1967: Julius Nyerere installs *ujamaa* in Tanzania

1989: Socialist countries in Eastern Europe begin to collapse

---

HISTORY

The Origins of Socialism: Early Utopian Socialism

In nineteenth–century England, then the world's most–developed state, just as liberalism was being reshaped to converge with the increasing social power and demands of the working class, socialism was also being reshaped to make it not just an idealist, but a real political movement. There was already a tradition of utopian, idealist thought running through the popular philosophy of the country on which to base socialist doctrines.

The roots of socialist thought, whether they be traced to Plato's *Republic*, Sir Thomas More's *Utopia* (1516), to Rousseau's *Discourses on the Origins of*

Inequality Among Mankind (1755), or Morelly's *Code of Nature* (1755), are invariably idealist. What all these works also have in common is a belief in the fundamental wrongness of private property. In the case of Plato (428–348 B.C.) that wrongness is seen as the cause of war, but at the same time he only envisions that a select group of people should forego private property and possessions and assume as "guardians" the direction of society.

In *Utopia*, More approvingly cites Plato's *Republic* for having argued for "an equal distribution of goods." But *Utopia* was written as a response to the break down of village life, the enclosure of lands for sheep pasturing, and the excessive punishments meted out to the large number of beggars, vagabonds, and thieves in the England of the early–sixteenth century. It was an attempt to devise a society in which poverty would be eliminated. In its attempt to eliminate poverty, like most communist attempts, it commences with the vilification of existing wealth and the power that accompanies it: "when I consider any social system that prevails in the modern world, I can't...see it as anything but a conspiracy of the rich to advance their own interests under the pretext of organizing society."

Code of Nature (1755) by the obscure Frenchman Morelly, asserts that "where no property exists, none of its pernicious consequences could exist," and "if you were to take away property, and the blind and pitiless self–interest that accompanies it you would cause all the prejudices and errors that they sustain to collapse." Like *Utopia*, this communist vision is frugal, meticulous, tedious, and draconian:

> Every citizen between the ages of twenty and twenty–five without exception, will be required to do agricultural work...In every occupational group, there will be one master for every ten or twenty workers, and it will be his task to instruct them, inspect their work...at the age of thirty, every citizen will be allowed to dress according to his taste...The senators and chiefs are authorized by this law to punish all excesses in this manner...Young people between the ages of twenty and thirty will be dressed uniformly with each occupation...every citizen will have both a work suit and holiday suit...Every citizen will be married as soon as he has reached the marriageable age...

During the upheavals of the English Civil War and revolution of the seventeenth century, some of these ideas actively came to the fore. Indeed, Oliver Cromwell, when pursuing his political ascendancy, had to suppress the Levellers (English radicals of the 1640s). But the eclipse of both Cromwell and the radicals permitted the evolution of the constitutional monarchy after the 1688 Restoration and the subsequent development of a prosperous commercial society. In

France, however, the absolutist *ancien* regime survived and in it utopian socialist opposition festered.

The French Revolution of 1789 and Its Aftermath

Morelly's *Code* contained many of the core elements of later communists—egalitarianism (belief in equal political, economic, and social rights), a sagacious bureaucracy, principles of rotation, prohibition of private property, and the requirement that all work. But it was Gracchus Babeuf (1760–1797) who is generally heralded as being the first systematic defender of modern communism. Babeuf, who was tried for conspiracy and executed during the French Revolution, saw his communist ideas as the natural progression of the Enlightenment. It was, he said at his trial, the philosophical poisons of Mably, Helvetius, Diderot and, most importantly, Rousseau which had corrupted him. For him, communism was a means for ending injustice.

In the *Manifesto of Equals* Babeuf wrote, "We declare ourselves unable any longer to tolerate a situation in which the great majority of men toil and sweat in the service and at pleasure of a tiny minority." "Men of all classes" should "be accorded the same rights in order of succession to property" and "an absolutely equal portion of all the goods and advantages that can be enjoyed in this mean world." And in the *Analysis of the Doctrine of Babeuf*, written by his followers, the egalitarianism of the Constitution of 1793 was invoked against the wealthy: "The revolution is not finished, because the rich are absorbing all goods and are exclusively in command, while the poor are toiling in a state of virtual slavery." The way out of this class division was to make everyone work: "no one has ever shirked this duty without having thereby committed a crime."

What these thinkers had in common was a failure to present a serious economic analysis of what a communist system would entail. Rather, a moral critique was combined with an economic critique and a solution which entailed a revolution in economic activity was presented as if it were guaranteed to reform human nature. Nevertheless, what they also had in common was an emphasis on relieving the suffering of the poorest classes by restricting property rights. This became the core doctrine of socialism.

Social Democracy

During the earlier part of the twentieth century, all the advanced states experienced the rise of such Social Democratic movements with the achievement of the more or less universal franchise. The result was a transfer of demands from the political sphere concerning representation in the deliberations of the state—much of which was achieved at the end of the First World War—to arguments about the purposes for which the state should be used.

The common form of the expression of Social Democracy was a democratic electoral coalition pursuing social rights to add to the political gains already won for the masses. Social Democratic parties were achieving Parliamentary representation by the 1890s and the first Social Democratic government in the world was formed in the semi–sovereign, self–governing British colony of Queensland (Australia) in 1899. Shortly thereafter, Social Democrats began to seriously influence political agendas everywhere. By bargaining for their electoral support with the reforming British Liberal government of 1906–1911 they achieved a significant part of their social agenda. In Australia, the Labour Party, founded in 1891, formed national governments of its own before the First World War and implemented modest reforming programs that either dismayed or astonished European observers of the day. Elsewhere Social Democrats put pressure on Rightist governments to accommodate to their agenda, as in Germany. That agenda emerged from the social composition of industrial society and included pensions, a decent wage, health care, holiday leave, and education.

Social democracy has no outstanding political theoreticians, although a body of literature derives from a variety of political, economic, and philosophical tracts. In the political sphere, among the most developed came from Britain and the Fabian Socialists, including: William Morris (1834–1896), who wrote *Why I Am a Socialist* in 1884; Sidney and Beatrice Webb; the playwright George Bernard Shaw (1856–1950), driving force behind the formation of the Fabian Society in 1884 and writer in 1928 of *The Intelligent Woman's Guide to Socialism and Capitalism*; the author and novelist H.G. Wells (1866–1946) in Outline of History, 1920; and the academic Harold Laski (1893–1950) who was on the executive at different times, of both the Fabian Society and the British Labour Party, as well as the author of *Communism* in 1927; and the politicians of the British Labour Party.

In October 1883 a socialist debating group was formed in London and called themselves the Fabian Society, after the Roman General Quintus Fabius Maximus, who advocated weakening the opposition by harassing operations rather than becoming involved in pitched battles. The Fabians came to include intellectuals like Eleanor Marx, J.A. Hobson, George Bernard Shaw, Clement Attlee, Ramsay MacDonald, Emmeline Pankhurst, and H.G. Wells.

These Fabian socialists argued for the pursuit of a vaguely defined form of socialism—which certainly included more state ownership of the economy, higher taxes and more welfare benefits—by using an elected Labour government to legislate for an extension of the egalitarian principle from the political to the economic and social sphere.

The Fabians believed that capitalism had created an unjust and inefficient society and they aimed to reconstruct it more rationally; early discussions included "How Can We Nationalise Accumulated Wealth?" But they rejected revolutionary socialism and wanted society to move to a socialist society painlessly. They tried to convince people by rational argument and they produced pamphlets to this end.

In 1889 they published Fabian Essays—with chapters written by George Bernard Shaw and Sidney Webb, among others—which sold extremely well. Fabian members traveled widely, giving lecturers on "Socialism." They founded a new university, the London School of Economics (LSE), in 1895, to teach political economy along socialist lines. Later, they decided to establish a distinct Labour group in Parliament.

The Fabians adopted similar attitudes to the German Marxist revisionists but were an upper–middle–class intellectual group. They became famous through publishing. These middle–class Fabians rejected revolutionary tactics and were more interested in practical politics and gains to be made through contacts in the international socialist movement, trade unions, and cooperative movements.

In Germany similar arguments were evolved by the previously mentioned Marxist Social Democratic Party, led by Kautsky and Bernstein, before it was twice destroyed—by the 1914 War and then by the Nazi regime. In France, a similar process witnessed the development of the Popular Front Left government of the 1930s, which was in turn to be destroyed by internal conflict with the Right and between competing socialist groups, and later by the Nazi blitzkreig.

In the economic realm, the dominant Social Democratic theoretician became a British academic, John Maynard Keynes (1883–1946). Keynes had achieved some distinction by warning, in *The Economic Consequences of the Peace* in 1919, that the punitive peace imposed on Germany, including reparations, would lead to the disruption and dislocation of the international economy, as eventually occurred. By later advocating what amounted to greater state intervention in the running of a capitalist economy in his *General Theory of Employment, Interest and Money*, 1936, Keynes gave theoretical legitimacy to the political aspirations of the Social Democrats. For a generation after the Second World War, they were to use this to great advantage and construct Social Democratic societies in capitalist Europe and, to a much lesser extent, in North America.

The U.S. had been created as a liberal state and grew rapidly at a time when liberal rather than socialist ideas were in the ascendancy. The resulting popular antagonism towards the state in part explains why no socialist movement of any significance developed in the U.S. In 1906 the German sociologist Werner Sombart asked, "Why is there no socialism in America?" The ethnic divisions among the newly immigrant working class during the rapid industrialization of the late nineteenth century, the strength of religious sentiment, and the high level of geographic and social mobility, all made class solidarity and socialist ideology difficult to achieve in the U.S. The great mass movements in opposition to unbridled capitalism—1890s' Populism, then Progressivism, and finally the 1930s' New Deal—all failed to ignite a mass socialist movement. Socialist candidates by the end of the twentieth century routinely achieved only one percent of the Presidential vote.

National unity for Americans was not constructed on the basis of ethnic solidarity or Social Democratic ideals, but on the ideology of American "particularism," which stressed liberal values and opposition to an interventionist state. Americanism, and with it the legend of the frontier and then upward social mobility, was an alternative ideology to socialism, which it transcended. The communist party in the U.S. was the result of the amalgamation of even smaller Russian immigrant–based sects. Periodically, small socialist parties existed on the slim pickings of intellectuals, migrants, labor unions and protected industry, but as David Mosler and Bob Catley argued in *Global America: Imposing Liberalism on a Recalcitrant World*, the U.S. remained determinedly liberal.

In Australia and New Zealand Social Democratic movements had already achieved considerable successes and these were consolidated during the early twentieth century. The Australian Labour Party was founded in 1891 and formed governments in Queensland in the 1890s and nationally before the First World War. The New Zealand Labour Party was created in 1916 and took power in 1935. In both countries the state was expanded deeply into the ownership of capital and the regulation of the economy—arguably to an extent much greater than other capitalist societies by the 1930s. Keynes' doctrines were quickly adopted by the labor political leaderships in both countries, and were only jettisoned following their inflationary impacts of the 1970s.

In the philosophical sphere, the egalitarian project of the Social Democrats was only to achieve its full expression when the movement itself was mature and arguably past its apogee, in the form of John Rawls' major work *A Theory of Justice* in 1971. In this, he influentially argued for a public policy principle, "the original position" which demanded a common status outcome be blindly pursued for all.

THEORY IN DEPTH

Classical Socialism

The same focus was found in the work of Claude Henri Saint–Simon (1760–1825), who saw in Christianity the means to call an easing between social divisions. He wrote, in *The New Christianity: Dialogues Between a Conservative and an Innovator* (1825), that "God gave only one principle to men: that He commanded them to organise their society in such a way as to guarantee to the poorest classes the promptest and most complete amelioration of their physical and moral existence." Like Jean Marie Condorcet, who wrote *Sketch for a Historical Picture of the Progress of the Human Mind* (1795), and Anne Robert Jacques Turgot, the physiocrat financial official who authored *Reflexions sur la Formation et la Distribution Richesses* (1766), Saint–Simon shared the belief that human society was progressing.

But progress for Saint–Simon was not primarily about intellectual evolution and the application of ideas to society, as it largely was in Condorcet, but instead entailed the increasing complexity and productivity of social organization and technology. History was conceived of as a series of stages of technological and sociological advances.

What Saint–Simon brought to this perspective was the promise of social fulfilment in a unified, administrative industrial society: science, industry, and the fine arts were seen as conspiring to form a social unity which if rightly administered would bring peace and prosperity to all. In Saint–Simon, the twentieth century bureaucratic cast of mind with its faith in a planned society found its nineteenth century antecedent, as can be gauged from his phrase, later repeated by German socialist Friedrich Engels (1820–1895): *that the government of persons will be replaced by the administration of things.*

Pierre–Joseph Proudhon In France, it was Pierre–Joseph Proudhon (1809–1865) who played the most important intellectual role in contributing to actual working class politics. Proudhon's *What is Prop-*

Pierre–Joseph Proudhon. (The Library of Congress)

erty? (1840) formulated what socialists and communists had all in one way or another been saying, when he answered: "It is theft." But Proudhon also incurred the wrath of communists by arguing:

> Communism is oppression and slavery....communism violates the sovereignty of the conscience and equality: the first, by restricting spontaneity of mind and heart, and freedom of thought and action; the second, by placing labor and laziness, skill and stupidity, and even vice and virtue on an equality in point of comfort.

For Proudhon, liberty was to be found by combining communism and property. But that combination, in his hands, became a plea for a society essentially composed of small–scale property holders, enjoying an interest–free credit system, and each working their land. Thus, while he insisted that he (just like Saint–Simon had done and Marx would do) was merely a messenger who knew the direction of history, his vision, as Marx all too easily saw, was built around a fundamental agrarian anachronism, which was more likely to appeal to the then social conditions of a still mostly agrarian France than industrial England or America.

Karl Marx and Nineteenth Century German Socialism

Karl Marx (1818–1883) dominated German intellectual socialist thought. Marx was a German law student whose philosophical studies of politics, history, and political economy became a search for the true meaning of human nature and history. After he had realized that German philosopher Ludwig Feuerbach (1804–1872) had understood that man is a "species being," and that is the clue to his nature, he went on to find the answer in *The Economic and Philosophical Manuscripts* of 1844 to "the riddle of history." It was communism. Only in a communist society could the powers of man's species be unlocked.

Marx would later dispense with any talk about liberating the whole people, and let the "working class" become the agent of historical destiny. Marx became obsessed with one thing—the elimination of private interests and property. Having discovered that history as it had hitherto been experienced was the expression of class conflict, as he wrote in the *Communist Manifesto* (1848), he came to see all social relations and institutions as pathologically infected by the existence of private interests. He then fled for refuge to liberal England.

Marx developed his ideas into a theory which came to be known as marxism. He declared that within marxism there would be no division of labor, no property, no law, no money, no state, no religion, and no alienation. That property, law, the division of labor, the state, and religion were not the artefacts of capitalist society but the very elements which emerge wherever there is any moderately large–scale, settled social organization or nation did not bother Marx or his followers. Indeed, when the occasion arose they would denounce the very idea of a nation as a repressive ideological construction.

Marx believed that the elimination of all known forms of social organization, apart from voluntary communal cooperation, would provide so much abundance that alienation stemming from the division of labor, capitalist oppression, and poverty would be eliminated. But he persistently attacked the Saint–Simonians, who were engaging in voluntary non–violent, social cooperative experiments for being utopians and idealists. Marx believed he had proof that capitalism would break down, but before it had done that it would sufficiently socialize and expand the means of production so that socialism, through marxism, would occur. Throughout his life Marx believed that communism is "not an ideal to which reality will have to adjust itself. We call communism the real movement which abolishes the present state of things."

Marx's followers ranged themselves against "idealists" even when, later, Joseph Stalin (1879–1953) made speech after speech declaring communism was an act of will, and of faith; even af-

ter the Italian communist Antonioni Gramsci (1891–1937) had said that socialism was a religion; and even when communist states imprisoned and executed people merely for the ideas they held. Marxism became essentially a Last Judgment doctrine that provided moral orientation for a social group, the intelligentsia, who had lost faith in the gods of religion and mere ethics and were themselves largely lacking in political power. When Marx repeatedly pointed to the scientific rigor of his analysis, even though he did not do one single model study of the mechanics of a modern large scale economy under marxism, he was really making a moral point.

Marxism was also the modern way of making philosophers rulers, at least notionally. This helps explain its popularity among them. But they could rule with a clear egalitarian conscience. For the whole enterprise of Marxism was to reproduce in secular society the religious dream of a life including the attainment of equality. The whole moral force of marxism lay in its promise of the elimination of inequalities by its elimination of classes.

In Russia, under Vladimir Lenin (1870–1924), Marx's political idealism was advanced as scientific and inevitable, in part, so that Marxists could also be free to grab power any way they could in the name of the working class, without moral scruples. The entire legitimacy of the enterprise involved Marxists in a moral substitution racket: the critics and opponents of Marx or the communist party were the enemies of the working class; and the enemies of the working class were the enemies of humanity; and all future generations would live in peace and prosperity if only the communists would be victorious. Since the stakes were so high, Marxists could not be bound by moral scruples. Furthermore, Marx had shown that morals were simply the ideological expression of class interests. Thus, Marxists became extremely ruthless.

Ferdinand Lassalle

While Marx fulminated in exile in London, in Germany, Ferdinand Lassalle (1825–1864), President of the General German Workers Association, lay the foundation for the German Socialist Party. Like Marx, Lassalle identified the interests of humanity with the interests of the working class. This class, he wrote in *The Working Class Program* of 1862, is:

> ...the disinterested class of the community, which sets up and can set up no further exclusive condition, either legal or actual, neither nobility nor landed possessions, nor the possession of capital, which it could make into a new privilege and force upon the arrangements of society. We are all working men in so far as we have the will to make ourselves useful in any way to the community.

The corollary of the belief that the self–interest of the working class would converge with the interest of society as a whole was the belief that the self interest of the upper class had to be at the expense of the nation's development. This too was close to Marx.

But there was one significant difference between them: Lassalle saw the state in positive terms and in this respect provided a cornerstone of Social Democracy. He believed that the state could be transformed by the political participation of the working class.

For Lassalle, like Johann Fichte (1762–1814), author of *Critique of All Revelation* (1792), and Georg W.F. Hegel (1770–1831), the German theorist of the state, the State thus would become the cornerstone of a nation's economic and moral development. Lassalle argued:

> It is the State, whose function is to carry on this development of freedom, this development of the human race until its freedom is attained. The State is this unity of individuals into a moral whole, a unity which increases a million–fold the strength of all the individuals who are comprehended in it, and multiplies a million times the power which would be at the disposal of them all as individuals.

> The object of the State, therefore, is not only to protect the personal freedom and property of the individual with which he is supposed according to the idea of the Bourgeoisie to have entered the State. On the contrary, the object of the State is precisely this, to place the individual through this union in a position to attain such objects, and reach such a stage of existence as they never could have reached as individuals; to make them capable of acquiring an amount of education, power, and freedom which would have been wholly unattainable by them as individuals.

This concept of the state, while far removed from *laissez–faire* liberalism, is not much different from the idealist social liberal conception of the state advanced by English philosopher T.H. Green (1836–1882). By the end of the century, Eduard Bernstein (1850–1932), the leading German socialist politician, had acknowledged that the extremist Marxian roots of social democracy were no longer legitimate. Socialism was a matter of parliamentary democracy and evolution.

English Fabian Socialism

Much the same conclusion had been reached by the English Fabian Socialists, who also believed in the historical inevitability of socialism (but not in either the necessity or desirability of class war). In 1894 the Fabian socialist Sidney Webb (1859–1947) proclaimed in *English Progress Toward Social Democracy* "that there is no anti–socialist party in England," and that, "England is already the most Socialist of all European communities." The Fabians were convinced

Beatrice Potter Webb. (The Library of Congress)

that they saw the future and that it was socialist. The leading English Fabian intellectuals, like Sidney Webb and his wife Beatrice (1858–1943), as well as playwright George Bernard Shaw, believed, like the Germans Bernstein and Kautsky, that socialism could and would be achieved by peaceful and parliamentary means.

This did not mean they were necessarily opposed to other methods being used, if appropriate. After Stalin had taken complete control of the Soviet Union by 1931, for example, they believed that that future had been realized. In 1935, the Webbs published the laudatory *Soviet Communism: A New Civilization.* Like many other socialist observers of the Soviet barbarity, the Webbs saw what they were shown and what they wanted to see. The Soviets had a whole industry for showing Western sympathizers what they desired, a Russian industry that started ironically with the Potemkin villages of Catherine the Great (1729–1796), who used building frontages with nothing behind. The Chinese communists later demonstrated their communes in similar light.

For socialists in Europe and North America at that time, and indeed later, the debate was not really about collectivism or individualism. As the philosophical debates among Western intellectuals swung to the Left in the 1930s and Social Democracy assumed a near dominant position after the Second

BIOGRAPHY:

Sidney Webb and Beatrice Potter Webb

At the core of the Fabian Society were Sidney Webb (1859–1947) and his wife, Beatrice Potter Webb (1858–1943). Beatrice was a leading Fabian and in 1892 married Sidney Webb, a socialist economist and politician. The Webbs were at the center of British intellectual and political life during the late nineteenth and early twentieth centuries. They wrote books on trade unionism and industrial democracy and founded *The New Statesman*. Parts of Beatrice's voluminous diary were written by Sidney during their world tours of 1898 and 1911 and their Soviet tour in 1932. Sydney was also a member of the London County Council and an MP. In his Presidential Address to Labour Party Conference in 1923, he referred to "The inevitability of gradualness." In 1929 he was made Lord Passfield by the British Labour government. She was also very energetic in the pursuit of their policies. In her Minority Report to the 1909 Commission on the Poor Laws, for example, she produced one of the first charters for a comprehensive social security scheme of state pensions and a welfare state that emerged later in Europe.

Beatrice Potter Webb wrote prodigiously. Her works include: *Cooperative Movement in Great Britain*, 1891; *Wages of Men and Women: Should They be Equal?*, 1919; *My Apprenticeship*, 1926; and *Our Partnership*, 1948. She also wrote numerous books and articles with Sidney, including: *History of Trade Unionism*, 1894; *Industrial Democracy*, 1897; and, most notoriously, *Soviet Communism: A New Civilization?*, 1935.

Together, the Webbs also wrote numerous studies of industry in Britain, alternative economic policies, and pamphlets for political reform. They believed that rent applied to capital as well as to land and that the state should acquire this rent. Their later admiration of Soviet Russia stemmed partly from Stalin's ability to acquire this rent. They tried to influence public opinion in this direction by the selective education of the powerful, including themselves, who would lead these reforms in government. They only later extended their appeal beyond the intelligentsia. This narrow appeal led some Fabians, such as G.D.H. Cole and H.G. Wells, to break with the Fabians.

The Fabians rapidly declined in the 1930s, when the Webbs' admiration of Soviet Russia seemed excessive. In any case, the power of the British Labour Party and trade unions made them seem redundant, although Sidney Webb did write the famous Clause Four of the Labour Party charter, committing it to a socialist policy. They also lost control of the LSE and their intellectual influence during the 1930s was overshadowed by the Keynesian Revolution. Finally, many of the reforms they had advocated were undertaken during and after the Great Depression, as Karl Popper described in *The Open Society and Its Enemies*. In the 1940s, following the famous 1942 *Beveridge Report*, a comprehensive welfare state was established in Britain, perhaps finally vindicating Beatrice Potter Webb.

World War, the issue became whether collectivism could be conducted within a liberal democratic framework. In the 1940s, Left academics argued whether the rights and liberties of people which had been won through political conflict could still be guaranteed by an independent judiciary, or whether the collective will of the socialist state had the power and right to do whatever it willed.

The major argument that emerged concerned the appropriate agency for achieving this transition to the socialist state. The Social Democratic, Fabian, or Labour parties were subjected to two critiques. On the one hand, and deriving from Left critiques of Social Democratic organizations, of which V. Gordon Childe's (1892–1923) *How Labour Governs* remains among the best, was the idea of the "embourgeousification" of Social Democratic politicians. In this process, which the Australians call "Duchessing," the Social Democratic leadership becomes hopelessly corrupted and incapable, and indeed unwilling to make the transition to socialism.

On the other hand, Robert Michels (1876–1936), in *Political Parties: A Sociological Study of the Oligarchical Tendencies of Modern Democracy*, after long observation of the German Socialist Party, then the largest of its kind in the world, concluded that as such organizations were subjected to the "Iron Law of Oligarchy." They ceased to be agents of socialist transition and became instead bureaucracies with a life form of their own. This proved to be an almost clairvoyant analysis of the forces which were to drive socialist parties in power, and therefore of the kinds of state they would create.

Marxism

In *Das Kapital* (1863), Marx believed he had proven there was a central contradiction within capitalism, between capital and labor, which would necessarily lead to the break down of the system. The false premise was that all value derived from one source: the power of labor. The entrepreneurial role of the capitalists and the interplay between consumer and the marketplace were ignored entirely. Marx asserted that the capitalist class could not create value and that value was like a congealment of labor power that could be measured on an homogenous time scale of man/hours. He then argued that while the capitalist class lives off labor power, the drive for profits leads the capitalists to discover labor displacing technologies. The technologies, however, do not generate profits, the workers do. Capitalism is thus a system devouring itself as the capitalists ruthlessly exploit labor which will revolt against and destroy them.

Marx held that the struggle between labor and capital must lead to massive poverty and a technology all geared up and ready to go to progress, but unmanned because it can not be used profitably by the capitalist class. Perceiving this contradiction, the working class will seize power, run the factories, and society will then be governed by need rather than profit. Marx believed that the contradiction would play itself out in the most advanced industrialized countries because that would be where the technologies were most advanced, and thus where the workers would lead the revolution.

This theory was wildly out of line with what actually happened in the industrialized world. Friedrich Engels saw the living conditions of English working men and women improve on a scale unprecedented in history. When writing a new Preface to his *The Conditions of the English Working Class* (1844), he had to concede this and offered the highly implausible explanation that the discovery of gold in California had a great deal to do with it.

Marx himself, who had always insisted that capitalism was the precondition of socialism, abandoned a semblance of consistency when he conceded to Russian socialists that it might be possible in Russia to bypass the capitalist phase on the way to socialism.

The lack of concern for political organization to Marx and Engels stemmed from their remoteness from any genuine revolutionary struggle. In England, they were largely left alone to get on with their writings and go to small political meetings, where the rhetoric of revolution was strong but they were in a thoroughly secure liberal state. In the less liberal backlands of Russia, revolutionary politics meant something altogether different: it was life and death. The lack of development of civil society in Russia went hand in hand with the lack of development of a tolerant state resting on pluralist institutions. Ideas in Russia had invariably come from France and Germany; but the political ideas that were still being circulated and taken seriously among the Russian intelligentsia were the ideas that were undergoing significant transformation in Europe as the working classes gained increasing economic and political power.

In industrialized England, the trade union movement created its own parliamentary Labour party, which at first allied with the Liberals to achieve legislative successes before 1914, and then formed its own government in the late 1920s. But in Russia, the lack of an industrial proletariat meant that there was no strong socio–political base to moderate the radical dreams of the intelligentsia.

The intelligentsia could speak on behalf of the Russian masses precisely because the masses were mostly illiterate peasants whose very livelihoods were not conducive to mass political organization. Thus, the ideas of Marx, twisted and developed by Lenin into Marxism–Leninism, could have more impact. There was less chance of their being dissolved and defused within the actual political experience of the group they purported to represent; and there was less chance of them becoming Social Democratic. Marx and Engels were radical democrats and eschewed secret political organizations because they could openly denounce capitalism in tolerant Britain. In Russia radical political ideas could only exist within clandestine political activity.

What had been instigated as a supposed materialist approach to power revealed itself more and more as an attempt to consolidate the ideas of a people, to control every thought that could be uttered. When Stalin succeeded Lenin, he pulled Russia even further way from socialist ideals into communism. Stalin not only interfered in music and literature, he also determined the truth to be followed in the sciences of linguistics, anthropology, biology, and physics. The extremism of Lenin and Stalin provided a dead end for human emancipation. This posed the issue of whether alternative socialist forms might better serve.

THEORY IN ACTION

Social Democracy, 1945–1975

The political rise of the Social Democratic movement was achieved in the developed states in the late 1940s, and was maintained for three decades thereafter. It derived from three main sources: a call for using the state as a re–distributive mechanism; the intellectual ideas of socialism; and the economic ideas of state intervention associated with the doctrines of John Maynard Keynes.

The Great Depression of the 1930s had an impact on political programs everywhere in the developed world. The level of employment became an important issue, and since classical *laissez–faire* liberalism appeared to have little to alleviate the situation in the short term, it faced political defeat everywhere. In its place, the movements which struggled for supremacy included fascism, communism, and social democracy. The fascists had already triumphed in Italy and the Nazis seized power in Germany. During the next decade much of Europe progressively came under fascist regimes, who used state economic intervention and terror to increase economic activity. Their communist opponents had control only in the Soviet Union, where the state ownership of the economy enabled avoidance of the Depression at great cost to human liberty.

In the other advanced societies some form of social democracy became more influential, although at differing rates of growth. In the U.S., President Franklin Roosevelt (1882–1945) reversed generations of liberal economic doctrines to inaugurate the "New Deal" with its emphasis on public works programs and welfare measures to stimulate economic activity. In Australia and New Zealand the welfare state was extended. In Britain the Depression only started to recede with the rearmament program of the 1930s, but the political impact of mass unemployment later changed the political landscape fundamentally. In France the Popular Front governments also pushed the Social Democratic program in a society close to civil war and soon to be rather easily defeated.

The end of the Second World War heralded the triumph of Social Democracy. The classical liberal ideas about an uncontrolled market economy seemed unsustainable in light of the experience of the depressed 1930s. The fusion of these tendencies produced the post–war dominance of Social Democratic governments.

In Britain, the Labour Party led by Clement Atlee (1883–1967) formed a majority government from 1945 to 1951, and spent those years nationalizing many British industries and creating the welfare state. The principles involved were straightforward. The state would run the commanding heights of the economy which were then defined as being the railways, road transport, electricity, water and gas supplies, and, more controversially, the steel industry. It also increased the rate of progressive taxation—particularly income tax—to pay for a greatly expanded system of welfare services, which included age pensions, a national health system, education, and unemployment benefits. It also adopted Keynes economic ideas to justify a progressive expansion in the size of the state and its anti–cyclical policies of running what should have been occasional deficits, which proved to be almost permanent.

In Australia the Labour governments of 1941–1949, under John Curtin and Ben Chifley, also laid the basis for state–directed industrialization. As Bob Catley described in *Globalising Australian Capitalism* (1996), in addition to forms of the Social Democratic program which British Labour introduced, in Australia the government also induced forced industrialization. This involved protecting and fostering domestic industry, including a new automobile industry, and building new industries through state financing, like the massive hydro–electricity generating scheme in the Snowy Mountains.

In New Zealand, the Labour government had been in power since 1935 and under Prime Minster Michael Savage introduced the world's first welfare state. There, again, state ownership of key industries—like the extensive railway system—was augmented by state regulation and protection of industry and a high, progressive level of taxation to finance a wide welfare program.

In liberated Europe, the Anglo–Americans sponsored Social Democratic–style regimes designed at first to crush the social forces which had sustained fascism. In most of Western Europe, Social Democratic parties expanded state intervention in the economy along much the same lines as British Labour. This program sometimes went even further as industries owned by wartime collaborators or bankrupted by war damage, were brought into the public sector. These included banks, automobile manufactures, and even aerospace companies.

Although not all the Social Democratic parties stayed in power—indeed the Conservatives led by Winston Churchill returned in Britain in 1951 and Robert Menzies led the Liberals back in Australia in 1949—the impact of their doctrines remained strong until the late 1970s. In the three decades that followed the war economic growth was strong, the business cycle was minimal, and the role of the state in economic management, redistribution of resources, and the running of welfare programs was extended.

International similarities The essential characteristics of Social Democracy were similar throughout Europe. The welfare expenditure of the state and its programs were steadily expanded to provide standard services to all citizens regardless of income or other status. These services included: in most countries education at least to secondary and often University level; universal health care; aged pensions and unemployment benefits; training and re–training programs for labor to adjust to economic change; public housing for rental; universal no fault insurance; sick and vocational leave; and, depending on the case, subsidized transport, holidays, sporting, and care facilities for the infirm, abandoned, or aged. These services were funded by a high rate of at first progressive income taxation—which is heaviest on higher incomes—and then by a wide–ranging sales tax in the form of a Value Added Tax (VAT) as the European Union expanded.

These services were often supplemented by an extensive system of State Owned Enterprises (SOEs), which might include employee representation in the management structure at all levels. SOEs were typically operated in the transport, hospital, energy, utility provision, and even major manufacturing sectors like automobile, steel, banking, and aerospace.

In the developed countries outside Europe, these tendencies towards Social Democratic regimes were also evident. In the U.S. the state sector grew, most notably in the welfare services under Democratic administrations in the 1960s, although the U.S. never became a truly Social Democratic society. In Australia and New Zealand the state share also expanded further under labor governments in the mid–1970s.

The effect of the encroachment of the democratic socialist state on the liberal capitalist order was at first positive. Wages and other entitlements for workers who provided the electoral support for these regimes, gradually rose. Unemployment generally fell to almost zero and the trade cycle was flattened by Keynesian demand management techniques involving budget deficits and rapid money supply growth. The size of the state also increased as a proportion of the national economy. In addition, even in those sectors of the economy where SOEs were not evident, the level of state regulation of private enterprise rose progressively to match diverse social democratic demands about labor conditions, employment levels, environmental protection, and product quality. The

European Union even devised a Social Charter, which encouraged its member states to pursue these options.

Asian Socialism

Socialist ideas took a wide variety of forms in Asia. These varied from communism in China, after the Revolution of 1949, and North Korea and Vietnam, through a mix of Fabian ideals and indigenous traditions in India, to the heavily Trotskyite–influenced organizations which prospered in Sri Lanka in the 1950s and 1960s.

India India adopted a unique socialist model, which involved a commitment to small scale peasant farming along traditional Indian lines as advocated by the independence agitator and mystic Mahatma Gandhi (1869–1948). Alongside this, the more modernist elements in the Indian independence movement, associated with the dominant Congress Party and the ascendant family of Pandit Nehru (1861–1931), also encouraged the development of heavy industry. Much of this was privately owned and state protected, but much also came into the state infrastructure sector as State Owned Enterprises. This hybrid project was strengthened after 1960 by establishing an economic relationship with the Soviet Union. It had a mixed success in terms of both economic growth and political egalitarianism until it was abandoned for more market–oriented structures in 1991 after the Soviet Union collapsed.

Sri Lanka In Sri Lanka a promising socialist model and welfare state was established in the 1950s, but fell prey first to declining prices for its exported commodities, notably tea, and then a protracted and extremely ferocious civil war in 1975. The vaguely socialist (and extremely corrupt) Guided Democracy of President Sukarno in Indonesia was terminated by a military regime which, after 1966, eliminated the physical presence of socialist forces.

Burma Burma became independent from Britain in 1948. It then adopted a socialist direction and isolated itself from the several military conflicts that ravaged Southeast Asia during the Cold War. It also declined from one of the richest countries of the region to one of the poorest, while similar and neighboring Thailand achieved more rapid growth with a more open economy. During this period Burma's dominant politician was Ne Win.

Ne Win's 1962 coup was to establish "Burmese Socialism" by military rule, based on a one–party political system. Ne Win held the chairmanship of the

BIOGRAPHY:

Ne Win

Born in 1911, Ne Win abandoned his original name in 1941 when he joined a nationalist military group opposing British rule and supported by Japan. He became commander of the Burmese Independence Army in 1943, but later turned against the Japanese. After Burma's independence from Britain in 1948, he became Home and Defense Minister. During this time many of the minority nationalities of Burma established regional independence from the ineffective central government.

In 1958, Ne Win deposed prime minister U Nu. U Nu returned and served from 1960 to 1962, but Ne Win removed him again in a coup. By 1971, he had transformed Burma into a one–party state led by the Myanmar Socialist Programme Party. Under the new constitution adopted in 1974, Ne Win became President, and remained Party head until 1988.

After 1988 Ne Win slipped into obscurity as the democratic opposition, rallied by Aung San Suu Kyi, grew stronger. The result of Ne Win's policy of cultural isolation and economic self–sufficiency had been the steady impoverishment of a nation rich in resources. Although the country avoided the wars that plagued the surrounding region, Burma's own precarious internal security and insurrections has been a major drain on national revenues.

In October 2001, Ne Win was admitted to a Singapore hospital with a terminal illness.

Burma Socialist Programme Party and remained in effective political control of the country until 1988, when he resigned after admitting to economic mismanagement in the face of mounting popular discontent. The reason for Burma's impoverishment was the implementation of a socialist system of state planning and controls. Foreign trade was closed and foreign investment forbidden in the 1960s. Most industrial enterprises were brought into public ownership. The trade in rice was regulated and the price fixed to satisfy consumers, thereby discouraging increases in production. Ownership of land cultivating rice was

strictly controlled. The arbitrary nature of the political and judicial system gave no incentive for private investment, either domestic or foreign, and economic stagnation set in. People knew Burma was missing the Asian economic miracle by retaining a socialistic economy.

In 1988 mass demonstrations for free elections led to a massacre of student activists—in which 20,000 were killed—and a complete military takeover, although Ne Win remained a power behind the scenes. The ruling *junta* was at first called the State Law and Order Restoration Council (SLORC) but later called itself the State Peace and Development Council (SPDC).

Burma, which was officially renamed Myanmar in 1989, held free multiparty elections in May, 1990. The military junta's political front overwhelmingly lost the election but refused to hand over power. The opposition leader, Aung San Suu Kyi, who easily won the election, maintained her opposition. She supported a democratic state and a market economy. She was held under house arrest for next six years—until July of 1995—and then re–detained in September of 2000. Her supporters are routinely harassed or jailed. Aung Sang Suu Kyi was awarded the Nobel Peace Prize in 1991.

Nonetheless, SLORC made some efforts to open and liberalize the economy and even joined the Association of South East Asian Nations in 1999. But it stepped back from liberalization as it became clear that this might threaten its already fragile power base. Burma is the world's second–largest producer of illicit opium (after Afghanistan), with an estimated potential production in 1999 of 1,090 metric tons. This helps sustain its poor still partly socialist economy.

Burma pursued a heavily regulated economic system under Ne Win's socialist regime. It now has a mixed economy with private activity dominant in agriculture, light industry, and transport, but with substantial state control over activity, mainly in energy, heavy industry, and the rice trade. Government policy in the 1990s aimed at revitalizing the economy after three decades of socialist planning. Private activity increased in the early to mid–1990s, but then began to decline. Published estimates of Burma's foreign trade are greatly understated because of the volume of black–markets, illicit drugs, and border trade—particularly in opium. It has failed to achieve monetary and fiscal stability or provide a transparent legal system for business to operate. Burma remains a poor Asian country and living standards for the majority of Burmese have not improved over the past several decades.

By the 1990s, indeed, the path to modernization for most Asian societies appeared best illuminated by the economic structures of liberalism, which had displaced socialist doctrine over much of the continent.

African Socialism

Socialism was also taken to Africa by European–educated independence movement leaders and was long linked to Julius Nyerere of Tanzania. He began as an anti–colonial African nationalist, demanding the independence of Tanganyika, a United Nations trusteeship under British administration. Nyerere helped form the Tanganyika African National Union in 1954, and when the country became independent in 1961, Nyerere became Prime Minister and then President in December 1962. In 1964 it united with Zanzibar to form Tanzania, one of the poorest countries in the world.

Nyerere was born of peasants in a remote village, educated by Catholic missionaries, and went to Edinburgh University in Scotland. He was clever, educated, and very articulate. His commitment, then, to nonviolence and socialism made him not just an icon in his own country but in the wider world. Nyerere developed a Christian socialist ideology designed to organize a new society where there were hardly the rudiments of modern physical structures. He believed that poor Tanzanians could transform their country into a new model in which both traditions and British imperial legacies could be jettisoned.

Nyerere had visions of a village–based socialism in which modern techniques, such as the use of tractors and fertilizers, could be managed by village teams and used in communal fields, with the village selling and buying from the wider economy on a cooperative basis. He was inspiring but too often inspired the wrong policies. He was self–righteous and held dogmatically strong convictions. Since his opinions could not be challenged at the ballot or by a free press, his ideas were never effectively challenged. Nyerere inaugurated three platforms: a cultural system based on the Swahili language; a political system based on the one–party state; and an economic system based on an African approach to socialism, *ujamaa* (familyhood).

The cultural policy based on Kiswahili was the most durable. Tanzania became one of the few African countries to use an indigenous language in parliament and as the primary language of national business. Kiswahili was promoted in politics, administration, education, and the media. It became a major instrument of nation–building, the most lasting of Nyerere's legacies. Tanzanians hold Swahili, the national lan-

Julius Nyerere in 1977. (AP/Wide World Photos)

guage, above other languages, a factor that has helped prevent Tanzania from disintegrating into tribal conflict which has torn other African countries apart.

The political experiment of the one–party state produced exciting political theory but bad political practice. Nyerere tried to unify Tanzanians through the instrument of the one party state, under his Chama Cha Mapinduzi (CCM) party. He thought he knew best and took short cuts in judicial procedures that ended up incarcerating his opponents without trial in miserable conditions. The theory that the one–party state could be as democratic as the multiparty system and was more culturally suited to Africa, was intellectually stimulating but merely excused Nyerere's long period of rule. Tanzania became a multiparty state only after he left office in 1985.

Nyerere defined *ujamaa* as the basis of African socialism: "*ujamaa* is familyhood and an attitude of the mind that is needed to ensure people care for each other's welfare," he said. "In traditional African society, the people take care of the community and the community takes care of them, without exploiting each other." Under *ujamaa* the people were encouraged to move into "familyhood" villages, which formed the cornerstone of Tanzanian socialism. *ujamaa* did help Tanzanians to gain access to primary and secondary education irrespective of their religion, ethnicity, or economic status.

***Implementation of* ujamaa** He began his economic experiments in the early 1960s by making urgent appeals to his people. The economic experiment of *ujamaa* was launched with the Arusha Declaration on Socialism and Self–Reliance in 1967. It was greatly admired by some Western intellectuals and the governments of such Social Democratic countries as Sweden, Norway, and Denmark. By the early 1970s he decided he had preached enough and ordered peasants to move into collective villages. This uprooted people who had sometimes farmed the same scattered plots of land for hundreds of years. Some moved voluntarily, but others had to be pushed. Villagers were herded together where there was often no running water, good agricultural land, or roads.

By June 1975, 9.1 million people—or 65 percent of Tanzania's entire population—lived in about 7,000 villages. The implementation of *ujamaa* was largely completed in 1976. But the rapid rate of imposition of the scheme and the disruption of traditional agriculture caused social and economic problems for the country. For example, "Operation Maduka," was designed to replace private retailers with cooperatives. This was begun early in 1976, but its implementation caused distribution problems and shortages and the operation was slowed down.

Some problems were the result of *ujamaa*'s poor implementation. During the villagization program in 1971, people were forced to leave their homes and set up what were more like concentration camps than traditional African villages. But the villagization program did help the provision of social services by the government as the people settled together and shared schools and hospitals. But the *ujamaa* policy, under which private properties were nationalized, was extremely disruptive and did not produce rapid economic development. One result was that Tanzania soon became riddled with state industries, state banks, state plantations, and state marketing boards, all of which lost money.

Education in the villages, greatly assisted by foreign aid, had some success. Tanzania achieved a literacy rate of about 91 percent, the highest in Africa.

The Arusha Declaration had about twenty years in which to deliver results. By 1985, disenchantment was widespread and the end was near. Far from Tanzania being self–reliant, it was more dependent on aid than ever. Nyerere admitted that even in his home village *ujamaa* had not taken hold. In the end he was forced to abandon *ujamaa*, but considerable damage had been done. Since socialist *ujamaa* had left the country poorer, so liberalization, privatization, and the market were adopted to reform it. Nyerere's African

socialist economic policies were failures. *ujamaa* and villagization had kept Tanzania backward.

Nyerere blamed economic difficulties on inherited poverty, appalling weather, world recessions, awful neighboring regimes like Idi Amin in Uganda, and war in southern Africa for such continuous failures. Also, after he started supporting the southern African liberation movements in Angola, Zimbabwe, Namibia, and South Africa and his country paid a heavy price. But the hard task of developing policies that ensured that Tanzania worked well and developed was sacrificed to socialist doctrine. When he stepped down from power in 1985 his experimental socialist system, *ujamaa*, had clearly failed.

The African National Congress A more promising socialist experiment has been provided by The African National Congress (ANC), which took power in South Africa in 1994 and overthrew White rule and apartheid. The ANC was formed in 1912 to unite the African people and spearhead the struggle for fundamental political, social, and economic change. The ANC achieved a decisive democratic breakthrough in the 1994 elections, where it was given a firm mandate to negotiate a new democratic Constitution for South Africa. The new Constitution was adopted in 1996. The ANC was re–elected in 1999 to national and provincial government. This was Africa's best chance for socialist development, since the previous racist regime had used statist methods to create an industrialized economy, an appropriate base for a socialist society.

In 1994 the ANC adopted the Reconstruction and Development Programme (RDP) as the basic policy framework guiding the ANC in the transformation of South Africa. Since the country is easily the most developed in Africa, the ANC had some realistic opportunity to pursue democratic socialist program. In fact, the economy has stalled, social dissonance and violent crime have risen quickly, and the government has had to severely modify its socialist policies with a view to reviving the economy—so far with limited success.

Arab Socialism

In the immediate aftermath of independence, the Arab world was also swept by ideas of socialist development. Arab socialism was heavily influenced by an emphasis on the Government, the Public Sector, and the use of State Owned Enterprises (SOEs). These ideas were first tried in Egypt under Gamel Abdel Nasser (1918–1970) in the 1950s, and then given considerable support from the 1970s by the increases in the revenues of some Arab states provided by hefty

Gamel Abdel Nasser (left), riding in cavalcade with Muhammad Naguib. (Hulton/Getty Liaison Agency)

oil price increases, as well as the involvement of the Soviet Union during the period of its strategic expansion, 1970–1985. The role of the state in the national economies of the Arab countries was as an economic agency and regulating body.

As an economic agency the state influenced resource allocation and acted as an investor and producer of goods and services. In the production of goods and services, the state often replaced, competed with, or shared with the private sector in these activities. State Owned Enterprises represented the basic instrument of state engagement in the field of economic activities. As a regulatory agent, the state also intervened in the activities of the private sector, mixed sector, cooperatives, and foreign–owned enterprises.

As in many other developing countries, in the Arab countries the state played a central and pivotal role in their national economies from independence until the 1990s. The centrality of the state in the national economies was not peculiar to the Arab countries of the Middle East and North Africa, and it came about gradually as a consequence of the interaction between many international, regional, and national factors.

Influence of the National Charter   After a series of nationalizations from the mid 1950s, including the Suez Canal, Egypt embarked on a program of social

reform on the basis of "Arab Socialism," which was introduced in the "National Charter" of 1962. According to the ideology of Arab Socialism, the whole society was expected to rally behind the government, which would, it was claimed, pursue the interests of all. This was translated into public ownership of public services, commercial activities (such as banking and insurance), communications, heavy, large and medium–sized industries, and of foreign trade. In Egypt the best–known case was the Suez Canal. A set of "socialist laws" were enforced, to put into practice what was envisaged by the Charter and by Arab Socialism.

Soon the influence of such developments in Egypt began to emerge in other Arab countries, namely Syria and Iraq. With the formation of United Arab Republic (UAR) between Syria and Egypt (1958–1961) all Syrian banks and insurance companies and three industrial enterprises were fully nationalized, and twenty four others were partially nationalized in June 1961. Though most of these nationalizations were lifted after the end of the UAR, more nationalizations and re–nationalizations took place in 1964 and 1965.

In Iraq, many "socialist laws" were enforced in July 1964 to increase the role of public sector to facilitate economic planning and implement government policies, and also (it was hoped) to accelerate the economic development of the country. A new "Economic

Organization" was created intending to develop the national economy by virtue of its activities in the public sector. All banks, both national and foreign, were nationalized in 1964.

Elsewhere in the Arab World, other regimes and rulers became committed to strong government expansion into the public sector. After Algeria gained independence in July 1962, attention was directed towards the nationalization of banks and of farms formerly owned and managed by the French settlers. The land of Algerians who had collaborated with the French regime prior to independence were confiscated in 1964. Socialist policies expanded elsewhere as the Ba'ath socialist party recaptured power in Iraq in 1968, Muammar Al–Qaddafi (1942–) overthrew the monarchy in Libya in 1969, and a Marxist group came to power in South Yemen in 1969.

These socialist trends were not peculiar to radical regimes. In Tunisia, for example, the 1960s was characterized as the decade of "state–led industrialization" where the state established more than eighty public sector industrial enterprises, producing everything from sugar and clothes to phosphates and tractors. Extensive nationalization of private and industrial enterprises was also undertaken in the Sudan into the 1970s. By the end of the 1960s, the public sector enterprise had consolidated its position in many, but not all, Arab countries. This second stage ended with increased involvement of the state in various aspects of economic life.

The third phase ran during the 1970s to the early 1980s, a period of extreme liquidity in the oil–producing states, and brought with it mixed developments among the Arab countries at large and within some of the new industrial enterprises owned by the state. What emerged were many joint ventures in the oil and other sectors, as well as the establishment of many inter–governmental and non–governmental organizations. This development in itself meant increasing the role and importance of the state even beyond the political boundaries of the particular country concerned.

But by the 1980s many Arab socialist countries, particularly those without oil revenues, found their economies deteriorating, external debt increasing, the balance of payment's worsening, the budgetary deficit rising, and that they were financially unable to sustain the expansion of the public sector. This had happened in spite of the development boom in the oil rich Arab countries.

Calls for change   One of the first initiatives against the state–dominated economy in the Arab countries took place, again, in Egypt in the mid–1970s, with the

development of the *Infitah*, or policy of the "open door." The then–President and Nasser's successor, Anwar el Sadat (1918–1981), issued the October Paper in 1974 according to which legislation was introduced to provide incentives for private investment (domestic and foreign), to open foreign trade to private companies, to eliminate most controls on workers' emigration, and to reduce government control over the agricultural and industrial sectors. This was designed to end the stagnation into which Arab socialism had taken Egypt.

During this phase, many Arab countries began the process of structural adjustment. But this attempt was abandoned in the following year due to the ensuing price increases and the social unrest that followed those measures. Then, in October 1980, Morocco embarked on a second stabilization program and concluded an agreement with the IMF in which the food subsidies were reduced.

By the early 1980s, the public sector domination phase had reached the end. A privatization and liberalization phase had begun, and this continued until the twenty first century. The public sector and many state–owned enterprises have been on the retreat and Arab socialism went on the defensive. Developments at the international, regional and national levels encouraged the move towards privatization, and consolidated the position of its advocates.

At the international level, the calls for privatization of public enterprise became stronger into the 1980s with Margaret Thatcher (1925–) in power in Great Britain and Ronald Reagan (1911–) in the U.S., and they influenced the IMF and the World Bank. The outbreak of the international and mostly Third World debt crisis in 1982, and the need to re–schedule the debt, made it easier for these institutions to insist on Stabilization and Structural Adjustment Programmes to be implemented by those countries seeking their assistance. Many governments found it impossible to continue with their increasing budgetary deficits. This was coupled with further declines in export revenues due to the deterioration of commodity export prices, terms of trade, and shrinking markets. A continuing decline in foreign aid donations after the Cold War and falling private foreign capital inflows made the situation even worse for many countries with fragile economies.

The collapse of the former Soviet Union furnished advocates of privatization in the Arab countries with an unprecedented argument, and thus provided support for the move toward privatization both there and worldwide. These dramatic developments also had a direct impact on the Arab and other Third World countries, who had relied on the Soviet bloc for economic assistance and cooperation. Assistance ended and their former Soviet bloc aid donors began to compete with them for Western aid, private capital investment, and officially supported export guaranties.

Socialism in Australia and New Zealand

The British colonized Australia and New Zealand in a lengthy process that started in 1788 with a British convict settlement at what is now the city of Sydney. Overland exploration and further coastal settlements then produced seven colonies that became self–governing in the 1850s. In 1901 the six Australian colonies formed the Commonwealth of Australia and in 1907 New Zealand became an independent Dominion. At the beginning of the twentieth century these two countries were famous for the success of their socialist experiments.

Whereas the U.S. Constitution had been written at a time when liberalism was a dominant ideology among English–speaking intellectuals and politicians, Australia and New Zealand formed their political structures when socialism was a doctrine sweeping Britain.

The early years of Australia's history comprised a parliamentary contest between the growing power of the Australian Labor Party (ALP) and the dominant social liberals led by Alfred Deakin (1856–1919). The result was an interventionist state, which regulated foreign trade through tariffs, set and enforced wage rates for workers, and controlled immigration. Later, the federal and state governments extended their ownership of businesses to encompass ports, banks, utilities, and shops. During the 1930s depression this was further developed into the state's regulation of many agricultural products, including wheat and wool, by marketing boards.

Not surprisingly, the development of nearby New Zealand took a similar path. While the New Zealand Labour Party was only formed twenty–five years after the ALP in 1916, it arguably became even more dominant. In 1935 the First New Zealand Labour government was formed and, in addition to introducing similar regulatory agencies to Australia, developed what may have become the world's first welfare state by 1949. Its measures included a complete free education system, universal health care, and pension provisions for the aged, unemployed, and infirm.

These socialist experiments were widely admired in Europe and attracted the attention and visits of socialist intellectuals, including Albert Metin, later French Minister for Labour who wrote the admiring *Socialism Without Doctrines*, and the Fabian Socialist Webbs, who left behind *The Webb's Australian Diary*. Needless to say, Lenin was scathing about the collaborationist nature of these socialist parties and quickly established opposing communist parties in the 1920s, which attracted only limited support. Visiting Americans, like author Mark Twain (1835–1910), were also less impressed by what they regarded as these excessively statist societies, as David Mosler and Bob Catley describe in *America and Americans in Australia*.

Australia and New Zealand were secure, social democratic societies for their White colonists, with extensive welfare systems and short hours of work. These conditions were underpinned by extremely democratic political systems, which were the first to give the vote to women. They were also rather intolerant of their indigenous communities, to whom socialist doctrines did not extend. In the mid–1970s both countries elected Labour governments, led by Gough Whitlam and Norman Kirk (1923–1974), who in many respects extended these Social Democratic regimes to include indigenous peoples.

The considerable affluence of these societies was underpinned by the efficient production of primary commodities—like wheat, wool, meat, and minerals—on territory newly discovered or conquered from indigenous peoples. During the 1960s and 1970s prosperity was maintained only with increasing difficulty, as the price of these commodities became less assured and markets more difficult to access. Both countries faced difficult economic problems in the 1980s, including stagflation and external trade deficits.

In the 1980s, both countries started to dismantle their statist and social democratic economic structures and joined the movement towards liberalization. In both cases, these reforms were undertaken by Labour governments. International trade was deregulated, economic regulatory agencies were dismantled, and many state–owned enterprises were privatized. Although the two countries often followed different polices, the pursuit of liberalizing reform was common to both. They continued to face difficulties in reorienting their economies to meet the challenges of the global economy of the twenty first century, but neither could be properly described any longer as socialist in structure.

The Neo Liberal Counter–Revolution, 1975–1991

In the mid–1970s the developed countries of the Organisation for Economic Cooperation and Development (OECD) underwent a severe economic dislocation. It was easily the worst since 1945. During the deep recession of 1974–75 the social democracies of Western Europe, Japan, North America and Australasia experienced increased inflation, negative growth, a large jump in unemployment and, for most, a severe imbalance in their domestic fiscal and foreign trade accounts. This became known as the crisis of stagflation.

There ensued a long intellectual debate about the causes of this problem. The OECD officials attributed the crisis to a series of singular events, which coincided and were unlikely to be repeated in that form. In some instances this was true, including the sharp rise in oil prices which the exporting states had been able to achieve by the coincidence of an Arab–Israeli War and a prolonged OECD dependence on that commodity. But there were also criticisms of the policy reactions of the OECD countries and indeed of their policy regime structures, which seemed for long unable to deal with the problems that had emerged. In particular, an old critique of Social Democracy emerged in a new guise.

Liberals had long held that the extension of the state into the economy and its resultant politicization would endanger the operation of economic calculation and damage the maintenance of economic prosperity. They had maintained this critique throughout the long post–war boom during which Social democracy had been extended in the manner previously indicated throughout much of the developed world. While growth was maintained, the liberal critique was broadly ignored. It then re–emerged as an explanation of the problem of stagflation and a policy recommendation for its resolution. Neo–liberalism revived in the Anglophone world and the U.S. economist and Nobel Prize winner Milton Friedman (1912–) became its most–celebrated advocate.

Friedman and the liberals argued that inflation was essentially the product of a rapid growth in the supply of money. Since money was a commodity, if it flooded the market its price would drop and all other prices, expressed in money terms, would rise. This had happened in the mid–1970s throughout the OECD. The solution was to arrest the growth of the money supply. Policy makers gradually took this on board into the 1980s and inflation receded. Corollaries of this policy, however, included stopping the growth of the state sector, abandoning budget deficits, deregulating domestic economies and foreign trade, and, later, privatizing SOEs. All these policies were adopted to varying degrees in the OECD states during the 1980s.

The result was winding back of the Social Democratic regimes. This was not undertaken at a similar pace or with the same intensity in each state. In the English–speaking countries, the liberal reforms of Social Democracy went furthest. In Great Britain, where arguably the crisis of stagflation hit deepest, Margaret Thatcher was elected Conservative Prime Minister in 1979 and while in office during the next eleven years wound back the level of state regulation and subsidies, the size of the state–owned sector, the power of the labor unions, and the commitment to full employment. The next Labour government under Prime Minister Tony Blair, elected in 1997, did not overturn these basic reforms.

In less–populated English–speaking countries—Canada, Australia, Ireland, and New Zealand—similar processes occurred. In each, SOEs were privatized, economies and markets deregulated, trade restrictions abolished, and the size of the state sector reduced. In general, this group of countries entered the twenty–first century with the smallest state sectors and the highest growth rates of the OECD countries. But they mostly retained a modest socialist structure, consistent with providing a social safety net for their citizens.

The developed countries of Western Europe were also influenced by these trends, but did not undertake the reforms nearly as far. They became known as the "Social Charter" capitalist counties who continued to subscribe to the European Union Charter on labor regulation and welfare provision. They retained large welfare systems, many SOEs, a state sector of up to half their economies, and extensive provisions and benefits to labor. Perhaps as a result, at the start of the twenty first century these countries had slower growth rates and higher unemployment levels than their Anglo–Saxon counterparts.

Collapse of the Soviet Union

As the heartland of Social Democracy was undergoing reform, so the countries of Communist socialism effectively collapsed. After the Second World War, Soviet–style communism had expanded into Eastern Europe and east Asia. Centered on the Soviet Union, it then created an alternative system of states based on the model created by Stalin in the 1930s. In the ensuing conflict with the West, known as the Cold War, its doctrines were then extended into many Third World countries, such that by the late 1970s it appeared a formidable social formation indeed. Nonetheless, within a decade it faced economic decline, geographic contraction, and finally, strategic defeat.

The collapse of the Soviet Union and its system took place in three phases. First, the client and allied regimes of the Soviet bloc were abandoned and their subsidies withdrawn in the late 1980s, thereby precipitating an economic crisis in many of them. Secondly, the Soviet garrisons and political guarantees to the puppet regimes of Eastern Europe were withdrawn in 1989, and all of the regimes of the "Peoples Democracies" collapsed almost immediately. Thirdly, the Soviet Union itself disintegrated into fifteen non–communist states in December, 1991.

The collapse of the Soviet Union was accelerated by the strategic confrontation and arms race opened by Ronald Reagan in the early 1980s, which the Soviet Union found itself unable to afford. But it could not compete because its economic and political structures were frozen in the socialist forms of the 1930s, implicitly created by nineteenth–century doctrines. The rigidity of the Soviet planning system made it unable to adapt to new technologies and processes. Its political dictatorship made it unable to change and provide the mechanisms for economic transformation. By the 1980s, Soviet communism was too conservative and rigid to survive. The liberal reforms of Mikhail Gorbachev in the late 1980s were insufficient to save it, but enough to generate its demise.

This marked the end of the long socialist experiment that had begun in 1917. The Soviet Union had effectively and/or ideologically underpinned the other variants of socialism, which had been created throughout the world in the period following the Revolution. The support that the Soviet state had provided—financially for communist parties, ideologically for philosophers, politically for activists, economically for state planners and SOE managers, and militarily for revolutionaries—disappeared. With it went one of the most significant props that the socialist movement had had since its modern incarnation two centuries earlier.

Certainly, socialist states continued to exist after 1991, but their utility as a model for continuing progress for the doctrine was greatly diminished by their character. The People's Republic of China was a poor Third World country, although it demonstrated impressive rates of growth. But by 2001 it was clear that these had been achieved by abandoning socialist doctrines and adopting market mechanisms, deployed in the revealing phrase "socialism with Chinese characteristics."

ANALYSIS AND CRITICAL RESPONSE

In theory, socialism is a political theory with the best of intentions—the elimination of private property and the sharing of economic resources. However, it has been difficult to maintain because it goes against the concepts of freedom and individuality. Not many people want to be forced to move into farming villages or turn their crops over to the government instead of selling them on an open market. All forms of socialism run into problems when they are put into action. "The social democracy form of socialism is difficult to maintain because it runs head on into the political pressure of democracy—which replaces abstract issues of fairness with the practical calculations of interest–group politics—and the economic pressure of open markets," wrote Victoria Postrel in a 1999 issue of *Reason* magazine. Moreover, socialism has a hard time shaking the negative associations brought on by the experiments in Soviet Russia and Third World countries. Too many versions of socialism take over areas of everyday life beyond economics.

The Problems With African and Arab Socialism

Why did Julius Nyerere's African Socialist policy of *ujamaa* fail in Tanzania? The problem essentially stemmed from the fact that Marxist doctrines assumed that socialism would be implemented in already developed societies. Many of the former colonies of the Third World were in fact very poor and often dominated by primary production with low levels of education and labor productivity. In these circumstances, socialist programs deriving from European circumstances had to try to produce a more egalitarian society and develop the economy at the same time. These were often difficult objectives to reconcile. Tanzania was and is one of the poorest countries in the world and faced this dilemma.

Nonetheless, in the 1960s and 1970s Tanzania gained much political respect, chiefly due to Nyerere's political ideas. He was personally uncorrupted by fame or position and remained throughout his life self–effacing and unpretentious. Since Nyerere's death in 1999 the positive aspects of *ujamaa*, particularly enhanced national unity, has received more credit, even from Ali Hassan Mwinyi, Nyerere's successor who abandoned socialism and began liberalization in 1985. Tanzania is one of the very few African countries that has not experienced serious tribal conflict.

Of course, *ujamaa* was not the only form of socialism that ran into problems. Egypt was a prime example of an economy ruined largely by its own self–destructive Arab Socialist policies. In 1979, with the conclusion of the Israel–Egypt peace treaty, there were predictions and expectations of large–scale Middle East trade; multinational infrastructure projects; joint ventures involving Egyptian, Israeli, and American or European investors; technology transfers; and a reallocation of resources from the military to civilian pursuits. But for various reasons, many unrelated to the Camp David agreements, since the 1980s the Egyptian economy has stagnated and per capita income has declined.

The poor performance of the economy, especially in the first half of the 1990s, was particularly disconcerting, in view of the massive financial aid which Egypt received in those years. A major part of Egypt's $50 billion debt was cancelled; interest rates were lowered and payments reduced on the remaining debt; and "Official Development Assistance" from various industrialized countries was raised from $1.8 billion in 1989—before the Gulf War—to $5.7 billion in 1990 and $10 billion in 1992. Egypt's economic problems stem largely from the legacy of "Arab Socialism" instituted by President Nasser in the 1960s. The state–owned industries, especially in manufacturing, suffered from gross inefficiency, over–manning, and very low productivity and profitability.

The loss–making state–owned firms were a serious drain on the treasury. Nasser guaranteed jobs to all university graduates and demobilized soldiers in the civil service or in state–owned enterprises. This policy was continued by Sadat and by his successor Hosni Mubarak (1929–) during the 1980s. Subsidies were expanded under Sadat and maintained by Mubarak. Price controls, foreign exchange regulations (including multiple–exchange rates), wage policies, and other measures added more distortions to the economy. Egyptian corruption did not begin with Arab Socialism, but Nasser's policies multiplied the opportunities and inducements. And the wide gap between the few rich and the many poor widened to dangerous dimensions, fuelled by widespread corruption.

Since 1991 Egypt has made some important monetary and fiscal changes in addition to alterations in its foreign exchange controls but it has been reluctant to embark on a large–scale privatization program to get rid of the bloated and very costly public sector enterprises. Politically powerful interests who benefit from "milking" the public sector oppose privatization plans. The public sector workers and managers fear that privatization would be followed by massive dismissals. As a result, about two–thirds of industrial production, together with oil extraction and refining remains in the public sector. Egyptian efforts to liberalize the economy have been very limited.

There was a similar problem in the Soviet Union, as well in other socialist countries. In the early twenty–first century, China faces the daunting prospect of either privatizing its SOEs, with the re-

sulting labor shedding and fear of political destabilization, or having the rest of the economy carry a socialist and inefficient millstone around its neck. Another problem is the massive public payroll common to socialist economies, involving literally millions of employees with little or nothing to do. Egypt has four million public servants comprising 23 percent of the labor force and another eight percent employed by public sector enterprises. In the public sector it is virtually impossible to sack anybody and labor laws also make it very difficult to dismiss private sector employees. This results in low productivity, financial losses, and depressed incomes. In the years since the conclusion of the peace agreements between Israel and Egypt in 1979, economic progress has been slight. Egypt is a modernized and more populous, but stagnant, Pharaonic state.

Socialism in the Third World has proven to be a difficult project. The Again, Marxist–Socialist doctrine assumed that capitalism would develop a country before socialism took it over, and socialists found their own doctrines only partly useful for providing a model for rapid development in undeveloped Third World countries. Indigenous socialism fell back on public ownership and collectivized land, which often impeded economic growth. The state forms which Third World socialists utilized, were almost uniformly dictatorial. By the twenty first century socialist regimes in the Third World were commonly reverting to the market as a means of escaping the problems their doctrines had devised. A similar pattern was evident in the more developed societies.

The Future: Socialism under Globalization

At the end of the Cold War in 1991 the doctrines of socialism faced considerable problems. The Soviet bloc had disintegrated because of its own failures to produce a viable alternative structure to democratic liberal capitalism. In the social democracies of Europe and elsewhere they had been exposed to a vigorous attack by the revival of the liberal critique. The remaining communist states were adopting liberal oriented reforms. In the Third World privatization and de–regulation was replacing statist, socialist development models almost everywhere. It seemed that the high tide of socialism had passed.

This process was accompanied by the evolution of a substantial international economy in a process often referred to as "globalization." The global economy was the manifestation of international market transactions increasingly overtaking those that had been nation based. A growing section of national economies become locked into a global trading structure rather than being confined to their own domestic market. States found that a growing proportion of their economies were devoted to foreign trade; that more of their capital markets were derived from foreign investors; that more of their own investments went into other economies; that more of their commodities were international brand name products; and that a growing proportion of their labor forces were internationally mobile.

This was a process that derived form three sources. First, the U.S. had been a determined sponsor of an international regime designed to produce a free market in capital, products, and culture for most of the twentieth century and after 1991 pursued it energetically as the only remaining superpower. Next, technological change increasingly permitted the global organization of production, distribution and exchange. This was evident in cheaper transport systems, including bulk carriers, containerization, and wide–bodied jetliners; in better data transmission, which created a global finance market; and in enhanced communications involving the fax, mobile phones, and the Internet. And finally, the only alternative economic system collapsed with the Soviet Union and its major successor state, the Russian Federation, became an advocate of liberal capitalism, not social democracy.

By 2001 these processes were creating a global economy. The institutional agencies of globalization, particularly the U.S. Treasury, the World Trade Organization, the World Bank and the IMF, promoted a state regime policy structure which was known as the "Washington Consensus." As David Mosler and Bob Catley describe in *Global America*, this involved free trade, deregulation, privatization of government assets, free movement for capital and investment, and, by the late 1990s, transparent representative government. This program contrasted sharply with the doctrines of socialism which—whatever its claims to internationalism—had evolved as an intellectual guideline for state policy makers.

At the dawn of the twenty–first century, it appears that socialism is an idea whose time has come and gone. However, many writers remind us that history comes and goes in cycles, and it was not even a century ago that philosophers and world leaders spoke of the coming death of capitalism. "The thesis that the end of socialism does not have a historical basis," states James Petras in a 1992 issue of *Canadian Dimension*. "At best, it is a reflection on a moment of retreat and reversals." And yet, it remains to be seen if and how socialism can adapt and survive into its

third century as a serious competitor to other political ideas and social formations.

TOPICS FOR FURTHER STUDY

- How do Marxism and Fabian socialism compare?
- Why and how did the doctrines of socialism became popular in Australia but not in the United States?
- Is socialism is an appropriate doctrine for Third World countries? Why or why not?

BIBLIOGRAPHY

Sources

Berki, R.N. *Socialism,*. Needham, Massachusetts: Prentice Hall, 1995.

Catley, Bob. *Globalising Australian Capitalism,* Cambridge University Press, 1996.

Mosler, David, and Bob Catley. *Global America: Imposing Liberalism on a Recalcitrant World,* Praeger, 2000.

Petras, James. "A Leftist Resurgence" in *Canadian Dimension*, March 1992 (vol. 26, no. 2). Canadian Dimension Publication, Ltd., 1992.

Postrel, Virginia. "After Socialism" in *Reason*, November 1999 (vol. 31, issue 6). Reason Foundation, 1999.

Further Readings

Hayek, F.A. *The Road to Serfdom,* 1944. A critical evaluation of the application of socialist doctrines to prosperous capitalist economies by one of the leading critics of socialist thought.

Lipset, Seymour Martin and Gary Marks. *It Didn't Happen Here: Why Socialism Failed in the United States,* W.W. Norton & Co., 2001. An explanation of why socialism as an ideology and a movement has been weaker in the United States than arguably any other developed country.

Morris, William. *Why I Am a Socialist,* 1884. Morris was the precursor of the Fabian Socialists in Britain, and this is one of the most forceful statements of a committed Democratic Socialist.

Sassoon, Donald. *One Hundred Years of Socialism: The West European Left in the Twentieth Century,* New Press, 1998. A clear account of the recent history of socialist movements in Western Europe.

SEE ALSO

Communism, Marxism, Utopianism

Totalitarianism

OVERVIEW

Political systems are often categorized according to the degree of freedom they afford their citizens or according to their degree of their responsiveness to citizen input. Democracies allow the most input; totalitarian systems stand at the extreme opposite end of the continuum. They offer the least amount of freedom and pay the least amount of attention to the voice of the people. In fact, as the name implies, totalitarian governments try to control the totality of human experience. A true totalitarian ruler attempts to take charge not only of the public life of the people, but also their personal and emotional lives. Until the advent of modern forms of travel, communication, and coercion, it would have been impossible to contemplate the total control of anything but a very small group of people. But, with mass media, electronic surveillance equipment, and prisons and torture facilities boasting the efficiency of advanced industrial operations, totalitarianism seemed within the grasp of leaders such as Hitler, Stalin, and Mao—men with a limitless desire for control. Totalitarianism is a form of government that emerged only in the twentieth century. So rapid was its rise, that by 1940, many people in Europe and America feared that totalitarianism might be able to overwhelm democratic peoples and governments. That fear proved to be unjustified because, by the end of the twentieth century, no country in the world practiced a full–blown totalitarian form of governance.

WHO CONTROLS GOVERNMENT? Dictator

HOW IS GOVERNMENT PUT INTO POWER? Overthrow or Revolution

WHAT ROLES DO THE PEOPLE HAVE? Devote life to dictator and the state

WHO CONTROLS PRODUCTION OF GOODS? The state

WHO CONTROLS DISTRIBUTION OF GOODS? The state

MAJOR FIGURES Friedrich Nietzsche; Adolf Hitler

HISTORICAL EXAMPLE OF GOVERNMENT Egypt, 1952–present

CHRONOLOGY

c. 2600–2200 B.C.: Egyptian Old Kingdom is ruled by pharaohs.

c. 1700 B.C.: Hammurabi rules.

c. 1028 B.C.: The Chou Dynasty controls northern China.

1507–1547: Henry VIII of England reigns as king of England.

1740–86: Frederick II, also known as Frederick the Great, rules as king of Prussia.

1821: Frederick Hegel writes *The Philosophy of Right*.

1883: Friedrich Nietzsche writes *Thus Spake Zarathustra*.

1939: Getulio Vargas is placed in power by the Brazilian military.

1948: The Purified Nationalist Party wins the parliamentary elections in South Africa.

1952: Gamal Nasser takes power in Egypt through a coup.

1979: The Ayatollah Khomeini establishes an Islamic theocracy in Iran.

Before the rise of totalitarianism in the 1920s and 1930s, even the most powerful and oppressive governments would have been classified as authoritarian rather than totalitarian. Authoritarian governments acted in arbitrary and autocratic ways, but they did not attempt to exert control over every facet of people's lives. In the 1500s, 1600s, and 1700s, a number of authoritarian regimes in Europe were headed by monarchs claiming absolute authority. Generally, however, they did not pretend to exercise absolute power or control. Almost to the end of the twentieth century, many Latin American regimes were headed by military leaders who ruled in a highly authoritarian manner. But, they did not try to intervene in the daily lives of citizens with the same degree of intensity characteristic of totalitarian governments. In Asia, for thousands of years, powerful monarchs and military rulers demanded compliance from their people. Like many other authoritarian leaders throughout history, they re-

quired absolute obedience from the people and they exercised the absolute power of life or death over their subjects. But, until the emergence of Maoism in China, they demanded compliance only in a limited portion of their subjects' lives and they used the sword only against people who posed a direct threat to their sovereignty or wealth.

At the beginning of the twenty–first century, most authoritarian governments were concentrated in the Middle East and Asia where monarchies and strong men or strong women continued to hold sway. In many of these authoritarian systems, for example Iraq, powerful leaders hoped to increase the wealth and military power of their countries without having to cope with the turmoil they believed accompanies political openness. To a large extent, those leaders cared little about the private sentiments of the people, as long as the people did not publicly oppose the policies of government.

HISTORY

The Ancient World

The ancient world was marked by a number of very large–scale states that exercised unchallenged control over some aspects of their peoples' lives. In ancient Egypt, Mesopotamia, and China, powerful dynasties were able to use their power to mobilize vast numbers of people to participate in extensive public works schemes. Complex irrigation systems, enormous monuments, and large–scale agricultural operations were some of the projects that provided the economic and political foundations for these ancient empires. The social and psychological distance between the leaders and the common people was so great that the rulers could claim near divine power and stature. The authoritarian nature of these rulers' governments enabled them to provide their subjects with a level of security and economic well being otherwise unattainable at the time. Peoples of the ancient world could not increase their productive capacity through highly advanced technologies and machines that came only with the modern industrial revolution. But, the coordination they achieved by offering obedience to a despotic ruler allowed them to focus their energies in ways that resulted in astonishing material and social achievements.

The ancient despotic regimes were limited to regions where people were forced to settle in close proximity and where they had little chance to live elsewhere. For example, in ancient Egypt and Mesopotamia, people had to remain close to the major rivers in order to farm. This reality made it easier for rulers to exert tighter control over their subjects. What sets the ancient despotic regimes apart from modern totalitarian systems is the fact that the ancient governments never sought to mobilize the people politically. Ordinary people were expected to be nonpolitical and uninvolved in the ceremonies and rituals of the capital and the court. Common people were required to work for the state, not to identify with or have affection for the regime.

Although Ancient Greece witnessed the rise of democracy in Athens, many city states, and even Athens at times, were ruled by authoritarian regimes. Sometimes the regimes were headed by tyrants, leaders who had seized power and who had the power of life and death over their subjects. In Sparta, the entire citizen population between the age of twenty and thirty was mobilized into military groups called "phalanxes." The demands of these groups controlled an individual's entire life. The men lived in barracks, took common meals, and were forbidden to marry. Many Greeks admired the strength and discipline of Sparta that enabled its people to defend themselves effectively and to exert their control over neighboring regions.

Ancient Rome functioned as a republic for more than 400 years before the republican form of government gave way to an autocratic imperial structure. The transformation came in response to internal tensions and external challenges. As the Roman city–state expanded to dominate all of what is now Italy and then extend its control over the entire Mediterranean region, ambitious generals wielded increased power. Competing with the Senate, a body composed of hereditary aristocrats, the generals based their authority on an appeal to the masses. Although the Republic would not have measured up to the standards of modern democracies, Rome moved even more decisively to authoritarian rule with the establishment of the Empire under Augustus, who ruled from 27 B.C. until his death in 14 A.D. But, even under the emperors, Rome functioned as an authoritarian not as a totalitarian system. In large part, that was true because the Roman Empire regarded itself as a society governed by laws that protected the rights of the citizens. Furthermore, at least some of the emperors believed strongly in the need to submit themselves to the rules of virtue and morality. No matter how powerful their office, such men regarded themselves as servants and protectors of the people.

The Middle Ages

In the Middle Ages, many European rulers thought of themselves as following in the footsteps of the great leaders of Rome. Virtue and law were now

Frederick the Great of Prussia (Corbis-Bettmann)

defined by the church rather than by an appeal to ancient traditions or Roman gods. But the concept of ruling according to higher principles remained an important theoretical concept. While the claim to rule on behalf of natural law or divine ordination imposed moral restrictions on political behavior, medieval leaders made no concession to the voice of the people.

By the fifteenth century, a shift in rhetoric and practice took place. Starting with the Renaissance, princes and even churchmen in Italy regarded themselves as unchecked by morality, rules, or the people when it came to political behavior. The only limits on a prince was competition from other ambitious leaders or the threat of revolt from an oppressed citizenry. Morality was no longer an important constraint regulating political conduct.

After about 1500, early European nation states increasingly were ruled by powerful autocratic leaders who attempted to impose linguistic, religious, and political uniformity over divided societies. Assertive monarchs such as Henry VIII of England, his daughter Elizabeth I, and Louis XIV of France; divine right kings such as James I and Charles I of England; and enlightened despots such as Catherine the Great of Russia and Frederick II of Prussia struggled to build the foundations of strong states. While their sometimes ruthless tactics resembled those of Renaissance rulers, their goals were the creation and protection of nations or empires, not just self promotion and personal power.

The Eighteenth and Ninteenth Centuries

Frederick the Great, who ruled Prussia from 1740 to 1786, is one example of these autocratic rulers. Frederick focused much of his energies on developing Prussia as a strong military state with a highly professional bureaucracy. The military and the bureaucracy served as two of the most important sources of his extensive authoritarian power. A man of the Enlightenment, Frederick attempted to rule according to the highest principles of reason. To some extent, he embodied the principles of Aristotle's ideal monarchy, where one individual ruled for the good of the whole. Although Frederick did not consult citizen voices, he tried to rule in a way that would benefit the people. Some of the benevolent and progressive measures he introduced in Prussia were the abolishment of using torture on criminals, strict prohibitions against bribing judges, the establishment of state–supported elementary schools, and the promotion of religious tolerance. On his own vast personal estates, which he owned as a feudal lord, he did away with capital punishment, reduced the amount of time peasants had to spend working for him instead of for themselves, and introduced scientific farming and forestry practices that increased production. In the nineteenth century, Otto von Bismarck, the autocratic German Chancellor continued in the tradition of Frederick. During his tenure in office from 1871 until 1890, Bismarck introduced many progressive social programs while working tirelessly to unify Germany and strengthen his country's military power.

The Modern World

In the twentieth century, a new kind of autocracy emerged. Using the tools of modern transportation, communication, surveillance, and psychology, men such as Stalin, Hitler, Mussolini, and Mao were able to control millions of peoples' lives in ways that would have been unthinkable or impossible in previous centuries. The political innovations of these men introduced a new type of governing that was given the label "totalitarian." Vicious, aggressive, and ideological, totalitarianism created its own morality. Mobilizing their citizens through propaganda and thought control, totalitarian leaders appeared to be intent on dominating other parts of the world as well as reshaping their own countries. In every case, totalitarian leaders were aggressively anti–democratic and anti–religious. They allowed no space for individual thought or criticism. Consequently, they allowed no room for an appeal either to individual liberties or to supernatural truth.

By the end of World War II, totalitarianism had collapsed in Germany and Italy. With the death of Stalin in 1953, totalitarianism in the form of Stalinism began to give way to authoritarianism in the Soviet Union as well. A similar pattern obtained in China after the death of Mao in 1976. In the Soviet Union, especially by the time Mikhail Gorbachev came to power in 1985, even authoritarianism came to be regarded as increasingly dysfunctional. At the beginning of the twenty–first century, authoritarian systems persisted in the Middle East; some parts of Asia such as China, Malaysia, and Vietnam; and Cuba. But, authoritarianism was increasingly under a shadow. South Africa, a racially divided nation governed in accordance with the principles of apartheid, voluntarily shifted to complete democracy in 1994. Even Iran, a nation run as a theocracy (where God is the ultimate ruler) was shifting to a pattern of incorporating popular opinion into government policy.

Iran Iran is illustrative of two important types of contemporary authoritarianism, one the more conventional modernizing authoritarianism, the other an authoritarianism guided by a fundamentalist ideology. The latter form has seemed especially threatening to people in the west. From 1941 until 1979, Iran was governed by an autocratic monarchy under Shah Muhammad Reza Pahlavi. Accepting military and economic aid from the United States, the Shah set about to modernize his nation. A key part of his policy was limiting the influence of the imams, Muslim clerics who had great authority over the lives and thoughts of the people. Although Iran witnessed rapid economic growth that dramatically transformed the cities and greatly strengthened the country's infrastructure, not everyone benefited from the changes. Small shopkeepers, small farmers, and ordinary workers sometimes found life to be more difficult. Furthermore, the westernization that accompanied the economic changes was not welcomed by the conservative and largely Shiiti Muslim population. Iranians who were troubled by what was happening in their country often blamed the United States for America was the Shah's main supporter. However, because Iran operated as an authoritarian regime, the voices of citizen disapproval had no constructive outlet.

The Ayatollah Ruhollah Khomeini, an exiled radical Islamic cleric, took advantage of the growing discontentment to incite a revolution that succeeded in overthrowing the Shah in 1979. Now, Iran was governed by a new type of authoritarianism, a theocracy. Religious leaders, who interpreted God's will as revealed in the Koran, came to play a major role in politics. Mullahs (clerics) sat as powerful members of parliament. A

Council of Guardians, Iran's supreme court, was a body of clerics who used the Koran, not the constitution, as the ultimate authority. Around the country, the Islamic Republican Party, the official party of the revolution, depended on clerics a party agents. At the top of the entire system, the Ayatollah Khomeini had the final word. And his word was based upon his concept of what God told him to say or do. Consequently, the Ayatollah's pronouncements could not be challenged.

The highly authoritarian nature of the Islamic Republic was evident in its internal and external policies. Internally, the Ayatollah's government moved harshly against dissidents. Intellectuals, people associated with the Shah's government, opposition politicians, and military leaders were arrested, imprisoned, and executed. People feared speaking against the regime and people feared conducting their private lives in ways that contradicted the mullahs' strict interpretation of Islamic law. Women, especially, were objects of religious supervision and control. Externally, Iran pursued an aggressive and militant policy. The United States, as the former backer of the Shah, was regarded as an especially "evil" state and labeled the "Great Satan" by the Ayatollah. In November of 1979, Iranian radicals stormed the American Embassy and took 52 people hostage. These people were held until January of 1981. Saudi Arabia, a conservative and, in the Ayatollah's view, apostate state, was also a target of Iranian anger. In 1987, the Ayatollah called for the overthrow of the Saudi government. Iran also conducted a protracted and bitter war with its neighbor Iraq. Although Iraq began the conflict—hoping to grab a piece of Iranian territory during the turmoil of the revolution—Iran regarded the conflict as a jihad or holy war.

As is characteristic of all fervent ideological or theological revolutions, the people and the country of Iran could not sustain the political intensity for long. Isolated internationally, suffering from economic decline internally, and facing increasing grumbling from moderate Iranians who wanted a more open political system, Iran's government moved back to the center. The first shift was from a rigid theocratic authoritarianism to a more pragmatic authoritarianism that relaxed the enforcement of religious laws and allowed for more openness of expression. This happened almost immediately after the death of the elderly Ayatollah in 1989. By the year 2000, Iran had installed a decidedly more moderate government that came to power as a result of relatively free and fair elections. While the majority of Iranians likely were content to be governed according to the principles of Islamic law, they desired more flexibility in how those laws were interpreted and they wanted more room to offer input to the government.

Ayatollah Khomeini, raising his hand to a crowd of supporters.

As the twenty–first century got under way, people in the West feared a dangerous conflict with an irrational Middle Eastern world filled with radical Islamic fundamentalists. A common concern was that these fundamentalists would set up governments filled with fanatics guided by a very narrow and xenophobic understanding of the Koran. The example of Iran suggests that enthusiasm for theocracy lasts about one generation. In the end, more pragmatic concerns push a nation to a more moderate, less authoritarian, and less aggressive form of government.

THEORY IN DEPTH

Terms such as authoritarianism and totalitarianism have been the subject of intense debates among many political scientists. Two sets of questions dominate this discussion. One revolves around the issue of definitions. What exactly is an authoritarian regime? What exactly is a totalitarian system? How are they the same and how do they differ? Is totalitarianism merely an extreme manifestation of authoritarianism or is it a fundamentally new and different phenomenon? Because definitions in a dictionary, encyclopedia, or text book are just reflections of the way both ordinary people and scholars use words, there is no precise or definitive explanation of the words. A second set of questions deals with the origins, functioning, and goals of authoritarian and totalitarian regimes. What caused them to emerge? How do they operate? And, what do the leaders and subjects in such systems hope to achieve?

Defining Authoritarianism and Totalitarianism

Monarchies, oligarchies, dictatorships, military juntas, and tyrannies are all top–down systems in which the influence and will of the political elite vastly outweighs any input from citizens. A monarchy is ruled by a king or queen who took power because of heredity. In the modern world, most monarchs are symbols of national unity rather than people with real power. Oligarchies and military juntas are ruled by a small group of leaders, in the one case civilian, in the other military. Both may have come to power through extra–legal means. Dictatorships and tyrannies are both forms of one–person rule and in both cases the leader may have come toppled a previous government through force. In the modern world, both are regarded as pejorative titles.

Systems also differ according to the degree of control exercised by the leaders. For the purposes of this essay, authoritarian and totalitarian systems will be treated as variants of the large number of governments, both historical and contemporary, that privilege the voice and power of political leaders over the voice and power of the people. In theory, monarchies, oligarchies, dictatorships, military juntas, and tyrannies could fall into either category. There is disagreement among scholars about the precise nature of the difference between authoritarianism and totalitarianism. But, there is a general consensus that totalitarianism seeks far greater control over people's lives. In contrast to totalitarian governments that accept no restrictions to their power, authoritarian systems are limited by their ability or desire to exert control over citizens. Frequently, these limitations are supported by long tradition and incorporated into law. Even very powerful authoritarian governments may operate within the framework of a constitution or a well–defined legal system. Many authoritarian systems allow people relative freedom in the area of religion, cultural life, or economic affairs. Authoritarian governments may respond very harshly if people try to involve themselves in politics. However, so long as citizens are obedient and do not openly challenge government policies, actions, and decisions, they may be left alone. Some authoritarian governments even tolerate rather pointed criticisms so long as those concerns

are voiced in private or not expressed in a way that might incite widespread opposition. Totalitarian systems, on the other hand, attempt to extend their control and influence into every corner of people's lives. Through massive propaganda they even endeavor to dominate people's minds and emotions. For an authoritarian government, what people think in private may matter very little. For a totalitarian system, every aspect of life must be molded by the state.

Why Authoritarianism and Totalitarianism?

In addition to defining the two types of regimes, the study of authoritarian and totalitarian systems also examines their origins, functions, and goals. Sometimes they emerged out of a need to protect against disorder, decline, or disaster. The threat of enemy attack, an economic crisis, or a period of great social upheaval may cause a society to turn to strong leadership thought to have the ability to deal with great problems. Such leadership may insist that it needs exceptional powers and freedom of action to defend society against grave danger. The views of the leaders may be tolerated or even supported by a frightened, impoverished, or disoriented populace. This type of regime is more conservative in nature and is trying to protect the status quo. At other times, authoritarian or totalitarian governments may arise because the political elite and/or the people want to create a new society. This vision might reflect the desire for economic growth, social modernization, racial purity, political reform, or territorial expansion. In contrast to an authoritarian leader, who will be more restrained in his or her goals, a visionary totalitarian ruler seeks a complete and fundamental restructuring of an entire intellectual, social, political, economic, and military order.

Totalitarian and authoritarian regimes differ according to the degree of popular support or agreement they seek or demand. Authoritarian systems, in fact, may avoid mobilizing popular support for fear that public enthusiasm can be unmanageable. For example, during World War I, the tsarist government of Russia was reluctant to encourage public sentiment in support of the war effort. Top Russian officials worried that intense popular emotions could easily turn against the government itself. For many authoritarian systems, a passive and inactive citizenry is best. Totalitarian governments, however, insist on constant, public, and frenetic expressions of support and loyalty. Totalitarian systems organize vast public rallies and engineer massive voter turnouts in order to show the depth and breath of popular attachment to the leaders and their vision.

Plato

Convinced of the need for order, control, and hierarchy, thinkers in the Ancient World developed philosophical justifications for authoritarian regimes. Philosophers held that wisdom and virtue were not distributed equally throughout an entire population. Only a very few people had the capacity to rule well. Plato (428–348 B.C.) and Aristotle (384–322 B.C.) differed in their approaches to epistemology (methods of knowing and arriving at truth) and in their view of how much power should be invested in a ruler. But, both men believed that societies functioned best when governed by one virtuous and wise person (or very small group of people). Drawing on the model of the human body, Plato and Aristotle claimed that individual human beings were better off when the mind (reason and rationality) controlled both the spirit (ambition and drives) and the appetites (physical desires and lower passions). Plato and Aristotle said that in the same way the mind provided order, moderation, and harmony for the human body, the virtuous autocrat provided those qualities for the body politic.

Just as different parts of the body exhibited different qualities, so too society was composed of people with different skills and abilities. The governance of society should be entrusted not to everyone, as in a democracy, but only to those with the ability to lead. Plato stated this more starkly than Aristotle. Plato believed in absolute truth that existed prior to and outside human experience. This truth was not invented or changeable. For Plato, the best society was the society governed according to the principles of eternal truth. Plato contended that truth was accessible only to a few people. In his famous allegory of the cave, he likened human beings to men sitting in a large cave. With their backs to the cave's entrance, the men could see only the back wall. The cave was illuminated by a source of light coming from behind the men who were unable to turn around and actually see the light. Behind the men, between them and the light, puppet–like figures moved back and forth casting shadows on the wall of the cave. Throughout their entire existence, the vast majority of the seated men had never left the cave. Therefore, they had never seen anything but the shadows. They had never seen the true light; they had never seen the actual objects and animals represented by the puppets; and they had never even seen the puppets. Plato suggested that human beings were like the captives in the cave. Except for a very few who were able to go outside the cave, most saw reality and truth in a very indirect and shadowy manner. But, as in the cave, a few people in real life would be able to escape the limits of ordinary understanding. This small minority would be able to see

Plato.

reality as it truly is, not just its imperfect reflection. Such people, argued Plato, had both a right and an obligation to rule.

Plato's concept of an extremely hierarchical and elitist pattern of leadership reflected what he observed in ancient Greek society where most people were not allowed to participate in politics. Like his fellow Greeks, Plato was convinced that the large majority of people—slaves, foreigners, women, and children—were incapable of making important decisions. Their proper role was to submit meekly to the dictates of their superiors. Plato's distrust of the people went much deeper than his disdain for the aforementioned non–citizens. He even believed that most citizens, and in his day citizens were a distinct minority of society, could not be trusted with government. Plato wrote that citizens who were workers and farmers were too ignorant and crude to be trusted with ruling. In general, he thought those who governed only should come from a hereditary ruling class.

Plato's authoritarian emphasis regarding *who* should rule was consistent with his description about *how* rulers ought to govern. He believed censorship and physical force were needed to protect society against disrespect and disorder. For example, he said government should not permit the use of stories from early Greek mythology because the accounts told by people like Homer presented the gods as immoral and prone to excess. Such stories would not be good influences on the people. Rather, the government should only allow narratives that taught self–discipline and obedience. Plato also held that it would be necessary for the leaders to lie to the people in order control their thoughts and actions. Just as a doctor might need to withhold the truth from a patient, so too the rulers would need to reshape the truth for the citizens who could not be trusted to deal with complex or difficult problems.

Comparing different systems of government, Plato said that authoritarian regimes were best. Nevertheless, Plato recognized that not all authoritarian governments were beneficial. He recommended monarchies and aristocracies, systems where governance was concentrated into the hands of a single virtuous person or in the hands of a very few virtuous people. But, he condemned despotisms, oligarchies, and plutocracies as systems that glorified war, money, fame, or the expression of raw passion. Plato viewed democracies, systems run by the uneducated and the poor majority, as undesirable. He regarded them as agreeable forms of anarchy that degenerated into despotism when people could no longer tolerate the chaos and aimlessness that reigned when a government merely catered to the selfish desires of the masses. Although heartless and cruel, the despot offered strength, order, and direction. Such control was preferable the self–serving instability of democracy.

Aristotle

While Plato believed he had developed his ideas about politics through a process of pure logic, Aristotle was more inclined to look at the real world to determine what worked and what did not. Nevertheless, like Plato he was deeply influenced by the social prejudices of his era. Closely associated with the Macedonian ruling family, Aristotle worked as the teacher of Alexander the Great. Aristotle agreed with Plato that men of virtue and high status were the best suited for ruling over society. In observing nature and society, Aristotle concluded that everything had its appropriate place in a predetermined hierarchy. Corruption was simply a situation when things were out of place. In the political world, corruption occurred with inferiors ruled superiors. Like Plato, Aristotle thought that wise and virtuous leaders were analogous to the mind in the human body. The body functioned best when the mind was in control; so too a society worked best when men of superior status were in control. Just as slaves, females, and animals were happier and better off when they are under the direction of a wise master, Aristotle thought, society was better off when an elite group managed political affairs. Aristotle did insist that the rulers treat their subjects with kindness

and affection. But, he saw this friendship as the type of condescending benevolence similar to that a Greek citizen might feel toward his domestic animals, children, or wives.

Aristotle refined and simplified Plato's categories of government. He listed three forms of good government: kingship or royalty, aristocracy, and constitutional (a generic name for a system in which all citizens governed). These three forms were characterized by virtue, the ability to make wise and just decisions on behalf of the entire society. The three good types could degenerate into three bad forms: tyranny, oligarchy, and democracy. These three unjust forms were characterized by self–interest. Thus, a tyranny sought the interest of the single ruler, an oligarchy privileged the concerns of the wealthy minority, and a democracy was concerned only about the immediate needs of the unruly or unthinking masses of the poor.

To some extent, Aristotle gave even greater scope than did Plato for the authoritarian rule of a virtuous individual. If such a person could be found, Aristotle said that his kingly reign would provide the best type of government. In fact, such a person should not be constrained by any law since he would embody virtue in such a complete form that no other person or statute would be able to provide superior guidance, advice, or criticism. Aristotle did, however, recognize that such an individual could be dangerous. He stated that a completely virtuous person should either be made ruler for life or expelled from society. Although Aristotle shared Plato's distrust of a government in which all citizens could participate, he conceded that a limited form of democracy might be best. He accepted the idea that involving the people might make the government more stable and more effective. Comparing government to a feast, he said even thought the guests might not cook as well as the chef, they were certainly in a good position to evaluate the work of the chef. While Aristotle wanted a man of virtue in charge of the government, he was willing to make a place for the voice of common citizens. By that concession, Aristotle took an important step away from authoritarianism.

From ancient times until well after the end of the Middle Ages, most political theorists accepted the notion that government needed to be firmly in the hands of an authoritarian leader. Christian thinkers, who dominated the development of political theory after the time of Constantine (died in 337 A.D.), borrowed their basic ideas from Plato and Aristotle. Although they substituted the word of God for the authority of reason, they tended to agree that the society required a powerful leader whose rule was unchallenged by the voice of the people. Some Christian political philosophers emphasized the idea that human evil required a strong state. Augustus, Bishop of Hippo from 395 until his death in 430, even went so far as to claim that the harshness of an authoritarian state was a justifiable punishment for people's sin. Defending a ruler's authority by appealing to an external, immutable, and unquestionable standard, Augustus believed that only a select few, or even just one individual, could claim the right to know and exercise the authority that came from God. Ordinary subjects had no right to provide input.

Alfarabi

In the Muslim world, the political philosopher Alfarabi (c. 870–950) developed a similar political philosophy. Attempting to harmonize Islam and classical Greek political ideas, he drew heavily from Plato. Like Plato and Augustus, Alfarabi taught that there was a ultimate source of truth above human beings. To create a good government, one had to know this truth. Only then was good legislation possible. Only then was virtuous political action possible. In Alfarabi's view, it was critically important that a government's founder, initial law–makers, and successive leaders were faithful to divinely ordained truth. Adherence to eternal truth, not deference to the will of the people was essential for good government. Without a strong and good leader, a people would focus on their immediate, selfish concerns. In his book *The Virtuous City*, Alfarabi said that a good political system was guided by reason. In such a regime, people come together cooperatively, live virtuously, act nobly, and achieve happiness. But, Alfarabi said such a government required discipline and guidance. Only a few individuals had the ability and the proper upbringing to provide such leadership. Most people know the truth only imperfectly, and even then only after having had the truth explained to them by people with more wisdom and insight. Consequently, in a virtuous regime, a few will rule and the vast majority will acquiesce.

Throughout the Middle Ages, most political thinkers saw authoritarian rule as the best form of government. Some went so far as to suggest that even an unjust or predatory ruler could not be questioned. A bad ruler was legitimate because God must have selected a tyrant in order to punish a disobedient society. The authority of the ruler was complete. Yet, many pre–modern political philosophers called on the ruler to act kindly and gently, to rule the people with the love of a father. However, they also admonished leaders to punish evil with the strength of a father.

St. Thomas Aquinas

Thomas Aquinas (1225–74) believed that both deductive reason and evidence from the real world sup-

ported the idea of a single authoritarian leader. Using logic, Aquinas argued that just as God was the sole ruler in the spiritual world and just as the soul was the only ruler of an individual, so too people living in community should be led by one person, a king. Drawing on the evidence of actual observation, Aquinas concluded that people were social beings, not individuals who lived in isolation. If people were to live together, they needed direction. Without strong leadership, society would splinter and fall apart.

Not only did medieval philosophers such as Aquinas believe authoritarian rule was best, they were strongly opposed to revolt even if against an unjust ruler. While Aquinas agreed that a tyrant could not claim legitimacy, he seemed to suggest that only God had the right to remove an evil ruler. To people considering revolt, Aquinas pointed out that they could not be assured of success. If the uprising failed, the people would face severe reprisal and suffer even more than before. Even if the people succeeded in removing the tyrant, the society could easily descend into chaos. Or, the people could end up with an even worse tyrant. In spite of his strong support for authoritarianism, Aquinas agreed that a ruler had an obligation to work for the common good, to promote peace, and to overcome dissension within the community. Although he was unwilling to sanction the removal of a tyrant, he suggested that kings should be held accountable by a constitution. In holding those views, he was somewhat ahead of his time.

Dante Alighieri

Dante Alighieri (1265–1321), also believed an authoritarian system would best serve society. Known for his vivid descriptions of heaven and hell in *The Divine Comedy*, Dante developed his political ideas in *De monarchia* (1310). Referring to the concept that there is only one God over the universe, one head of a family, and one mind directing the body, Dante used the same arguments employed by Aquinas. Like Aquinas, he asserted that the authoritarian ruler should be a servant, not a tyrant. A staunch admirer of the ancient Roman Empire, Dante suggested that the entire world should be brought under the control of one authoritarian leader. The result, he said, would be universal peace. According to Dante, a world government under a single ruler would fulfill the promise of the angels who had announced the birth of Jesus by singing "Peace on Earth."

Niccolà Machiavelli

Niccolò Machiavelli (1469–1527) introduced a radical notion that removed moral restrictions on a

Thomas Hobbes. *(Archive Photos, Inc.)*

ruler's authority. Machiavelli said a ruler's only obligation was to maintain power. By making that argument, Machiavelli rejected the ancient and medieval views that a ruler deserved to be in office because of natural virtue, because of a superior understanding of justice, or because of God's will. It might seem that Machiavelli had weakened authoritarianism by undermining the foundational intellectual structures that had been used to justify the system. However, he strengthened authoritarianism by destroying the limits to a ruler's actions. For Machiavelli, what gave legitimacy was a ruler's own ability to exert power. Consequently, Machiavelli removed any religious or philosophical barriers against cruelty or deviousness on the part of a prince. But, while Machiavelli is often regarded as the father of the theory that the pursuit of power must be a leader's only goal, it must be recalled that he frequently reminded rulers of the need to win the loyalty and affection of the people. Without their support, a leader's power would erode and a ruler could fall. This need to keep the support of the people tempered the inclination to move from a benevolent authoritarianism to tyranny.

Thomas Hobbes

The British scholar Thomas Hobbes (1588–1679) was one of history's most articulate and persuasive champions of authoritarian government. Hobbes lived during an extremely turbulent time in European history when the authority of the church, the state, and philosophy were all being challenged. The Reformation had unleashed religious wars, Spain and England were locked in conflict—in fact Hobbes was born in the same year the British defeated the Spanish Armada—and England itself faced a long civil war that resulted in the beheading of King Charles I in 1649. An unapologetic supporter of royal power, Hobbes argued for a strong state whose powers could not be undermined by the people.

Seeking to apply logical mathematical and scientific principles to the study of politics, Hobbes rejected any Platonic or Aristotelian notion that some people are more virtuous and, therefore, more fit to rule. Like Machiavelli, he dismissed any appeal to innate reason or religion as justifications for authoritarian rule. But, instead of weakening a ruler's authority by removing traditional arguments supportive of kings or aristocrats, Hobbes greatly strengthened a ruler's claim to power.

Plato, Aristotle, and most medieval thinkers had based their defense of strong government on the belief in the inequality—intellectual, moral, spiritual—of human beings. Because of inequality, Plato and Aristotle held that a gifted or chosen individual (or perhaps a small elite group) had both a right and an obligation to govern in an autocratic fashion. Hobbes, however, believed in the near equality of all human beings. Although he acknowledged that some people were more powerful, more courageous, and more intelligent, he noted that even the weakest could find ways to kill or rob the strongest. For Hobbes, the underlying reality about all society was that every person experienced two closely linked emotions: a desire for power and a fear of death. The desire for power resulted in a savagery that led everyone to harbor a justifiable fear of being attacked, robbed, and destroyed. Hobbes described an imaginary "state of nature" to explain what life would be like if people were simply left to their own devices. Without the rules and protections of government, people would be in a perpetual state of war against each other. As a result, they could not conduct business, develop an intellectual or artistic life, organize society, or ever feel safe. Life would be "solitary, nasty, brutish, and short."

Thomas Hobbes believed the only way for people to escape the profound danger posed by their own brutal ambitions was for the people to covenant together and turn over all power to a sovereign. This transaction had to be both complete and irrevocable. The agreement or covenant—Hobbes called it a social contract—was made among the people themselves; the ruler had no part in arranging for the bargain that gave him complete power. As a result, the covenant could not undone by the people because they freely had relinquished all their rights to the ruler in an unconditional manner. Although Hobbes conceded that the sovereign might be an assembly (for example, something similar to the British Parliament), he believed a single monarch was best. In any case, the sovereign had to be indivisible and absolute.

In Hobbes' view, the sovereign could commit no injustice, the sovereign could not be punished or removed, and the sovereign had the right to use any means thought necessary to ensure peace and security. In the pursuit of order and security, the sovereign had a right to control the content of books and opinions, make laws at will, and hear and judge all legal cases. Hobbes recognized that government might, at times, make the people miserable. But, he argued that such misery was unavoidable and should be accepted.

The nature of Hobbes' authoritarian views are especially clear when he explained the relationship between government and the individual. Hobbes gave no room for questioning or challenging the government. He rejected the idea that a private individual had a right to rely on his or her conscience as a measure of good and evil. Only the law of the state could provide that standard. Therefore, Hobbes said it was not a sin to go against one's conscience if conscience came into conflict with the law. Education, discipline, and correction must be used by the sovereign to prevent people from advancing their own private judgements opposing official orthodoxy. While citizens must obey the law, the sovereign stood above the law. Hobbes reasoned that if the sovereign stood under the power of the law, then sovereignty would be diminished. Writing about wealth, Hobbes said that citizens had a right to protect their property against other citizens. But, they had no absolute right to any property needed by the sovereign.

Hobbes believed the power and authority of the sovereign should never be limited or divided. Any diminution of government sovereignty put the people at risk because their only security rested in the ability of the state to keep both internal and external peace. At one level, Hobbes' ideas apply equally to democratic and authoritarian states. Even in the most open modern democracies people are not free to disobey the law, take the law into their own hands, avoid paying taxes, or set up separate governments within a country. But, Hobbes is more justly regarded as a strong defender of authoritarianism than of the sovereignty of democratic systems. Certainly, he himself was uncomfortable with democratic sentiments. In spite of his support of an overwhelmingly strong government, Hobbes stopped short of totalitarianism.

MAJOR WRITINGS:
Leviathan

In his book *Leviathan* (1651), Hobbes described what life would be like without a strong government. He wrote,

During the time men live without a common power [i.e. an authoritarian ruler] to keep them all in awe, they are in that condition which is called war: and such a war as is of every man against every man...In such condition, there is no place for industry, because the fruit thereof is uncertain; and consequently no culture of the earth; no navigation or use of commodities that may be imported by sea; no commodious building;...no arts; no letters; no society and, which is the worst of all, continual fear, and danger of violent death; and the life of man, solitary, nasty, brutish, and short.

People should be free, he asserted, to live where they wished, pursue the jobs they selected, raise their children as they chose, determine who would inherit their wealth, and engage in commerce without government interference.

Frederick Hegel

The German Frederick Hegel (1770–1831), an admirer of Frederick the Great, returned to a more platonic notion of government and political authority. One of the most influential German philosophers of the nineteenth century, Hegel believed that the world was guided by an "Absolute Spirit" that he equated with Reason or an impersonal God. Throughout the millennia of human history, the Absolute became ever more visible and concrete. While earlier generations had thought of the Absolute in a spiritualized and rudimentary form, modern people had a much greater ability to see the Absolute clearly. While previously people had come into contact with the Absolute through God and religion, now they could see the Absolute concretely manifested in the state. For Hegel, there was no higher good in human society that a strong and just government.

For people in the twenty–first century who are inclined to think of government as oppressive, intrusive, or inefficient, Hegel's views seem peculiar.

BIOGRAPHY:

Friedrich Nietzsche

Friedrich Nietzsche was raised in a devout Protestant family in Germany. His father, who had gone insane, died in 1849, when Friedrich was five years old. A brilliant student, Nietzsche became an atheist when he attended university in Bonn and Leipzig. Even before he had completed his doctorate, he was appointed a professor at the University of Basel in 1869. Claiming to be the descendent of Polish nobility, he attempted to present himself as a person of elevated importance and vision. Severe health problems, perhaps psychosomatic, forced him to resign his university post in 1879. Addicted to opium, a drug he took to combat severe migraines, he fell into insanity in 1889. Although he published a number of writings during his lifetime, his sister edited and published much of his work after his death in 1900. An ardent anti–Semite, she reshaped his ideas by emphasizing Nietzsche's anti–Jewish concepts and sentiments.

Twenty–first century people must remember that Hegel lived after a period of great political and social turmoil marked by civil, religious, and expansionary wars. The emergence of powerful constitutional monarchies that brought peace, progress, and prosperity in the 1700s was regarded by Hegel as a near miraculous advancement. Hegel contrasted the state with the family and with civil society (business and community relationships and organizations). In the family setting people demonstrated support and respect for every member no matter how weak or unproductive, for example small children. But, they did not extend that to people who were not related to them. In business relationships, people reached out to everyone regardless of kinship. But, they do so in a very selfish and competitive manner. Only in the state, Hegel said, was everyone included and everyone treated with care.

In Hegel's view, by far the best state was the kind of stable, authoritarian regime he observed in his native Prussia. Ruled by a strong constitutional monarch, Prussia provided a proper balance between freedom and order. In his *Philosophy of Right* (1821), Hegel

argued that people were truly free only when they fulfilled their duties to their fellow citizens. Hegel, who had witnessed the excesses of the French Revolution and of Napoleon, was skeptical of democracy and of imperial populism. He was also critical of the more cautious British form of democracy. By extending too much power to the voters, he said the British were flirting with a system that gave too little attention to duty and discipline. By increasing the authority of Parliament—a body beholden to the people—the British had eroded the ability of the monarchy to preserve the equilibrium between freedom and order. As a result, Hegel feared Britain would descend into mob rule.

Hegel grounded his argument for a strong authoritarian system in an appeal to the existence of superhuman Divine guidance that was gradually inspiring humans to create more perfect forms of government. He also grounded his argument in the claim that the Absolute desired the highest order of freedom for human beings. Thus, Hegel was a strong advocate of a benevolent authoritarianism. He should not be regarded as a precursor to Nazi totalitarianism. True, he supported the idea of a very strong ruler. But, he believed such a leader was guided by a reasonable higher purpose and that the purpose of government was justice for all citizens.

Friedrich Nietzsche

A more likely intellectual precursor to modern totalitarianism was the German thinker Friedrich Nietzsche (1844–1900). A brilliant, but emotionally unstable individual, Nietzsche challenged the fundamental values of western civilization. He rejected rationalism, democracy, and religious love and compassion. In his view, those values merely promoted and protected the weak and unworthy. Reason, democracy, and religion upheld the ideas of good and evil, brotherhood, and pity for the disadvantaged. Using Darwin's logic of natural selection, Nietzsche argued that such "virtues" simply safeguarded the most useless and despicable characteristics of the human race. Laws, social customs, and religion were designed for the benefit of the least desirable human qualities. In Nietzsche's view, true humanity glorified strength and power, not impotence and restraint.

In his book *Thus Spake Zarathustra* (1883), Nietzsche described a prophet named Zarathustra who lived alone in the mountains before returning to civilization in order to teach and enlighten his fellow human beings. Arriving in town, he entered a market where people had gathered to watch a man dance on a rope. Zarathustra told the people that their concepts of happiness, reason, virtue, justice, good and bad, pity, and self–satisfaction were merely obstacles to true freedom, power, and life. Lightening, frenzy, and passion were the stuff of real human life. Such life would come with a Superman (*Ubermencsh*). To Zarathustra's disappointment, the people laughed and said they wanted to see the rope dancer, not the superman. In other words, they were content with a fake replica of a true hero. Zarathustra compared the people to fleas, blinking but not seeing. Like fleas, ordinary people had no vision, no capacity to struggle for excellence, and no desire for anything beyond immediate material and social comforts. People only wanted to be part of a herd, to be equal, to be the same, to be entertained, to be reconciled.

In his disdain for morality based on compassion, kindness, and self–sacrifice, Nietzsche laid the groundwork for a tyrant such as Hitler. In *The Antichrist*, Nietzsche wrote:

> What is good? Everything that heightens the feeling of power in man, the will to power, power itself. What is bad? Everything that is born of weakness. What is happiness? The feeling that power is growing, that resistance is overcome. [The true human being should seek] not contentedness but more power; not peace but war; not virtue but fitness....What is more harmful than any vice? Active pity for all the failures and all the weak.

A true Superman would not be bound by any constraints of custom, law, pity, or equity. Such constraints only stood in the way of authentic human achievement. Rejecting the limitations of religion or conventional ethics, Hitler exalted strength and power. Not only did Hitler admire Nietzsche, his troops sometimes carried copies of Nietzsche's writings.

Vladimir Lenin

Perhaps the most cogent twentieth–century defense of authoritarianism was written by Vladimir Lenin in *What Is To Be Done* (1902). Lenin argued that a dictatorial form of government was justified during and immediately after a period of Community revolution. A highly disciplined, secretive, and small clique of determined party activists would lead the people through a successful revolution. Afterwards, the same group would defend the revolution against its internal and external enemies. Nevertheless, Lenin regarded this strong system of government as a temporary necessity. Furthermore, the dictatorship had an historical and ideological obligation to rule on behalf of the proletariat (working class) and never for its own interests. While Lenin's failed to set up safeguards against the abuse of power, he certainly would not have favored the totalitarian regime Stalin built on the organizational and intellectual foundations Lenin established.

German philosopher Friedrich Nietzsche.

(Archive Photos, Inc.)

THEORY IN ACTION

Authoritarian governments have been the most common political systems throughout most of human history. With the exception of the United States and England, almost all countries in the world were ruled by authoritarian systems even into the twentieth century. Although sometimes regarded as anachronistic or inefficient, authoritarian governments generally were not considered as political mistakes until World War II. Even then, only the most extreme authoritarian forms, such as Nazism in Germany and Stalinism in the Soviet Union, were renamed as totalitarian and were condemned as evil or uncivilized.

Italy

Italy was the first modern country to experiment with what became known as Fascism. After World War I, Italy fell under the spell of ex–journalist Benito Mussolini (1883–1945) who began the ultra nationalistic Fascist movement. Suffering from the aftermath of World War I and disillusioned with the ineffectiveness of democracy, Italians turned to a strong, charismatic leader who promised to restore their fortunes and their glory. Although a former socialist, Mussolini had no deep commitment to any

Benito Mussolini (left) and Adolf Hitler marching side by side, 1939. (Archive Photos, Inc.)

ideology except Italian nationalism. In 1919, he formed *Fasci di Combattimento* (combat groups) to build support for a new political movement that promised to strengthen and glorify the nation. The Latin term *fascina* refers to a bundle of sticks. Individually they are weak; tied together they are unbreakable).

Mussolini founded his combat groups at a time when peasants had attempted to confiscate land and when some workers had taken over factories. His call for order appealed to large industrialists, wealthy landowners, and the lower middle class who feared labor unions, socialism, and communism. Mussolini

also garnered support from unemployed, including returning soldiers from World War I. Mussolini reached out to this growing segment of the population who were aimless and hopeless. Providing them with the security and identity that came from wearing a uniform and participating in mass rallies, Mussolini mobilized them by making them feel that they belonged and had power. Relying on black–shirted thugs drawn from the ranks of the disillusioned and unemployed, Mussolini used terror to intimidate opponents. Disgusted with the central government's ineffectiveness and lack of unity, the police stood by as his combat groups took control of Italian towns.

In the elections of 1921, Mussolini's Fascist Party won 35 of 535 seats in a badly divided parliament. On October 28, 1922, Fascists from all over the country marched on Rome in a show of force. Sympathetic to Mussolini, King Victor Emmanuel refused to authorize martial law to contain the Fascists. The King then asked Mussolini to form a new coalition government. With a toehold on power, Mussolini moved quickly to frighten or eliminate his opponents. In 1924, he assassinated a socialist member of parliament. Using a combination of political maneuvers, terror, and oratorical skills, Mussolini, known as *Il duce* (the chief), consolidated his control. After getting parliament to grant him extraordinary powers for a year, he moved to eliminate other parties, fill the bureaucracy with Fascist loyalists, and establish a Fascist militia and police managed by the Fascist Party and funded by the state. Lauding the virtues of the group over the individual, Mussolini promised to end civil conflict. He abolished labor unions, banned strikes and lockouts, and he organized workers, employers, and professionals into corporations. He also launched massive public works projects to encourage national pride and to provide employment for workers and contracts for businesses. Schools celebrated Fascist values and Mussolini encouraged a cult of personality. He also threatened or censored the press. Mussolini appealed to national pride by building an impractically large military and then using it to restore the Roman Empire. In 1936, he attacked Ethiopia and in 1939 he moved against Albania.

Once Hitler came to power, Mussolini allied himself politically with the German leader, not so much because he admired Germany, but because he so strongly detested democracy. His support for Hitler was never enthusiastic and Mussolini entered World War II on the side of the Nazis only after it appeared that Germany was winning the war. Militarily weak, Italy surrendered the Allied forces in September of 1943. For a time Mussolini headed a puppet government in northern Italy.

In the end, Mussolini failed to realize his dream of building a powerful nation in which the individual would be diminished and the state elevated. Terror, relentless propaganda, mass rallies, fiery speeches, appeals to the glory of the ancient Roman Empire, and external wars enabled him to construct the appearance of a strong state in which the Italian citizens supposedly found meaning and fulfillment. But, these proved to be a weak foundation upon which to construct a sound political system. In April of 1945, Mussolini was captured by Italian partisans and executed in Milan, the city where Fascism had begun.

Germany

In Germany, Adolph Hitler (1889–1945) presided over one of the most totalitarian systems of all history. Like Mussolini, Hitler exalted the state over the person. However, he added particularly noxious racial and militaristic elements to his doctrine. Hitler's ability to mobilize the total resources—economic, emotional, and military—of a nation may have been unparalleled in the history of the world. There are many similarities between the rise of Mussolini and Hitler. Disenchantment with democracy and economic hardship affected both German and Italy. However, the plight of Germany was much more severe. Defeated in World War I, Germany had been humiliated and overburdened by the terms of a very punitive peace treaty imposed by the Allies at Versailles. Not only did Germany have to pay reparations for having caused the war, German was also forced to disarm. Furthermore, the peace treaty demanded that Germany set up a new democratic government that came to be known as the Weimar Republic. The Weimar government proved absolutely ineffective. The result of the treaty of Versailles was enormous economic hardship, great hostility toward France and England, and deep antipathy toward democratic institutions. The situation was only made worse by the global economic depression that began in 1929. Massive unemployment, hyperinflation, an internal political crisis, and resentment toward neighboring countries caused the German people to look for a scapegoat and a savior. Hitler provided them with both.

After serving valiantly in World War I, Hitler returned to a disheartened and impoverished Germany. In Munich, he joined a racist, militarist party of malcontents. There, he polished his oratorical skills by condemning the Versailles treaty, the Weimar Republic, Communists, and Jews. By 1921, Hitler was selected as the leader of the National Socialist German Workers Party. He created a private army known as storm troopers (SA) who not only protected Hitler but violently disrupted meetings of other political groups. From the start, Hitler based his power on his ability to motivate an audience and on the use of illegal force against rivals. To a nation mired in humiliation and despair, Hitler preached the superiority of the German *Volk* (people). The cause of German's suffering, he said, had nothing to do with the German people themselves. Rather, Jews and Communists were to blame. Under a visionary leader, Hitler announced, the German people could regain the glory rightfully theirs as descendants of a proud and superior Aryan race. He said that a special spirit dwelled in this people, whose destiny was to dominate and rule less noble peoples. Hitler's ideas about racial superiority and anti–Semitism were not his own creation. Many people all over Europe harbored such sentiments.

After failing to take power through a coup—the infamous Beer Hall Putsch of 1923 which landed him in prison for a year—Hitler worked to enter government through the political process. Using the apparatus of the Nazi party, he attracted members and supporters though a newspaper, a youth organization, and a propaganda division. He also relied on the persuasive power of violence exercised by the SA and an elite private military force known as the SS. As head of the party and the military organizations, Hitler took the title of *Fuehrer* (leader). The Nazi party grew rapidly under his leadership, especially after the 1929 economic crisis created massive unemployment in Germany. Now, Hitler appealed to a broad segment of the German population, not just to social misfits and racial bigots. In September of 1930, the Nazis won 6.5 million votes and by January of 1933, Hitler was appointed as the Chancellor (prime minister) as head of a coalition government.

Hitler quickly consolidated his power. His SA and SS operatives attacked the meetings of other political parties. In February of 1933, the Reichstag (parliament) burned and Hitler blamed communists. In response to the fire, parliament granted him emergency powers and the constitution was suspended along with civil liberties. Now, the SA attacked communists, socialists, and liberals, thus intimidating and silencing political opposition. Government radio constantly warned of a communist conspiracy. After the passage of an Enabling Act granting his cabinet dictatorial powers for four years, Hitler moved to crush all potential sources of dissent. State assemblies were abolished and all regional government was brought under the direct supervision of the central Ministry of the Interior. Trade unions were put under strict government control. Hitler purged the civil service, universities, and the court system of all non–Aryans and dissenters. He decreed that the government could intervene in legal proceedings to stop cases or to adjust sentences considered too lenient. Furthermore, a new secret police, the Gestapo, began arbitrarily to arrest, torture, and imprison opponents of the regime. In 1936, the Gestapo officially was declared to be above the law. In an effort to stifle all independent voices, Hitler exerted great pressure against the Catholic and Protestant churches. In fact, he established a Reich Church that supported Nazi doctrines of racial superiority and that recognized Hitler as the Fuehrer. Radio and newspapers were censored and editors were required to be Aryans. Teachers, from elementary schools to universities, had to swear an oath of allegiance to the government. Hitler also exerted rigid control over the Nazi party and the army. Although not as extensive as Stalin's purges, Hitler's murderous attacks eliminated many top party and military officials in 1934.

While Hitler's totalitarian regime was not reluctant to use coercion, it also promised and delivered welcome benefits to the German people. Elaborate public celebrations and rallies restored pride in the nation and the people. Hitler's policies rebuilt the German economy. Public works projects, tax cuts for industries, and most of all rearmament returned millions of Germans to work. By 1936, the unemployment rate had dropped to one million people. Compared to the economic recovery rate in the rest of Europe and America, this was a phenomenal success. Hitler's success won the affection of the German people and the respect, even sometimes the admiration, of others in Europe or America.

Hitler's totalitarian vision included building the glory of Germany by territorial expansion and by conquering or exterminating supposed enemies of the state and of the German people. In 1938, he announced that Germany would rearm, thus making Germany the equal of England and France, and that he would bring all German peoples under his protection and rule. In that year he annexed Austria and German–speaking parts of Czechoslovakia. In 1939, claiming that the superior German race needed living space, he launched an attack on Poland and began World War II. Using the same argument, in 1941 he invaded Russia. His conquest of France in 1940 was justified, in part, as a necessary effort to save that country from the evils of democracy and racial impurity. Internally, Hitler pursued his policy of elevating the Aryan race by exterminating Jews, mentally handicapped people, Gypsies, and homosexuals. Although Hitler saw Nazism as a constructive ideology that would build a master race, his philosophy was nihilistic and ended with the military defeat of Germany in 1945.

The Soviet Union

In the Soviet Union, Joseph Stalin (1879–1953) ruled in a totalitarian manner. Drawing on the ideology of Marx and Lenin, Stalin insisted on controlling every aspect of his subjects' lives. Nevertheless, his totalitarianism was different from that of Hitler or Mussolini. While those two men exalted the state for its own sake, Stalin used totalitarian techniques to build and defend his country. To some extent, Stalin resembled his tsarist predecessors who faced difficult challenges. Like the tsars, Stalin had to bring unity to an empire of very diverse peoples, he had to develop the country economically, and he had to defend Russia's long and porous borders. Also, like the tsars,

Stalin wanted to increase his country's world standing and prestige. Stalin took over a country badly defeated in World War I and a country with no history of democracy. Autocracy, so extreme that it became totalitarian, was a natural step for Stalin and his cohorts.

A secretive, cunning, and ambitious man, authoritarianism fit Stalin's personality and nationalistic goals. Appointed General Secretary of the Communist Party in 1922, he took over full control when Lenin died in 1924. Previously regarded as a functionary rather than a visionary, he consolidated his position by appointing loyal supporters to key positions. One by one, he then vilified rival party leaders and had them removed from their positions and expelled from the Communist Party. Relying less on personal charisma than either Mussolini or Hitler, Stalin used the apparatus of the Communist Party and the government bureaucracy to exert control over politics, the economy, social life, education, culture, and religion.

Stalin regarded improving the economy and the military as his two main challenges. In the area of agriculture, he forcefully introduced mechanization and collectivization into a previously backward system. Forcing Russian peasants onto large state–managed or state–owned farms, Stalin transformed farming into an enterprise that took on many characteristics of industry. Division of labor, machines (tractors, combines, trucks), and enormous mono–culture fields were all intended to boast production and reduce the number of people needed for farm work. Stalin used the rural regions' excess food and surplus labor to support rapid industrialization in the cities of the Soviet Union. He was willing to use brutal force to achieve his goals. Millions of people were compelled to relocate to cities or to places such as Siberia where there was great potential for mining and forestry. Millions of peasants starved because the grain they produced was shipped to urban areas to feed factory workers or exported abroad to obtain hard currency. People who complained or resisted were eliminated or sent to prison camps run by the secret police. All over the country, forced labor was used in the construction of roads, railroads, canals, dams, bridges, and electrical lines.

Stalin's ultimate goal was to build an industrial base that could provide machinery for Soviet agriculture and provide equipment and transport for the Soviet military. In World War I, a pitifully weak infrastructure and industrial complex had left Russia so weak that soldiers went to war without adequate shoes, weapons, ammunition, or food. Stalin wanted to ensure that the Soviet Union did not face the same catastrophe ever again. With the help of reckless military decisions on the part of Hitler and the fierceness of

the Russian winter, Stalin's rebuilt Soviet military was able to withstand and defeat the German war machine in World War II. The Soviet victory was perhaps the decisive factor in bringing an end to World War II.

The cost of Stalin's totalitarianism was enormous. As many people died under Stalin as under Hitler. Between five to ten million peasants were killed or deported to Siberia. In 1932–1933, food shortages in the rural areas, shortages caused because the government commandeered too much grain, resulted in perhaps five million deaths, especially among women and children in the Ukraine. In 1950, an estimated ten million people were living in Siberian prison camps and during the entire period when Stalin ruled, twenty million people had been sent to Siberia. Dissent was not tolerated. People suspected of criticizing Stalin were arrested—often in the middle of the night—and tortured, imprisoned, or shot. Top party members or military generals did not escape Stalin's vindictiveness and suspicion. Leon Trotsky, a close associate of Lenin, was forced into exile and then killed by one of Stalin's agents in Mexico in 1940. Thousands were killed in the Great Purge of 1934 when innocent people were forced to confess disloyalty to the party and the nation.

While the sufferings and deaths were devastating to the nation, the intellectual conformity was also harmful. Artists and authors feared producing work that did not glorify Stalin, the Soviet state, heroic farmers or factory workers, or valiant soldiers. As a result, art and literature stultified. Economists, historians, sociologists, and philosophers felt equally constrained. Even though the hard sciences fared better, largely because they produced results with military or industrial applications, even disciplines such as physics had to be cautious. For example, uncomfortable with the ambiguity implicit in Einstein's theory of relativity, Stalin banned its teachings.

In spite of his brutality, when Stalin died in 1953, people wept openly on the streets of Moscow. A harsh tyrant, he was also regarded as a great patriot whose efforts had saved the Soviet Union from defeat in World War II. Not only had Stalin's strategies won the war, they also enabled the Soviet Union to rebuild after the war. Although the Soviet industrial capacity had been reduced by 50 percent during the war, the government's ability to conscript labor and direct resources made it possible for the country to regain its capacity to produce coal, steel, heavy equipment, and military hardware. By the 1960s, the Soviet Union was a superpower.

Soviet leaders after Stalin gradually relaxed their control of their citizens. While they continued to manage the economy through the use of five year plans, an openness to the west and a willingness to entertain a limited number of critical opinions began to transform the character of central authority. Mikhail Gorbachev, who took power in 1985, moved the Soviet Union decisively away from any vestiges of totalitarianism.

China

Following the victory of the communists in 1949, China constructed the twentieth century's fourth great totalitarian regime. Combining the fanatic emphasis on popular mobilization behind a charismatic leader that had characterized Italy and Germany with the extreme focus on economic development that preoccupied the Soviet Union, Mao Tse–tung (1893–1976), attempted to enlist a nation of 1 billion people to dedicate their lives to his vision. Like Italy, Germany, and Russia, China had no historical experience with a successful democracy. Furthermore, in the 1800s, China had been exploited and humiliated by the West, the cradle of liberalism and democracy. In the twentieth century, China was torn by civil strife among warlords. Then, in 1937 Japan invaded China. As a result of the upheavals of the nineteenth and twentieth centuries, the Chinese longed for a political system that would protect and develop their nation. Since the Chinese traditionally had regarded themselves as culturally superior to the rest of the world, the desire to restore their political fortunes was especially urgent.

After World War II, the Chinese communists gained control of the country. One of the defining events in the history of their movement had been the Long March which began in 1933. Surrounded by their enemies, the Nationalists, the Communists led by Mao Tse–tung had trekked for thousands of miles through remote mountains to avoid defeat. Although nearly 75,000 people are said to have died in the course of the march, those who survived came to believe that any obstacle could be overcome by sheer determination and courageous leadership. After 1949, the Communists applied the same discipline and resolve to restoring their nation.

The Communists faced an enormous challenge. Devastated by years of war and bad government, China was an impoverished country with little infrastructure and almost no industry. This created a theoretical problem for the communists since Marxism held that real revolution must be based on an uprising of an alienated and oppressed industrial worker class. Encouraged by Mao Tse–tung, the Chinese communists decided to create a revolution from the top down. Furthermore, they decided to base their revolution on the peasantry, a class that Marx considered to be po-

litically inactive or reactionary. At first, Mao and his associates tried to implement their reforms through relatively benign tactics. In 1949, they began land reforms by redistributing some of the land held by wealthy peasants. In 1952, they moved to collectivization, a scheme that encouraged peasants to pool their land voluntarily. These programs did not increase agricultural production or reallocate the land as much as the communists had hoped. Therefore, in 1958, Mao declared a guerrilla war against economic backwardness. During the Great Leap Forward, 120 million households were placed into about 25,000 People's Communes. These communes replaced the family, the village, and private economic enterprise. In an attempt to dramatically increase production, millions of peasants were organized into work teams terracing fields, building earthen dams, constructing roads, and making schools. Instead of using heavy earth moving equipment, the peasants accomplished these tasks with simple baskets, hoes, tampers, and shovels. In a highly publicized endeavor, the rural communes even built simple blast furnaces to produce pig iron.

This massive economic and social transformation was accomplished under the direction of communist party activists (cadres) who coaxed and coerced people into action. Although proclaimed an unqualified success, the Great Leap was actually a disaster. Unhappy peasants sabotaged some of the projects; in order to meet production targets for making pig iron, peasants sometimes melted down metal tools; and floods and droughts ruined crops from 1959 until 1961. Nevertheless, many top communist party officials believed the Great Leap had been a success because commune managers and local bureaucrats distorted their annual reports so as not to be shamed before their superiors.

The Cultural Revolution Undaunted by the shortcomings of the Great Leap, Mao mobilized the people for a Cultural Revolution that took place from 1966 until 1969. While the Great Leap had been designed to transform the economy, the Cultural Revolution was intended to conquer traditional Chinese culture that emphasized looking to the past and to the elders for guidance. Traditional Chinese culture had also valued private economic gain that advanced either an individual or a family. Convinced that such perspectives blocked the road to progress, Mao encouraged young people to criticize all people in authority except people in the army. Teachers, government administrators, scientists, and even very senior communist party leaders were challenged and humiliated by waves of youth known as Red Guards travelling around the country. Carrying copies of Mao's sayings in little red books, they threw the country into chaos for much of the late 1960s. During the Cultural Revolution, university education came to a standstill and prominent leaders in business, education, and government were forced to work in menial jobs in factories or in the communes. For example, Deng Xiaoping (1904–1997), the general secretary of the party's Central Committee and China's future leader, had to work in a restaurant. So great was the humiliation, that a number of people committed suicide. Mao's goal was to reinvigorate the revolutionary spirit that he thought was needed to eradicate old habits of thought that prevented China from attaining its potential. He also wanted to prevent creeping tendencies toward the individualistic inclinations of capitalism. Just as the Long March had hardened an older generation of communists, the Cultural Revolution would toughen the younger generation. In Mao's view, revolution would need to be permanent. Only then could "capitalist roaders" be thwarted.

In actuality, the Cultural Revolution plunged the country into chaos. Only the intervention of the People's Liberation Army in 1969 restored order to the nation. Nevertheless, a number of highly placed Chinese leaders, including Mao's wife Jiang Qing, wanted to continue the fervor of the Cultural Revolution. When Mao died in 1976, a quarrel erupted between the radicals known as the Gang of Four and moderate pragmatists such as Zhou Enlai and Deng Xiaoping. The moderates, who prevailed in the end, believed that China could not be transformed through sheer will power and by ignoring global economic realities. Although claiming to revere Mao, they began to reorient the economy along the lines of the free market. Although remaining loyal to communism, Deng distanced the government from Mao. Deng said correct theory was less important than practical results. "It does not matter," he asserted, "whether the cat is black or white, so long as it catches mice." By the end of the twentieth century, China was no longer a totalitarian state. Some would even argue that it had ceased being an orthodox communist state because so much of the economy had been liberalized. However, China remained decidedly authoritarian. The ruling elite continued to exert tight control. Although they allowed a great deal of economic freedom, they continued to resist political freedom. In comparing the stability and prosperity of China with the instability and economic decline evident in Russia, the twenty–first–century Chinese leadership believed it was fully justified in insisting on authoritarian control.

Egypt

In the Middle East, Egypt is one modern state exhibiting many characteristics of authoritarianism. Au-

thoritarianism seems natural both to Egypt's leaders and citizens. Going back thousands of years to the time of the Pharaohs, Egypt has been led by exalted rulers far removed from the masses. Even in the twentieth century, the Egyptian political system presents the leader as a father figure who guides, disciplines, and rewards. The Egyptian president is the center of a network of power and decision making. The rank and power of other people within the system are determined by their proximity to the president. Some Egyptian presidents cultivated a cult of personality. Gamal Abdel Nasser (1918–1970), who ruled from 1952 until 1970, was known as "Father Gamal," "Destroyer of Imperialism," and "Hero of Heroes." Less charismatic, Anwar Sadat (1918–1981), president from 1972 until 1981, encouraged the use of titles such as "Hero of the Crossing," and "Hero of Peace."

The great authority of Egypt's chief executive is facilitated by the low level of political awareness on the part of the rural masses known as *fellahs*. More than 50 percent of the nation's people live in self–contained peasant villages. Concerned primarily about local issues, these people often knew little of national politics. While government must be careful not to offend the fellah population, the peasants have minimal direct impact on policy.

Rather than competitive elections, the *coup d'é tat* and presidential appointment have served as the way to assume power in Egypt. The leadership team controlling Egypt throughout the last half of the twentieth century has had close links the group that came to power through a military coup in 1952. The 1952 coup was not a popular revolution, but the work of a small military clique acting "on behalf of the nation." These leaders saw discipline, not democratic participation, as the best way to advance Egypt. To them, economic development and national power have been far more important than popular political participation.

Modern Egyptian presidents run the government as a general would run an army. The president initiates all major legislation, conducts foreign policy (Sadat negotiated the Camp David Accords in complete secrecy), runs the army, and issues decrees that have the authority of law. The president can call a public referendum to amend the constitution, can be elected to an unlimited number of six–year terms, and can invoke "emergency powers" to override the constitution in times of threat to the country. He also controls the security offices, controls the nation's dominant political party, and removes and reassigns high–level officials to prevent them from building a base of support. The Egyptian presidents do listen to the opinions of close advisors and they consider the debates of the National Assembly. Then, they personally make decisions that the bureaucracy and the military are required to implement. Under Hosni Mubarak (1928–), the group of advisors has been expanded to include more than senior government and military figures. Newspaper editors, business leaders, university and religious leaders, heads of chambers of commerce are among the people with whom he consults regularly. This move suggests that authoritarianism, unlike totalitarianism, can build a foundation upon which democracy eventually could stand.

In Egypt's authoritarian climate, opposition parties are fragmented and extremely weak. At times, Egyptian presidents have banned or severely controlled the parties. In general, parties are used by the president to mobilize support; they are not primarily intended to debate, challenge, articulate interests, or present viable candidates for election. The National Democratic Party, the government party, controls about 75 percent of the seats in the National Assembly. Because no parties are allowed to form on the basis of class, region, or religion, Islamic parties are prohibited. Such parties would pose the greatest threat to the authoritarian dominance of the ruling party.

Brazil

In Latin America, Brazil is but one of many countries that have been governed by authoritarian regimes. Like Egypt, Brazil has an authoritarian history and authoritarian neighbors. Also, like Egypt, Brazil has been pursuing ambitious development and modernization goals. This environment makes it easier to consider authoritarianism as natural, normal, and practical. The largest and most powerful nation in Latin America in area, population, and gross national income, Brazil was ruled by authoritarian leaders from its inception as a nation until 1985 when a military junta handed power back to elected civilian officials.

Brazil began its existence as an autocracy. First colonized by Portugal, the country was dominated by Europeans who had no intention of encouraging democracy. Unlike North American settlers, who believed in limited government, the importance of the individual, and capitalism, Portuguese and Spanish settlers looked to military strongmen—*caudillos*—as the people best suited to direct social, economic, and political affairs. From 1807, Brazil was governed as a monarchy until that form of government was toppled by a military coup in 1889. Although military leaders periodically turned over government to popularly elected presidents, such leaders ruled in an autocratic fashion. Furthermore, the army was quick to step in anytime it felt the country was becoming unstable. Over the years, the chief goal of the Brazil's authoritarian leaders has been to maintain order. A second

important goal has been economic development and modernization. Liberty and equality were not regarded as essential. Maintaining order and encouraging economic progress are tasks that Brazil's governing elite has not often been willing to entrust to the uncertainties and instabilities of democracy. Since the 1920s, this ruling elite has been composed of the middle class business people and progressive military officers. These two groups believed they needed to band together to impose reform and modernization on their nation. They believed they were acting on behalf of the people and in opposition to conservative elements in Brazil that stood in the way of progress.

The presidency of Getulio Vargas (1883–1954) is one example of authoritarian rule in Brazil. Installed after the military seized power in order to prevent a civil war sparked by rival politicians, Vargas ruled from 1930 until 1945. Although he actually stood for election in 1933, he refused to leave office at the end of his term in 1937. Suspending the constitution, he governed as a benevolent, but fascist dictator. As an authoritarian ruler he banned political parties, he curtailed freedom of the press, and he organized society into representative groups that supposedly spoke for the people. Thus, instead of participating in politics through democratic institutions that they established or joined freely, business people, landowners, workers, and bureaucrats communicated with government through organizational leaders selected by the president of the country. Vargas did not, however, use his powers only in regressive ways. He pushed for labor reforms including the recognition of labor unions, minimum wages, and a limited work week. He also supported land reform and the nationalization of natural resources. In addition, he greatly expanded the public school system. These are measures the more conservative elements of society, including the church and wealthy land owners, had opposed.

Vargas' administration was followed by nearly 20 years of democracy. But, even that democracy was established by military decree after army generals organized a coup in 1945. Then, in 1964, the military again engineered a coup after becoming disgusted with the corruption and ineffective economic policies of popularly elected presidents. Now, instead of using the façade of a civilian president, either elected or appointed, the military ruled Brazil themselves. During their tenure, the Brazilian military government stressed economic growth and stability. Rather than attempting to manage the economy directly, they appointed civilian technocrats. In order to stimulate industrialization, they secured large foreign loans and attracted significant amounts of foreign investment. Under the guidance of the military and their economic experts, Brazil became a major exporter of primary products such as soybeans, iron ore, and copper. Brazil also produced manufactured goods, mainly for third world markets. The sale of automobiles, airplanes, small arms, and construction (for example building dams in Iraq and Angola) all contributed to Brazil's economic miracle. Brazil's economy grew at a rate of about 10 percent per year until the mid–1970s. But, the miracle came at the expense of workers and the poor whose salaries were controlled and whose public services were curtailed. Any real criticism of official economic policies was suppressed. Placing restrictions on the press, running roughshod over human rights, and eliminating political opponents on both the right and the left, Brazil's military government prevented open opposition to the technocrats' economic programs.

In the end, however, the Brazilian military leaders lost faith in authoritarian rule. Gradually, they turned away from the use of torture, opened the door for competing political parties, and allowed the press, labor unions, and the church to criticize government policies. By the mid–1970s, the military junta permitted local elections. But, it was an economic crisis in the mid–1980s that brought an even greater political shift. In the 1980s, the high price of oil on world markets and the $100 billion debt the country incurred in order to invest in economic modernization placed an unacceptable strain on Brazil's economy. The economic strain resulted in an enormous increase in resentment toward the military leaders. Increasingly they decided they would be better off without the burdens of governing. Consequently, in 1985, the military allowed country–wide elections and Brazil returned to democracy.

ANALYSIS AND CRITICAL RESPONSE

Although by the end of the twentieth century, there were no defenders of totalitarianism, a number of advocates for authoritarianism remained. In the Middle East and Asia—notably China— authoritarian leaders claimed the destabilizing side effects of modernization required the steady hand of powerful authoritarian government. Many authoritarian leaders wanted to introduce economic liberalization and at the same time shield their societies from the political turmoil they feared would accompany rapid economic and social transition. Democracy, they argued, was not up to that task. In fact, in the 1960s, 1970s, and 1980s, many policy makers and political theorists in the United States supported that perspective. Somewhat

ironically, development experts in democratic America regarded autocratic models, for example Brazil's military regime, as successes. Development theorists held that the key to meaningful development was the implementation of bold economic, educational, and social reforms *and* the use of a strong authoritarian governments to control any dissent from people who did not benefit from the "improvements." Some Americans suggested that democracy was too weak a political system to achieve real progress in the modern world. Consequently, both in Vietnam and in Central America, the United States government promoted economic and social development at the same time it supported strongmen dictators. That policy was repeated elsewhere in Africa and Asia.

As the twenty–first century began, however, there was a growing consensus around the world that, in the long run, authoritarianism was unworkable. The main problem with authoritarianism was that by not allowing informational feedback through the democratic process, the system was unable to correct mistakes. Also, authoritarianism, especially if applied to the economic realm was simply too complicated. For decades the Soviet Union had attempted to manage the entire economy through central planning offices located in Moscow. Although central planning promised efficiencies and a more rational allocation of national resources, in the end it proved ineffective and unworkable. The Chinese communists came to the same realization. Thus, by the 1990s, both China and Russia had moved away from centralized control of the economy.

By the year 2000, it was evident that efforts to bring economic progress come into conflict with attempts to exert authoritarian control over civil society. In the modern world, openness is essential for economic development. The Internet, faxes, satellite TV, cell phones, and international travel that are required to remain competitive in the economic realm make it impossible for vibrant economies to close out the world and control thought. Modern governments have discovered that it is impossible to contain popular opinion and dissent unless they force their people to live in a completely insular fashion. Cambodia under Pol Pot, North Korea under Kim Sung II, and Afganistan under the Taliban chose that path with disastrous economic consequences. The result is poverty and eventual political collapse.

Because of the interconnected nature of the modern world, especially in the economic domain, the pattern has been that totalitarian or theocratic governments move gradually away from the excesses of centralized control to a milder form of authoritarianism mixed with democracy. In the Soviet Union, the

KGB actually promoted reform and openness because intelligence experts understood the outside world and realized that the Soviet Union would be left behind economically and technologically if their system remained overly autocratic.

George Orwell

While many twentieth–century professors and government experts have challenged the practicality of non–democratic systems, the best known and most influential modern critic of authoritarianism and totalitarianism was neither a political scientist nor a policy maker. That person was a socialist novelist who took the pen name George Orwell. Orwell (1903–1950) did more than anyone else in the twentieth century to shape popular notions about the dehumanizing effects of overly controlling government systems. In his novels *Animal Farm* (1945) and *1984* (1949), Orwell painted a vividly grim picture of totalitarian regimes. Stalin's Soviet Union was the obvious target of both books, but Orwell was also concerned that milder forms of government, even Britain's, could become oppressive while presenting a front of benevolence.

Born in India, where his father worked for the British colonial administration, Orwell returned to England for his secondary education. He did not attend university, but instead spent time working for the colonial police in India and living with the poor in London and Paris. A socialist, his goal was to learn about the plight of the underprivileged and to develop his skills as a writer. In 1936, he went to Spain to fight on the side of the socialists against the dictator Francisco Franco. Back in England, he worked as an editor and writer until he died of TB in 1950.

1984 describes a dreary totalitarian society. The year is 1984, far in the future from when Orwell wrote. The place is England, now called Airstrip One, part of vast country named Oceania (England, North America, South Africa, and Australia). Two other huge countries, both totalitarian as well, rule the rest of the world. At all times, one of the countries, although never the same one, is Oceania's ally, the other its mortal enemy. The book's main character, Winston Smith, is a writer in the Ministry of Truth. Winston's job is to rewrite records such as old newspaper articles so that they conform to whatever the government says is the truth. In Oceania, the thought and actions of party members are molded and closely monitored by the state. In every room, a TV screen spews forth a constant barrage of propaganda while a hidden camera spies on an individual's every activity. As in the Soviet Union, where pictures of Stalin were ubiquitous, portraits of Big Brother were ever in view. The goal of government was to make every person believe that Big Brother loved and cared for them and to believe, in turn, that they loved Big Brother.

Orwell's portrayal of Oceania bore all the traits of twentieth century totalitarianism. Thought control (either through peaceful propaganda or the violence of the Thought Police), purges, forced confessions, spying, torture, mass rallies, and compulsory citizen activities were all designed to shape the hearts and minds of an unthinking population. Doublespeak, a language that called forced labor "joycamps" and labeled the War Department, the Ministry of Love, twisted falsehood into truth. If Big Brother said two plus two equaled five, people were obligated to accept that as fact. An external enemy also served to unify the people in support of Big Brother. The constant struggle against an enemy enabled government to justify the country's low standard of living and tight economic rationing imposed by the authorities. Mandatory Two Minute Hate drills and a more formal Hate Week against Oceania's foes were used by government to divert people's attention away from the dismal realities of their own life.

While Winston Smith was a low–level party member, as in the Soviet Union the great majority of Oceania's population were not party members. The "proles"—the term was an obvious reference to the proletariat or working class—lived in oppressive poverty. Although Big Brother did not attempt to monitor their thought or actions with the same degree of intensity as for party members, the proles had no time or energy to think about politics. Work, easy sex, and mindless entertainment filled their days.

George Orwell's *1984* has been read by millions of readers around the world. Even people with little knowledge of political theory or government policies came to regard totalitarianism as dismal, cruel, aggressive, and hypocritical. Although claiming to govern for the good of the people, totalitarian leaders were exposed by Orwell as self–serving predators. In Orwell's view, not only did they insist on political obedience, they extracted the very humanity of their victims. Clearly, George Orwell intended to condemn Soviet, and also German, totalitarianism. Nevertheless, the fact that Airstrip One is England indicates that he was issuing a prophetic warning to the people of his own country. Totalitarianism could be in their future. And, they could be brainwashed to love it.

Hannah Arendt

On the academic front, the German political thinker Hannah Arendt (1906–1975) did the most to define totalitarianism and to claim it as an entirely novel and evil political phenomenon. Focusing on Nazism in Germany and Communism in Russia, she claimed that Hitler and Stalin had introduced an entirely new type of political system that previously had not existed. Totalitarianism, she argued, developed out of the breakdown of social structures and ideals that had characterized Europe in the nineteenth century. With the chaos of World War I, the economic crisis following the war, the migration of millions of people, and the decline of stable political systems, the citizens of Europe were plunged into hopelessness and deep anxiety. They felt profoundly lonely, rootless, and superfluous. To them, the world seemed both meaningless and inexplicable. Furthermore, the people had no faith that their leaders would be able to do anything to remedy the tragic emptiness that so dominated their lives.

According to Arendt, totalitarianism offered a suicidal solution for the grim void of post–World War I Europe. People such as Hitler and Stalin provided people with direction and meaning. Both Hitler and Stalin embodied evil in a form so radical and absolute that they introduced political forms unlike anything the world had ever experienced before. The evil of Nazism, Arendt argued, surpassed the evil of any previous regime. This evil was more than just an exaggerated self–interest, greed, lust for power, cowardice, or resentment. The evil of Nazi totalitarianism was an unmitigated passion for destruction (nihilism). First, the Nazi's believed they needed to completely destroy the existing world in order to create the new world to which they aspired. Second, by exercising the power of destruction, the Nazis demonstrated their own unlimited power. Why, Arendt, asked did the Nazis need the death camps and why did they engineer the Holocaust? Certainly not for any rational political or military advantage. From a practical point of view, the death camps were a liability. But, as a symbol of complete power and domination, the death camps served the Nazi's aims. The death camps allowed the Nazis to treat others as sub–human and to inflict infinite revenge on other human life. By their despicable acts, the Nazis were attempting to escape their own feelings of smallness and impotence. Ordinary people responded in a supportive way because they too wanted to escape their weakness.

Because both the Nazi leaders and the followers lost their ability to see the humanity in those they classified as sub human, they were able to extinguish those people without any feelings of remorse or discomfort. Just as the vast power difference between humans and insects allows most people to kill such creatures with no thought, so too the Nazis were able to kill undesirables in a routine, meticulous, and unemotional

BIOGRAPHY:
Hannah Arendt

Born in Germany in 1906, Hannah Arendt was a brilliant philosophy student. Arendt received her doctorate from the University of Heidelberg in 1928. Among her teachers was Karl Jaspers, a scholar who focused much of his work on the issue of human freedom. A Jew, Arendt left Germany in 1933, the year Hitler came to power. Arendt lived in France until 1941 when she moved to the United States where she would be out of the reach of Nazi authorities. In America she taught at the University of Chicago and the New School for Social Research in New York. Deeply troubled by what she saw in Russia and Germany, Arendt devoted her life to teaching and writing about the topics of totalitarianism and freedom. In her view, totalitarianism was a new and evil reality that had not existed before the twentieth century. Hannah Arendt's most famous book was *The Origins of Totalitarianism* first published in 1951. Arendt died in 1975.

manner. While the Nazis exterminated people such as Jews and Gypsies, they effectively destroyed the humanity and individuality of all the German people. For Arendt, one of the ways to prevent totalitarianism was to encourage free citizens to participate in politics. Citizens who took an active role in the political realm would not allow a totalitarian regime to control their minds, emotions, and conscience. They would not lose themselves to a state trying to obliterate the humanity of all its subjects.

Carl Friedrich and Zbigniew Brzezinski

Although many social scientist are critical of the highly moralistic tone of Arendt's writing, they are virtually unanimous in their belief that totalitarianism is immoral and that authoritarianism is impractical in today's complex and interconnected world. A classic definition of totalitarianism and authoritarianism, a definition contained in book written in the 1950s, still expresses the antipathy most contemporary scholars feel toward non–democratic systems. In their frequently cited book *Totalitarian Dictatorship and Autocracy* (1956), Carl Friedrich and Zbigniew Brzezinski attempted to provide a more neutral and less ide-ologically loaded definition of authoritarianism and totalitarianism. However, they label the cluster of characteristics that identify totalitarian regimes as a "syndrome." Thus, like Arendt, they say that non–democratic governments are diseased or aberrant political phenomenon.

According to Friedrich and Brzezinski, totalitar-ian regimes exhibit the following: first, an official ide-ology that every citizen is expected to accept in their outward behavior and inner belief. Second, a single mass party led by a single individual. Leaders of this party serve as exalted and unchallenged interpreters of the truth. Third, a highly organized police system that uses modern technology to terrorize and spy on the population. Fourth, centralized supervision, con-trol, and censorship of the mass media. Fifth, a ban on private citizens possessing weapons or explosives. Sixth, central control of the economy through highly structured regulation or direct ownership. Explicitly and implicitly, the Friedrich and Brzezinski list con-demned totalitarianism as a violation of fundamental human rights. Humans, they suggested, were not crea-tures to be manipulated or tools to be use in the pur-suit of some larger end. Individual human being counted more than any cause, no matter how noble.

Looking at the Friedrich and Brzezinski list, one could argue that non–totalitarian governments, espe-cially in times of crisis, exhibit some of the same char-acteristics. Such thinking merely highlights the fact that totalitarian regimes are simply harsh exaggera-tions of authoritarian systems. While authoritarian sys-tems allow some space for independent private and even civic thought and activity, totalitarian govern-ments do all they can to consume and control the to-tality of their citizen's existence. While authoritarian leaders may want to restructure society and change cultural values, totalitarians rulers aspire to impose transformations so sweeping that the old is completely eradicated. While authoritarian governments tolerate no open disagreement, totalitarian regimes require ac-tive obedience and acclimation. The Friedrich and Brzezinski list also suggests that even democratic sys-tems could move in that direction. That was George Orwell's fear.

TOPICS FOR FURTHER STUDY

- Look at the Divine Right Kings or the Enlight-ened Despots of early modern Europe. Did the solid administrative, legal, and bureaucratic struc-tures put in place by such monarchs provided a

needed foundation for the subsequent emergence of democracy?

- Why are most of the contemporary world's func-tioning monarchies in the Middle East?

- Look at the connection between religion and au-thoritarianism or totalitarianism. Does religion limit a ruler's authority and power (because there is a higher power) or does religion strengthen a leader's power (because now the leader can claim to speak for God)?

BIBLIOGRAPHY

Sources

Arendt, Hannah. *The Origins of Totalitarianism,* San Diego, New York, and London: Harcourt Brace Jonvanovich, 1951.

Aristotle, *Politics,* in Ebenstein, William and Alan Ebenstein. *Great Political Thinkers, Plato to the Present,* New York: Har-court College Publishers, 2000.

Ebenstein, William and Alan Ebenstein. *Great Political Thinkers, Plato to the Present,* New York: Harcourt College Publishers, 2000.

Friedrich, Carl J., and Zbigniew K. Brzezinski. Totalitarian Dic-tatorship and Autocracy, *New York: Frederick A. Praeger, 1956.*

Magstadt, Thomas M. *Nations and Governments, Comparative Politics in Regional Perspective,* New York: St. Martin's Press, 1998.

Nietzsche, Friedrich, *Thus Spake Zarathustra,* in Ebenstein, William and Alan Ebenstein. *Great Political Thinkers, Plato to the Present,* New York: Harcourt College Publishers, 2000.

Orwell, George. *1984,* New York: Harcourt, Brace and Com-pany, 1949.

Plato. *The Republic,* in Ebenstein, William and Alan Ebenstein. *Great Political Thinkers, Plato to the Present,* New York: Har-court College Publishers, 2000.

Further Readings

Aburish, Said K. *The Rise, Corruption and Coming Fall of the House of Saud,* New York: Saint Martin's, 1995. An Arab's critical evaluation of how the Saudi authoritarian regime serves its own needs rather than those of the people.

Bakhash, Shaul. *The Reign of the Ayatollahs: Iran and the Is-lamic Revolution,* San Bernardino, California: Borgo Press, 1991. Detailed account of the internal political maneuvering that went on inside the Ayatollah Khomeini's Iran.

De Klerk, F.W. *The Last Trek — A New Beginning,* New York: St. Martin's Press, 1999. First–hand account by South Africa's last authoritarian President. De Klerk oversaw his nation's tran-sition to democracy.

Deutscher, Isaac. *Stalin: A Political Biography,* New York: Vin-tage Books, 1960. Older, but classic study of Stalin that de-scribes him more as an autocratic Russian nationalist than as an expansionist and revolutionary communist.

Hunter, Wendy. *Eroding Military Influence in Brazil: Politicians against Solider*, Chapel Hill, North Carolina: University of North Carolina Press, 1996. Study of the tension between democracy and authoritarianism in Brazil. Hunter suggests that the desire of politicians for money and power helped the erode the power of the military.

Springborg, Robert. *Mubarak's Egypt: Fragmentation of the Political Order*, Boulder, Colorado: Westview Press, 1989. Discussion of the difficulties of maintaining control in Egypt.

SEE ALSO

Communism, Fascism, Nationalism

Utopianism

OVERVIEW

From the writings of ancient Greece to the most recent films of Hollywood, people have tried to imagine how the ideal community might look. Each description of the perfect state not only expresses the hopes of the author, but also carries with it an implied criticism of current systems. As analyses of the imperfections of contemporary governments and explorations of the possibilities for future systems, utopianism has led to reform, revolution, and a number of experimental communities designed to test models of ideal states. Cultures all over the world from the classical age to the present, from Jewish and Christian and Moslem traditions, have produced utopias. Most utopian literature and community experimentation, however, is associated with the West. Utopias and their alter egos, dystopias, reflect not only specific concerns about how governments and people interact, but also an overarching hope that change can make institutions and individuals better.

WHO CONTROLS GOVERNMENT? State supported by the people

HOW IS GOVERNMENT PUT INTO POWER? Cooperative founded by dissatisfied group

WHAT ROLES DO THE PEOPLE HAVE? Tolerate differences; conform if needed

WHO CONTROLS PRODUCTION OF GOODS? The people, managed by state

WHO CONTROLS DISTRIBUTION OF GOODS? The people, managed by state

MAJOR FIGURES Sir Thomas More; Robert Owen

HISTORICAL EXAMPLE The Farm

HISTORY

The word *utopia* first appeared in Thomas More's (1478–1535) book of the same name, published in 1516. More coined the term by combining the Greek words for "not" (*ou*) and "place" (*topos*), thus creating a word that meant "nowhere." This name captured the essence of More's endeavor. He wished to describe

CHRONOLOGY

c. 360 B.C.: Plato completes his *Republic*, the first true utopian work.

1516: Thomas More coins the term "utopia" in his book of the same name.

1623: Tommaso Campanella completes *City of the Sun.*

1656: James Harrington completes his *Commonwealth of Oceana.*

1776: Ann Lee founds a Shaker settlement in Watervliet, near Albany, New York.

1825: Robert Owen founds an experimental cooperative society in New Harmony, Indiana.

1841: John Humphrey Noyes founds the socialist Oneida Community in Putney, Vermont.

1844: Brook Farm in West Roxbury, Massachusetts, becomes a Fourierist phalanx.

1888: *Looking Backward,* by Edward Bellamy, appears.

1932: Aldous Huxley completes *Brave New World* and launches the era of the dystopia.

1971: Stephen Gaskin and 320 self–described San Francisco "hippies" create The Farm in Summertown, Tennessee.

1974: Robert Nozick's *Anarchy, State, and Utopia* appears.

---

in detail a place that did not exist, that was located in no physical spot—but that might be, and could be, and should, represent the ideal place to which every real location might aspire. Utopia could be found only in the imagination, in the mind's eye.

Although the word originated with More, the idea of utopia wasn't new. The first precursors of the utopian thinkers were known as prophets. They criticized contemporary culture, its excesses and inequalities, and contrasted what existed to what might one day be—the end of oppression, the reign of peace, and the unity of people across every conceivable economic and social boundary. One of the earliest of these utopian thinkers was Amos. Born in the eighth cen-

tury B.C., Amos was a shepherd and fruit gatherer, and he railed against the corruption of the elite classes in Israel and their misuse of honest laborers. According to the Torah and Old Testament, he predicted that the aristocracies such as the one in Israel would fall and the bounty of the lands would rest in the hands of the honest and faithful Jews. His message was two–fold: religious and ethical. Only those of the right faith and lifestyle would reap the benefits of a golden age.

Similar thinkers followed, such as Hosea, Jeremiah, and Ezekial. Perhaps most noteworthy was the Israeli courtier/councilor of the late 700s B.C., Isaiah. Like those who had come before him, Isaiah denounced the corruption of the ruling class and the emptiness of most religious practice, predicting the fall of the current system and the preservation of a faithful, moral few. He then described the peaceful kingdom that would follow; according to Isaiah 2:4 in the Revised Standard Version of the Old Testament, the people "shall beat their swords into plowshares, and their spears into pruning hooks; nation shall not lift up sword against nation, neither shall they learn war any more."

These early prophets paved the way for a tradition of religious thinkers who described utopias marked by love, service, humility, and worship of a common deity. In the first century A.D., according to the New Testament, Jesus spoke of a Kingdom of God on Earth. Augustine (354–430 A.D.) wrote about a City of God, and Savonarola (1452–1498) preached of an ideal theocratic state. Some of these Judeo–Christian thinkers believed the perfect world they described would come to pass; others described the ideal land as an exercise to show what areas of their system needed to be changed. Other spiritual traditions such as Taoism, Theraveda Buddhism, and medieval Islam also had their own comparable precursors to utopianism as well. Both kinds of thinkers, those who foresaw a literal paradise and those who used it as a foil for their own era, led the way for later forms of religious utopian thought and action.

Plato and the Utopian Republic

The golden age of Greece provided the first real utopian work in the form of Plato's (428–348 B.C.) *Republic*. Written in the fourth century B.C., *The Republic* was a political work meant not only to sketch out an ideal form of government, but, in doing so, to highlight the problems Plato saw in contemporary Greece. Plato's solution for the inequalities of wealth and status was a state in which wealth was evenly distributed and individuals were divided into three groups: artisans; warriors; and the guardians, the spe-

BIOGRAPHY:

Plato

The author of the first true work of utopianism, *The Republic*, is also one of the most influential philosophers in history. In 407 B.C., Plato became the student and friend of the most visible and controversial Greek thinker of the day, Socrates. Eight years later, Socrates was convicted of corrupting youth and teaching religious heresies; he was given poisonous hemlock to drink for his execution. The death of Socrates affected Plato deeply; Plato wrote many of his works as dialogues, such as the *Apology*, the *Crito*, and the *Phaedro*, among others, and in these the former student cast the late Socrates in a key role as the champion voice of reason. Plato lived at the court of Dionysius, Tyrant of Syracuse for a time and then returned to Athens to found the Academy, where he taught philosophy and mathematics until his death.

Plato's earliest written works described the ideas of Socrates regarding virtue, knowledge, and happiness. As Plato's own ideas matured, his writings focused on the questions of how to know and how to live. He believed the universe possessed its own internal harmony, and he wanted to build a philosophical scheme that paralleled and explained the rationality of the universe. This led him to the notion of ideal forms. Ideas, he argued, were independently real, regardless of correspondence to objects we can see. Likewise, every object, every thing, corresponded to an ideal form of that thing, far more real than the fleeting existence of the object in our realm. For example, according to Plato, a chair is but a shadow of the Ideal Chair that embodies true Chairness in the realm of ideas.

If what we see in the temporal realm is an anemic copy of the ideal form of an object or system, then what does that ideal form look like? Plato penned his *Republic* in the effort to explain what the ideal form of a government—in other words, utopia—might look like. He tried to systematize the state as a mirror of the harmony that he believed existed somewhere else. In Plato's "Allegory of the Cave," he compared the realm of ideas to a sunlit world that threw shadows on the wall of a dark cave; those chained in the cave saw only the shadows and believed that these shadows represented the real world, rather than a pale comparison of it. In his *Republic*, Plato tried to turn away from the shadows on the cave wall and see the real community in the sunlight. The product was the very first work of utopian political theory.

---

cial leadership class trained from childhood to rule. In short, Plato advocated an aristocratic communism to guide the life of a *Republic.*

Plato's *Republic* not only offered the first classic blueprint of a political utopia, but it also delved into the issue of the ideal personal life. This included the issues of sexual relations and parenthood. Though Plato afforded women more opportunities in his *Republic* than they had at the time in Greece, he expected men to comprise the guardian class, and even indicated that they should hold wives in common—as well as children, who would be raised apart from their biological parents. He even suggested such a group family would allow experimentation with selective breeding to take place to create the best leaders possible. Plato's concern not only with public structures but also with personal issues such as the family opened the door for future utopian thinkers to address the relationships between men, women, and children in their plans for the ideal world.

After Plato's *Republic*, many centuries passed before the next true utopian work, Thomas More's *Utopia*, appeared. The tendency to criticize contemporary ways of life and suggest better ones did not hibernate during this time, however. Philosophers, statesmen, religious leaders, and poets all noted their concerns for their political and social systems and their dreams for paradise. For example, classic Roman figures such as Virgil, Seneca, Tacitus, and Juvenal all complained of injustices and inequalities and longed for a natural, simple state that provided justice and plenty for all citizens. Augustine's *City of God* (approximately 412 A.D.) used the fall of Rome as a springboard for religious utopianism in the tradition of the early Jewish prophets.

By the Middle Ages, thinkers took the classical preoccupation with a "natural state" a step further and tried to determine what the state of nature looked like for humankind. John Wycliffe (c. 1328–1384), a British church and political leader, believed that the

Bronze bust sculpture of Plato. (The Library of Congress)

state of nature was communist in form, with all property held in common. John Ball (?–1381) agreed, and the social reformer took part in the radical Peasant Revolt in England before he was excommunicated by the church and drawn and quartered by the crown. His example moved utopian thought from the realm of ideas to the realm of action, and led the way for future utopians to try to put their visions of the ideal world into practice. The writings of Wycliffe and Ball later influenced William Morris, who named his work of socialist utopianism *The Dream of John Ball* (1888).

More Coins a Vision

More's *Utopia* (1516) launched a new literary genre and gave a name to it as well. More wrote the story as if its central character, sailor Raphael Hythloday, were real and had visited an actual, physical place called Utopia. At the time, so-called travel narratives of explorers' journeys were a popular form of literature. More therefore based his fictional account on the popular non-fictional works of the day, turning the travel narrative on its head to speak about what could be instead of what was. Hythloday's experience discovering the land, its people, and its systems, though fictional, made key points about labor, justice, education, and religion in society. The Utopians believed the goal of life was happiness, but they recognized that true happiness came from moderate and worthy ac-

tivities such as work and study, and not false pleasures such as excessive wealth or empty status. Framing the critique and challenge within a fantastical story gave More greater philosophical freedom than if he had written a book criticizing his king and country.

More's book sprung from the humanist tradition of the era, which celebrated the human capacities of reason and rationality, and urged individuals to contemplate truth to better themselves inside and out. More inspired a series of others to write similar works describing imaginary paradises, their systems, and the types of people who could maintain them. These sixteenth- and seventeenth-century European utopias harnessed the new methods of the Scientific Revolution as well as the new theologies of the Reformation to examine the nature of the good life and the perfect state. François Rabelais' description of the Abbey of Thélème in *Gargantua* (1532), Tommaso Campanella's *City of the Sun* (approximately 1602), Francis Bacon's *New Atlantis* (1627), and James Harrington's *The Commonwealth of Oceana* (1656), among others, followed from the example of More's *Utopia*.

Political theory of the era had a direct impact on the utopias produced during the time. Theorists such as Hugo Grotius (1583–1645), Thomas Hobbes (1588–1679), and John Locke (1632–1704), for example, wrote extensively about two particular ideas: the social contract and natural law. The social contract was a shorthand way of describing the mutual duties and responsibilities of the government and the governed. The consent of the governed, or the citizens, legitimized the authority of the government. This consent was based on an understanding of what the government would do for the governed, and, likewise, what the citizens owed in terms of obedience to the state. This implied contract could be broken if one side failed to live up to expectations, however; for example, if the citizens agreed to place themselves under a particular government so it could protect their lives and property, and in turn it abused the citizens' rights and property, then the contract was broken, and the citizens had the right to revolt against the state. The idea of the social contract influenced a number of utopian visions, particularly among the experimental communities.

Natural Law Theory

Likewise, natural law theory also influenced the formation of utopian works and experiments. Natural law theory looked back to an earlier time—literal or metaphorical—before the development of so-called civilization to imagine how the earliest humans ordered themselves into societies. Some theorists such as Thomas Hobbes believed that humans in nature were violent, greedy, and irrational, and the state had to set up mechanisms to control the base instincts of its citizens. In contrast, philosophers like John Locke believed that human nature allowed for peaceful, co-operative relationships between individuals, and the state's chief responsibility was to try to maintain the freedom that would allow individuals to recapture this state of nature again. Utopians fell on both sides of the issue, but more tended to agree with Locke's more optimistic assessment of the natural law. As a result, many utopias described populations as natural, un-touched, or uncorrupted by civilization, enjoying life in an Eden–like atmosphere.

Social contract theory and natural law theory helped to usher in a new era in the West. The era of revolutions—namely the American War of Independence (1775–1783) and the French Revolution (1789–1799)—and the theorists who helped to inspire them led to a new wave of utopian thinkers and works, especially in France. Utopian socialists and political reformers/revolutionaries such as François Noel Babeuf (1764–1797), Étienne Cabet (1788–1856), Comte Henri de Saint–Simon (1760–1825), and Pierre–Joseph Proudhon (1809–1865) not only wrote, but also worked to make their views become reality. Their combination of agitation and activism led to a new era in utopian thought; not only would utopians write about their views, but they would develop communities in which their ideas could be put into practice, showcases for their theories in action. Although utopian thought existed and exists throughout the world, the West, and in particular the United States, offer strikingly vivid examples of utopian communities in action.

Ann Lee and the Shakers

Ann Lee (1736–1784), also known as Ann the Word or Mother Ann, was the chief leader of the Shakers, a Christian sect that broke away from the Quakers and developed utopian communities based on their unique theology. The Shaker movement, also known as the United Society of Believers in Christ's Second Appearing, or the Millennial Church, began with a Quaker revival in England in 1747 and grew under the initial leadership of James and Jane Wardley. Ann Lee, however, took the group from England to the United States and established an exclusive, utopian Shaker settlement.

Lee came from humble beginnings in Manchester, England. Illiterate and poor, Lee worked in cotton factories and as a cook. She married blacksmith Abraham Stanley in 1762. In approximately 1770, Lee claimed to have a vision that changed her life and the lives of many others forever. She said she received a revelation that the Second Coming of Christ had taken place within her; she was the embodiment of the holy on earth, the female incarnation of God who fulfilled Her role as mother just as Jesus had suggested God's fatherhood. This vision, along with the abilities she claimed such as speaking in tongues and performing miracles, gave Lee authority not only as a religious leader but as a divine figure as well.

The teachings of Lee, however, included the complete equality of the sexes and the holiness of celibacy, and both ideas seemed radical to the eighteenth–century English mainstream. She was even imprisoned for a time for her beliefs. Eventually, Lee realized that the Shakers had to find a way to pursue freely the ideal community. She decided to follow a vision and take a faithful few to North America and begin a Shaker colony there. In 1776, she founded Watervliet, near Albany, New York. After her death in 1784, the Shaker impulse toward building utopian colonies continued to grow. By 1826, there were eighteen American Shaker communities in a total of eight states, each organized into groups, or families, of thirty to ninety people who owned property communally.

Lee is an important figure for organizing the first Shaker communities, as well as for emphasizing gender equality in a utopian setting. Her message had staying power: the Shakers outlived Lee by more than 230 years—unusual for a group that practiced celibacy. Though Shaker communities are all but extinct today, their vision of balance, simplicity, and equality in the ideal world survives through their signature architecture, furniture, and crafts.

Charles Fourier

One of the first theorists to inspire communities based on his utopian thought was Charles Fourier (1772–1837), known as the father of utopian socialism, the most visible French utopian thinker, and the inspiration for a series of celebrated experimental utopian communities. Many of his concerns about the mechanization, dehumanization, and class schism of society previewed concerns later raised by critics of the Industrial Revolution. His belief in channeling humans' natural passions to achieve social harmony, and the practical means he suggested for achieving it, became known as Fourierism.

Unlike communist utopians, who believed the state needed to own all means of production in the economy, Fourier accepted a few of the tenets of capitalism, including some private property ownership. He simply wanted a well–ordered agricultural society,

Lithograph of Charles Fourier. (The Library of Congress)

one based on cooperation and gender equality. Fourier devised with almost mathematical precision his plan for achieving harmony: the phalanx, an economic unit of 1,620 people who divided labor among themselves according to ability. He wrote and spoke about his blueprint for utopia, and followers and newspapers responded enthusiastically.

The Frenchman Fourier believed that natural human passions could be channeled to create social harmony. His prescription for this endeavor was quite specific: he believed the phalanx worked best to produce an organized, agricultural society. His teachings spread from France to the United States and resulted in The Society for the Propagation and Realization of the Theory of Fourier. Dozens of Fourierist communities developed according to the blueprint of the writer, including the highly visible Brook Farm.

Unfortunately, Fourier did not live to see his ideas applied in real settings. After his death, adherents such as Albert Brisbane and Horace Greeley transplanted Fourierism to the United States and in 1843 founded Phalanx, New Jersey, the first of almost thirty experimental communities based on Fourier's vision. Christian, but nonsectarian, these colonies organized themselves as cooperatives with equalized wages and supported themselves by the work of members and money from non–resident stockholders. The communities encouraged traditional values such as

monogamy and family, but also encouraged gender equality—several directors or presidents of Fourierist communities, in fact, were women.

The most successful symbol of Fourierism was Brook Farm, an experimental community in West Roxbury, Massachusetts. The community began in 1841 as a Unitarian venture but converted to a Fourierist phalanx in 1844. Brook Farm gained international celebrity status due to its membership, which included some of the era's intellectual elite, including Nathaniel Hawthorne, Ralph Waldo Emerson, Margaret Fuller, and Orestes Brownson. The Fourierist newspaper *Harbinger* began publication at Brook Farm as well. After the central building was destroyed by fire, the colony fell into economic hardship and eventually disbanded. Its fame lived on, however, in the works and lives of its former members.

Later Utopian Idealists

Other communities based on the political theories of utopian writers followed. Robert Owen (1801–1877) founded a cooperative rather than communist society in New Harmony, Indiana, in 1825. Among New Harmony's historical contributions were the first trade school, kindergarten, public school, and free library in the United States. John Humphrey Noyes (1811–1886) believed Fourier had highlighted real problems in contemporary systems, but Noyes disagreed with Fourier's conclusions about how to solve them. Noyes advocated the blend of religion and politics, arguing that socialism could not work without institutionalized faith, and a "complex marriage" that offered a form of polygamy and sharing of children in common. He founded the Oneida Community in Putney, Vermont, in 1841.

At the same time theorists were experimenting with communities that put their ideas into practice, religious groups established their own societies for the free exercise of their faiths. Between 1663, when Dutch Mennonites created a communitarian colony in the Delaware of today, until 1858, approximately 138 separate religious communities sprang up in North America. German Pietists, Shakers, and Hutterites, among others, founded long–lived towns and communities, some of which still exist today. However, the U.S. Civil War tore apart the fabric of the nation and brought a halt to the community–building impulse of the utopian movement. Few other utopian experiments took place.

By the time of the Industrial Revolution, utopian literature across the West began to resemble More's *Utopia* once again; works like Laurence Gronlund's *The Coöperative Commonwealth* (1884), Edward Bellamy's *Looking Backward* (1888), Samuel Butler's *Erewhon* (1891), William Morris's *News From Nowhere*, and H.G. Wells' *A Modern Utopia* (1905) described worlds that could be—often with solutions to the problems of labor, mechanization, overcrowding, and income that seemed to arrive hand–in–hand with a more urban and industrialized society. The reliance on science and economics typified these turn–of–the–century utopias.

The Dystopia

The twentieth–century experience with two world wars and a Cold War led to a new literary subgenre: the dystopia. Just as theorists wrote utopias to prove how good things could be if they were changed, authors of dystopias warned of how bad things could be if they were not changed. Aldous Huxley's *Brave New World* (1932), George Orwell's *1984* (1949), Ray Bradbury's *Fahrenheit 451* (1953), Anthony Burgess's *A Clockwork Orange* (1962), and Ursula Le Guin's *The Dispossessed: An Ambiguous Utopia* (1974) were early warnings of how anti–intellectual, despotic regimes might threaten individual liberties. Later dystopias dealt with specific issues such as racism, environmentalism, and ageism. Margaret Atwood's *The Handmaid's Tale* (1985) was one of many dealing with the problems of gender in society and government.

History seemed to run parallel to this change of literary tone. Optimistic experiments in communal living, especially during the 1960s in the United States, appeared to be overshadowed by the negative examples of other communities gone awry; leaders such as Charles Manson, Jim Jones, and others led their followers to acts of violence and self–destruction. Writers continued to use warnings as the main method of critiquing current practices. The advent of films from *Metropolis* (1926), *The Man From Planet X* (1951), and *Planet of the Apes* (1968) to *Mad Max* (1979), *Blade Runner* (1982), and *Dark City* (1998) further marked the century as the age of the dystopia.

Although the form of utopian thought has changed over time from religious imagery and political blueprint to fictional description and visual drama, one thing is clear: the impulse to describe what might be possible, and in the process to criticize what exists, is a long–lived urge that dates from antiquity to the present day. Theorists over time have expressed their desire for change in many ways. The ideal worlds they have desired have looked different across the years. One thing remains the same: dreamers of different nations and eras all have seen a glimpse of something better and tried in their own ways to bring their societies closer to the world of their dreams.

THEORY IN DEPTH

From the early days of the Hebrew prophets and Greek philosophers to the present era of novelists and movie makers, utopianism has never been a theory *per se* as much as a state of mind, a way of initiating a conversation about the manner in which people can live together best. The utopian thinkers themselves have disagreed widely on the political nature of the good life and espoused a number of different and even contradictory systems that might meet the need of given communities. Utopians fall into their category not so much because of what they seek specifically, but because of how they seek it. Rather than work for incremental reforms within systems, changing existing governments from the inside, utopian thinkers look outside of current models to what could take their places. Rather than reform what exists, utopians dream of replacing it with something new and different. The goals they have often put utopian theorists outside of the mainstream dialogue of political theory. Despite the isolated position of its adherents, utopianism has endured in one form or another for thousands of years.

Although the forms of utopianism are almost as numerous and unique as the individuals who have dreamed of utopias, several key strains of utopian thought appear over and over again; these ideal states involve religion, property, relationships, and past injuries. Any utopia might address several aspects of life—economic, social, personal—but each must have a central cause for its creation. The oldest form of utopia, which dates to the era of the Hebrew prophets in the eighth century B.C. and survives to this day, is the religious utopia.

Religious Utopias

By suggesting the right way to live, utopian thinkers automatically criticize the way of life in their time. If the contemporary systems worked perfectly, after all, then there would be no need to replace them with something else. The religious utopians believe that the practice of or return to a true faith is the heart of the ideal state. Theocracies, or governments led by spiritual leaders, often follow from this type of reasoning. The states of religious utopias often perform the same functions attributed to the church: leading worship of the God/gods, coordinating the rituals/ceremonies of the faith, instructing the people in the values of the faith, and policing the populace to enforce practice of the faith.

The Jewish prophets such as Isaiah believed the true faith existed, but people had fallen away from its practice. Their utopias consisted of a return to the traditional practices of Judaism and then the reward from God for their renewed obedience. They held systems and their followers accountable for the fact they had once known the true faith but had abandoned it. Utopia, then, was a return to a previously held practice, though it would be made better, perfected even, the second time around.

In contrast to this point of view, other religious utopian thinkers believed the true faith, or at least some key ingredient in it, was new. This recent revelation called for a different way of living and a new community to support it. These utopian leaders did not seek a return to old ways; they wanted a system that was entirely original. The Shakers, for example, began with a Quaker revival in England in 1747. Led first by James and Jane Wardley, and later by Ann Lee, who believed she was the reincarnation of Jesus Christ as a mother figure, the Shakers left England for Watervliet, New York, where they founded the first Shaker colony. Others followed. Though Christian in background, the Shaker utopia looked different than any other Christian community at the time: pacifism, communism, and celibacy, as well as confession to the dual—male and female—nature of God and the equality of the sexes typified these isolated colonies. While the Jewish prophets urged people to remember past teaching and build a perfect world upon it, Shakers urged people to accept a new revelation and build a perfect world on its new tenets. These two contrary impulses—returning to the old wisdom of the past and accepting the new wisdom of the present—formed the two sides to religious utopian thought.

Utopians and Property

A second historical strain of utopianism focuses on the question of property. The inequality of economic systems, the stratification of wealth, and the division of the rich and poor classes serve as repeating motifs in utopian literature. Consequently, many blueprints for a true utopia revolve around the question of property ownership. Many of the utopian works from More's *Utopia* (1516) to Bellamy's *Looking Backward* (1888) emphasize the fact that, although every citizen of the ideal state has everything he or she needs, none of the people are overly wealthy. This often is achieved by a kind of communalism in which major property such as agricultural fields or commercial factories are held in common by all citizens and usually managed by the government; therefore, socialist and communist utopias make up many of those preoccupied by the question of property.

Most of the utopians who have written or spoken about property have tended to treat the issue as a procedural matter rather than a natural one. In other words, they have suggested that, with the right structure for government, greed and need would be eliminated—the fault lies with the contemporary system, not the people in it. By taking this position, the theorists have not had to be concerned about the human nature of those who govern and distribute property; the assumption is that they will resist temptation and act fairly instead of using their positions for their own advantages. This forms the heart—or, according to critics, the vulnerability—of the property approach to utopianism.

Individual Relationships

Other utopian thinkers have focused less on issues of faith and property than those of individual relationships. For these people, government begins not in the public arena, but in the home; significant reform therefore begins not between the citizen and his or her government, but the individual and his or her family. One of the notions identified with utopianism is that of "free love"—meaning the pursuit of sexual relations outside of the traditional heterosexual conception of marriage. But many utopian thinkers were interested in more than simply experimenting with sexuality. They believed the historical monogamous couple and nuclear family created an impediment for the achievement of the ideal life.

Some utopian thinkers came to this conclusion from different directions. Plato's concern in his *Republic*, for example, was one of genetics. He wanted the brightest and best people possible to lead as guardians of his ideal state. By sharing wives and rearing children in common, Plato believed, the most intelligent of the citizens could experiment with mating in different combinations to produce the most gifted offspring possible. Plato's concern had little to do with feelings and emotions, and much to do with a calculated, if somewhat primitive, attempt at eugenics (improving the hereditary qualities of a race).

On the other hand, other utopian thinkers who have addressed the same kind of questions of sexual and familiar relationships did so for very different reasons. Their concern was not for the efficiency of selective breeding, but with the pleasure of unrestrained experimentation with intimacy. Charles Fourier and John Humphrey Noyes believed the traditional marriage and family would dissolve in favor of a complex family relationship based on caring for the group, the whole—multiple and/or revolving partnerships, as well as different forms of communal parenting, they believed, would take the place of the old ways of life. These lifestyles might be efficient, but, more to the point, they would also be exciting and pleasurable. In such utopias, happiness remained the chief objective of the utopian exercise. The counterculture revolution of the 1960s built on this foundation and added experimentation with drugs to the mix.

Still other utopian thinkers focused on issues beyond faith, property, and relationships. These theorists are concerned with historical patterns of injustice and/or wrongdoing and seek to undo specific errors of past systems by creating new ones. Pacifist responses to war, environmentalist responses to pollution, and feminist responses to discrimination offer examples of this kind of approach to building the ideal society. Perhaps the most obvious of these is the response to the rise of totalitarian states such as that of the former Soviet Union in the twentieth century; dystopias such as Huxley's *Brave New World* (1932), and Orwell's *1984* (1949) warned of what would happen in the future if changes were not made.

Advocates of civil rights and individual liberties contemplated how governments could limit themselves to preserve as much freedom as possible for their citizens. One example of a response to fears of "Big Brother" and its control over the path of individuals' lives is Robert Nozick's *Anarchy, State, and Utopia* (1974).

Utopian Literature

Utopianism as a political theory has had many manifestations—prophecy, revolution, reform—but two main legacies: utopias in literature and experimental communities. The literature of utopianism ranges from works of theory to fiction. The most sophisticated have drawn from theory and fiction to create lasting impressions of ideal worlds.

Plato   Plato's *Republic*, written in approximately 360 B.C., is considered the foundational work of utopianism. Authors as diverse as Thomas More in the sixteenth century and Aldous Huxley (1894–1963) in the twentieth century drew upon *Republic* when writing their own contributions to utopian thought. Plato believed that everything on earth was but a shadow of the ideal form of that object or idea; in his *Republic*, he tried to imagine and describe in detail the ideal form of the state. *Republic* featured Plato's late mentor, Socrates, discussing this perfect community with a number of characters and extolling the virtue of reason that guided it. Plato's paradise consisted of three classes, the lead of which was the guardian class. His utopia therefore was not a democracy, but an aristoc-

Engraving of Sir Thomas More. (The Library of Congress)

racy, led by those dedicated to reason, wisdom, and virtue:

> But the simple and temperate desires governed by reason, good sense, and true opinion are to be found only in the few, those who are the best born and the best educated. . . . Both the few and the many have their place in the city. But the meaner desires of the many will be held in check by the virtue and wisdom of the ruling few. It follows that if any city may claim to be master of its pleasures and desires—to be master of itself—it will be ours. For all these reasons, we may properly call our city temperate.

To create this leading class, Plato described a primitive version of selective breeding, including wife–sharing among the guardians, to produce the best human specimens possible. These children also benefit from the most advanced and carefully regulated education available, with everything from books to music carefully censored in order to feed the minds of the future leaders with the best material. In many ways, Plato built a political system in *Republic* that would avoid the suspicious anti–intellectualism of the Greek process that, years before, had sentenced Socrates to death for corrupting youth and spreading heresy with his philosophical teachings.

***More expands on the* Republic**   Thomas More's Utopia, published in 1516, built on the foundation of Plato's *Republic*. It copied many of the classic's

BIOGRAPHY:

Sir Thomas More

Thomas More coined the term "utopia" in his 1516 work of the same name. By the time of its publication, More already had built a reputation as a scholar and lawyer in England. His work brought him into contact with a number of luminaries such as Erasmus who formed a Christian humanist movement in the West. These thinkers valued rationality and religion, and sought ways to better themselves and humankind through philosophical inquiry. More joined these humanists, writing and translating a number of histories, prayers, poems, and devotional works.

His most famous publication, *Utopia*, described an ideal society based on reason. He located this society on an island in the so–called New World of North America. The book explored not only the community's system of government, but also the details of citizens' daily lives, from their poetry to their laws of divorce. More, himself a character in the book, acted as a lawyer would, at times cross–examining the traveler who encountered Utopia and his views on what he had found. Some historians have seen More's focus on orderly justice, peace, and equality in *Utopia*

as an influence on the later development of Anabaptism, Mormonism, and even communism.

More's work brought him to the attention of King Henry VIII of England, who took More into his service. In 1521, More was knighted; in 1529, he became Lord Chancellor. A combination of poor health and discomfort with Henry's failing relationship with the Catholic Church led More to resign in 1532. When Henry required his subjects to submit to his Act of Supremacy, which made Henry the head of the English Church instead of the Pope, the retired More could not go against his conscience and subscribe to the policy. Henry had him imprisoned on a charge of treason in 1534 and, a year later, executed. For his commitment to conscience and the Church, More was beatified in 1886 and canonized in 1935. His life remains a source of contemporary interest, as the multiple stage and screen versions of Robert Bolt's dramatic biography of More, *A Man For All Seasons*, prove. The 1998 film *Ever After: A Cinderella Story* brought More's work more clearly to mainstream attention by showing and quoting a battered copy of *Utopia* repeatedly as a blueprint for making the ideal world a reality.

---

ideas—for example, children were common property of the community in both—with a distinctly Christian twist absent from Plato's work. The success of More's venture spawned a wave of utopian works over the next century and inspired various religious and political movements from Mormonism to communism. Perhaps the greatest contribution of the work, however, was its very name, a new addition to the English language.

More's style also inspired future utopian authors in terms of tone. Wry, witty, and satirical, More wrote not as if exploring a theory in the abstract, but rather as if Utopia existed. This made his work interesting to a wide readership. He also maintained his sense of fun:

> Lines on the Island of Utopia by the Poet Laureate, Mr. Windbag nonsenso's sister's son: Noplacia was once my name That is, a place where no one goes; Plato's *Republic* I now claim To match, or beat at its own game; For that was just a myth in prose, But what he wrote of, I became, Of men, wealth, laws a solid frame, A place where every wise man goes: Goplacia is now my name.

Just as Plato had crafted his *Republic* in reaction to the contemporary system of Greece, More was moved to write about economics and justice after viewing the disparity of wealth and corruption of legal procedure in Tudor England. The English government that he subtly criticized in *Utopia* eventually took More's life when he would not submit to a law he believed was immoral and unjust—an ironic parallel to the death of Socrates that so haunted Plato.

Françoise Rabelais Many of the utopias that followed More's work suggested that so–called civilization corrupted many of the instincts humans needed to live with one another in peace and harmony. The more complicated and authoritarian governments became, some theorists argued, the less successful they were. To these thinkers, the state of nature, humans' original condition, possessed certain natural laws—individuals should not kill each other, for example—that made a more innocent time also a more successful one politically. Françoise Rabelais, in his "Abbey of Thélème" from the larger French comic masterpiece *Gargantua* (1532), described a utopia built on natural law with a populace of noble savages:

> These people are wild in the sense in which we call wild the fruits that nature has produced by herself and in her ordinary progress; whereas in truth it is those we have altered artificially and diverted from the common order that we should rather call wild. In the first we still see, in full life and vigor, the genuine and most natural and useful virtues and properties, which we have bastardized in the latter, and only adapted to please our corrupt taste. . . . Those nations, then, appear to me so far barbarous in this sense, that their minds have been formed to a very slight degree, and that they are still very close to their original simplicity. They are still ruled by the laws of Nature and very little corrupted by ours.

Like a Garden of Eden, Rabelais' Abbey was pristine, peaceful, and well ordered. Civilization could not better it, only corrupt it. Rabelais' "Abbey" offered one of the most visible utopias to be built on natural law theory. In contrast, Tommaso Campanella's *City of the Sun* (1623) reflected another trait in utopian literature of the era: the influence of the Scientific Revolution. The momentum of scientific thought inspired centrally planned and organized paradises built with almost mathematical precision. Campanella's utopia was no exception:

> The greater part of the city is built upon a high hill . . . It is divided into seven rings or huge circles named from the seven planets, and the way from one to the other of these is by four streets and through four gates, that look toward the four points of the compass. Furthermore, it is so built that if the first circle were stormed, it would of necessity entail a double amount of energy to storm the second; still more to storm the third; and in each succeeding case the strength and energy would have to be doubled; so that he who wishes to capture that city must, as it were, storm it seven times.

The repetition of significant numbers, as well as the vision of concentric circles and evidence of careful planning in this passage marks the City of the Sun as a product of the Scientific Revolution. Otherwise, Campanella's book read like something of an Italian version of Plato's *Republic*, making this key example of Italian utopianism also proof of the durability of Plato's vision.

James Harrington James Harrington's *Commonwealth of Oceana* (1656) was perhaps one of the most influential utopias ever written in terms of the political impact it had in its era. The Englishman Harrington described a political system based on land ownership. *Oceana* did much to advance Harrington's belief in the wide distribution of property to create invested citizens with a personal stake in the government, as well as a division of powers in the state and

a written constitution. Ultimately, Harrington's blueprints for the proper state influenced William Penn when founding the colony of Pennsylvania and the central figures in the American and French Revolutions.

In his epitaph of Oceana's Olphaus Megaletor, Harrington underscores the values of citizenship and Christianity that he believed formed the foundation of an ideal state. The great leader was "invincible in the field, inviolable in the faith, unfeigned in his zeal, immortal in his fame, the greatest of captains."

Edward Bellamy If James Harrington's *Commonwealth of Oceana* influenced the politics of its time, Edward Bellamy hoped his *Looking Backward* (1888), one of the most popular utopias of its era, would also change the world he knew. The American Bellamy feared the trends toward industrialization that he witnessed and wondered how mechanization, urbanization, and competition would affect human lives. His utopia included a government–controlled economy and a socialist state. In a postscript to his work, Bellamy not only explained why he designed his ideal state the way he did, but captured the optimistic spirit of utopianism in general:

> As an iceberg, floating southward from the frozen north, is gradually undermined by warmer seas, and, become at last unstable, churns the sea to yeast for miles around by the mighty rockings that portend its overturn, so the barbaric industrial and social system, which has come down to us from savage antiquity, undermined by the modern humane spirit, riddled by the criticism of economic science, is shaking the world with convulsions that presage its collapse. All thoughtful men agree that the present aspect of society is portentous of great changes. The only question is, whether they will be for the better or worse. . . . Looking Backward was written in the belief that the Golden Age lies before us and not behind us, and is not far away. Our children will surely see it . . .

***Huxley's* Brave New World** Interestingly enough, Bellamy wrote his utopia as a tale of time travel through the eyes of a contemporary viewing the world of the future. In this sense, Bellamy anticipated the rise of the science fiction utopia and dystopia. The groundbreaking pioneer of the science fiction dystopia was Aldous Huxley's *Brave New World* (1932). Huxley drew a dark picture of what would happen if the government grew in power and exercised increasing control over the lives of individuals—ironically, much the way Bellamy would have liked—and that system evolved to its ultimate conclusion: totalitarian tyranny. Chillingly, Huxley, through the character of the Controller, explained that the architects of subjugation would believe they were acting for the greater good of all.

Rather than describing the ideal state, Huxley made his point about the importance of limited government and individual liberty by describing the worst state possible and noting how the contemporary system might devolve into something like it. Instead of suggesting what to do to become like a utopia, Huxley implied what not to do to become like a dystopia. Huxley's highly successful work ushered in the era of the dystopia.

Although many of the twentieth–century works dealing with utopian themes have been dystopias, many from the genre of science fiction, one book reintroduced the idea of utopianism to the political theory community: Roberty Nozick's *Anarchy, State, and Utopia* in 1986.

Robert Nozick Born in Brooklyn in 1938, Robert Nozick was appointed to Harvard in 1965. His 1974 *Anarchy, State and Utopia* sent shock waves through the political theory community. In part his work answered the thesis of John Rawl's *A Theory of Justice* (1971), which outlined a concept of a just society. Rawls defended a kind of mixed economy socialism, with social policies/rules chosen behind a "veil of ignorance." Behind this veil, Rawls suggested, policy makers would act as if they were ignorant of their status in the community as they created policy, so that goods would be distributed fairly across race, gender, and class lines in a manner that always benefited the least advantaged group.

Nozick criticized the redistribution inherent in Rawls' proposals, defending each person's claim to his or her own using a natural rights argument reminiscent of early utopians. In fact, Nozick began his work in a state of nature, then asked whether there should be a state at all. In the end, Nozick argued for a "minarchist" state, a minimalist government for protection only. He argued completely from individual consent–based morality; according to his rules, for example, a state could not tax, because that would be analogous to forced labor. In his words, "[The minarchist state] allows us, individually or with whom we choose, to choose our life and to realize our ends and our conception of ourselves, insofar as we can, aided by the cooperation of other individuals possessing the same dignity. How *dare* any state or group of individuals do more. Or less."

According to John Gray in *Liberalism* (1986), Nozick was successful in "reclaiming for the liberal tradition the utopian vision which virtually all liberals (except [Friedrich] Hayek) had rejected as uncon-

genial to the pluralism demanded by the liberal ideal." Nozick asserted that the minimal state would provide the framework for a meta–utopia in which individuals might join together to form communities of free entry and exit, competing for members. Within these smaller associations, members might choose to contract away certain rights in favor of receiving certain services. Thus a communist association, a cooperative community, and an anarchist colony all might coexist. With the option of exit ever–present, however, each association would be forced to remain true to its contract and accountable to its members. Nozick pioneered the exodus of other minarchists into public view—for example, John Hospers, chairman of the University of Southern California Philosophy Department and 1972 National Libertarian Party candidate for the U.S. presidency, and Tibor Machan, philosophy professor and author—and brought the serious philosophical discussion of utopia back into fashion.

In his book, Nozick imagines a world of competing states with different systems and only one coordinating principle: free entry and free exit. In this utopian vision, Nozick imagined individuals choosing what amount of state authority, what form of government, they liked best. No one state could abuse the rights of its people, because citizens would leave for a more palatable alternative. Just as Nozick offers a view of a world free from totalitarian regimes, others imagine worlds free of bigotry, sexism, violence, and environmental crisis.

In his work, Nozick imagined utopia to be not a specific community, but rather an overarching, minimal state that offered "playing rules"—free entry, free exit—that would allow smaller experimental communities to evolve and compete for members. The diversity of possibilities available in this model over time has since inspired a new dialogue among political theorists.

In a sense, the open–endedness of Nozick's view of utopia, and his willingness to abandon central control in favor of spontaneous order, added a new dimension to the view of utopia. He raised the bar from static, complete notions of "the perfect state" by arguing that the perfect state would be many ever–changing societies impossible to predict. As the twenty–first century begins, the hopefulness of utopian political theory endures, but remains overshadowed by the dystopian vision of filmmakers and genre authors. Television, in the guise of science fiction hits such as *Dark Angel* (2000), has continued this trend.

Of course other utopias have shaped the course of the political theory as well. From Plato to Huxley and beyond, from Greece and Italy to France and the United States and elsewhere, all of the great utopias and dystopias have shared an underlying optimism that their suggestions or warnings might change the world for the better.

The one resounding commonality among all of the approaches to the ideal world is that of optimism. By discussing, illustrating, and even experimenting with their visions of paradise, the utopian thinkers not only criticized what they found to be wrong with their contemporary political systems, but also believed those systems could be changed. Whether motivated by the doom they saw ahead or the paradise they dreamed of, these theorists were dedicated to the proposition that things could be better than they were. Some believed the world would improve if individuals embraced a particular faith. Others believed equality of property or opportunities in personal relationships were necessary for positive change. Still others believed that paradise meant the solution to one problem, the righting of an historical wrong. Their conclusions remain as different as the eras in which they originated. Utopianism is less about the ends, however, than the means of achieving them. What unites utopian thinkers is not the detail of a given system, but the optimism and imagination to envision that system in place, working as planned, successful and enduring.

THEORY IN ACTION

Utopia, the ideal "nowhere" sought by writers and revolutionaries and reformers, has meant different things to different people, and thus has been acted upon in very different ways. The ancient Greek legends of Atlantis, a continent of advanced, peaceful, enlightened people who had achieved their own utopia before a natural disaster submerged their land beneath the sea, so inspired seekers and scientists that searches for the physical remains of the place continue to this day, as if pinpointing the ruins on a map might make the possibility of achieving a new paradise on earth more possible. Likewise, the stories of El Dorado, a utopian city built of gold somewhere in South America, spawned exploration of the continent by colonizing European nations beginning in the sixteenth century. The goal of discovering an ideal community motivated nations in a way that simple internal reform—building a more ideal community—could not.

Others seemed to know that paradise had no earthly address. Plato nursed anger and resentment toward the government of Greece that had executed his

beloved teacher Socrates, and Thomas More watched with wariness the state of England that eventually executed him. Neither philosopher expected to find Atlantis or El Dorado on earth. To them and others like them, utopianism in practice meant using the motif of an ideal community as a foil, a literary device, to contrast the way things should be with the way things were. The ultimate goal was not the discovery or creation of the described paradise, but the betterment of the current system and the attitudes and values that supported it. Dystopians such as Huxley and Orwell represented the other side of this impulse, using negative examples of how a terrible state might behave to warn readers and promote reform. This literary—and today, also cinematic—form of utopianism stretches from the fourth century B.C. to the twenty–first century, and continues to produce political critique for our systems.

Other utopian thinkers found the need for reform much too urgent to write works of fiction and theory and hope that their messages eventually touched sympathetic readers. For them, change had to come immediately. These utopians became fervent, and sometimes violent, revolutionaries. For example, Babeuf had a vision of equality for all citizens of France. Though he supported the French Revolution, he did not believe that the first wave of change it brought to the nation beginning in 1789 went far enough to create this quality. He published criticisms of the government, was imprisoned, and emerged even more dissatisfied with the state. He therefore created the Conspiracy of the Equals, a secret organization focused on overthrowing the fledgling new French government and instituting a utopian communist regime in which all people would share the economy's products equally. Babeuf's plans required violent upheaval, and he was eventually captured and executed for his plots before they became reality. His method of devising revolutionary cells for the distribution of information became the blueprint for the organization of revolutionary, freedom fighter, and terrorist groups even today. For Babeuf and others, achieving utopia meant not only reform, but also revolution.

The Shakers

The Shakers, led by Ann Lee (known as Mother Ann), took up residence near Albany, New York in September, 1776, and began creating the first Shaker community. The people benefited from the revivalistic interest created by the phenomenon of the Great Awakening. These protracted revivals, which occurred widely in the Middle and New England colonies, commonly exhibited the same dramatic characteristics that were seen among the Shakers. Thus, people on the

Shakers dancing during a prayer meeting. *(Corbis Corporation)*

frontier were less likely to be scandalized by religious emotionalism. As the revival fires cooled, the Shaker community continued to attract those who ardently looked for signs of the Second Coming.

Shaker villages consisted of separate buildings for eating, working, and sleeping. Everything was separated by gender—the buildings even had different stairways for men and women. This was probably done so men and women would have as little contact as possible, which would make it easier to honor to rules of celibacy. Schools and shops were shared among the people, while some "families" controlled their own small money–making ventures, such as crops.

Though their unusual religious practices were always a curiosity (their name comes from the way they jumped and shook during prayer and worship), it was Shaker doctrines, such as the condemnation of marriage, and Ann Lee's messianic claims, which caused the greatest controversy. As the Americans fought England for independence, the Shakers' pacifism was misunderstood, resulting in imprisonment for several members of the community. Events gradually improved when local citizens began to object to the mistreatment of the Shakers, believing that such actions betrayed the ideals of the new republic. (Generations later, during the Civil War, Shakers would provide food and relief to both Union and Confederate troops.)

The six months following the release of the jailed Shakers was a period in which the Shakers were allowed to practice their faith unmolested. Mother Ann and two disciples set out on horseback on a preaching mission that would last more than two years. This mission was of tremendous importance to Shaker history—several new communites were established in New England.

Unfortunately, the mission was marred by repeated acts of mob violence in which several Shaker leaders were horsewhipped. Ann herself was dragged out of a dwelling and thrown into a carriage where she was mocked by abusive citizens.

When Mother Ann and her company finally returned home, the violence of the New England mission left her in a weakened condition, and she never fully regained health. She died on September 8, 1874.

Before her death, Ann passed the reins of leadership to James Whittaker. Unlike Lee, Whittaker had a great gift for organization and, under his leadership, the movement prospered. He urged all the Shaker communities to implement communal living and common ownership of property as demonstrated in the New Testament.

In spite of her convictions concerning celibacy, which doomed the Shakers to eventual extinction, Anne Lee was in many ways a progressive eighteenth–century women who made a significant impact on the world. She was a pioneer for justice and equality. The Shakers were among the first in America to advocate pacifism, abolition of slavery, equality of the sexes, and communal ownership of goods. The Shakers also made contributions to American culture beyond that of ideology—they were the first people in the United States to produce commercial seed, and invented the circular saw, metal pen points, and the first commercially successful washing machine.

Robert Owen and Cooperative Utopia

For the pioneer of a social movement, Robert Owen had very inauspicious beginnings. With little formal education to his credit, Owen began working in the textile business at age ten. But by the time he was 23, Owen had worked his way up to be a successful cotton manufacturer in Manchester, England, and read widely enough to compensate for his lack of schooling. In 1800, he moved to New Lanark, Scotland, where he became a co–owner of the mills once owned by his father–in–law.

Owen used the opportunity afforded by the mill town to put his fledgling theories into practice; he reorganized the community—which included profit stores, competitive schools, and organized sanitation—into a model of a self–sufficient, cooperative agricultural–industrial community, in which enterprises were owned and operated for the benefit of those using their services. As working conditions bettered, profits increased. Owen's influence spread and even instigated the Factory Act of 1819, a reform bill targeting the conditions of businesses like the one in which Owen worked as a child.

With the success of his community in Scotland, Owen suggested that other similar utopian experiments be conducted elsewhere. In 1825, followers organized New Harmony in Indiana after Owen's model—coincidentally, New Harmony had been founded ten years earlier as another kind of utopian experiment by German Separatists who practiced communism and celibacy. The overhauled, Owenite experimental colony gained widespread attention when it became a cultural and educational center, boasting some of the era's leading intellectuals as residents. The town boasted the nation's first kindergarten, public school, free library, and equal instruction for boys and girls. The experiment ended in 1828 because of internal conflict.

Owen's base of support shifted from the upper class to the working class as he published various works such as *New View of Society; or, Essays on the Formation of Character* (three volumes from 1813 to 1814) and *Report to the County of Lanark* (1821), which revealed his disinterest in religion and his desire to transform society and its institutionalized system of privilege. For a time he worked with labor unions and suggested that they join forces with cooperative societies, but the union movement proved too disposed toward violence for Owen, who wanted change to come through peaceful means. For the last decades of his life, Owen wrote and lectured about his belief that environment shaped individuals and cooperative societies, in particular, improved character. His life's work, in his writings and in the communities such as New Lanark and New Harmony, secured Owen's place as the father of cooperative utopian thought.

The Oneida Community

Many explorers, writers, and revolutionaries can be considered utopians. The groups seem to share little in common, but all are united by the idea that the government could be bettered. The most visual example of utopianism in action is that of the experimental communities, colonies created as experimental tests of utopian theory. Even among this subset of utopianism, however, many differences arise. Some communities came together due to faith. Others united over interests in property, personal relationships, or historical wrongs associated with issues of race, gender, the environment, and/or individual liberty. Groups such as the Oneida Community, founded in 1841, and The Farm, founded in 1971, reflect different sides of the experimental utopian community.

The Oneida community existed from 1847 to 1881 in New York. This faith–based group evolved from the religious teachings of John Humphrey Noyes (1811–1886), a Christian preacher who believed in the ultimate perfectibility of humanity. His theology of Perfectionism brought him ridicule from other mainstream Protestants, but also drew a faithful band of followers that eventually agreed to set up a colony apart from nonbelievers. After being forced to flee other areas due to the controversial nature of their faith, Noyes and his adherents finally established the Oneida community. The practices of the Perfectionists—including group marriage, a form of polygamy, and economic communism—followed from Noyes's teaching of how to attain communion with Christ and, ultimately, sinlessness.

The Oneida experience exemplifies the pattern of many religious utopian experiments. The first year's population was a mere 87, but it increased to 205 at the height of the colony's popularity. All members met nightly for community business meetings and worked and reared children in common. Women attained rights equal to those of men. But the society was exclusive, closed to the outside, and the community's practices didn't spread to the surrounding area.

Eventually, internal dissension forced Noyes to leave the United States for Canada. In the absence of the community's governmental and theological cornerstone, the community disintegrated. What was left of the group abandoned any utopian pretense and became a joint stock company. Factories producing paper products, plastic goods, and the famous Oneida silverware are the lasting legacy of the community. The formula of an iconoclastic, charismatic religious leader and followers who join together apart from the mainstream, maintain their faith and its corresponding practices for a while, but eventually lose interest seems the standard pattern for religious utopian experiments in action.

The Farm

Other utopian communities are not tied so directly to their founders as leaders or focused on attaining a single end—in the case of Noyes and Oneida, human perfection—but, instead, are developed as responses to certain concerns and dedicated to the journey as well as the end goal. For example, Stephen Gaskin (1935–) and 320 self–described San Francisco "hippies" created The Farm in Summertown, Tennessee, in 1971. They agreed on certain principles—nonviolence and environmentalism, for example—but shared no common vision regarding religion or economics. The community developed organically, meeting challenges as they arose. The adaptiveness of this approach allowed the colony to survive. Membership skyrocketed to 1,200 by 1980, but now remains a steady 250.

Some members earn money outside of the community in nearby towns; others work with internal community businesses, now reaching a global audience through the Internet. Some members live a vegetarian lifestyle; others eat meat. Some members take part in a communal economic experiment known as The Second Foundation; others maintain private property ownership. The anti–violence, pro–environment atmosphere of The Farm remains intact, however, and the fact that members interact with the outside world allows The Farm's experiment to affect life outside the utopia. In fact, The Farm's use of solar power, organic farming, and spiritual midwifery, among other things, has brought international attention. Nonetheless, the world has not changed to look like The Farm. The experiment may be considered successful by many criteria, but The Farm remains an exception to the rule of contemporary society.

Utopian thinkers in turn have sought to socialize the economy and free it of government involvement, give power to all equally and reserve it for a chosen few, honor one gender over another and give both genders the same authority. Just as there are as many utopias as there are utopian thinkers, there is no satisfactory way to categorize utopianism in practice. Historically, however, a pattern does emerge of when certain kinds of utopian action became more prevalent than others, especially in the West. The eighth century B.C., for example, contained mostly religious utopian thinkers who relied on oration to communicate their messages. The sixteenth century offered many literary utopias presented as travel narratives to contrast with current systems. The eighteenth century brought revolutionaries who longed to see immediate change. The nineteenth century yielded experimental communities that put theory into practice, at least for a time. The twentieth century brought dystopias that warned what might happen if systems did not reform. Of course in each era, overlap exists. But even within each era of utopian action, the utopias themselves, the blueprints for a better world, remained as unique as the individuals who conceived of them.

ANALYSIS AND CRITICAL RESPONSE

In many ways it is difficult to analyze utopianism, for it has been many things to many people across the ages. How can Plato's *Republic*, a staple of Western literature for more than 2,000 years, be considered a failure? How can François Noel Babeuf's abortive attempt to overthrow the French government be considered a success? And how can these two examples of utopianism in action be considered comparable at all? Nonetheless, the open–endedness of the theory aside, there can be legitimate criticisms and compliments made with regard to utopianism.

Perhaps the most obvious criticism of utopianism is the underlying uncertainty of whether the ideal community is, in fact, real. The most visual illustration of this uncertainty is the image of Spanish conquistadors searching South America for El Dorado, or contemporary oceanographers trying to pinpoint the lost city of Atlantis. Does paradise exist? Though it seems that the legends of beautiful societies of learning, peace, and eternal health were but a foil for the current day's problems, a device to critique existing governments and peoples, some continue to experience the urge to tie utopia to a geographical location. If utopias cannot be mapped, seen, and touched, does this make the idea of them

BIOGRAPHY:

Aldous Huxley

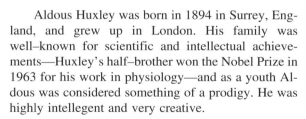

Aldous Huxley was born in 1894 in Surrey, England, and grew up in London. His family was well–known for scientific and intellectual achievements—Huxley's half–brother won the Nobel Prize in 1963 for his work in physiology—and as a youth Aldous was considered something of a prodigy. He was highly intelligent and very creative.

Eton and Oxford–educated Huxley left his native England to live in the United States, where he became one of the most famous novelists of the twentieth century. Though nearly blind since his late teens, Huxley was remarkably prolific and produced a number of works, many of which set the standard for the modern dystopia. Huxley's dark humor and natural cynicism grew with age and his increasing pessimism with the direction the world was taking. His *Brave New World* (1932) served as perhaps the best example of his dystopian thought and opened the door for George Orwell's *1984* (1949) and the era of the dystopia.

Huxley's novels displayed his deep background in utopian literature. In *Brave New World*, for example, he describes "soma," a psychedelic drug used to control citizens—a term lifted from Thomas More's *Utopia* (1516). His dystopias like *Brave New World* and *Ape and Essence* (1948) satirized earlier science fiction utopias as well—such as H. G. Wells' *A Modern Utopia* (1905) and *Men Like Gods* (1923)—by turning their premises upside down, showing how societies based on scientific principles alone develop into sterile, empty worlds of many means but no ends. *Brave New World* explored a caste society in which

emotions are repressed, relationships are hollow, and humans are genetically altered to fit preexisting classes while the totalitarian 10 World Controllers serve the stability of the citizens while protecting their own self–interest. *Ape and Essence* painted a devastating picture of a depraved humanity in a United States after atomic and bacteriological warfare.

His one attempt at a true utopia, 1962's *Island*, described a peaceful community in the Indian Ocean whose peace rested on the dual pillars of Tantric Buddhism and drugs. *Island* did not reflect the passion of Huxley's other works, however, and did not bring similar attention to the author. Huxley met the greatest success commercially and intellectually when he explained the terror of the world that might be created—the antithesis of paradise—if society did not change. Mechanization, materialism, violence, sexism, and, above all, the willingness to surrender individual liberty and responsibility for stability and efficiency, according to Huxley, led in the opposite direction of true utopia. His body of work became one of the foundational currents in contemporary science fiction and the model for twentieth–century dystopian literature.

In the last years of his life, Huxley experimented with mysticism and drugs such as LSD. He died on November 22, 1963, the same day President John F. Kennedy was assassinated. His influence is felt in the world of literature and beyond. The rock group The Doors took its name from Huxley's novel *The Doors of Perception*.

---

and their systems less viable? Many sixteenth–century writers described their utopias in the form of travel narratives, as if the authors themselves had visited concrete, three–dimensional locations and then simply reported on their findings. Yet these places were fiction only. The uneasy tension between literal and metaphorical readings of utopian works remains a difficulty of the theory. If the fabled utopias don't really exist, then what does that mean for those who would institute the reforms suggested by them?

This question leads to a second problem with utopianism: its abstract nature. Especially in the case of

utopian prophets and writers, who discussed the ideal society and its attributes in a vacuum, utopias remained in the realm of ideas only. Few utopian thinkers of this sort explained how to move current systems toward attaining the attributes of paradise. Communities that enjoyed enlightened leaders and no poverty sounded wonderful, but how could people get there from where they were with their fallible, unsatisfactory states? By relying on the image of a utopia, thinkers did not have to explain what reforms needed to be made or how they could be achieved. This means that many of the potential changes utopian thinkers might have brought never found their way to actual practice.

The Problems of Utopias

Even when some utopian thinkers experimented with actual communities and tried to implement their ideas, members often proved to be the theories' own worst enemies. By making utopian communities exclusive, cut off from the larger world around them, community members ensured that their reforms never influenced mainstream culture. To be fair, some groups, such as the Shakers, remained apart for reasons of self–defense; their practices inflamed outsiders and sometimes led to acts of animosity and even violence. Others remained separate for fear of contamination from the outside world. Regardless of the reasons, though, insularity meant that any reforms the communities made lived and died within the community walls and never had the opportunity to affect the larger world. While open communities still exist, exclusivity was a tenet of many utopian experiments.

These communities often revolved around a central figure—an Ann Lee or a John Humphrey Noyes—especially if religion provided the foundation for the utopia and the leader held specific theological authority. The first problem with this is that, in some communities, the life span of the experiment paralleled the life span of the leader. When the leader died, so, too, did the utopia. This meant that the experiment did not last long enough to experience growth and maturity, and its message rarely had any lasting impact. Surely in the ideal world the truth the members sought would be more permanent, less transient than the life of a man or a woman.

The power of these experimental community leaders, coupled with the isolation of the colonies, also leads to another potential downfall of utopian thinking: the cult of personality. One contemporary example illustrates this well. Jim Jones (1931–1978) was a Protestant minister in the United States, preaching particularly in Indianapolis, Indiana, and Ukiah and San Francisco, California. After officials began to investigate his alleged misuse of church money, Jones convinced a thousand of his followers to go to Guyana with him and create an experimental utopian community named Jonestown, after its leader. At one level, the community did seem Eden–like; its members came from different races, classes, and age groups to form a cooperative, faith–based, self–sufficient community in the wilds of an exotic land. But if the charismatic Jones had power before, it was doubled after his followers left the larger world behind in favor of the insulated settlement. Eventually, the paranoid Jones convinced his followers to commit mass suicide in 1978, and he followed by taking his own life. Many members went to Guyana in the hopes of developing an alternative community that would serve as an example to the rest of the world; the experimental paradise devolved into a cult of personality that ended up costing more than 900 lives. Certain utopian visions can lead to dangerous cults of personality with the potential for violence.

A Vision of Hope

The impact of these tragic utopias is the exception, however, and not the rule. In fact, the chief criticism of utopian thought is not that it has dangerous outcomes, but rather that it is rarely acted upon. If no society recreates Plato's *Republic* or More's *Utopia,* does this mean that the authors failed in their utopian quest? The saving grace of the utopian impulse is not in the details, but in the big picture. The one thing that unites all forms of utopianism, from sermons to literature to communities, is hope. None of the utopian theorists would have bothered with lengthy books or dangerous revolutions or challenging community experiments if they believed that the system in which they found themselves could not be changed for the better. Some might not have given their audience blueprints for how to implement their ideas, but all assumed that criticizing the status quo and/or suggesting what kind of better world could exist was a worthy use of their time. Even the dystopians with their gloomy and even frightening predictions of the future voiced their concerns so individuals had the time to make things better. The utopians believed ideas mattered and progress was possible. The question of what those ideas were, and what was meant by progress, pales in comparison to the realization that all utopians were and are, at heart, optimists. Over 2,000 years of unbroken optimism about the political process in all its forms and functions is a remarkable legacy for any theory.

TOPICS FOR FURTHER STUDY

- Consider several of the utopian works. How did women's roles change from Plato's *Republic* to later works such as Bellamy's *Looking Backward*?

- What about the United States made it the most successful launching ground for experimental utopian communities?

- Which utopian theorists were most associated with the American and French revolutions? How did the revolutions affect their ideas of the perfect society?

• Consider recent books and films. In what ways has science fiction influenced utopianism in the twentieth and twenty–first century?

BIBLIOGRAPHY

Sources

Andrews, Charles M., comp. *Famous Utopias: Being the Complete Text of Rousseau's Social Contract, More's Utopia, Bacon's New Atlantis, Campanella's City of the Sun.* New York: Tudor, 1901.

Bellamy, Edward. *Looking Backward*: 2000–1887. New York: Hendricks House, n.d.

Clute, John, ed. *Science Fiction: The Illustrated Encyclopedia.* New York: Dorling Kindersley, 1995.

Clute, John, and Peter Nicholls, eds. *The Encyclopedia of Science Fiction.* New York: St. Martin's Griffin, 1995.

Eliav–Feldon, Miriam. *Realistic Utopias: The Ideal Imaginary Societies of the Renaissance, 1516–1630.* Oxford: Clarendon Press, 1982.

The Farm. Available at http://www.thefarm.org/.

Gray, John. *Liberalism.* Minneapolis: University of Minnesota Press, 1986.

Guarneri, Carl J. *The Utopian Alternative: Fourierism in Nineteenth–Century America.* Ithaca: Cornell University Press, 1991.

Harrington, James. *The Commonwealth of Oceana and A System of Politics.* J. G. A. Pocock, ed. New York: Cambridge University Press, 1992.

Hayden, Dolores. *Seven American Utopias: The Architecture of Communitarian Socialism, 1790–1975.* Cambridge, MA: The MIT Press, 1976.

Holloway, Mark. *Heavens on Earth: Utopian Communities in America, 1680–1880.* 2nd edition. New York, Dover, 1966.

Huxley, Aldous. *Brave New World.* Reprint edition. New York: HarperPerennial Library, 1998.

Kraut, Richard, ed. The Cambridge Companion to Plato. Cambridge: Cambridge University Press, 1992.

Kumar, Krishan. *Utopianism.* Minneapolis: University of Minnesota Press, 1991.

Laidler, Harry W. *Social–Economic Movements: An Historical and Comparative Survey of Socialism, Communism, Co–operation, Utopiansm; and Other Systems of Reform and Reconstruction.* New York: Thomas Y. Crowell Company, 1947.

Manuel, Frank E. and Fritzie P. Manuel, *Utopian Thought in the Western World.* Cambridge, The Belknap Press of Harvard University Press, 1979.

Miller, David, ed. *The Blackwell Encyclopedia of Political Thought.* Cambridge, Blackwell, 1991.

Moment, Gairdner B. and Otto F. Kraushaar, eds., *Utopias: The American Experience.* Metuchen, NJ: The Scarecrow Press, 1980.

More, Thomas. *Utopia.* Ralph Robinson, trans. London: A. Constable, 1906.

Nozick, Robert. *Anarchy, State and Utopia.* New York: Basic Books, 1974.

Plato, *The Republic.* B. Jowett, trans. New York: Tudor Publishing, 1892.

White, Frederic R., ed. *Famous Utopias of the Renaissance.* New York: Hendricks House, Inc, 1955.

Wiener, Philip P., ed. *Dictionary of the History of Ideas: Studies of Selected Pivotal Ideas.* Volume IV. New York: Charles Scribner's Sons, 1973.

Further Readings

Andrews, Edward D. *People Called Shakers: A Search for the Perfect Society.* Mineola, NY: Dover, 1994. This work looks at the origin and ideology of the Shakers, as well as examining the everyday life of Shaker society.

Baker, Robert S. *Brave New World: History, Science, and Dystopia.* New York: Twayne Publishing, 1989. This book analyzes the key points and ideas of Huxley's classic novel.

Horrox, Rosemary, and Sarah Rees Jones, ed. *Pragmatic Utopianism: Ideals and Communities, 1200–1630.* Cambridge, Cambridge University Press, 2001. This book examines the meaning and practice of Utopia in the medieval and early Renaissance world.

Huxley, Aldous. *Brave New World Revisited.* Reprint edition. New York: HarperPerennial Library, 2000. One of the most brilliant minds of the century analyzes the issues related to his landmark novel two decades after its publication.

Royle, Edward. *Robert Owen and the Commencement of the Millennium: A Study of the Harmony Community.* Manchester: Manchester University Press, 1998. A look at the life of Robert Owen and his New Harmony utopian vision.

SEE ALSO

Communism, Pacifism, Socialism

Glossary & Master Index

Glossary

A

amnesty: An act of government by which pardons are granted to individuals or groups who have violated a law.

anarchism: The political theory that advocates all forms of government as wrong and unnecessary and promotes a society based on noncoercion and free from all forms of political authority.

antiquity: Ancient times, particularly any time before the Middle Ages (c. 450–c. 1500).

apartheid: The policy of political, social, and economic segregation and discrimination based on race. The political system in South Africa throughout most of the twentieth century.

Articles of Confederation: The compact made among the thirteen original U.S. colonies to form the basis of their government. Prepared in 1776, the Articles were adopted by all states in 1781. The Articles of Confederation provided for a relatively weak national government, leaving most power at the state level. They were replaced by the U.S. Constitution in 1789.

asceticism: The belief that extreme self–denial allows access to the divine.

atomism: The branch of political study that stems from the idea that institutions form only because of individuals.

Austrian School: A group of twentieth–century intellectuals who used economic arguments to defend classical liberalism.

authoritarianism: A political theory based upon the idea of the concentration of power in a ruler or rulers who do not have a direct responsibility to the people they govern. The people, in turn, must offer complete obedience to the government.

autocracy: A system of government in which all authority and power is placed in one individual.

B

bolshevik: A member of an extreme faction within the Russian Social Democratic Labor Party that seized control of the government and ushered in the Soviet age. The bolshevik message was peace, land reform, and worker empowerment, expressed in the slogan, "Land, Peace, and Bread."

bourgeoisie: The middle class consisting largely of businessmen and businesswomen; in Marxist theory, the bourgeoisie is opposed to the working class.

buddhism: A religion involving reincarnation, or a continuous cycle of rebirth, until the soul achieves the highest form of enlightenment, or nirvana.

bushido: Eastern term for a code of values and aesthetics followed by knights during the Middle Ages (c. 450–c. 1500).

C

caliph: The male leader of Islam.

capital: Wealth, including money and property.

capitalism: An economic system based on private ownership of industries, and supply and demand, where suppliers sell products for profit and buyers determine which products they will purchase at what cost.

checks and balances: A system, particularly in government, where equal branches must cooperate with each other, oversee each other, and enforce and support each others' decisions according to established rules.

chivalry: Western term for a code of values and aesthetics followed by knights during the Middle Ages (c. 450–c. 1500).

civic nationalism: Nationalist feelings and actions based on shared appreciation and respect for key political values.

collectivism: The system of control of production and distribution by the people together, supervised by a government.

communism: A political, economic, and social theory that promotes common ownership of property for the use of all citizens. All profits are to be equally distributed and prices on goods and services are usually set by the state.

compound federalism: A model of federalism where interdependent governments overlap in authority.

conservative: A political philosophy that generally favors state over federal action, and opposes regulation of the economy, extensive civil rights legislation, and federally funded social programs.

copperhead: In the United States during the Civil War, a person from the North who aligned himself or herself with the South.

Crusades: Religious wars waged from 1096 to 1291 by Christians to recapture the Holy Land (present day Palestine) from the Muslims.

Cultural Revolution: A series of reforms in China started by Mao Tse–tung in 1965 to eliminate opposition in China's institutions and leadership. It brought about social and economic trouble.

D

daimyo: Japanese term for a lord of the feudal system during the Middle Ages (c. 450–c. 1500).

demesne: Under the feudal system, the land a lord set aside for his own use.

democracy: A form of government in which the power lies in the hands of the people, who may govern directly, or govern indirectly by electing representatives.

despot: An oppressive ruler with absolute powers.

dystopia: A place or political state characterized by fear and dehumanization.

dual federalism: A model of federalism where different levels of government have separate spheres of authority; issues are either of national or state concern, and are mutually exclusive.

E

Enlightenment: A period during the seventeenth and eighteenth centuries when European philosophers stressed the use of reason as the best method for learning the truth. During this time, also called the Age of Reason or the Age of Rationalism, extensive intellectual activity took place, including the publication of several encyclopedias and numerous treatises on philosophical, political, and social topics.

enracinement: A theory which suggests the existence of a mystical link between a country's living and dead citizens, placing great emphasis on the importance of a nation to uphold the traditions and values of their ancestors.

ethnic nationalism: Nationalist feelings and actions based on concepts of shared ethnic identity.

eugenics: The science of improving hereditary qualities of a species or breed by controlling or altering genetic material.

European Union: A treaty–based organization of fifteen European nations that advocates political and economic cooperation. Includes Austria, Belgium, Denmark, Finland, France, Germany, Greece, Ireland, Italy, Luxembourg, The Netherlands, Portugal, Spain, Sweden, and the United Kingdom.

executive branch: In the United States, the branch of government charged with administering the laws and policies of the nation or state. In contrast, the legislative and judicial branches of government have the respective powers of creating and interpreting the laws.

F

fascism: An extreme political philosophy that holds nation and race above the individual, advocating a government with absolute power vested in the leader.

federalism: The system of government in which the power of government is distributed between a central authority and its constituent units (for example, states).

Federalist Papers: A famous and influential series of articles believed to be written by Alexander Hamilton, John Jay, and James Madison. The Federalist Papers were published during the period that ratification of the U.S. Constitution was being debated, in an attempt to justify and explain the Constitution.

feudalism: A political and economic system practiced during the Middle Ages (c. 450–c. 1500), in which a lord governed and protected self–sufficient states. In return for the land and protection he offered peasants, or serfs, the serfs were expected to pay the lord fees-either money (taxes), services, or goods.

fief: A collection of several manors that was governed and protected by a lord under feudalism.

Fourierism: A form of socialism advocated by Charles Fourier that accepted a few of the tenets of capitalism, including some private property ownership. Fourierism called for a well–ordered agricultural society, one based on cooperation and gender equality.

Fourteen Points: U.S. President Woodrow Wilson's version of a peace settlement for World War I, the speech emphasized the goals of the United States. The Fourteen Points were to have:open agreements among nations; freedom of the seas; free international trade; reduction of national armaments; impartial adjustment of colonial claims; evacuation of Russian territory; evacuation of Belgium; evacuation of French territory and the return of Alsace–Lorraine to France; readjustment of Italian frontiers; autonomy for Austria and Hungary; evacuation of Romania, Serbia, and Montenegro, and security for the Balkan states; self–determination of the peoples of the Turkish empire; independence for Poland; and formation of a general association of nations.

G

glasnost: In the Soviet Union, Mikhail Gorbachev's policies of openness regarding social problems.

globalization: The evolution of a substantial international economy which was the manifestation of international market transactions increasingly overtaking those that had been nation based.

government: The political and administrative system of a nation or state including legislative, executive, and judicial functions.

Great Leap Forward: A massive collectivization (government control) of agriculture and industry under Mao Tse–tung, which brought economic failure and a two–year famine to China in the late 1950s.

Great Society: Term used by U.S. President Lyndon Johnson during his administration (1963–1969) to describe his vision of the United States as a land without prejudice or poverty, that would be made possible by implementing his series of social programs.

I

imperialism: The theory, policy, and practice of extending a nation's power over new territories and their economies: individualism: A political theory advanced by anarchists that emphasized the emancipation of the individual from the political coercion of the state. Individualists believe that any time people are treated as collectives rather than different individuals, violence is done against them.

industrialization: The process of converting from an economy that is based primarily on agriculture and/or manual labor to one devoted to the manufacture of goods, with extensive use of heavy machinery.

J

jihad: A crusade, especially a Muslim spiritual war against nonbelievers.

judicial branch: The segment of government that protects citizens against excessive use of power by the executive or legislature and provides an impartial setting for the settlement of civil and criminal cases. In the United States, the judicial system is divided into state and federal courts with further divisions at those levels. State and federal courts are independent except that the Supreme Court of the United States may review state court decisions when a federal issue is involved.

junta: The group of military officials who rule a nation after overthrowing the previous regime.

K

Koran: The holy book of Islam, considered by Muslims to contain God's revelations to the prophet Muhammad.

L

laissez faire: An economic theory that proposes that governments should not interfere in their economies and that natural economic laws should guide the production and consumption of goods.

liberalism: A political philosophy that generally favors change and development of new ideas. Traditionally, U.S. liberals have pushed for political, economic, and social change to benefit individuals. In the twentieth century this has often included the expansion of the government's role on the every day life of Americans.

libertarianism: A political philosophy that advocates the rights of individuals and property, a government's obligation to protect property rights, and a limited constitution.

lebensraum: German for "living space," this specifically refers to Hitler's policy which advocated the eastward expansion of German territory.

legislative branch: The branch of government that makes or enacts laws. In the U.S. government, Congress is the legislative branch.

leninism: The political theory developed from Marxism by Vladimir Lenin, suggesting revolution by the working class.

M

Machiavellian: Characterized by cunning, duplicity, or bad faith in his or her attempts to gain political power. It is derived primarily from *The Prince* by Niccoló Machiavelli, which presents an amoral theory of governing.

Magna Carta: Signed by King John of England in 1215. Ensured personal liberty and asserted the rights of the individual; important to the development of the British constitutional system, or government based on written laws.

Marshall Plan: Formally known as the European Recovery Program, a joint project between the United States and most Western European nations under which $12.5 billion in U.S. loans and grants was expended to aid European recovery after World War II (1939–1945). Expenditures under the program, named for U.S. Secretary of State George C. Marshall, were made from fiscal years 1949 through 1952.

marxism: An economic and political system based on economic equality and cooperation instead of competition.

McCarthyism: In the United States, the anticommunist scare of the early 1950s. Senator Joseph McCarthy of Wisconsin headed a committee investigating communist influence in the United States from the late 1940s to the early 1950s. Begun as a legitimate investigation, the committee began questioning individuals about their activities with little or no evidence that they had been involved in communist activities. The excesses of the committee and McCarthy created widespread suspicion and hysteria concerning national security. McCarthy was censured by the Senate in 1954 and the committee's activities were severely restricted.

medieval: Relating to the Middle Ages (c. 450–c. 1500).

menshevik: A member of a faction of the Russian Social Democratic party who believed in the gradual development of socialism by legislative means rather than revolution.

mercantilism: An economic system that stresses the goals of the national government rather than the individual, developed in Europe as the feudal system declined. The main economic system in Europe during the sixteenth, seventeenth, and eighteenth centuries, this system required the national government to strictly control businesses to meet certain objectives, such as exporting more goods to other countries than importing goods from other countries.

mercenary: A person who is hired to work for another, often as a soldier fighting for a foreign nation. The sole motivation for the individual is money.

Miranda rights: In the United States, police must tell a suspect during arrest that he or she has some given rights, even during arrest: "You have the right to remain silent; anything you say can and will be used against you in court. You have the right to consult with a lawyer; if you cannot afford a lawyer, one will be appointed for you."

monarchy: A system of government in which ruling power is based upon heredity, as in a king or queen; powers can vary from absolute to in name only.

muckrakers: Journalists who use newspapers as a means of attacking injustice, exposing abuses, and circulating information about misconduct to the general public. The term was popularized in the late 1800s when some American journalists began to stray from reporting news events and started investigating and writing about prominent people and organizations. Concerned with exposing corruption in both business and politics, they helped raise awareness of social, economic, and political ills. Their work led to a number of reforms and legislative changes.

mutualism: A theory put forth by Pierre–Joseph Proudhon that advocated the cooperation of industrial and agricultural communities and the commercial use of labor checks instead of money; labor checks, Proudhon thought, would represent how much labor went into the production of a given product, and thus would assure that the exchange rate of products would be determined by the labor they represent, to the benefit of the workers.

N

nation-state: The concept that territorial boundaries, political authority, and the composition of a population inhabiting a territory should coincide, theoretically with the population all belonging to the same homogeneous nation. Few nation–states actually fit this strict definition, since nearly all states in the twenty–first century are composed of a multiplicity of peoples from many national groups.

nationalism: Strong, sentimental feelings about one's own country and a patriotic fervor directed toward advancing the national interest. Nationalism can be the driving philosophy behind social movements that can both infect and inspire large numbers of people living in the same geographical region to attack other groups or countries for the anticipated benefit of one's own interests. By the 1700s, several countries, notably England, France, and Spain, had developed as "nation–states," groups of people with a shared background who occupy a land that is governed independently.

Nazism: A political doctrine developed by the National Socialist German Workers' Party, under the leadership of Adolf Hitler. At first "Nazi," which is an abbreviation for the name of the party, was considered a negative term; but eventually it was adopted by party members. It was based on three philosophies: extreme nationalism, anti–Semitism, and anticommunism.

neolithic revolution: The movement started in approximately 10,000 BC in which humans first implemented farming technology. The revolution led humans to settle and create political units capable of organizing political, administrative, economic, and military power on a large scale.

New Deal: The name given to U.S. President Franklin Roosevelt's plan to save the American nation from the devastating effects of the Great Depression. His programs included direct aid to citizens and a variety of employment and public works opportunities sponsored by the federal government. It began shortly after his inauguration in 1933.

nihilism: A belief in the necessity of destruction, especially of existing political or social institutions, for future growth and change.

nullification: A political doctrine which holds that state governments are sovereign in their own territory, and therefore have the ability to ignore and even block the enforcement of federal laws which they do not approve of. This controversial theory had many supporters in the early nineteenth century United States, but was largely discredited by the Civil War.

O

objectivism: The theory pioneered by novelist Ayn Rand that states individuals' efforts and ability serve as the sole source of genuine achievement; all individuals' highest moral end is their own happiness, and any notion of a group threatens all people as individual rights–bearers.

oligarchy: Any system of government in which a small elite group holds the ruling power.

P

perestroika: Mikhail Gorbachev's policy of economic and governmental reform instituted in the 1980s when he was the leader of the Soviet Union.

phalanx: Also phalanstery. A group of the followers of Fourierism, living communally in a self–sustaining environment.

polis: A small, independent, and distinctive political community or city in Ancient Greece.

polity A nation's form of government.

populism: A belief in the rights, wisdom, and virtues of average citizens. A political philosophy that advocates on behalf of common people as opposed to favoring the interests of industry.

pork barrel: Funds appropriated for local projects that are not critically needed. As an example, members of the U.S. Congress generally do not question other members' pork barrel legislation for fear their own local projects could be defeated.

primordialism: The concept that the quest for ethnic identity and solidarity is rooted physically in the human animal.

Prohibition: In the United States, the sale, manufacture, or transportation of alcoholic beverages was made illegal by constitutional provision between 1920 and 1933. The rapid repeal of this provision showed the unpopularity of this ban.

proletariat: The working class, especially those who do not produce their own goods.

Q

"Qu'est–ce qu'une nation?" ("What is a nation?"): The landmark lecture given by Ernest Renan in 1882 which raised questions about the origins of nations and the nature of their identity.

R

Red Scare: A period during U.S. history (late 1940s to early 1950s) of great fear of communists, heightened by the actions of Senator Joseph McCarthy and his senate committee.

Renaissance: The European era from the end of the Middle Ages (c. 1500) to the beginning of modern times (c. 1750), characterized by a revival in art, philosophy, and literature.

S

samurai: A warrior class in feudal Japan, they ruled over local peasants and defended their manor houses.

Scramble for Africa: The conquest and partition of the African continent by numerous European nations which took place mainly in the nineteenth century.

sedition: Rebellion against a governing authority.

separation of powers: The cornerstone of U.S. government wherein power is divided among three branches of government—the executive, legislative, and judicial. Officials of each branch are selected differently, have different responsibilities, and serve different terms. The separation of power is not absolute, however, due to the system of checks and balances.

Shakers: A religious group founded in the 1770s which was characterized by communal living, separation by gender, and the sharing of resources. The Shakers were among the first in America to advocate pacifism, abolition of slavery, equality of the sexes, and communal ownership of goods.

social contract theory: An idea developed by Thomas Hobbes that civil government rests on the consent of the governed.

social darwinism: The theory that one gains advantage over others due to genetic superiority.

socialism: An economic and political system based on the idea of communal ownership of industry, either by the state or by the workers themselves.

spoils system: A system wherein elected officials award their supporters with appointments to federal jobs, often without any consideration given to the qualifications of the people thus appointed. Developed from the phrase "to the victor go the spoils."

squadristi: Fascist squads, composed mainly of disillusioned Italian ex–servicemen, who increasingly took on a paramilitary role and favored the use threats and terror to achieve Mussolini's goals.

squire: A knight in training, usually an adolescent of noble blood. In the feudal social rank the squire would rank just below the knight.

structural violence: Norwegian peace theorist Johann Galtung's term for violence indirectly caused by oppressive social, political, and economic structures and discriminatory practices.

suffrage: The right to vote.

suzerain: A feudal lord to whom vassals had to pay allegiance and money or goods.

syndicalist: A follower of a political movement that advocates bringing industry and government under the control of labor unions. The goal is thought to be achievable through the use of strikes, sabotage, and other such actions.

T

territorial democracy: The theory that geographic divisions within a nation ensures a degree of neutrality and equality at the national and local levels.

theism: Belief in a higher power, such as a god or gods.

theocracy: A system of government in which the ruler or rulers are supposed to be governing by divine guidance.

totalitarianism: A political philosophy that advocates taking charge not only of the public life of the people, but also their personal and emotional lives.

Treaty of Versailles: Peace agreement which officially ended World War II in 1919. Many historians feel that the harsh conditions the treaty imposed upon Germany were partly responsible for the rise of Hitler and the Nazis.

tyranny: An oppressive government in which absolute power is held by one individual.

U

ujamaa: A form of socialism implemented in Tanzania by Julius Nyerere in 1967. The policies included families moving into villages and sharing schools and hospitals.

utopia: An ideal or perfect place or political state; from the novel of the same name written by Sir Thomas More in 1516.

utopianism: Belief in a political system of an ideal society, in which men and women are treated equally, land is owned communally, politicians are honest, and religious commonplace. Based upon the ideals presented by Sir Thomas More.

V

vassal: In the feudal system of the Middle Ages (c. 450–c. 1500), anyone who was under the protection of another and therefore owed and gave that person allegiance and payment of some kind for providing safety. Peasants were always vassals to a lord of a manor (a self–sufficient estate) or a feudal lord (a lord of several manors). A lord of a manor was himself a vassal to the feudal lord. Feudal lords then became vassals of kings.

vizier: A high–ranking official in a Muslim country, in particular the Ottoman Empire.

X

xenophobia: The fear or dislike of anything foreign, especially people.

Index

Index

Sharp, Gene, 270–271
Siddhartha, 260
South Africa, 272–273
Stoics, 261
Suu Kyi, Aung San, 269
teachings of Jesus, 259
Thoreau, Henry David, 262–263
Tolstoy, Leo, 263–264
Tutu, Desmond, 257
twentieth century, 255–256
Victim Offender Reconciliation
    Programs (VORP), 273
Vietnam War, 256–257, 267–268
Walensa, Lech, 257
World War II, 274–275
See also Imperialism; Socialism;
    Utopianism
Palestine, 246–247
Pan–Africanism, 248–249
Parastatal companies, 295–296
Party affiliation, 64
Patron–client system, *277–299*
    accountability, 297
    adaptability, 296–297
    Adrian IV, Pope, 285–286
    advantages, 296–298
    Africa, 282–284, 287–288, 294–296,
        296–297
    ancient, 278–281, 284–285
    Aquinas, Thomas, 287
    Argentina, 291–292, 297–298
    Asia, 290
    Auyero, Javier, 297–298
    Bentham, Jeremy, 288–289
    compatibility, 297
    Daly, Richard J., 297
    Doe, Samuel, 294
    economies of affection, 289–290
    Great Britain, 281
    Greece, 279–281, 284–285
    Hyden, Goran, 289–290
    India, 290
    Indonesia, 290
    Japan, 290–291
    John of Salisbury, 285
    Kenya, 295
    legend of Kuaba, 287–288
    Liberia, 294
    Machiavelli, Niccolò, 281, 288
    Marcos family, 290
    Mexico, 293–294
    Middle Ages, 281, 285–287
    Mobutu Sese Seko, 294–295
    Moi, Daniel Arap, 295
    Nehru family, 290
    Old Testament, 278–279, 284
    parastatal companies, 295–296
    Perón, Juan and Eva, 291–292
    Phillipines, 290
    political theory's lack of attention
        to, 284
    political philosophers' challenges
        to, 288–289

problems, 296
Rawls, John, 289
Roman Empire, 281
Rousseau, Jean–Jacques, 288
Salampasu, 282
spoils system, 281–282, 297
stability, 297
Suharto family, 290
Taylor, Charles, 294
Tolbert, William, 294
tribute, 283
Tubman, William, 294
Tweed, William Macy, 297
United States, 281–282, 297
Zaire, 294–295
See also Communism; Feudalism;
    Populism; Republicanism;
    Socialism
Paul, Ron, 206
Peacemaking, 272–273
People's Party. *See* Populist Party
Pepin the Short, 131–132
Perón, Juan and Eva, 291–292, 310–311
Perot, H. Ross, 306, 313, *314*
Perpetual Peace (Kant), 168, 262
Phillipines, 290
Philosophy of Right (Hegel), 372
Plato
    authoritarianism, 367–368
    capitalism, 22
    communism, 44
    eugenics, 394
    Marxism, 212
    republicanism, 324–325
    utopianism, 388–389, *390, 394,* 395
Plekhanov, Georgy, 310
PNF (National Fascist Party), 91, 98–102
Poland, 257
Poleis, 318–319
*Policraticus: Of the Frivolities of
    Courtiers and the Footprints
    of Philosophers* (John of
    Salisbury), 139
*Politica: Politics Methodically Set Forth
    and Illustrated with Sacred
    and Profane Examples*
    (Althusius), 112
Political parties, 65, 114, 122
    See also Individual parties
*Politics Among Nations: The Struggle
    for Power and Peace*
    (Morgenthau), 166
Politics (Aristotle), 319, 320
Populism, *301–316*
    agrarian populists, 303–304, 307,
        309–310, 311–312
    anti–Washington, 305–306
    Argentina, 310–311
    Baum, Frank L., 314–315
    Bryan, William Jennings, 308–309
    Buchanan, Pat, 306
    conservatives, 305–306
    core beliefs, 306–307

economics, 302–304, 307–309,
    314–315
Gompers, Samuel, 304
grass–roots nature of, 307–308
Herzen, Aleksandr, 310
interpretations, 312–314
Jackson, Andrew, 302–303
Jefferson, Thomas, 302
labor concerns, 304
Latin America, 310–311
Littlefield, Henry M., 314–315
Perot, H. Ross, 306, 313, *314*
Plekhanov, Georgy, 310
rule by the people, 306
ruling elite, 306, 312
Russia, 309–310
temperance movement, 304
United States, 302–309, 311–314
Viguerie, Richard, 309
Wallace, George, 305–306, 309
Wonderful Wizard of Oz, The,
    314–315
xenophobia, 306, 312, 314
Populist Party, 68, 304, 311–312
Portugal, 93–94, 163
*Practical Details in Equitable
    Commerce* (Warren), 8–9
Precaria, 130–131
Prescott, William, 167
Presidential election of 2000, 79
PRI (Institutional Revolutionary Party),
    293–294
Price determination, 23
Primordialists, 237–238
Prince, The (Machiavelli), 281, 288
Privatization, 33–34, 354, 358
Profit, 29
Progressive Movement, 68, 117
Propaganda, 96, 99–101, 103–104
Property ownership
    anarchism, 8–9, 10
    capitalism, 23–25
    liberalism, 176–178, 190
    libertarianism, 202
    Marxism, 219
    utopianism, 394, 397
    See also Economics; Wealth
Proportional representation, 184–185
Proudhon, Pierre–Joesph, 4, 9–10, 343
Prussia, 122, 364
Public Choice School of Economics, 201

Q

Qing Dynasty, 151–152
Quakers and pacifism, 262
"Qu'est–ce qu'une nation?" (Renan), 239

R

Rabelais, Françoise, 396–397
Rabin, Yitzhak, *246*